D0874520

HIGASHIMURA
a, Akiko.
lyfish.

Princess Jellyfish 09
Akiko Higashimura

DEAREST READERS!

AH, WHAT A LONG
SERIALIZATION THIS HAS BEEN!
NOW WE'VE FOUND
OURSELVES AT THE
FINAL VOLUME OF TEARS!
DEAREST READERS,
I HOPE YOU KEEP CHASING
THE THINGS YOU LOVE
AND KEEP ENJOYING LIFE—
FROM NOW UNTIL FOREVER!
AMARS FOREVER!

-AKIKO HIGASHIMURA

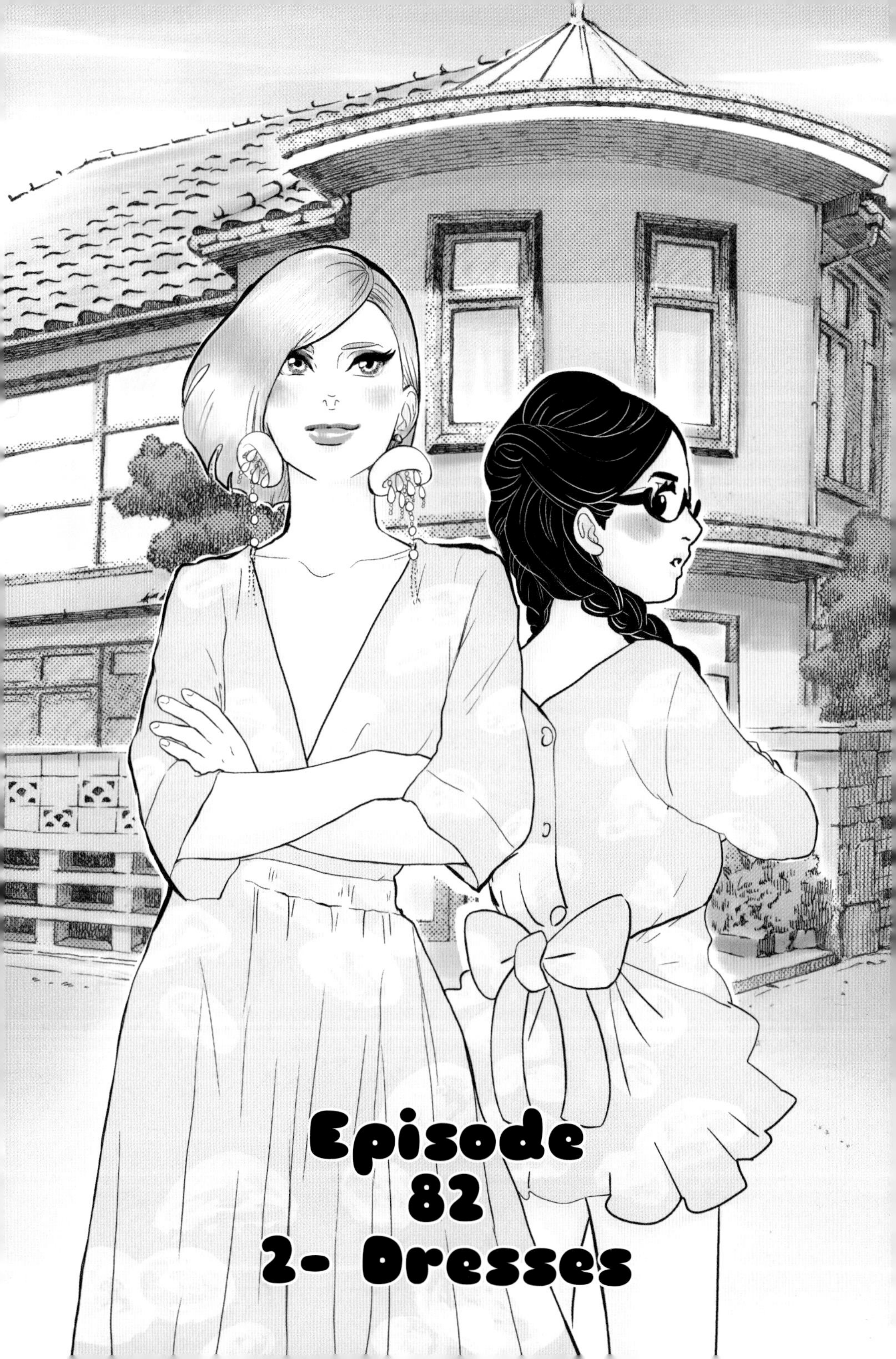
Episode
82
2- Dresses

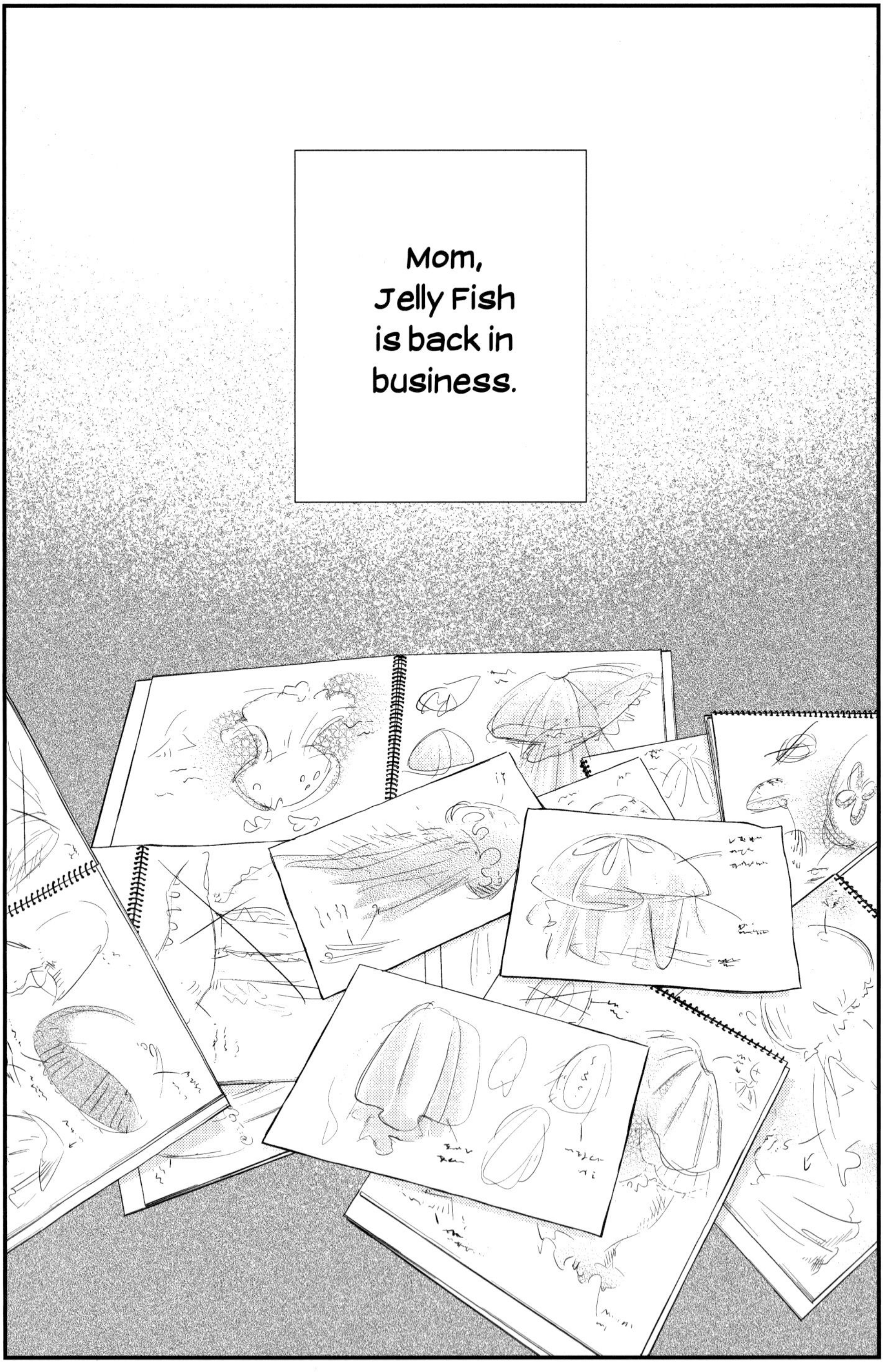
Mom,
Jelly Fish
is back in
business.

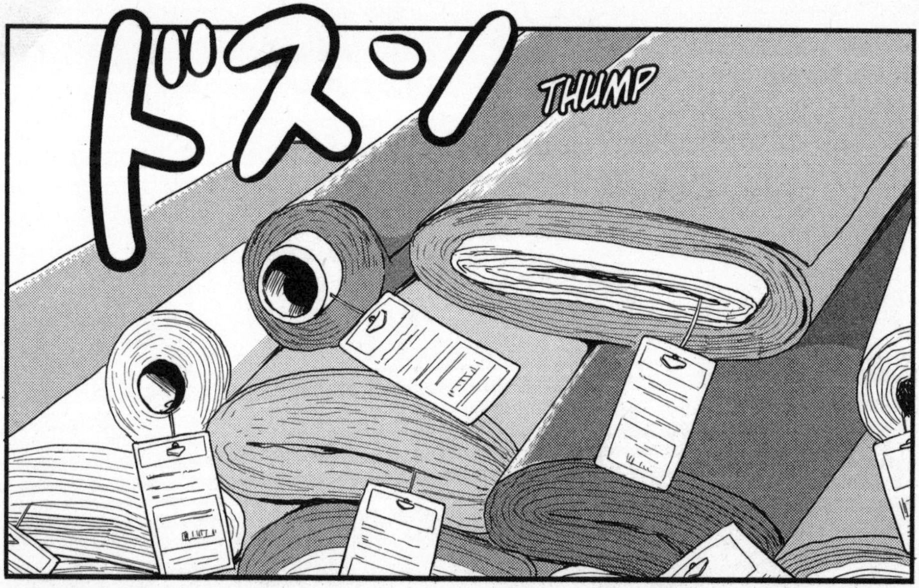
ドスン
THUMP

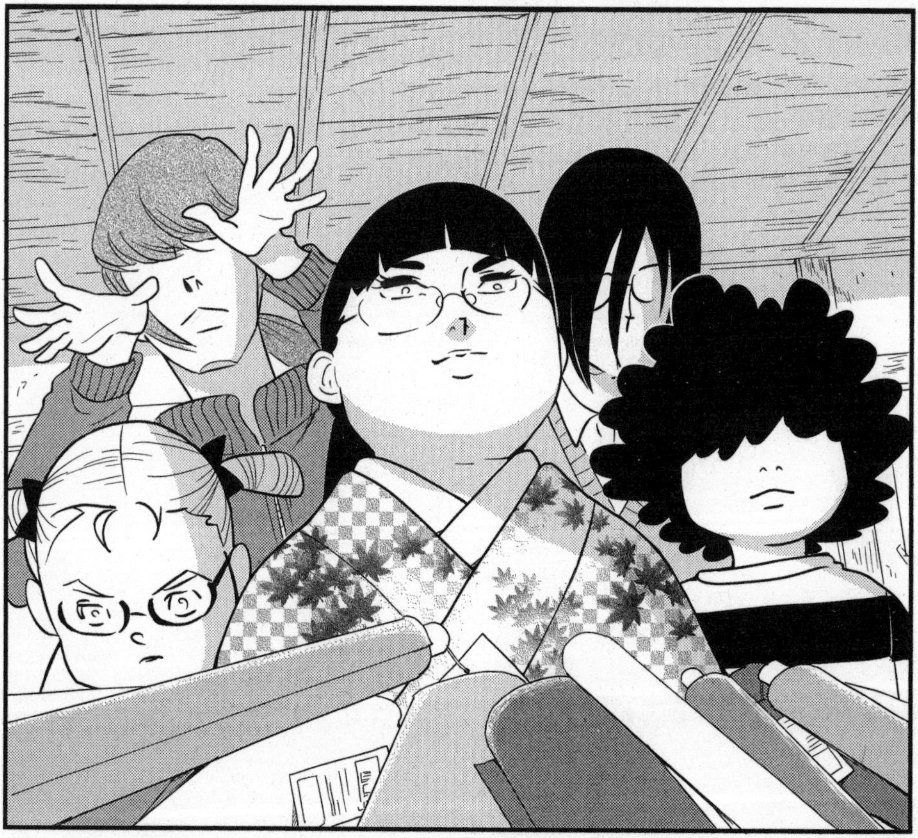

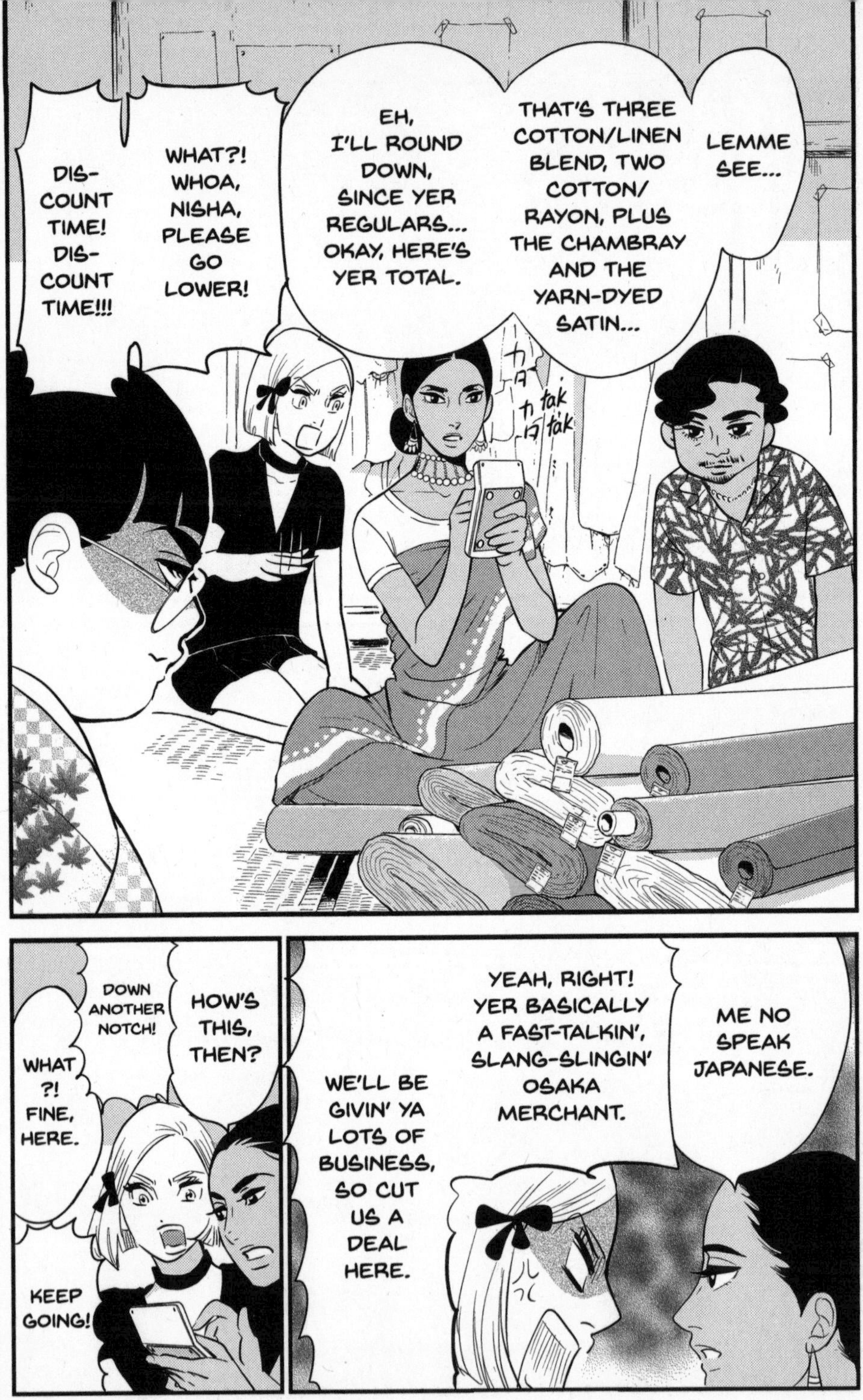
LEMME SEE...
THAT'S THREE COTTON/LINEN BLEND, TWO COTTON/ RAYON, PLUS THE CHAMBRAY AND THE YARN-DYED SATIN...
EH, I'LL ROUND DOWN, SINCE YER REGULARS... OKAY, HERE'S YER TOTAL.
WHAT?! WHOA, NISHA, PLEASE GO LOWER!
DIS-COUNT TIME! DIS-COUNT TIME!!!
tak
tak
ME NO SPEAK JAPANESE.
YEAH, RIGHT! YER BASICALLY A FAST-TALKIN', SLANG-SLINGIN' OSAKA MERCHANT.
WE'LL BE GIVIN' YA LOTS OF BUSINESS, SO CUT US A DEAL HERE.
HOW'S THIS, THEN?
DOWN ANOTHER NOTCH!
WHAT?! FINE, HERE.
KEEP GOING!

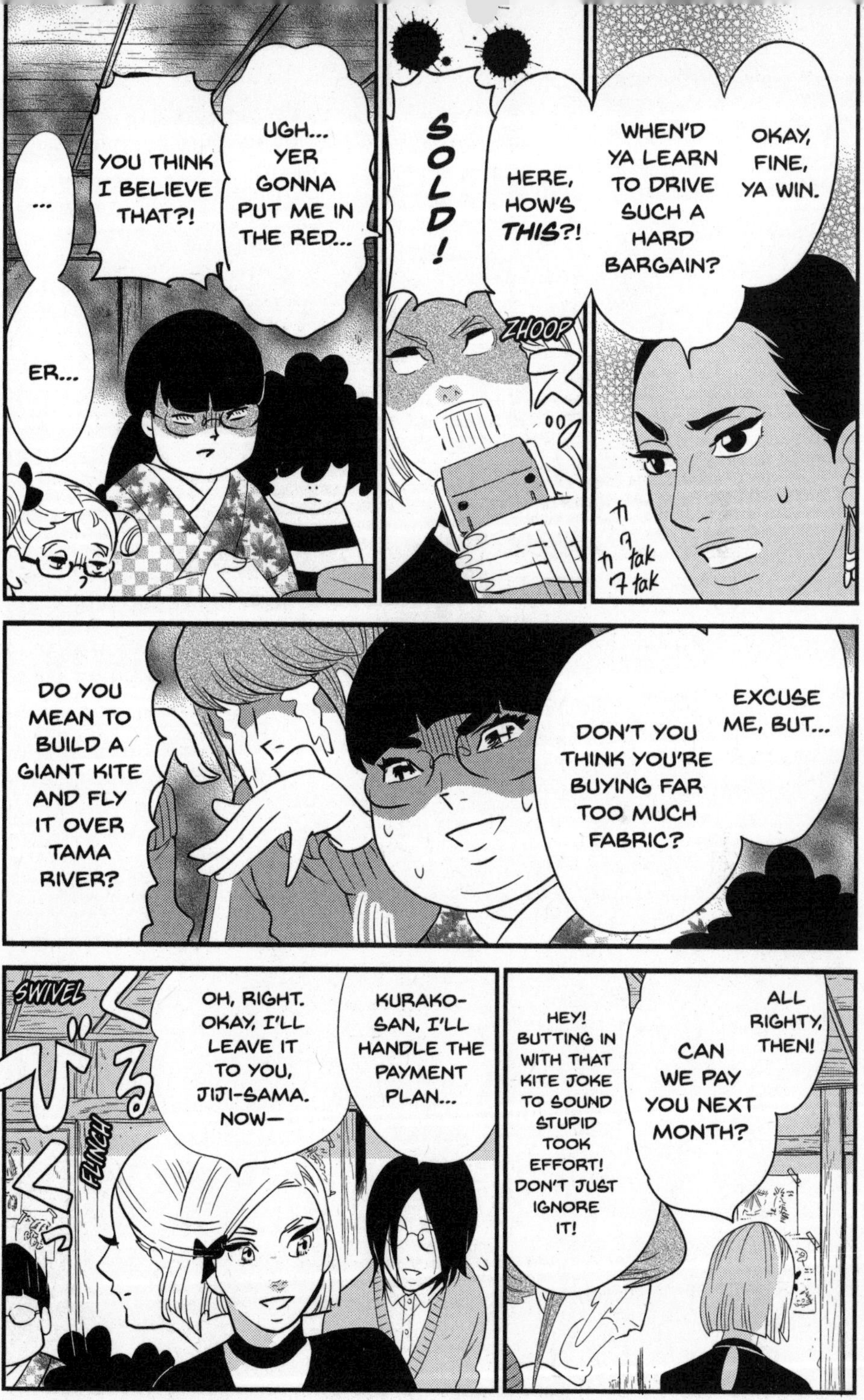
OKAY, FINE, YA WIN.
WHEN'D YA LEARN TO DRIVE SUCH A HARD BARGAIN?
tak tak
HERE, HOW'S THIS?!
SOLD!
ZHOOP
UGH... YER GONNA PUT ME IN THE RED...
YOU THINK I BELIEVE THAT?!
...
ER...
EXCUSE ME, BUT...
DON'T YOU THINK YOU'RE BUYING FAR TOO MUCH FABRIC?
DO YOU MEAN TO BUILD A GIANT KITE AND FLY IT OVER TAMA RIVER?
ALL RIGHTY, THEN!
CAN WE PAY YOU NEXT MONTH?
HEY! BUTTING IN WITH THAT KITE JOKE TO SOUND STUPID TOOK EFFORT! DON'T JUST IGNORE IT!
KURAKO-SAN, I'LL HANDLE THE PAYMENT PLAN...
OH, RIGHT. OKAY, I'LL LEAVE IT TO YOU, JIJI-SAMA. NOW—
SWIVEL
FLINCH

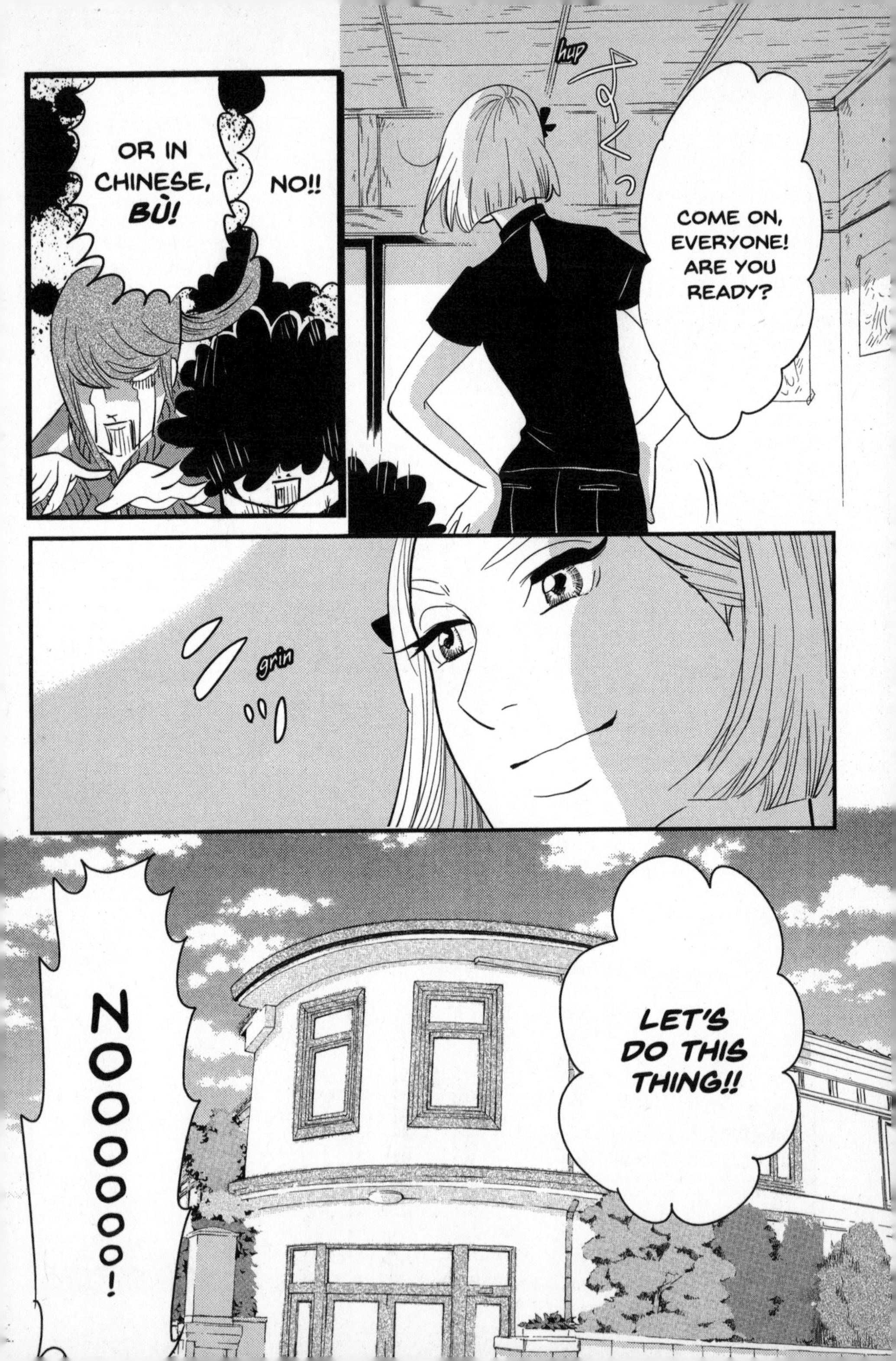
hup
COME ON, EVERYONE! ARE YOU READY?
NO!!
OR IN CHINESE, BÙ!
grin
LET'S DO THIS THING!!
NOOOOOOO!

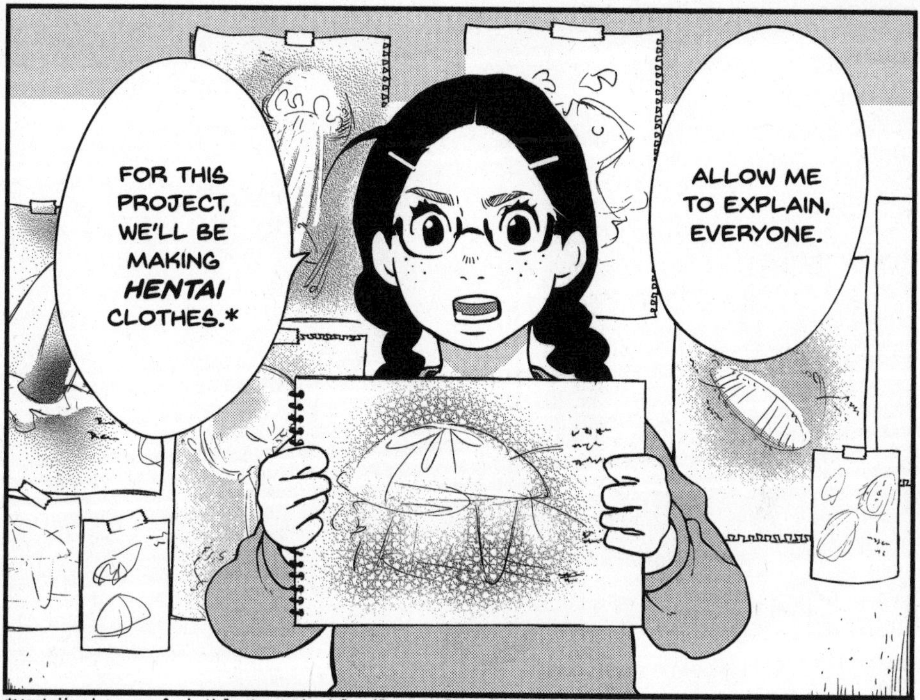
ALLOW ME TO EXPLAIN, EVERYONE.
FOR THIS PROJECT, WE'LL BE MAKING **HENTAI** CLOTHES.*

*Hentai is a homonym for both "metamorphosis" and "pervert."

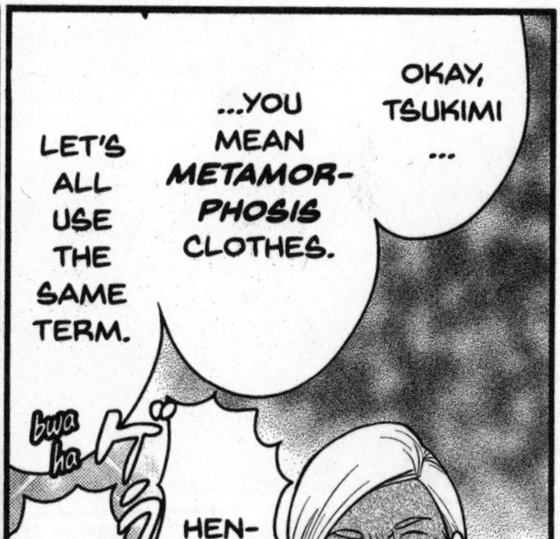
OKAY, TSUKIMI ...
...YOU MEAN **METAMOR-PHOSIS** CLOTHES.
LET'S ALL USE THE SAME TERM.
bwa ha
HEN-TAI!
HENTAI CLOTH-ES!
ha ha

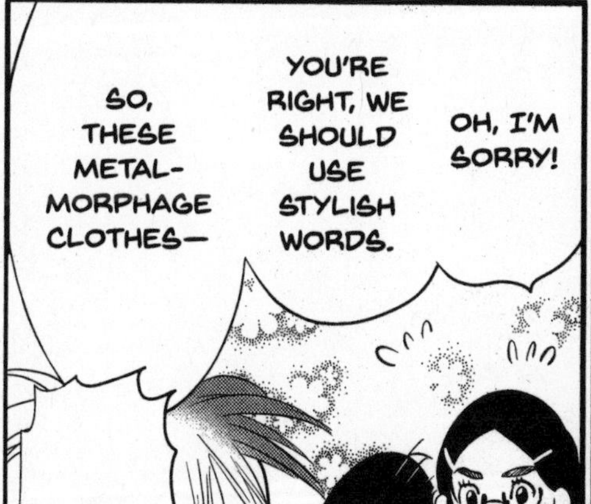
OH, I'M SORRY!
YOU'RE RIGHT, WE SHOULD USE STYLISH WORDS.
SO, THESE METAL-MORPHAGE CLOTHES—
IT'S NOT METAL! **META**-MORPHO-SIS!

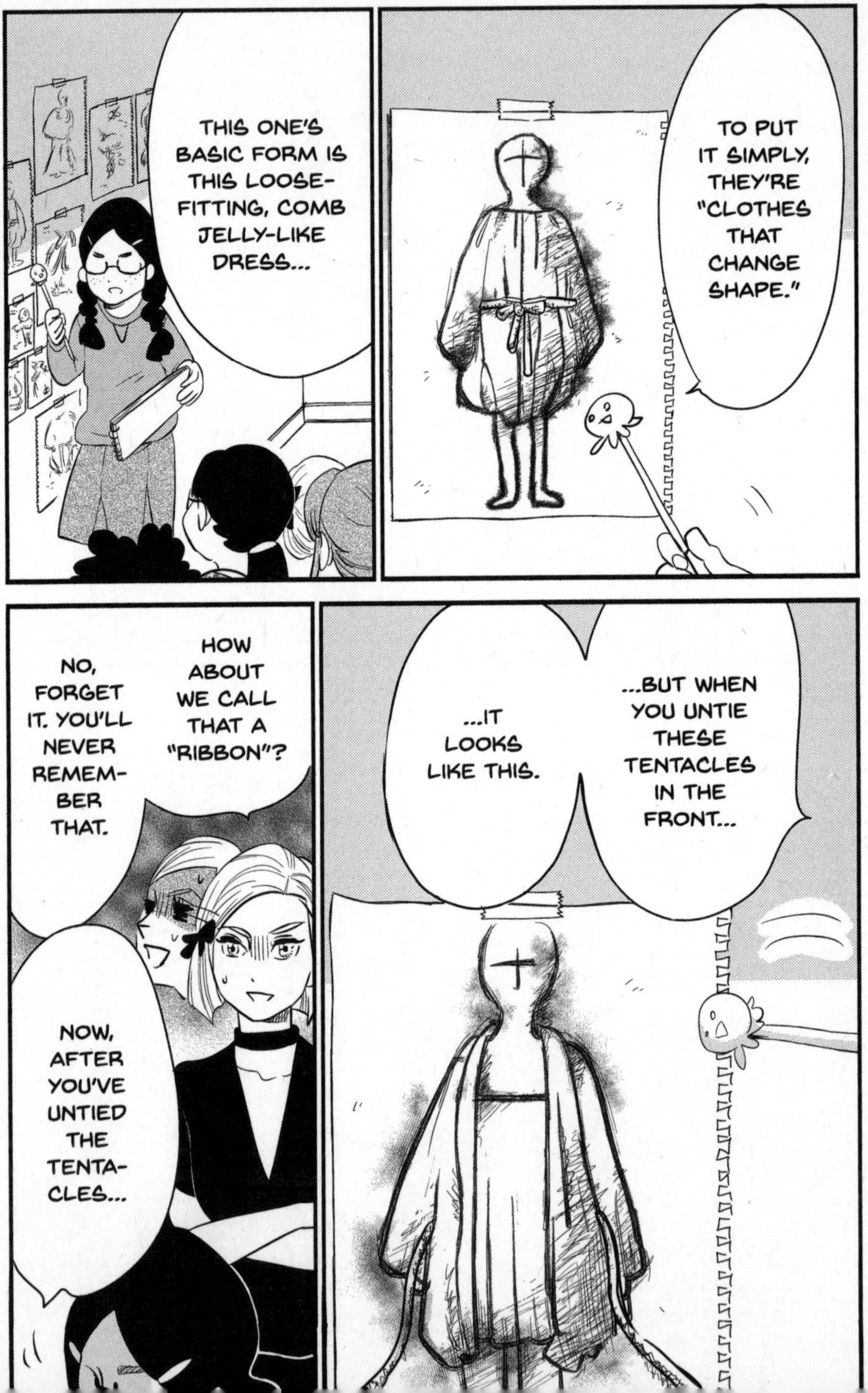
TO PUT IT SIMPLY, THEY'RE "CLOTHES THAT CHANGE SHAPE."
THIS ONE'S BASIC FORM IS THIS LOOSE-FITTING, COMB JELLY-LIKE DRESS...
...BUT WHEN YOU UNTIE THESE TENTACLES IN THE FRONT...
...IT LOOKS LIKE THIS.
HOW ABOUT WE CALL THAT A "RIBBON"?
NO, FORGET IT. YOU'LL NEVER REMEMBER THAT.
NOW, AFTER YOU'VE UNTIED THE TENTACLES...

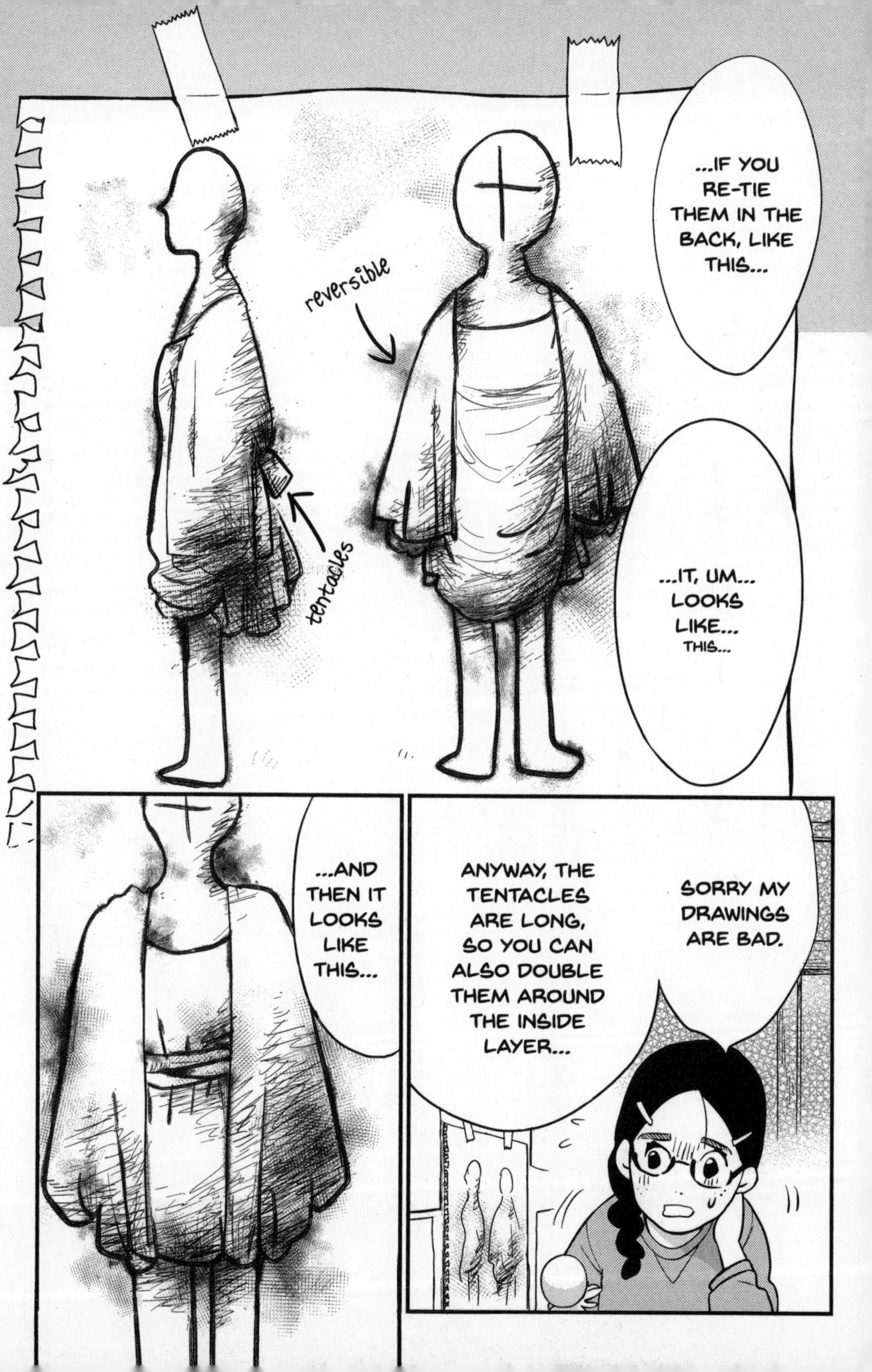
...IF YOU RE-TIE THEM IN THE BACK, LIKE THIS...
...IT, UM... LOOKS LIKE... THIS...
reversible
tentacles
SORRY MY DRAWINGS ARE BAD.
ANYWAY, THE TENTACLES ARE LONG, SO YOU CAN ALSO DOUBLE THEM AROUND THE INSIDE LAYER...
...AND THEN IT LOOKS LIKE THIS...

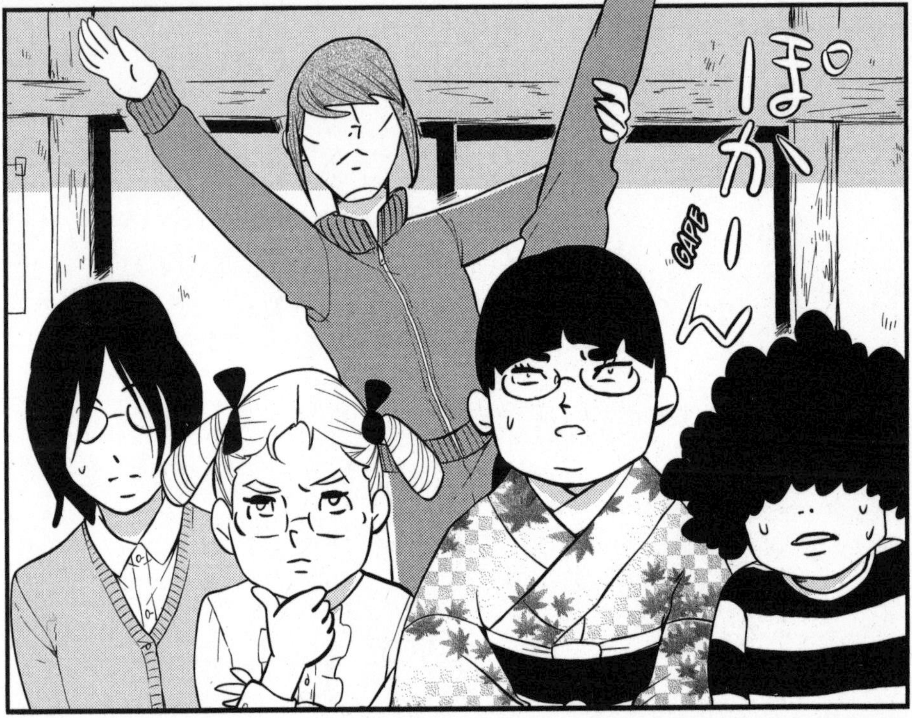
ぽかーん
GAPE

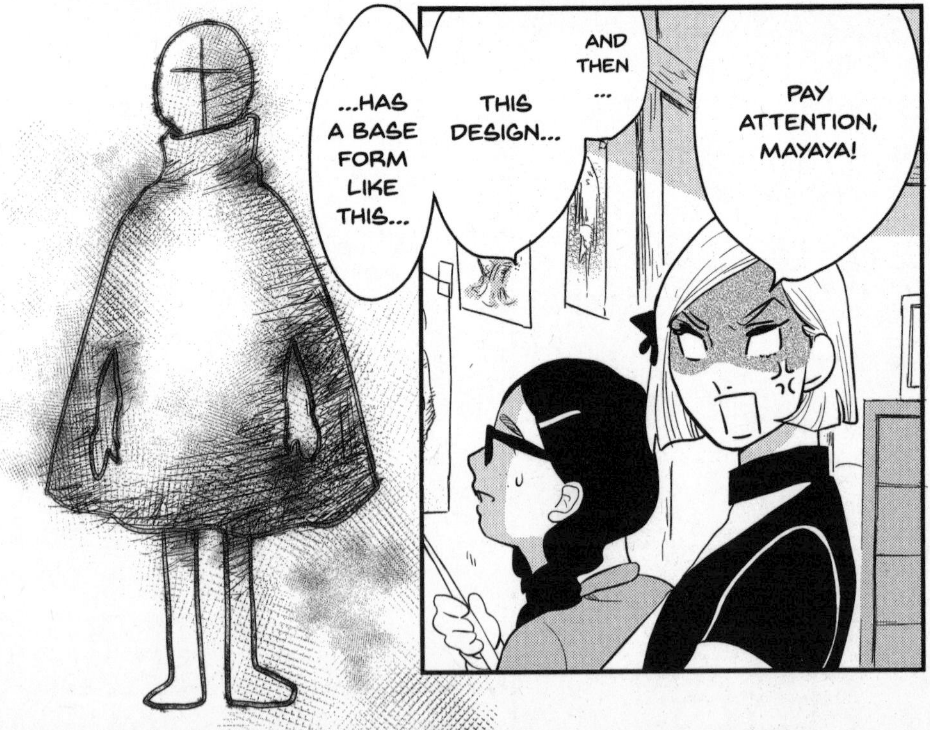
PAY ATTENTION, MAYAYA!
AND THEN ...
THIS DESIGN...
...HAS A BASE FORM LIKE THIS...

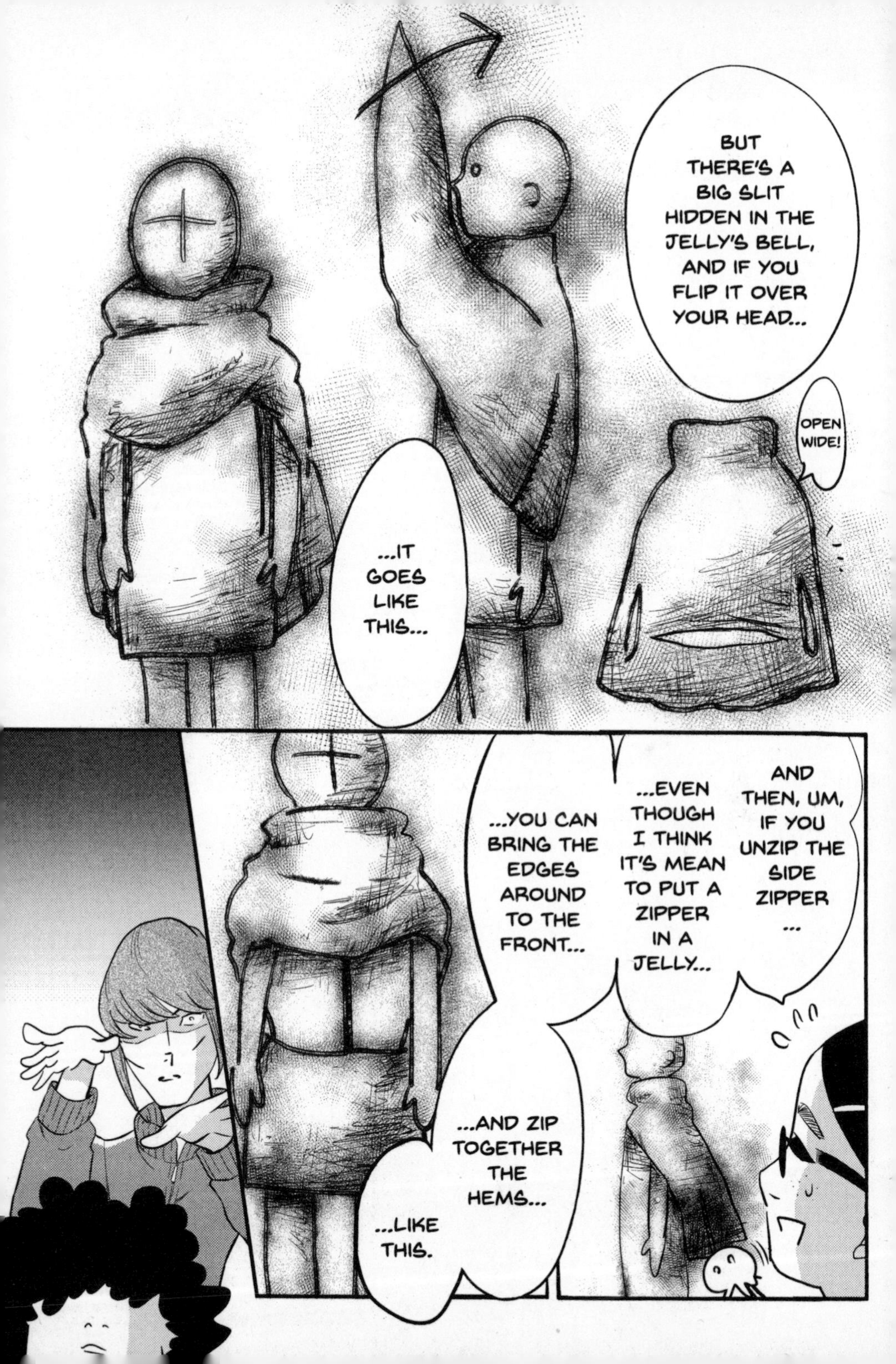
BUT THERE'S A BIG SLIT HIDDEN IN THE JELLY'S BELL, AND IF YOU FLIP IT OVER YOUR HEAD...
OPEN WIDE!
...IT GOES LIKE THIS...
AND THEN, UM, IF YOU UNZIP THE SIDE ZIPPER ...
...EVEN THOUGH I THINK IT'S MEAN TO PUT A ZIPPER IN A JELLY...
...YOU CAN BRING THE EDGES AROUND TO THE FRONT...
...AND ZIP TOGETHER THE HEMS...
...LIKE THIS.

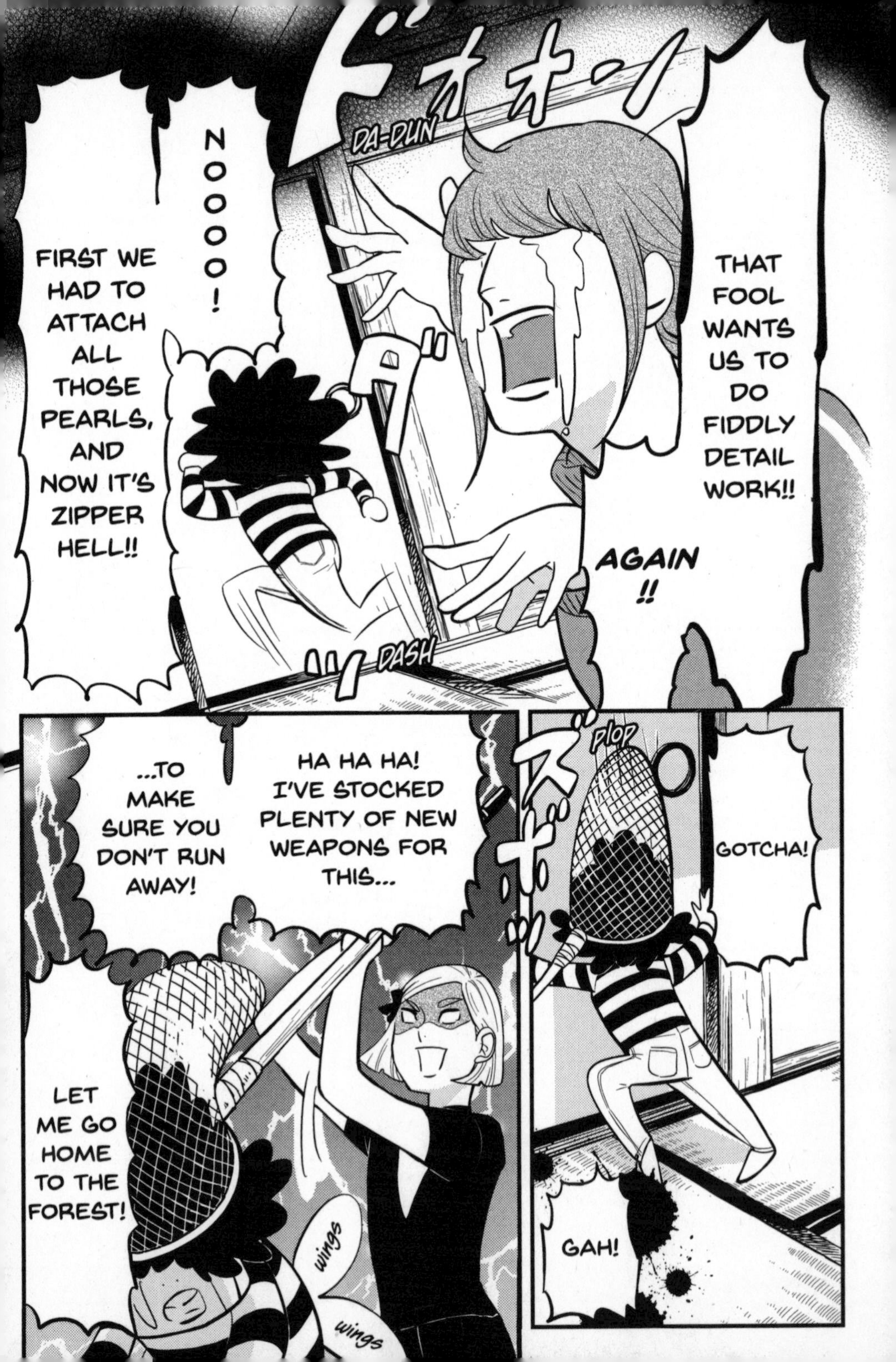

DA-DUN
THAT FOOL WANTS US TO DO FIDDLY DETAIL WORK!!
AGAIN!!
NOOOOO!
FIRST WE HAD TO ATTACH ALL THOSE PEARLS, AND NOW IT'S ZIPPER HELL!!
DASH
plop
GOTCHA!
GAH!
HA HA HA! I'VE STOCKED PLENTY OF NEW WEAPONS FOR THIS...
...TO MAKE SURE YOU DON'T RUN AWAY!
LET ME GO HOME TO THE FOREST!
wings
wings

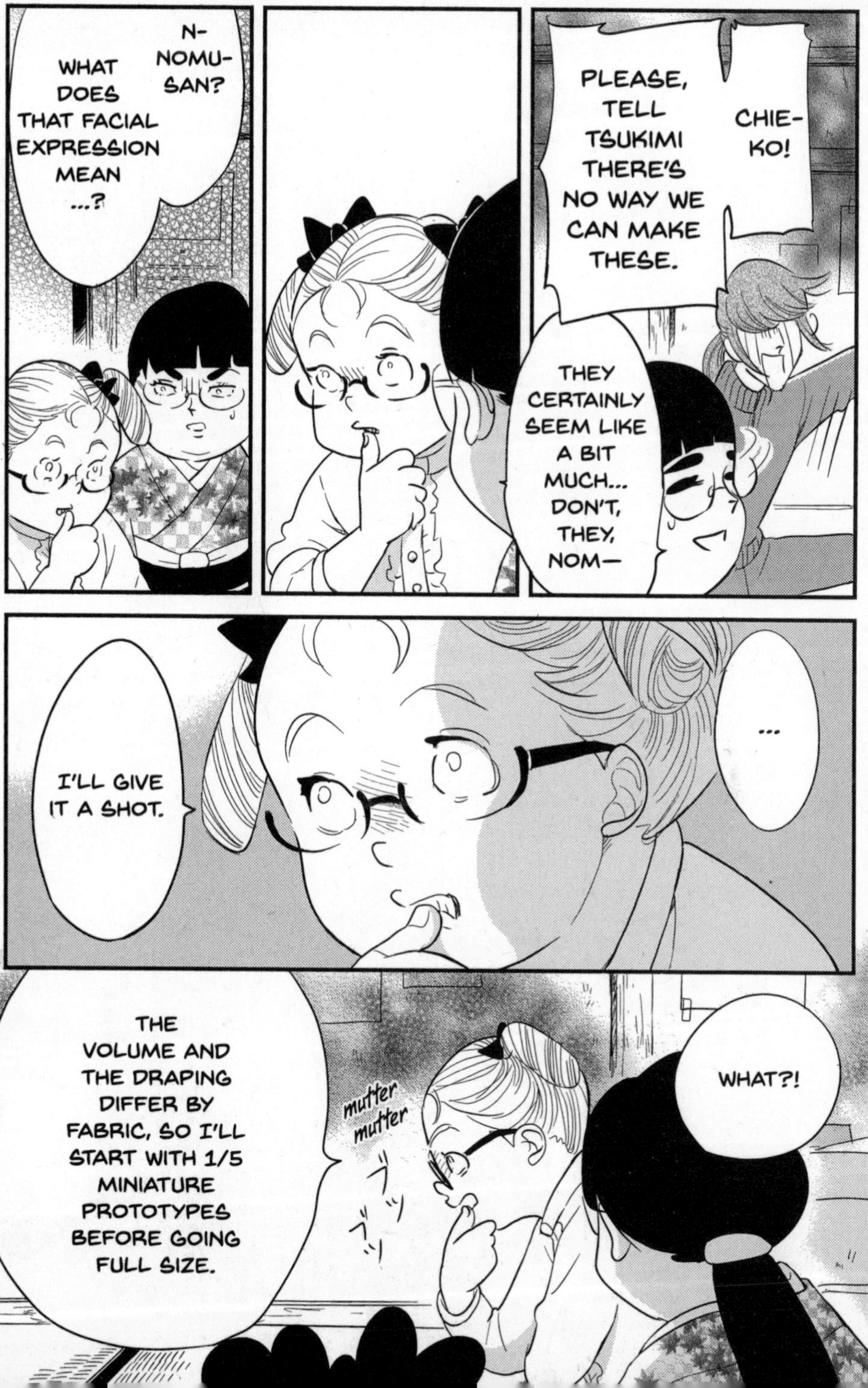
CHIE-KO!
PLEASE, TELL TSUKIMI THERE'S NO WAY WE CAN MAKE THESE.
THEY CERTAINLY SEEM LIKE A BIT MUCH... DON'T, THEY, NOM—
N-NOMU-SAN?
WHAT DOES THAT FACIAL EXPRESSION MEAN ...?
...
I'LL GIVE IT A SHOT.
WHAT?!
mutter mutter
THE VOLUME AND THE DRAPING DIFFER BY FABRIC, SO I'LL START WITH 1/5 MINIATURE PROTOTYPES BEFORE GOING FULL SIZE.

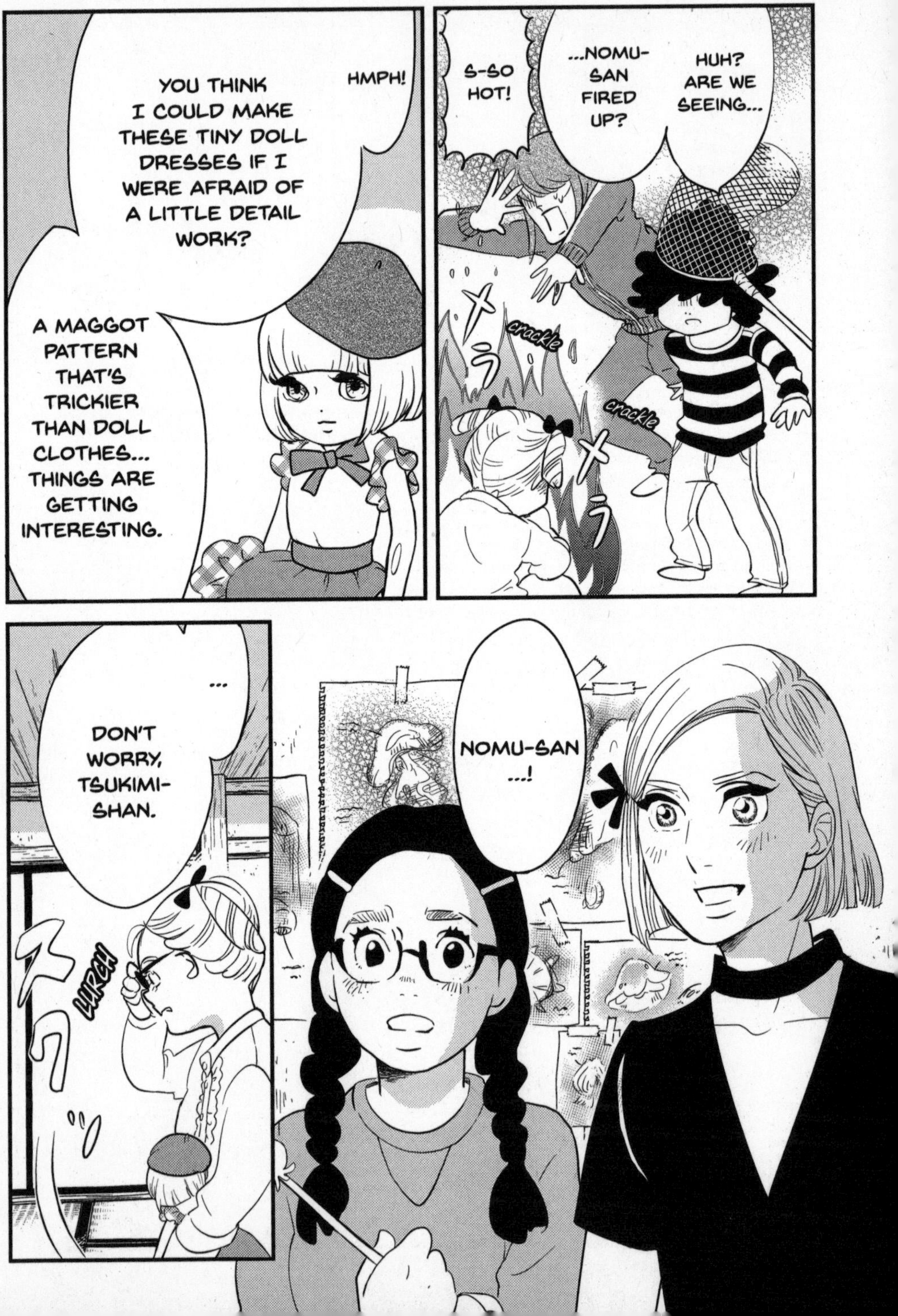
HUH? ARE WE SEEING...
...NOMU-SAN FIRED UP?
S-SO HOT!
crackle
crackle
HMPH!
YOU THINK I COULD MAKE THESE TINY DOLL DRESSES IF I WERE AFRAID OF A LITTLE DETAIL WORK?
A MAGGOT PATTERN THAT'S TRICKIER THAN DOLL CLOTHES... THINGS ARE GETTING INTERESTING.
NOMU-SAN ...!
...
DON'T WORRY, TSUKIMI-SHAN.
LURCH

SORRY, NOMU-SAN, BUT THAT WORDING IS ALL KINDS OF WRONG... COULD YOU PUT IT DIFFERENTLY?

I'LL HAVE ALL YOUR PERVY MAGGOT PATTERNS DONE IN 24 HOURS.

shff

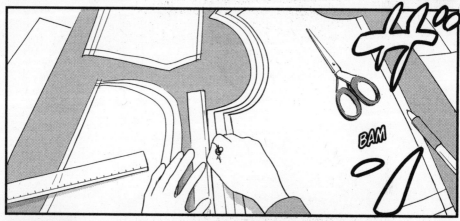

BAM

Mom...

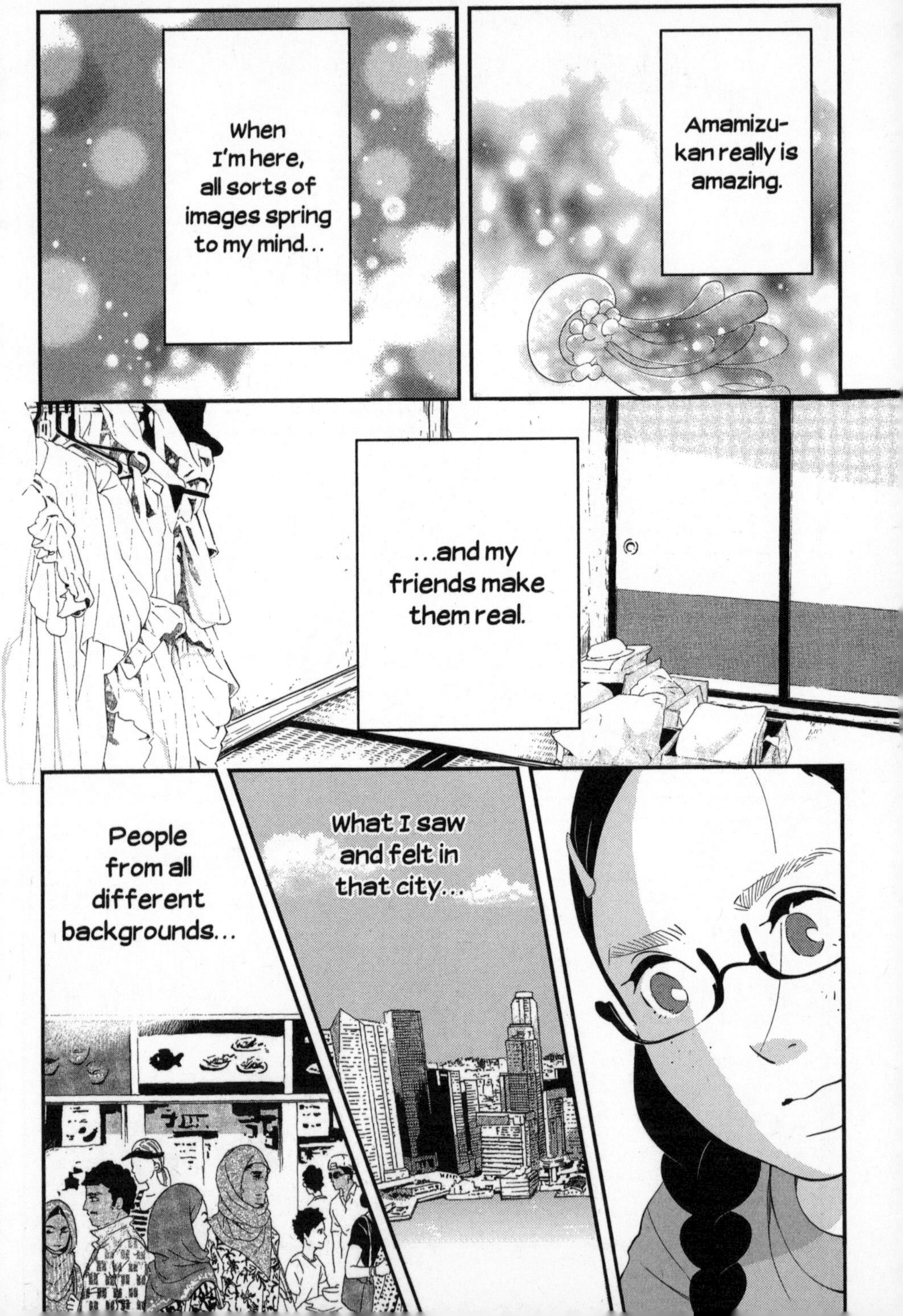
Amamizu-kan really is amazing.
When I'm here, all sorts of images spring to my mind...
...and my friends make them real.
What I saw and felt in that city...
People from all different backgrounds...

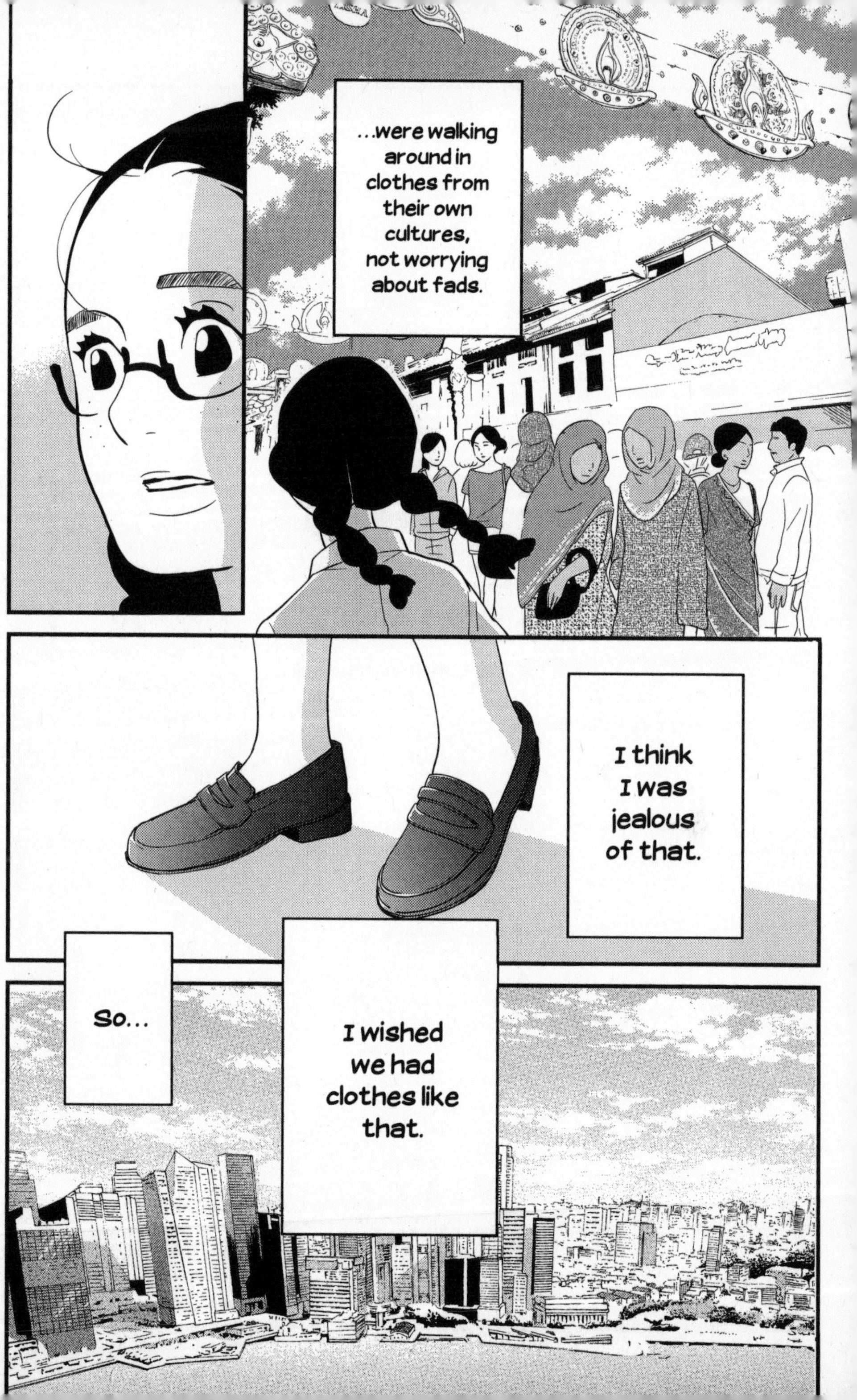
...were walking around in clothes from their own cultures, not worrying about fads.
I think I was jealous of that.
So...
I wished we had clothes like that.

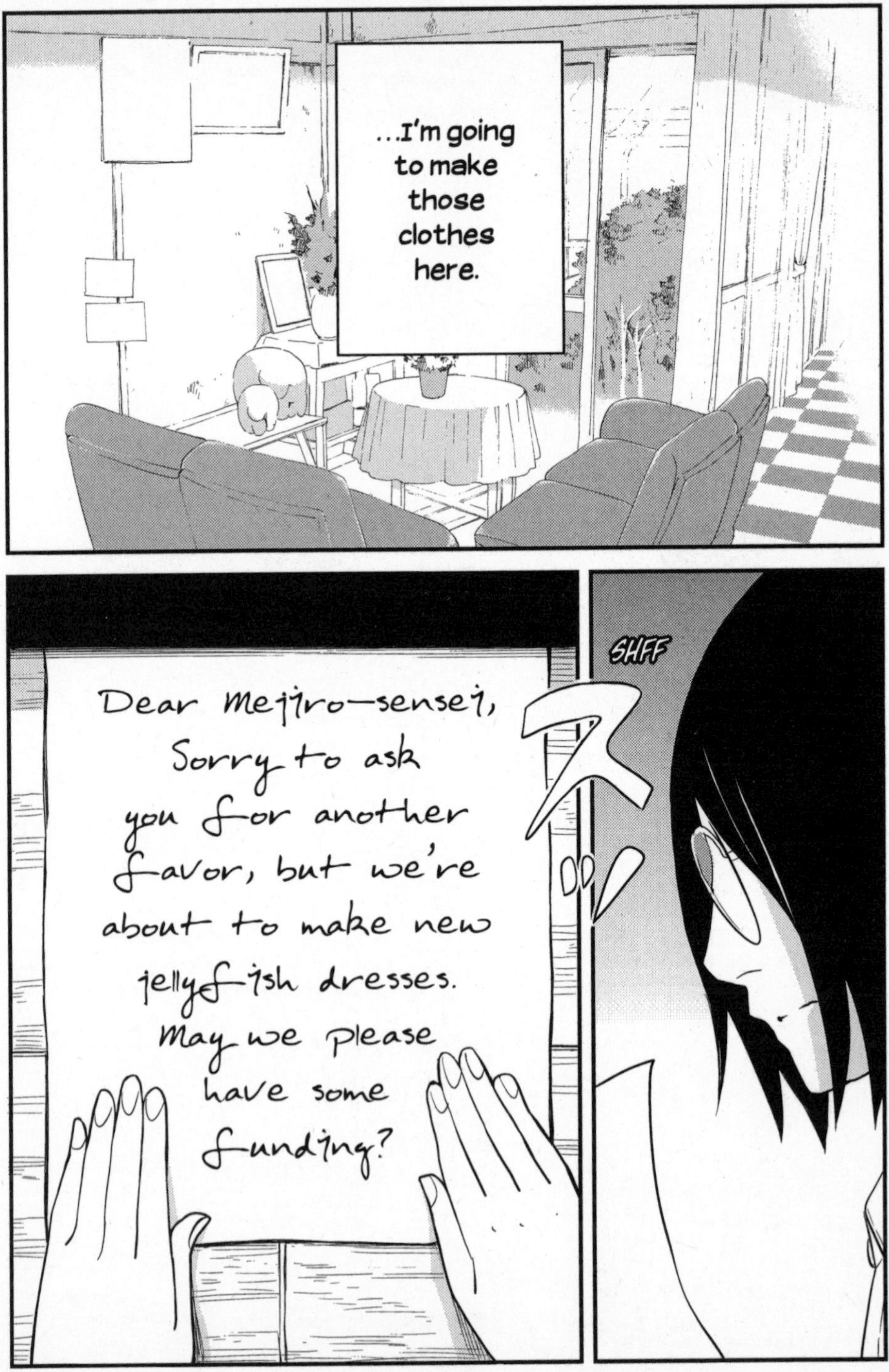
...I'm going to make those clothes here.
SHFF
ス
Dear Mejiro-sensei,
Sorry to ask you for another favor, but we're about to make new jellyfish dresses.
May we please have some funding?

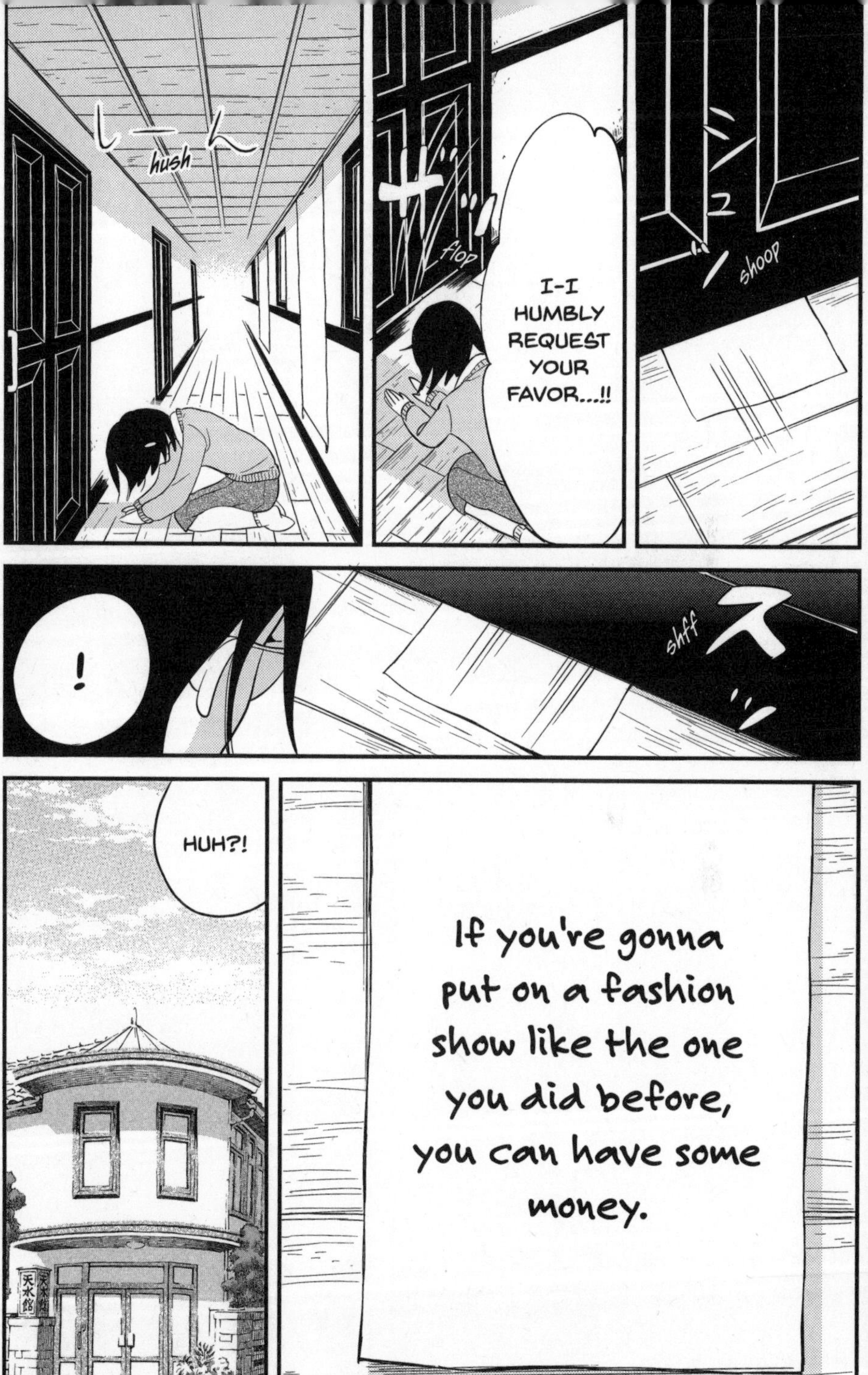

shoop
flop
I-I HUMBLY REQUEST YOUR FAVOR...!!
hush
shff
!
If you're gonna put on a fashion show like the one you did before, you can have some money.
HUH?!
天水館

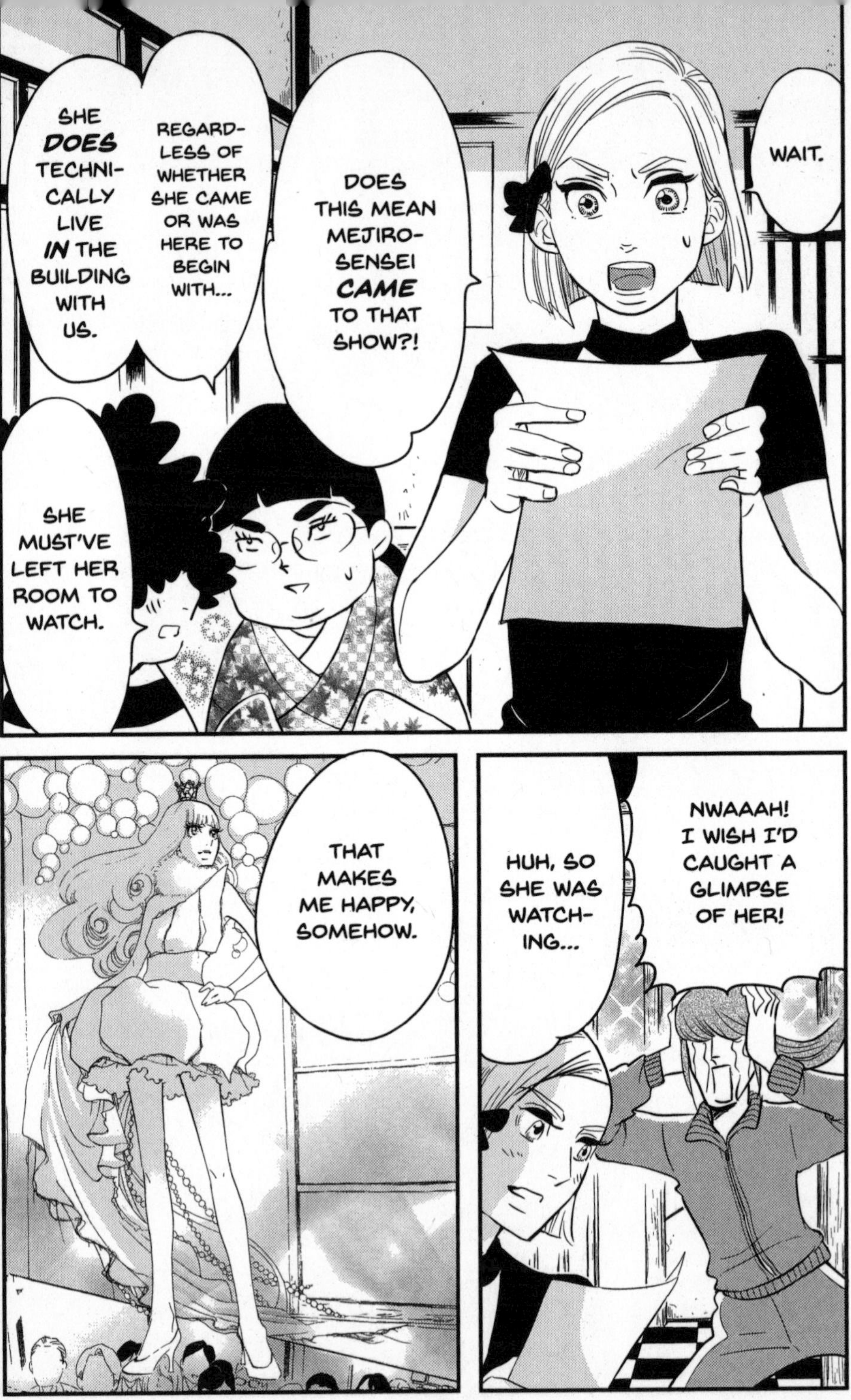
WAIT.
DOES THIS MEAN MEJIRO-SENSEI **CAME** TO THAT SHOW?!
REGARDLESS OF WHETHER SHE CAME OR WAS HERE TO BEGIN WITH...
SHE **DOES** TECHNICALLY LIVE **IN** THE BUILDING WITH US.
SHE MUST'VE LEFT HER ROOM TO WATCH.
NWAAAH! I WISH I'D CAUGHT A GLIMPSE OF HER!
HUH, SO SHE WAS WATCHING...
THAT MAKES ME HAPPY, SOMEHOW.

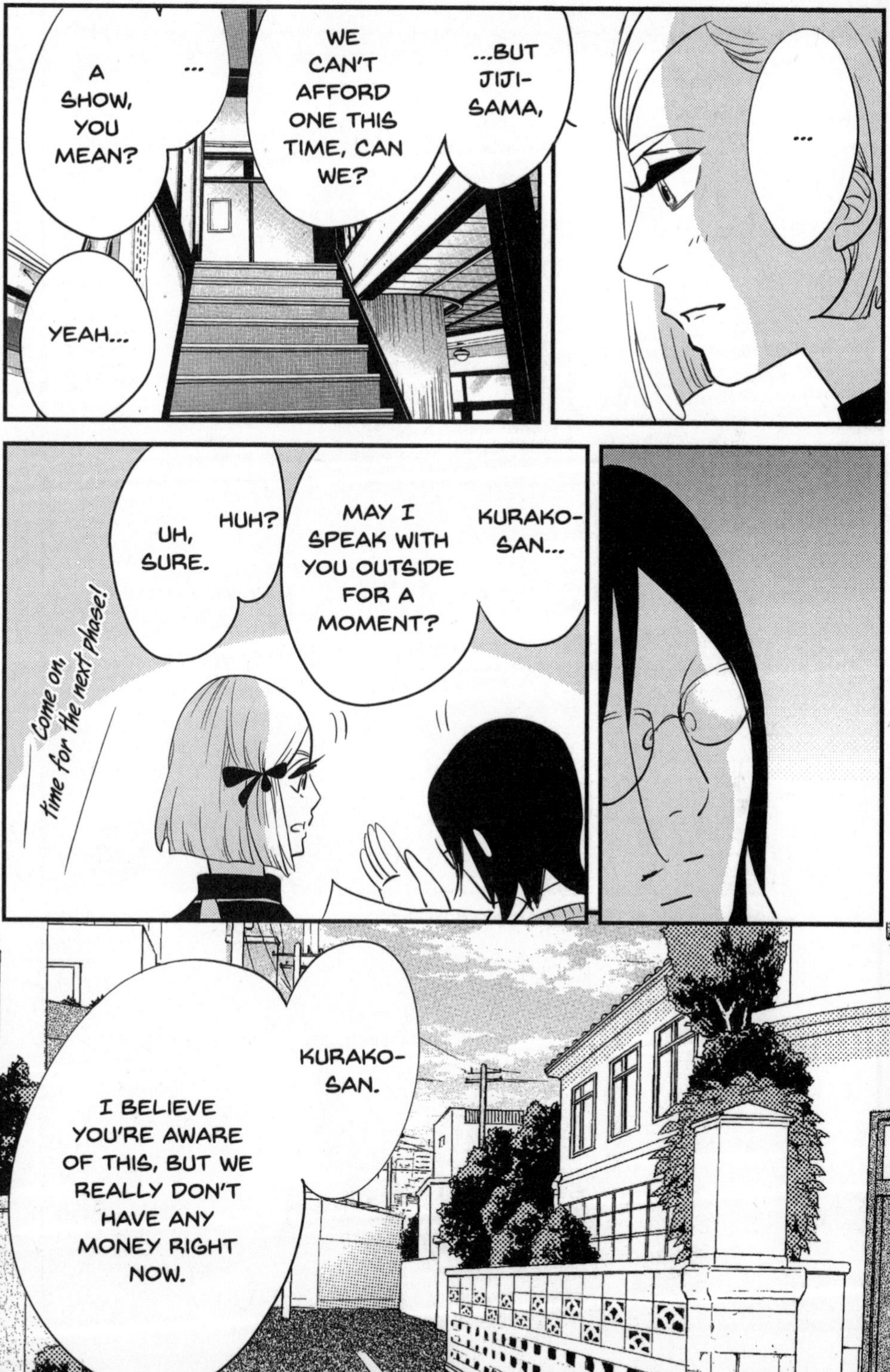
...
...BUT JIJI-SAMA,
WE CAN'T AFFORD ONE THIS TIME, CAN WE?
...
A SHOW, YOU MEAN?
YEAH...
KURAKO-SAN...
MAY I SPEAK WITH YOU OUTSIDE FOR A MOMENT?
HUH?
UH, SURE.
Come on, time for the next phase!
KURAKO-SAN.
I BELIEVE YOU'RE AWARE OF THIS, BUT WE REALLY DON'T HAVE ANY MONEY RIGHT NOW.

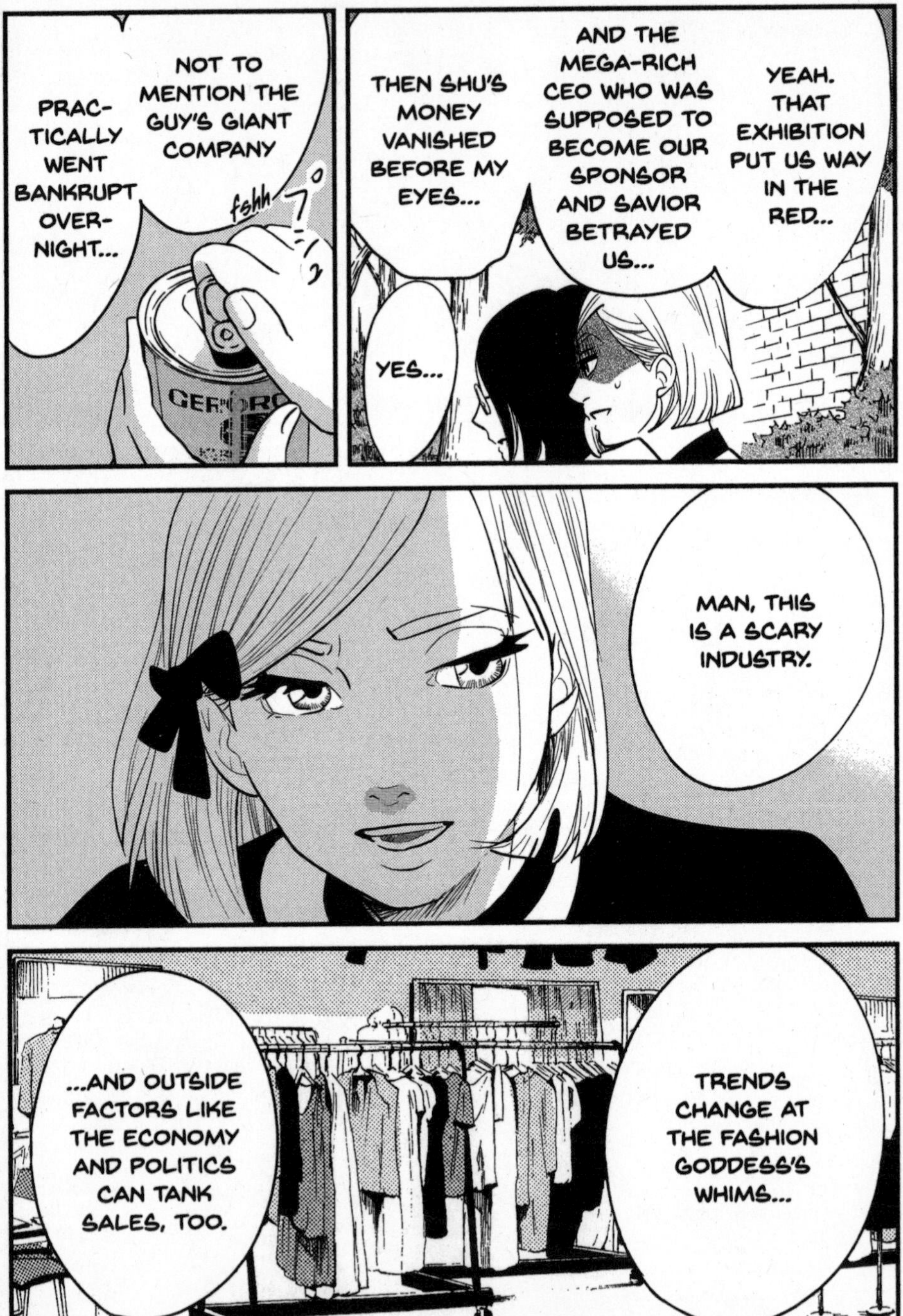
YEAH. THAT EXHIBITION PUT US WAY IN THE RED...
AND THE MEGA-RICH CEO WHO WAS SUPPOSED TO BECOME OUR SPONSOR AND SAVIOR BETRAYED US...
THEN SHU'S MONEY VANISHED BEFORE MY EYES...
YES...
NOT TO MENTION THE GUY'S GIANT COMPANY
PRAC-TICALLY WENT BANKRUPT OVER-NIGHT...
fshh
MAN, THIS IS A SCARY INDUSTRY.
TRENDS CHANGE AT THE FASHION GODDESS'S WHIMS...
...AND OUTSIDE FACTORS LIKE THE ECONOMY AND POLITICS CAN TANK SALES, TOO.

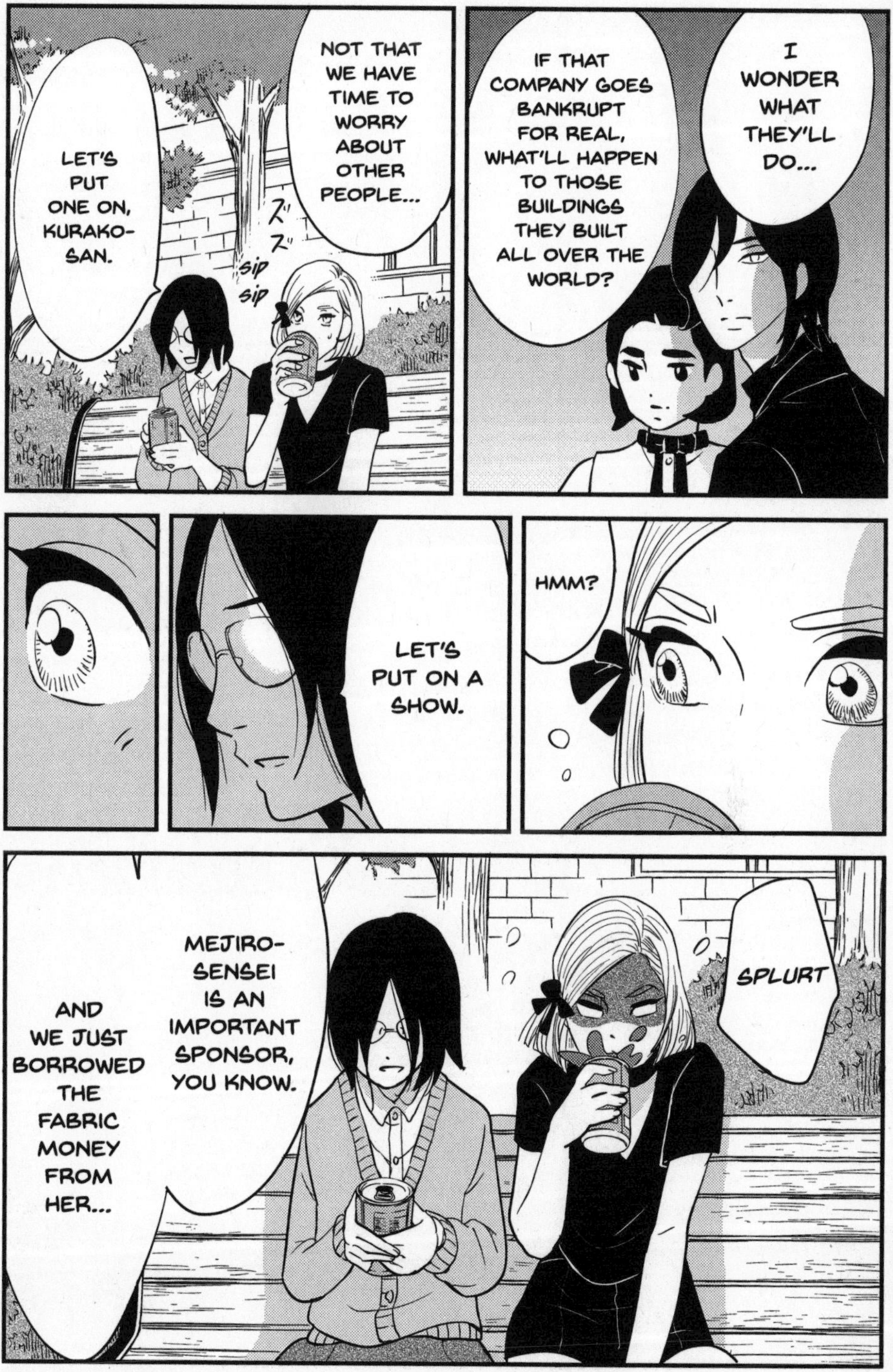
I WONDER WHAT THEY'LL DO...
IF THAT COMPANY GOES BANKRUPT FOR REAL, WHAT'LL HAPPEN TO THOSE BUILDINGS THEY BUILT ALL OVER THE WORLD?
NOT THAT WE HAVE TIME TO WORRY ABOUT OTHER PEOPLE...
ズズ
sip sip
LET'S PUT ONE ON, KURAKO-SAN.
HMM?
LET'S PUT ON A SHOW.
SPLURT
MEJIRO-SENSEI IS AN IMPORTANT SPONSOR, YOU KNOW.
AND WE JUST BORROWED THE FABRIC MONEY FROM HER...

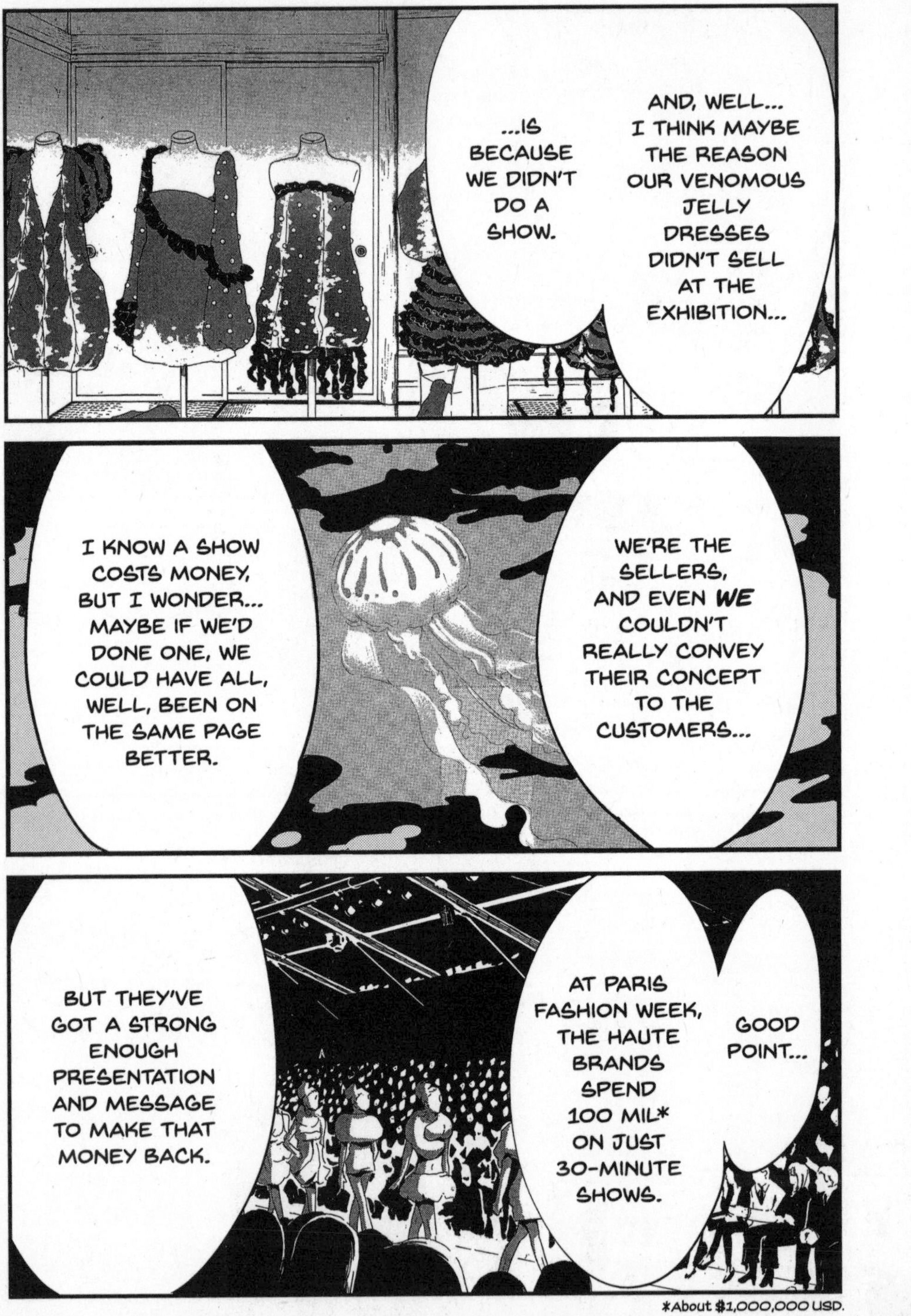
AND, WELL... I THINK MAYBE THE REASON OUR VENOMOUS JELLY DRESSES DIDN'T SELL AT THE EXHIBITION...
...IS BECAUSE WE DIDN'T DO A SHOW.
WE'RE THE SELLERS, AND EVEN *WE* COULDN'T REALLY CONVEY THEIR CONCEPT TO THE CUSTOMERS...
I KNOW A SHOW COSTS MONEY, BUT I WONDER... MAYBE IF WE'D DONE ONE, WE COULD HAVE ALL, WELL, BEEN ON THE SAME PAGE BETTER.
GOOD POINT...
AT PARIS FASHION WEEK, THE HAUTE BRANDS SPEND 100 MIL* ON JUST 30-MINUTE SHOWS.
BUT THEY'VE GOT A STRONG ENOUGH PRESENTATION AND MESSAGE TO MAKE THAT MONEY BACK.

*About $1,000,000 USD.

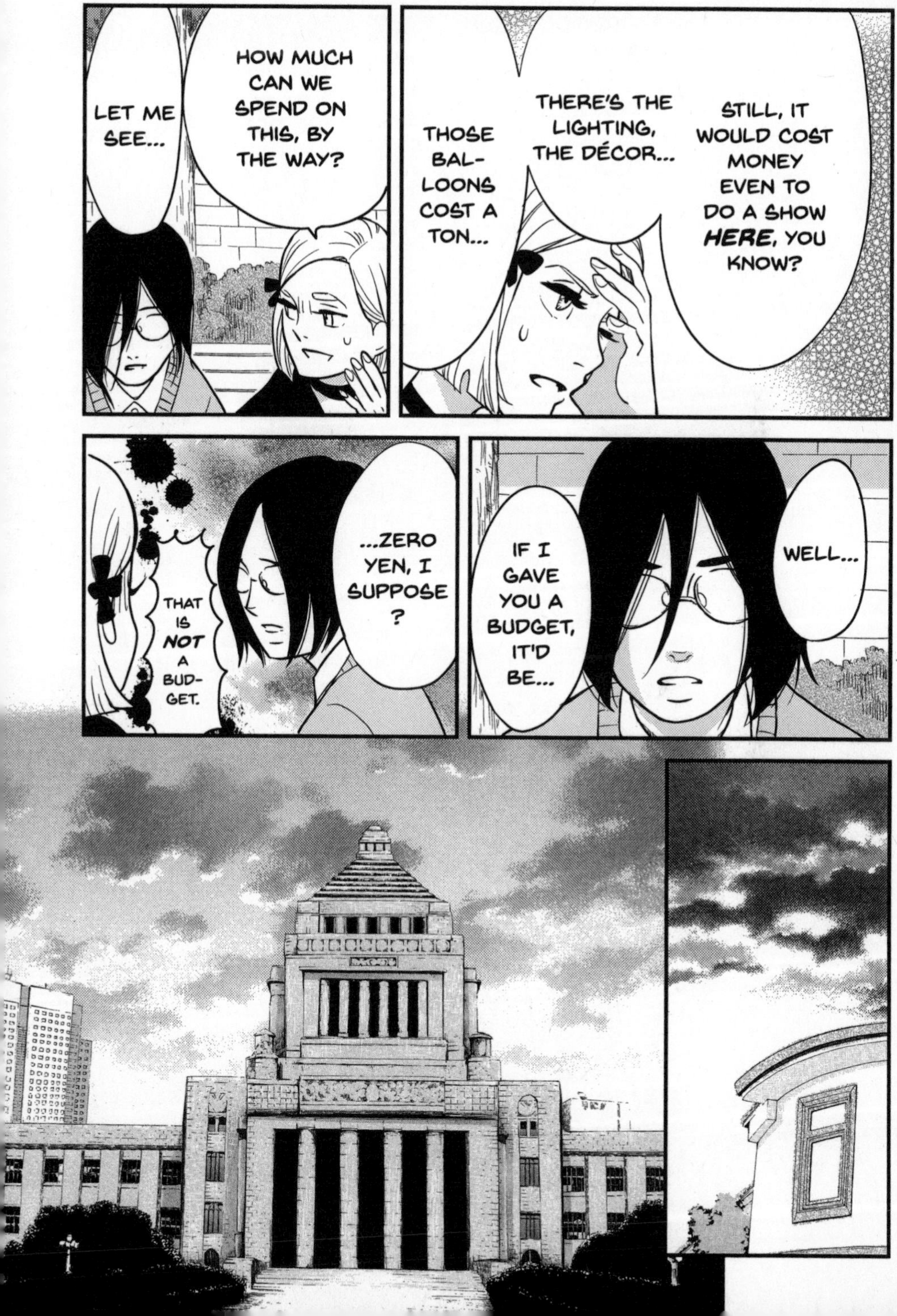
STILL, IT WOULD COST MONEY EVEN TO DO A SHOW **HERE**, YOU KNOW?
THERE'S THE LIGHTING, THE DÉCOR...
THOSE BAL-LOONS COST A TON...
HOW MUCH CAN WE SPEND ON THIS, BY THE WAY?
LET ME SEE...
WELL...
IF I GAVE YOU A BUDGET, IT'D BE...
...ZERO YEN, I SUPPOSE?
THAT IS **NOT** A BUD-GET.

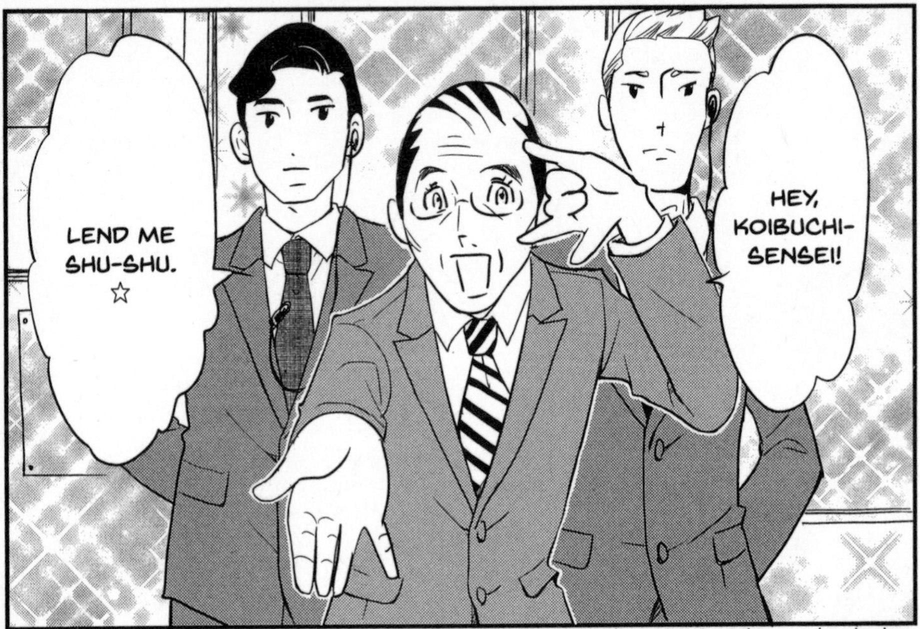
HEY, KOIBUCHI-SENSEI!
LEND ME SHU-SHU. ☆

*MEXT = the Ministry of Education, Culture, Sports, Science and Technology.

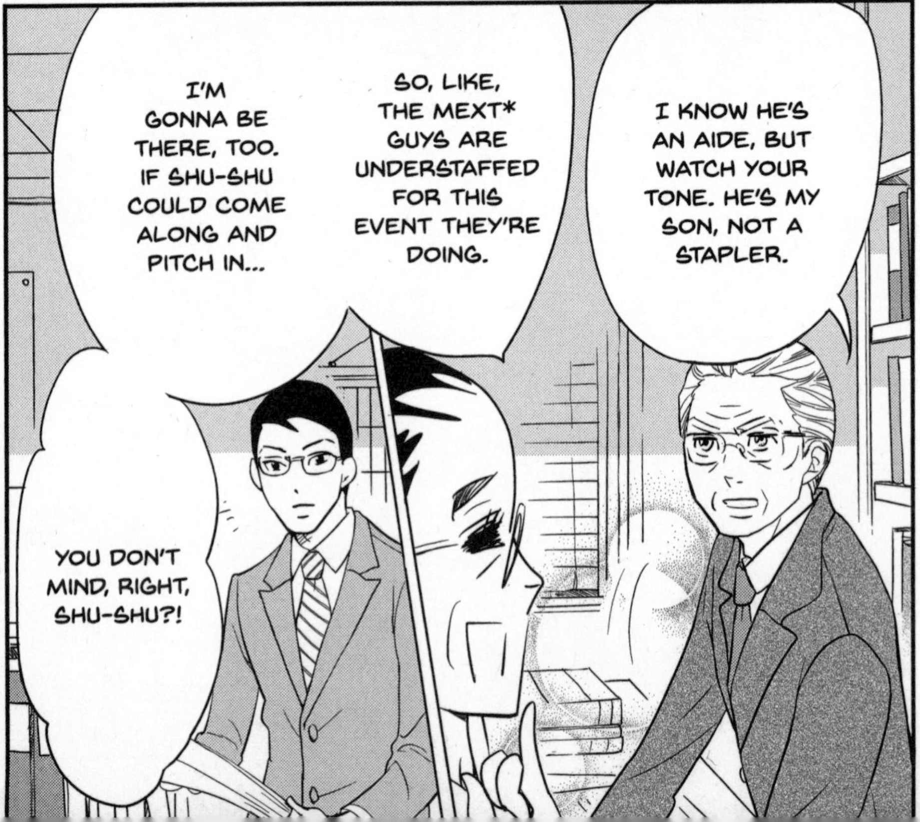
I KNOW HE'S AN AIDE, BUT WATCH YOUR TONE. HE'S MY SON, NOT A STAPLER.
SO, LIKE, THE MEXT* GUYS ARE UNDERSTAFFED FOR THIS EVENT THEY'RE DOING.
I'M GONNA BE THERE, TOO. IF SHU-SHU COULD COME ALONG AND PITCH IN...
YOU DON'T MIND, RIGHT, SHU-SHU?!

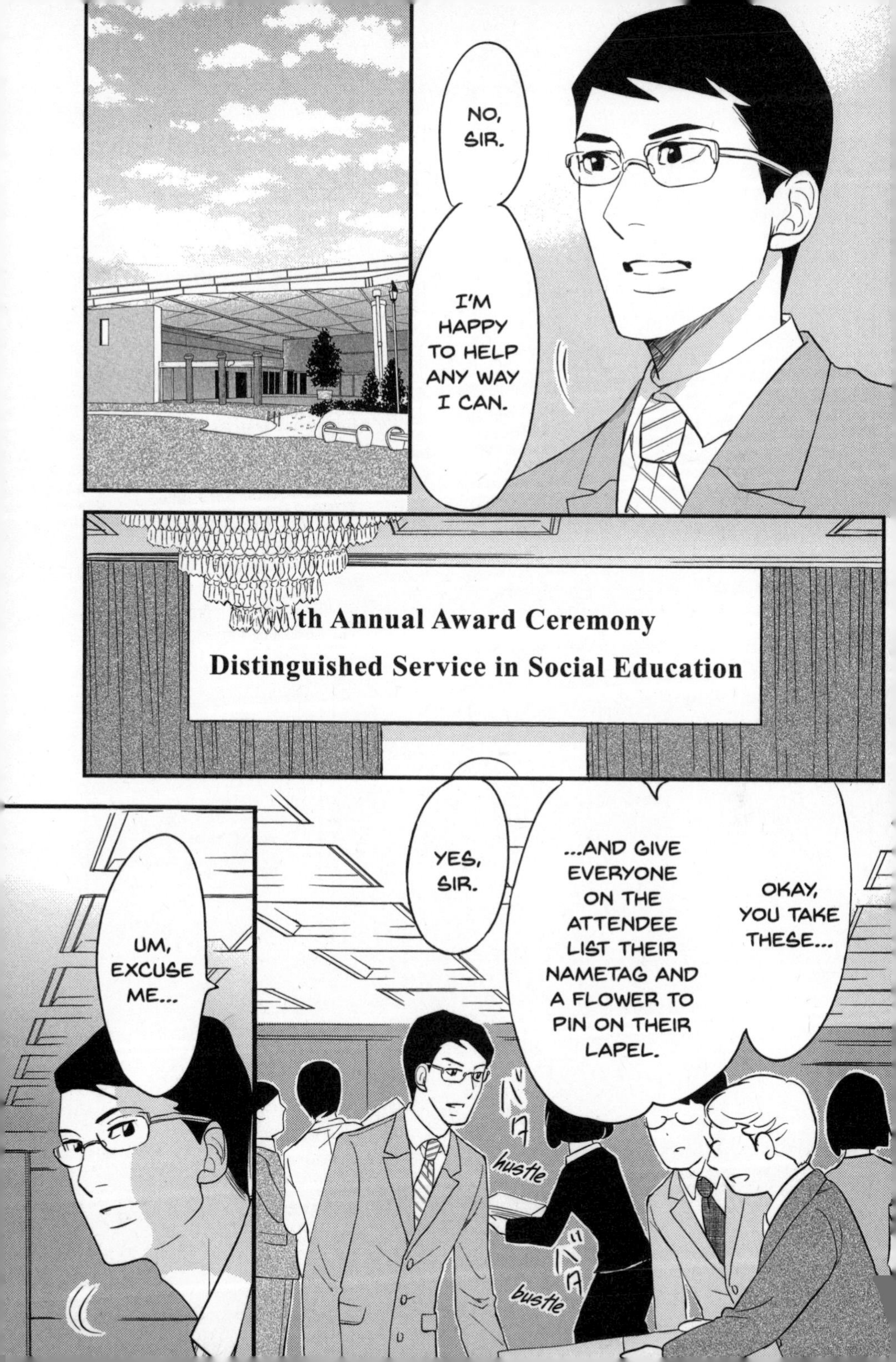
NO, SIR.
I'M HAPPY TO HELP ANY WAY I CAN.
th Annual Award Ceremony
Distinguished Service in Social Education
OKAY, YOU TAKE THESE...
...AND GIVE EVERYONE ON THE ATTENDEE LIST THEIR NAMETAG AND A FLOWER TO PIN ON THEIR LAPEL.
YES, SIR.
hustle
bustle
UM, EXCUSE ME...

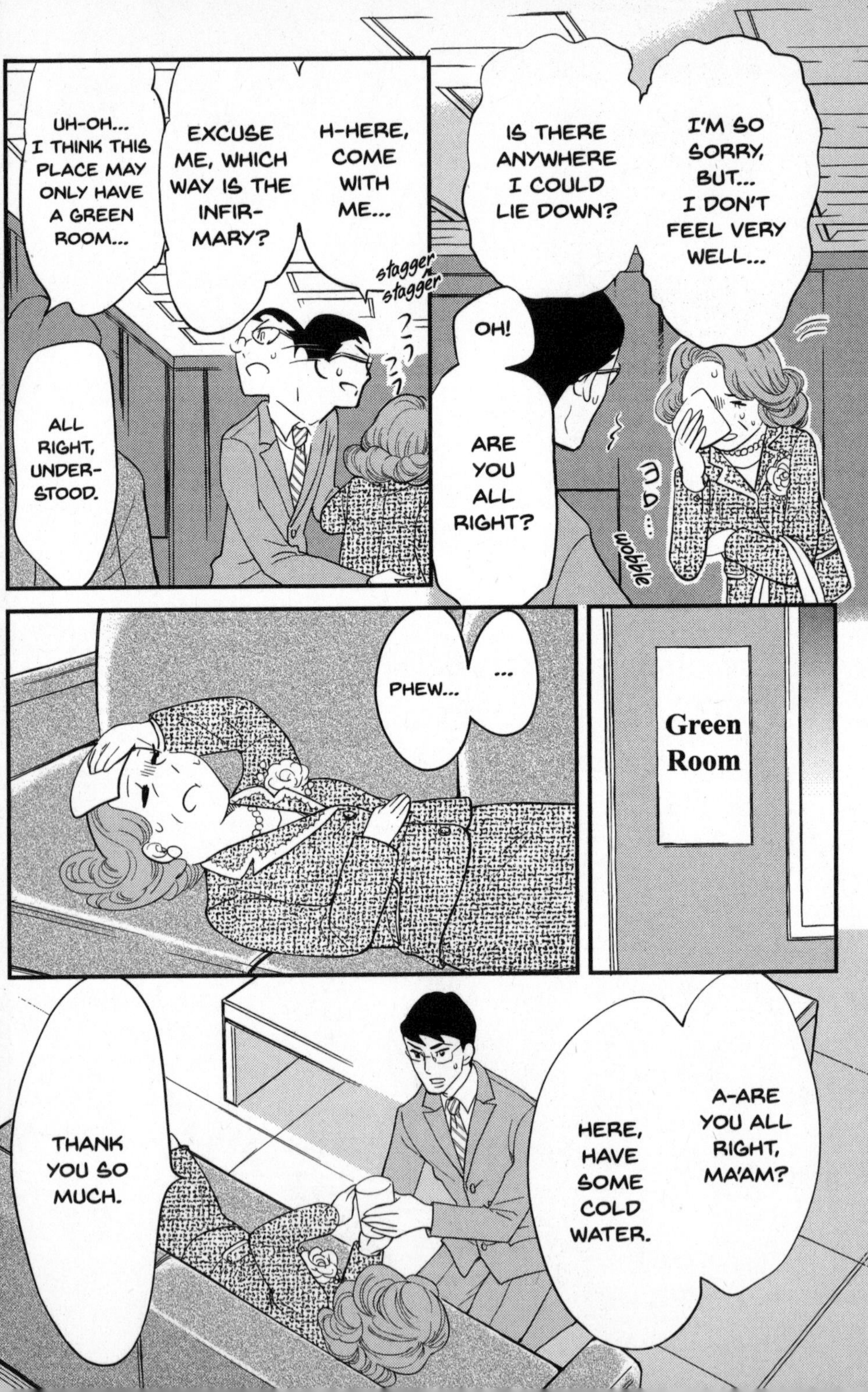
I'M SO SORRY, BUT... I DON'T FEEL VERY WELL...
IS THERE ANYWHERE I COULD LIE DOWN?
OH!
ARE YOU ALL RIGHT?
wobble
H-HERE, COME WITH ME...
EXCUSE ME, WHICH WAY IS THE INFIR-MARY?
stagger stagger
UH-OH... I THINK THIS PLACE MAY ONLY HAVE A GREEN ROOM...
ALL RIGHT, UNDER-STOOD.
Green Room
...
PHEW...
A-ARE YOU ALL RIGHT, MA'AM?
HERE, HAVE SOME COLD WATER.
THANK YOU SO MUCH.

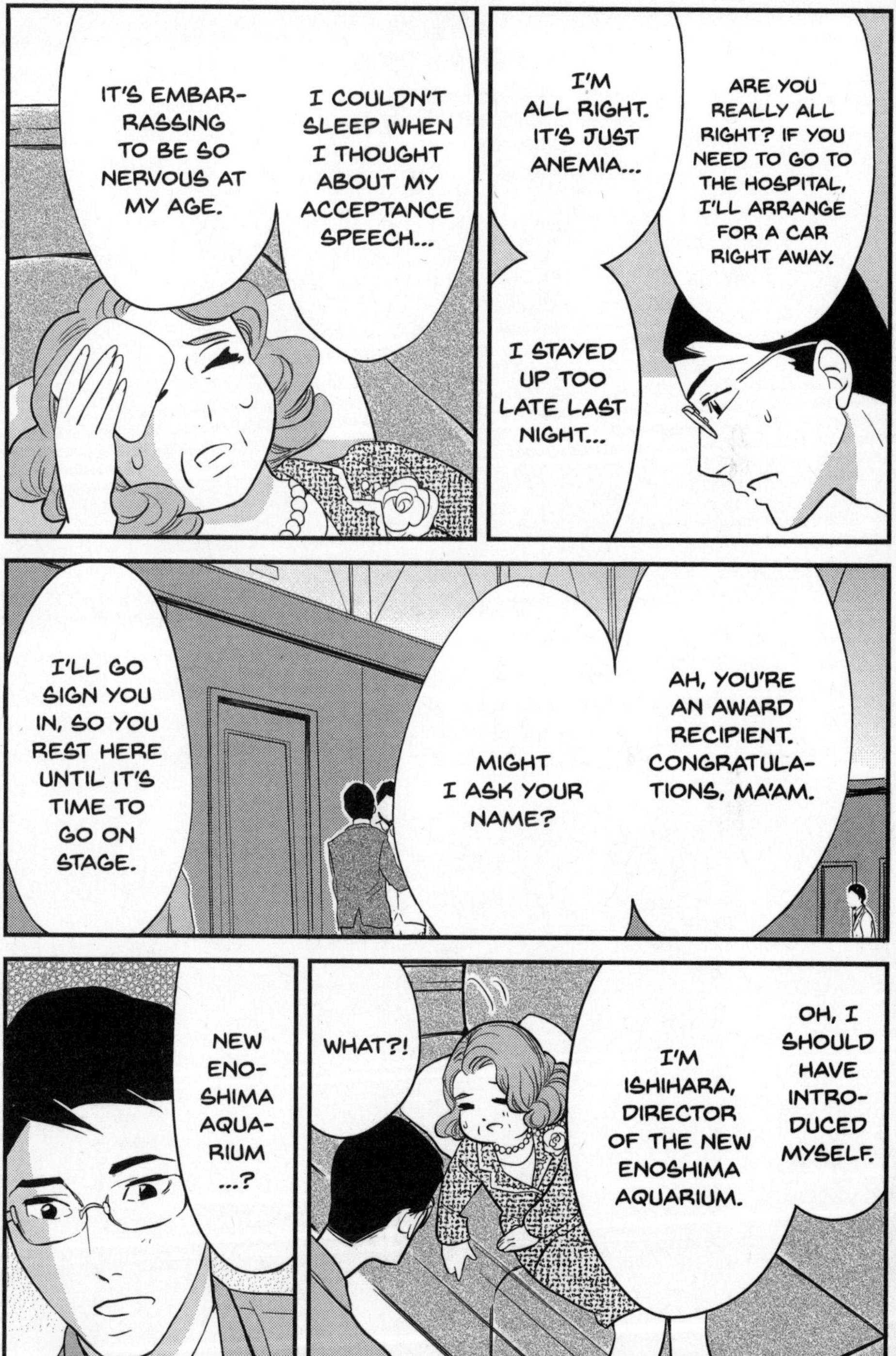
ARE YOU REALLY ALL RIGHT? IF YOU NEED TO GO TO THE HOSPITAL, I'LL ARRANGE FOR A CAR RIGHT AWAY.
I'M ALL RIGHT. IT'S JUST ANEMIA...
I STAYED UP TOO LATE LAST NIGHT...
I COULDN'T SLEEP WHEN I THOUGHT ABOUT MY ACCEPTANCE SPEECH...
IT'S EMBARRASSING TO BE SO NERVOUS AT MY AGE.
AH, YOU'RE AN AWARD RECIPIENT. CONGRATULATIONS, MA'AM.
MIGHT I ASK YOUR NAME?
I'LL GO SIGN YOU IN, SO YOU REST HERE UNTIL IT'S TIME TO GO ON STAGE.
OH, I SHOULD HAVE INTRODUCED MYSELF.
I'M ISHIHARA, DIRECTOR OF THE NEW ENOSHIMA AQUARIUM.
WHAT?!
NEW ENOSHIMA AQUARIUM ...?

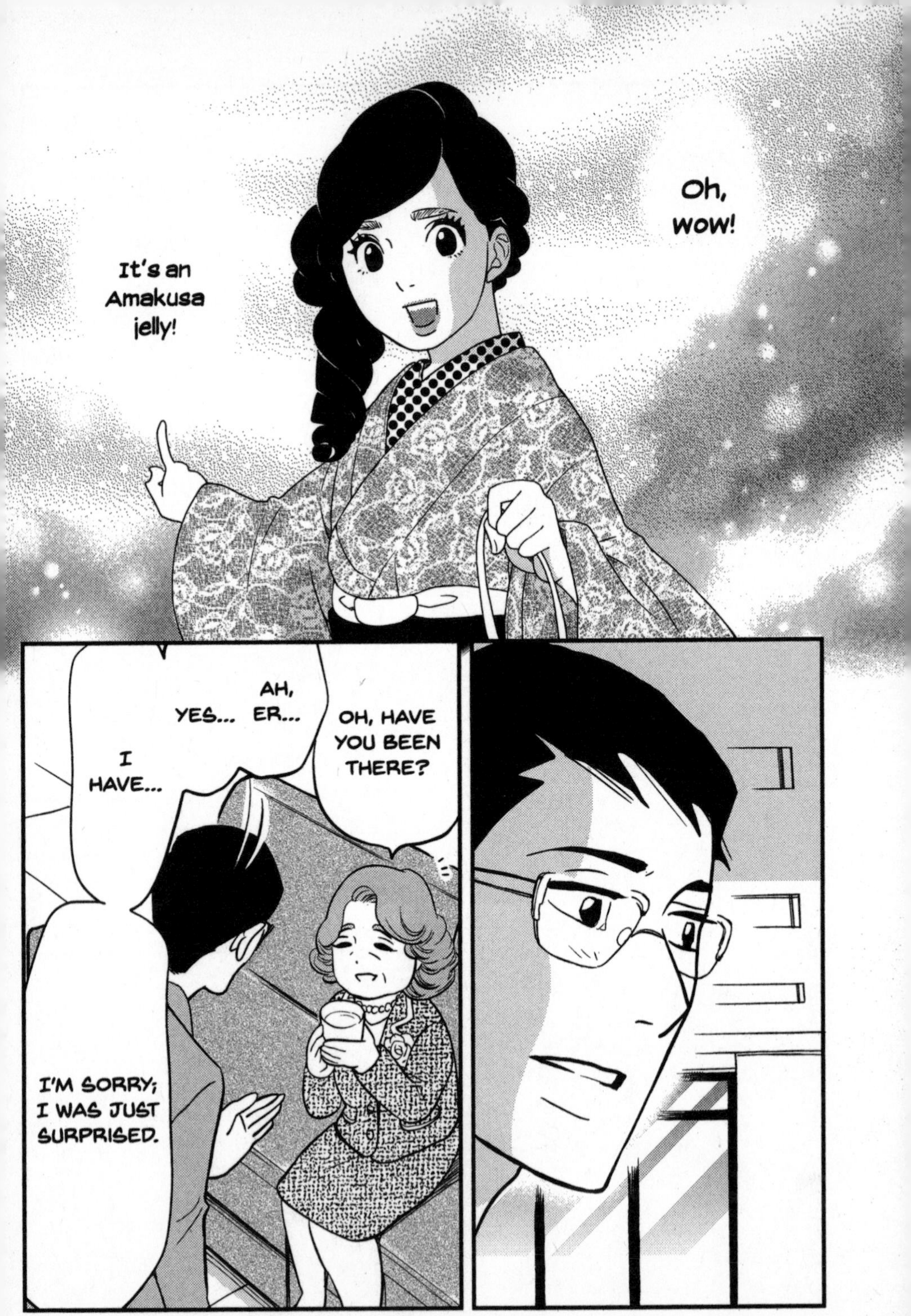
Oh, wow!
It's an Amakusa jelly!
OH, HAVE YOU BEEN THERE?
AH, YES... ER...
I HAVE...
I'M SORRY; I WAS JUST SURPRISED.

hurry scurry

W-WELL, I'LL GO SIGN YOU IN.

I'M SORRY FOR THE TROUBLE...

Distinguished Service in Social Education Award
New Enoshima Aquarium
Masami Ishihara, Director

flip

THE DIRECTOR...

...

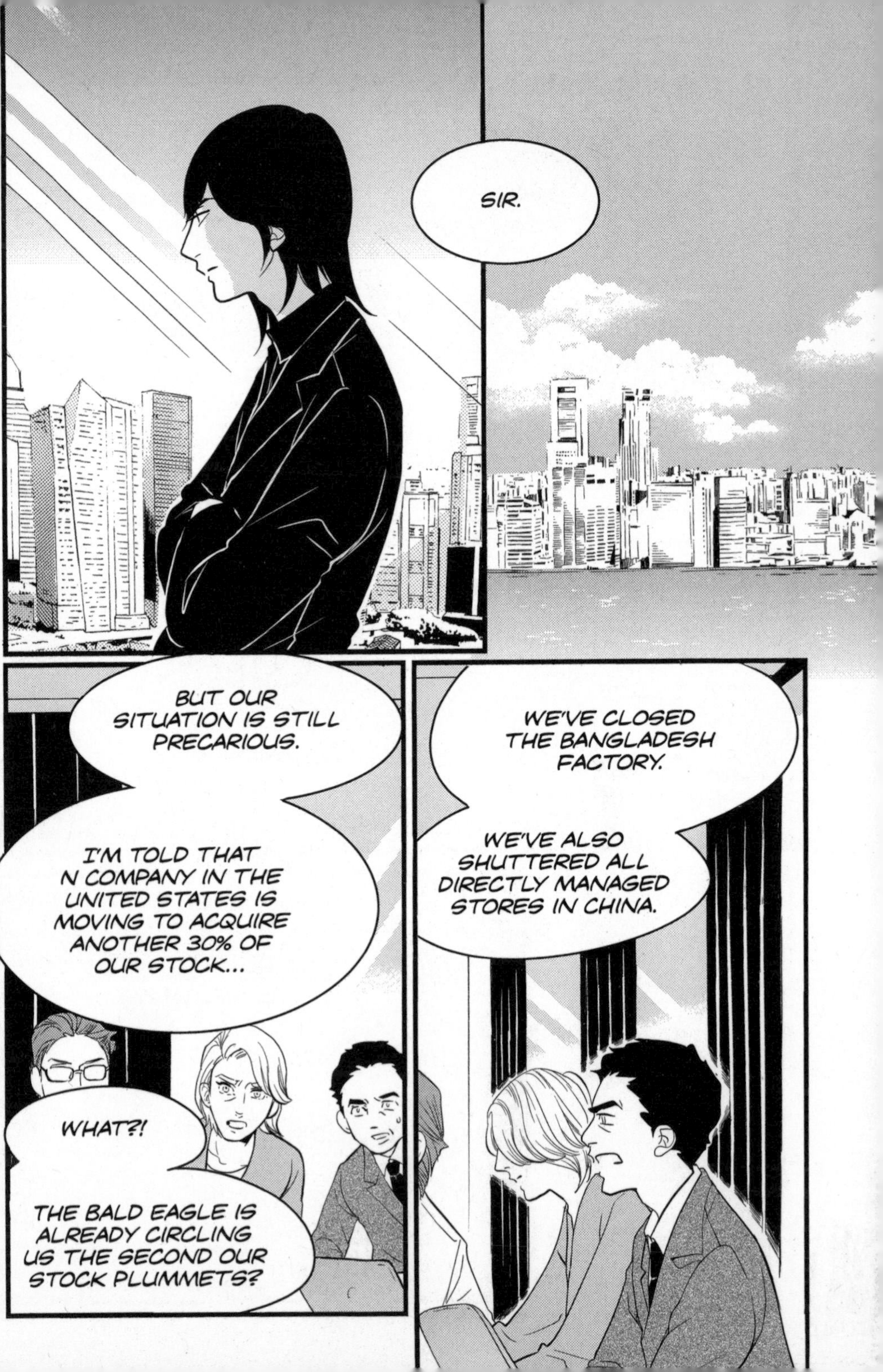
SIR.
WE'VE CLOSED THE BANGLADESH FACTORY.
WE'VE ALSO SHUTTERED ALL DIRECTLY MANAGED STORES IN CHINA.
BUT OUR SITUATION IS STILL PRECARIOUS.
I'M TOLD THAT N COMPANY IN THE UNITED STATES IS MOVING TO ACQUIRE ANOTHER 30% OF OUR STOCK...
WHAT?!
THE BALD EAGLE IS ALREADY CIRCLING US THE SECOND OUR STOCK PLUMMETS?

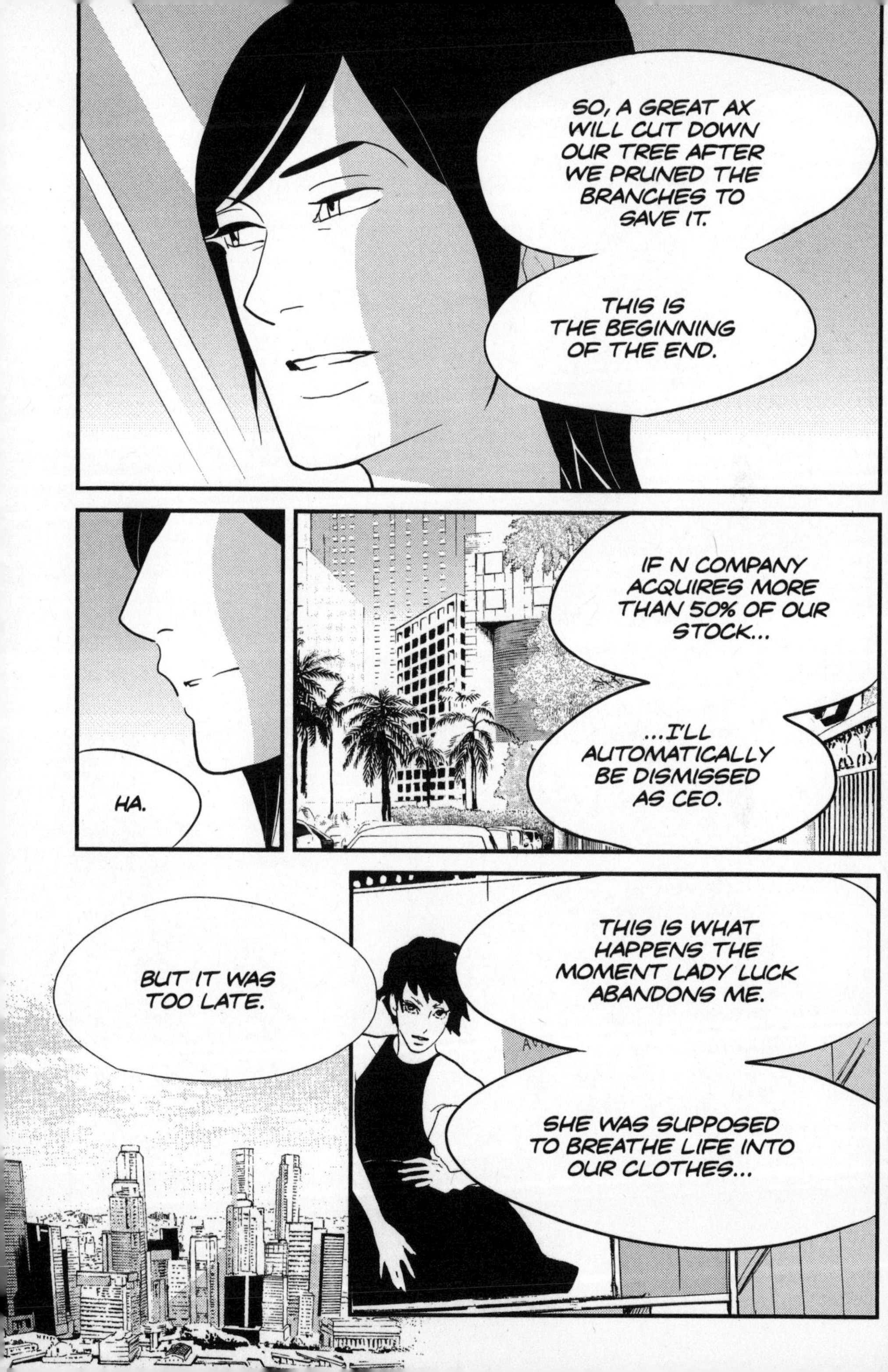
SO, A GREAT AX WILL CUT DOWN OUR TREE AFTER WE PRUNED THE BRANCHES TO SAVE IT.
THIS IS THE BEGINNING OF THE END.
IF N COMPANY ACQUIRES MORE THAN 50% OF OUR STOCK...
...I'LL AUTOMATICALLY BE DISMISSED AS CEO.
HA.
THIS IS WHAT HAPPENS THE MOMENT LADY LUCK ABANDONS ME.
SHE WAS SUPPOSED TO BREATHE LIFE INTO OUR CLOTHES...
BUT IT WAS TOO LATE.

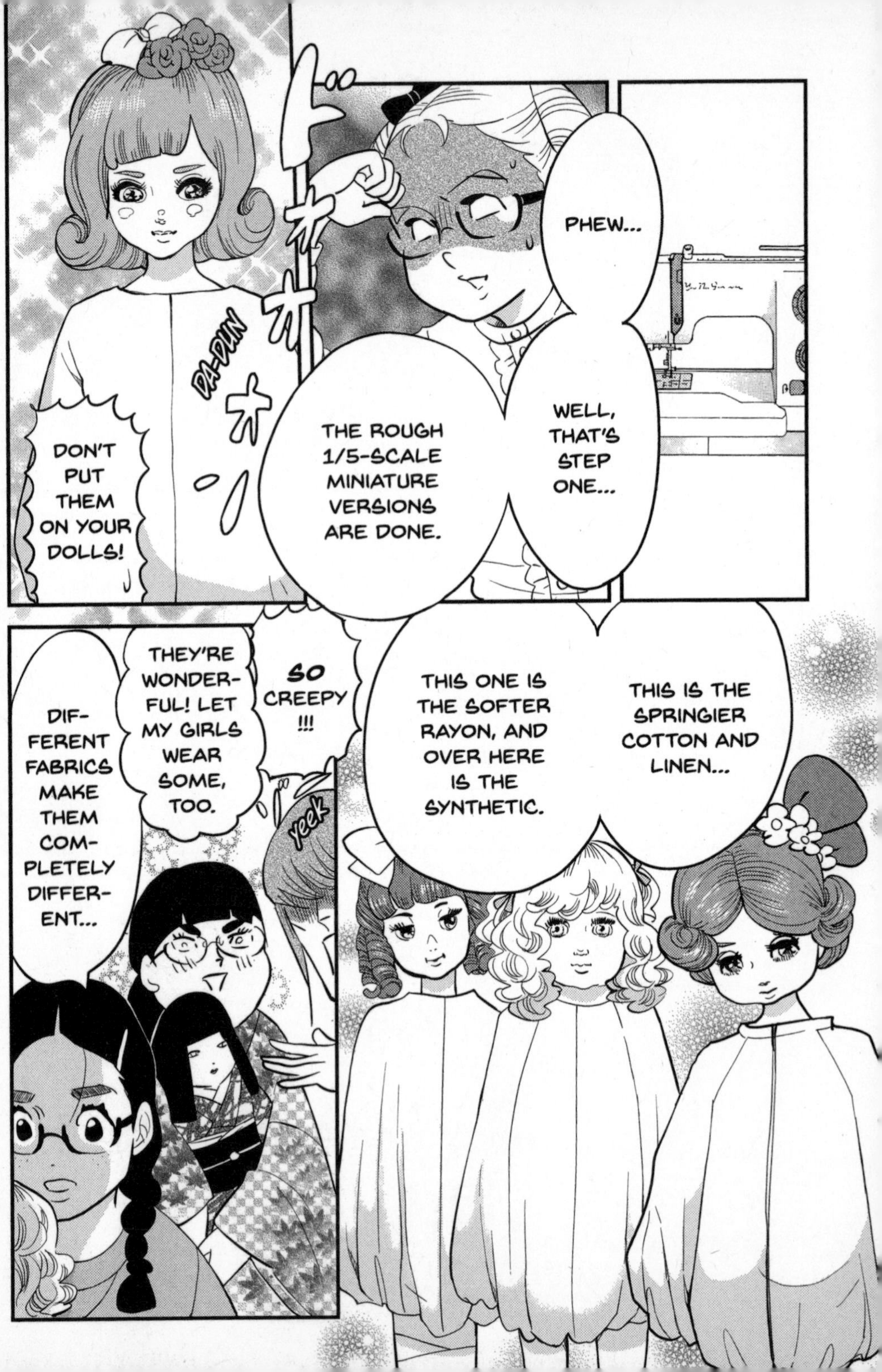

PHEW...
WELL, THAT'S STEP ONE...
THE ROUGH 1/5-SCALE MINIATURE VERSIONS ARE DONE.
DA-DUN
DON'T PUT THEM ON YOUR DOLLS!
THIS IS THE SPRINGIER COTTON AND LINEN...
THIS ONE IS THE SOFTER RAYON, AND OVER HERE IS THE SYNTHETIC.
SO CREEPY !!!
yeek
THEY'RE WONDER- FUL! LET MY GIRLS WEAR SOME, TOO.
DIF- FERENT FABRICS MAKE THEM COM- PLETELY DIFFER- ENT...

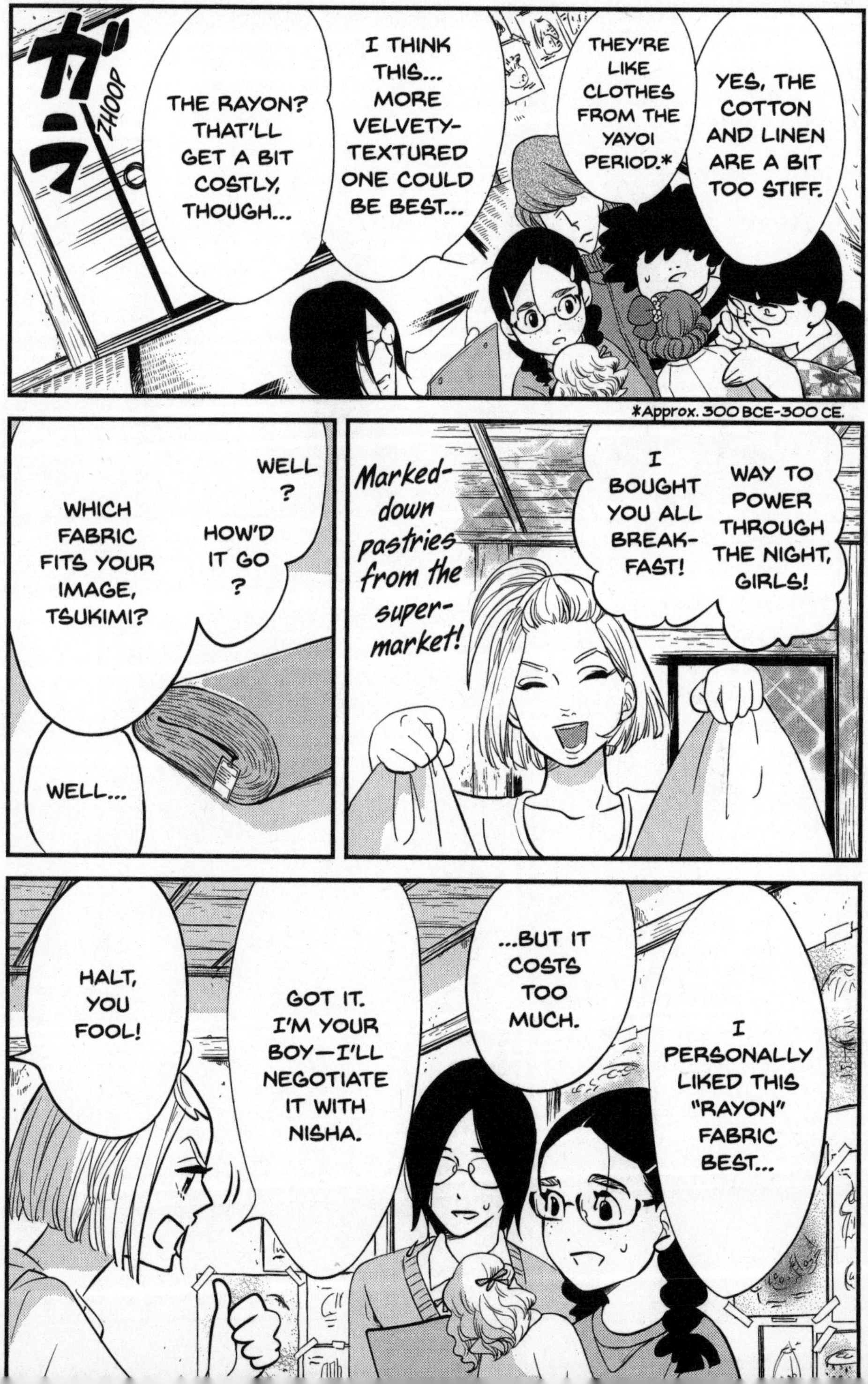
YES, THE COTTON AND LINEN ARE A BIT TOO STIFF.
THEY'RE LIKE CLOTHES FROM THE YAYOI PERIOD.*
I THINK THIS... MORE VELVETY-TEXTURED ONE COULD BE BEST...
THE RAYON? THAT'LL GET A BIT COSTLY, THOUGH...
ガラ ZHOOP
*Approx. 300 BCE-300 CE.
WAY TO POWER THROUGH THE NIGHT, GIRLS!
I BOUGHT YOU ALL BREAKFAST!
Marked-down pastries from the supermarket!
WELL?
HOW'D IT GO?
WHICH FABRIC FITS YOUR IMAGE, TSUKIMI?
WELL...
I PERSONALLY LIKED THIS "RAYON" FABRIC BEST...
...BUT IT COSTS TOO MUCH.
GOT IT. I'M YOUR BOY—I'LL NEGOTIATE IT WITH NISHA.
HALT, YOU FOOL!

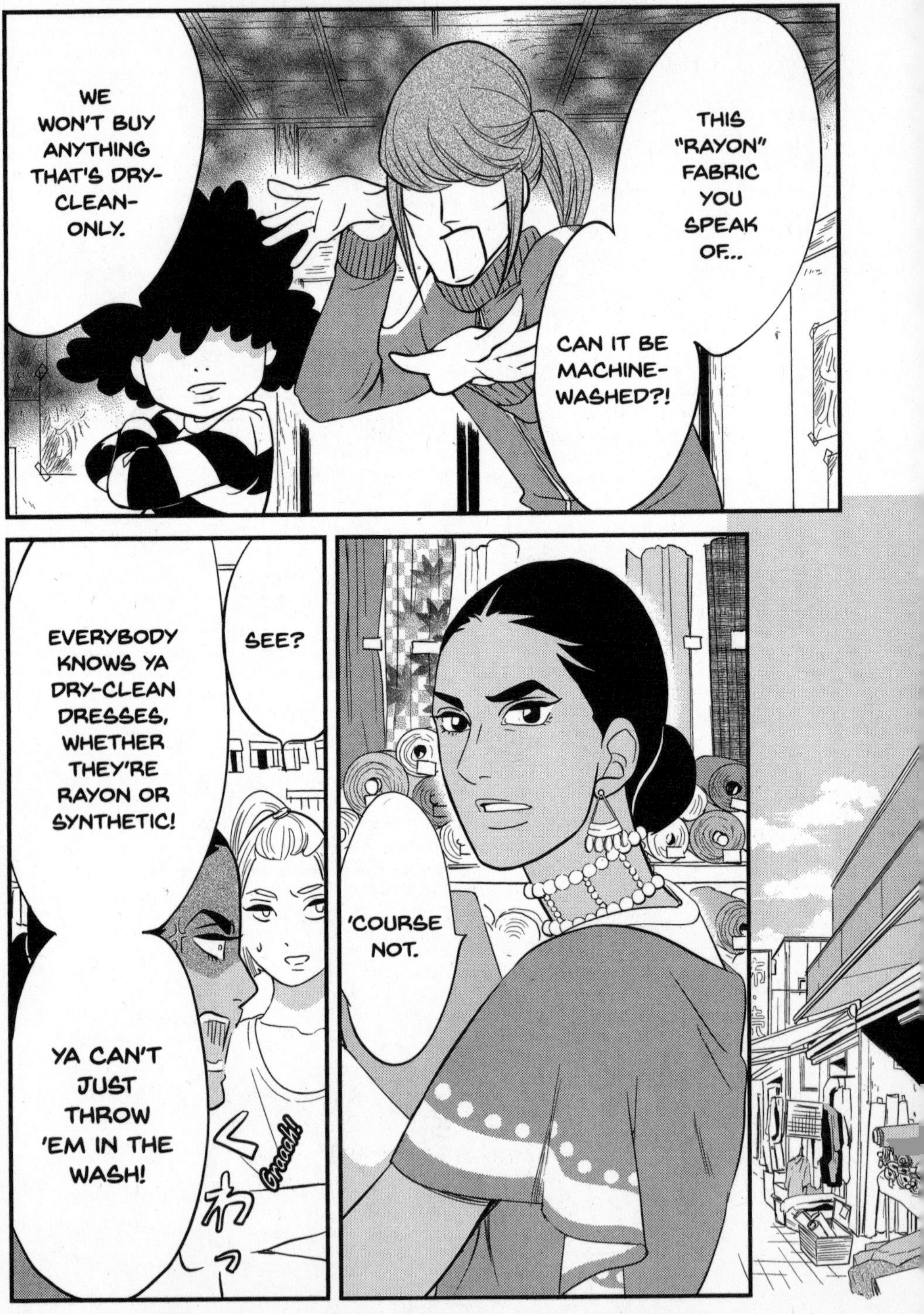
THIS "RAYON" FABRIC YOU SPEAK OF...
CAN IT BE MACHINE-WASHED?!
WE WON'T BUY ANYTHING THAT'S DRY-CLEAN-ONLY.
'COURSE NOT.
SEE?
EVERYBODY KNOWS YA DRY-CLEAN DRESSES, WHETHER THEY'RE RAYON OR SYNTHETIC!
YA CAN'T JUST THROW 'EM IN THE WASH!
Graaah!
くわっ

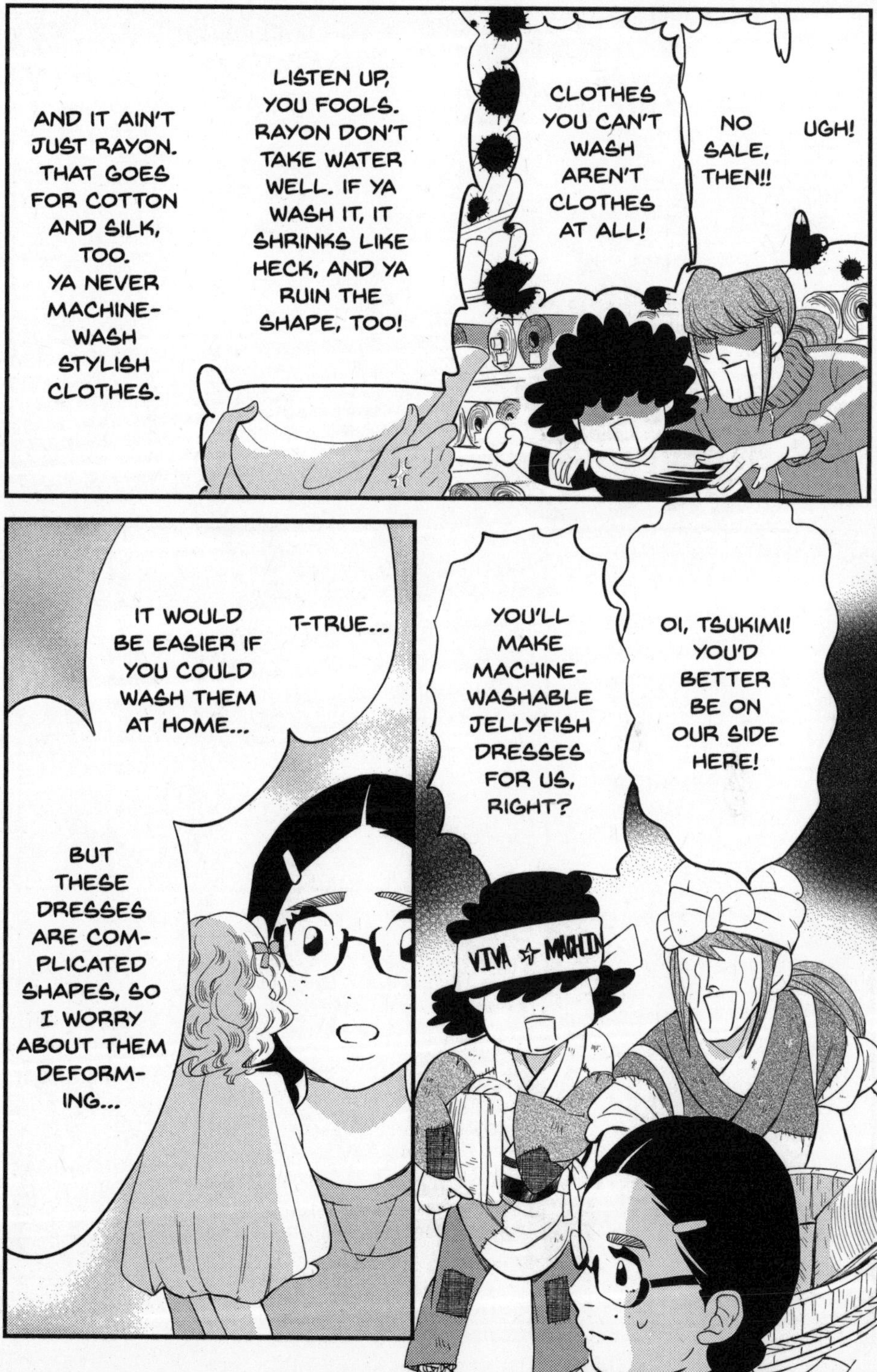
UGH!
NO SALE, THEN!!
CLOTHES YOU CAN'T WASH AREN'T CLOTHES AT ALL!
LISTEN UP, YOU FOOLS. RAYON DON'T TAKE WATER WELL. IF YA WASH IT, IT SHRINKS LIKE HECK, AND YA RUIN THE SHAPE, TOO!
AND IT AIN'T JUST RAYON. THAT GOES FOR COTTON AND SILK, TOO. YA NEVER MACHINE-WASH STYLISH CLOTHES.
OI, TSUKIMI! YOU'D BETTER BE ON OUR SIDE HERE!
YOU'LL MAKE MACHINE-WASHABLE JELLYFISH DRESSES FOR US, RIGHT?
VIVA ☆ MACHIN
T-TRUE...
IT WOULD BE EASIER IF YOU COULD WASH THEM AT HOME...
BUT THESE DRESSES ARE COM-PLICATED SHAPES, SO I WORRY ABOUT THEM DEFORM-ING...

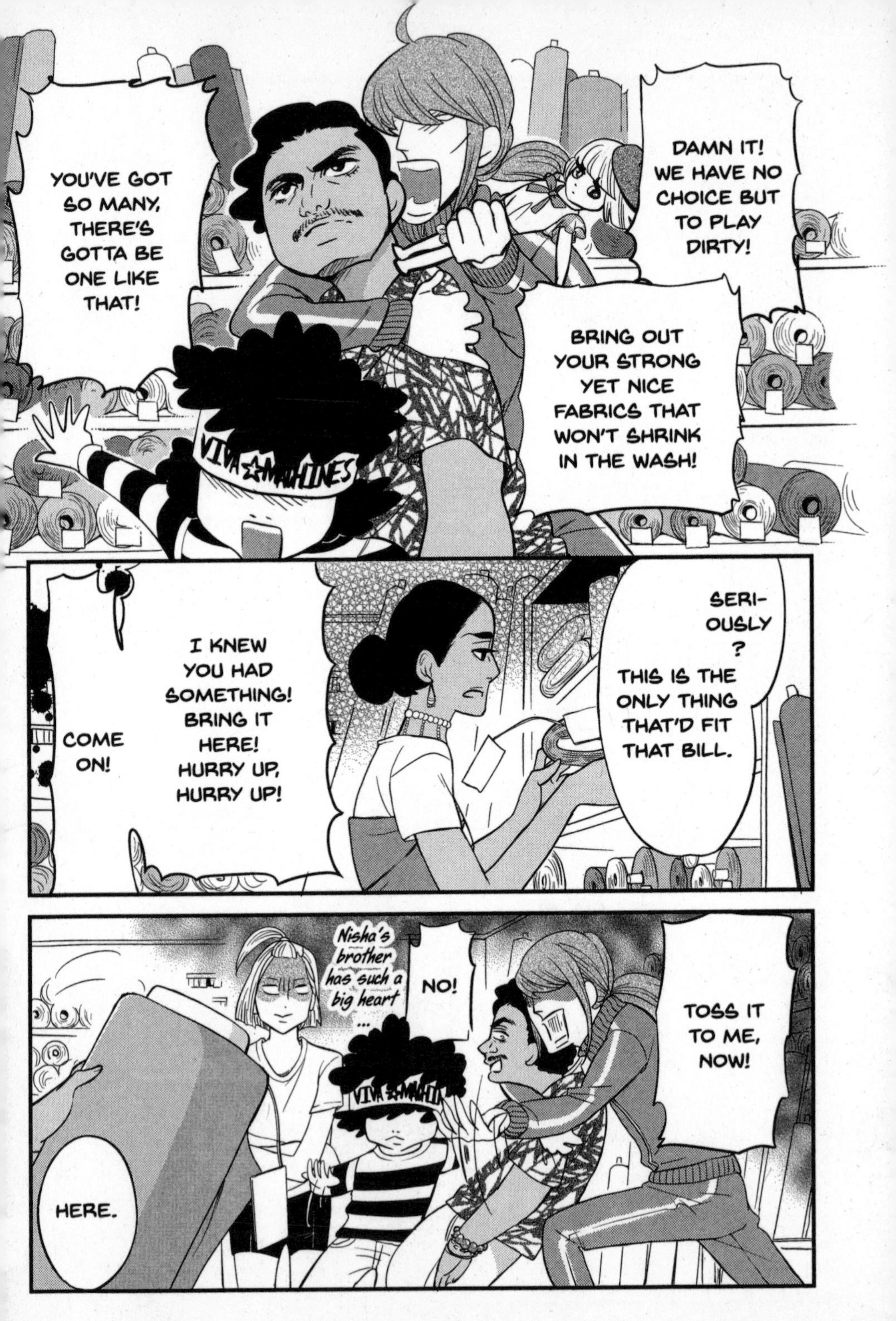
DAMN IT! WE HAVE NO CHOICE BUT TO PLAY DIRTY!
BRING OUT YOUR STRONG YET NICE FABRICS THAT WON'T SHRINK IN THE WASH!
YOU'VE GOT SO MANY, THERE'S GOTTA BE ONE LIKE THAT!
VIVA☆MACHINES
SERI-OUSLY?
THIS IS THE ONLY THING THAT'D FIT THAT BILL.
I KNEW YOU HAD SOMETHING! BRING IT HERE! HURRY UP, HURRY UP!
COME ON!
TOSS IT TO ME, NOW!
NO!
Nisha's brother has such a big heart...
HERE.

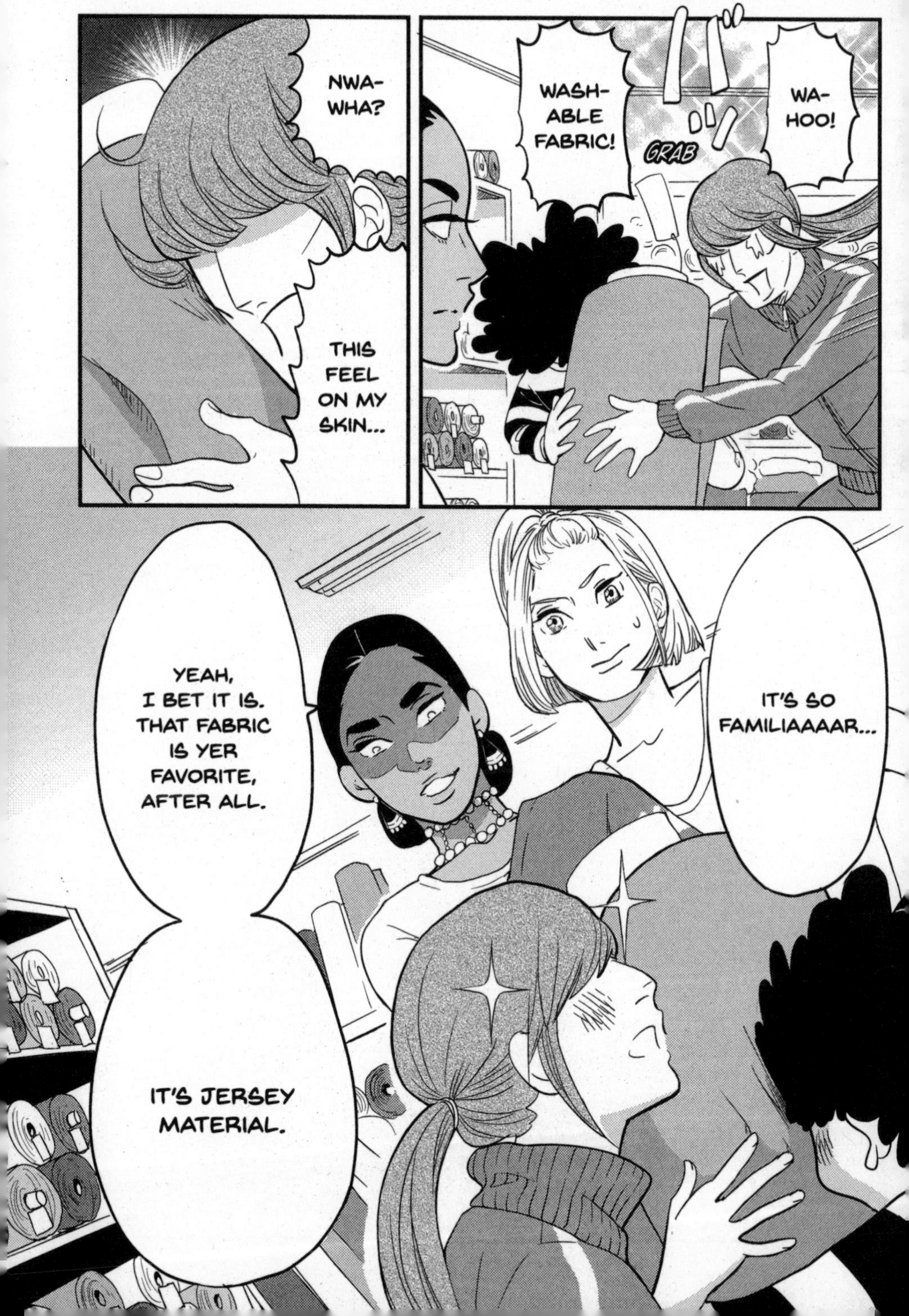
WA-HOO!
WASH-ABLE FABRIC!
GRAB
NWA-WHA?
THIS FEEL ON MY SKIN...
IT'S SO FAMILIAAAAR...
YEAH, I BET IT IS. THAT FABRIC IS YER FAVORITE, AFTER ALL.
IT'S JERSEY MATERIAL.

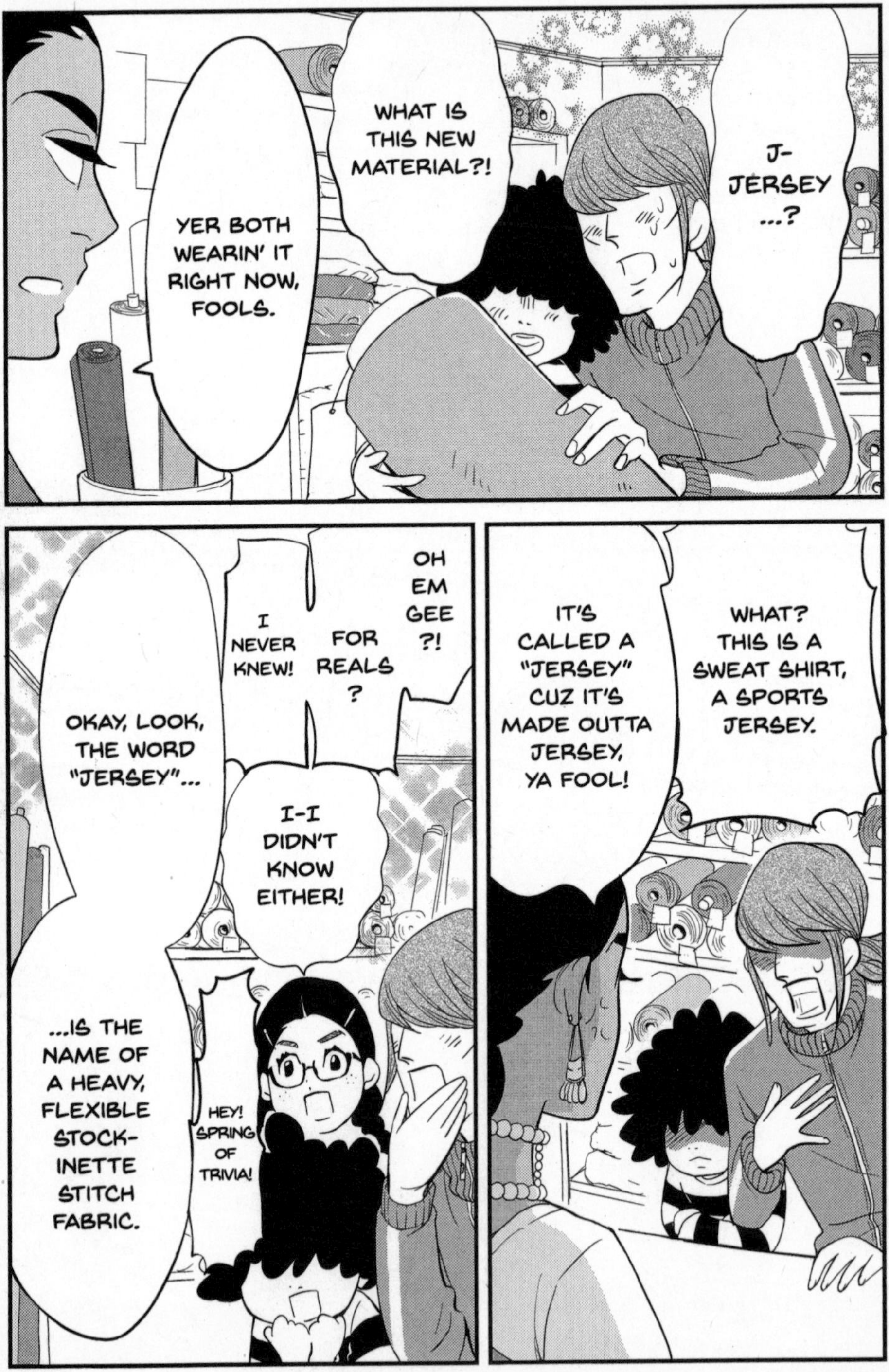
J- JERSEY ...?
WHAT IS THIS NEW MATERIAL?!
YER BOTH WEARIN' IT RIGHT NOW, FOOLS.
WHAT? THIS IS A SWEAT SHIRT, A SPORTS JERSEY.
IT'S CALLED A "JERSEY" CUZ IT'S MADE OUTTA JERSEY, YA FOOL!
OH EM GEE ?!
FOR REALS ?
I NEVER KNEW!
I-I DIDN'T KNOW EITHER!
OKAY, LOOK, THE WORD "JERSEY"...
HEY! SPRING OF TRIVIA!
...IS THE NAME OF A HEAVY, FLEXIBLE STOCK-INETTE STITCH FABRIC.

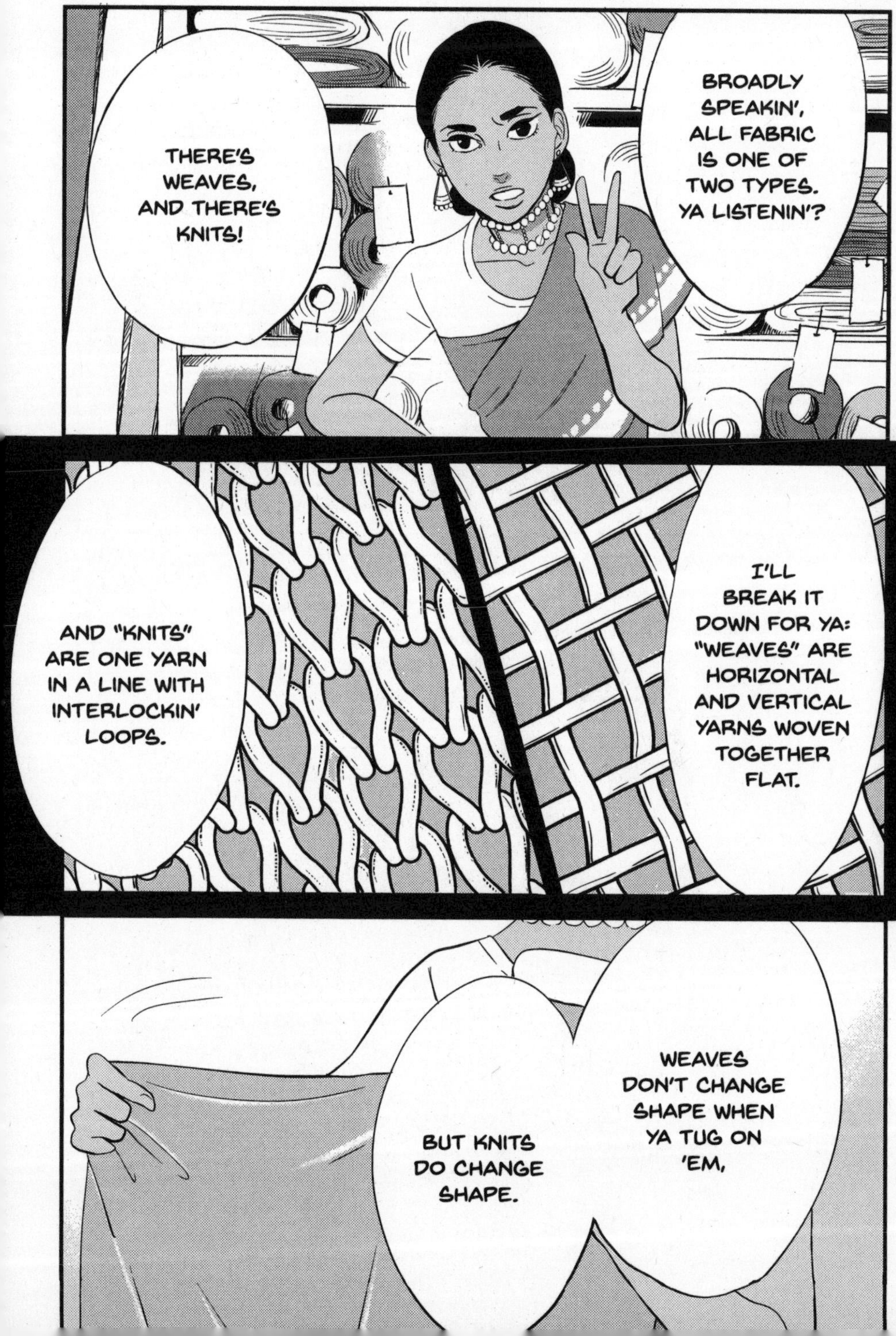

BROADLY SPEAKIN', ALL FABRIC IS ONE OF TWO TYPES. YA LISTENIN'?
THERE'S WEAVES, AND THERE'S KNITS!
I'LL BREAK IT DOWN FOR YA: "WEAVES" ARE HORIZONTAL AND VERTICAL YARNS WOVEN TOGETHER FLAT.
AND "KNITS" ARE ONE YARN IN A LINE WITH INTERLOCKIN' LOOPS.
WEAVES DON'T CHANGE SHAPE WHEN YA TUG ON 'EM,
BUT KNITS DO CHANGE SHAPE.

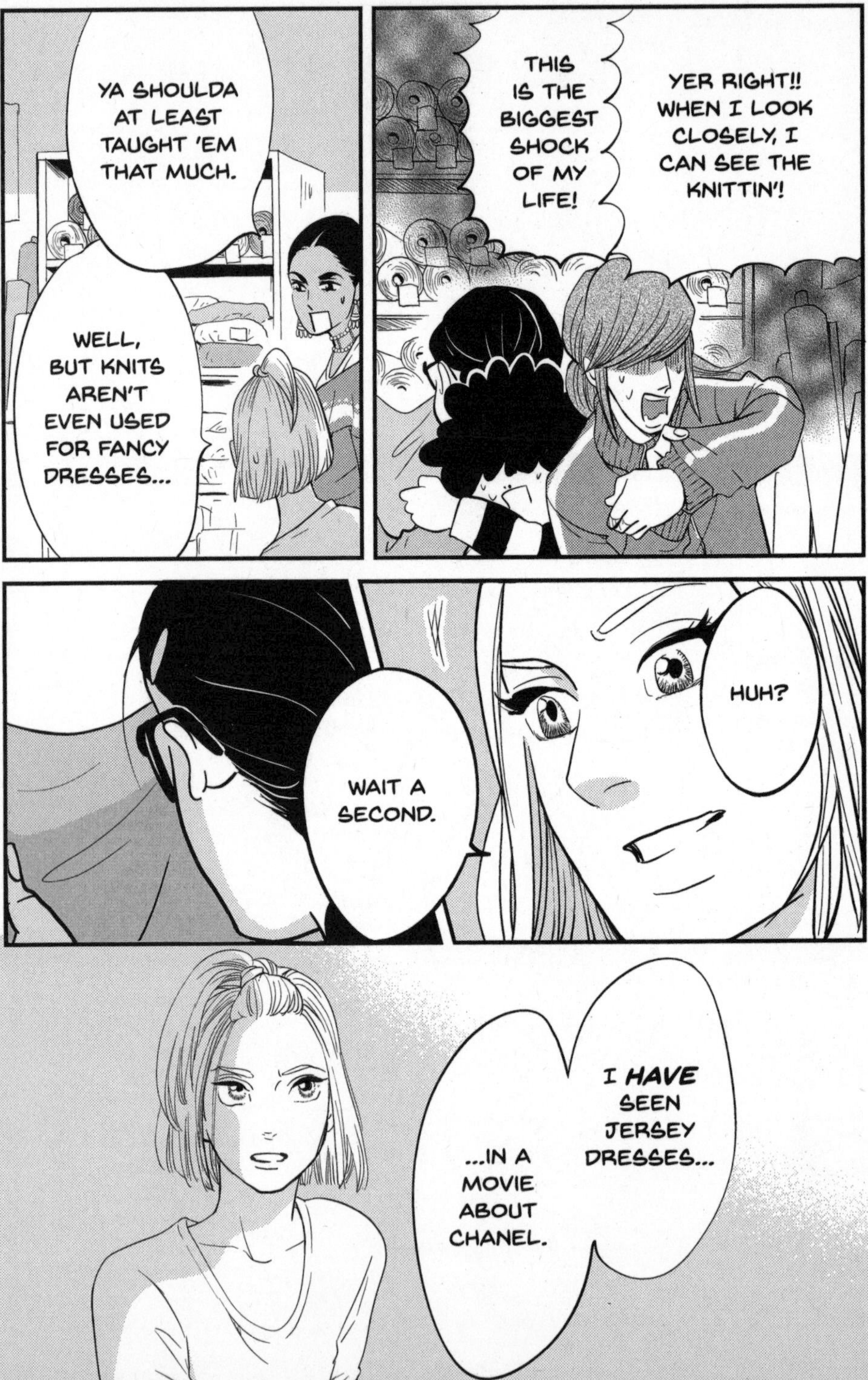
YER RIGHT!! WHEN I LOOK CLOSELY, I CAN SEE THE KNITTIN'!
THIS IS THE BIGGEST SHOCK OF MY LIFE!
YA SHOULDA AT LEAST TAUGHT 'EM THAT MUCH.
WELL, BUT KNITS AREN'T EVEN USED FOR FANCY DRESSES...
HUH?
WAIT A SECOND.
I *HAVE* SEEN JERSEY DRESSES...
...IN A MOVIE ABOUT CHANEL.

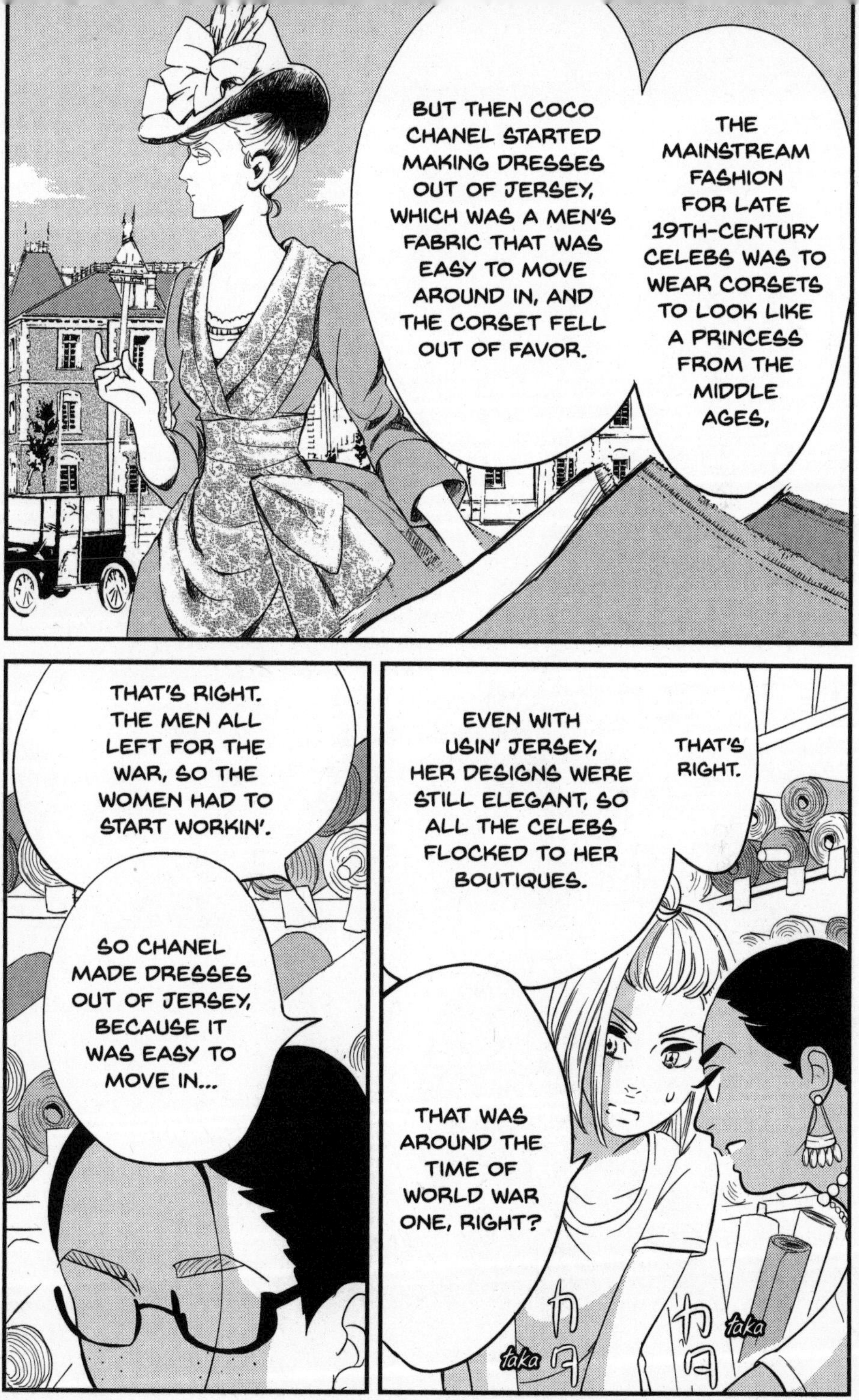
THE MAINSTREAM FASHION FOR LATE 19TH-CENTURY CELEBS WAS TO WEAR CORSETS TO LOOK LIKE A PRINCESS FROM THE MIDDLE AGES,
BUT THEN COCO CHANEL STARTED MAKING DRESSES OUT OF JERSEY, WHICH WAS A MEN'S FABRIC THAT WAS EASY TO MOVE AROUND IN, AND THE CORSET FELL OUT OF FAVOR.
THAT'S RIGHT.
EVEN WITH USIN' JERSEY, HER DESIGNS WERE STILL ELEGANT, SO ALL THE CELEBS FLOCKED TO HER BOUTIQUES.
THAT WAS AROUND THE TIME OF WORLD WAR ONE, RIGHT?
カタ taka
カタ taka
THAT'S RIGHT. THE MEN ALL LEFT FOR THE WAR, SO THE WOMEN HAD TO START WORKIN'.
SO CHANEL MADE DRESSES OUT OF JERSEY, BECAUSE IT WAS EASY TO MOVE IN...

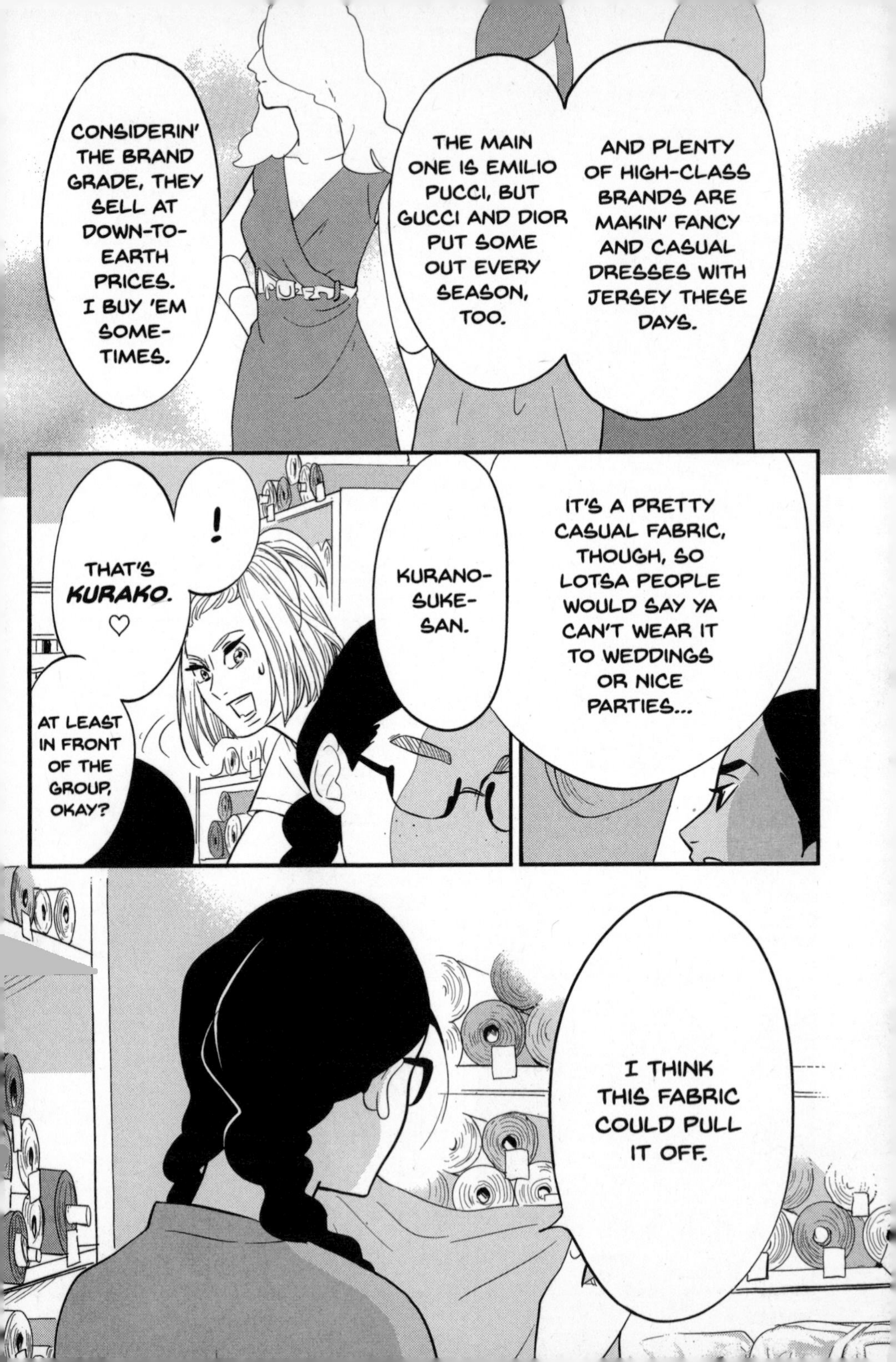
THE MAIN ONE IS EMILIO PUCCI, BUT GUCCI AND DIOR PUT SOME OUT EVERY SEASON, TOO.
AND PLENTY OF HIGH-CLASS BRANDS ARE MAKIN' FANCY AND CASUAL DRESSES WITH JERSEY THESE DAYS.
CONSIDERIN' THE BRAND GRADE, THEY SELL AT DOWN-TO-EARTH PRICES. I BUY 'EM SOME-TIMES.
IT'S A PRETTY CASUAL FABRIC, THOUGH, SO LOTSA PEOPLE WOULD SAY YA CAN'T WEAR IT TO WEDDINGS OR NICE PARTIES...
KURANO-SUKE-SAN.
!
THAT'S **KURAKO.** ♡
AT LEAST IN FRONT OF THE GROUP, OKAY?
I THINK THIS FABRIC COULD PULL IT OFF.

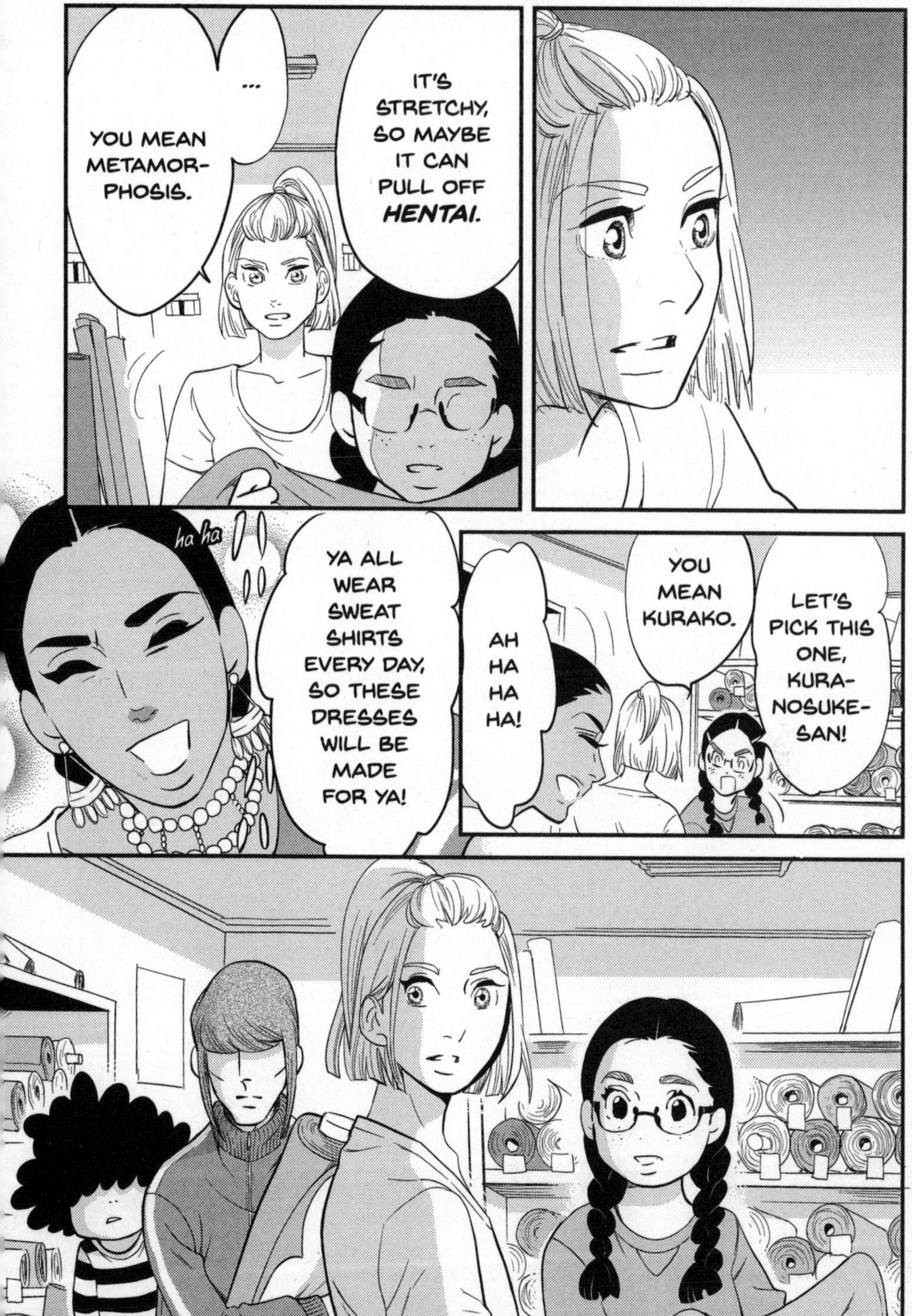
IT'S STRETCHY, SO MAYBE IT CAN PULL OFF *HENTAI.*
...
YOU MEAN METAMORPHOSIS.
LET'S PICK THIS ONE, KURANOSUKE-SAN!
YOU MEAN KURAKO.
AH HA HA HA!
YA ALL WEAR SWEAT SHIRTS EVERY DAY, SO THESE DRESSES WILL BE MADE FOR YA!
ha ha

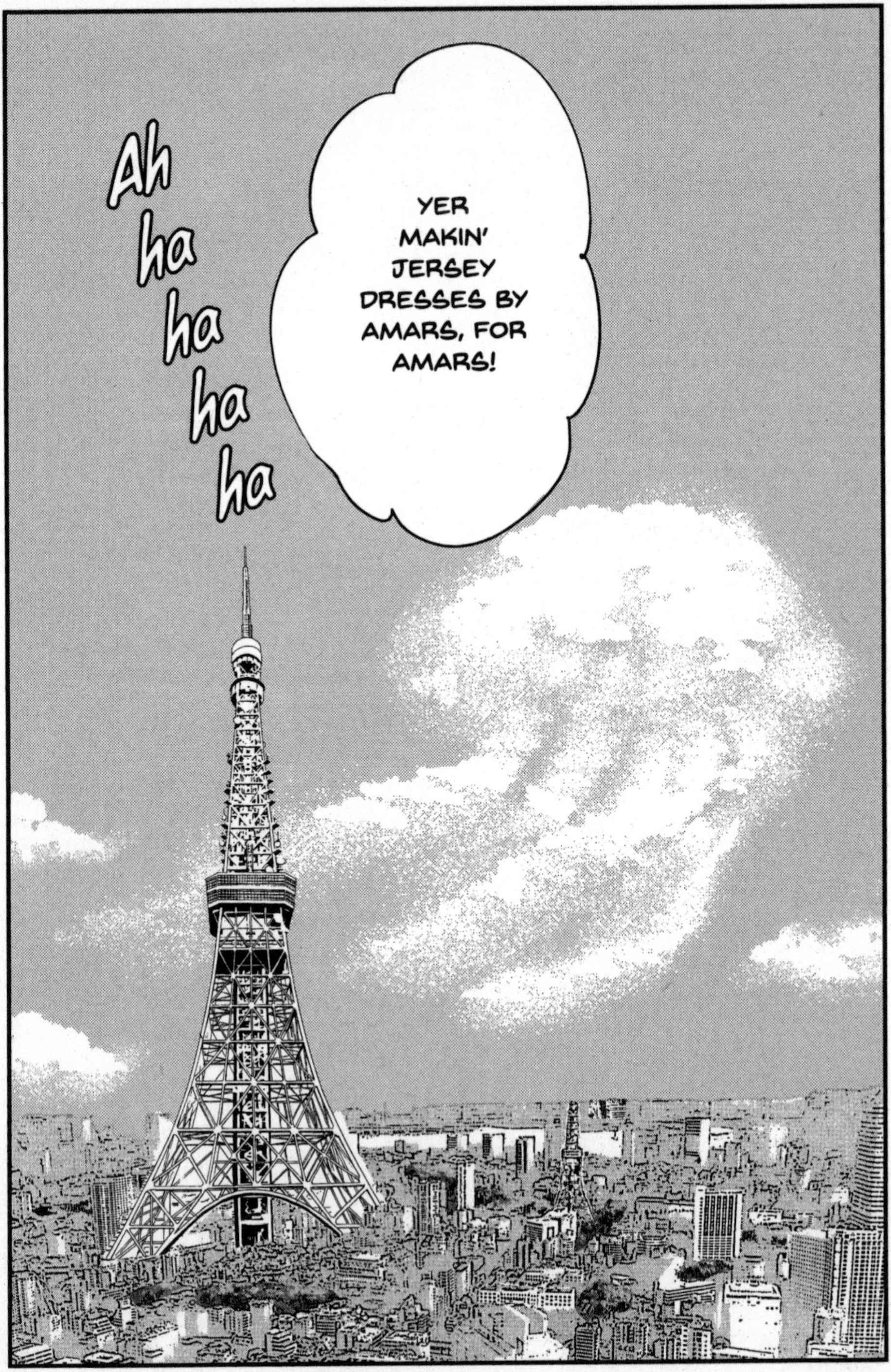
YER MAKIN' JERSEY DRESSES BY AMARS, FOR AMARS!
Ah ha ha ha ha

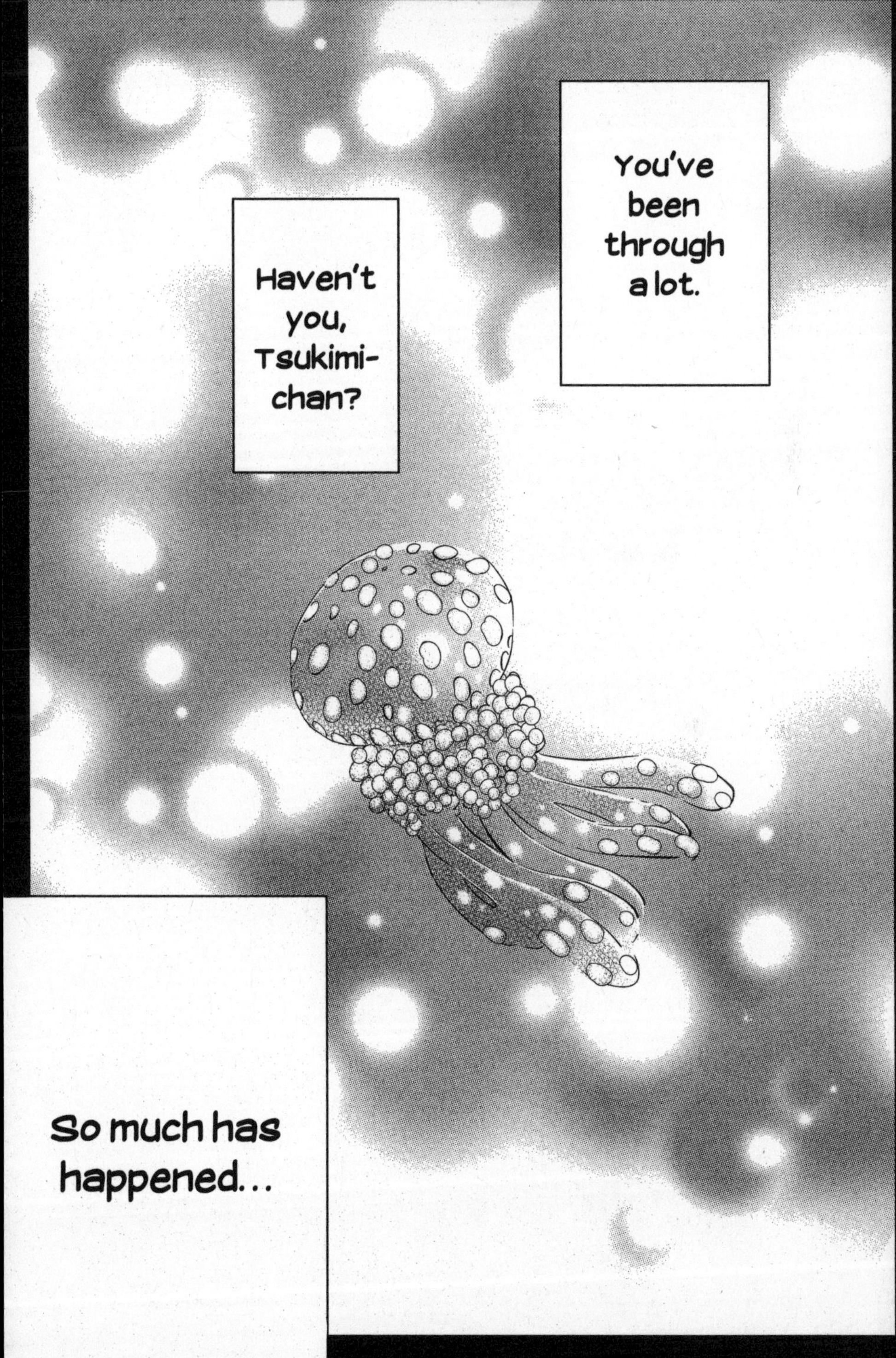
You've been through a lot.
Haven't you, Tsukimi-chan?
So much has happened...

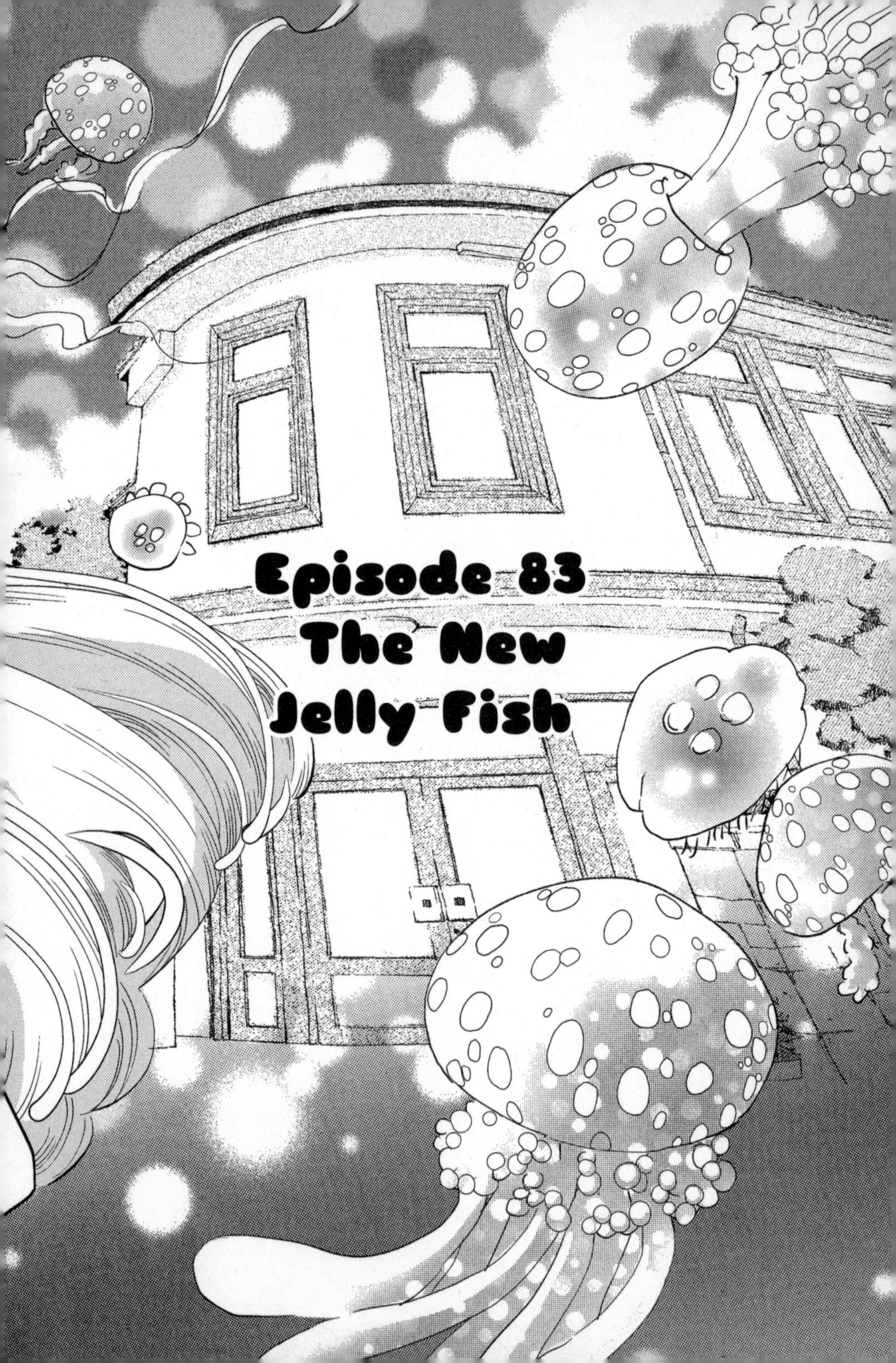
Episode 83
The New
Jelly Fish

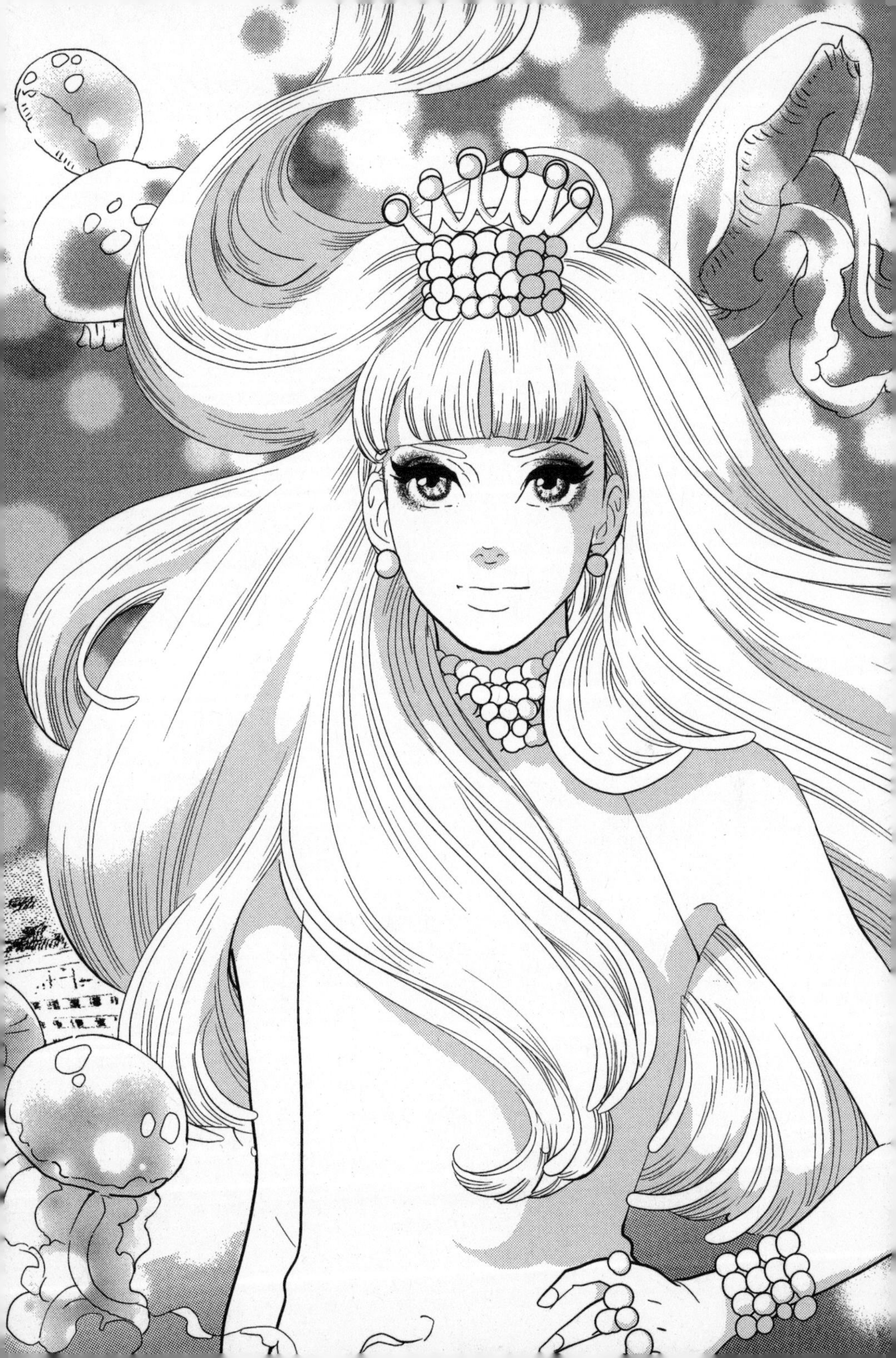

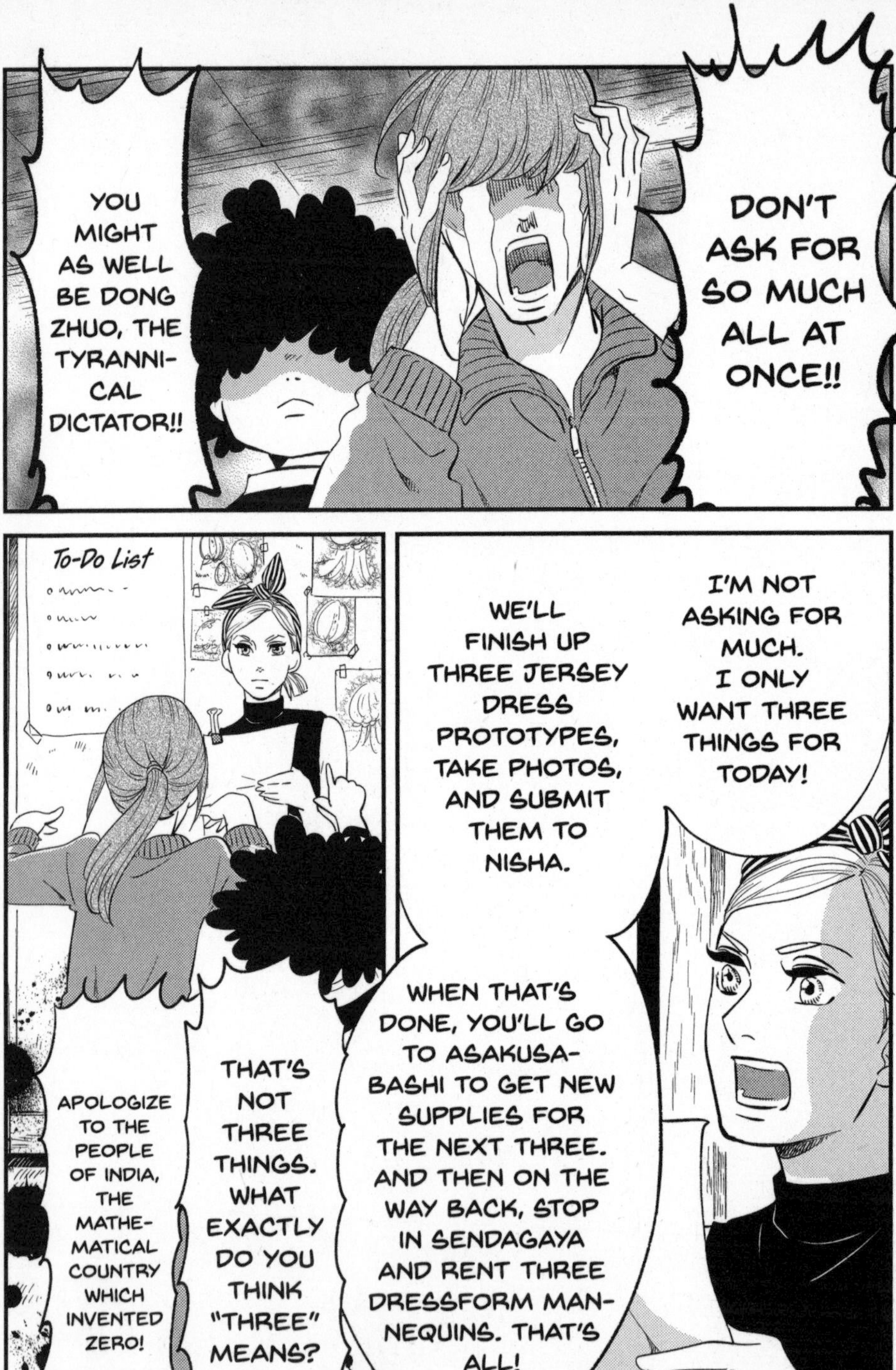
DON'T ASK FOR SO MUCH ALL AT ONCE!!
YOU MIGHT AS WELL BE DONG ZHUO, THE TYRANNI-CAL DICTATOR!!
I'M NOT ASKING FOR MUCH. I ONLY WANT THREE THINGS FOR TODAY!
WE'LL FINISH UP THREE JERSEY DRESS PROTOTYPES, TAKE PHOTOS, AND SUBMIT THEM TO NISHA.
WHEN THAT'S DONE, YOU'LL GO TO ASAKUSA-BASHI TO GET NEW SUPPLIES FOR THE NEXT THREE. AND THEN ON THE WAY BACK, STOP IN SENDAGAYA AND RENT THREE DRESSFORM MAN-NEQUINS. THAT'S ALL!
To-Do List
THAT'S NOT THREE THINGS. WHAT EXACTLY DO YOU THINK "THREE" MEANS?
APOLOGIZE TO THE PEOPLE OF INDIA, THE MATHE-MATICAL COUNTRY WHICH INVENTED ZERO!

OKAY, HANA-MORI-SAN APOL-OGIZED, SO WE'RE GOOD.

COME BACK WHEN YOU'RE DONE!

I'M SORRY.

NO WOR-RIES.

Don't sweat it.

NWAAH! THEY LOOK LIKE AN AUTOMATA EXHIBIT AT A DOLL MUSEUM!

THEY'VE BEEN WORKING HARD FOR TWO DAYS NOW, DOING SPECIALIZED STUFF ONLY THEY CAN DO.

WHY SHOULD **WE** HAVE TO RUN THIS TEDIOUS ERRAND?!

YOU GUYS, JUST LOOK AT CHIEKO AND NOMU-SAN OVER THERE.

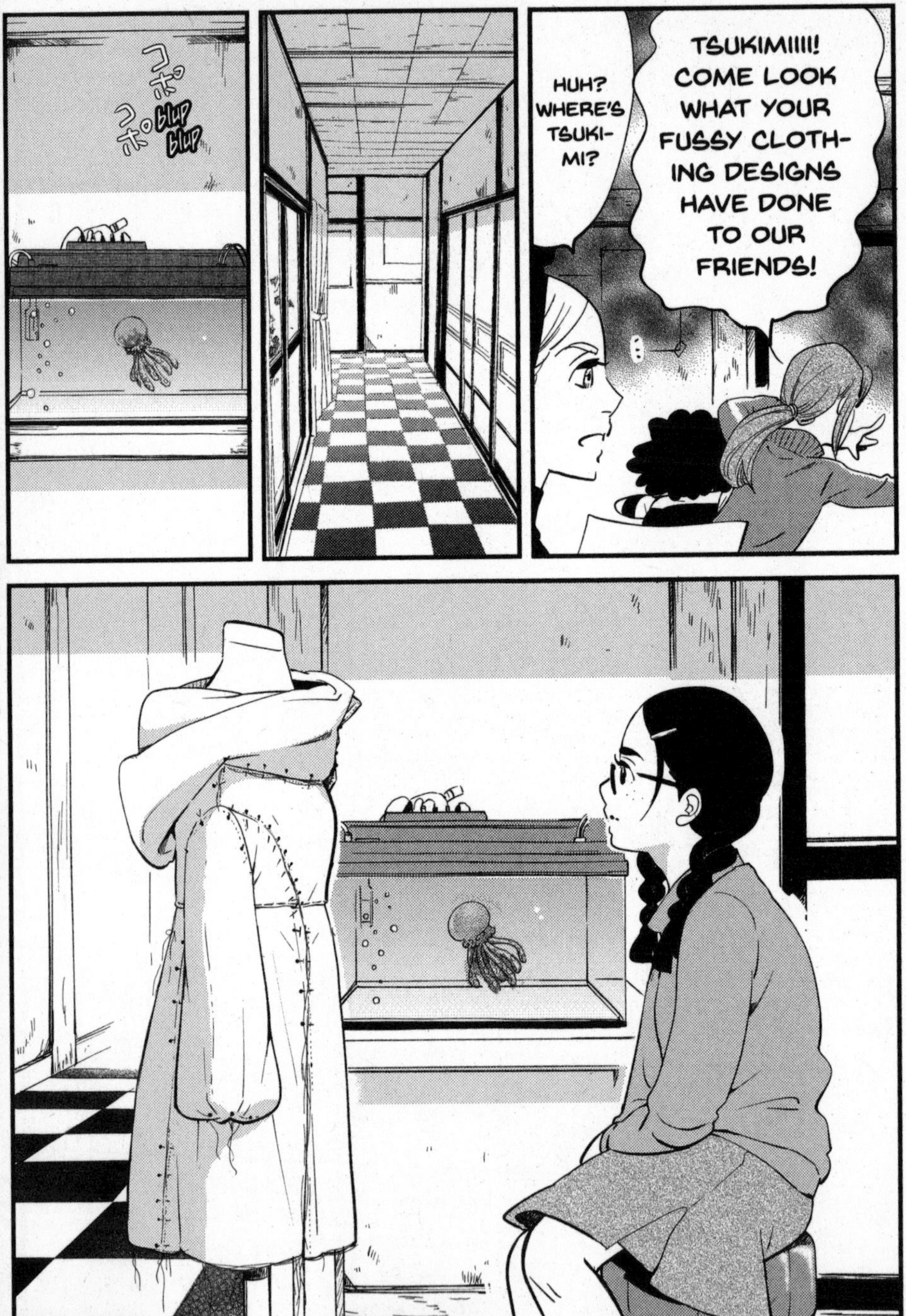
TSUKIMIIII! COME LOOK WHAT YOUR FUSSY CLOTHING DESIGNS HAVE DONE TO OUR FRIENDS!
HUH? WHERE'S TSUKIMI?
コポコポ
blup blup

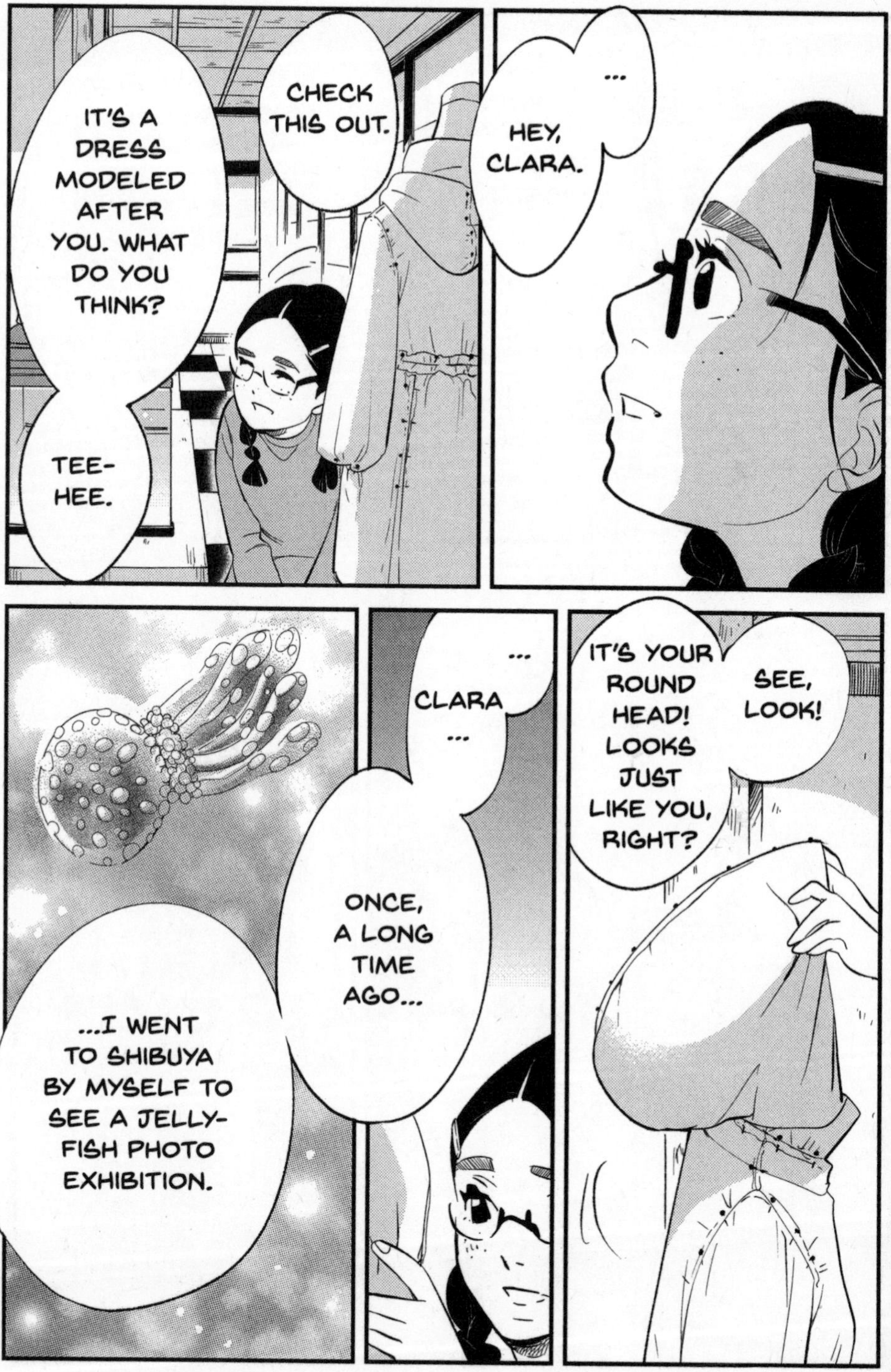
...
HEY, CLARA.
CHECK THIS OUT.
IT'S A DRESS MODELED AFTER YOU. WHAT DO YOU THINK?
TEE-HEE.
SEE, LOOK!
IT'S YOUR ROUND HEAD! LOOKS JUST LIKE YOU, RIGHT?
... CLARA ...
ONCE, A LONG TIME AGO...
...I WENT TO SHIBUYA BY MYSELF TO SEE A JELLY-FISH PHOTO EXHIBITION.

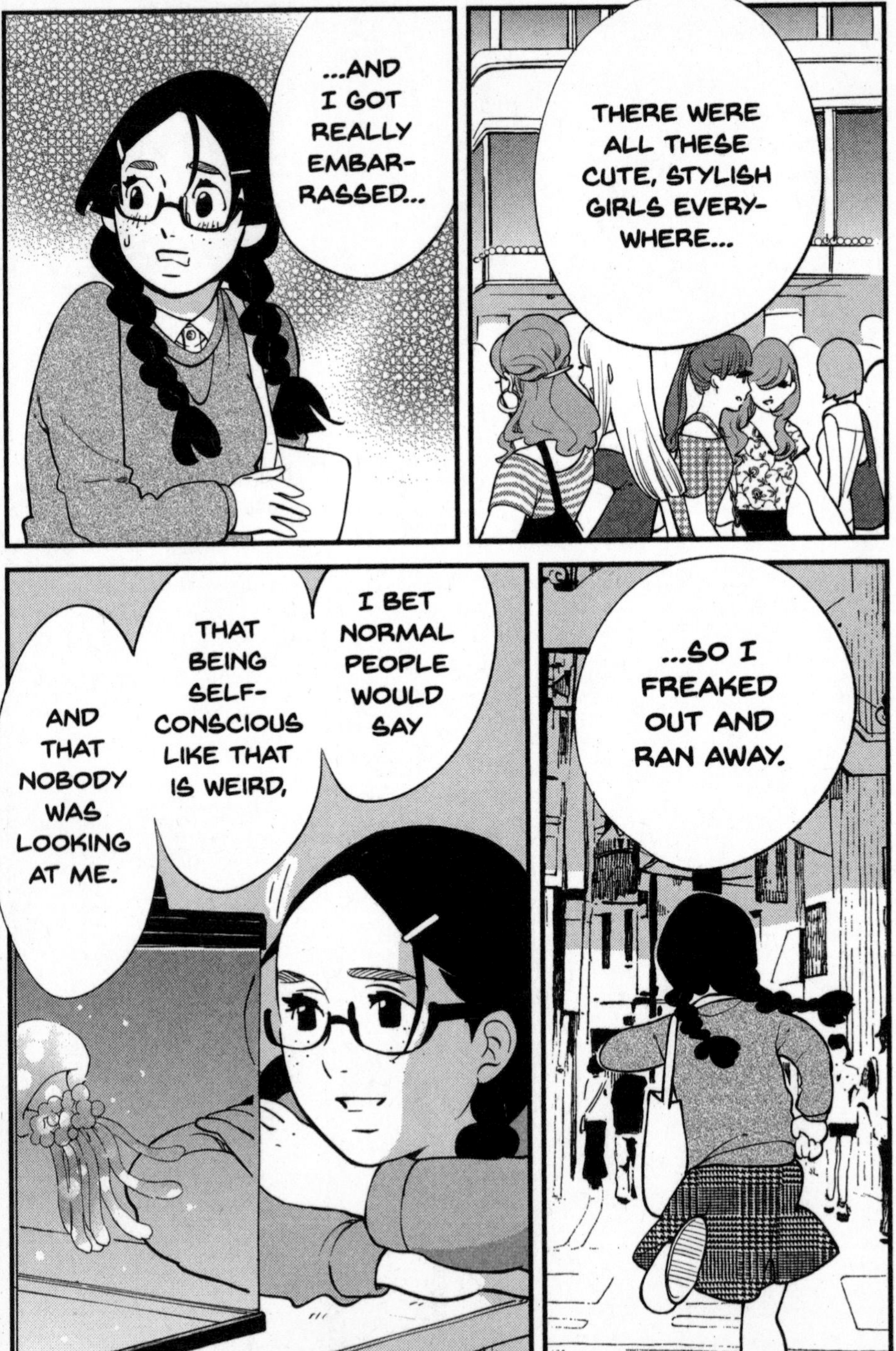
THERE WERE ALL THESE CUTE, STYLISH GIRLS EVERY-WHERE...
...AND I GOT REALLY EMBAR-RASSED...
...SO I FREAKED OUT AND RAN AWAY.
I BET NORMAL PEOPLE WOULD SAY
THAT BEING SELF-CONSCIOUS LIKE THAT IS WEIRD,
AND THAT NOBODY WAS LOOKING AT ME.

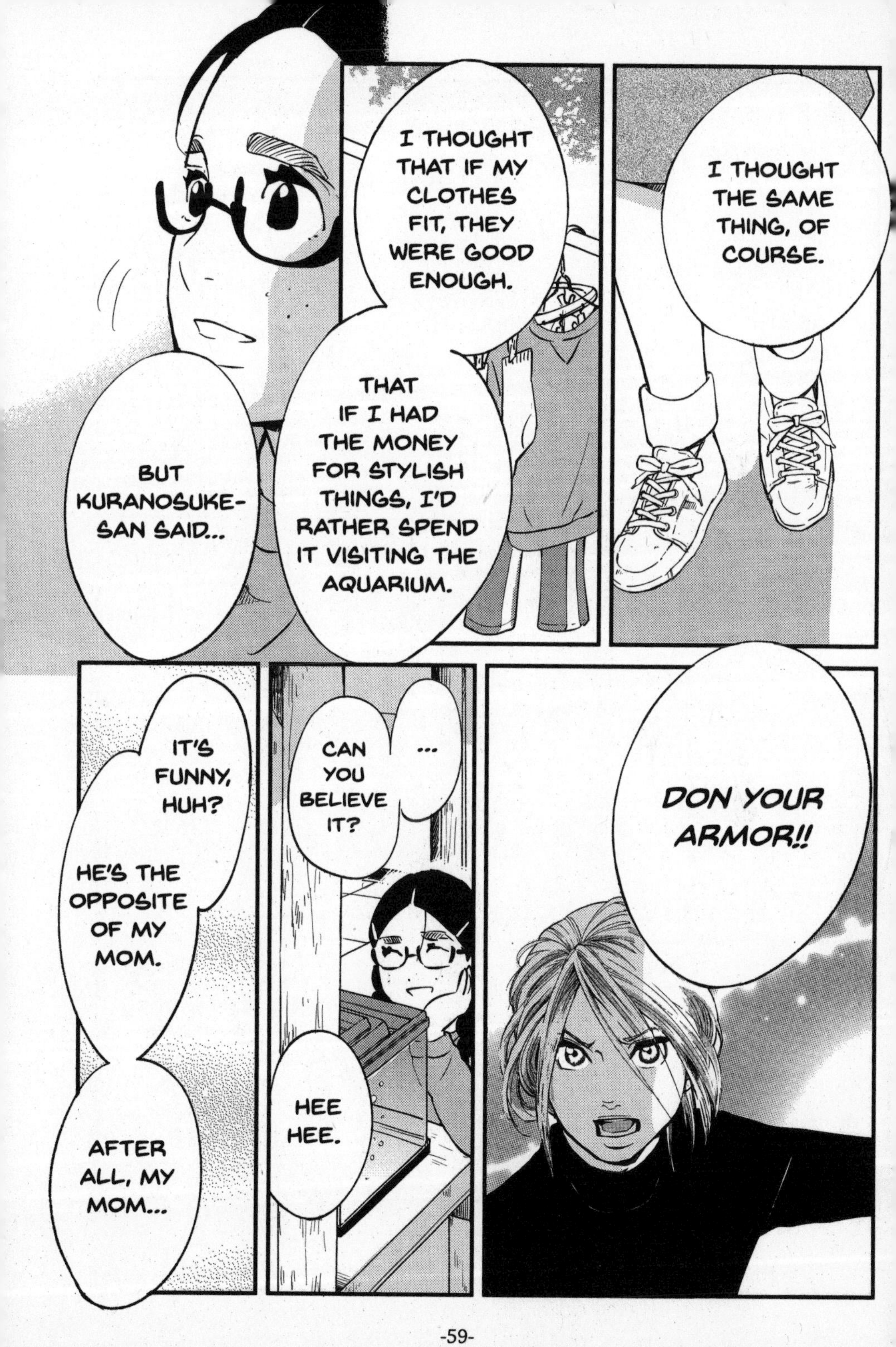
I THOUGHT THE SAME THING, OF COURSE.
I THOUGHT THAT IF MY CLOTHES FIT, THEY WERE GOOD ENOUGH.
THAT IF I HAD THE MONEY FOR STYLISH THINGS, I'D RATHER SPEND IT VISITING THE AQUARIUM.
BUT KURANOSUKE-SAN SAID...
DON YOUR ARMOR!!
...
CAN YOU BELIEVE IT?
HEE HEE.
IT'S FUNNY, HUH?
HE'S THE OPPOSITE OF MY MOM.
AFTER ALL, MY MOM...

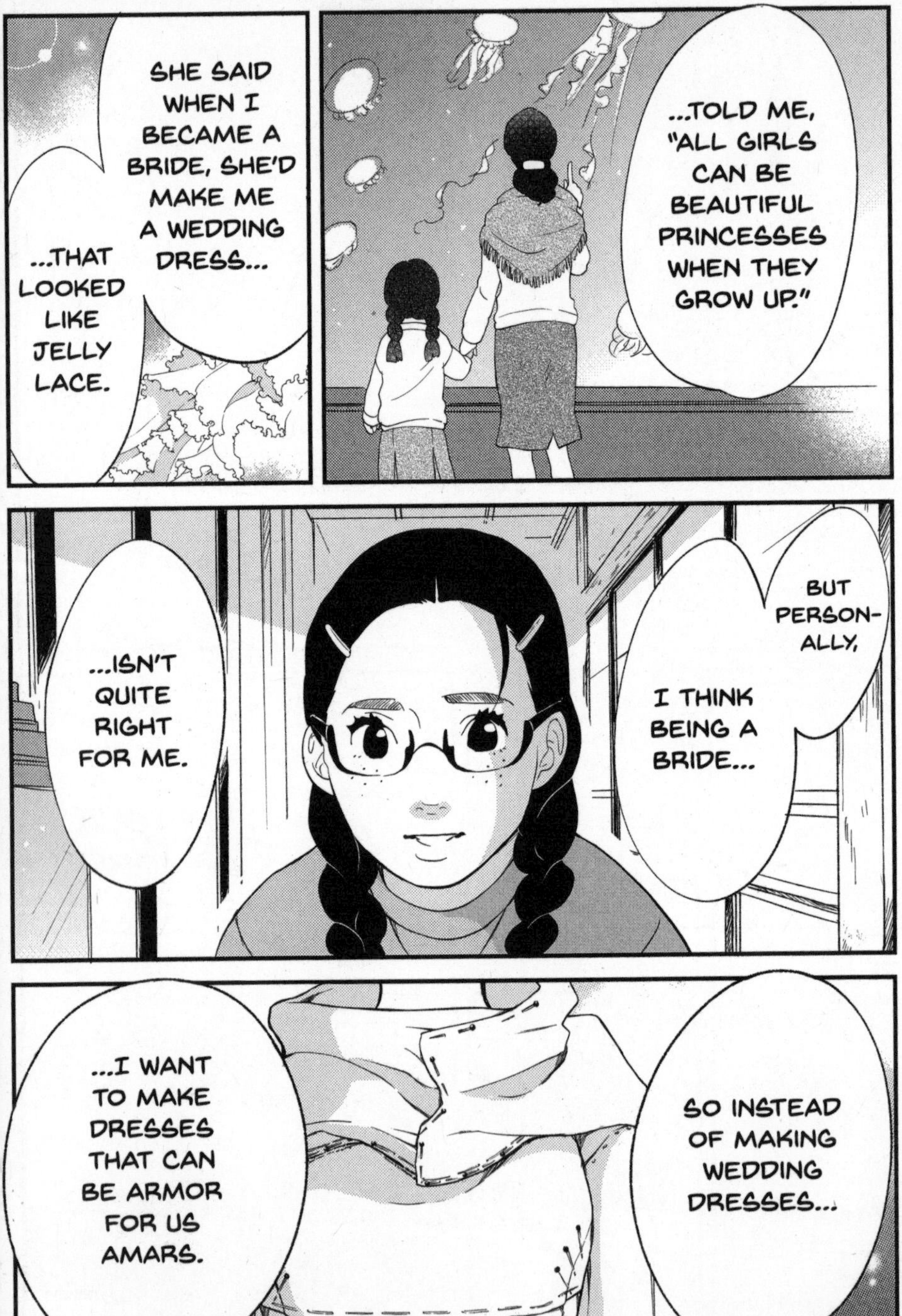
...TOLD ME, "ALL GIRLS CAN BE BEAUTIFUL PRINCESSES WHEN THEY GROW UP."
SHE SAID WHEN I BECAME A BRIDE, SHE'D MAKE ME A WEDDING DRESS...
...THAT LOOKED LIKE JELLY LACE.
BUT PERSON-ALLY,
I THINK BEING A BRIDE...
...ISN'T QUITE RIGHT FOR ME.
SO INSTEAD OF MAKING WEDDING DRESSES...
...I WANT TO MAKE DRESSES THAT CAN BE ARMOR FOR US AMARS.

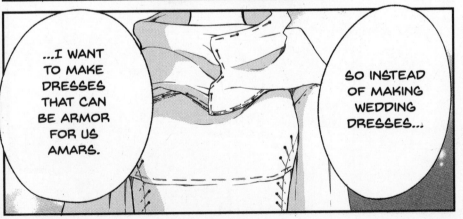

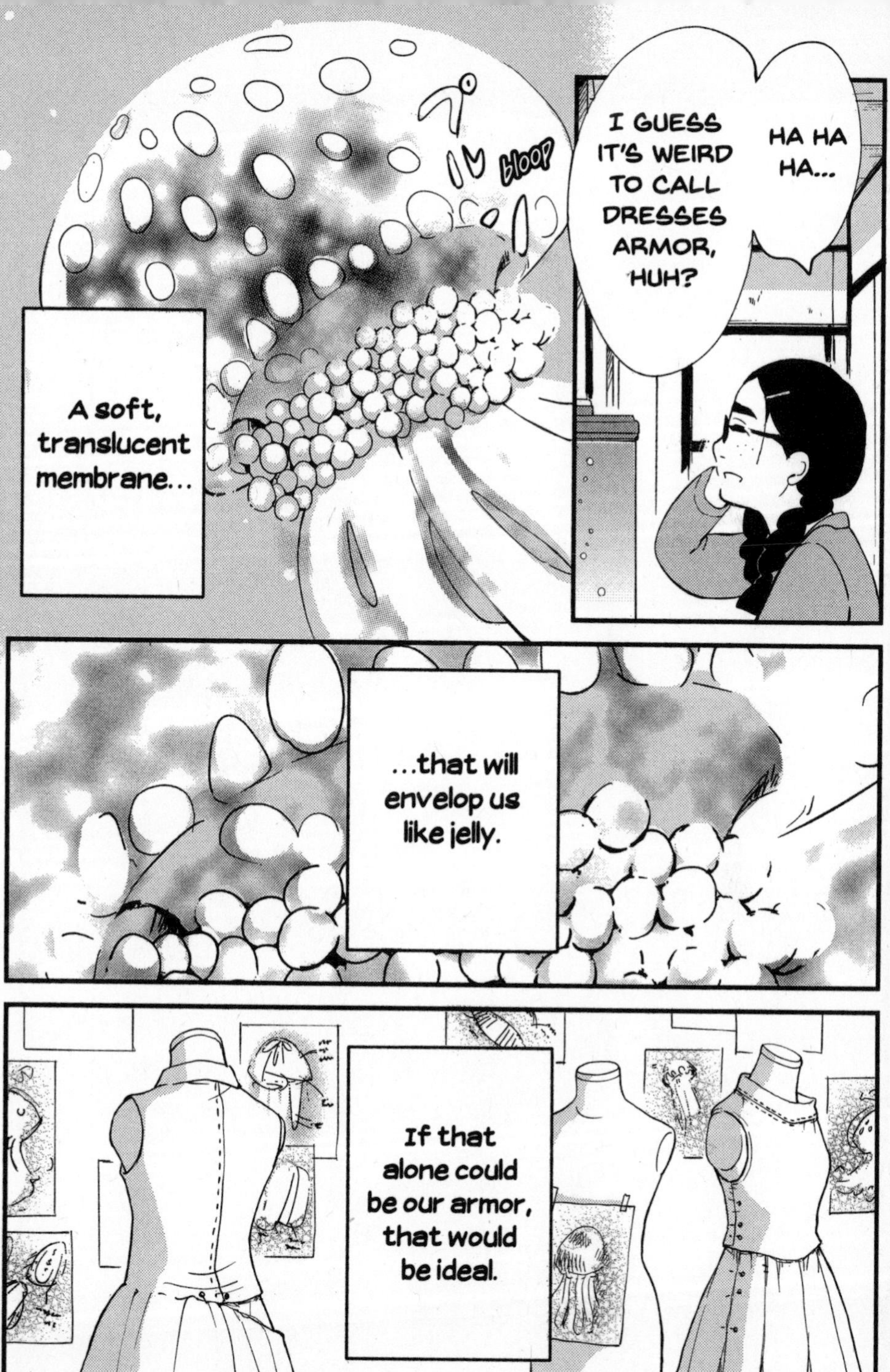

I GUESS IT'S WEIRD TO CALL DRESSES ARMOR, HUH?
HA HA HA...
bloop
A soft, translucent membrane...
...that will envelop us like jelly.
If that alone could be our armor, that would be ideal.

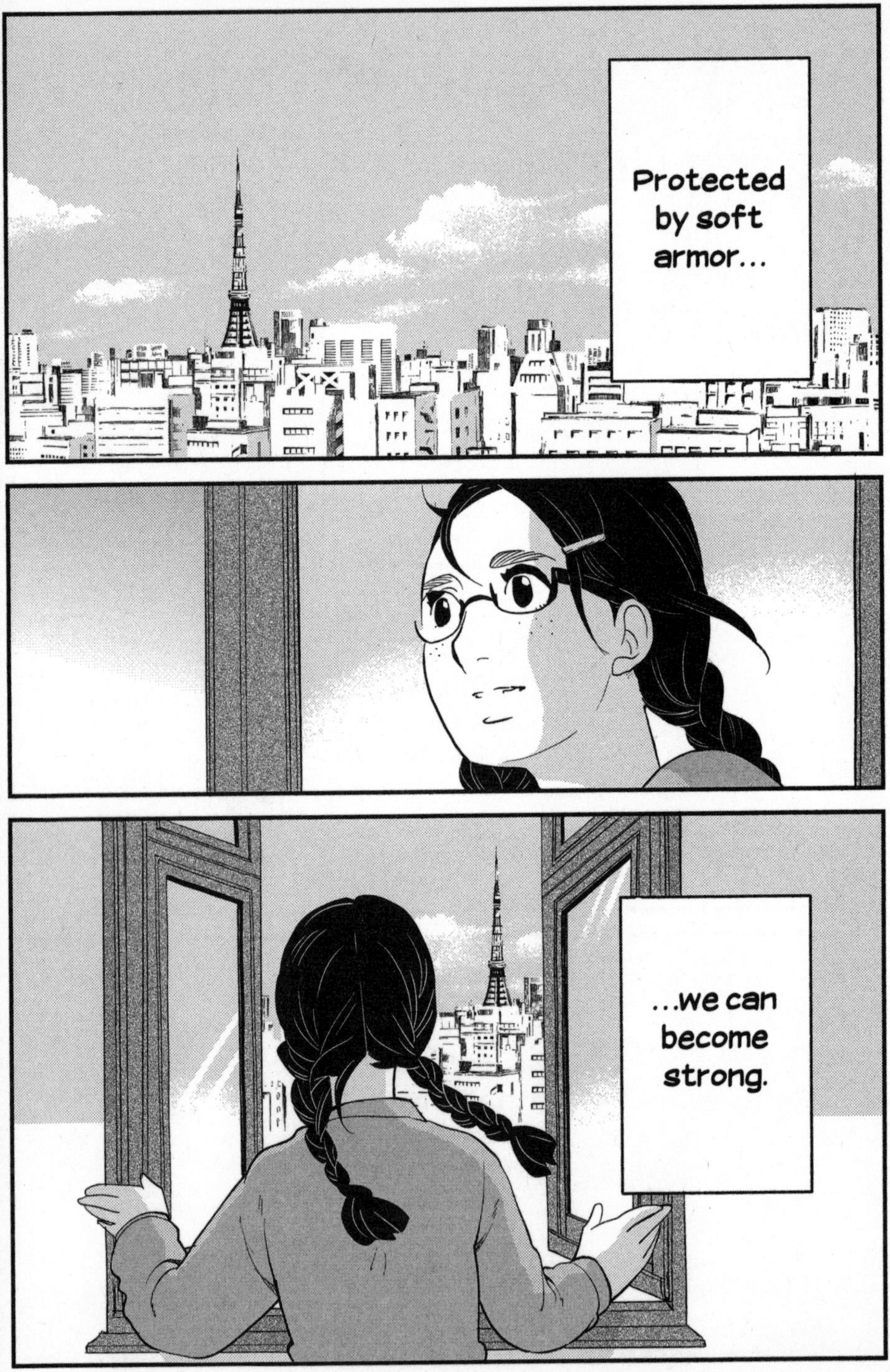
Protected by soft armor...
...we can become strong.

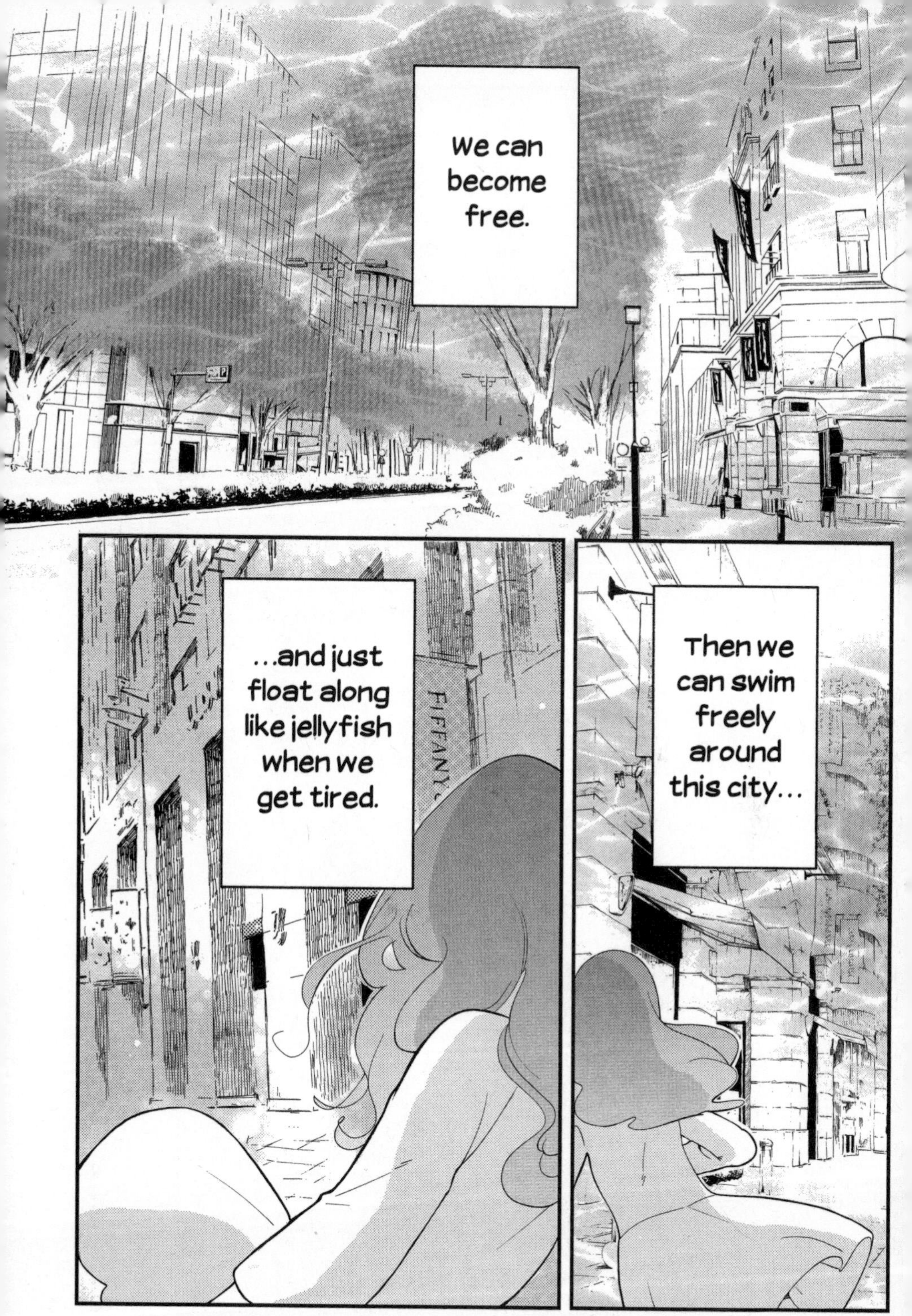
We can become free.
Then we can swim freely around this city...
...and just float along like jellyfish when we get tired.
FIFFANY

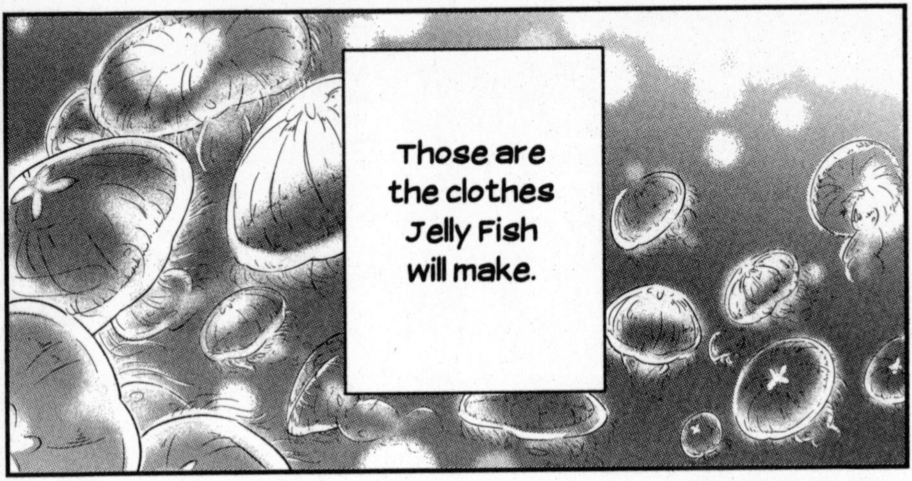
Those are the clothes Jelly Fish will make.

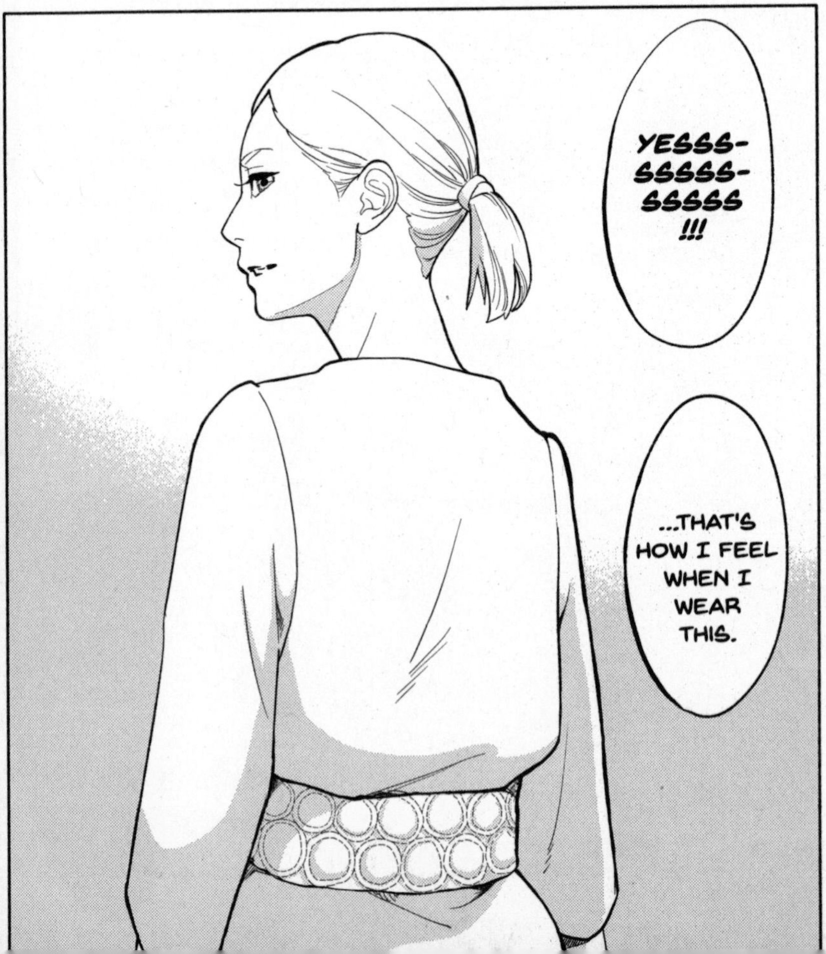
YESSS-SSSSS-SSSSS!!!
...THAT'S HOW I FEEL WHEN I WEAR THIS.

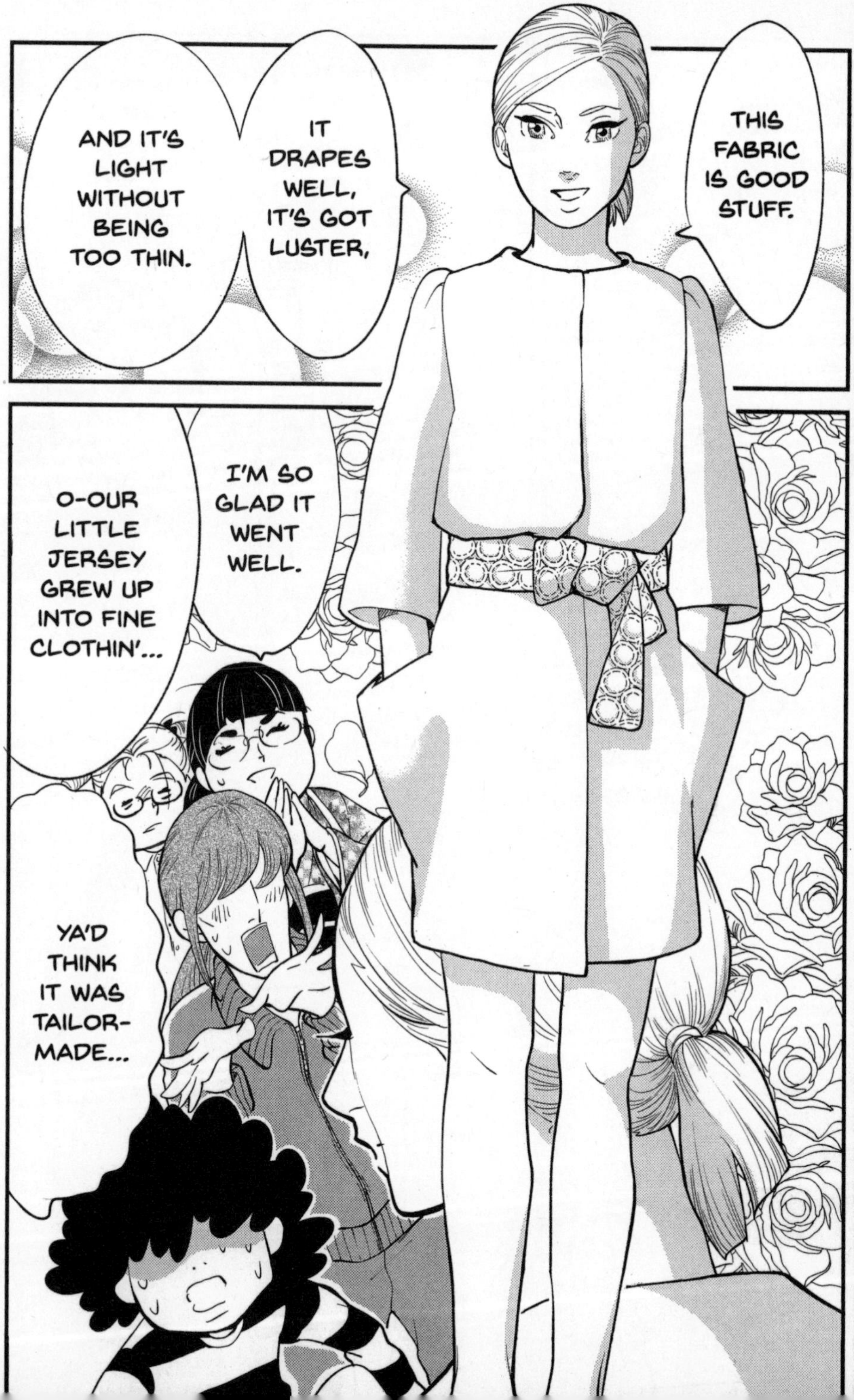
THIS FABRIC IS GOOD STUFF.
IT DRAPES WELL, IT'S GOT LUSTER,
AND IT'S LIGHT WITHOUT BEING TOO THIN.
I'M SO GLAD IT WENT WELL.
O-OUR LITTLE JERSEY GREW UP INTO FINE CLOTHIN'...
YA'D THINK IT WAS TAILOR-MADE...

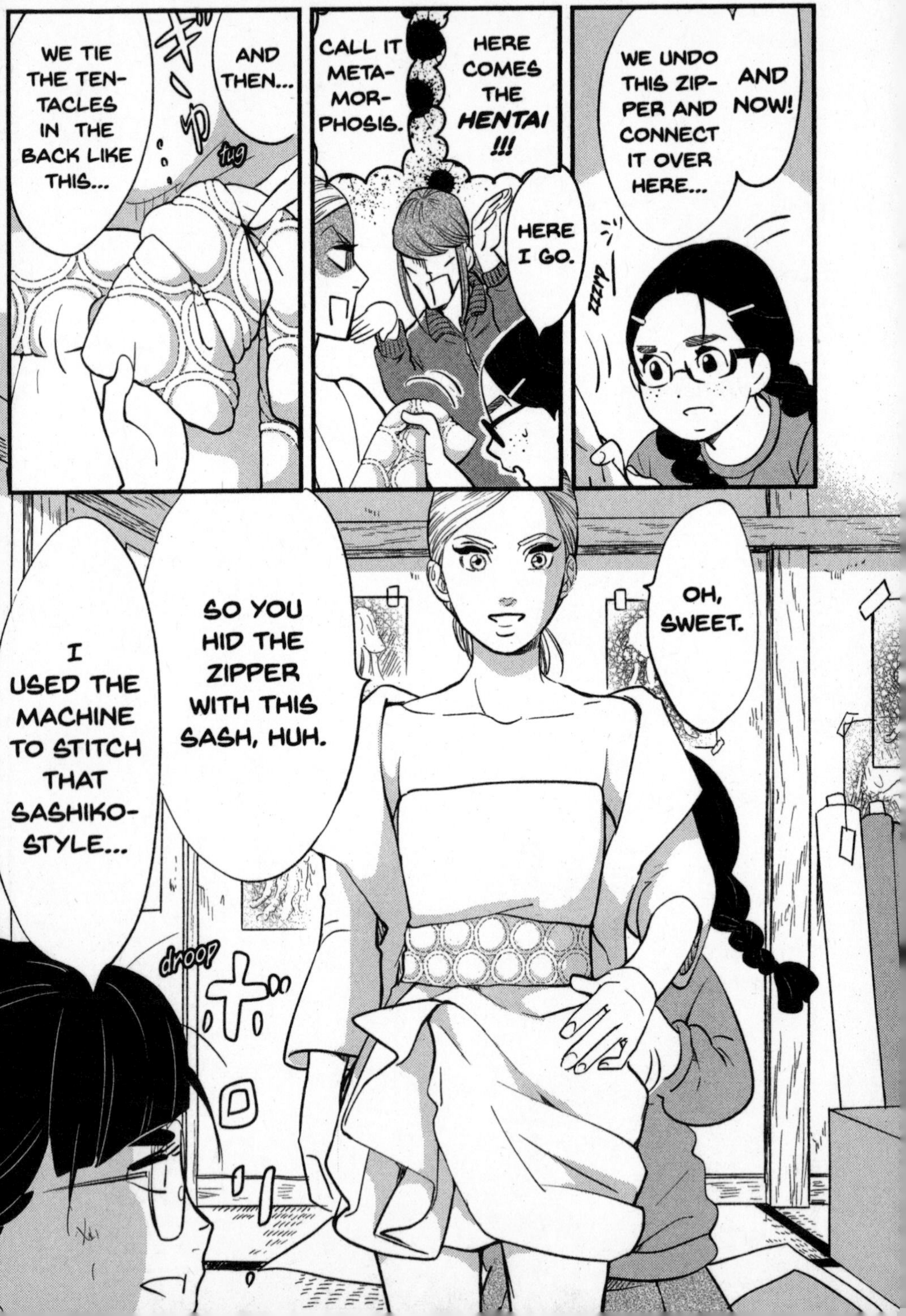
AND NOW!
WE UNDO THIS ZIPPER AND CONNECT IT OVER HERE...
ZZZZP
HERE COMES THE *HENTAI* !!!
CALL IT METAMORPHOSIS.
HERE I GO.
AND THEN...
WE TIE THE TENTACLES IN THE BACK LIKE THIS...
tug
OH, SWEET.
SO YOU HID THE ZIPPER WITH THIS SASH, HUH.
I USED THE MACHINE TO STITCH THAT SASHIKO-STYLE...
droop

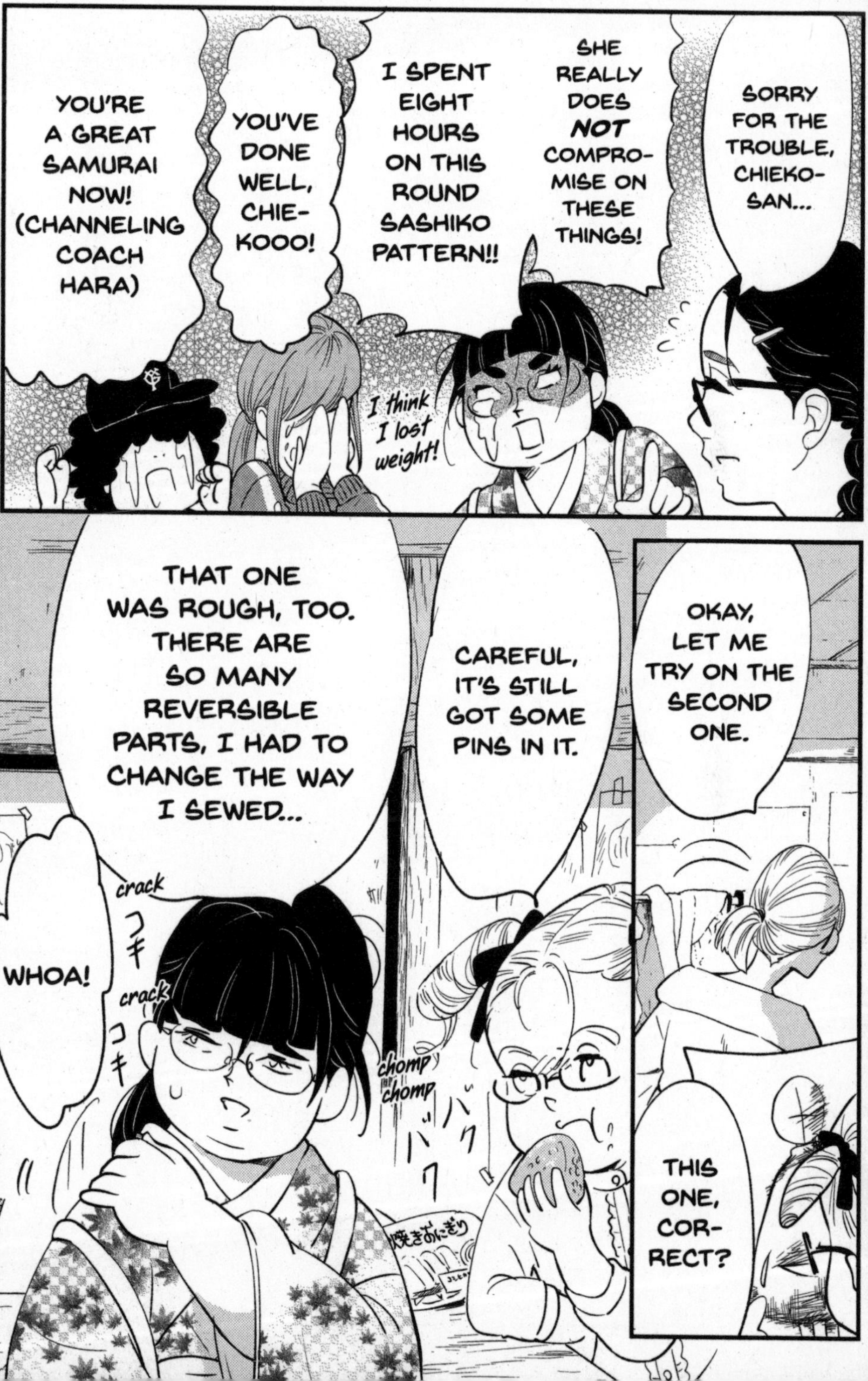
SORRY FOR THE TROUBLE, CHIEKO-SAN...
SHE REALLY DOES NOT COMPROMISE ON THESE THINGS!
I SPENT EIGHT HOURS ON THIS ROUND SASHIKO PATTERN!!
I think I lost weight!
YOU'VE DONE WELL, CHIE-KOOO!
YOU'RE A GREAT SAMURAI NOW! (CHANNELING COACH HARA)
OKAY, LET ME TRY ON THE SECOND ONE.
THIS ONE, CORRECT?
CAREFUL, IT'S STILL GOT SOME PINS IN IT.
chomp chomp
THAT ONE WAS ROUGH, TOO. THERE ARE SO MANY REVERSIBLE PARTS, I HAD TO CHANGE THE WAY I SEWED...
crack
crack
WHOA!

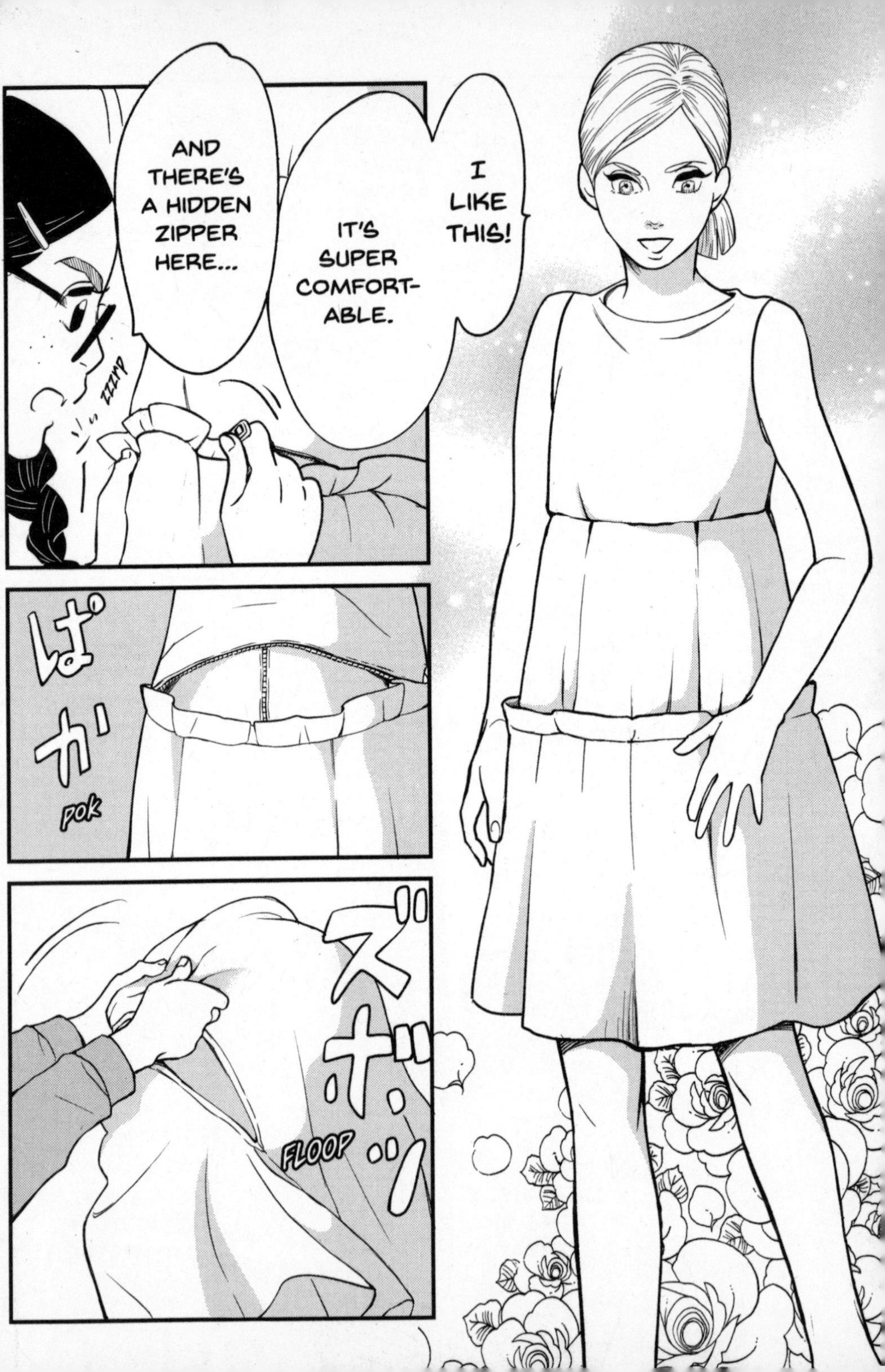
I LIKE THIS!
IT'S SUPER COMFORTABLE.
AND THERE'S A HIDDEN ZIPPER HERE...
ZZZRP
ぱか
POK
ズボッ
FLOOP

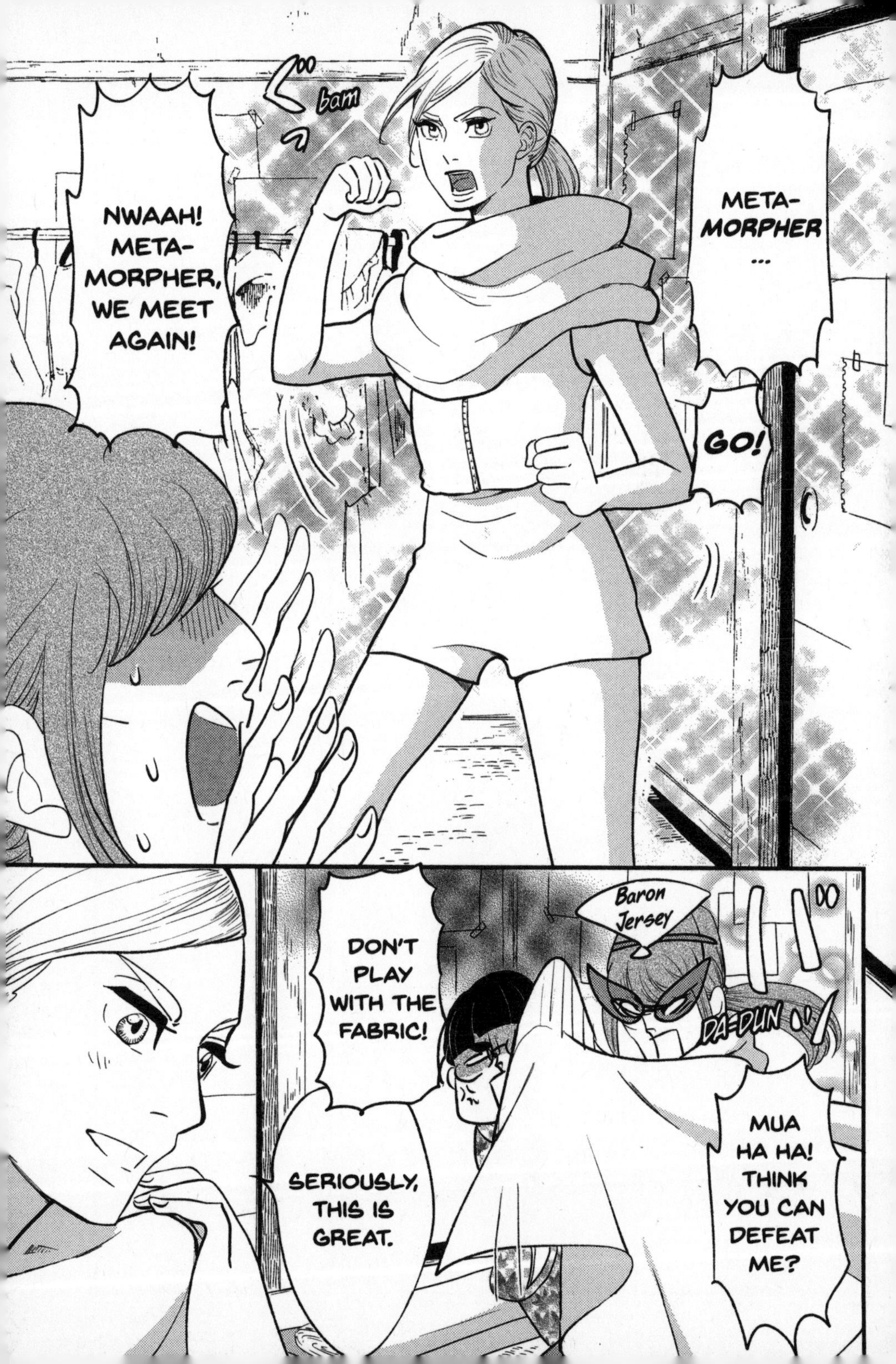
META-MORPHER ...
GO!
bam
NWAAH! META-MORPHER, WE MEET AGAIN!
DO
Baron Jersey
DA-DUN
MUA HA HA! THINK YOU CAN DEFEAT ME?
DON'T PLAY WITH THE FABRIC!
SERIOUSLY, THIS IS GREAT.

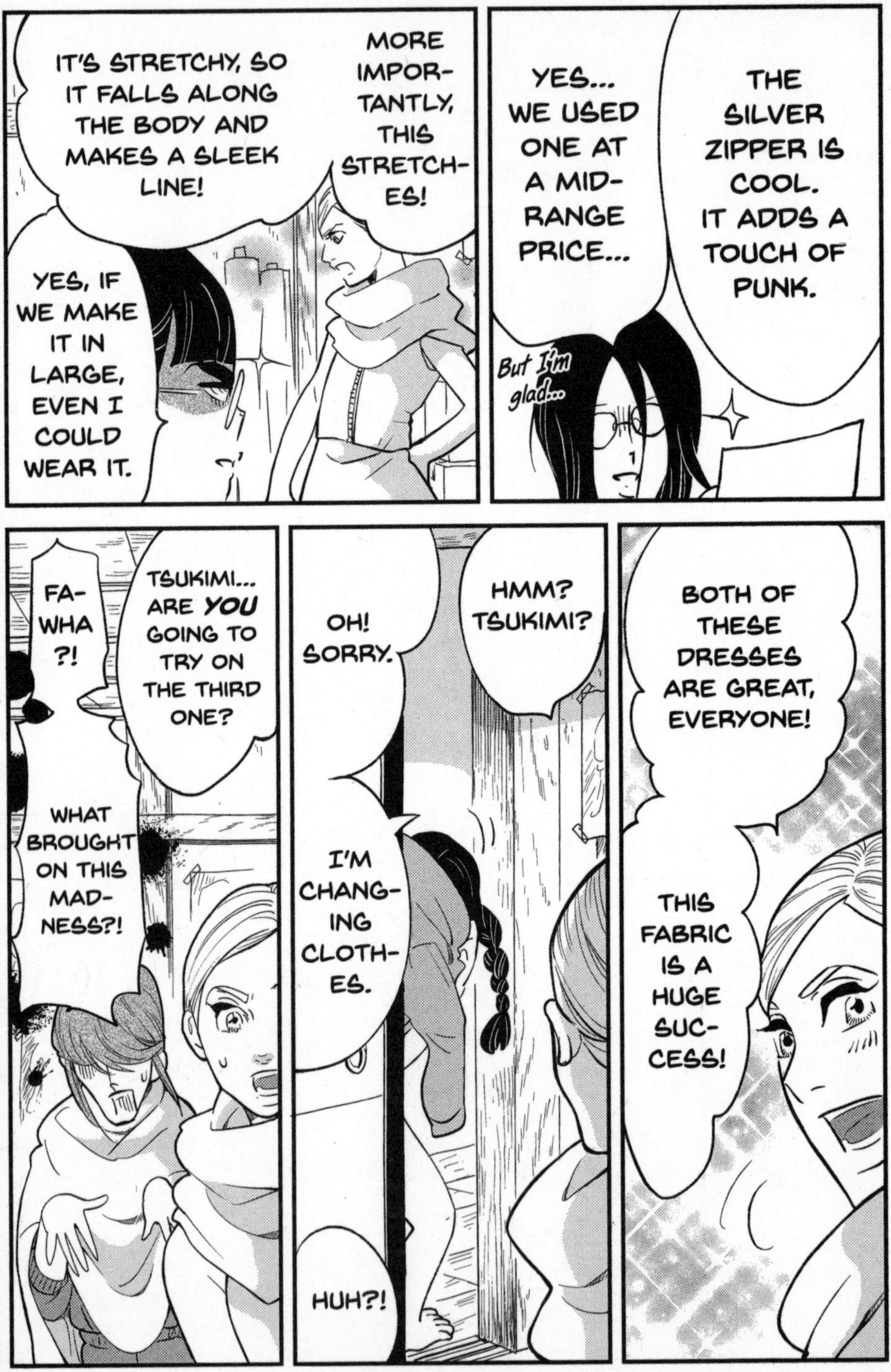
THE SILVER ZIPPER IS COOL. IT ADDS A TOUCH OF PUNK.
YES... WE USED ONE AT A MID-RANGE PRICE...
But I'm glad...
MORE IMPORTANTLY, THIS STRETCHES!
IT'S STRETCHY, SO IT FALLS ALONG THE BODY AND MAKES A SLEEK LINE!
YES, IF WE MAKE IT IN LARGE, EVEN I COULD WEAR IT.
BOTH OF THESE DRESSES ARE GREAT, EVERYONE!
THIS FABRIC IS A HUGE SUCCESS!
HMM? TSUKIMI?
OH! SORRY.
I'M CHANGING CLOTHES.
HUH?!
TSUKIMI... ARE *YOU* GOING TO TRY ON THE THIRD ONE?
FA-WHA?!
WHAT BROUGHT ON THIS MADNESS?!

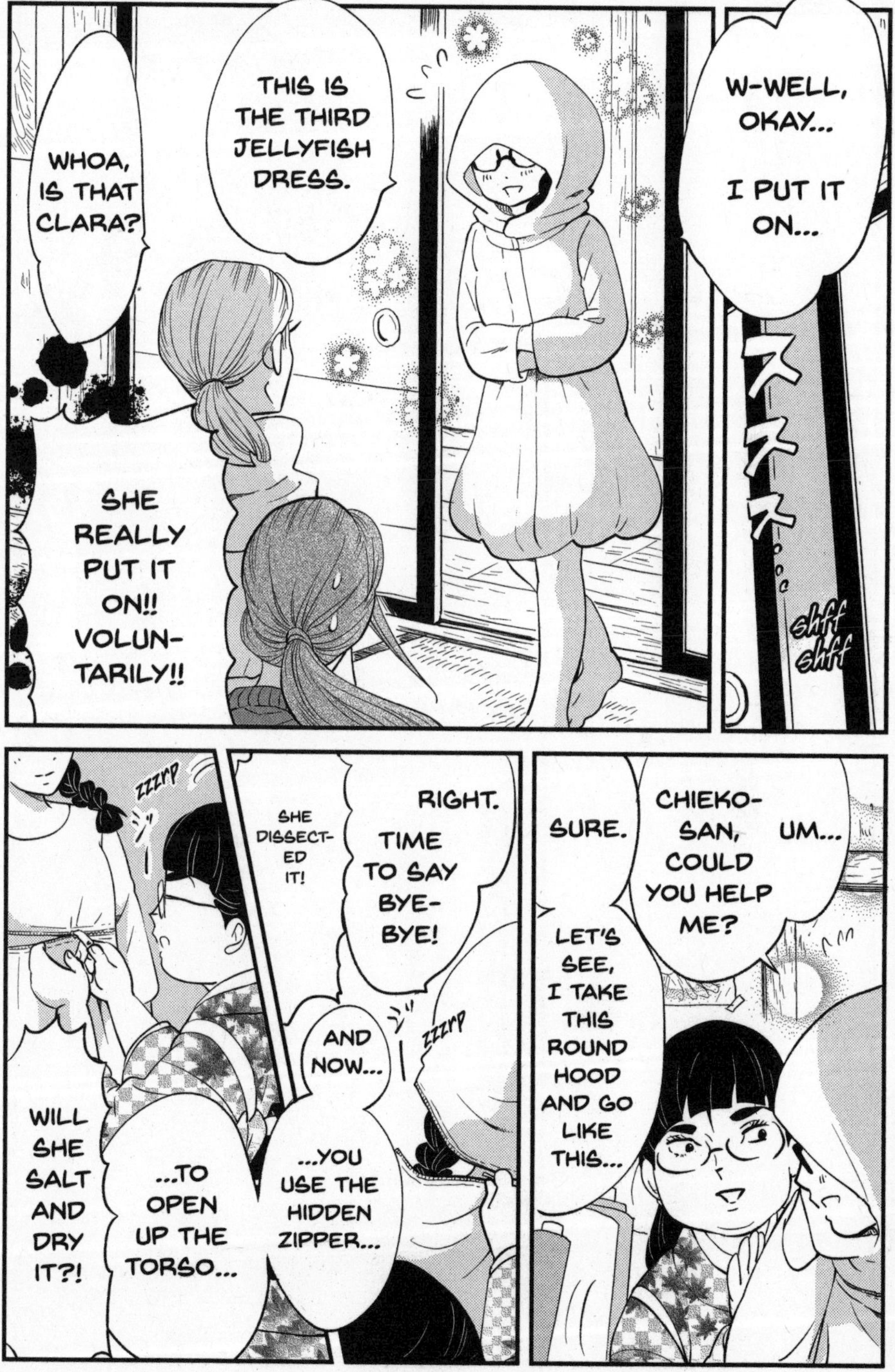
W-WELL, OKAY... I PUT IT ON...
shff shff
THIS IS THE THIRD JELLYFISH DRESS.
WHOA, IS THAT CLARA?
SHE REALLY PUT IT ON!! VOLUNTARILY!!
CHIEKO-SAN, UM... COULD YOU HELP ME?
SURE.
LET'S SEE, I TAKE THIS ROUND HOOD AND GO LIKE THIS...
RIGHT. TIME TO SAY BYE-BYE!
SHE DISSECTED IT!
AND NOW...
zzzrp
...YOU USE THE HIDDEN ZIPPER...
zzzrp
...TO OPEN UP THE TORSO...
WILL SHE SALT AND DRY IT?!

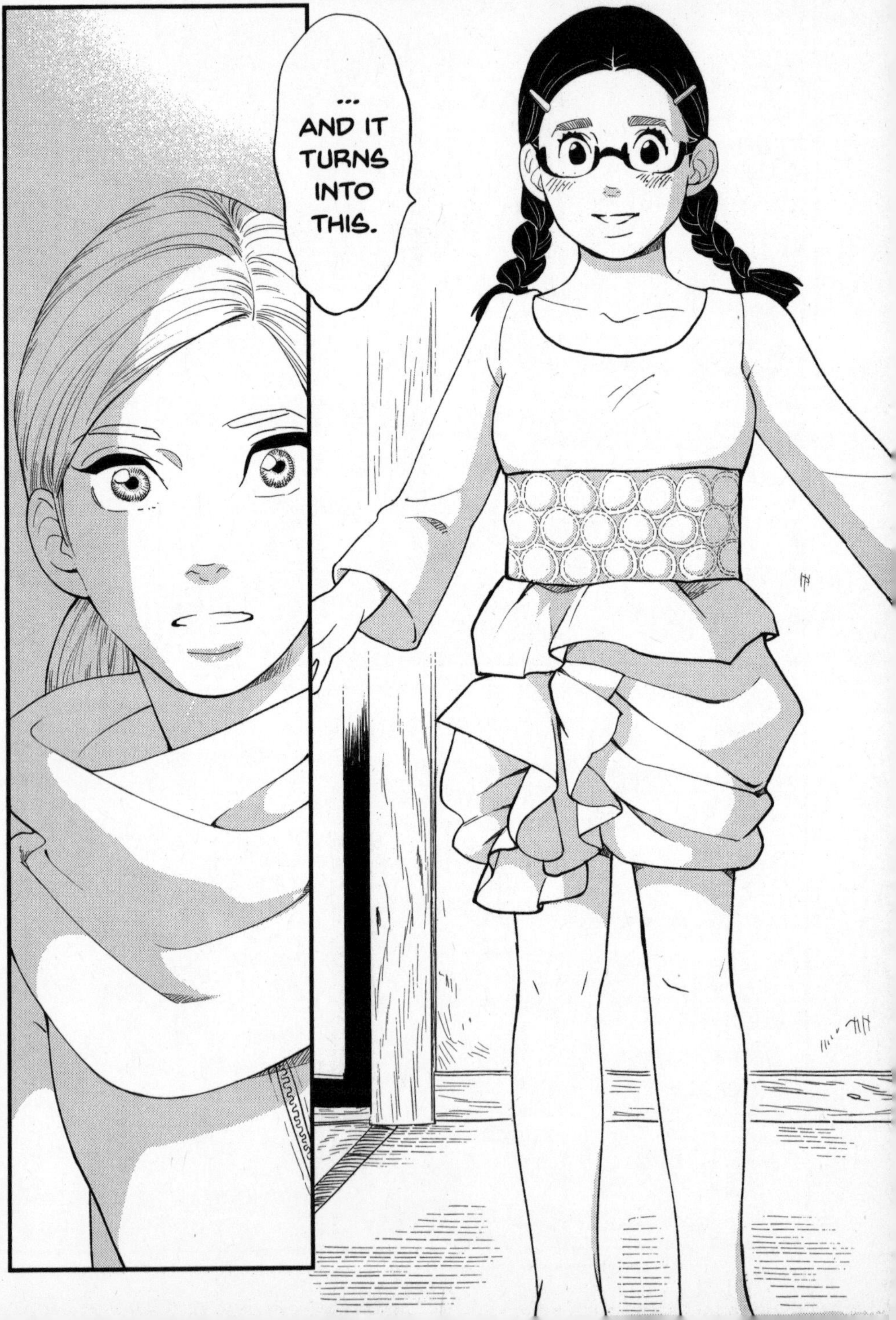
... AND IT TURNS INTO THIS.

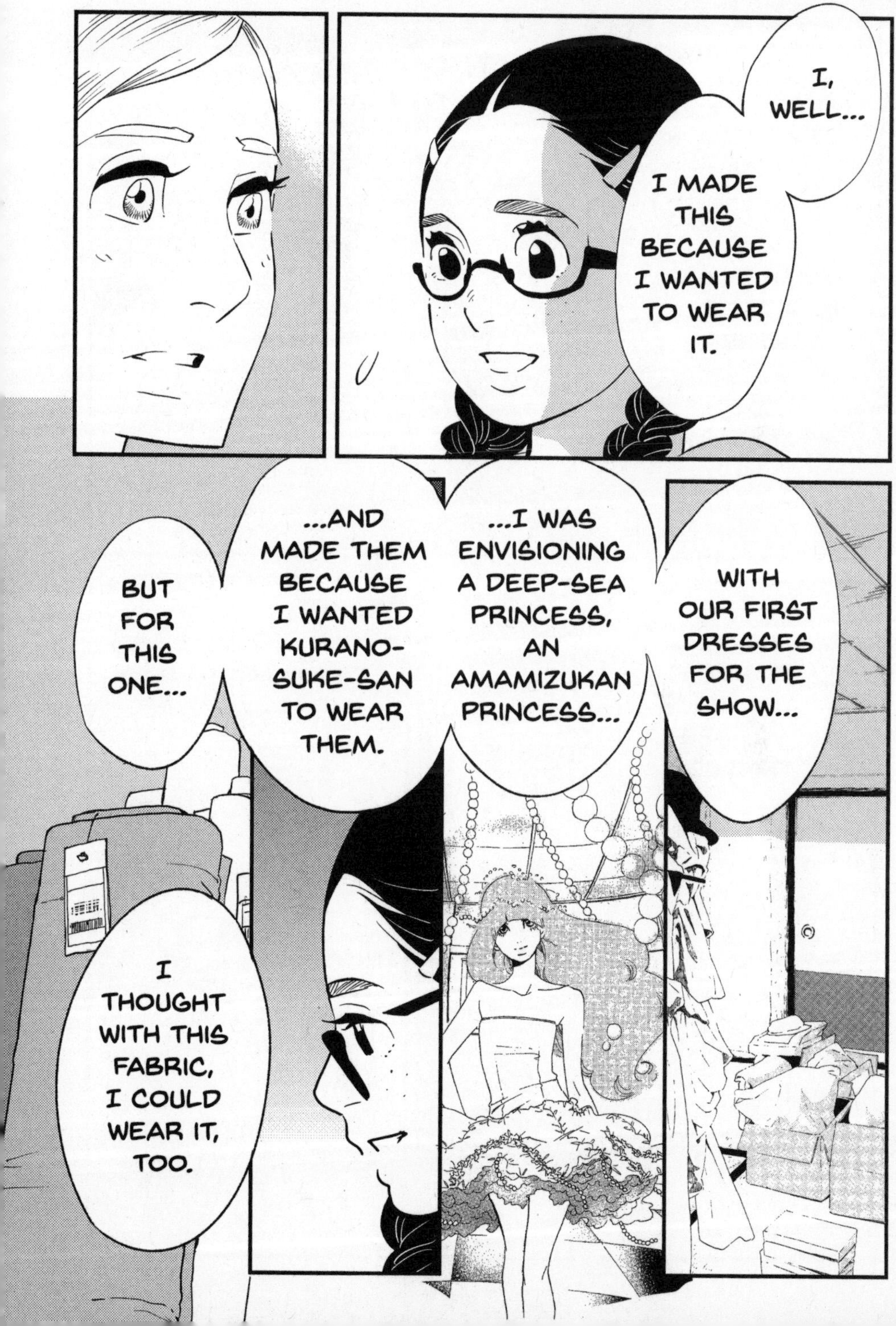
I, WELL...
I MADE THIS BECAUSE I WANTED TO WEAR IT.
WITH OUR FIRST DRESSES FOR THE SHOW...
...I WAS ENVISIONING A DEEP-SEA PRINCESS, AN AMAMIZUKAN PRINCESS...
...AND MADE THEM BECAUSE I WANTED KURANO-SUKE-SAN TO WEAR THEM.
BUT FOR THIS ONE...
I THOUGHT WITH THIS FABRIC, I COULD WEAR IT, TOO.

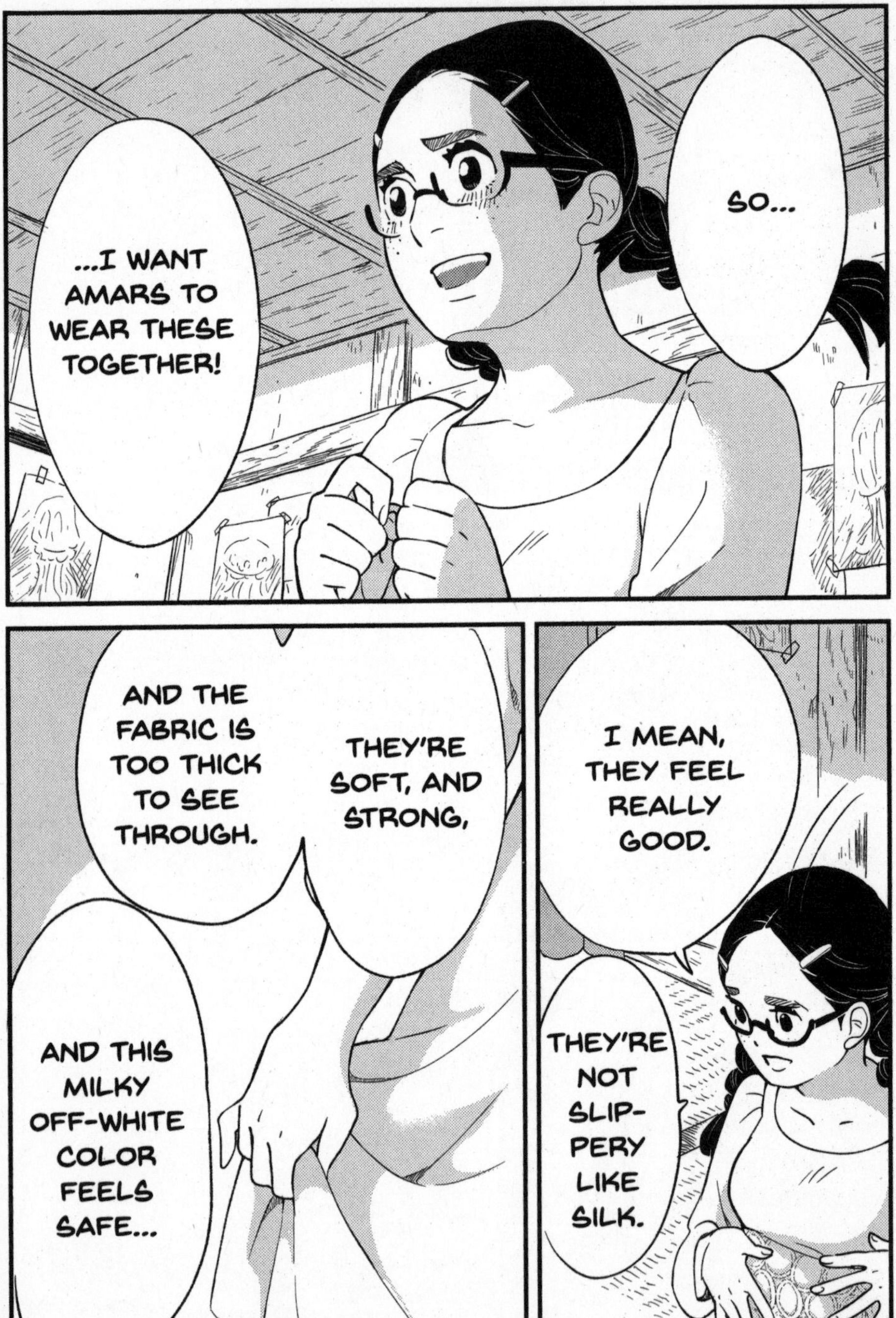
SO...
...I WANT AMARS TO WEAR THESE TOGETHER!
I MEAN, THEY FEEL REALLY GOOD.
THEY'RE NOT SLIP-PERY LIKE SILK.
THEY'RE SOFT, AND STRONG,
AND THE FABRIC IS TOO THICK TO SEE THROUGH.
AND THIS MILKY OFF-WHITE COLOR FEELS SAFE...

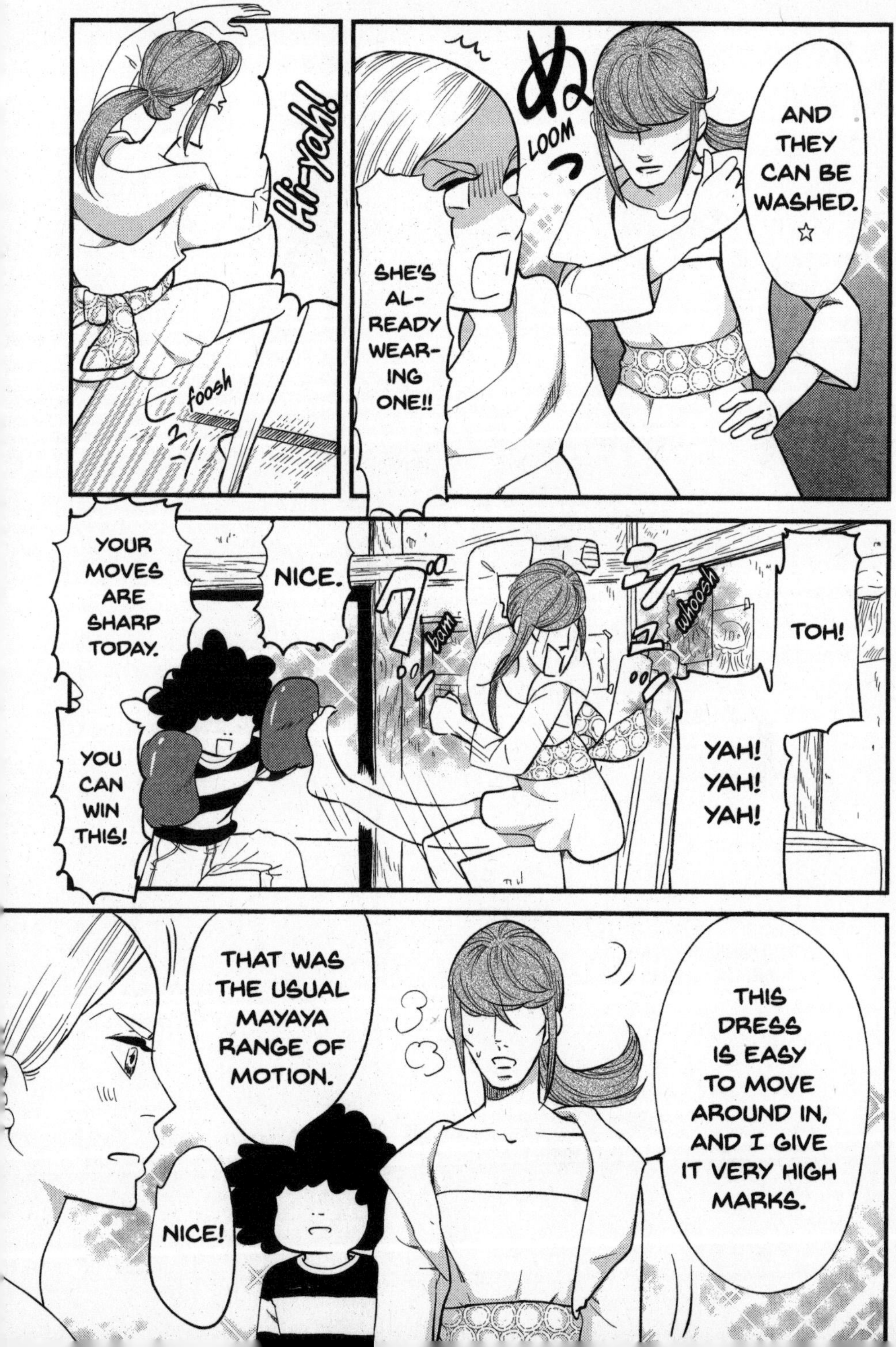
AND THEY CAN BE WASHED. ☆
ぬ
LOOM
SHE'S ALREADY WEARING ONE!!
Hi-yah!
foosh
TOH!
whoosh
YAH! YAH! YAH!
bam
NICE.
YOUR MOVES ARE SHARP TODAY.
YOU CAN WIN THIS!
THIS DRESS IS EASY TO MOVE AROUND IN, AND I GIVE IT VERY HIGH MARKS.
THAT WAS THE USUAL MAYAYA RANGE OF MOTION.
NICE!

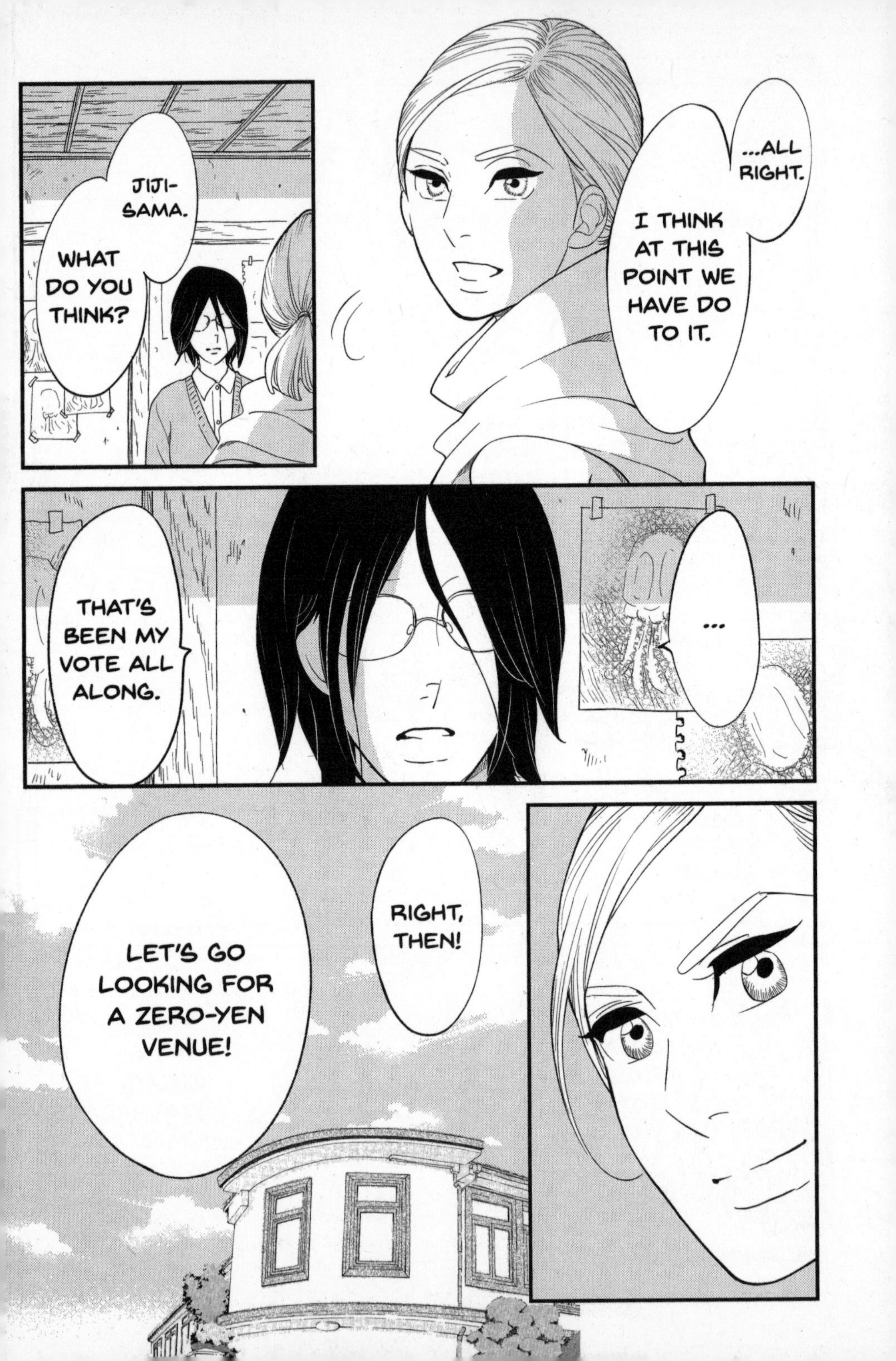
...ALL RIGHT.
I THINK AT THIS POINT WE HAVE DO TO IT.
JIJI-SAMA.
WHAT DO YOU THINK?
...
THAT'S BEEN MY VOTE ALL ALONG.
RIGHT, THEN!
LET'S GO LOOKING FOR A ZERO-YEN VENUE!

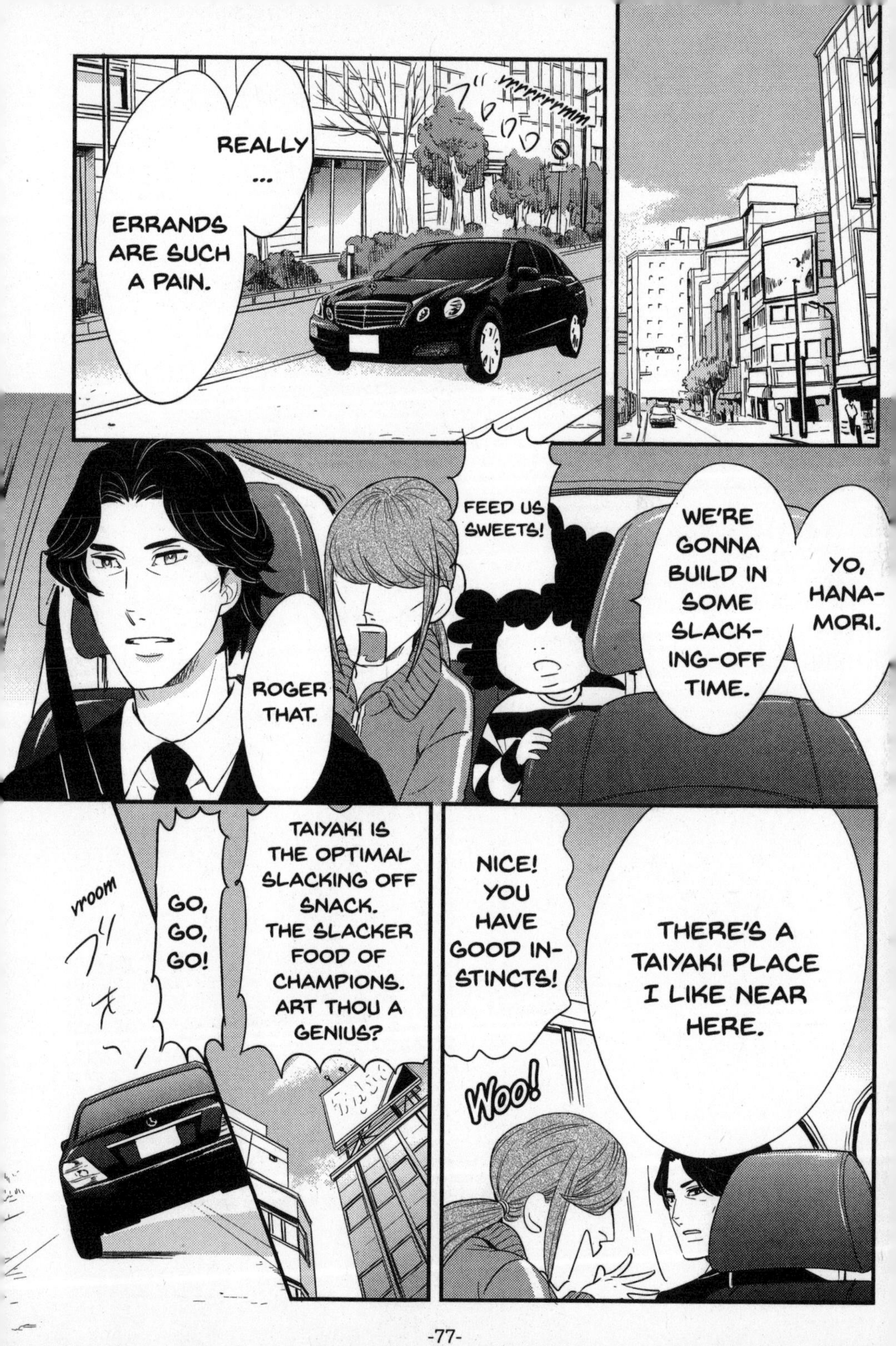
vrrrrrrrmm
REALLY ...
ERRANDS ARE SUCH A PAIN.
YO, HANAMORI.
WE'RE GONNA BUILD IN SOME SLACKING-OFF TIME.
FEED US SWEETS!
ROGER THAT.
THERE'S A TAIYAKI PLACE I LIKE NEAR HERE.
NICE! YOU HAVE GOOD INSTINCTS!
Woo!
TAIYAKI IS THE OPTIMAL SLACKING OFF SNACK. THE SLACKER FOOD OF CHAMPIONS. ART THOU A GENIUS?
GO, GO, GO!
vroom

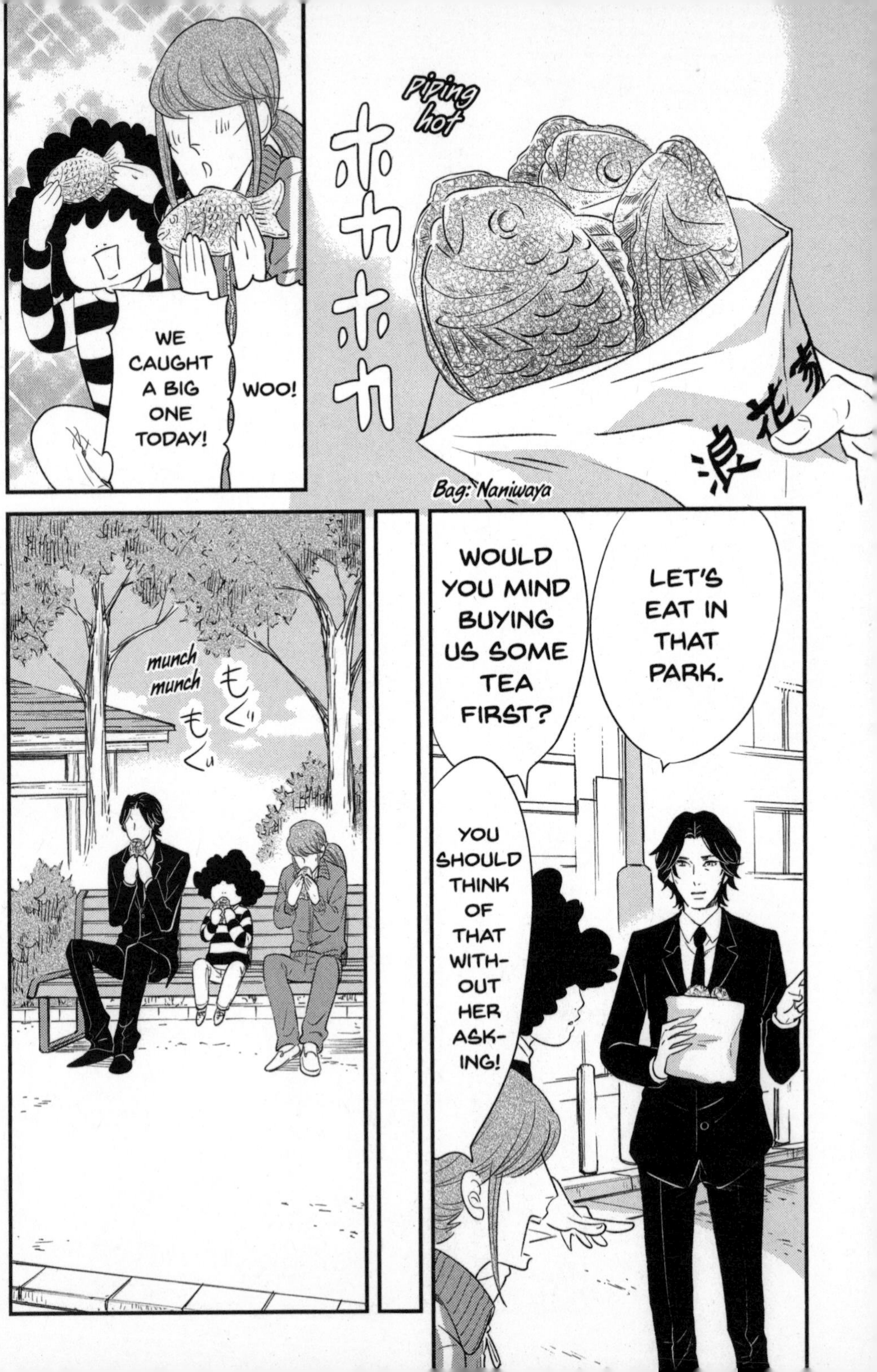
piping hot
ホカホカ
浪花
Bag: Naniwaya
WE CAUGHT A BIG ONE TODAY!
WOO!
LET'S EAT IN THAT PARK.
WOULD YOU MIND BUYING US SOME TEA FIRST?
YOU SHOULD THINK OF THAT WITH-OUT HER ASK-ING!
munch munch
もぐもぐ

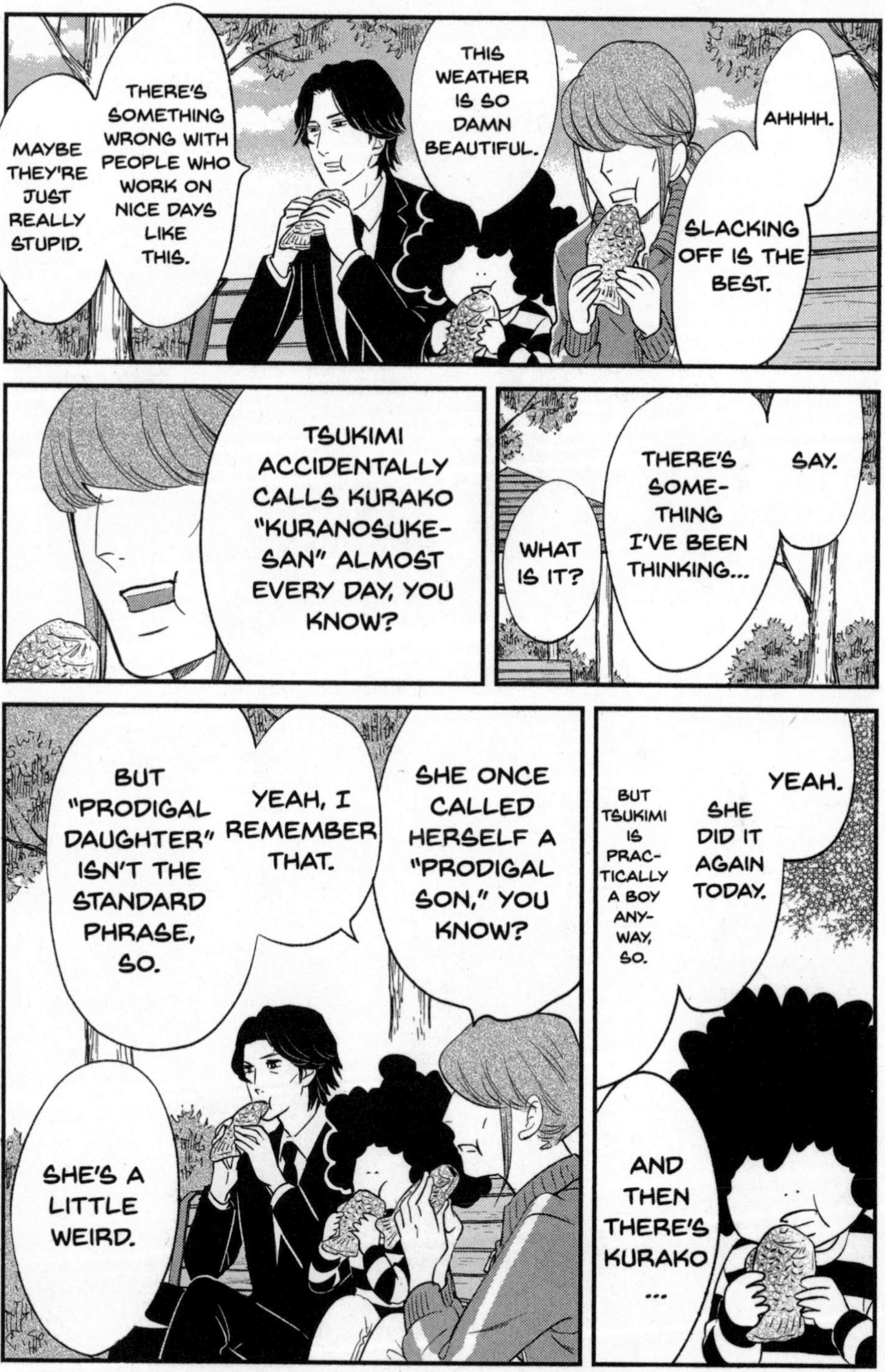
AHHHH.
SLACKING OFF IS THE BEST.
THIS WEATHER IS SO DAMN BEAUTIFUL.
THERE'S SOMETHING WRONG WITH PEOPLE WHO WORK ON NICE DAYS LIKE THIS.
MAYBE THEY'RE JUST REALLY STUPID.
SAY.
THERE'S SOME-THING I'VE BEEN THINKING...
WHAT IS IT?
TSUKIMI ACCIDENTALLY CALLS KURAKO "KURANOSUKE-SAN" ALMOST EVERY DAY, YOU KNOW?
YEAH.
SHE DID IT AGAIN TODAY.
BUT TSUKIMI IS PRAC-TICALLY A BOY ANY-WAY, SO.
AND THEN THERE'S KURAKO ...
SHE ONCE CALLED HERSELF A "PRODIGAL SON," YOU KNOW?
YEAH, I REMEMBER THAT.
BUT "PRODIGAL DAUGHTER" ISN'T THE STANDARD PHRASE, SO.
SHE'S A LITTLE WEIRD.

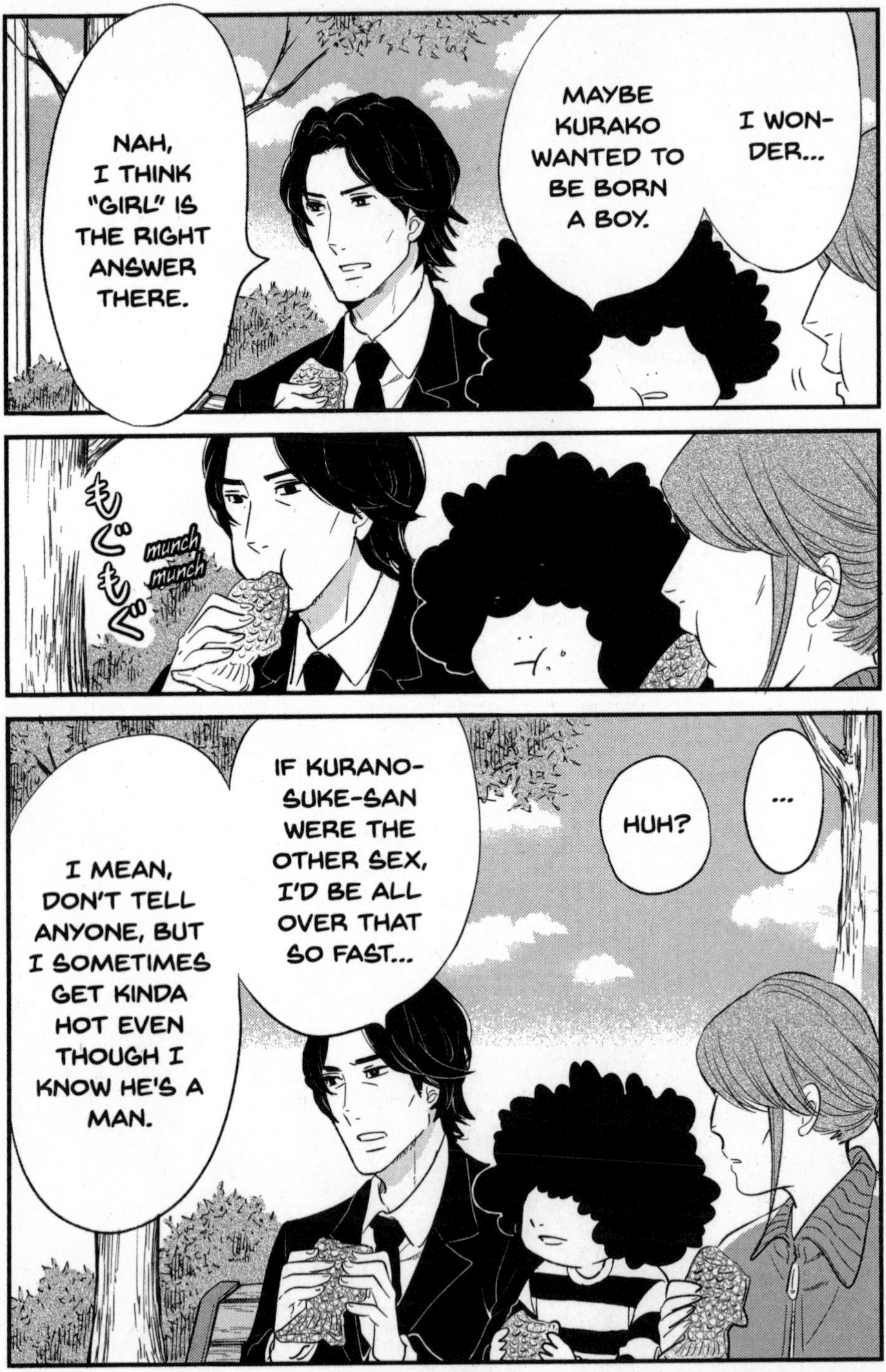
I WON-DER...
MAYBE KURAKO WANTED TO BE BORN A BOY.
NAH, I THINK "GIRL" IS THE RIGHT ANSWER THERE.
もぐもぐ
munch munch
...
HUH?
IF KURANO-SUKE-SAN WERE THE OTHER SEX, I'D BE ALL OVER THAT SO FAST...
I MEAN, DON'T TELL ANYONE, BUT I SOMETIMES GET KINDA HOT EVEN THOUGH I KNOW HE'S A MAN.

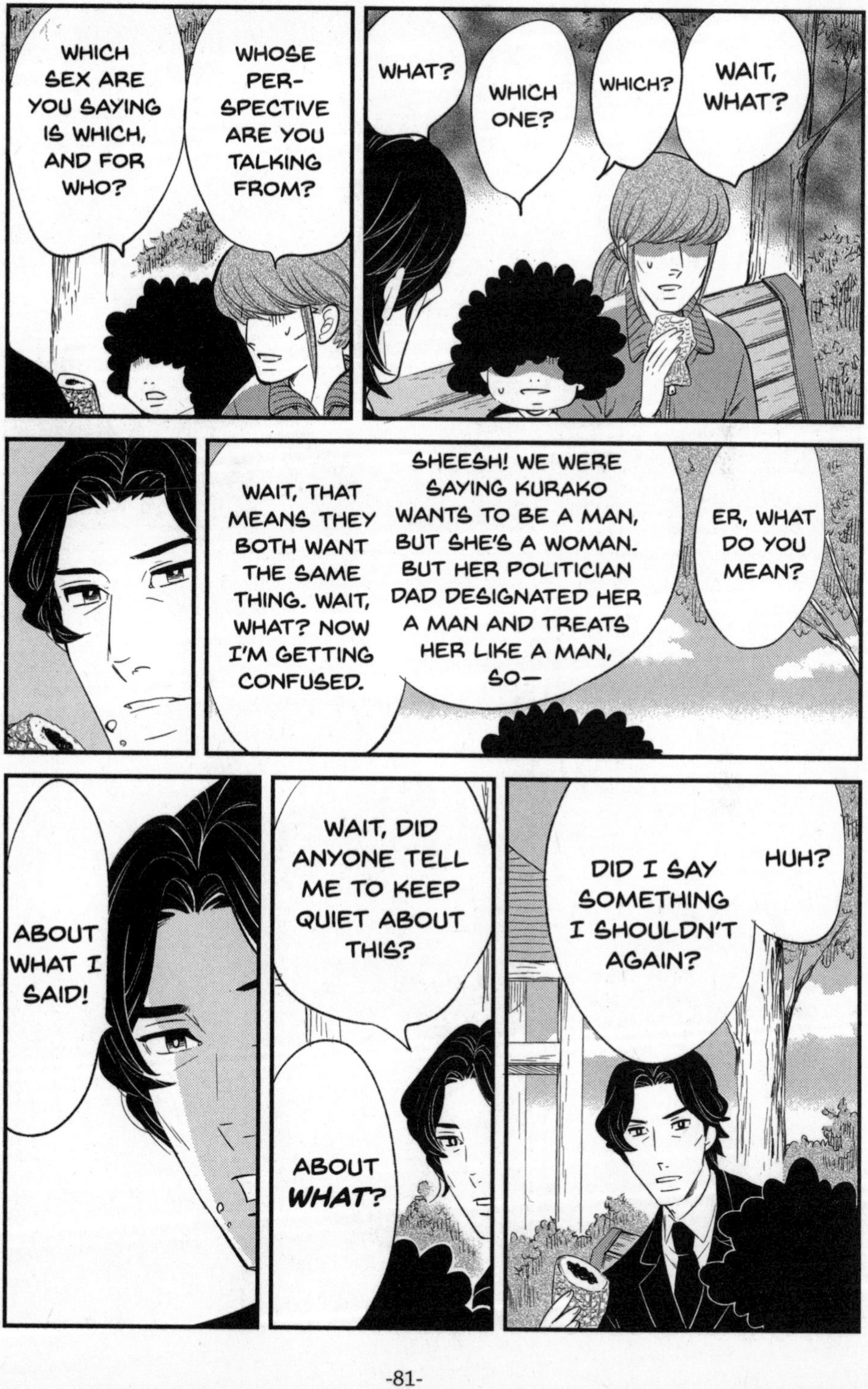
WAIT, WHAT?
WHICH?
WHICH ONE?
WHAT?
WHOSE PERSPECTIVE ARE YOU TALKING FROM?
WHICH SEX ARE YOU SAYING IS WHICH, AND FOR WHO?
ER, WHAT DO YOU MEAN?
SHEESH! WE WERE SAYING KURAKO WANTS TO BE A MAN, BUT SHE'S A WOMAN. BUT HER POLITICIAN DAD DESIGNATED HER A MAN AND TREATS HER LIKE A MAN, SO—
WAIT, THAT MEANS THEY BOTH WANT THE SAME THING. WAIT, WHAT? NOW I'M GETTING CONFUSED.
HUH?
DID I SAY SOMETHING I SHOULDN'T AGAIN?
WAIT, DID ANYONE TELL ME TO KEEP QUIET ABOUT THIS?
ABOUT *WHAT*?
ABOUT WHAT I SAID!

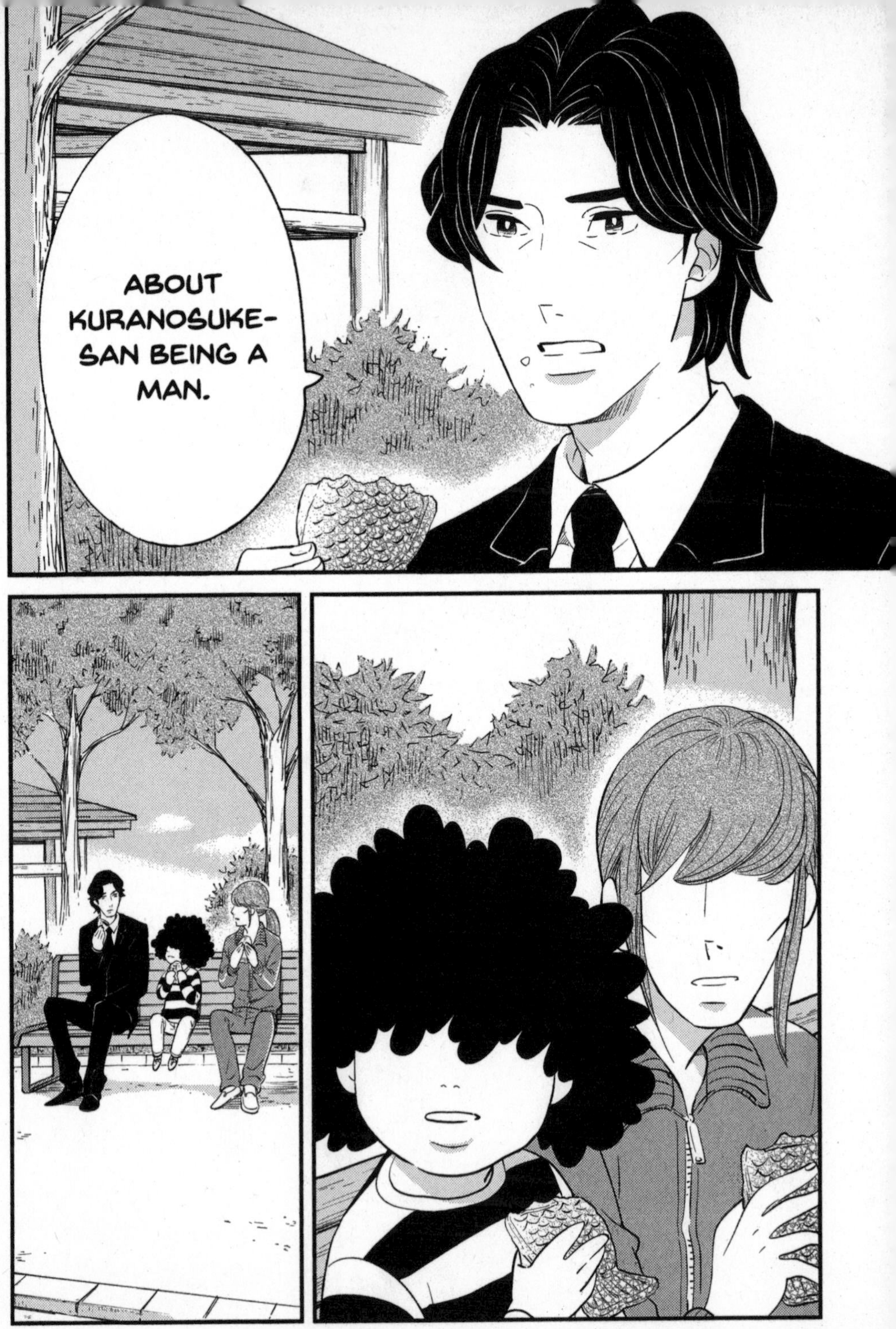

ABOUT KURANOSUKE-SAN BEING A MAN.

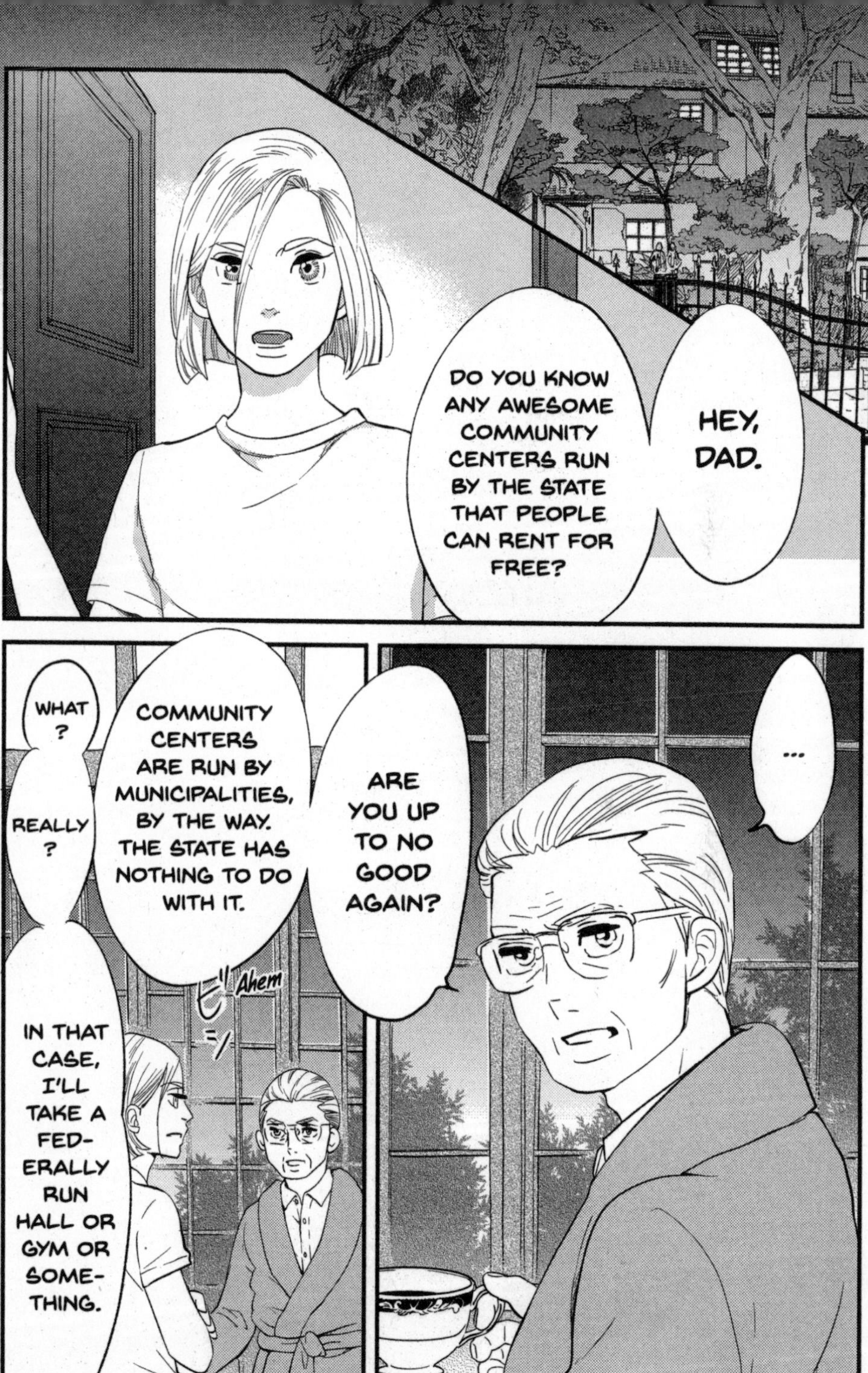
HEY, DAD.
DO YOU KNOW ANY AWESOME COMMUNITY CENTERS RUN BY THE STATE THAT PEOPLE CAN RENT FOR FREE?
...
ARE YOU UP TO NO GOOD AGAIN?
COMMUNITY CENTERS ARE RUN BY MUNICIPALITIES, BY THE WAY. THE STATE HAS NOTHING TO DO WITH IT.
Ahem
WHAT?
REALLY?
IN THAT CASE, I'LL TAKE A FED-ERALLY RUN HALL OR GYM OR SOME-THING.

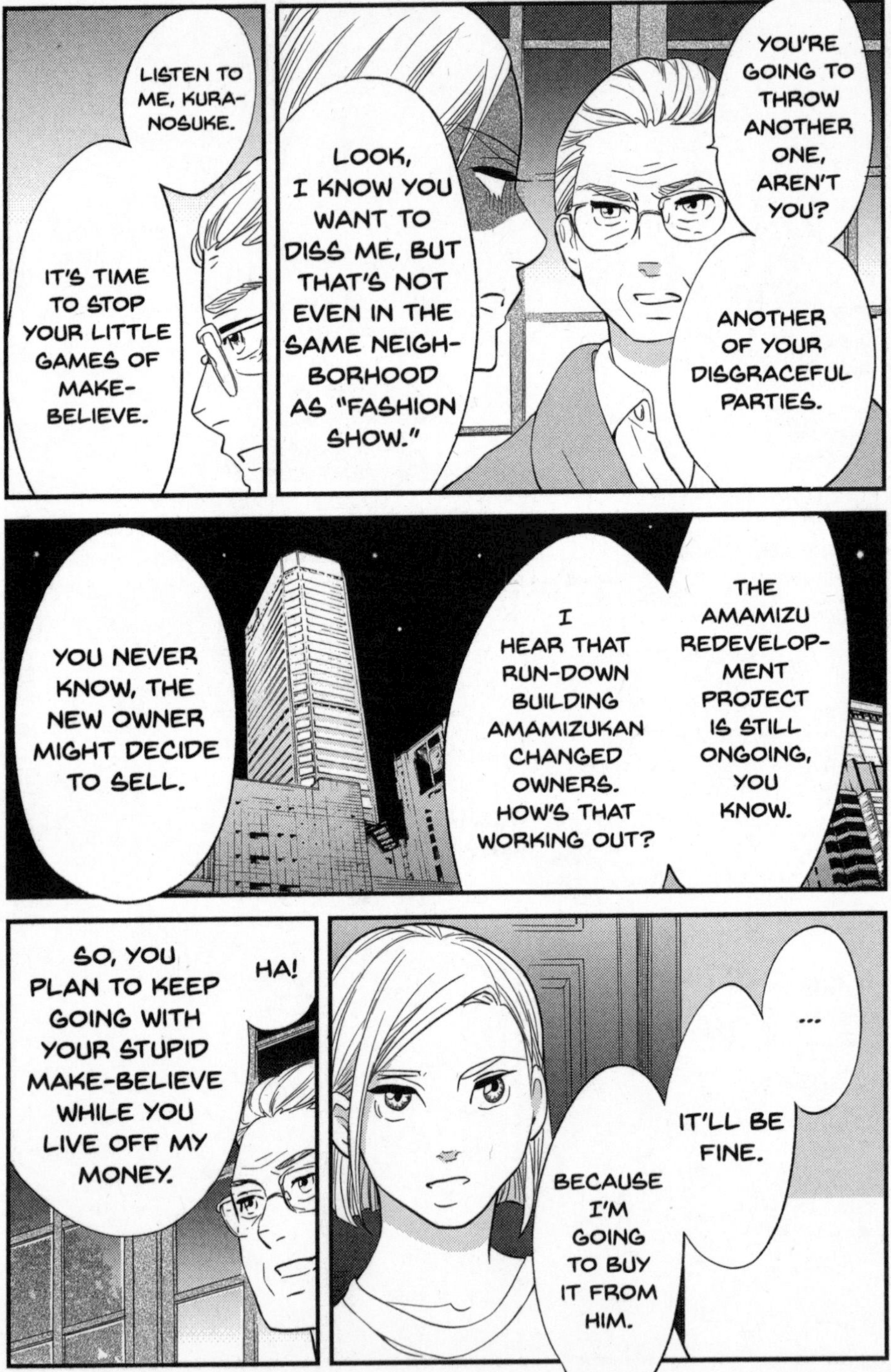
YOU'RE GOING TO THROW ANOTHER ONE, AREN'T YOU?
ANOTHER OF YOUR DISGRACEFUL PARTIES.
LOOK, I KNOW YOU WANT TO DISS ME, BUT THAT'S NOT EVEN IN THE SAME NEIGH-BORHOOD AS "FASHION SHOW."
LISTEN TO ME, KURA-NOSUKE.
IT'S TIME TO STOP YOUR LITTLE GAMES OF MAKE-BELIEVE.
THE AMAMIZU REDEVELOP-MENT PROJECT IS STILL ONGOING, YOU KNOW.
I HEAR THAT RUN-DOWN BUILDING AMAMIZUKAN CHANGED OWNERS. HOW'S THAT WORKING OUT?
YOU NEVER KNOW, THE NEW OWNER MIGHT DECIDE TO SELL.
...
IT'LL BE FINE.
BECAUSE I'M GOING TO BUY IT FROM HIM.
HA!
SO, YOU PLAN TO KEEP GOING WITH YOUR STUPID MAKE-BELIEVE WHILE YOU LIVE OFF MY MONEY.

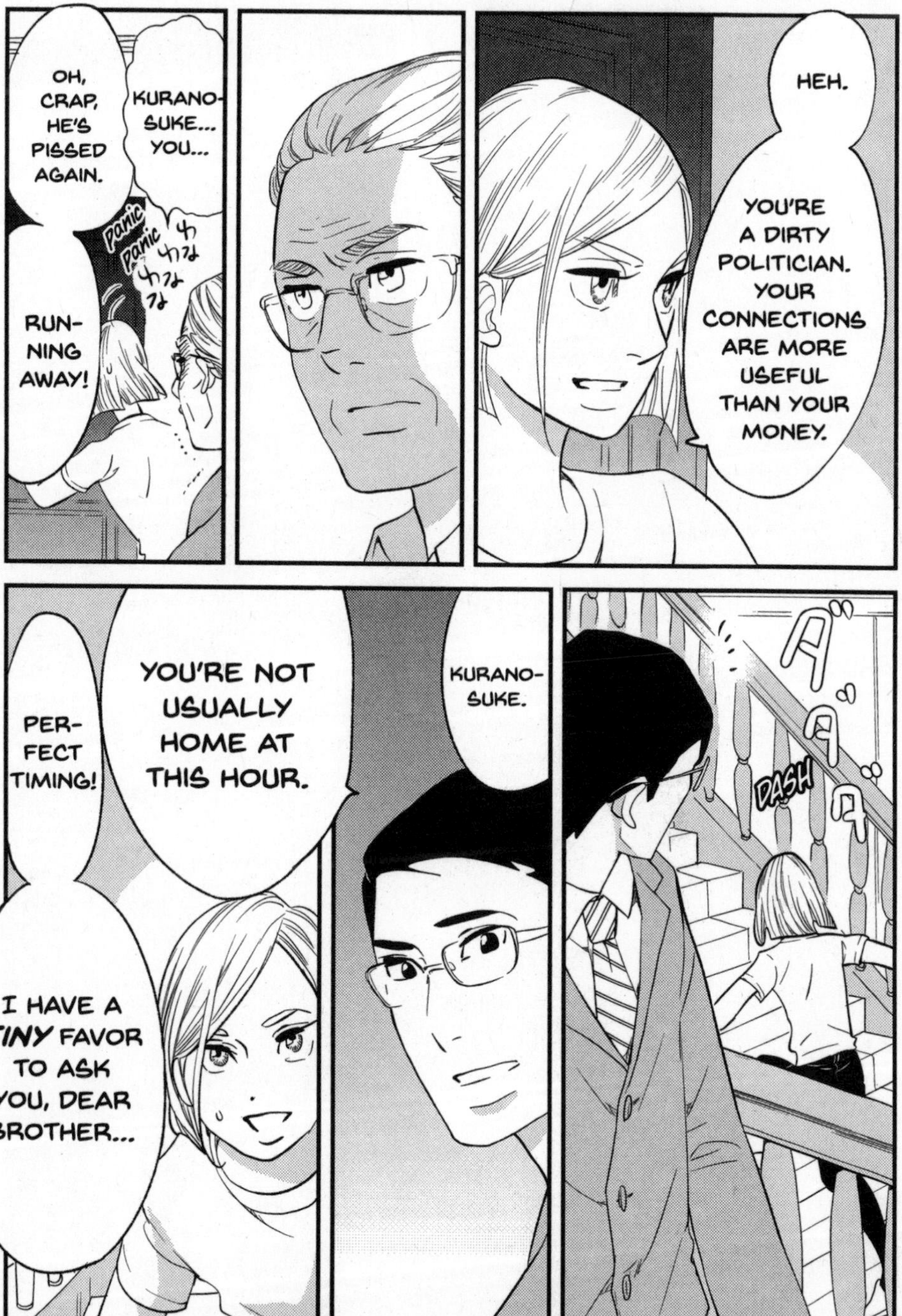
HEH.
YOU'RE A DIRTY POLITICIAN. YOUR CONNECTIONS ARE MORE USEFUL THAN YOUR MONEY.
KURANO-SUKE... YOU...
OH, CRAP, HE'S PISSED AGAIN.
panic panic
RUN-NING AWAY!
DASH
KURANO-SUKE.
YOU'RE NOT USUALLY HOME AT THIS HOUR.
PER-FECT TIMING!
I HAVE A TINY FAVOR TO ASK YOU, DEAR BROTHER...

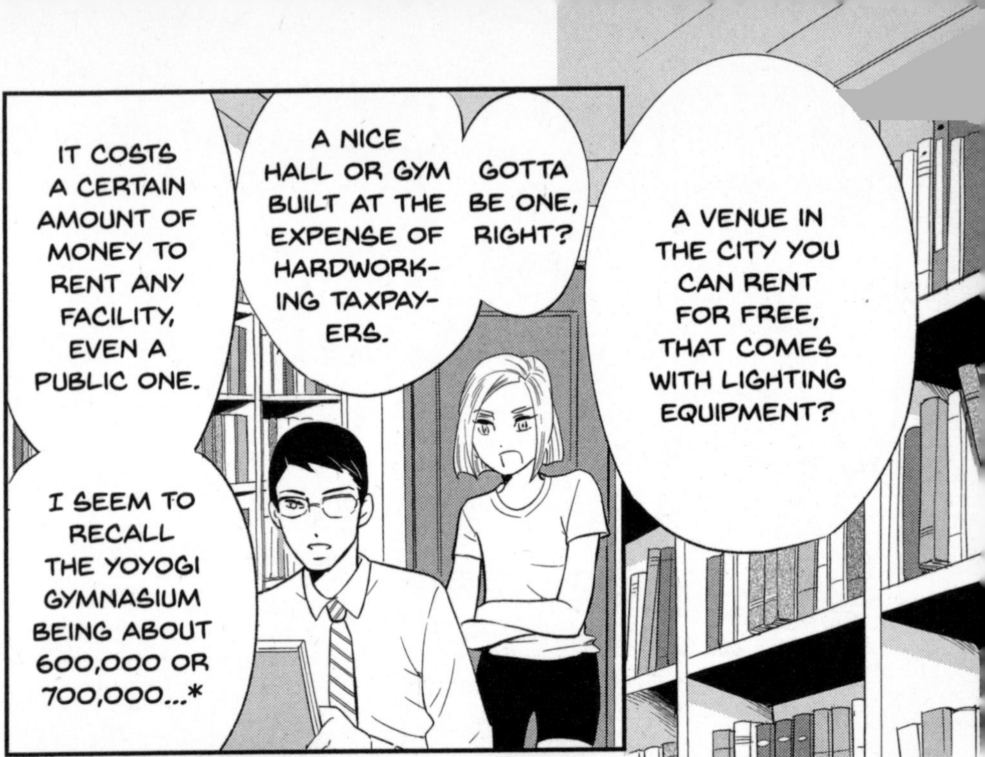
A VENUE IN THE CITY YOU CAN RENT FOR FREE, THAT COMES WITH LIGHTING EQUIPMENT?
GOTTA BE ONE, RIGHT?
A NICE HALL OR GYM BUILT AT THE EXPENSE OF HARDWORKING TAXPAYERS.
IT COSTS A CERTAIN AMOUNT OF MONEY TO RENT ANY FACILITY, EVEN A PUBLIC ONE.
I SEEM TO RECALL THE YOYOGI GYMNASIUM BEING ABOUT 600,000 OR 700,000...*

*About $6,000 or $7,000 USD.

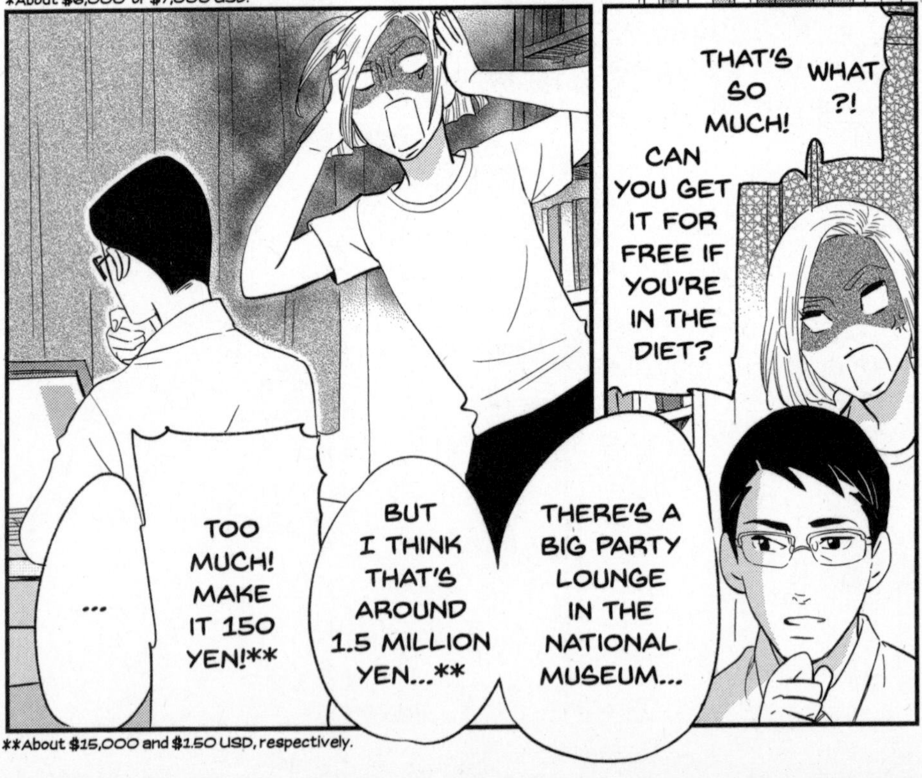
WHAT?!
THAT'S SO MUCH! CAN YOU GET IT FOR FREE IF YOU'RE IN THE DIET?
THERE'S A BIG PARTY LOUNGE IN THE NATIONAL MUSEUM...
BUT I THINK THAT'S AROUND 1.5 MILLION YEN...**
TOO MUCH! MAKE IT 150 YEN!**
...

**About $15,000 and $1.50 USD, respectively.

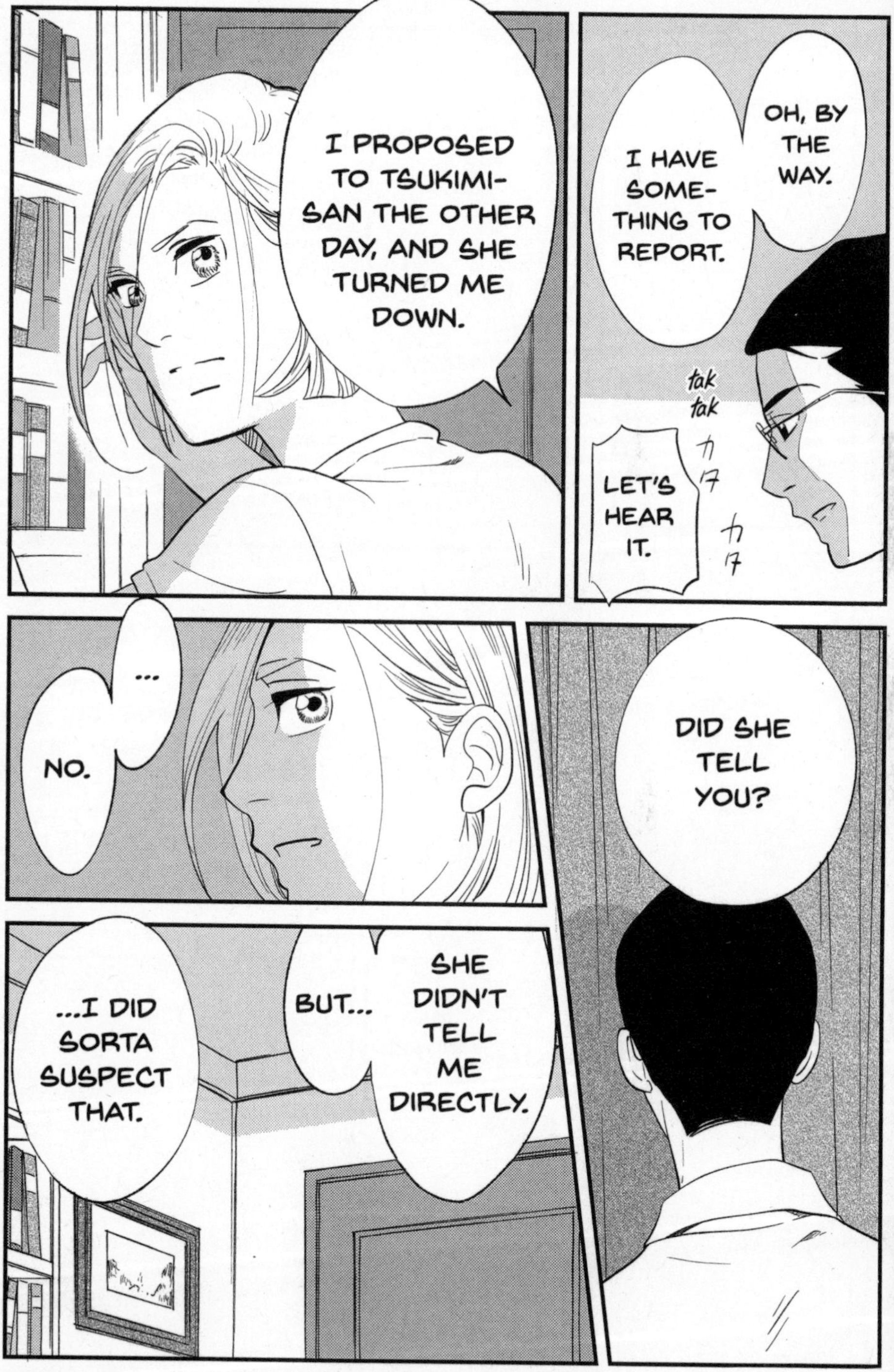
OH, BY THE WAY.
I HAVE SOME-THING TO REPORT.
tak tak
カタ
カタ
LET'S HEAR IT.
I PROPOSED TO TSUKIMI-SAN THE OTHER DAY, AND SHE TURNED ME DOWN.
DID SHE TELL YOU?
...
NO.
SHE DIDN'T TELL ME DIRECTLY.
BUT...
...I DID SORTA SUSPECT THAT.

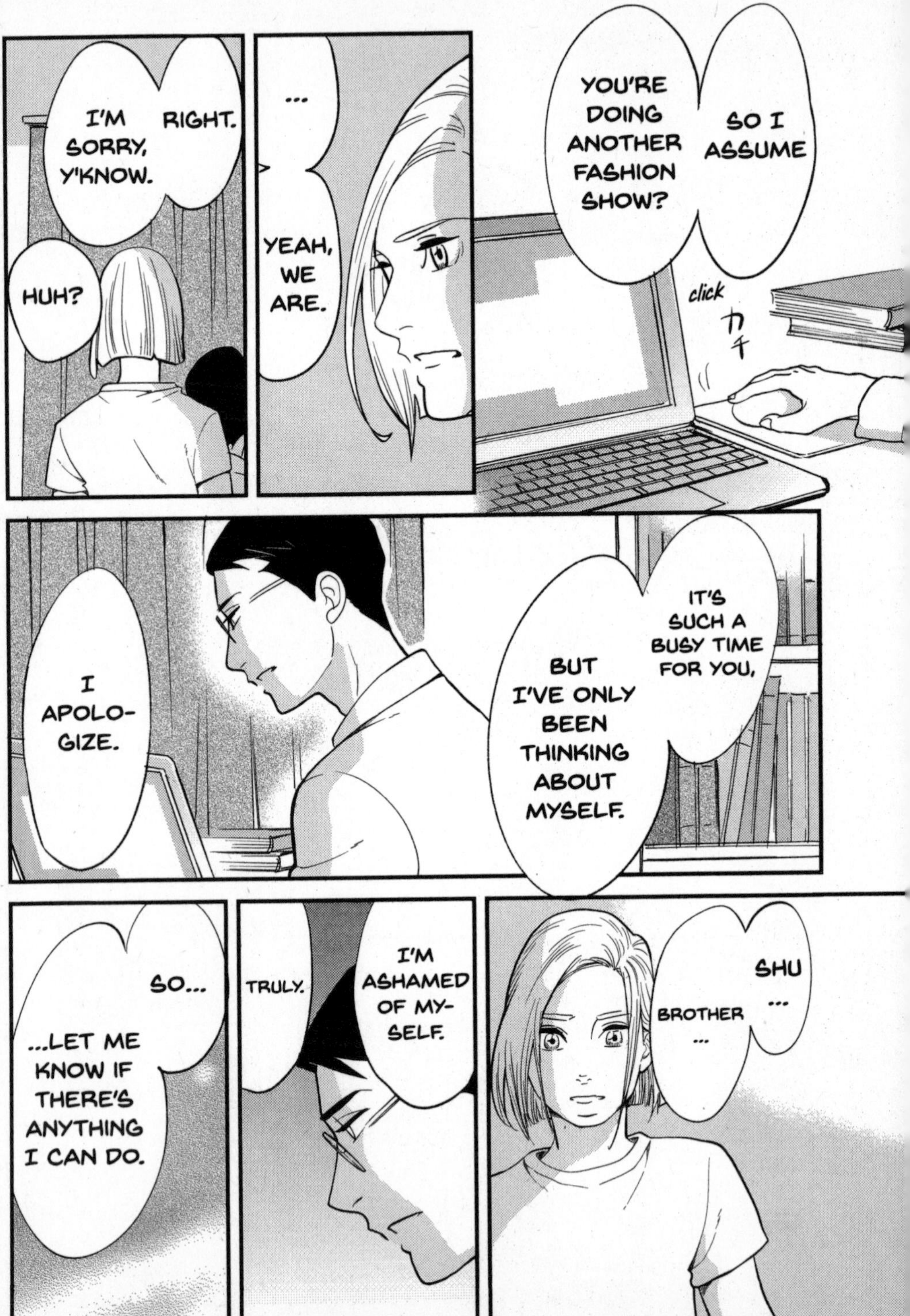
SO I ASSUME
YOU'RE DOING ANOTHER FASHION SHOW?
click
カチ
...
YEAH, WE ARE.
RIGHT.
I'M SORRY, Y'KNOW.
HUH?
IT'S SUCH A BUSY TIME FOR YOU,
BUT I'VE ONLY BEEN THINKING ABOUT MYSELF.
I APOLOGIZE.
SHU...
BROTHER...
I'M ASHAMED OF MY-SELF.
TRULY.
SO...
...LET ME KNOW IF THERE'S ANYTHING I CAN DO.

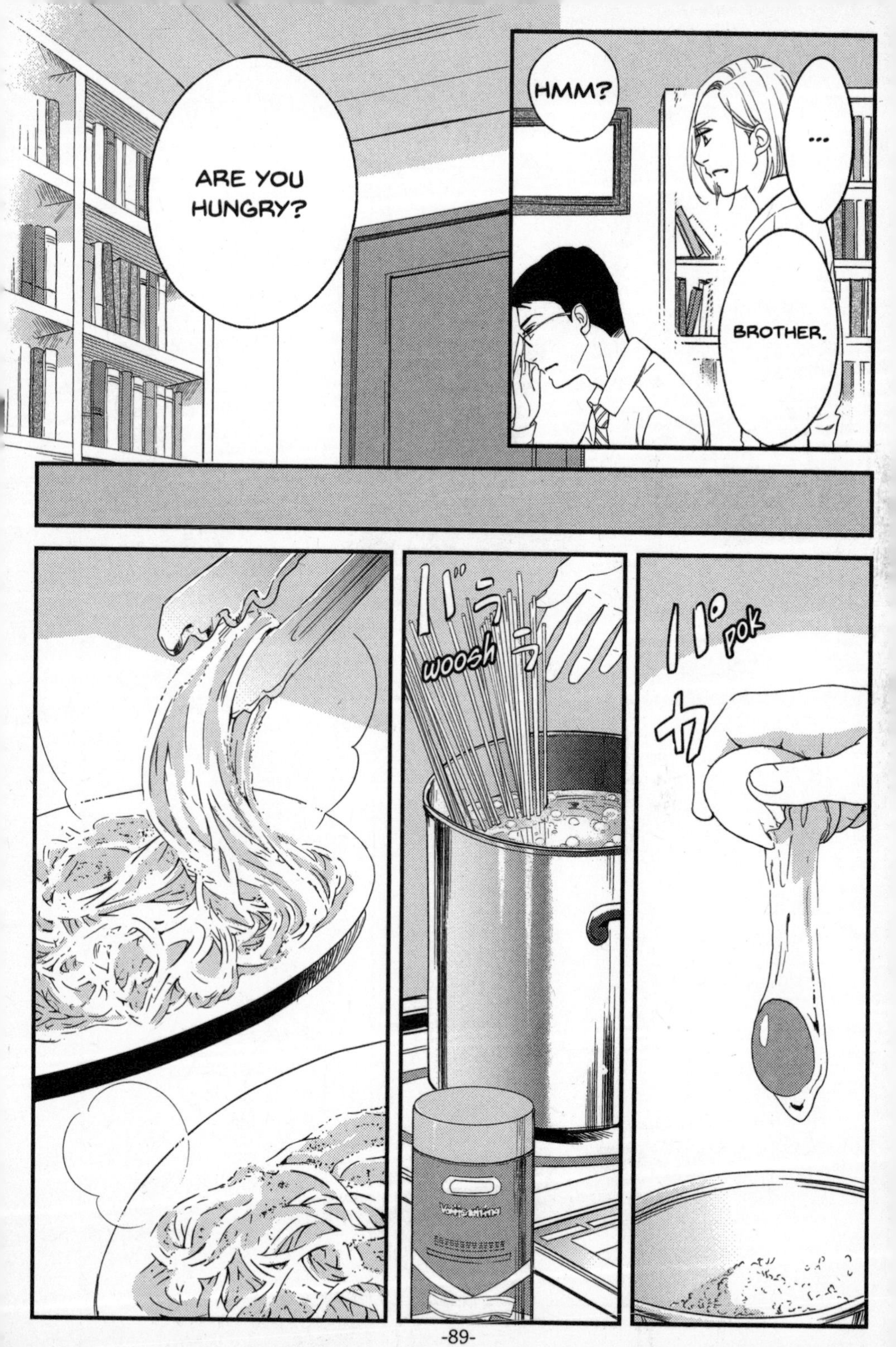
...
BROTHER.
HMM?
ARE YOU HUNGRY?
パカ
pok
バララ
woosh

PROB-
ABLY
NOT.

I CAN'T
TELL THE
DIFFER-
ENCE.

THERE WAS
NO PARMIGIANO-
REGGIANO, SO I
USED REGULAR
CHEAP CHEESE.

IT'S
GOOD.

HMM.

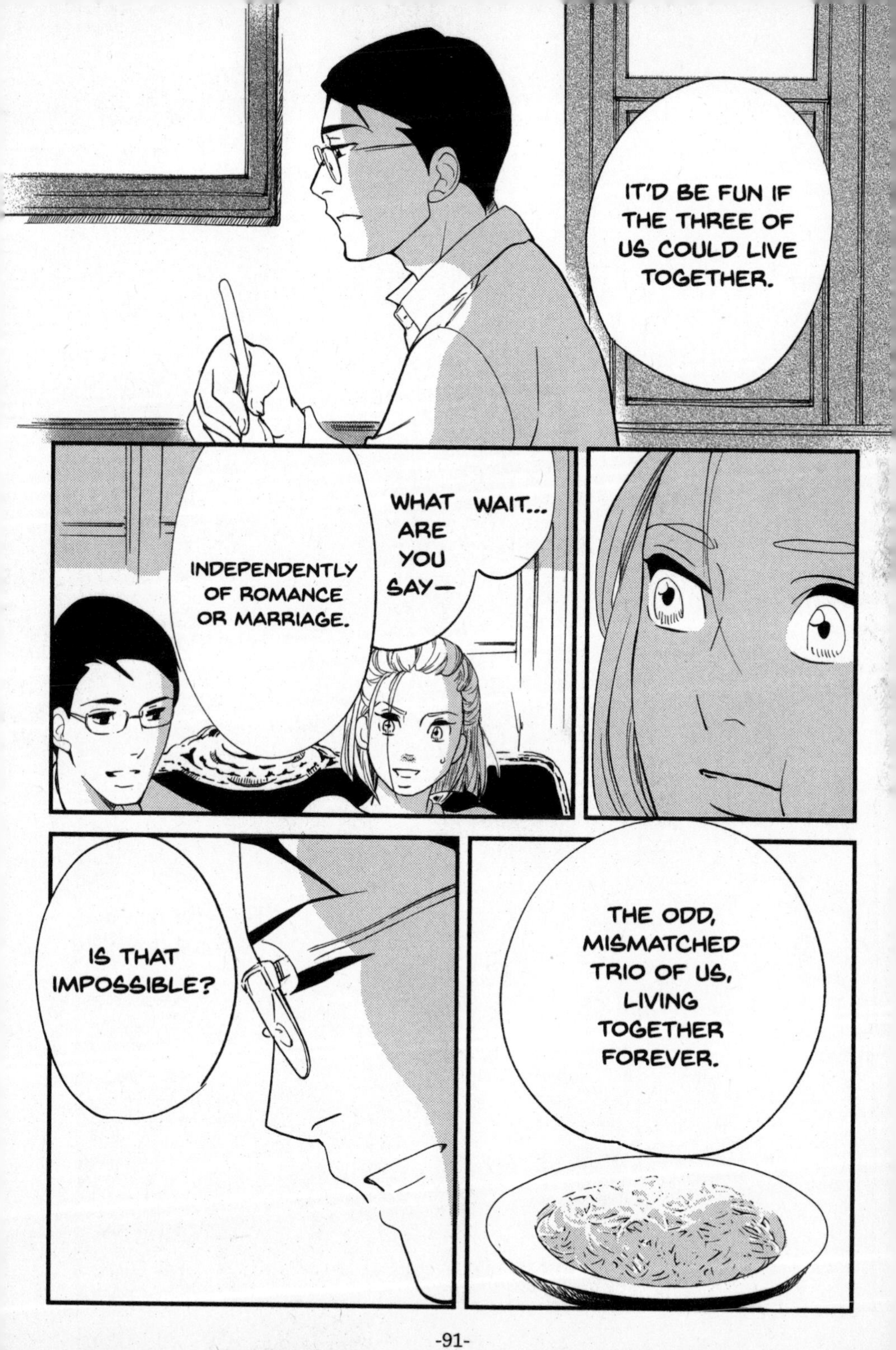
IT'D BE FUN IF THE THREE OF US COULD LIVE TOGETHER.
WAIT... WHAT ARE YOU SAY—
INDEPENDENTLY OF ROMANCE OR MARRIAGE.
THE ODD, MISMATCHED TRIO OF US, LIVING TOGETHER FOREVER.
IS THAT IMPOSSIBLE?

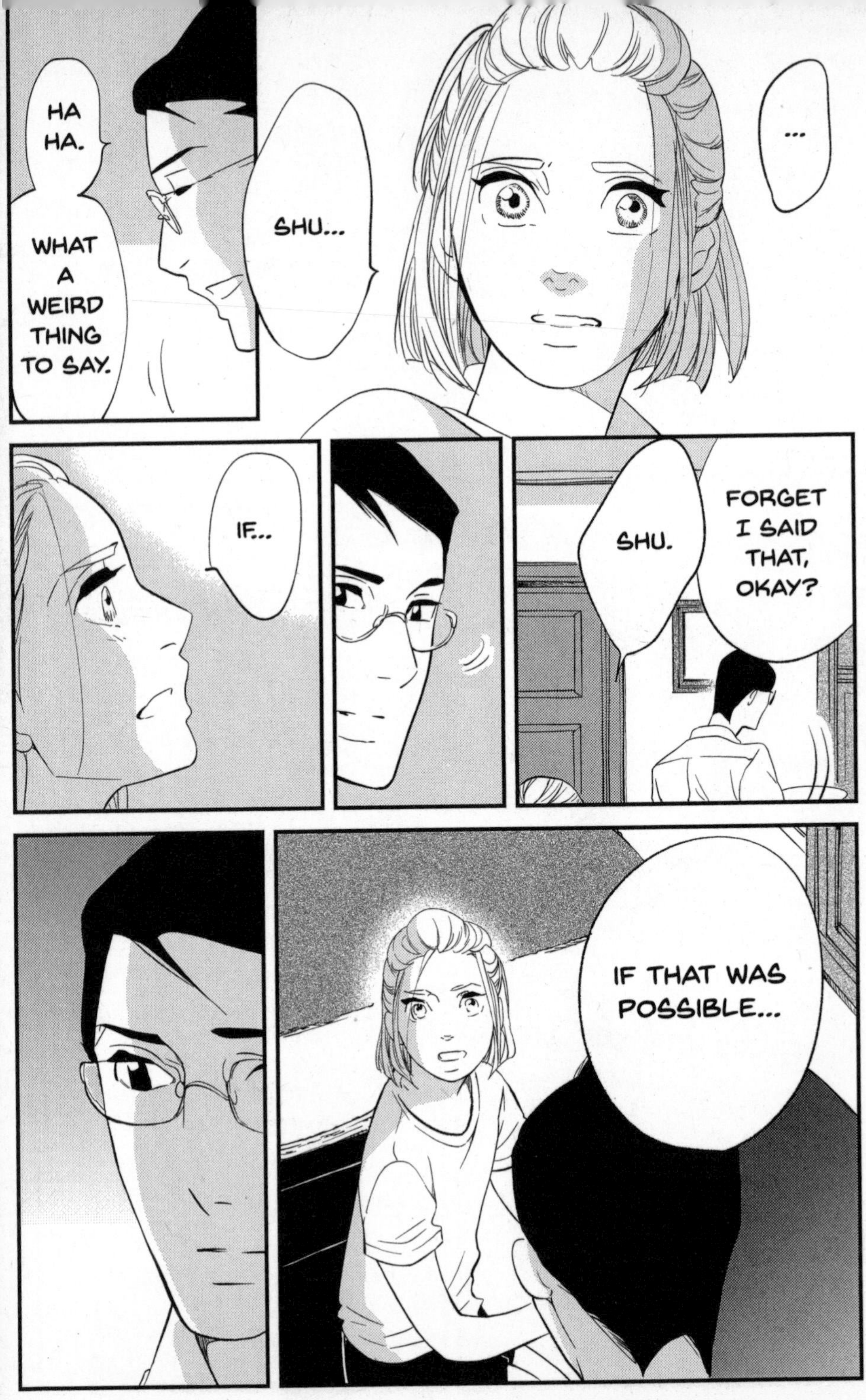
...
SHU...
HA HA.
WHAT A WEIRD THING TO SAY.
FORGET I SAID THAT, OKAY?
SHU.
IF...
IF THAT WAS POSSIBLE...

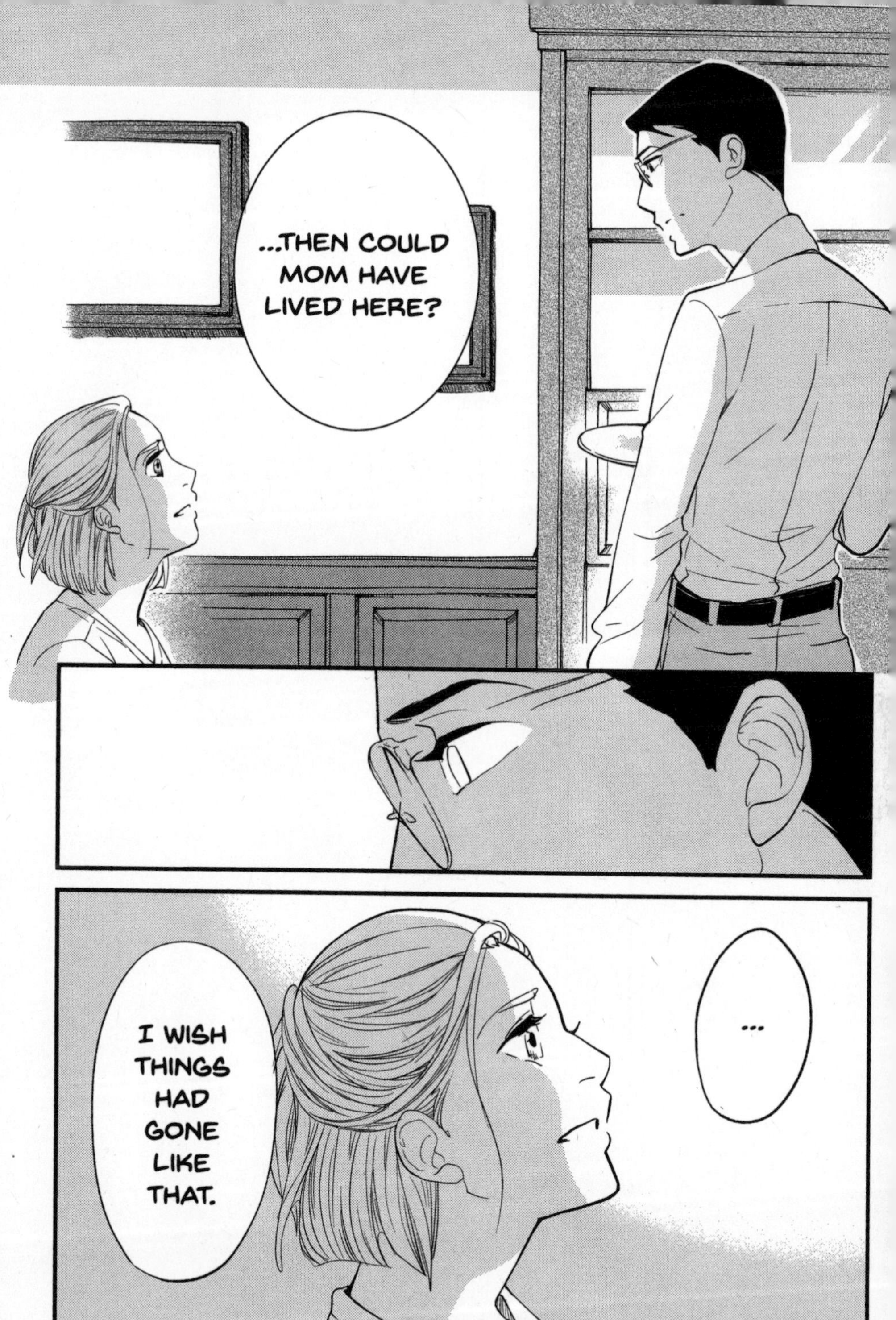
...THEN COULD MOM HAVE LIVED HERE?
...
I WISH THINGS HAD GONE LIKE THAT.

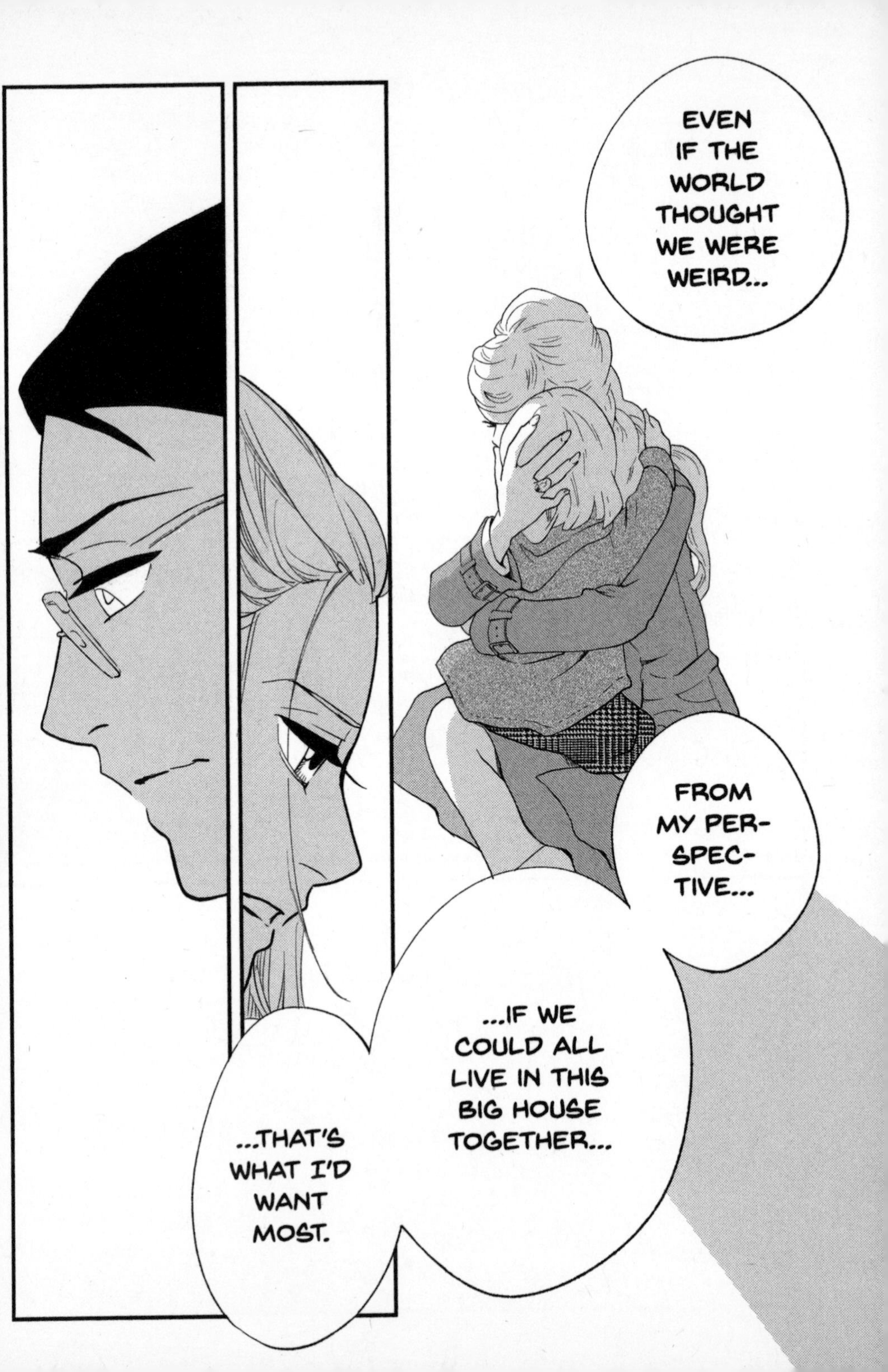
EVEN IF THE WORLD THOUGHT WE WERE WEIRD...
FROM MY PER-SPEC-TIVE...
...IF WE COULD ALL LIVE IN THIS BIG HOUSE TOGETHER...
...THAT'S WHAT I'D WANT MOST.

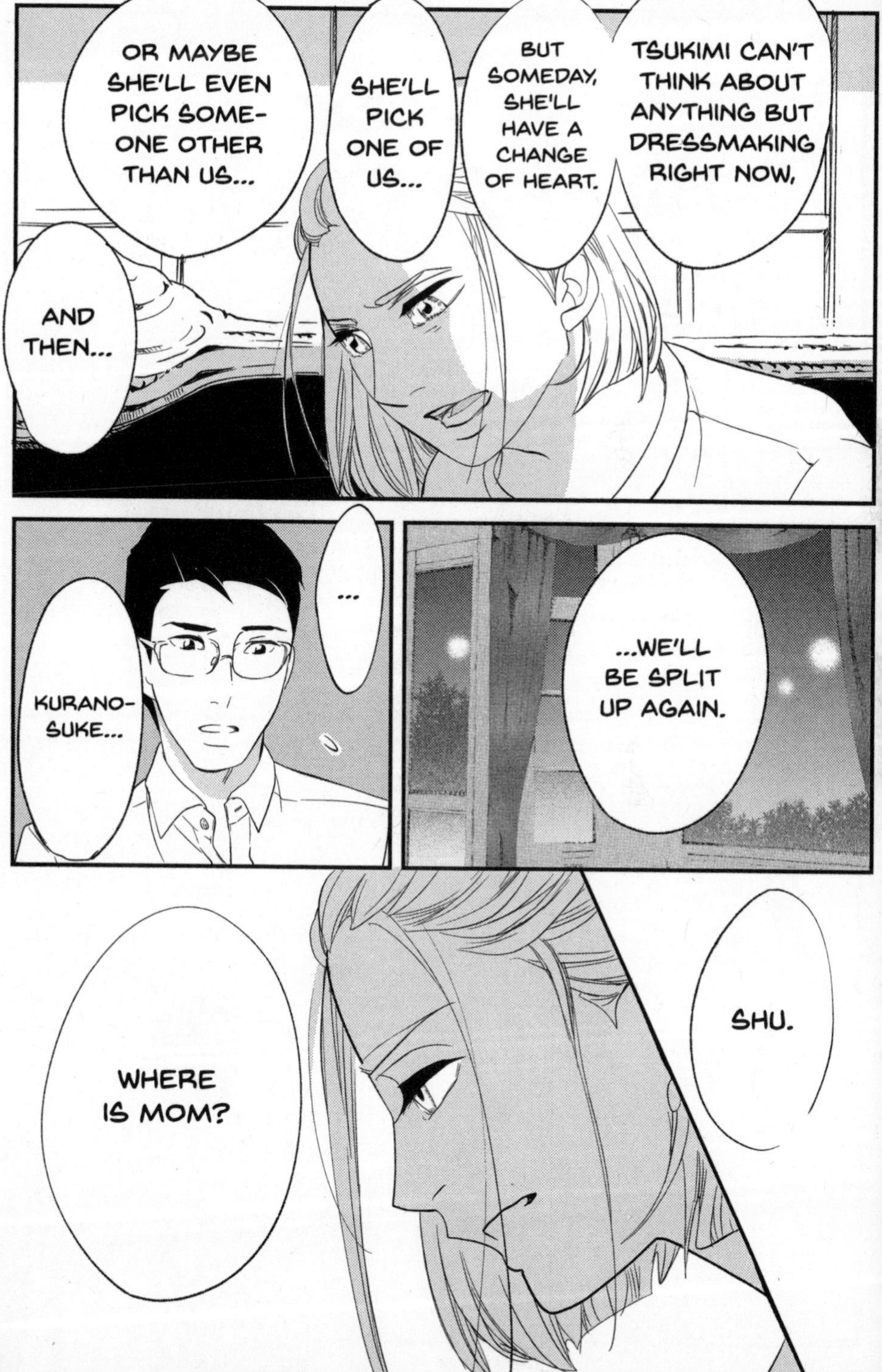
TSUKIMI CAN'T THINK ABOUT ANYTHING BUT DRESSMAKING RIGHT NOW,
BUT SOMEDAY, SHE'LL HAVE A CHANGE OF HEART.
SHE'LL PICK ONE OF US...
OR MAYBE SHE'LL EVEN PICK SOME-ONE OTHER THAN US...
AND THEN...
...WE'LL BE SPLIT UP AGAIN.
...
KURANO-SUKE...
SHU.
WHERE IS MOM?

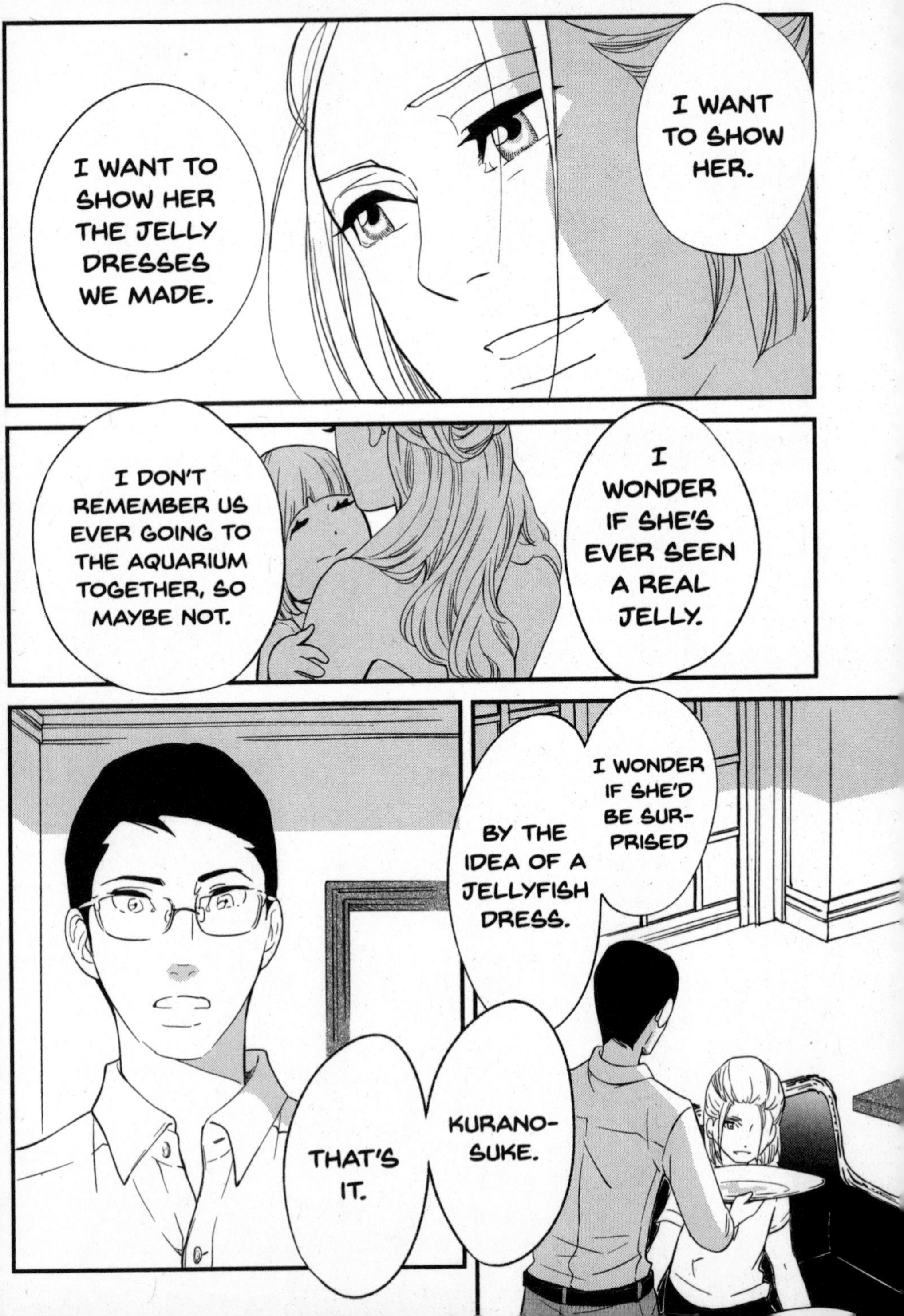
I WANT TO SHOW HER.
I WANT TO SHOW HER THE JELLY DRESSES WE MADE.
I WONDER IF SHE'S EVER SEEN A REAL JELLY.
I DON'T REMEMBER US EVER GOING TO THE AQUARIUM TOGETHER, SO MAYBE NOT.
I WONDER IF SHE'D BE SURPRISED
BY THE IDEA OF A JELLYFISH DRESS.
KURANOSUKE.
THAT'S IT.

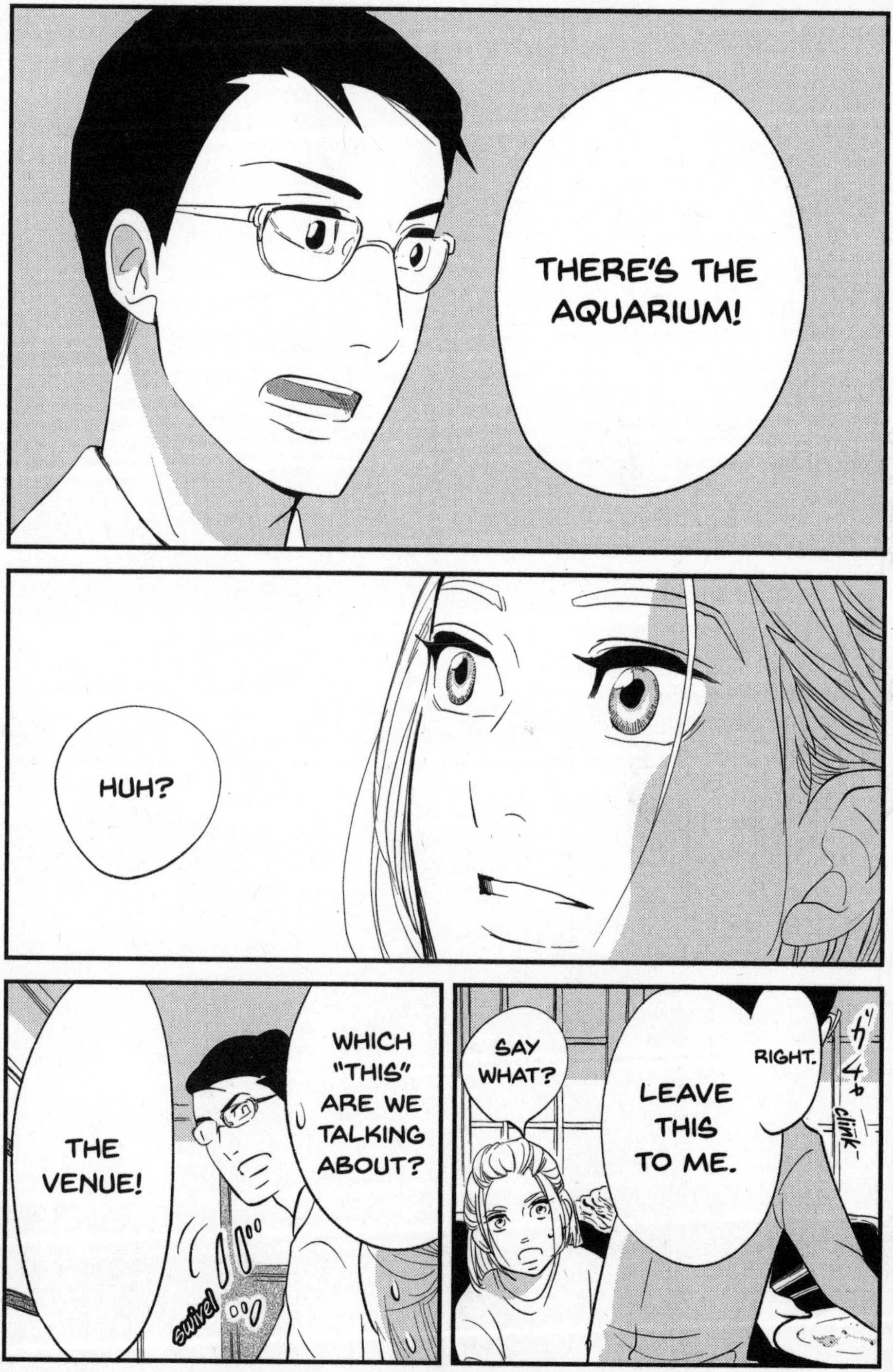
THERE'S THE AQUARIUM!
HUH?
clink
RIGHT.
LEAVE THIS TO ME.
SAY WHAT?
WHICH "THIS" ARE WE TALKING ABOUT?
THE VENUE!
swivel

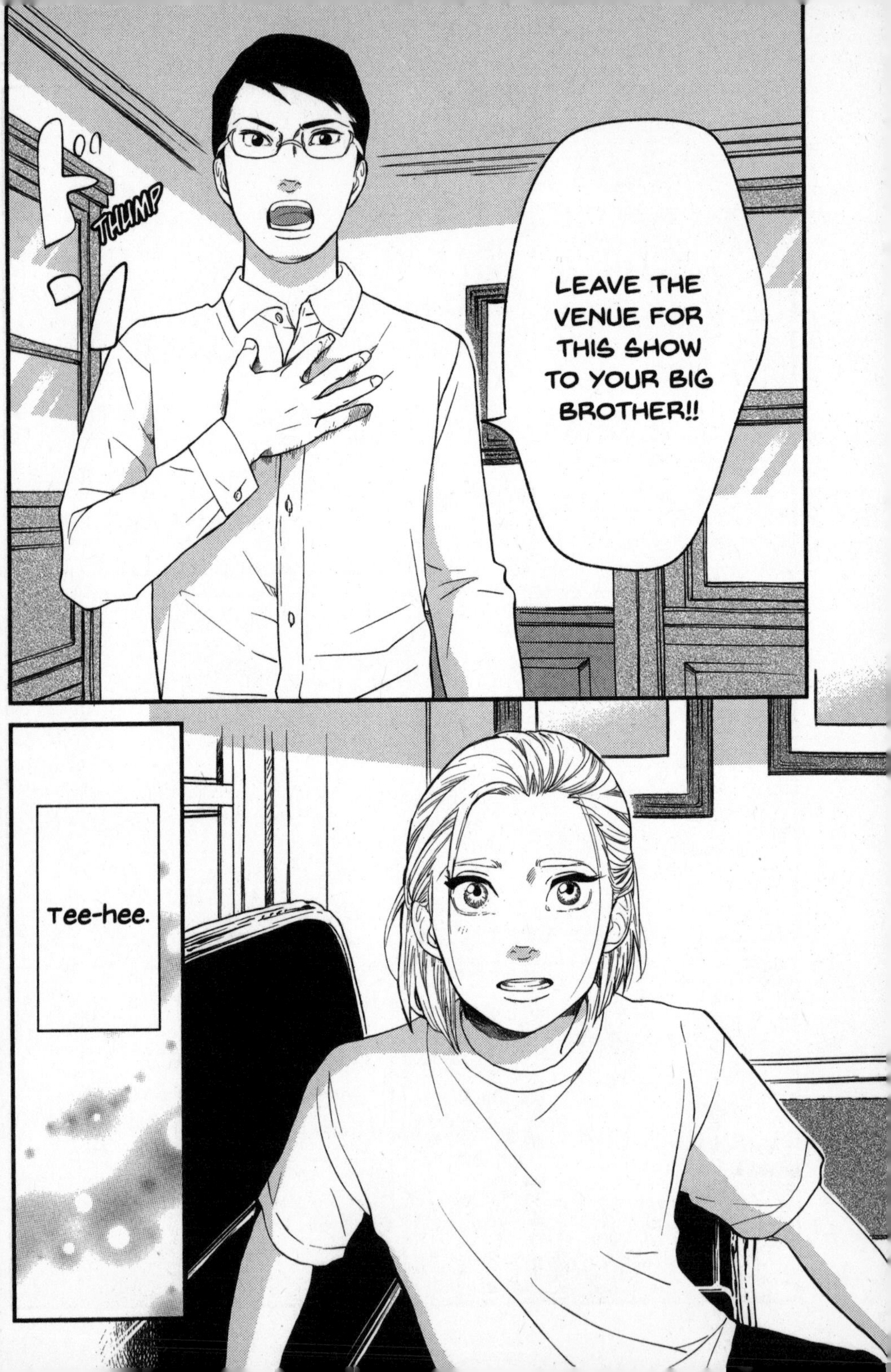
LEAVE THE VENUE FOR THIS SHOW TO YOUR BIG BROTHER!!
ドン
THUMP
Tee-hee.

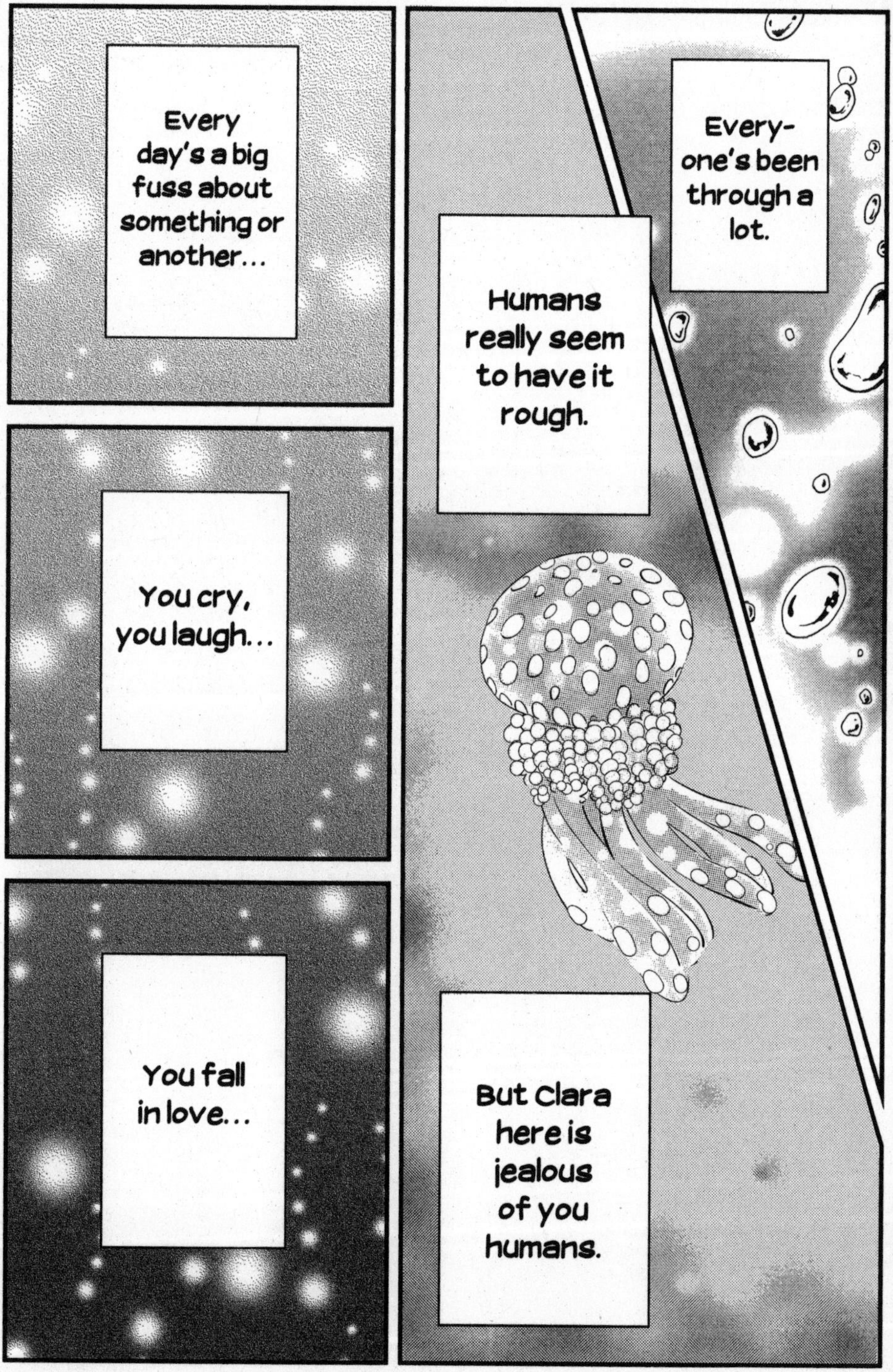
Every-one's been through a lot.
Humans really seem to have it rough.
But Clara here is jealous of you humans.
Every day's a big fuss about something or another...
You cry, you laugh...
You fall in love...

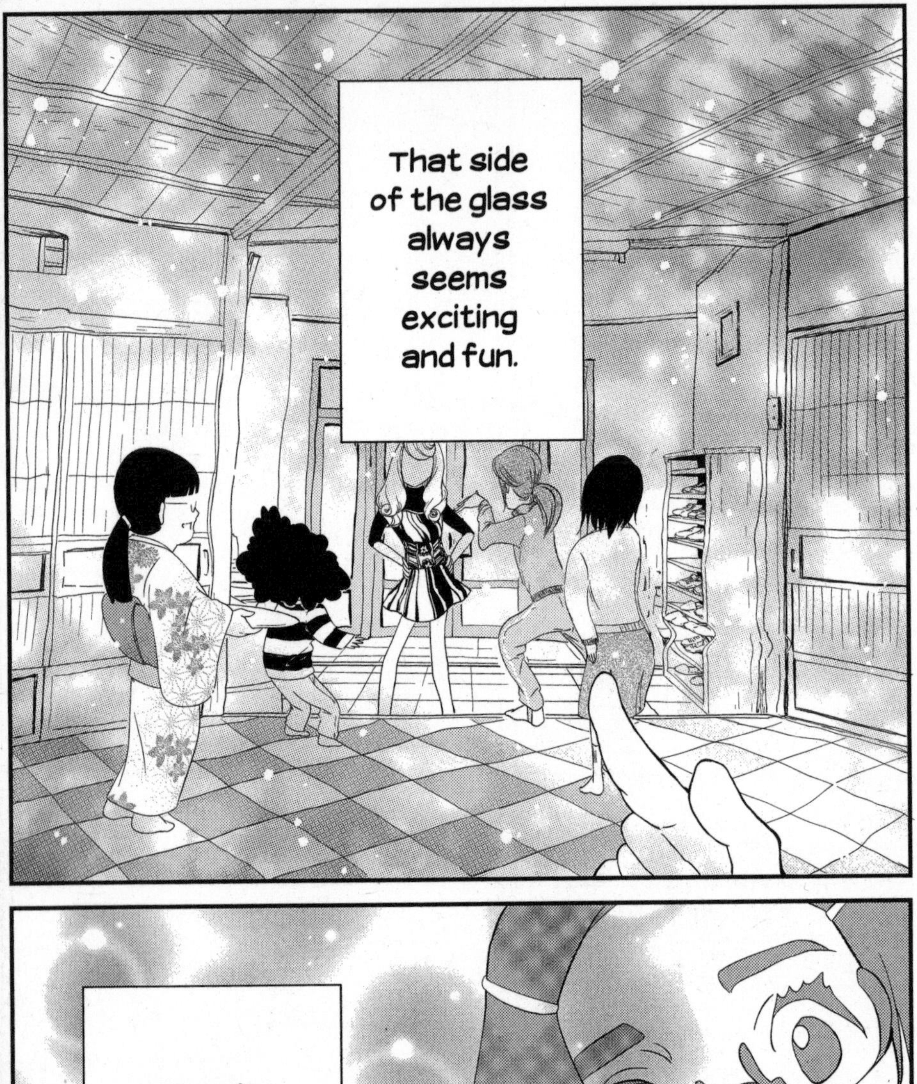
That side of the glass always seems exciting and fun.
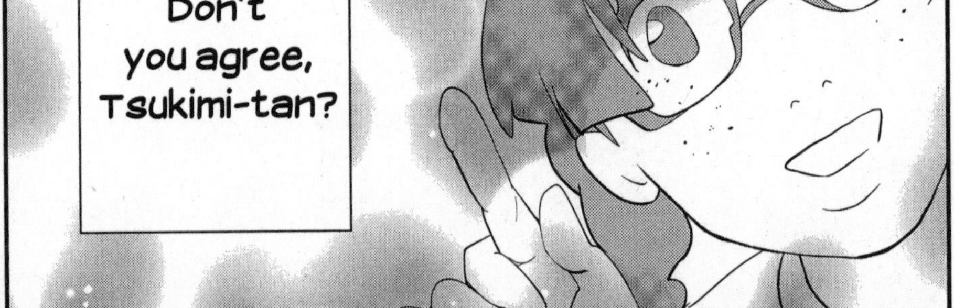
Don't you agree, Tsukimi-tan?

Final Episode
Princess Jellyfish

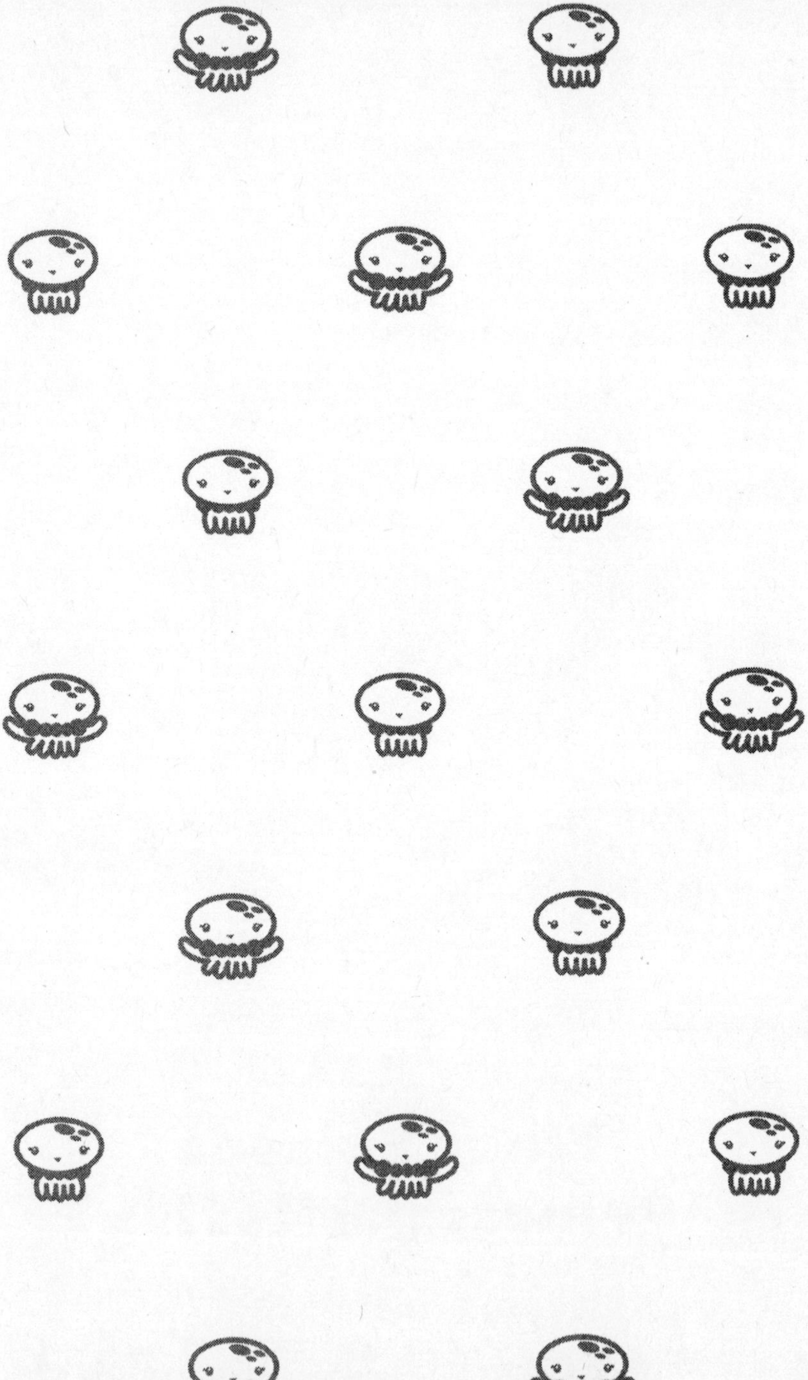

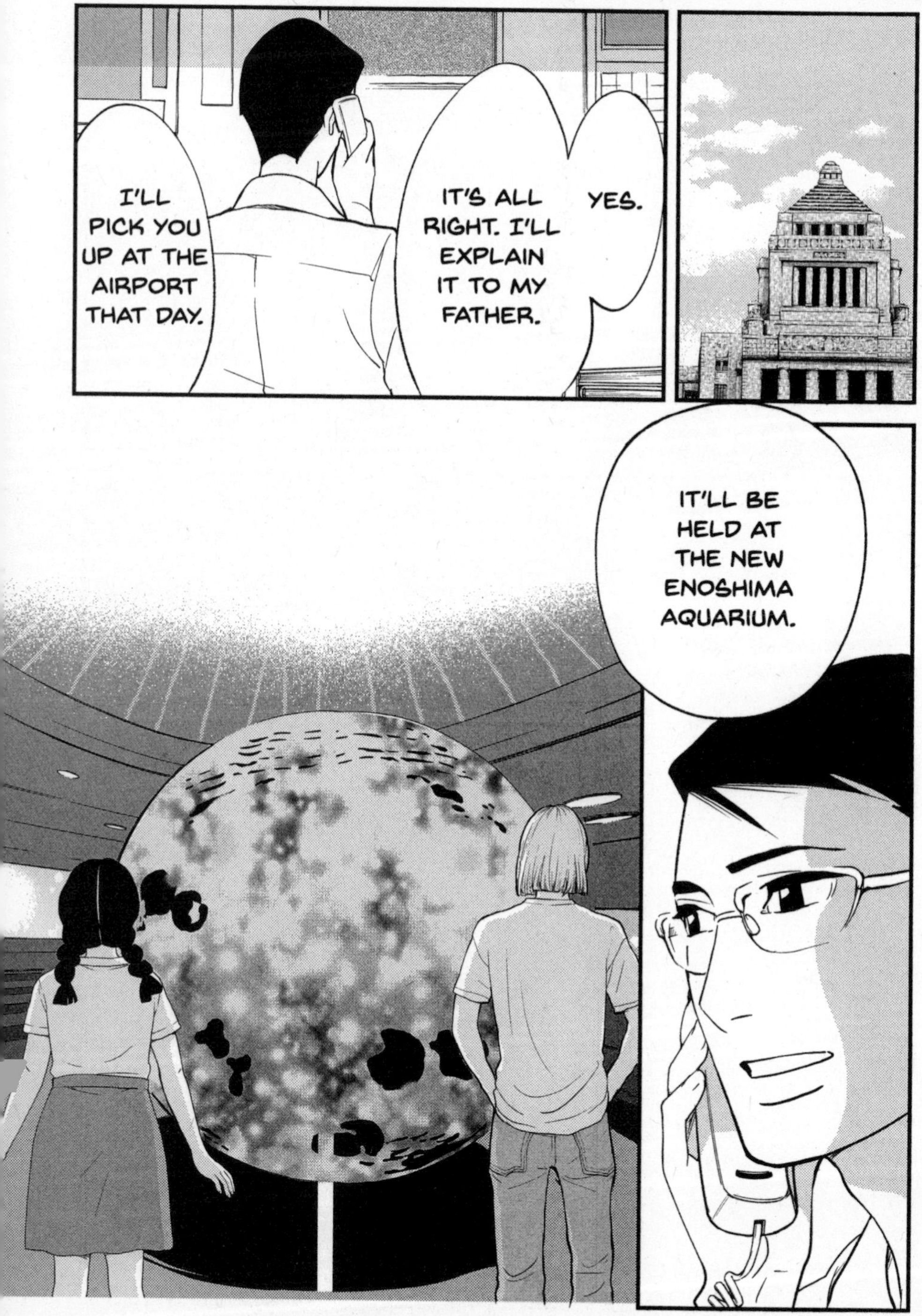
YES.
IT'S ALL RIGHT. I'LL EXPLAIN IT TO MY FATHER.
I'LL PICK YOU UP AT THE AIRPORT THAT DAY.
IT'LL BE HELD AT THE NEW ENOSHIMA AQUARIUM.

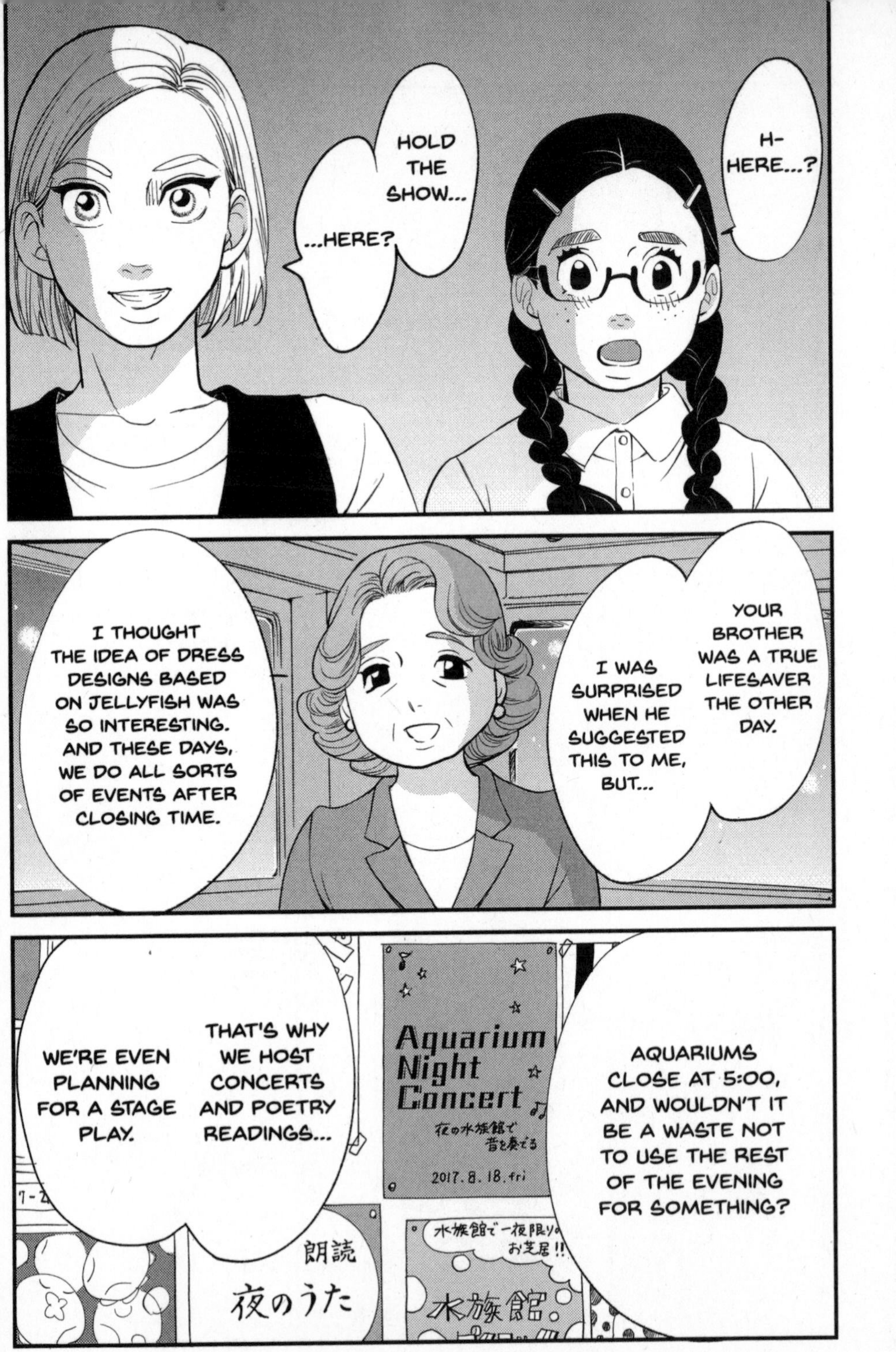
H- HERE...?
HOLD THE SHOW... ...HERE?
YOUR BROTHER WAS A TRUE LIFESAVER THE OTHER DAY.
I WAS SURPRISED WHEN HE SUGGESTED THIS TO ME, BUT...
I THOUGHT THE IDEA OF DRESS DESIGNS BASED ON JELLYFISH WAS SO INTERESTING. AND THESE DAYS, WE DO ALL SORTS OF EVENTS AFTER CLOSING TIME.
AQUARIUMS CLOSE AT 5:00, AND WOULDN'T IT BE A WASTE NOT TO USE THE REST OF THE EVENING FOR SOMETHING?
Aquarium Night Concert
夜の水族館で音を奏でる
2017.8.18.fri
水族館で一夜限りのお芝居!!
水族館
THAT'S WHY WE HOST CONCERTS AND POETRY READINGS...
WE'RE EVEN PLANNING FOR A STAGE PLAY.
朗読
夜のうた

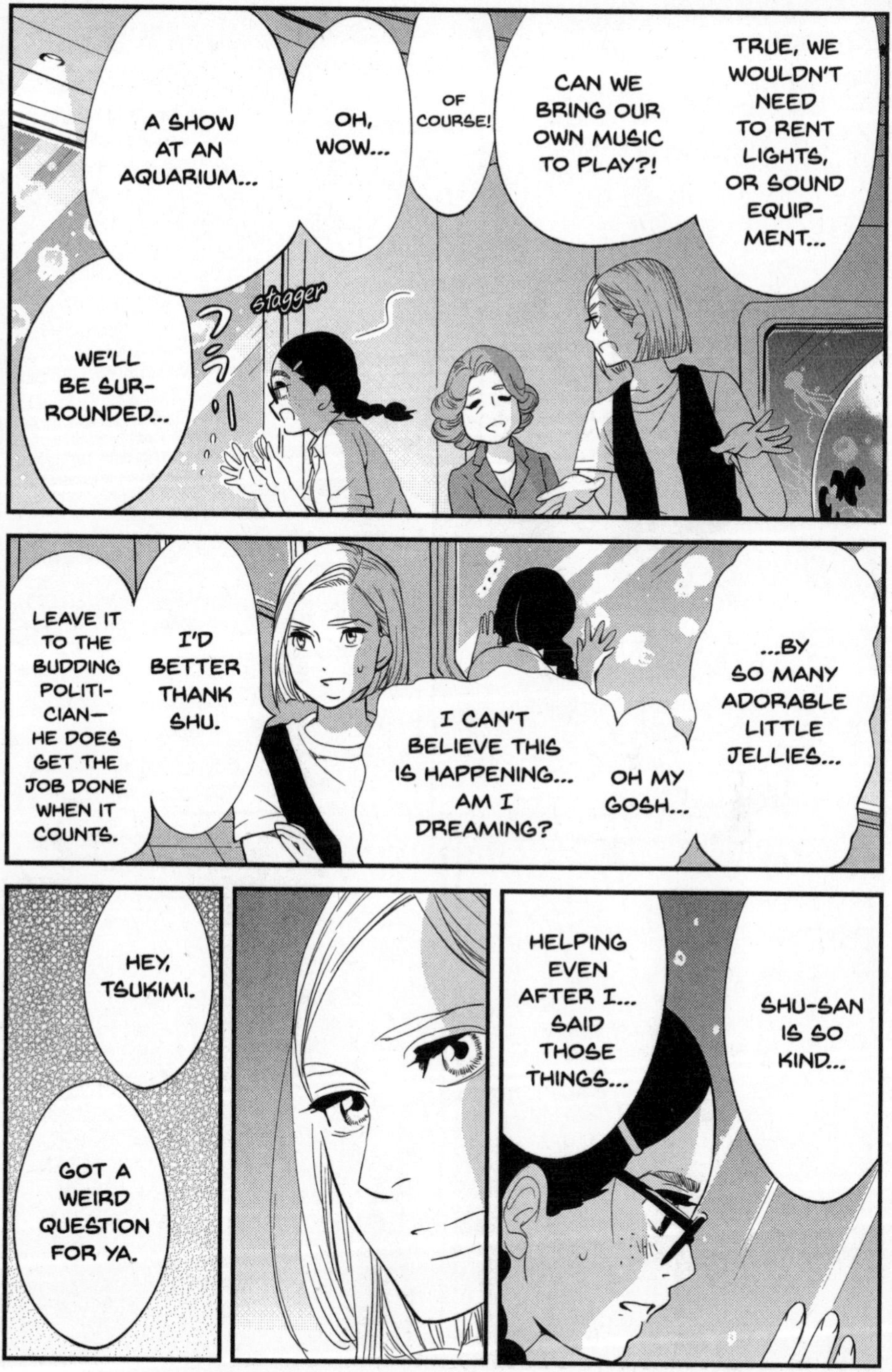
TRUE, WE WOULDN'T NEED TO RENT LIGHTS, OR SOUND EQUIPMENT...
CAN WE BRING OUR OWN MUSIC TO PLAY?!
OF COURSE!
OH, WOW...
A SHOW AT AN AQUARIUM...
stagger
WE'LL BE SURROUNDED...
...BY SO MANY ADORABLE LITTLE JELLIES...
OH MY GOSH...
I CAN'T BELIEVE THIS IS HAPPENING... AM I DREAMING?
I'D BETTER THANK SHU.
LEAVE IT TO THE BUDDING POLITICIAN—HE DOES GET THE JOB DONE WHEN IT COUNTS.
SHU-SAN IS SO KIND...
HELPING EVEN AFTER I... SAID THOSE THINGS...
HEY, TSUKIMI.
GOT A WEIRD QUESTION FOR YA.

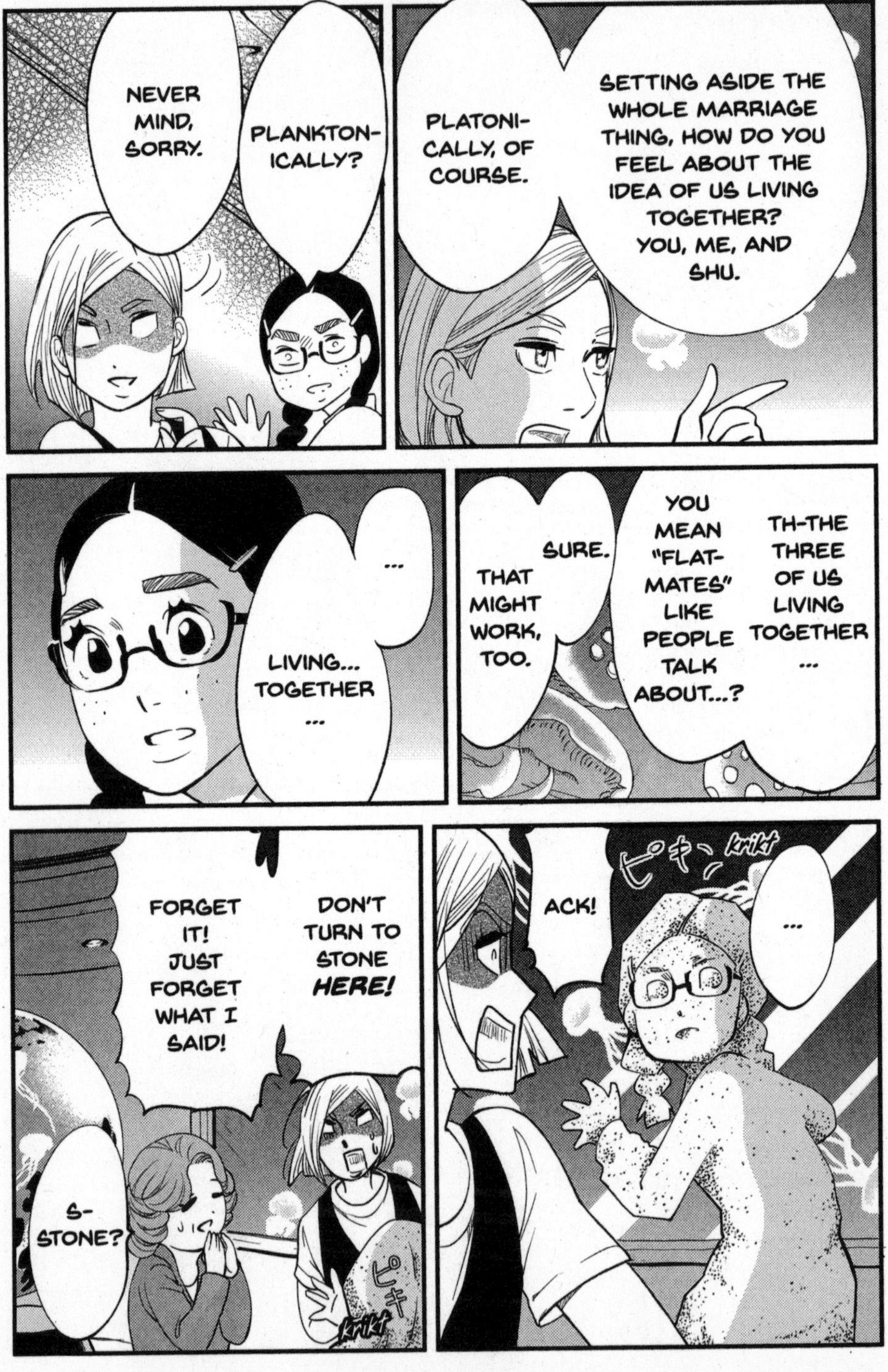

SETTING ASIDE THE WHOLE MARRIAGE THING, HOW DO YOU FEEL ABOUT THE IDEA OF US LIVING TOGETHER? YOU, ME, AND SHU.
PLATONI-CALLY, OF COURSE.
PLANKTON-ICALLY?
NEVER MIND, SORRY.
TH-THE THREE OF US LIVING TOGETHER ...
YOU MEAN "FLAT-MATES" LIKE PEOPLE TALK ABOUT...?
SURE.
THAT MIGHT WORK, TOO.
...
LIVING... TOGETHER ...
ピキ、 krikt
...
ACK!
DON'T TURN TO STONE *HERE!*
FORGET IT! JUST FORGET WHAT I SAID!
S-STONE?
ピキ krikt

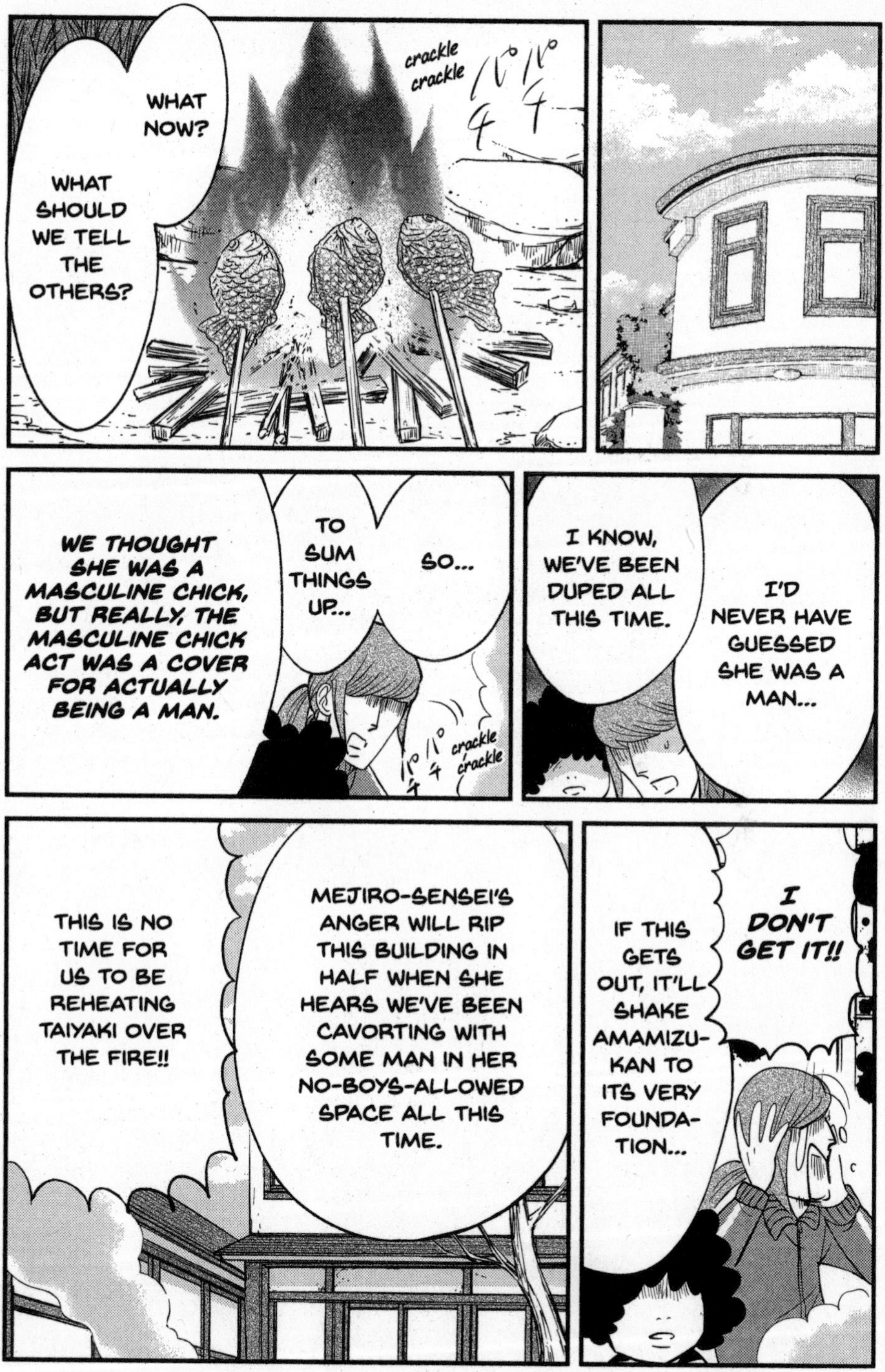

crackle crackle
パチパチ
WHAT NOW? WHAT SHOULD WE TELL THE OTHERS?
I'D NEVER HAVE GUESSED SHE WAS A MAN...
I KNOW, WE'VE BEEN DUPED ALL THIS TIME.
SO...
TO SUM THINGS UP...
WE THOUGHT SHE WAS A MASCULINE CHICK, BUT REALLY, THE MASCULINE CHICK ACT WAS A COVER FOR ACTUALLY BEING A MAN.
crackle crackle
パチパチ
I DON'T GET IT!!
IF THIS GETS OUT, IT'LL SHAKE AMAMIZU-KAN TO ITS VERY FOUNDA-TION...
MEJIRO-SENSEI'S ANGER WILL RIP THIS BUILDING IN HALF WHEN SHE HEARS WE'VE BEEN CAVORTING WITH SOME MAN IN HER NO-BOYS-ALLOWED SPACE ALL THIS TIME.
THIS IS NO TIME FOR US TO BE REHEATING TAIYAKI OVER THE FIRE!!

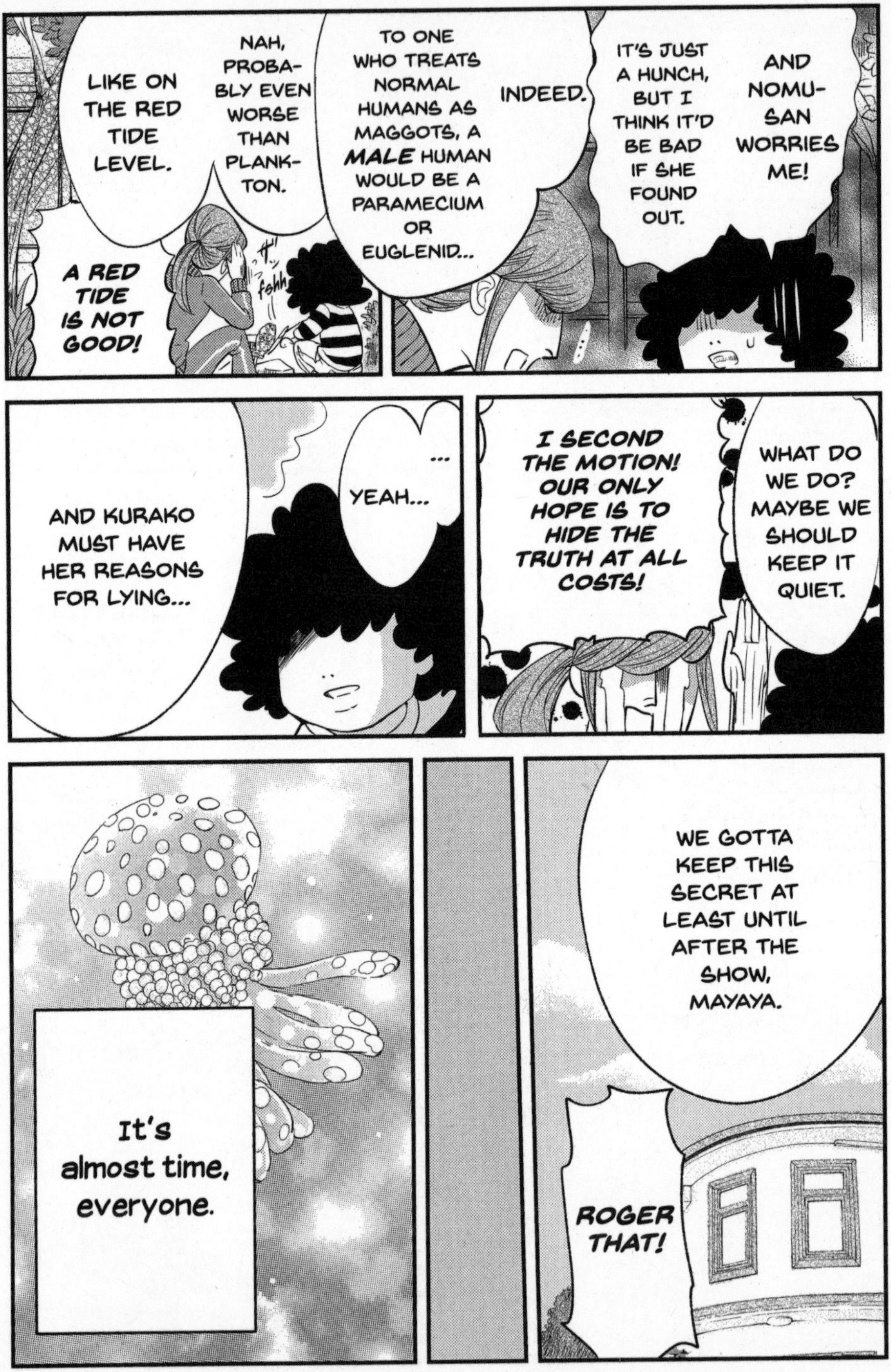
AND NOMU-SAN WORRIES ME!
IT'S JUST A HUNCH, BUT I THINK IT'D BE BAD IF SHE FOUND OUT.
INDEED.
TO ONE WHO TREATS NORMAL HUMANS AS MAGGOTS, A MALE HUMAN WOULD BE A PARAMECIUM OR EUGLENID...
NAH, PROBABLY EVEN WORSE THAN PLANKTON.
LIKE ON THE RED TIDE LEVEL.
fshh
A RED TIDE IS NOT GOOD!
WHAT DO WE DO? MAYBE WE SHOULD KEEP IT QUIET.
I SECOND THE MOTION! OUR ONLY HOPE IS TO HIDE THE TRUTH AT ALL COSTS!
... YEAH...
AND KURAKO MUST HAVE HER REASONS FOR LYING...
WE GOTTA KEEP THIS SECRET AT LEAST UNTIL AFTER THE SHOW, MAYAYA.
ROGER THAT!
It's almost time, everyone.

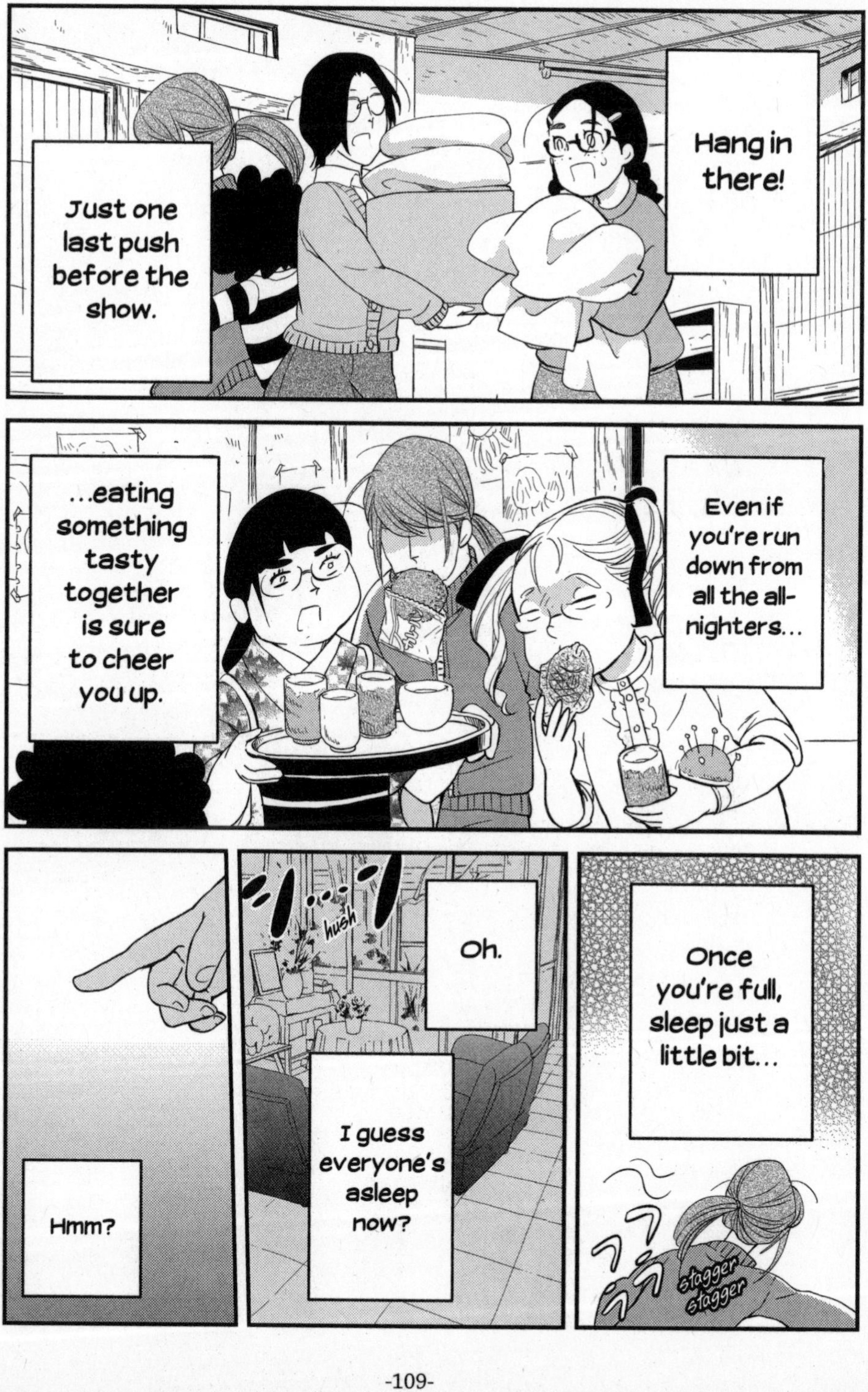
Hang in there!
Just one last push before the show.
Even if you're run down from all the all-nighters...
...eating something tasty together is sure to cheer you up.
Once you're full, sleep just a little bit...
stagger stagger
Oh.
hush
I guess everyone's asleep now?
Hmm?

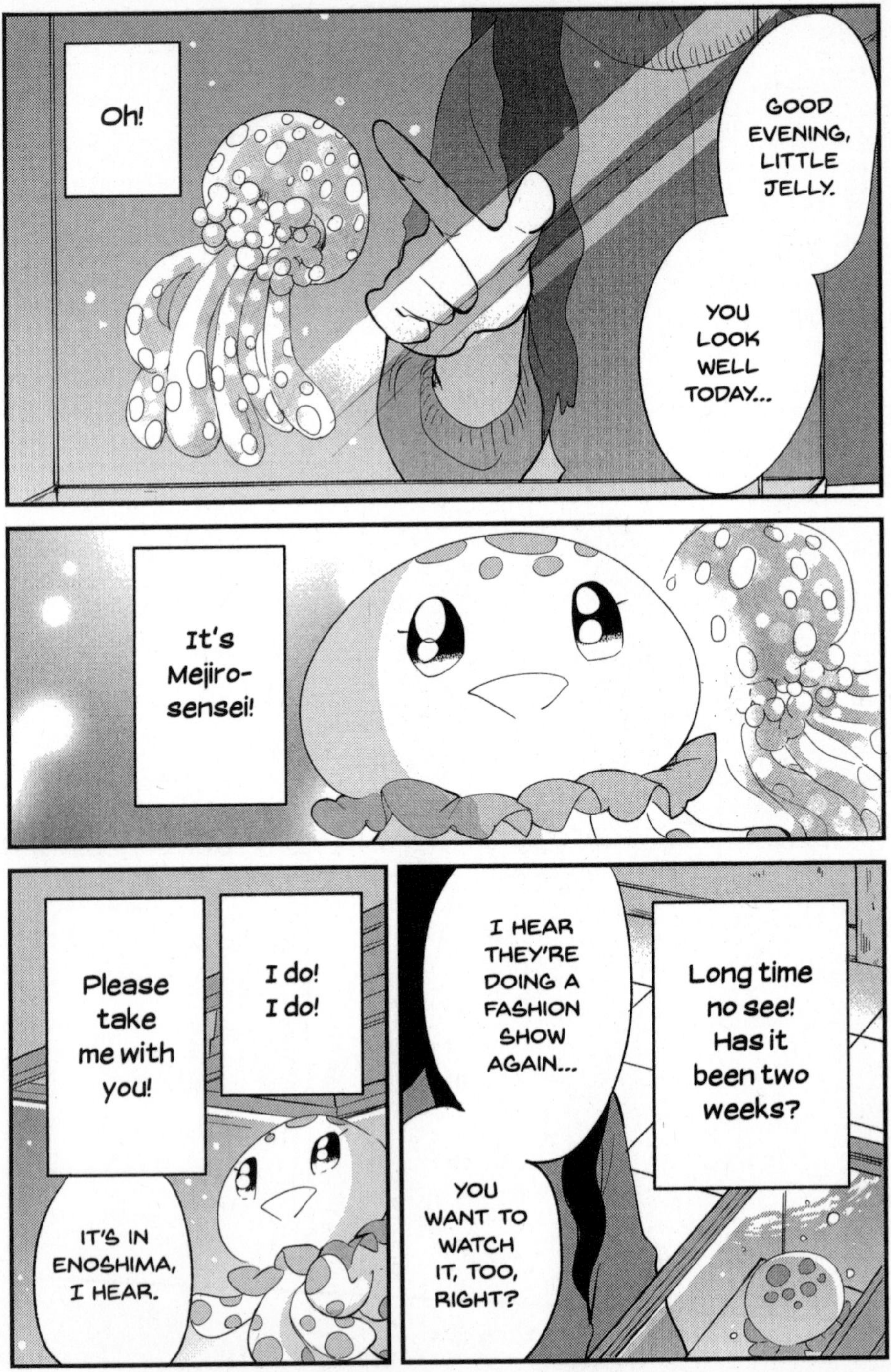
GOOD EVENING, LITTLE JELLY.
YOU LOOK WELL TODAY...
Oh!
It's Mejiro-sensei!
Long time no see! Has it been two weeks?
I HEAR THEY'RE DOING A FASHION SHOW AGAIN...
YOU WANT TO WATCH IT, TOO, RIGHT?
I do! I do!
Please take me with you!
IT'S IN ENOSHIMA, I HEAR.

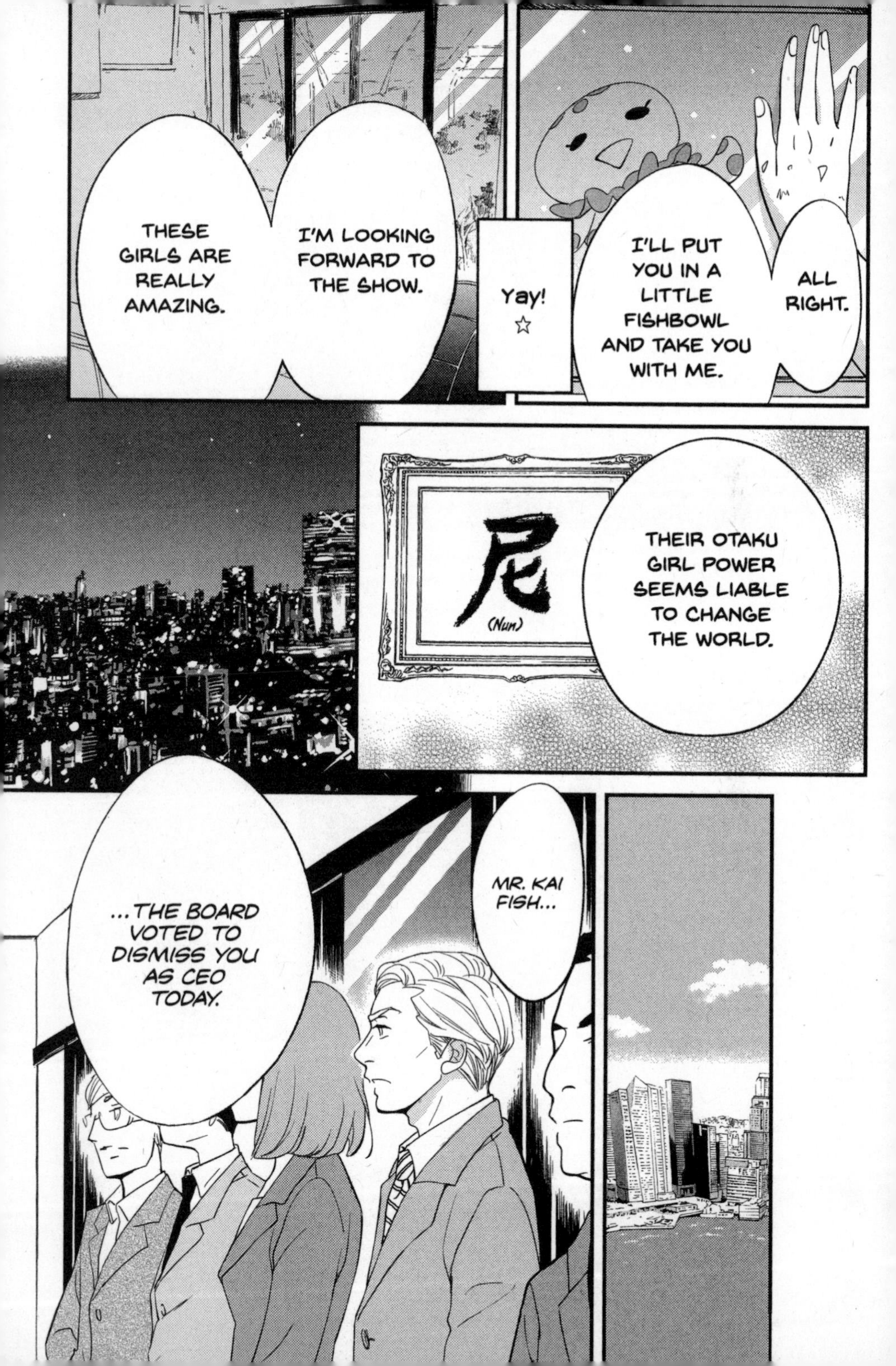
ALL RIGHT.
I'LL PUT YOU IN A LITTLE FISHBOWL AND TAKE YOU WITH ME.
Yay! ☆
I'M LOOKING FORWARD TO THE SHOW.
THESE GIRLS ARE REALLY AMAZING.
THEIR OTAKU GIRL POWER SEEMS LIABLE TO CHANGE THE WORLD.
尼
(Nun)
MR. KAI FISH...
...THE BOARD VOTED TO DISMISS YOU AS CEO TODAY.

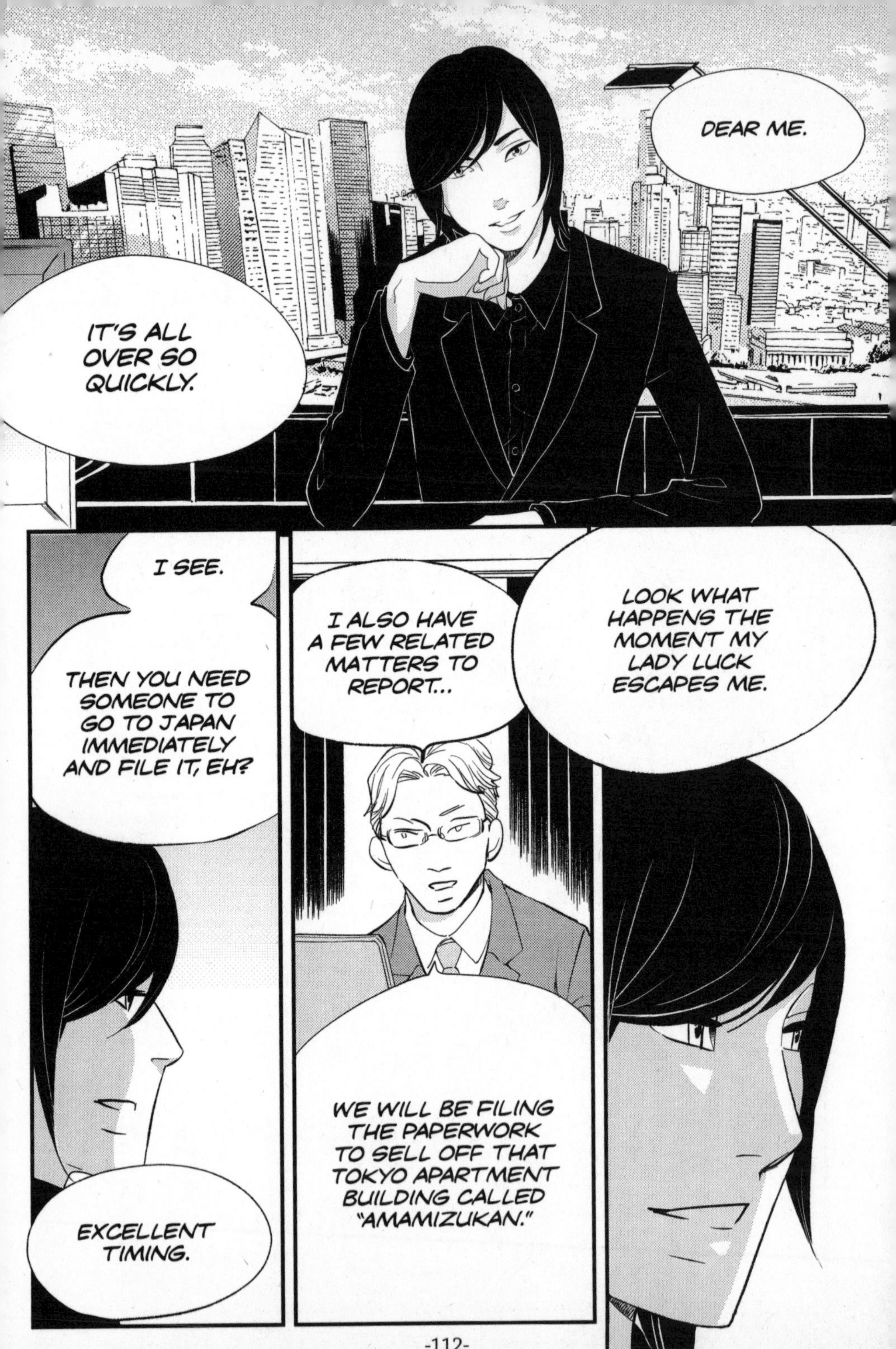
DEAR ME.
IT'S ALL OVER SO QUICKLY.
LOOK WHAT HAPPENS THE MOMENT MY LADY LUCK ESCAPES ME.
I ALSO HAVE A FEW RELATED MATTERS TO REPORT...
WE WILL BE FILING THE PAPERWORK TO SELL OFF THAT TOKYO APARTMENT BUILDING CALLED "AMAMIZUKAN."
I SEE.
THEN YOU NEED SOMEONE TO GO TO JAPAN IMMEDIATELY AND FILE IT, EH?
EXCELLENT TIMING.

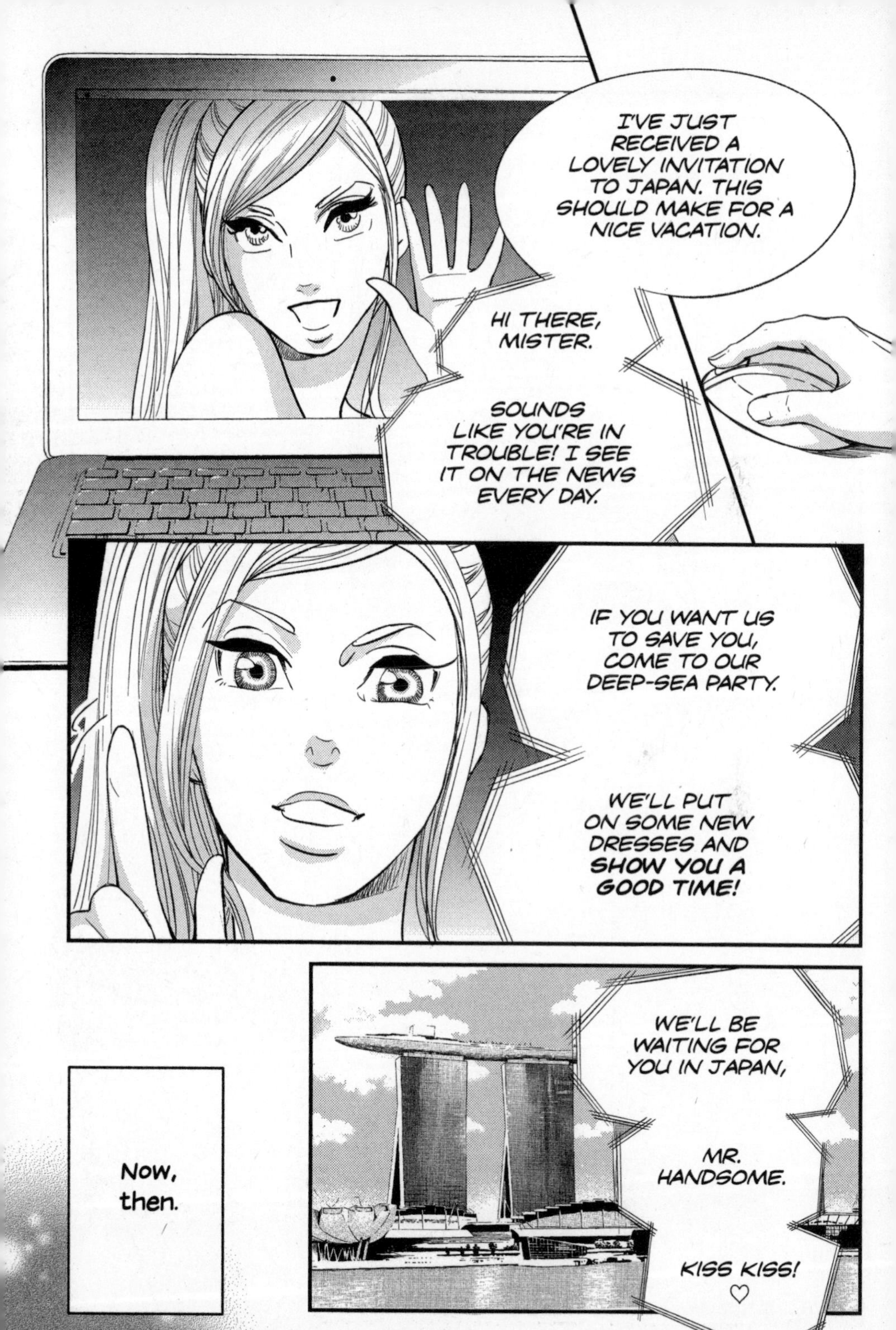
I'VE JUST RECEIVED A LOVELY INVITATION TO JAPAN. THIS SHOULD MAKE FOR A NICE VACATION.
HI THERE, MISTER.
SOUNDS LIKE YOU'RE IN TROUBLE! I SEE IT ON THE NEWS EVERY DAY.
IF YOU WANT US TO SAVE YOU, COME TO OUR DEEP-SEA PARTY.
WE'LL PUT ON SOME NEW DRESSES AND SHOW YOU A GOOD TIME!
WE'LL BE WAITING FOR YOU IN JAPAN,
MR. HANDSOME.
KISS KISS! ♡
Now, then.

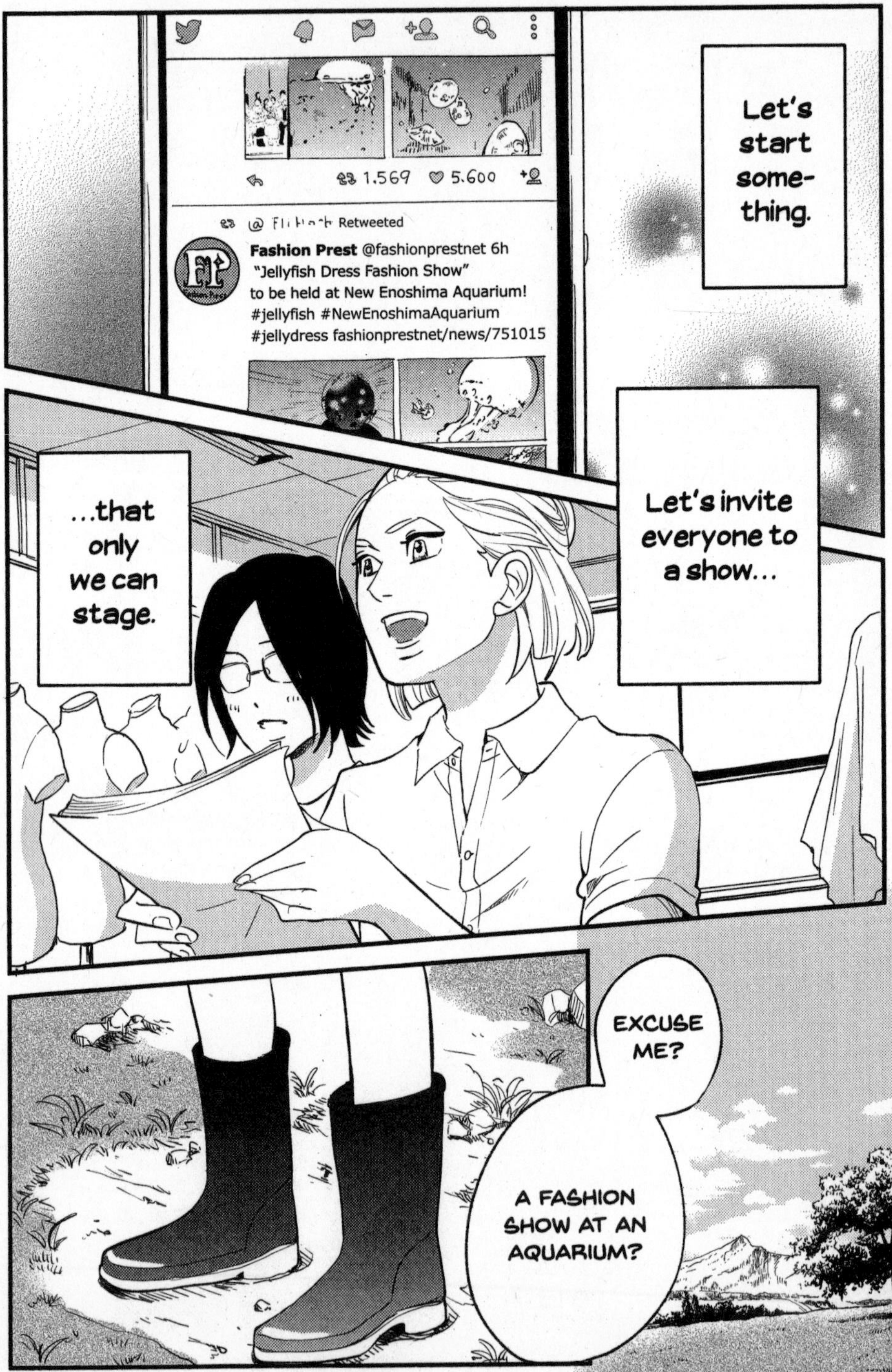

Let's start some-thing.
1.569
5.600
Retweeted
Fashion Prest @fashionprestnet 6h
"Jellyfish Dress Fashion Show" to be held at New Enoshima Aquarium! #jellyfish #NewEnoshimaAquarium #jellydress fashionprestnet/news/751015
Let's invite everyone to a show...
...that only we can stage.
EXCUSE ME?
A FASHION SHOW AT AN AQUARIUM?

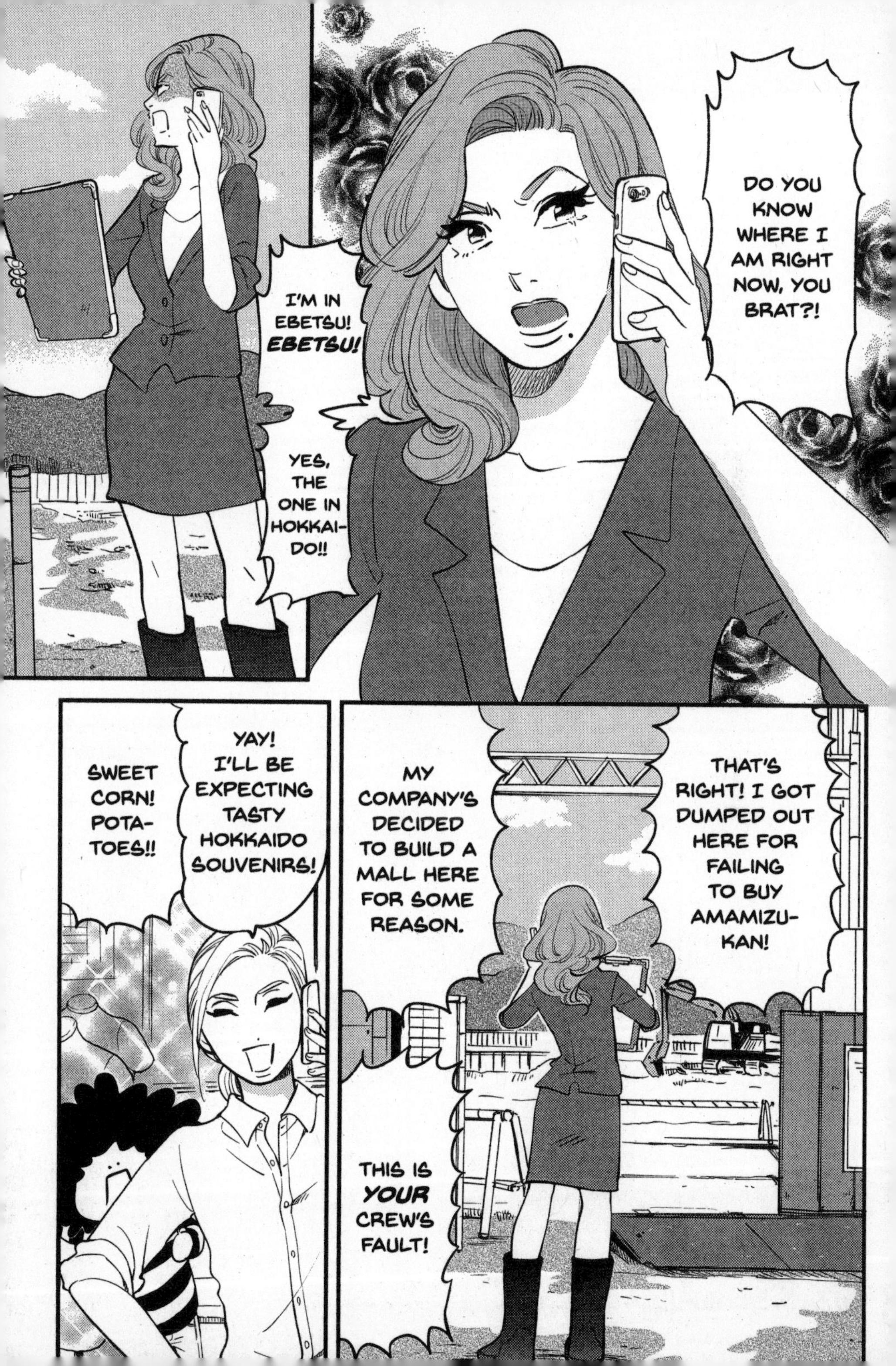

DO YOU KNOW WHERE I AM RIGHT NOW, YOU BRAT?!
I'M IN EBETSU! **EBETSU!**
YES, THE ONE IN HOKKAIDO!!
THAT'S RIGHT! I GOT DUMPED OUT HERE FOR FAILING TO BUY AMAMIZUKAN!
MY COMPANY'S DECIDED TO BUILD A MALL HERE FOR SOME REASON.
THIS IS ***YOUR*** CREW'S FAULT!
YAY! I'LL BE EXPECTING TASTY HOKKAIDO SOUVENIRS!
SWEET CORN! POTATOES!!

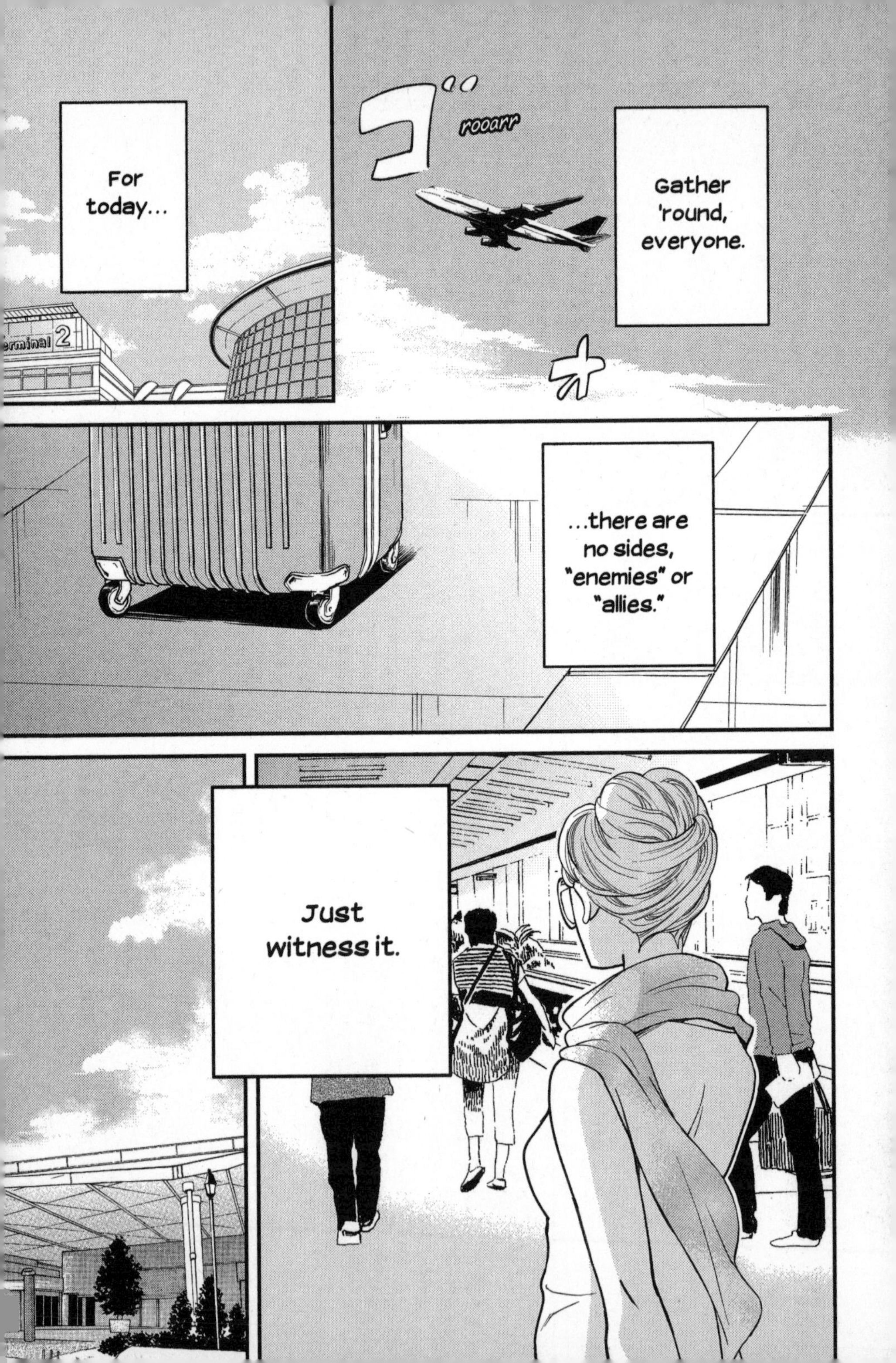
ゴ
rooarr
Gather 'round, everyone.
For today...
erminal 2
...there are no sides, "enemies" or "allies."
Just witness it.

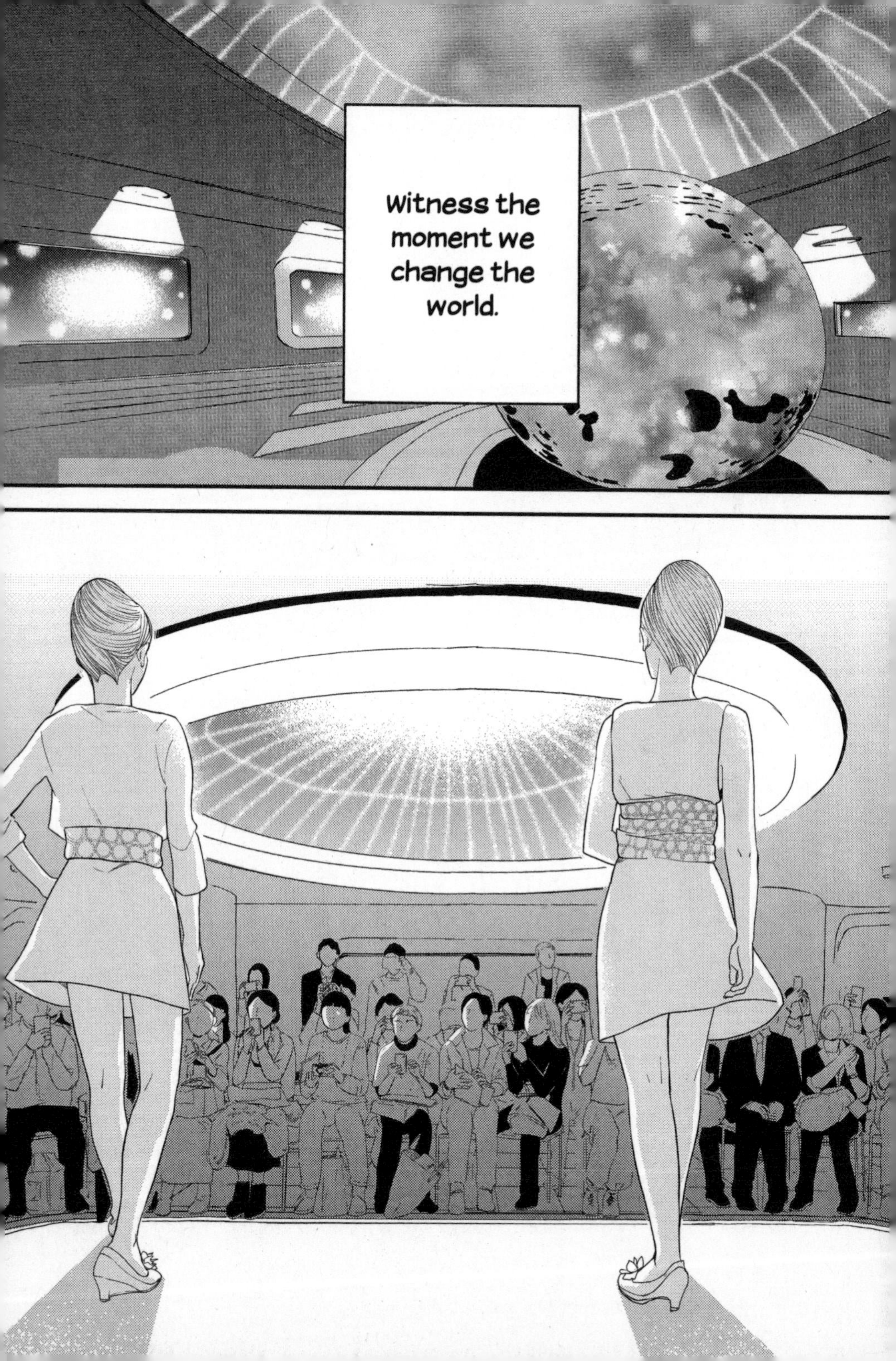
Witness the moment we change the world.

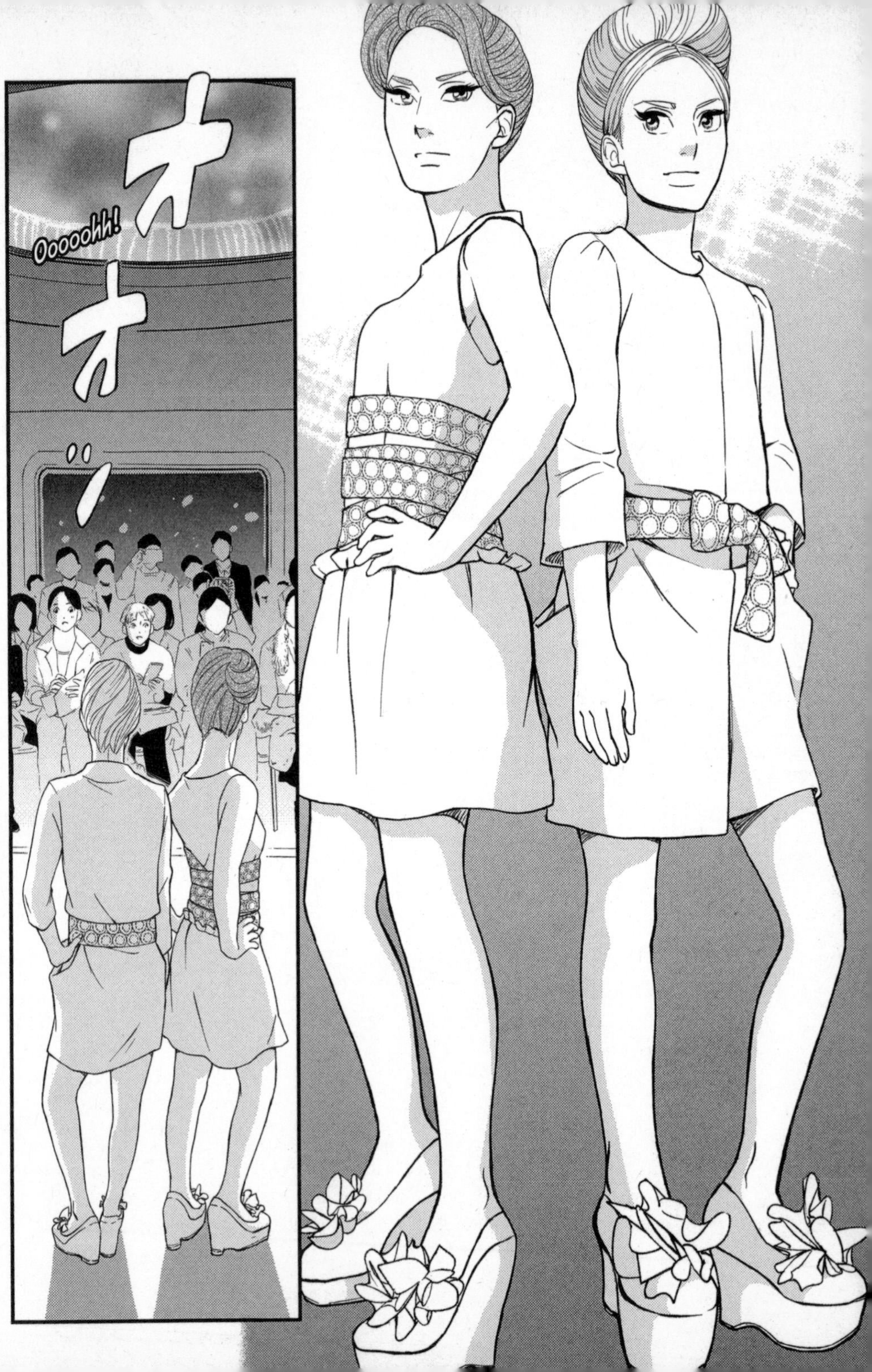
オオッ
Ooooohh!

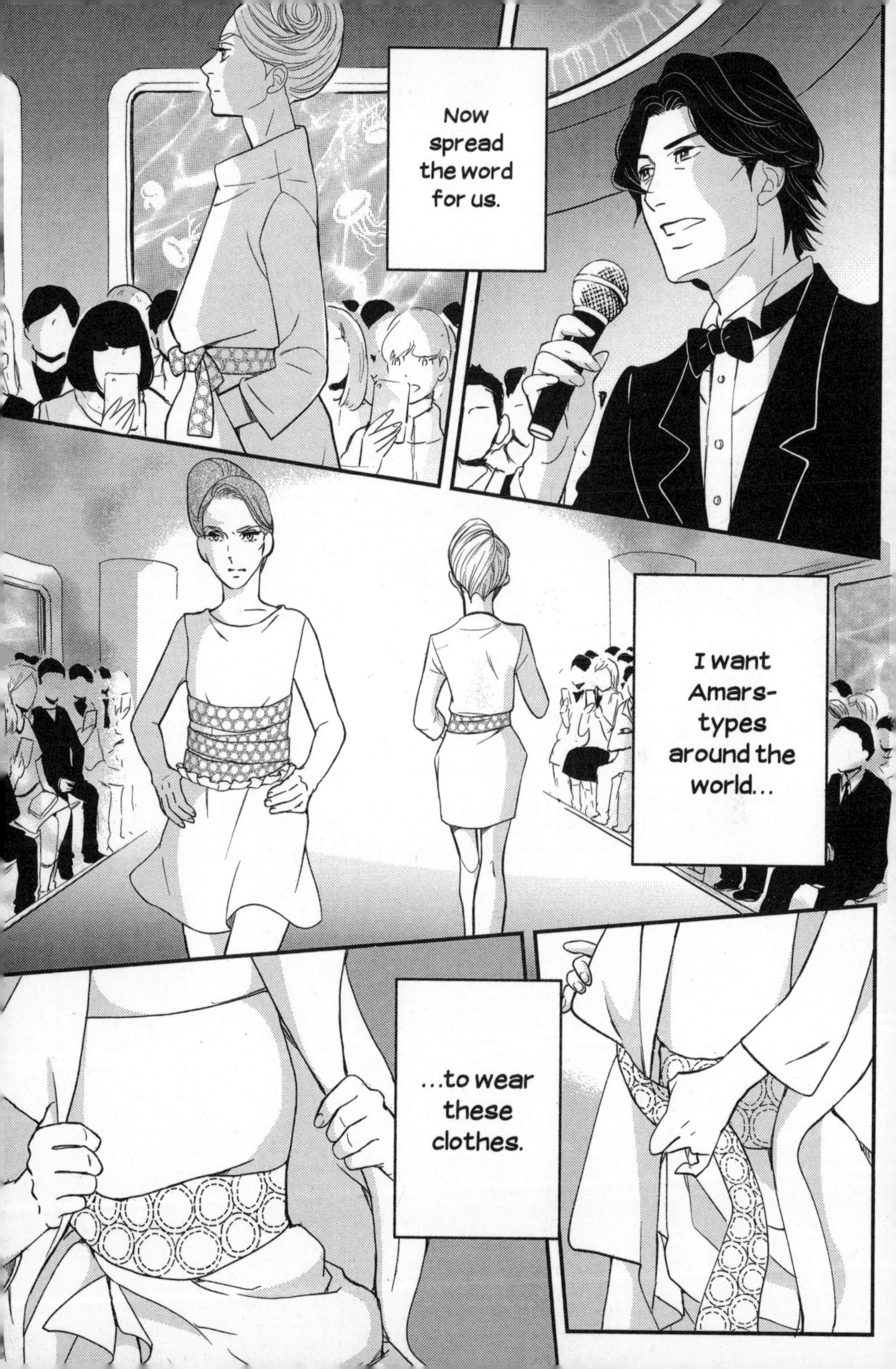
Now spread the word for us.
I want Amars-types around the world...
...to wear these clothes.

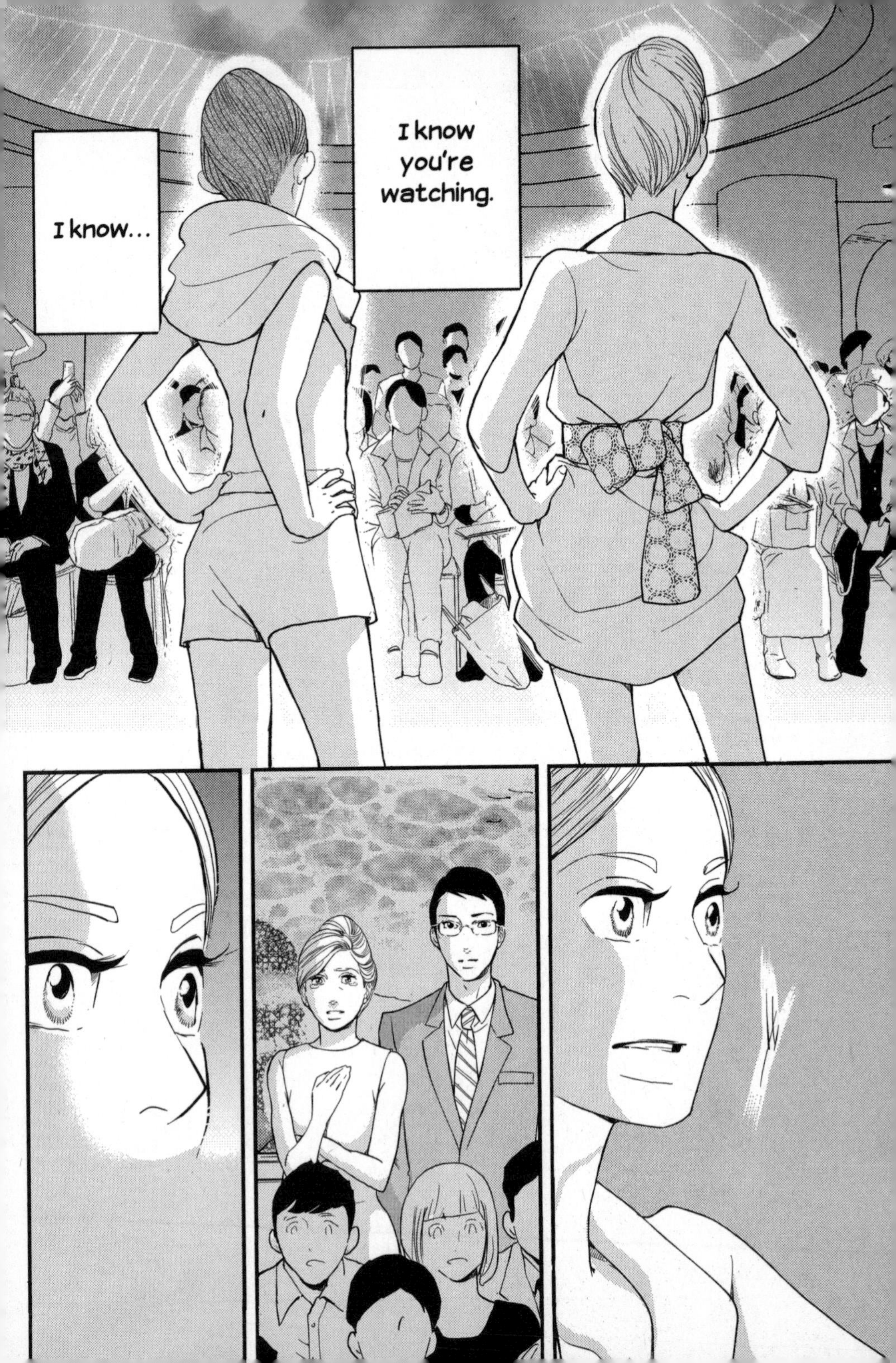
I know you're watching.
I know...

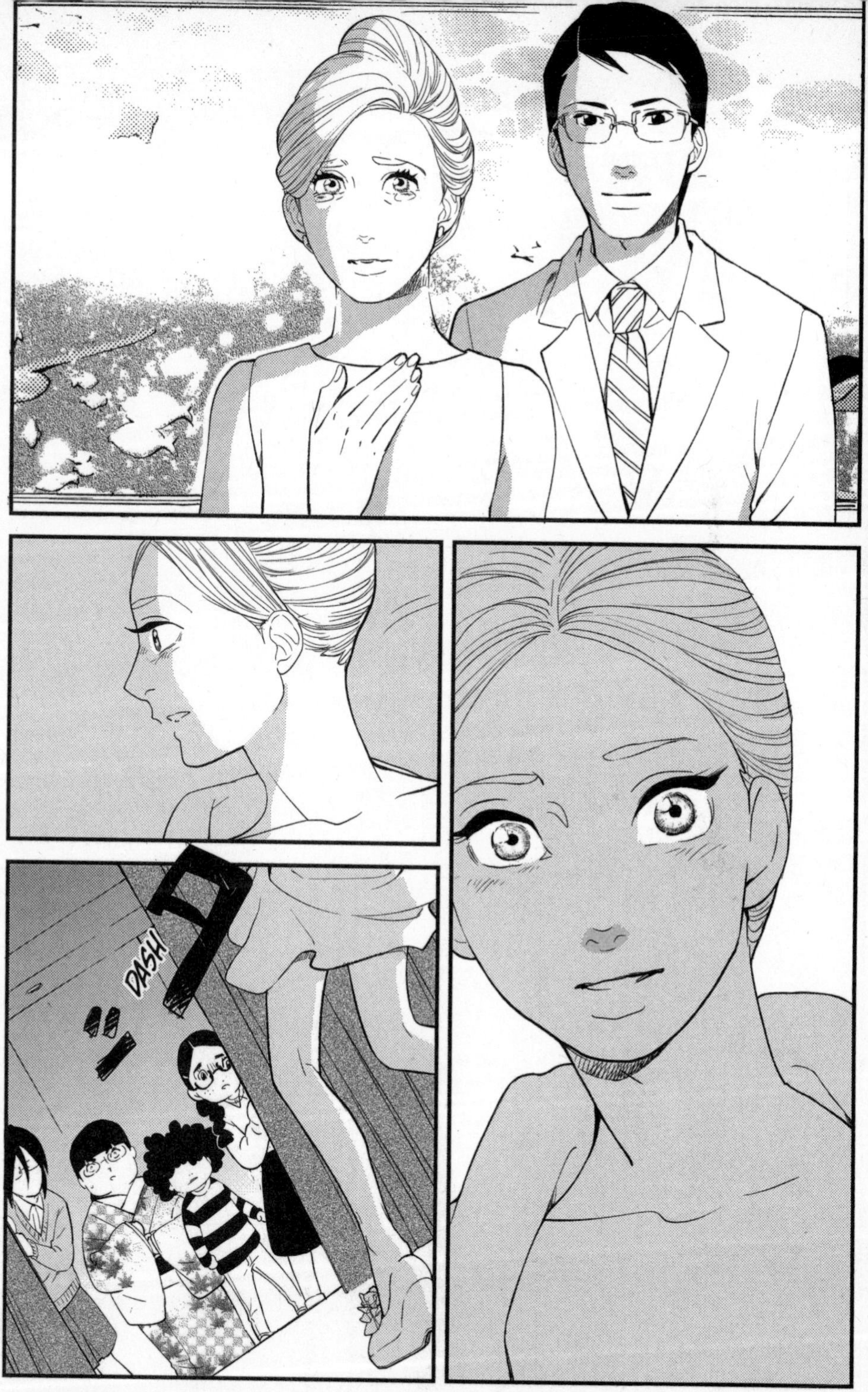
DASH

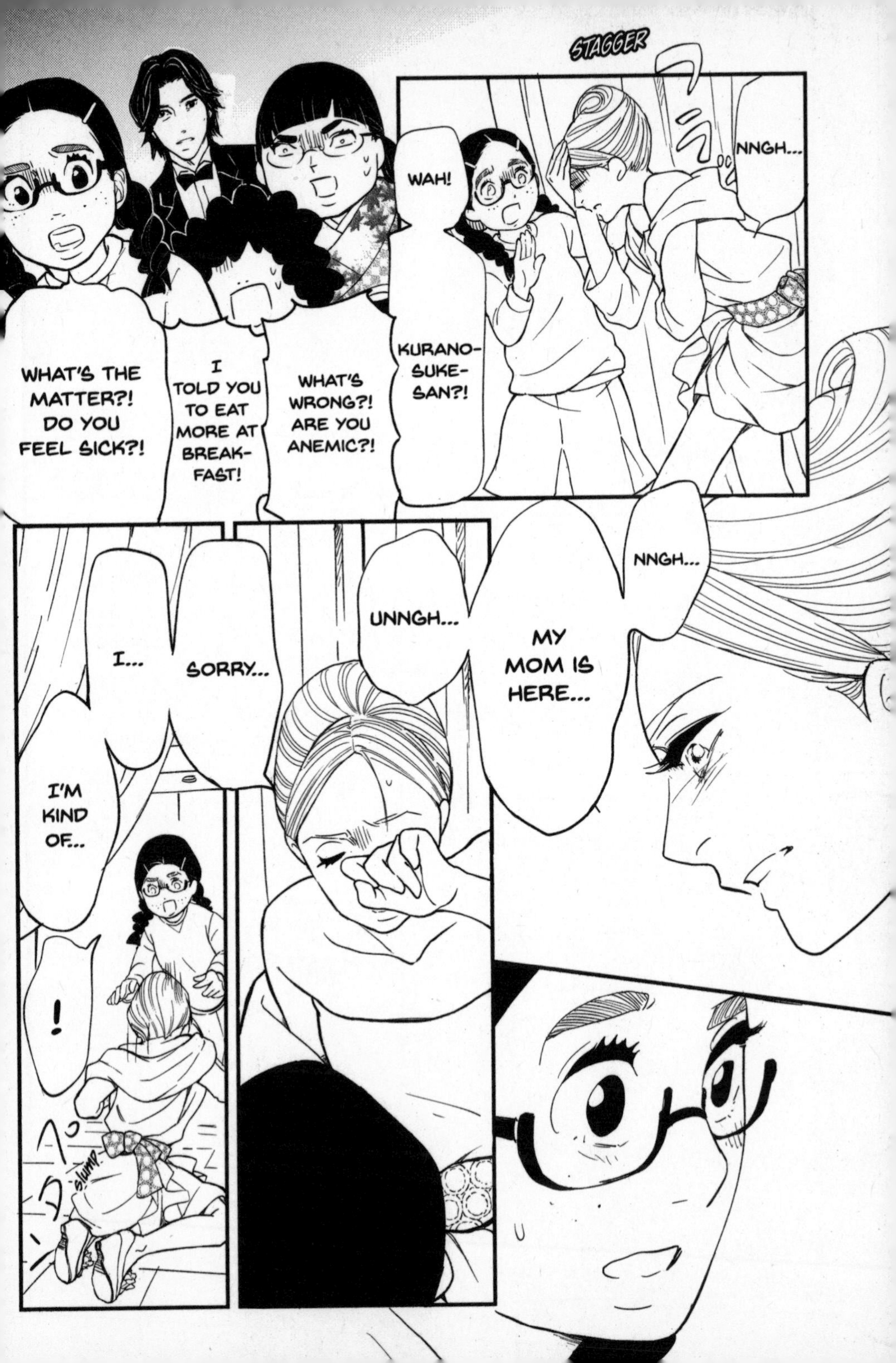
STAGGER
NNGH...
WAH!
KURANO-SUKE-SAN?!
WHAT'S WRONG?! ARE YOU ANEMIC?!
I TOLD YOU TO EAT MORE AT BREAK-FAST!
WHAT'S THE MATTER?! DO YOU FEEL SICK?!
NNGH...
MY MOM IS HERE...
UNNGH...
SORRY...
I...
I'M KIND OF...
!
slump

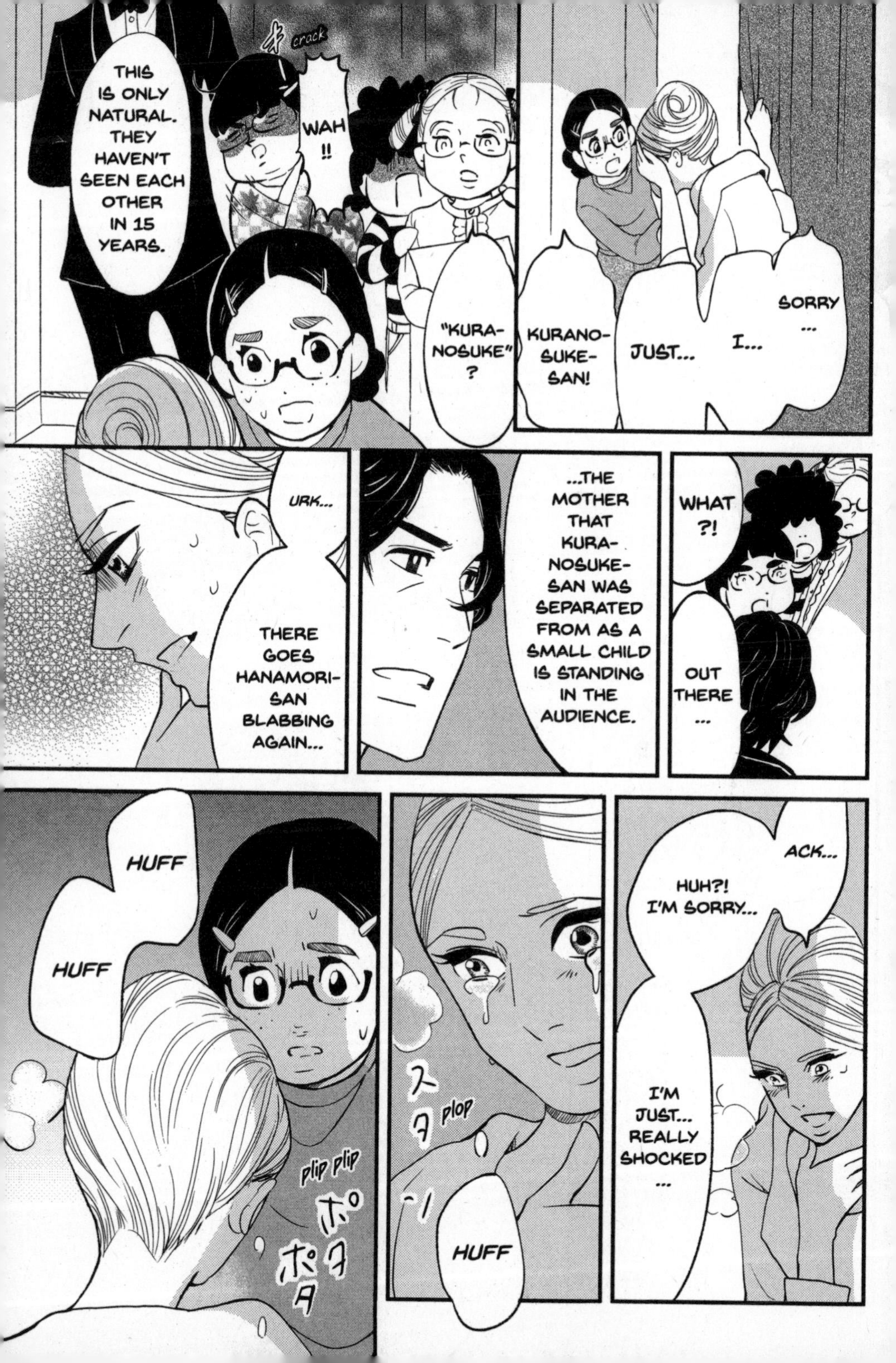
SORRY ...
I...
JUST...
KURANO-SUKE-SAN!
crack
WAH !!
"KURA-NOSUKE" ?
THIS IS ONLY NATURAL. THEY HAVEN'T SEEN EACH OTHER IN 15 YEARS.
WHAT ?!
OUT THERE ...
...THE MOTHER THAT KURA-NOSUKE-SAN WAS SEPARATED FROM AS A SMALL CHILD IS STANDING IN THE AUDIENCE.
URK...
THERE GOES HANAMORI-SAN BLABBING AGAIN...
ACK...
HUH?! I'M SORRY...
I'M JUST... REALLY SHOCKED ...
スタ plop
HUFF
HUFF
HUFF
plip plip ポタポタ

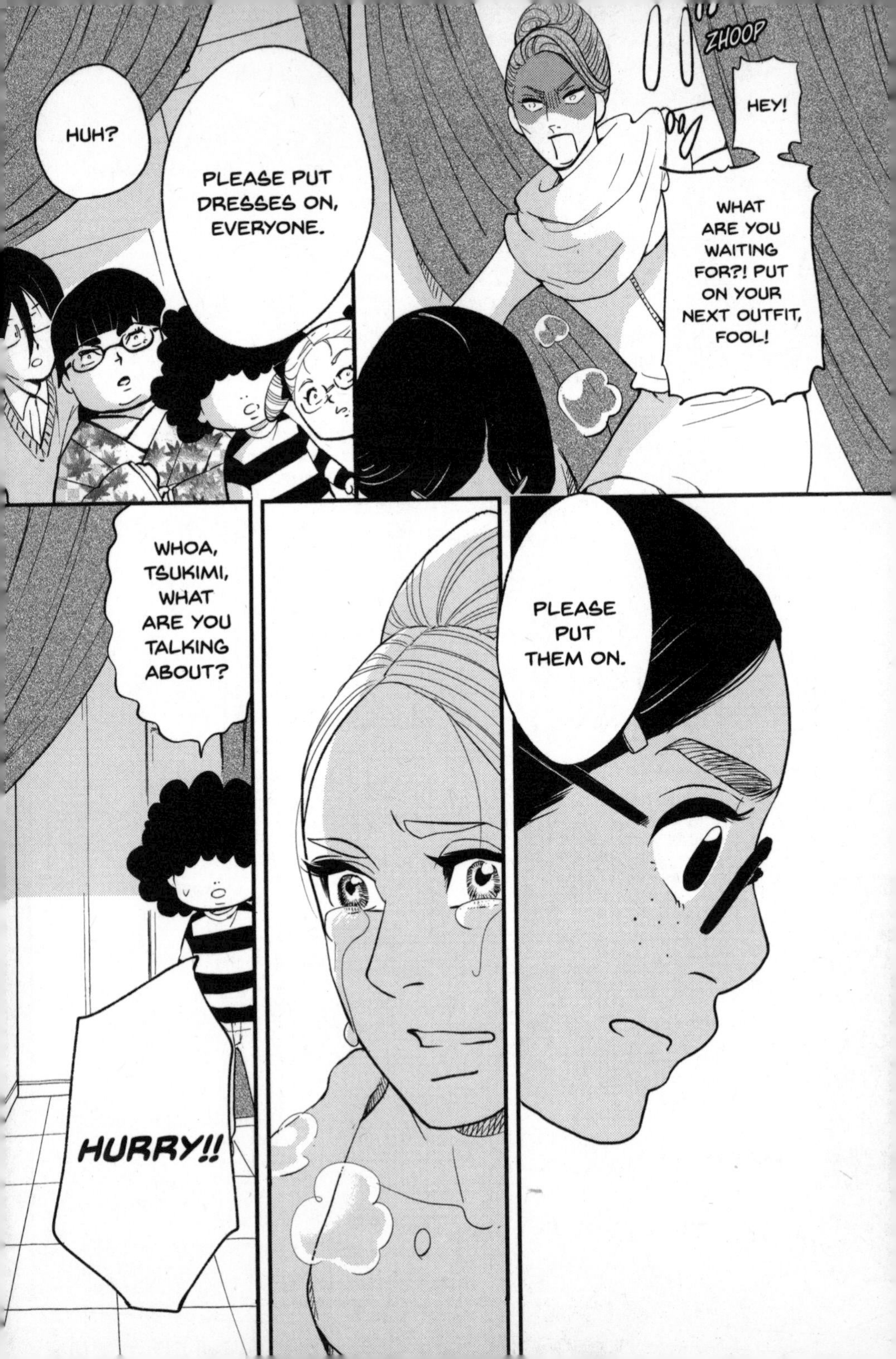
ZHOOP
HEY!
WHAT ARE YOU WAITING FOR?! PUT ON YOUR NEXT OUTFIT, FOOL!
PLEASE PUT DRESSES ON, EVERYONE.
HUH?
PLEASE PUT THEM ON.
WHOA, TSUKIMI, WHAT ARE YOU TALKING ABOUT?
HURRY!!

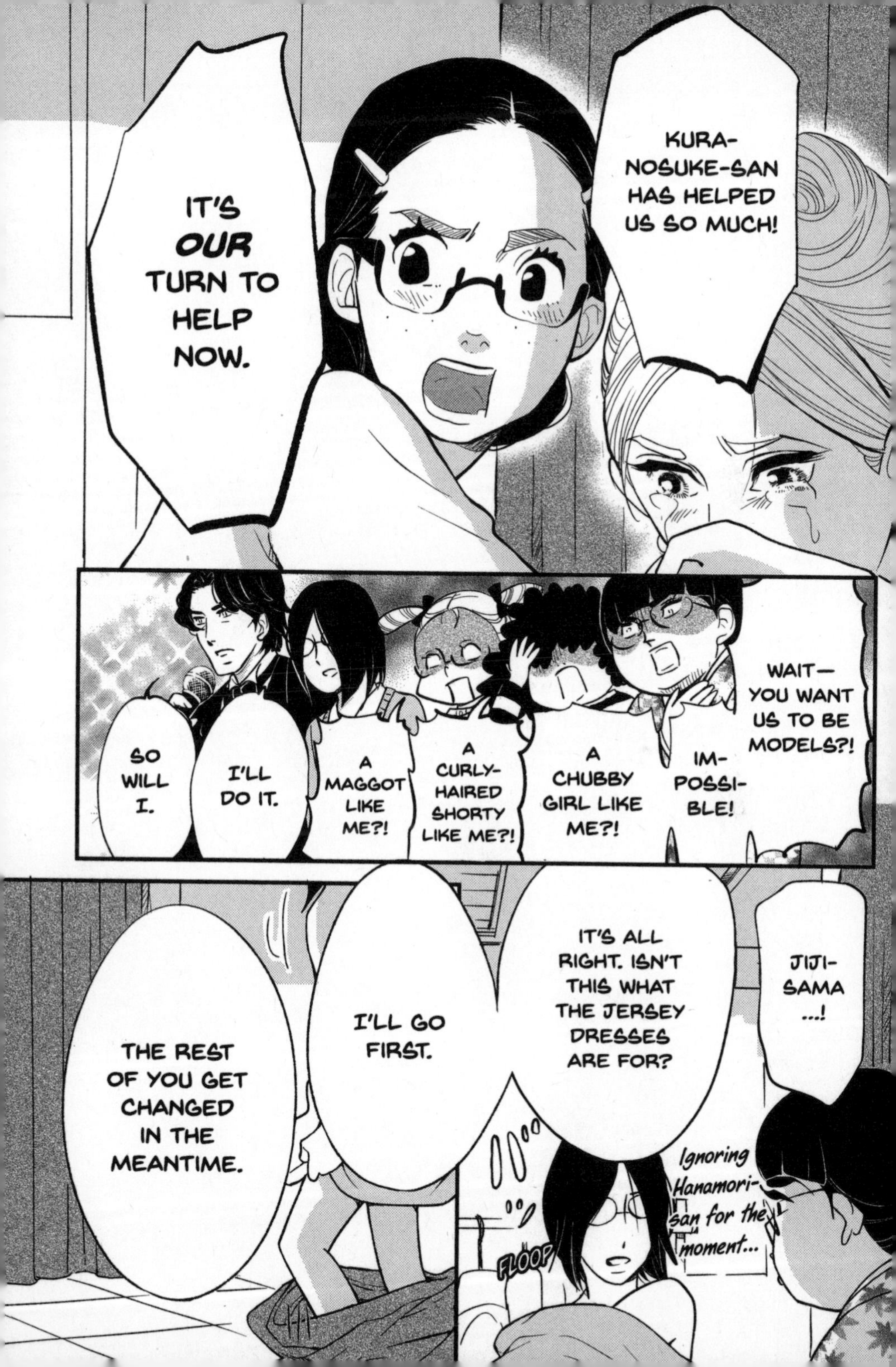
KURA-NOSUKE-SAN HAS HELPED US SO MUCH!
IT'S *OUR* TURN TO HELP NOW.
WAIT— YOU WANT US TO BE MODELS?!
IM-POSSI-BLE!
A CHUBBY GIRL LIKE ME?!
A CURLY-HAIRED SHORTY LIKE ME?!
A MAGGOT LIKE ME?!
I'LL DO IT.
SO WILL I.
JIJI-SAMA ...!
Ignoring Hanamori-san for the moment...
FLOOP
IT'S ALL RIGHT. ISN'T THIS WHAT THE JERSEY DRESSES ARE FOR?
I'LL GO FIRST.
THE REST OF YOU GET CHANGED IN THE MEANTIME.

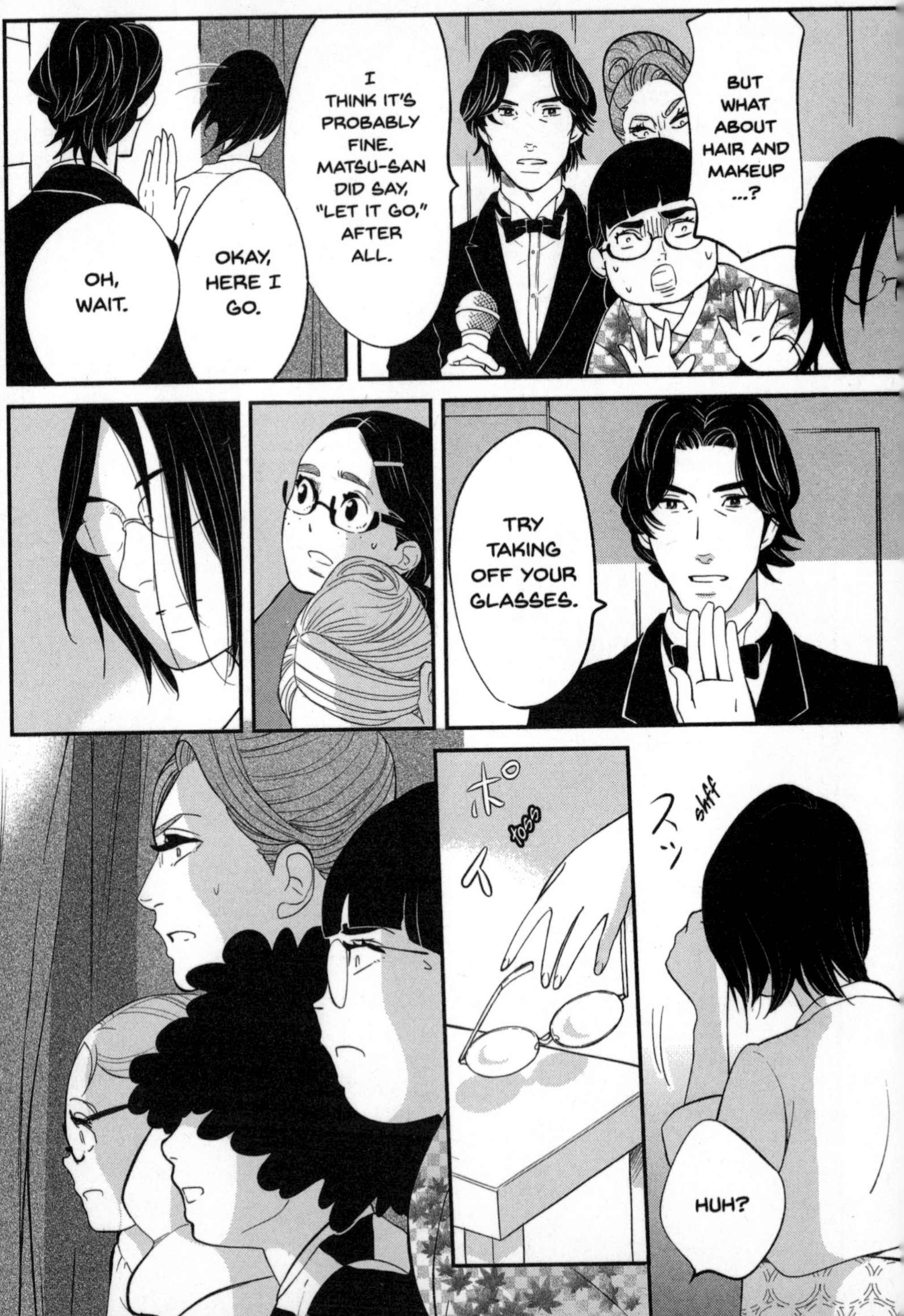
BUT WHAT ABOUT HAIR AND MAKEUP ...?
I THINK IT'S PROBABLY FINE. MATSU-SAN DID SAY, "LET IT GO," AFTER ALL.
OKAY, HERE I GO.
OH, WAIT.
TRY TAKING OFF YOUR GLASSES.
スッ shff
HUH?
ポイ toss

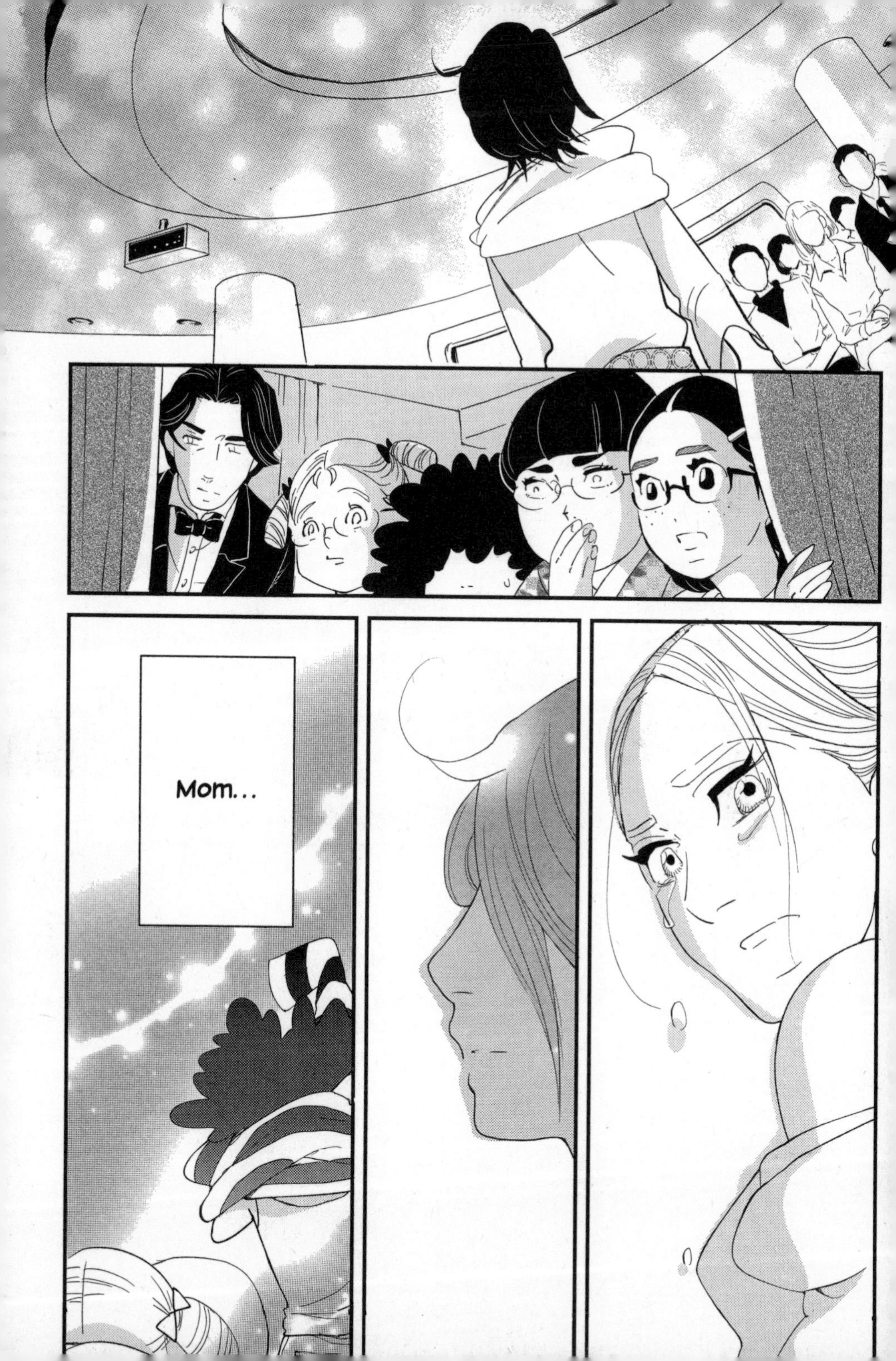
Mom...

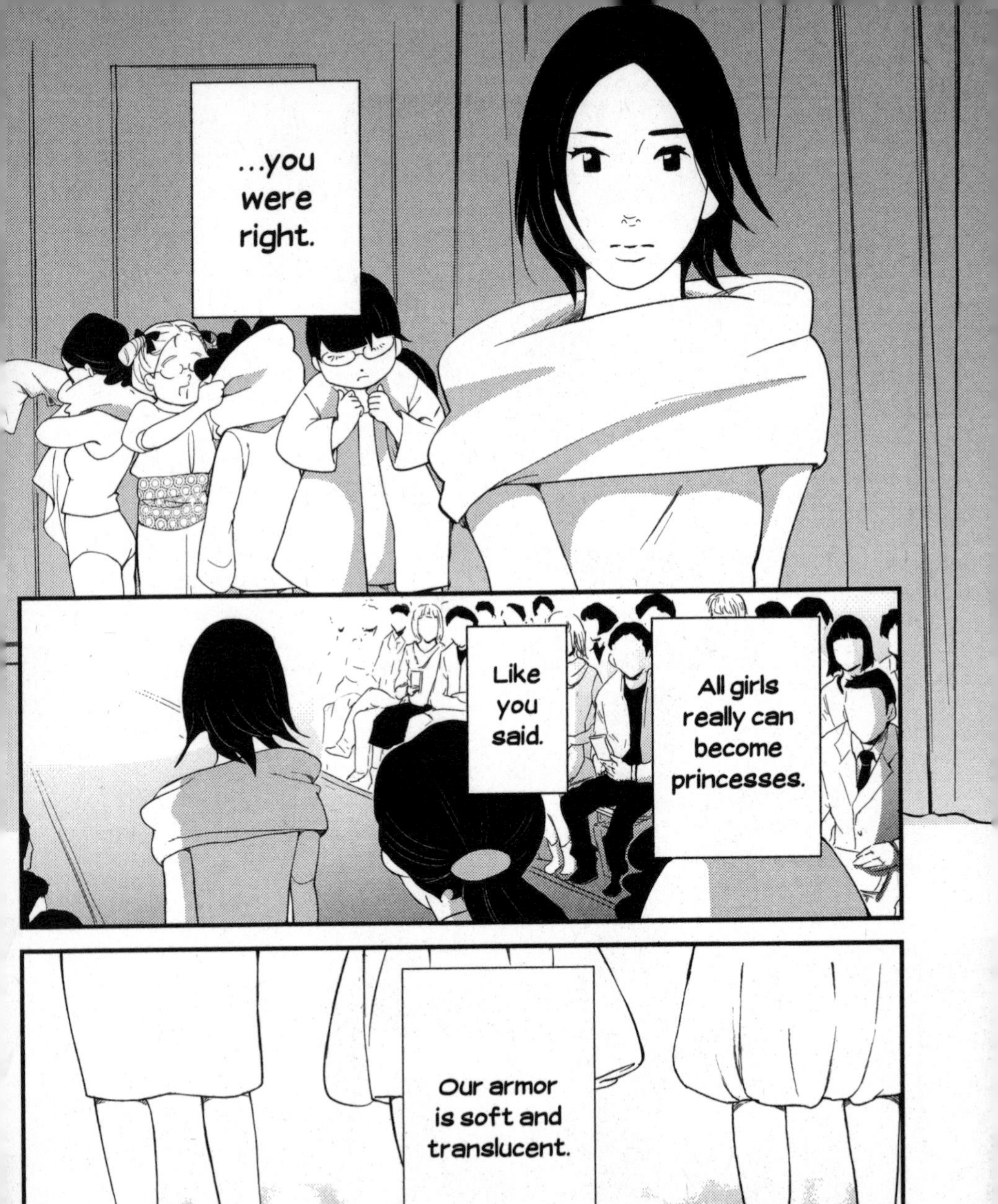
...you were right.
All girls really can become princesses.
Like you said.
Our armor is soft and translucent.

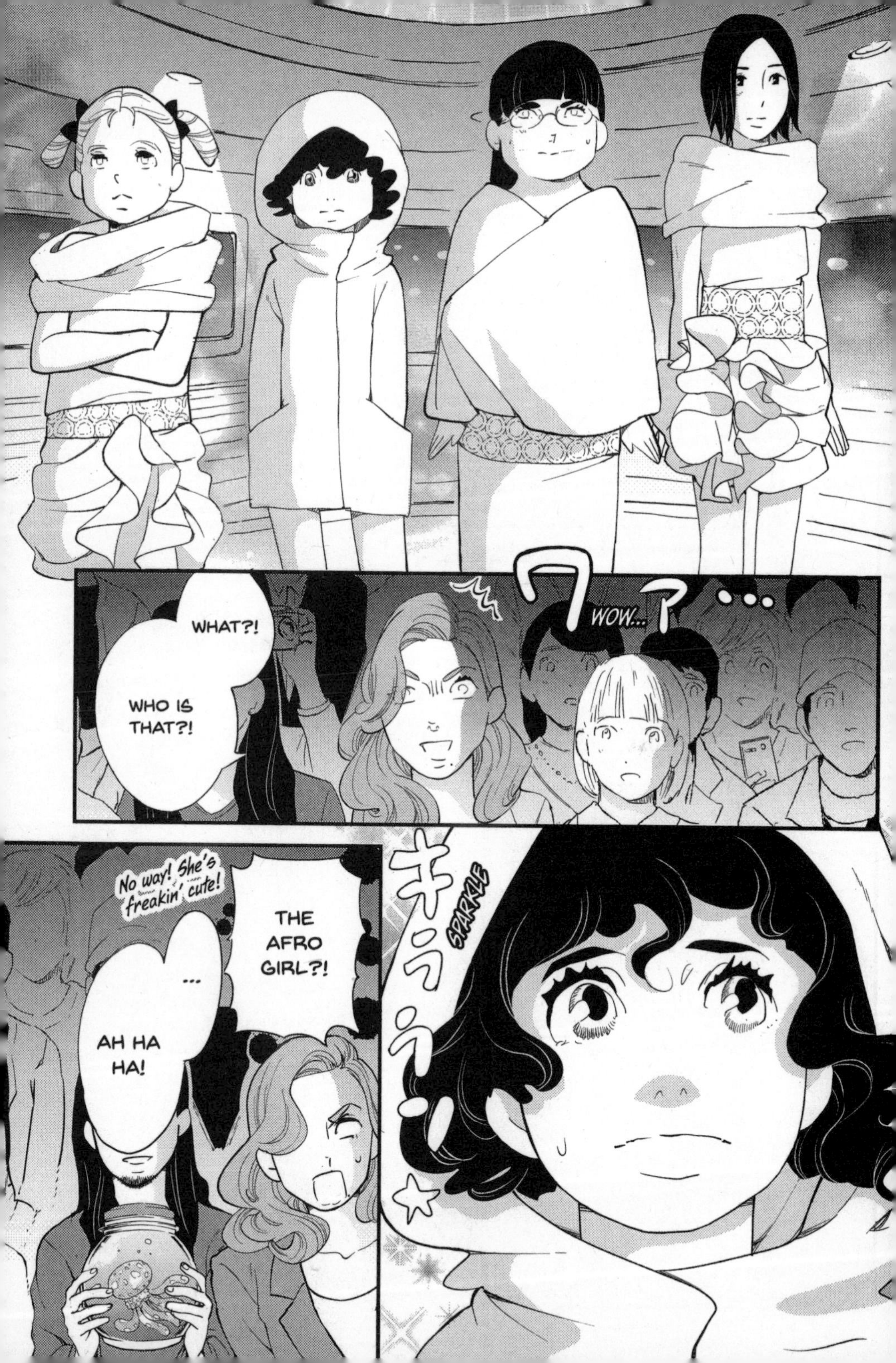

...
WOW...
WHAT?!
WHO IS THAT?!
SPARKLE
THE AFRO GIRL?!
No way! She's freakin' cute!
...
AH HA HA!

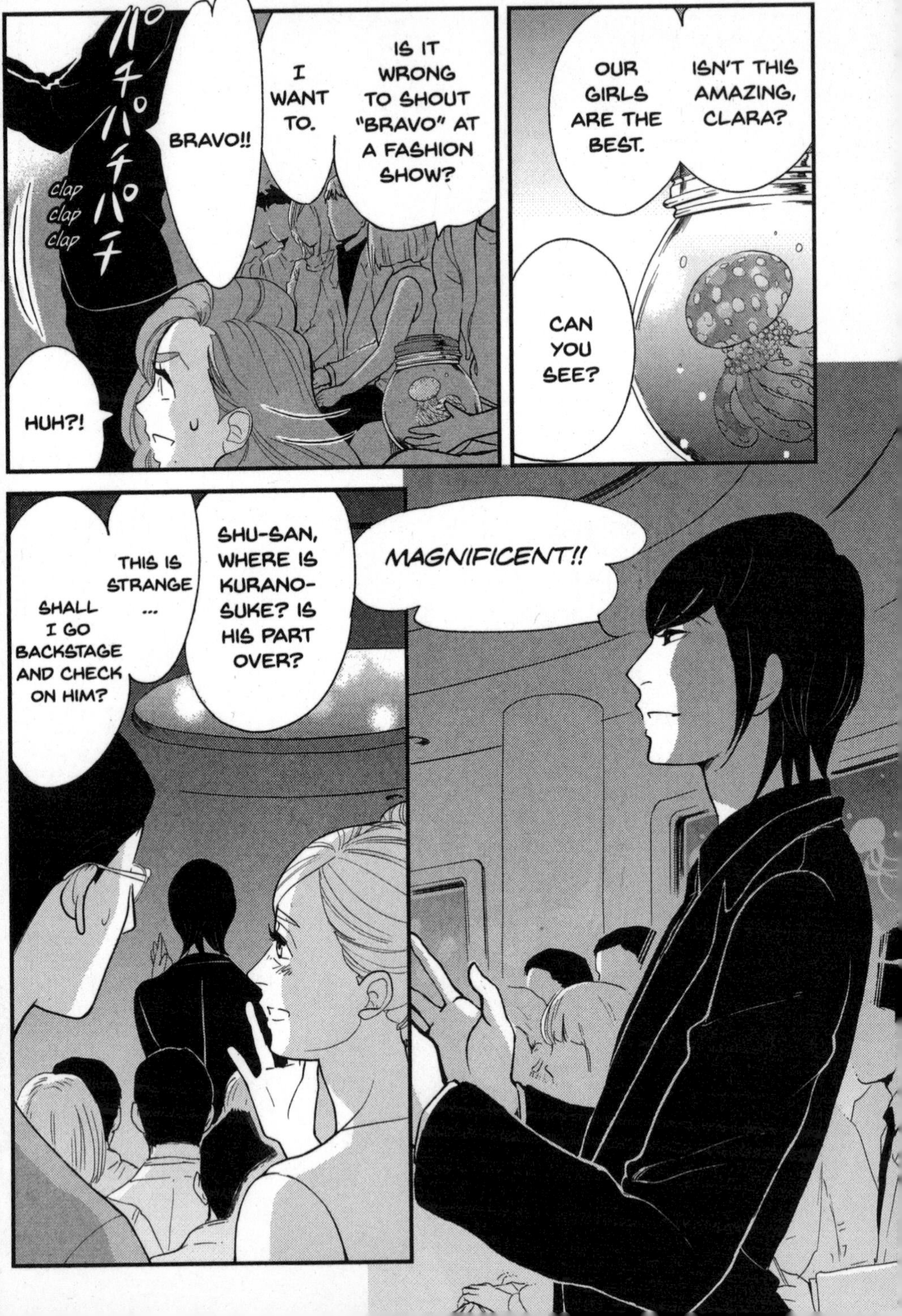
ISN'T THIS AMAZING, CLARA?
OUR GIRLS ARE THE BEST.
CAN YOU SEE?
IS IT WRONG TO SHOUT "BRAVO" AT A FASHION SHOW?
I WANT TO.
BRAVO!!
パチパチパチ
clap clap clap
HUH?!
MAGNIFICENT!!
SHU-SAN, WHERE IS KURANO-SUKE? IS HIS PART OVER?
THIS IS STRANGE ...
SHALL I GO BACKSTAGE AND CHECK ON HIM?

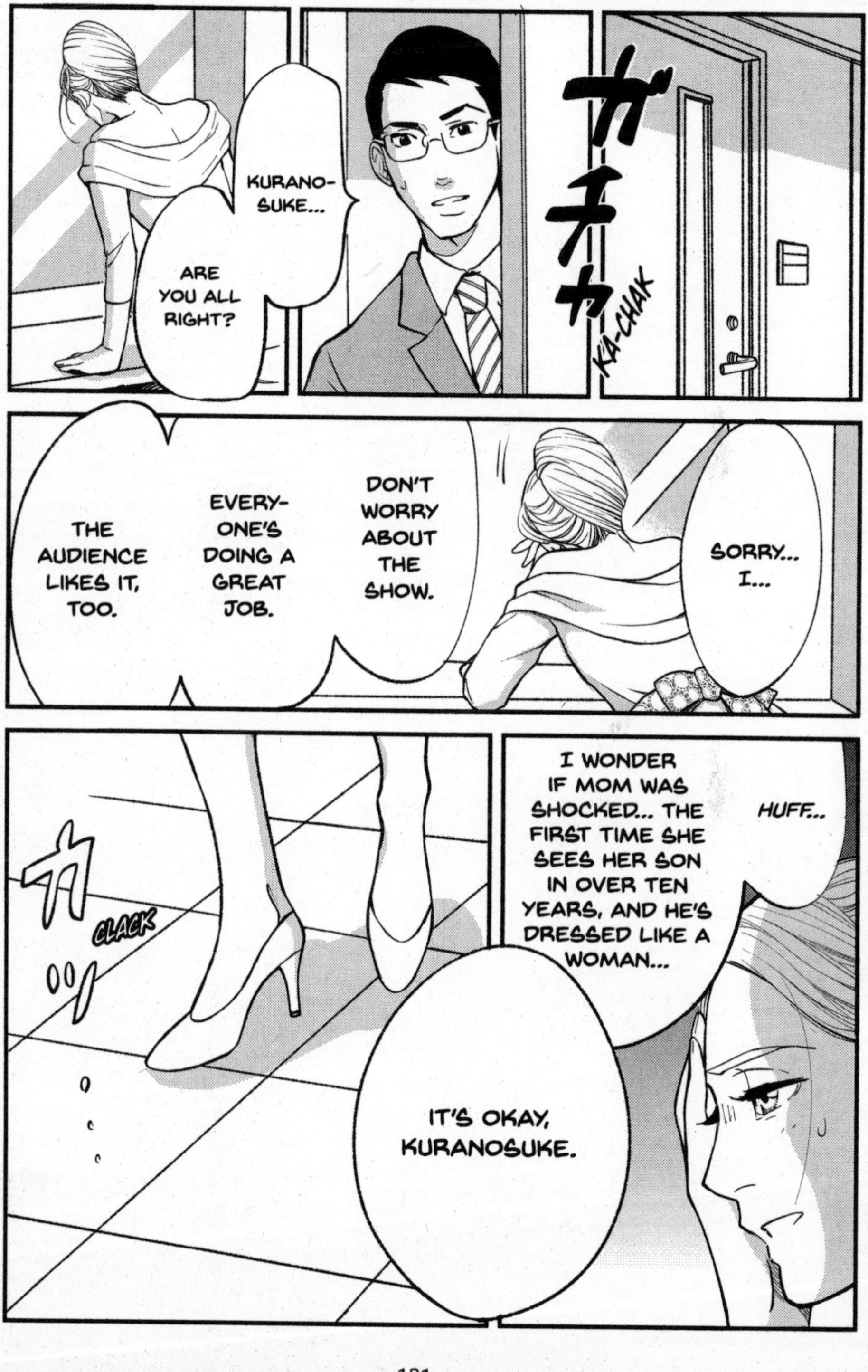
ガチャ
KA-CHAK
KURANO-SUKE...
ARE YOU ALL RIGHT?
SORRY... I...
DON'T WORRY ABOUT THE SHOW.
EVERY-ONE'S DOING A GREAT JOB.
THE AUDIENCE LIKES IT, TOO.
HUFF...
I WONDER IF MOM WAS SHOCKED... THE FIRST TIME SHE SEES HER SON IN OVER TEN YEARS, AND HE'S DRESSED LIKE A WOMAN...
IT'S OKAY, KURANOSUKE.
カ
CLACK

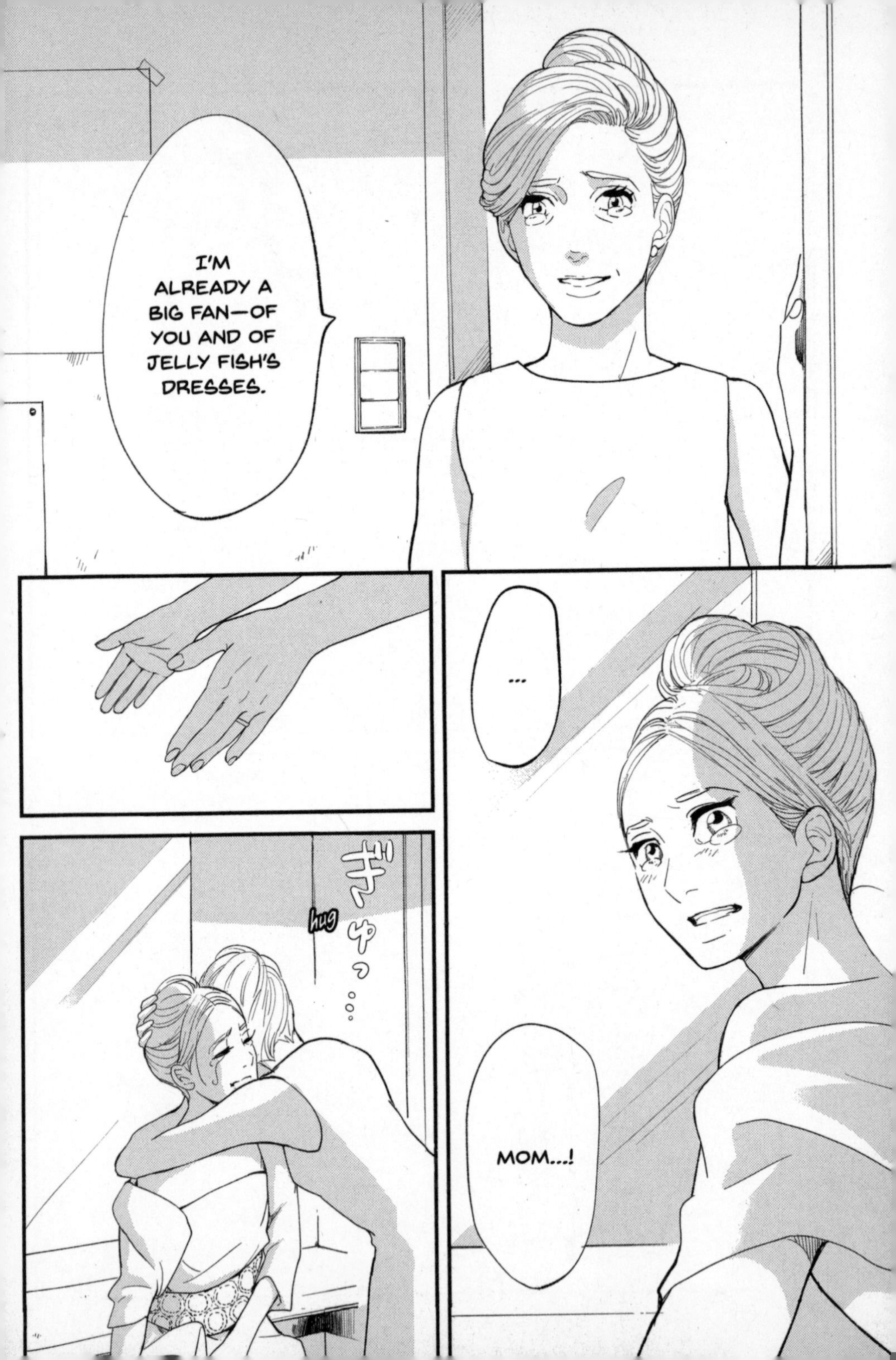
I'M ALREADY A BIG FAN—OF YOU AND OF JELLY FISH'S DRESSES.
...
MOM...!
ぎゅっ…
hug

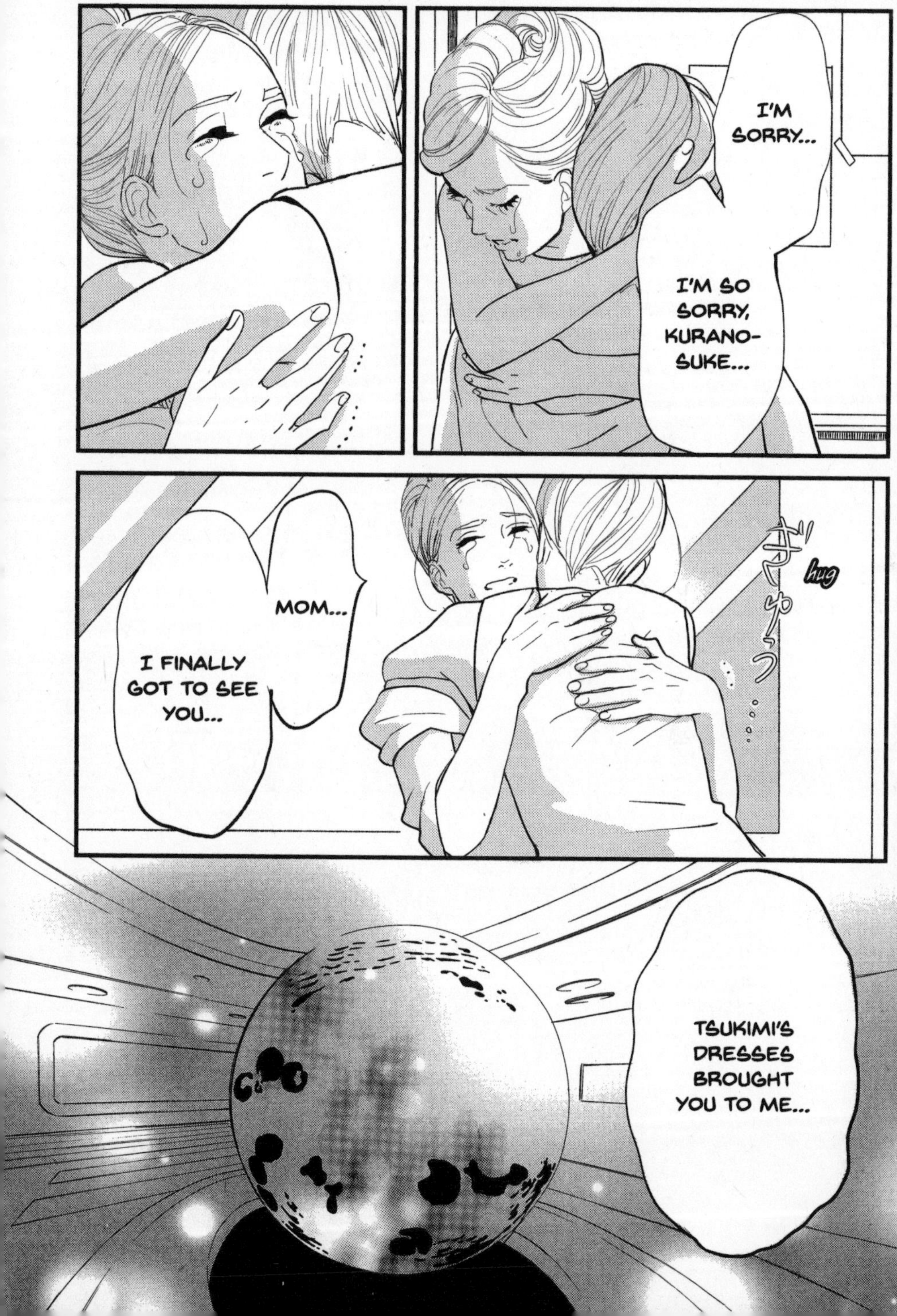
I'M SORRY...
I'M SO SORRY, KURANO-SUKE...
ぎゅっ...
hug
MOM...
I FINALLY GOT TO SEE YOU...
TSUKIMI'S DRESSES BROUGHT YOU TO ME...

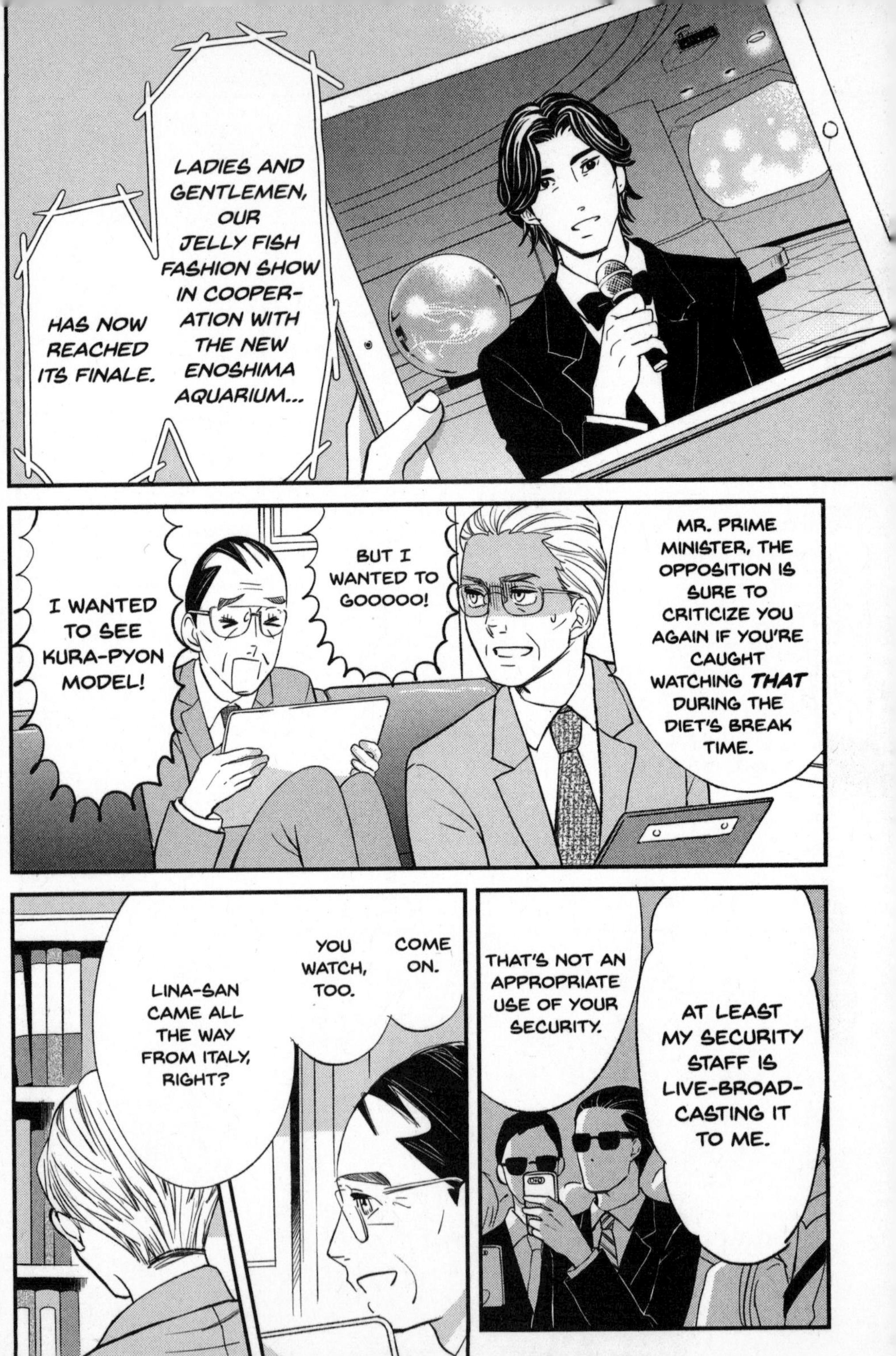
LADIES AND GENTLEMEN, OUR JELLY FISH FASHION SHOW IN COOPERATION WITH THE NEW ENOSHIMA AQUARIUM...
HAS NOW REACHED ITS FINALE.
MR. PRIME MINISTER, THE OPPOSITION IS SURE TO CRITICIZE YOU AGAIN IF YOU'RE CAUGHT WATCHING *THAT* DURING THE DIET'S BREAK TIME.
BUT I WANTED TO GOOOOO!
I WANTED TO SEE KURA-PYON MODEL!
AT LEAST MY SECURITY STAFF IS LIVE-BROADCASTING IT TO ME.
THAT'S NOT AN APPROPRIATE USE OF YOUR SECURITY.
COME ON.
YOU WATCH, TOO.
LINA-SAN CAME ALL THE WAY FROM ITALY, RIGHT?

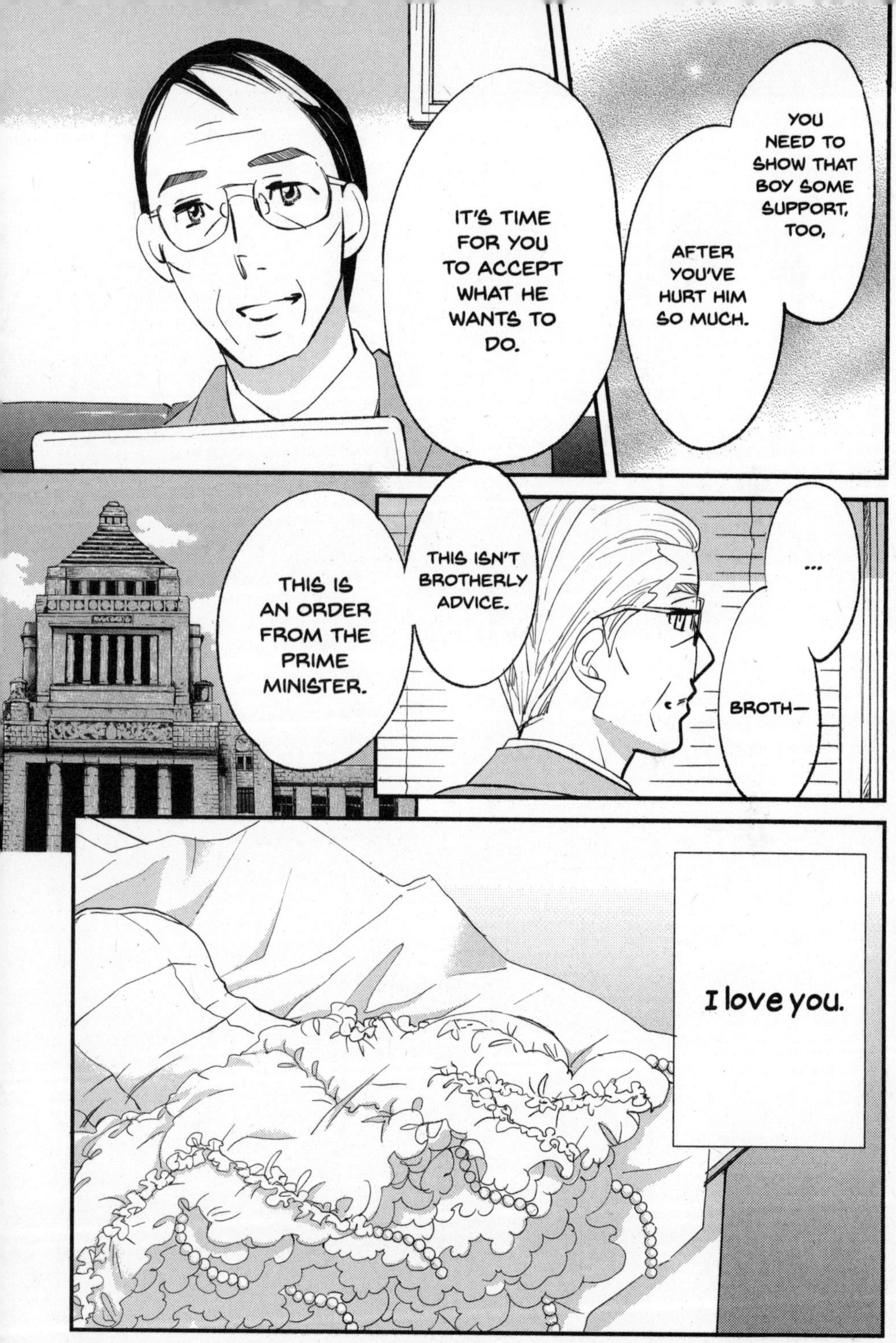
YOU NEED TO SHOW THAT BOY SOME SUPPORT, TOO,
AFTER YOU'VE HURT HIM SO MUCH.
IT'S TIME FOR YOU TO ACCEPT WHAT HE WANTS TO DO.
...
BROTH—
THIS ISN'T BROTHERLY ADVICE.
THIS IS AN ORDER FROM THE PRIME MINISTER.
I love you.

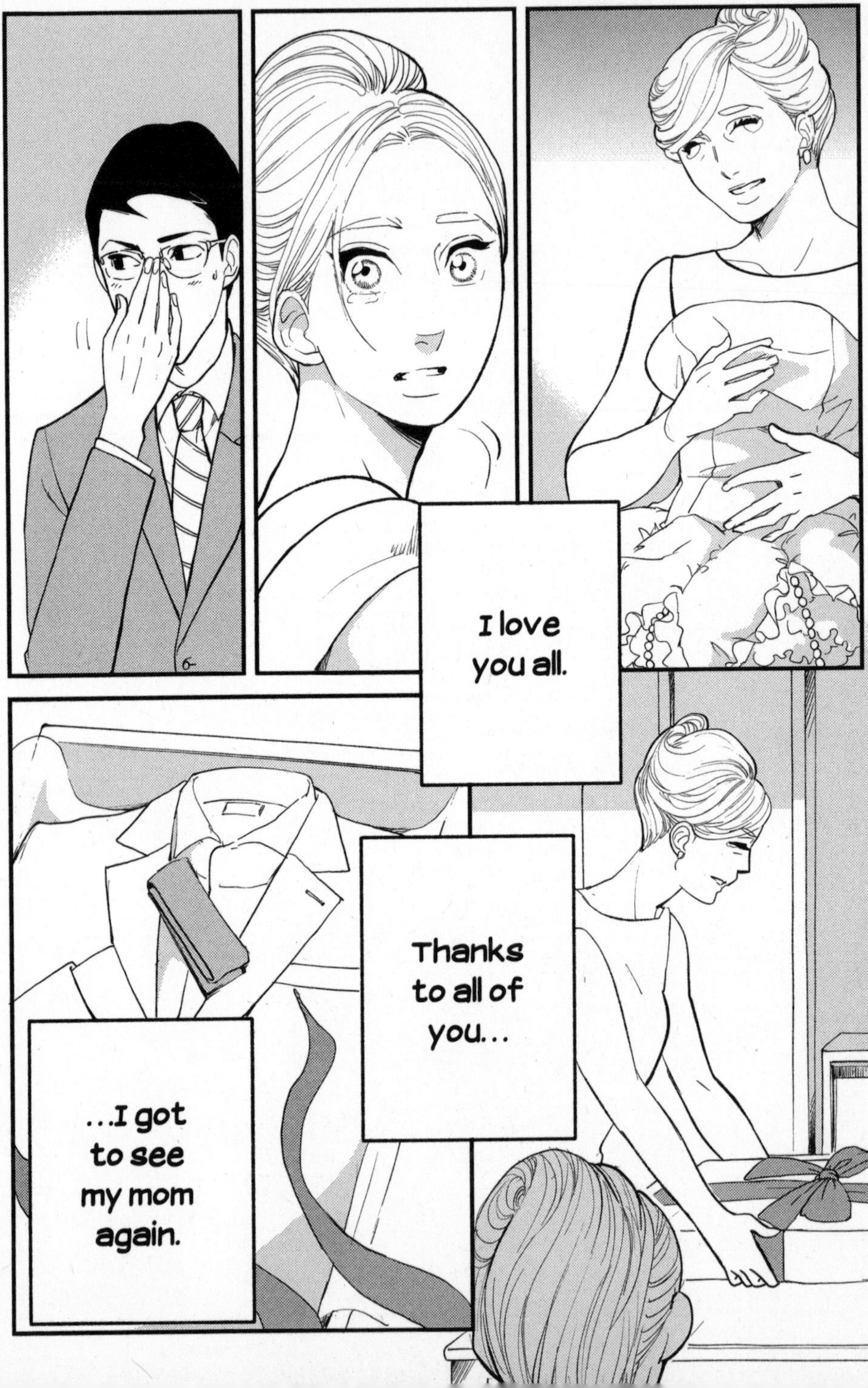
I love you all.
Thanks to all of you...
...I got to see my mom again.

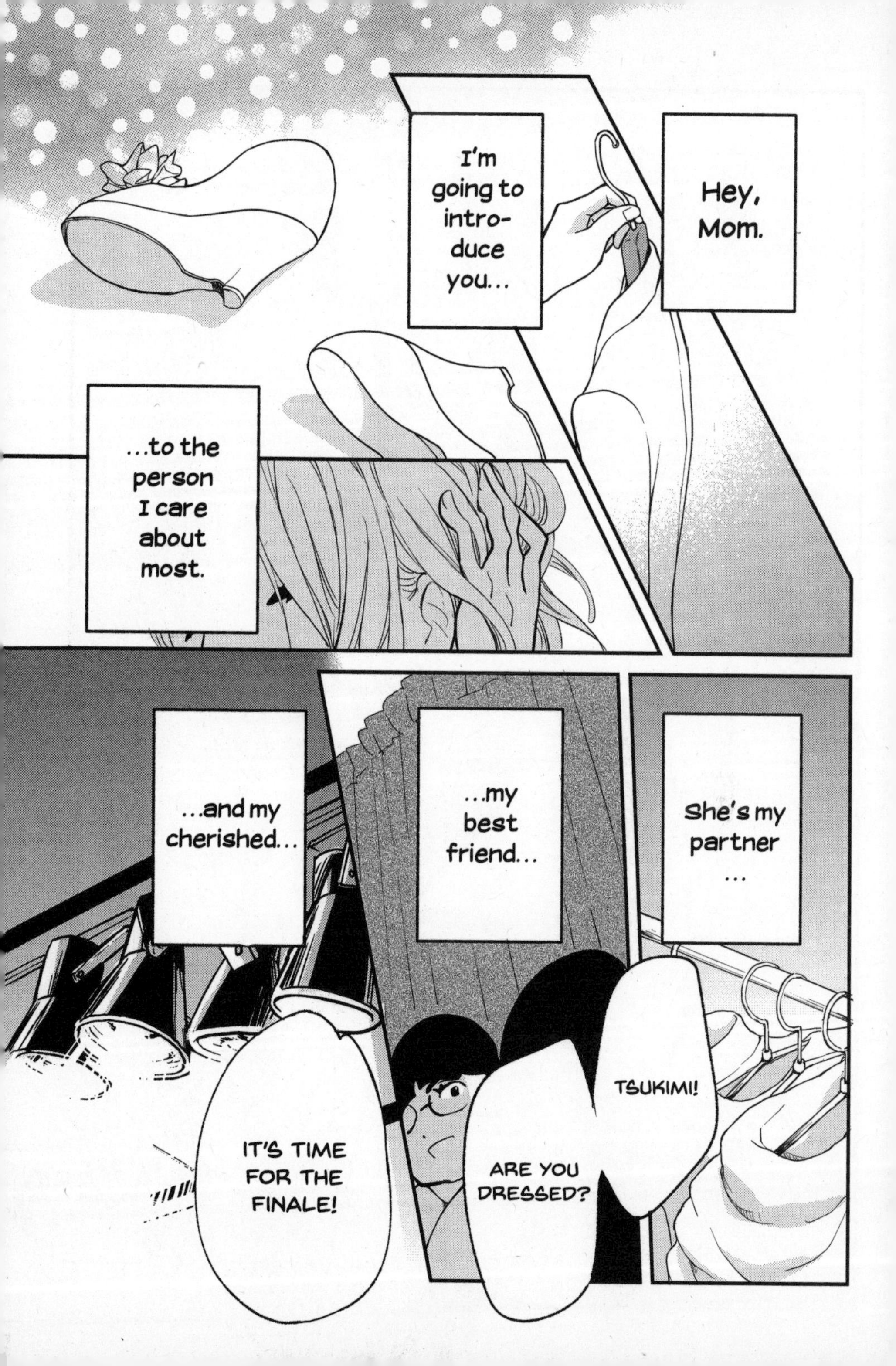
Hey, Mom.
I'm going to intro-duce you...
...to the person I care about most.
She's my partner ...
...my best friend...
...and my cherished...
TSUKIMI!
ARE YOU DRESSED?
IT'S TIME FOR THE FINALE!

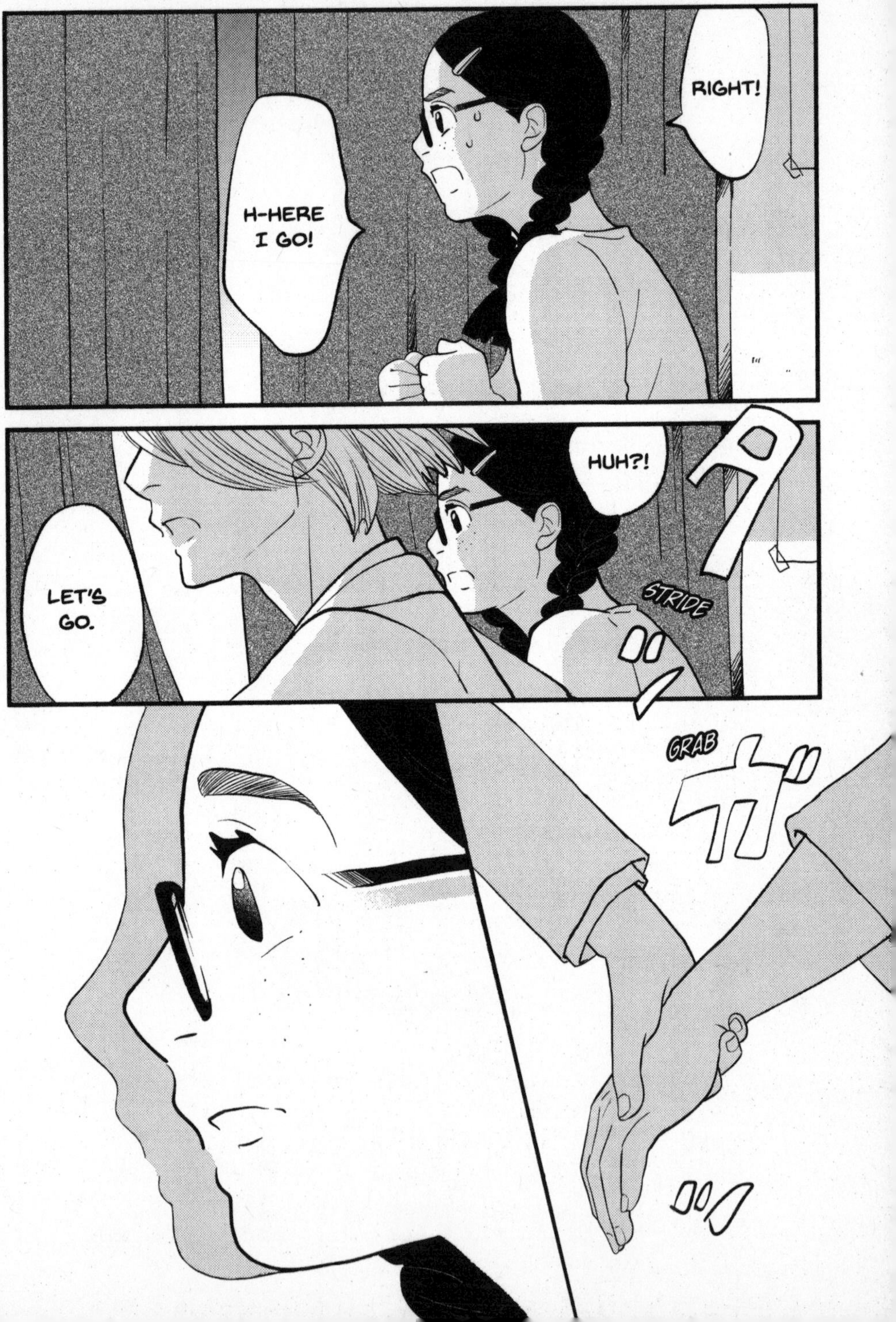
RIGHT!
H-HERE I GO!
HUH?!
STRIDE
LET'S GO.
GRAB

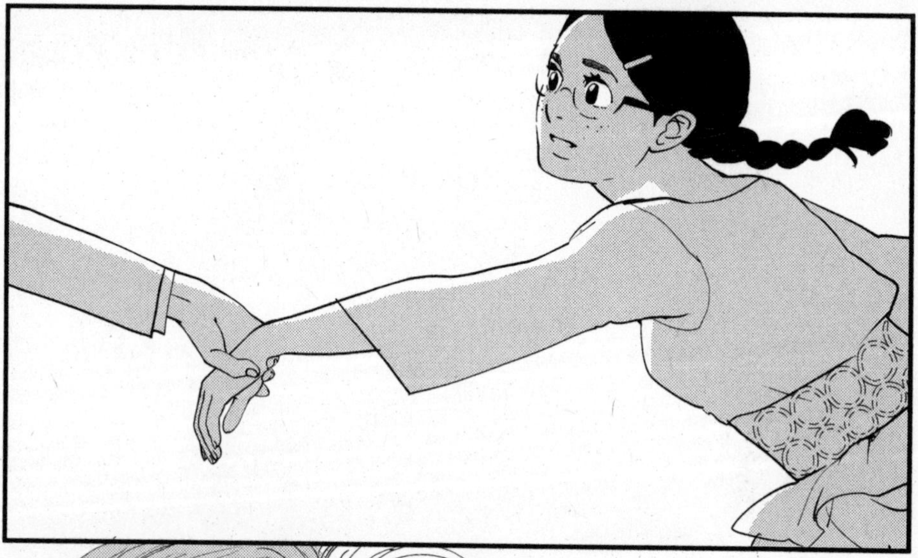
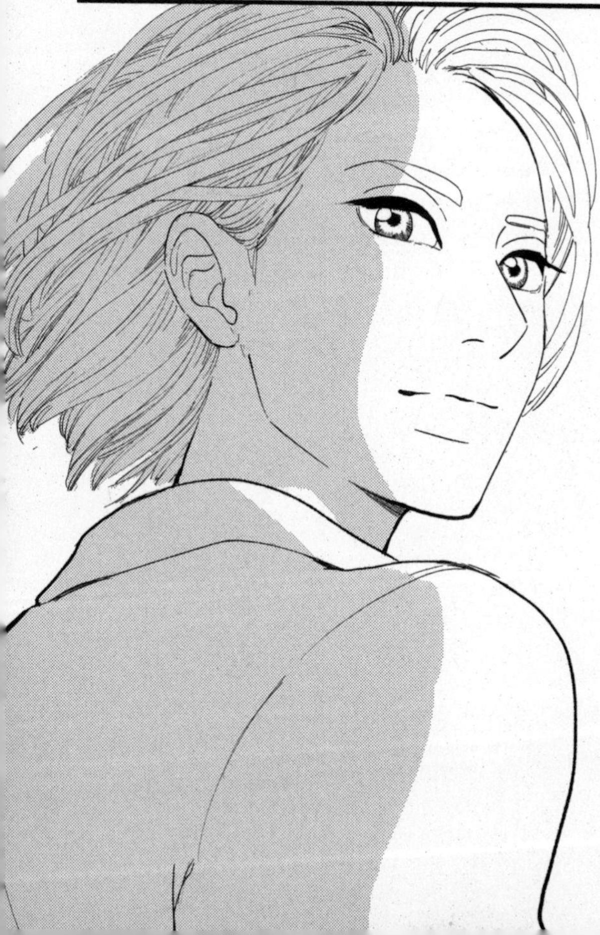

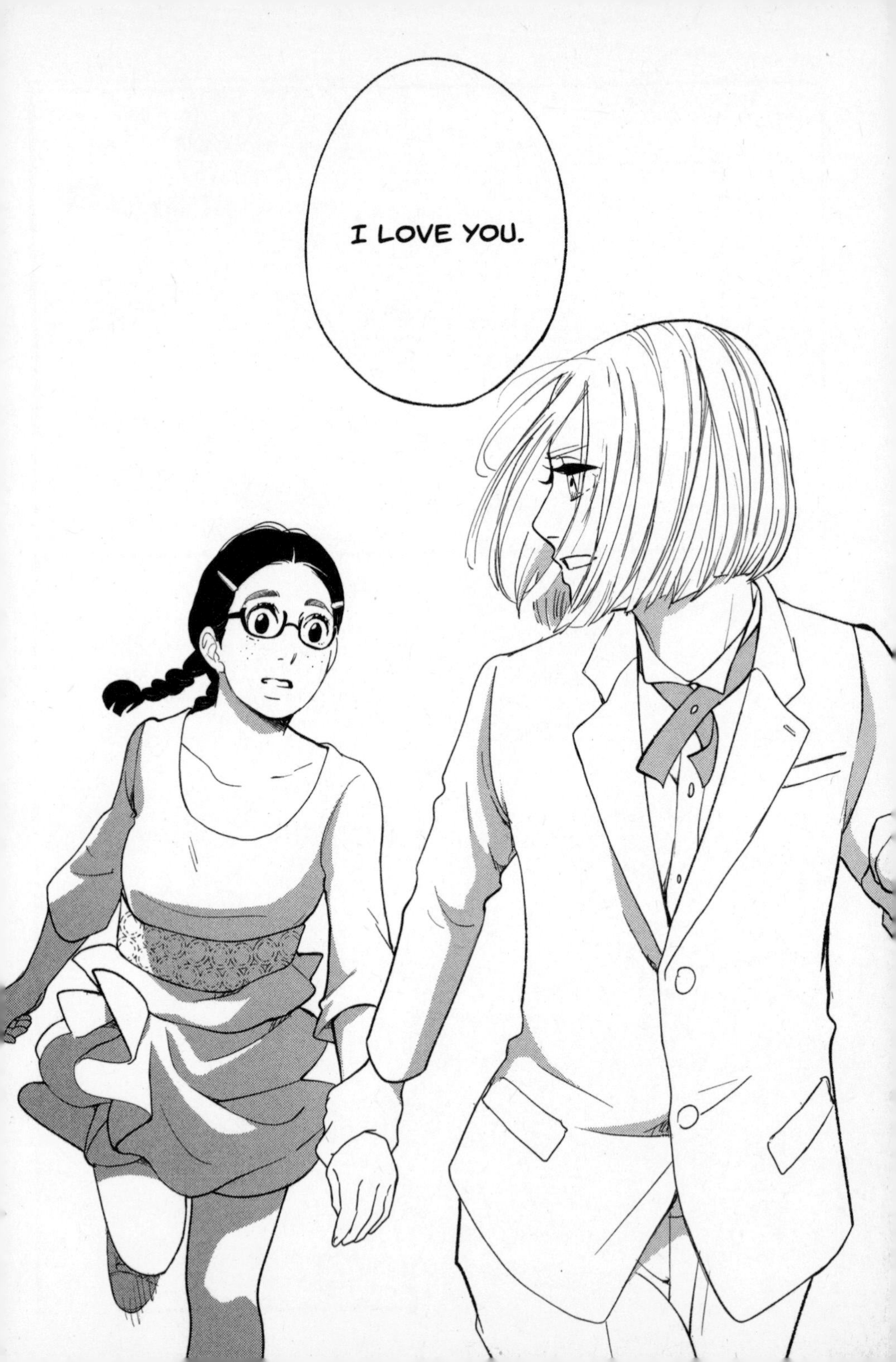
I LOVE YOU.

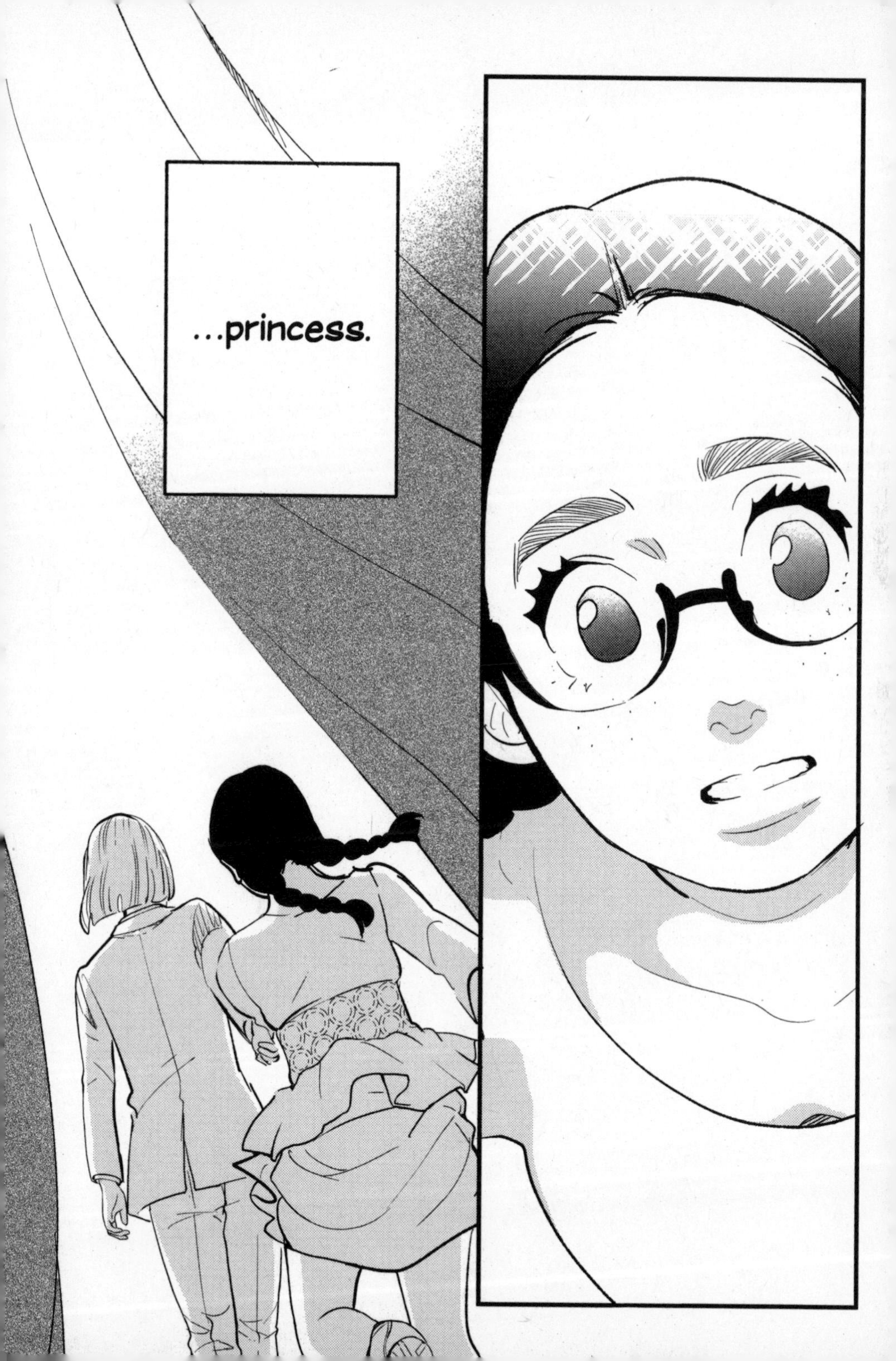
...princess.

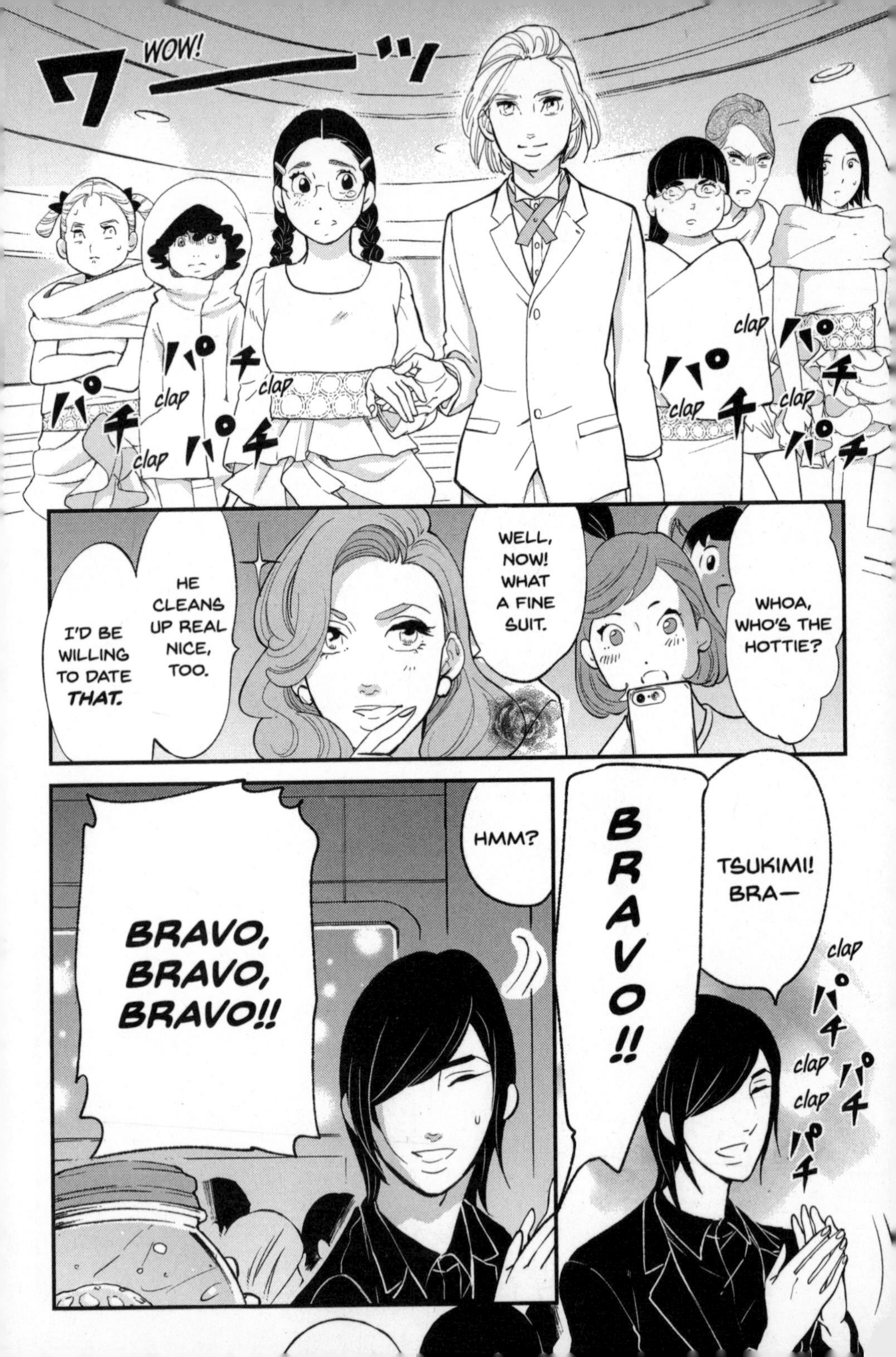
WOW!
ワーーッ
clap
clap
clap
clap
clap
clap
WHOA, WHO'S THE HOTTIE?
WELL, NOW! WHAT A FINE SUIT.
HE CLEANS UP REAL NICE, TOO.
I'D BE WILLING TO DATE *THAT.*
TSUKIMI! BRA—
BRAVO!!
HMM?
clap
clap
clap
BRAVO, BRAVO, BRAVO!!

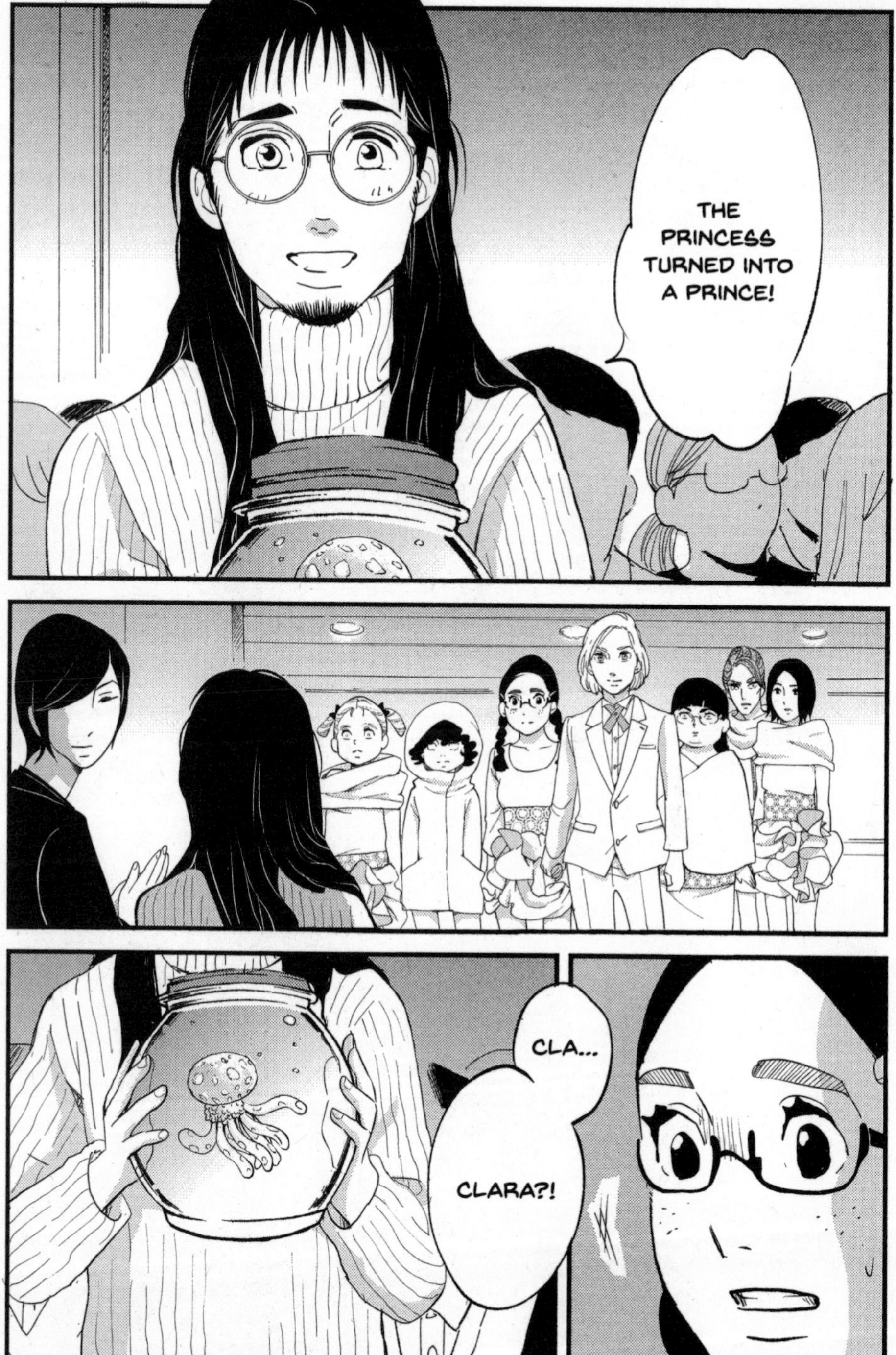
THE PRINCESS TURNED INTO A PRINCE!
CLA...
CLARA?!

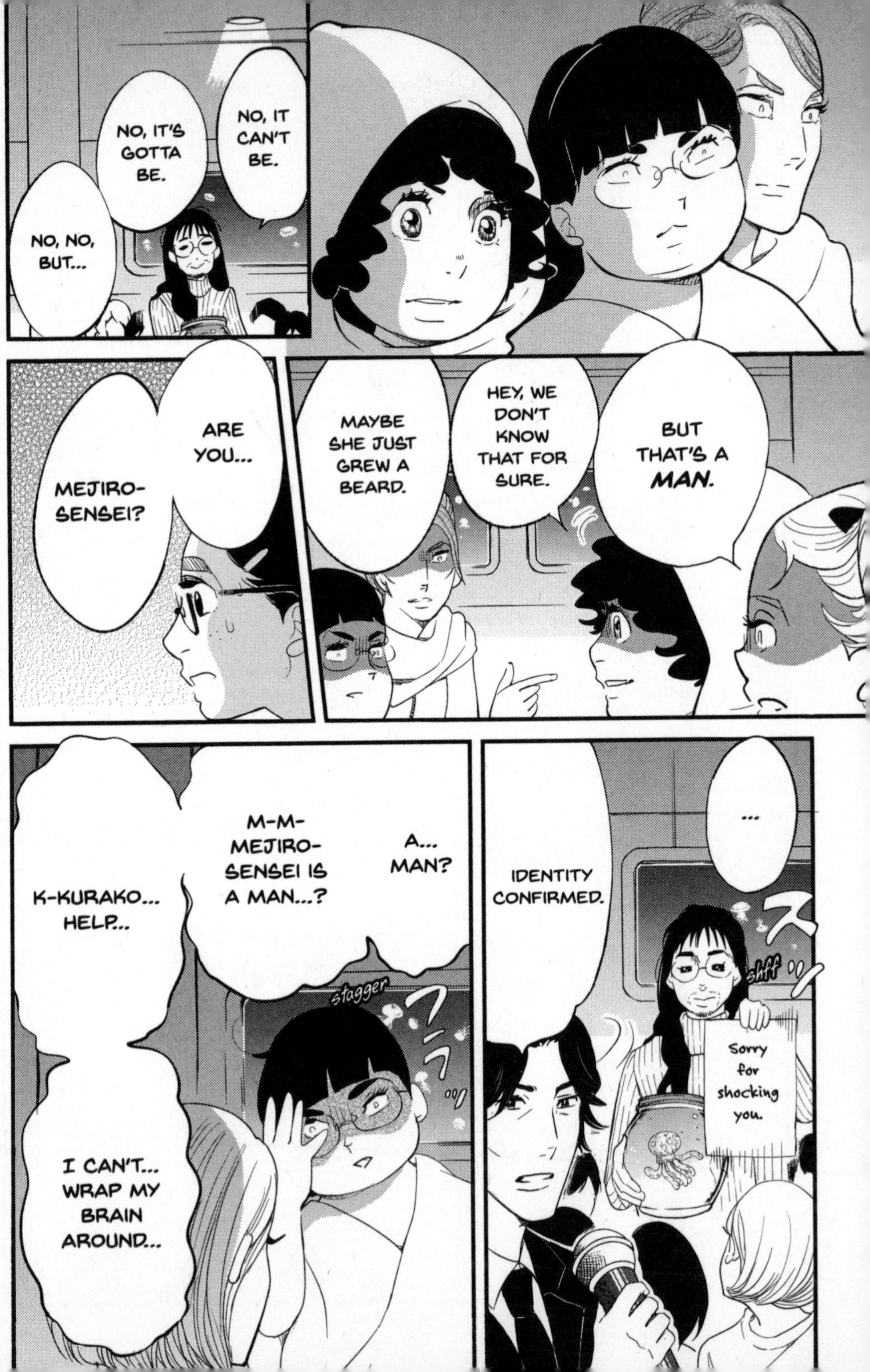
NO, IT CAN'T BE.
NO, IT'S GOTTA BE.
NO, NO, BUT...
BUT THAT'S A MAN.
HEY, WE DON'T KNOW THAT FOR SURE.
MAYBE SHE JUST GREW A BEARD.
ARE YOU...
MEJIRO-SENSEI?
...
IDENTITY CONFIRMED.
shff
Sorry for shocking you.
A... MAN?
M-M-MEJIRO-SENSEI IS A MAN...?
stagger
K-KURAKO... HELP...
I CAN'T... WRAP MY BRAIN AROUND...

I'M SORRY.
BUT I'M A
MAN, TOO.

I'M SORRY
FOR LYING
TO YOU ALL.

I'M A MAN...
BUT PLEASE,
LET ME STAY
FRIENDS WITH
YOU.

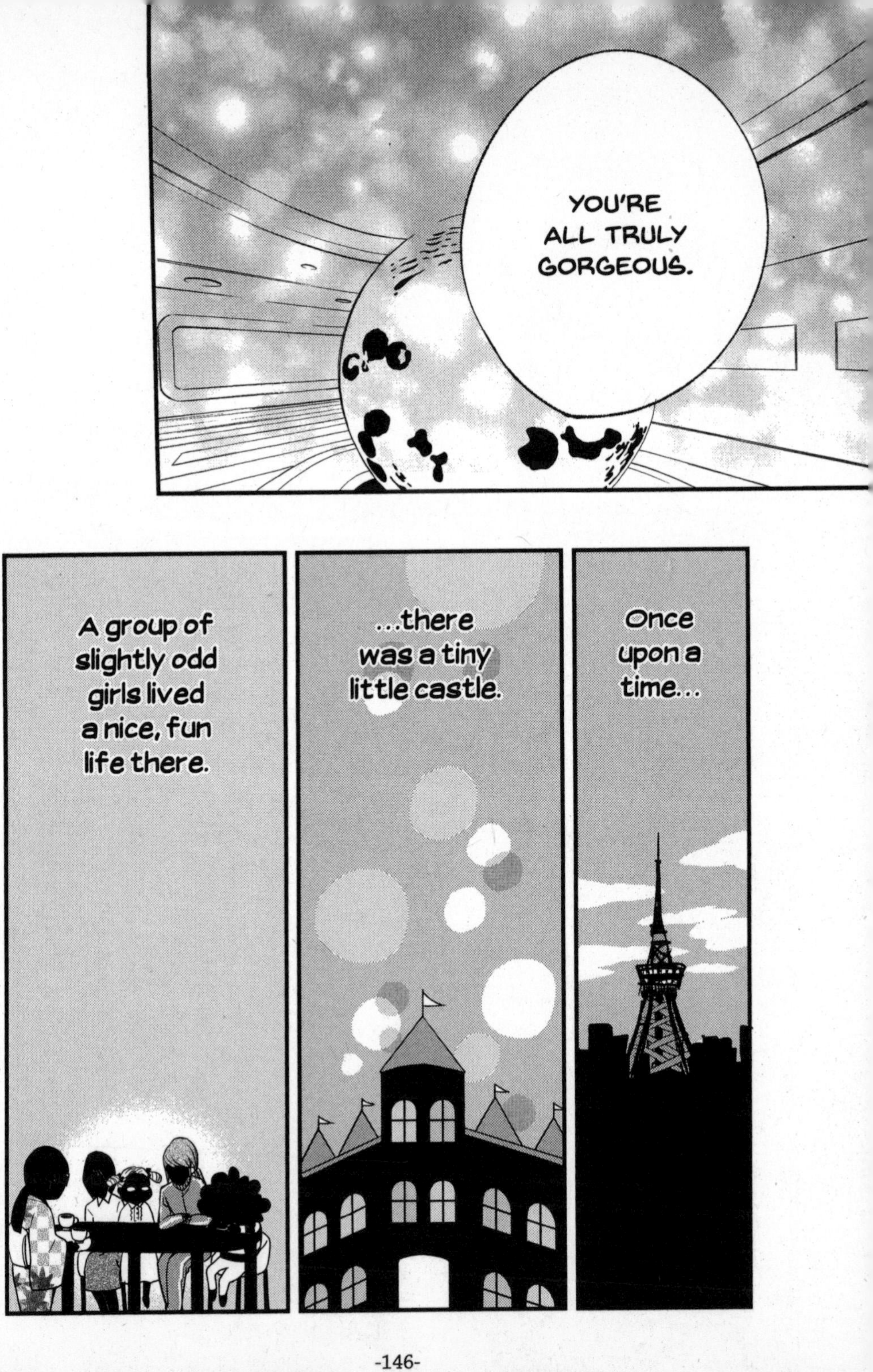
YOU'RE ALL TRULY GORGEOUS.
Once upon a time...
...there was a tiny little castle.
A group of slightly odd girls lived a nice, fun life there.

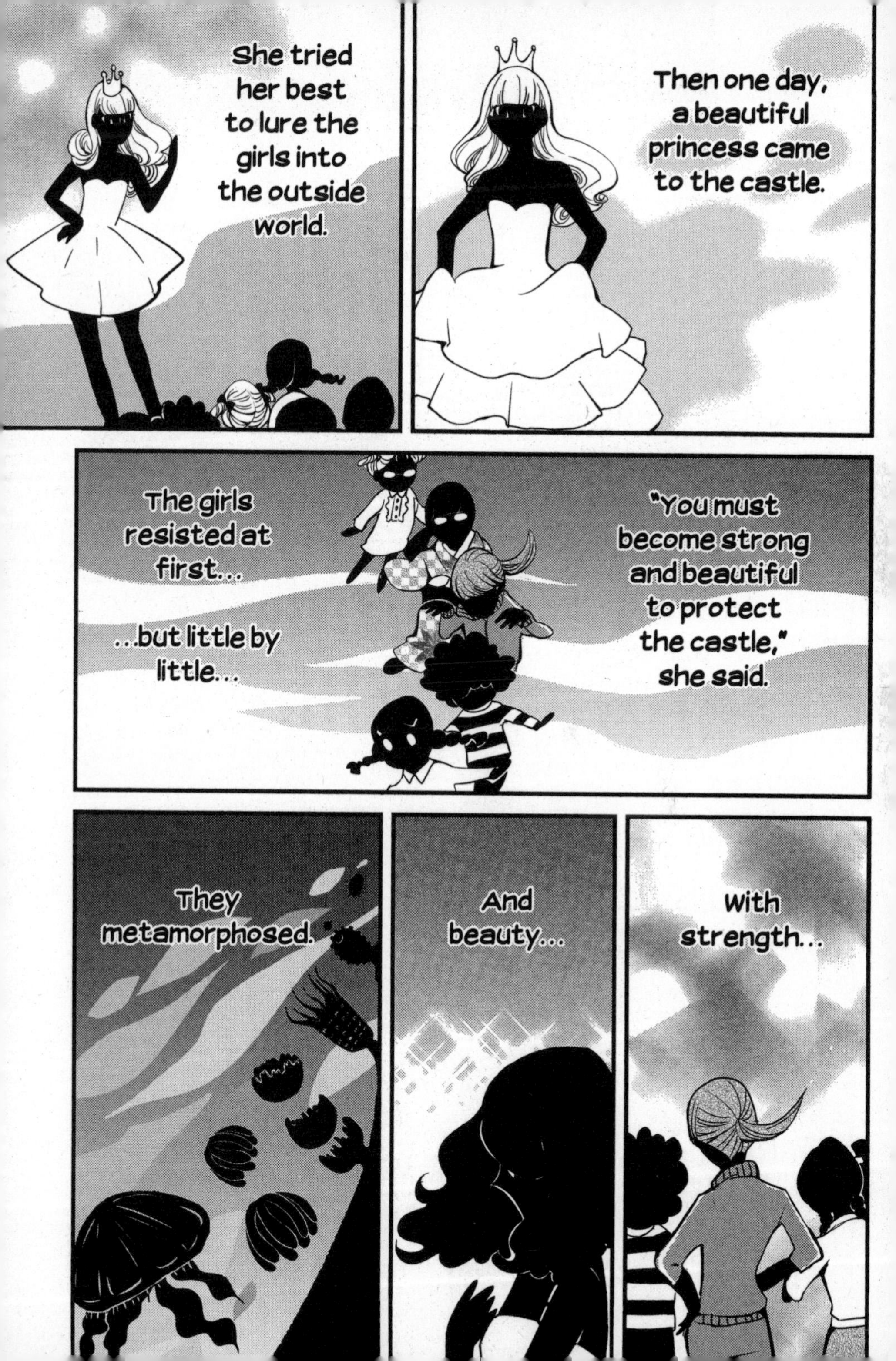
Then one day, a beautiful princess came to the castle.
She tried her best to lure the girls into the outside world.
"You must become strong and beautiful to protect the castle," she said.
The girls resisted at first...
...but little by little...
With strength...
And beauty...
They metamorphosed.

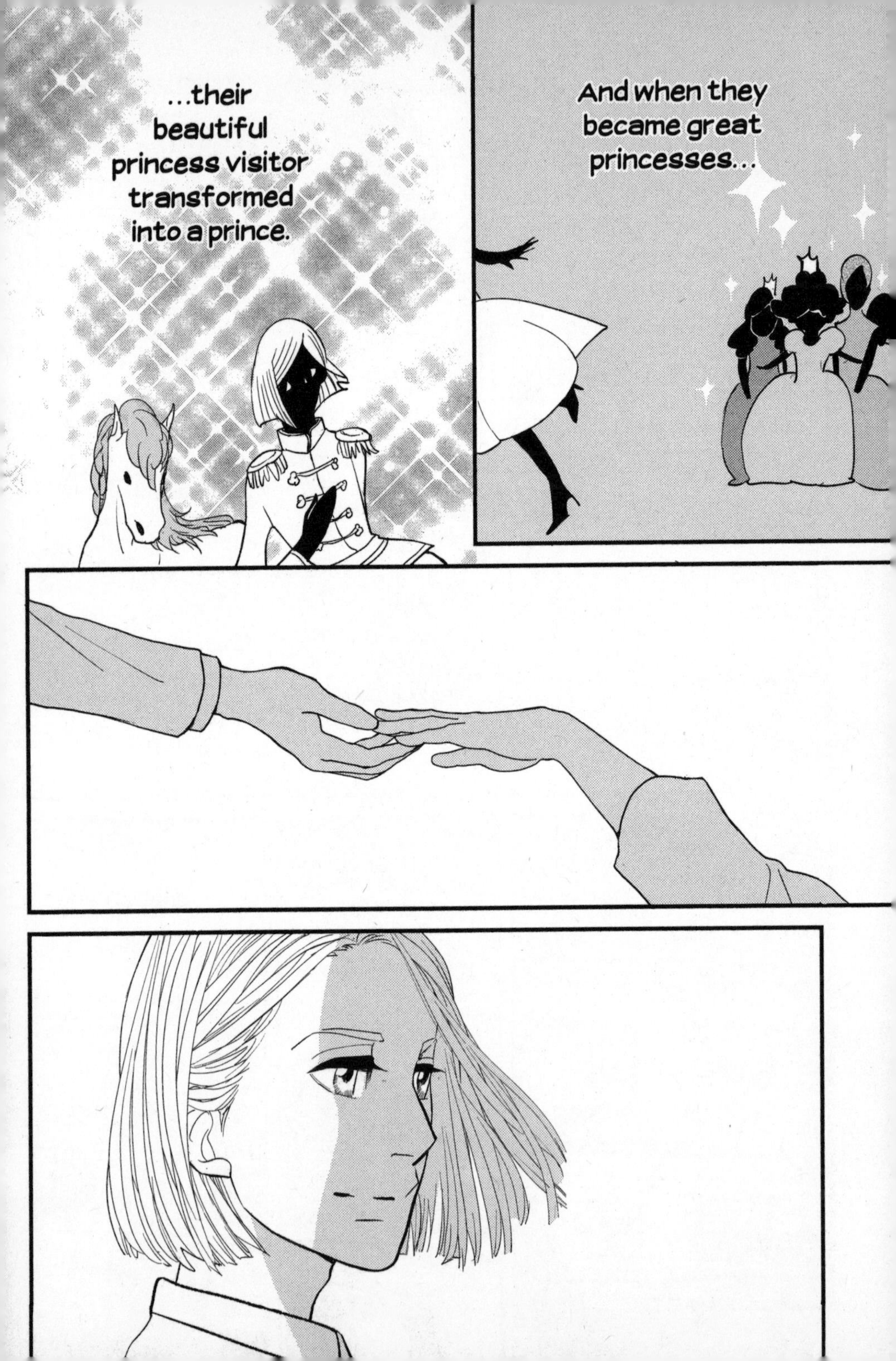
And when they became great princesses...
...their beautiful princess visitor transformed into a prince.

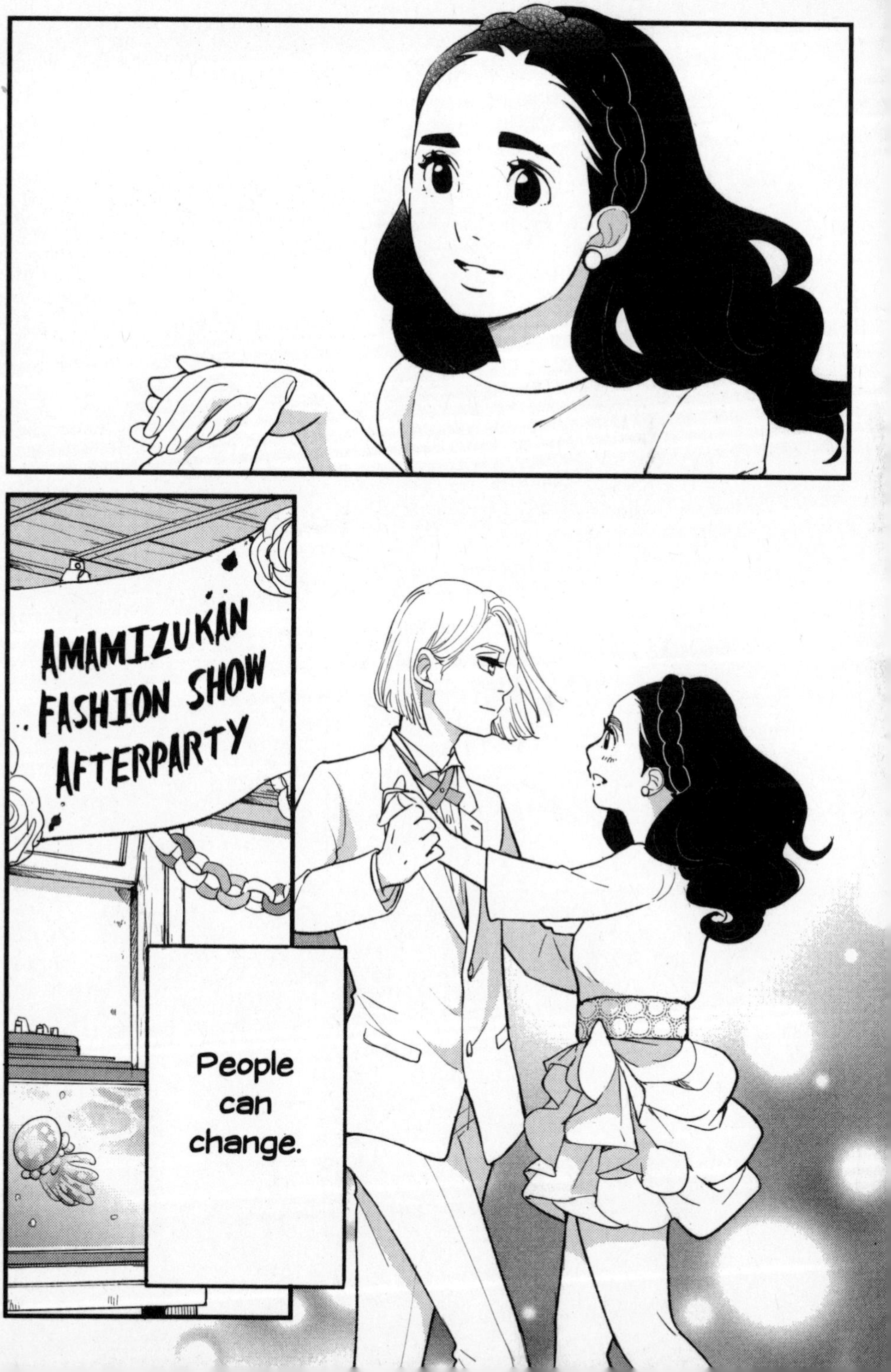
AMAMIZUKAN FASHION SHOW AFTERPARTY
People can change.

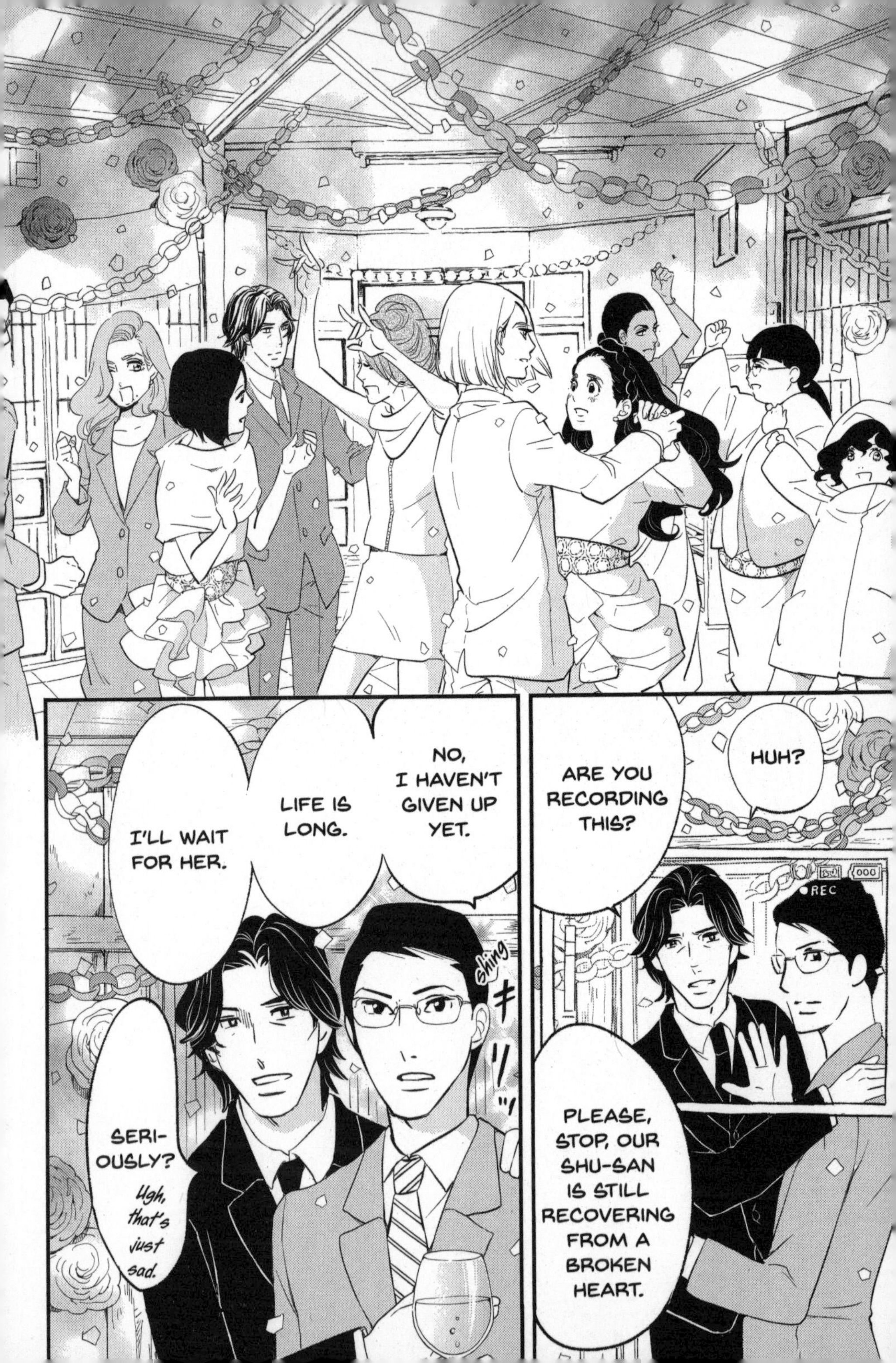

HUH?
ARE YOU RECORDING THIS?
REC
PLEASE, STOP, OUR SHU-SAN IS STILL RECOVERING FROM A BROKEN HEART.
NO, I HAVEN'T GIVEN UP YET.
LIFE IS LONG.
I'LL WAIT FOR HER.
shing
SERI-OUSLY?
Ugh, that's just sad.

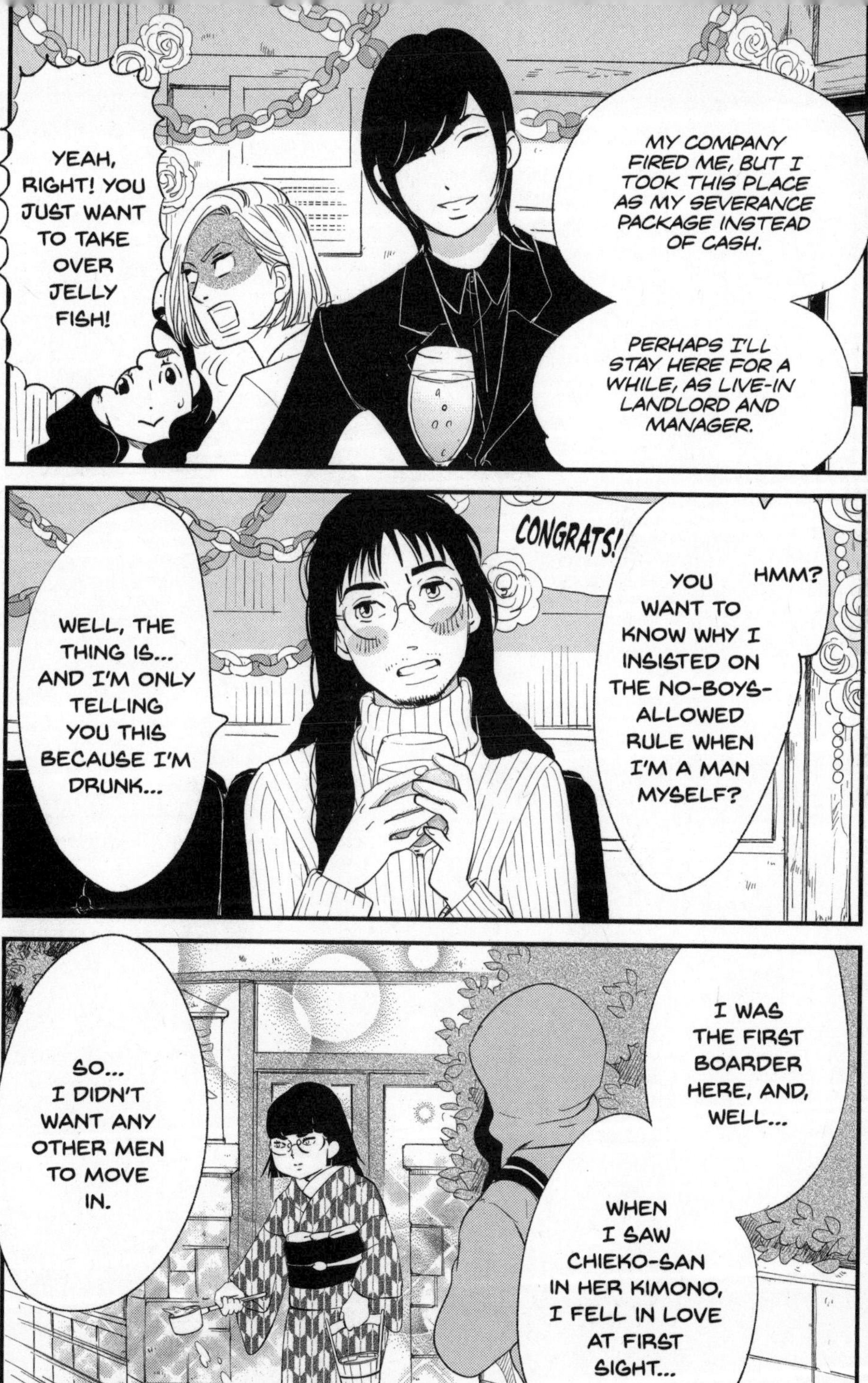
MY COMPANY FIRED ME, BUT I TOOK THIS PLACE AS MY SEVERANCE PACKAGE INSTEAD OF CASH.
PERHAPS I'LL STAY HERE FOR A WHILE, AS LIVE-IN LANDLORD AND MANAGER.
YEAH, RIGHT! YOU JUST WANT TO TAKE OVER JELLY FISH!
HMM?
YOU WANT TO KNOW WHY I INSISTED ON THE NO-BOYS-ALLOWED RULE WHEN I'M A MAN MYSELF?
CONGRATS!
WELL, THE THING IS... AND I'M ONLY TELLING YOU THIS BECAUSE I'M DRUNK...
I WAS THE FIRST BOARDER HERE, AND, WELL...
WHEN I SAW CHIEKO-SAN IN HER KIMONO, I FELL IN LOVE AT FIRST SIGHT...
SO... I DIDN'T WANT ANY OTHER MEN TO MOVE IN.

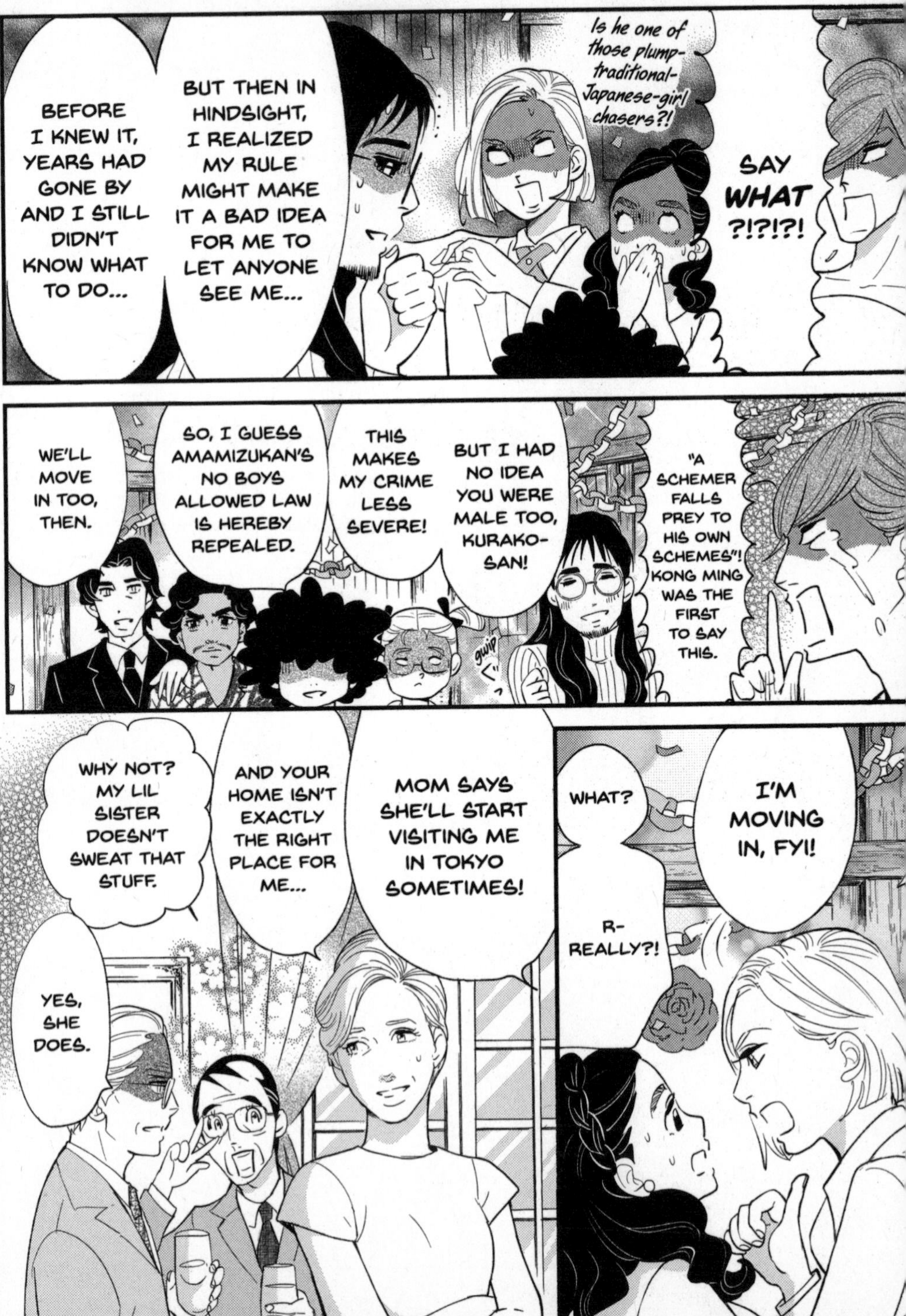
SAY WHAT ?!?!?!
Is he one of those plump-traditional-Japanese-girl chasers?!
BUT THEN IN HINDSIGHT, I REALIZED MY RULE MIGHT MAKE IT A BAD IDEA FOR ME TO LET ANYONE SEE ME...
BEFORE I KNEW IT, YEARS HAD GONE BY AND I STILL DIDN'T KNOW WHAT TO DO...
"A SCHEMER FALLS PREY TO HIS OWN SCHEMES"! KONG MING WAS THE FIRST TO SAY THIS.
BUT I HAD NO IDEA YOU WERE MALE TOO, KURAKO-SAN!
THIS MAKES MY CRIME LESS SEVERE!
gwip
SO, I GUESS AMAMIZUKAN'S NO BOYS ALLOWED LAW IS HEREBY REPEALED.
WE'LL MOVE IN TOO, THEN.
I'M MOVING IN, FYI!
WHAT?
R-REALLY?!
MOM SAYS SHE'LL START VISITING ME IN TOKYO SOMETIMES!
AND YOUR HOME ISN'T EXACTLY THE RIGHT PLACE FOR ME...
WHY NOT? MY LIL SISTER DOESN'T SWEAT THAT STUFF.
YES, SHE DOES.

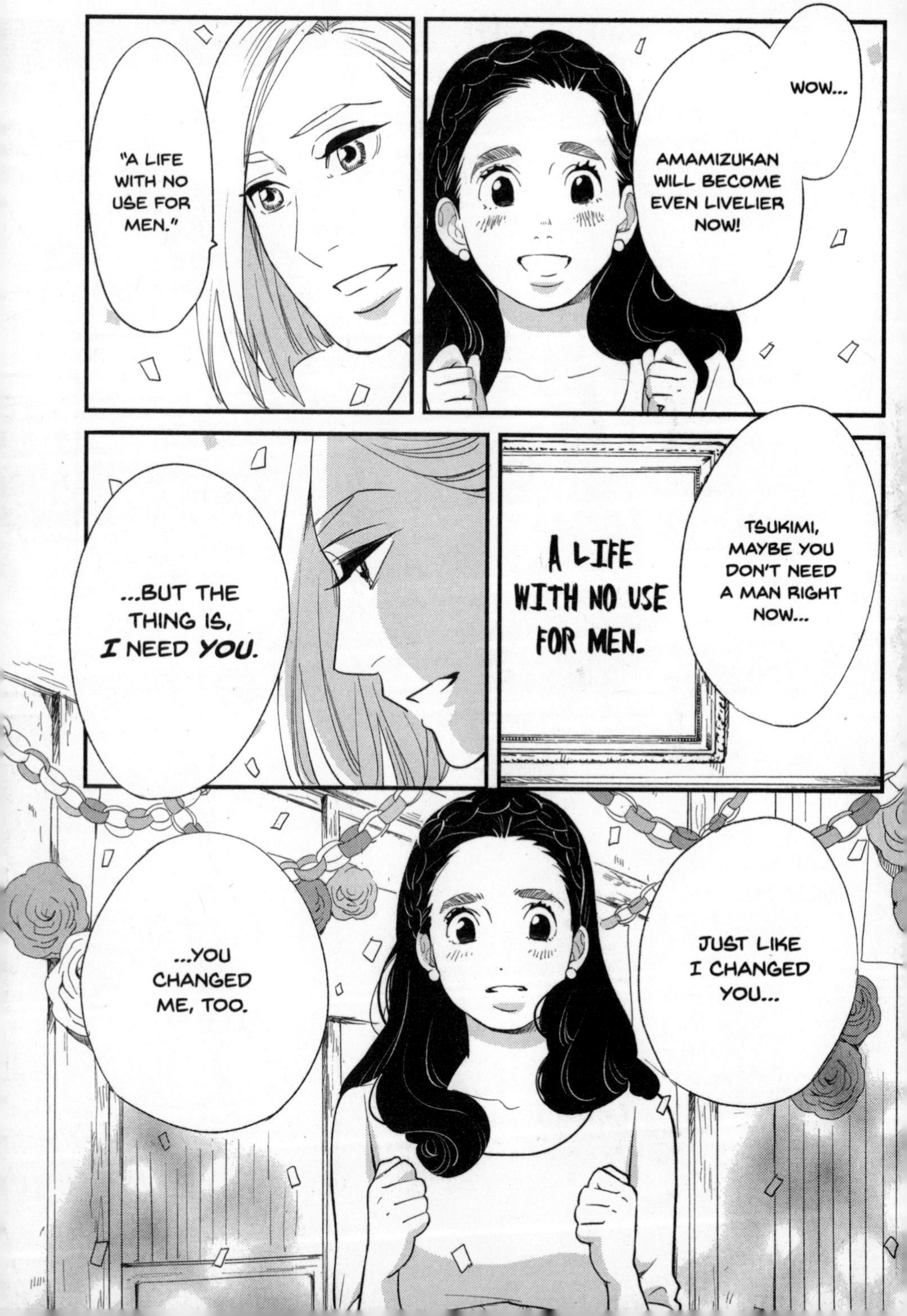
WOW...
AMAMIZUKAN WILL BECOME EVEN LIVELIER NOW!
"A LIFE WITH NO USE FOR MEN."
TSUKIMI, MAYBE YOU DON'T NEED A MAN RIGHT NOW...
A LIFE WITH NO USE FOR MEN.
...BUT THE THING IS, I NEED YOU.
JUST LIKE I CHANGED YOU...
...YOU CHANGED ME, TOO.

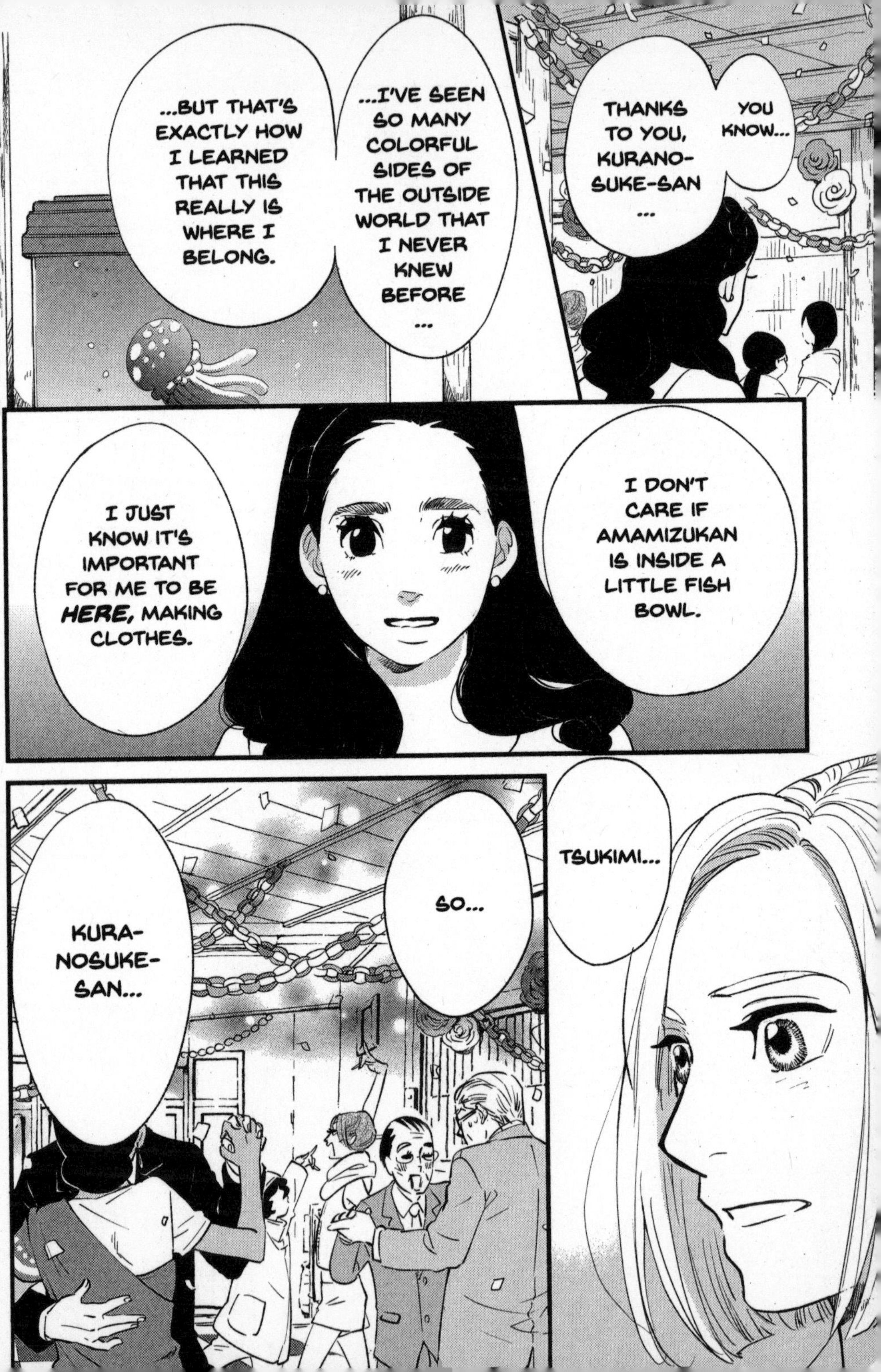
YOU KNOW...
THANKS TO YOU, KURANO-SUKE-SAN...
...I'VE SEEN SO MANY COLORFUL SIDES OF THE OUTSIDE WORLD THAT I NEVER KNEW BEFORE...
...BUT THAT'S EXACTLY HOW I LEARNED THAT THIS REALLY IS WHERE I BELONG.
I DON'T CARE IF AMAMIZUKAN IS INSIDE A LITTLE FISH BOWL.
I JUST KNOW IT'S IMPORTANT FOR ME TO BE *HERE,* MAKING CLOTHES.
TSUKIMI...
SO...
KURA-NOSUKE-SAN...

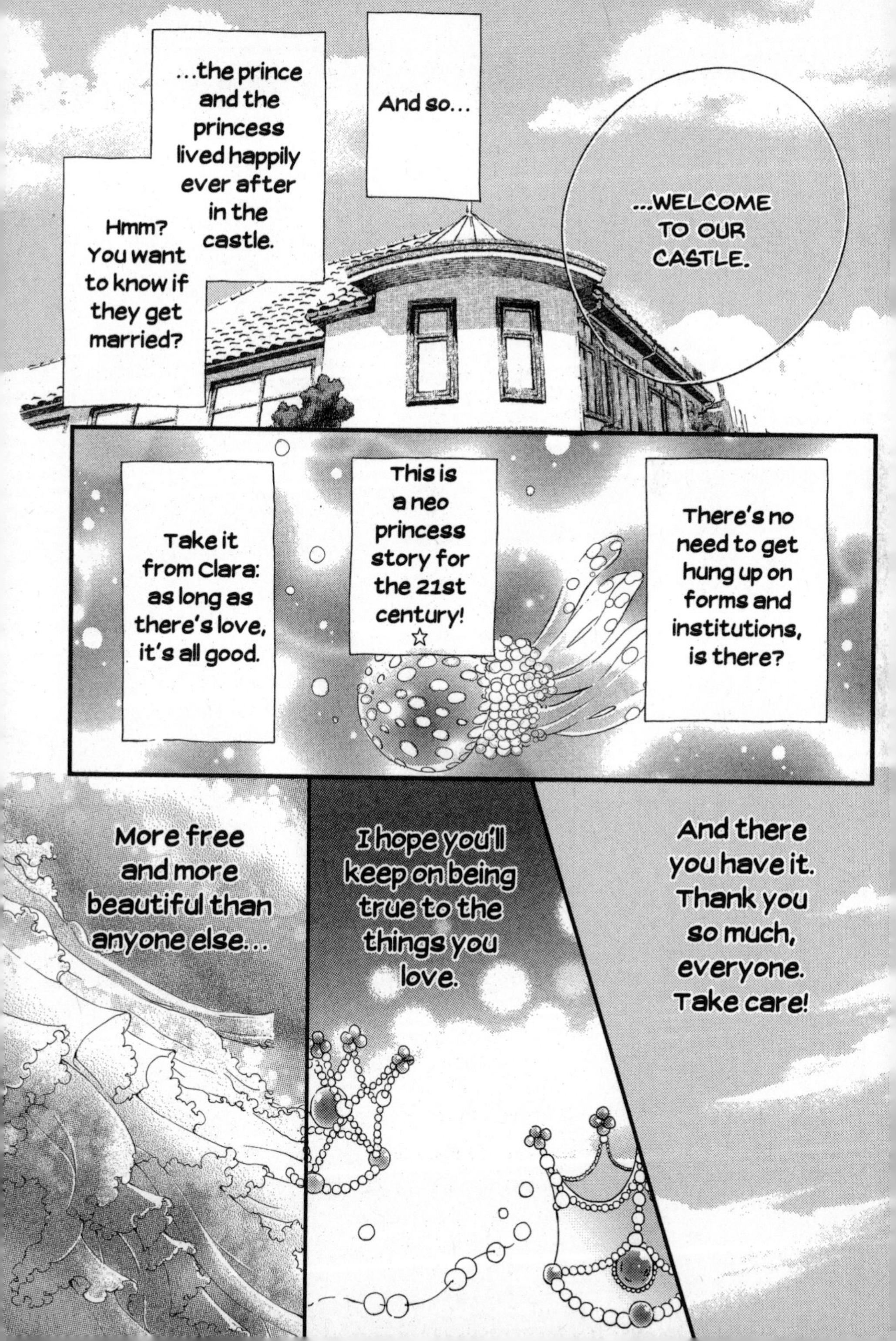
...WELCOME TO OUR CASTLE.
And so...
...the prince and the princess lived happily ever after in the castle.
Hmm? You want to know if they get married?
There's no need to get hung up on forms and institutions, is there?
This is a neo princess story for the 21st century! ☆
Take it from Clara: as long as there's love, it's all good.
And there you have it. Thank you so much, everyone. Take care!
I hope you'll keep on being true to the things you love.
More free and more beautiful than anyone else...

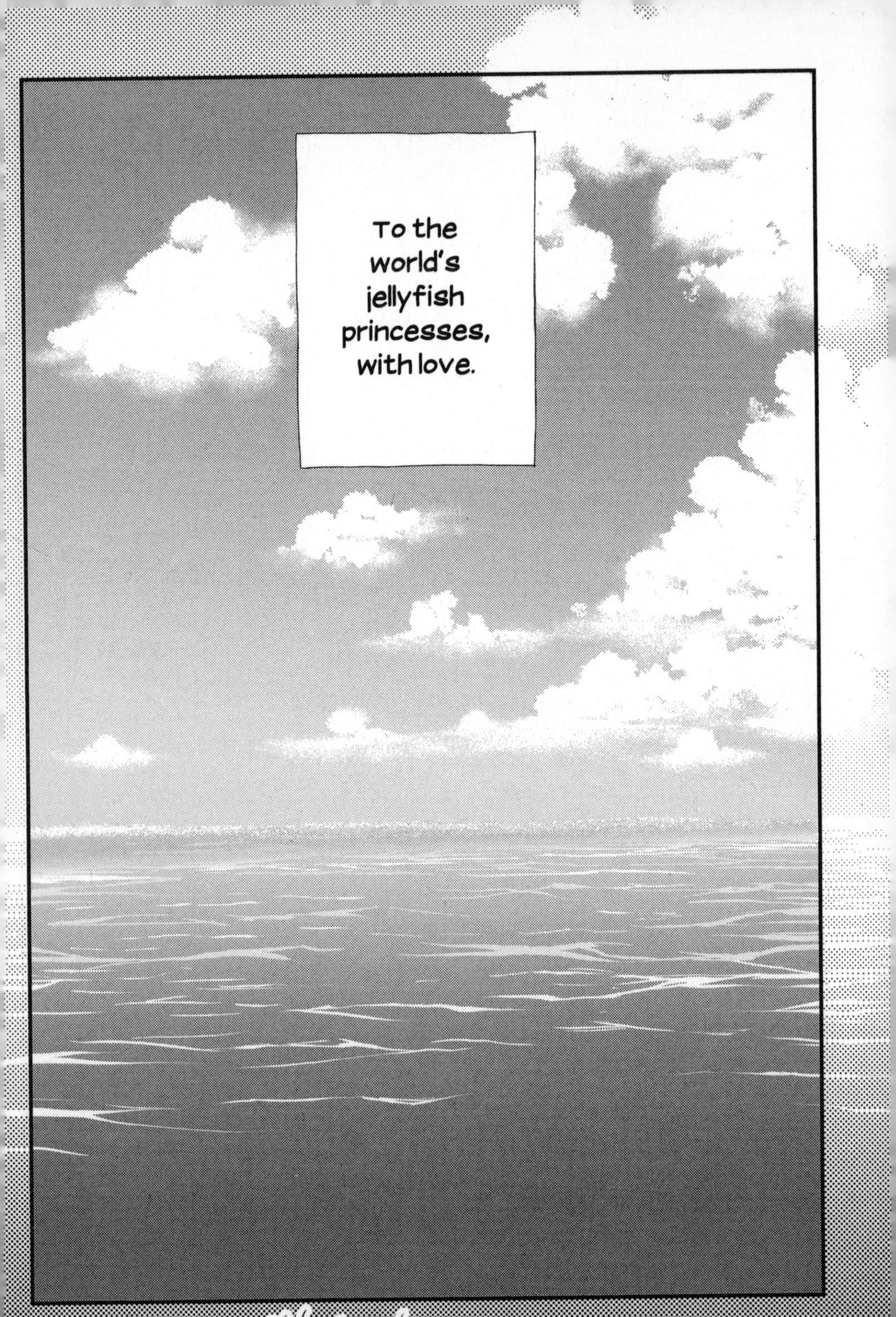
To the world's jellyfish princesses, with love.

2017. 8. 7. Akiko Higashimura <Princess Jellyfish/End>

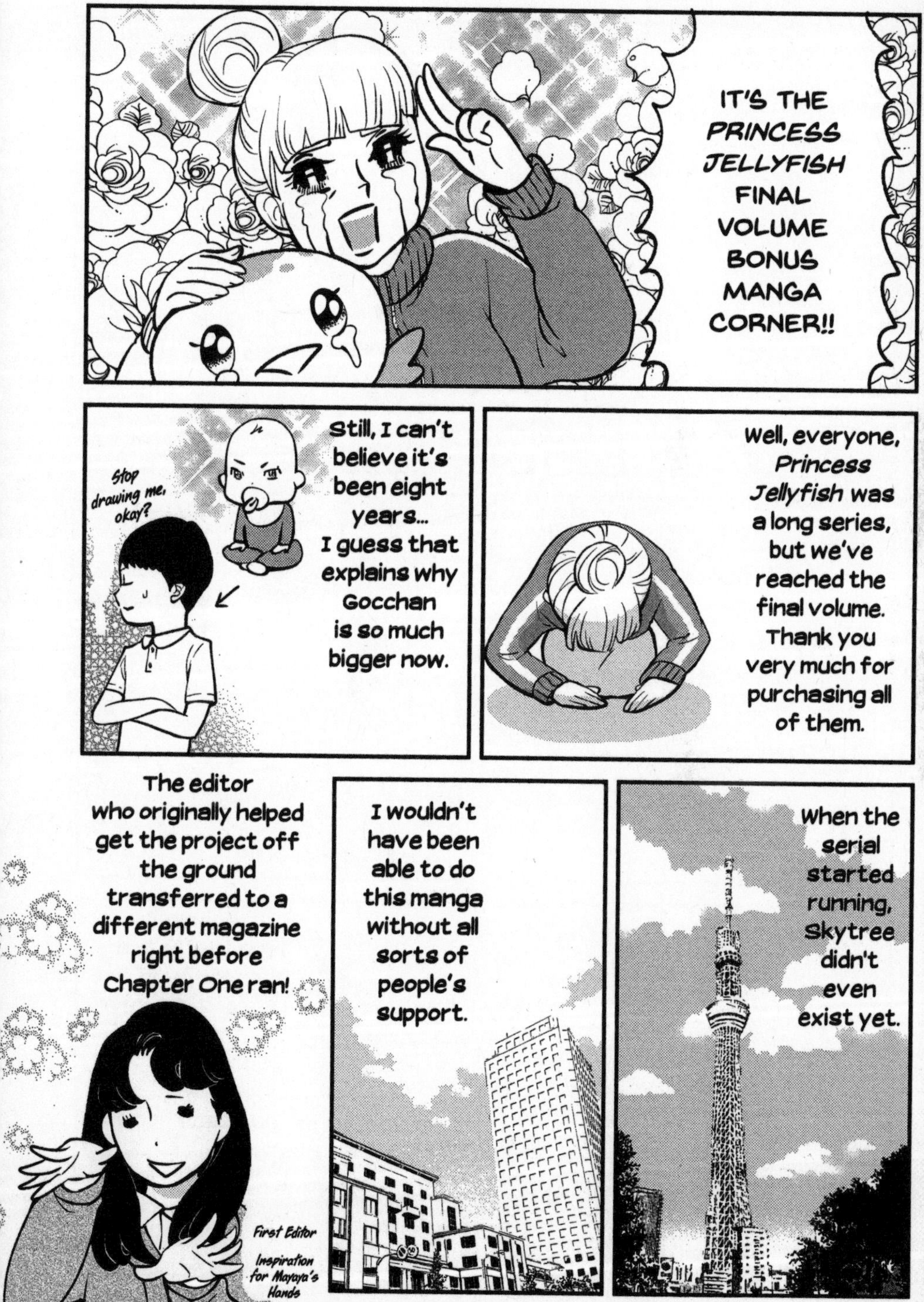
IT'S THE PRINCESS JELLYFISH FINAL VOLUME BONUS MANGA CORNER!!
Well, everyone, *Princess Jellyfish* was a long series, but we've reached the final volume. Thank you very much for purchasing all of them.
Still, I can't believe it's been eight years... I guess that explains why Gocchan is so much bigger now.
Stop drawing me, okay?
When the serial started running, Skytree didn't even exist yet.
I wouldn't have been able to do this manga without all sorts of people's support.
The editor who originally helped get the project off the ground transferred to a different magazine right before Chapter One ran!
First Editor
Inspiration for Mayaya's Hands

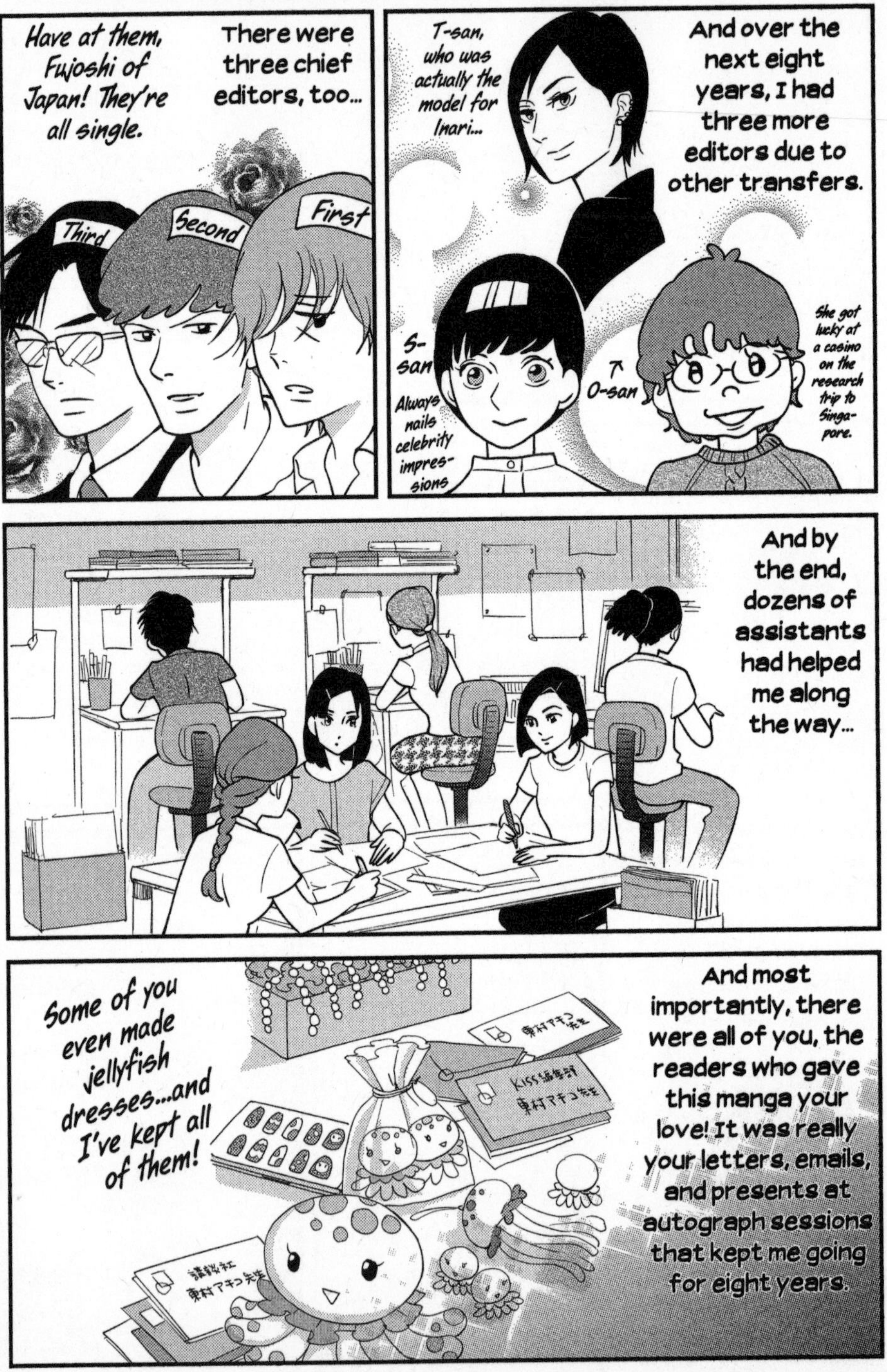
And over the next eight years, I had three more editors due to other transfers.
T-san, who was actually the model for Inari...
She got lucky at a casino on the research trip to Singapore.
O-san
S-san
Always nails celebrity impressions
There were three chief editors, too...
Have at them, Fujoshi of Japan! They're all single.
First
Second
Third
And by the end, dozens of assistants had helped me along the way...
And most importantly, there were all of you, the readers who gave this manga your love! It was really your letters, emails, and presents at autograph sessions that kept me going for eight years.
Some of you even made jellyfish dresses...and I've kept all of them!
東村アキコ先生
KISS編集部 東村アキコ先生
講談社 東村アキコ先生

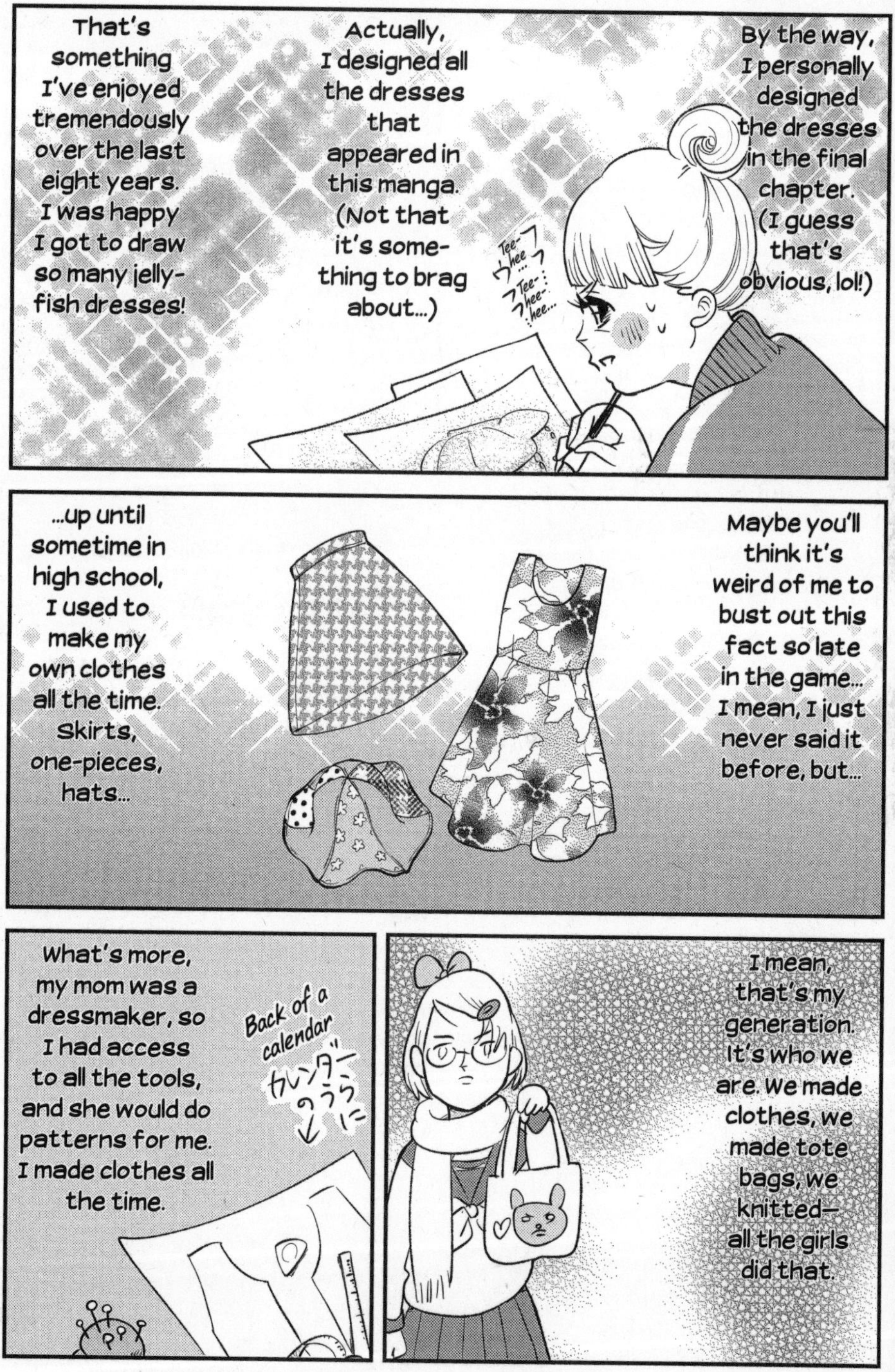
By the way, I personally designed the dresses in the final chapter. (I guess that's obvious, lol!)
Tee-hee... Tee-hee-hee...
Actually, I designed all the dresses that appeared in this manga. (Not that it's some-thing to brag about...)
That's something I've enjoyed tremendously over the last eight years. I was happy I got to draw so many jelly-fish dresses!
Maybe you'll think it's weird of me to bust out this fact so late in the game... I mean, I just never said it before, but...
...up until sometime in high school, I used to make my own clothes all the time. Skirts, one-pieces, hats...
I mean, that's my generation. It's who we are. We made clothes, we made tote bags, we knitted— all the girls did that.
What's more, my mom was a dressmaker, so I had access to all the tools, and she would do patterns for me. I made clothes all the time.
Back of a calendar
カレンダーのうらに

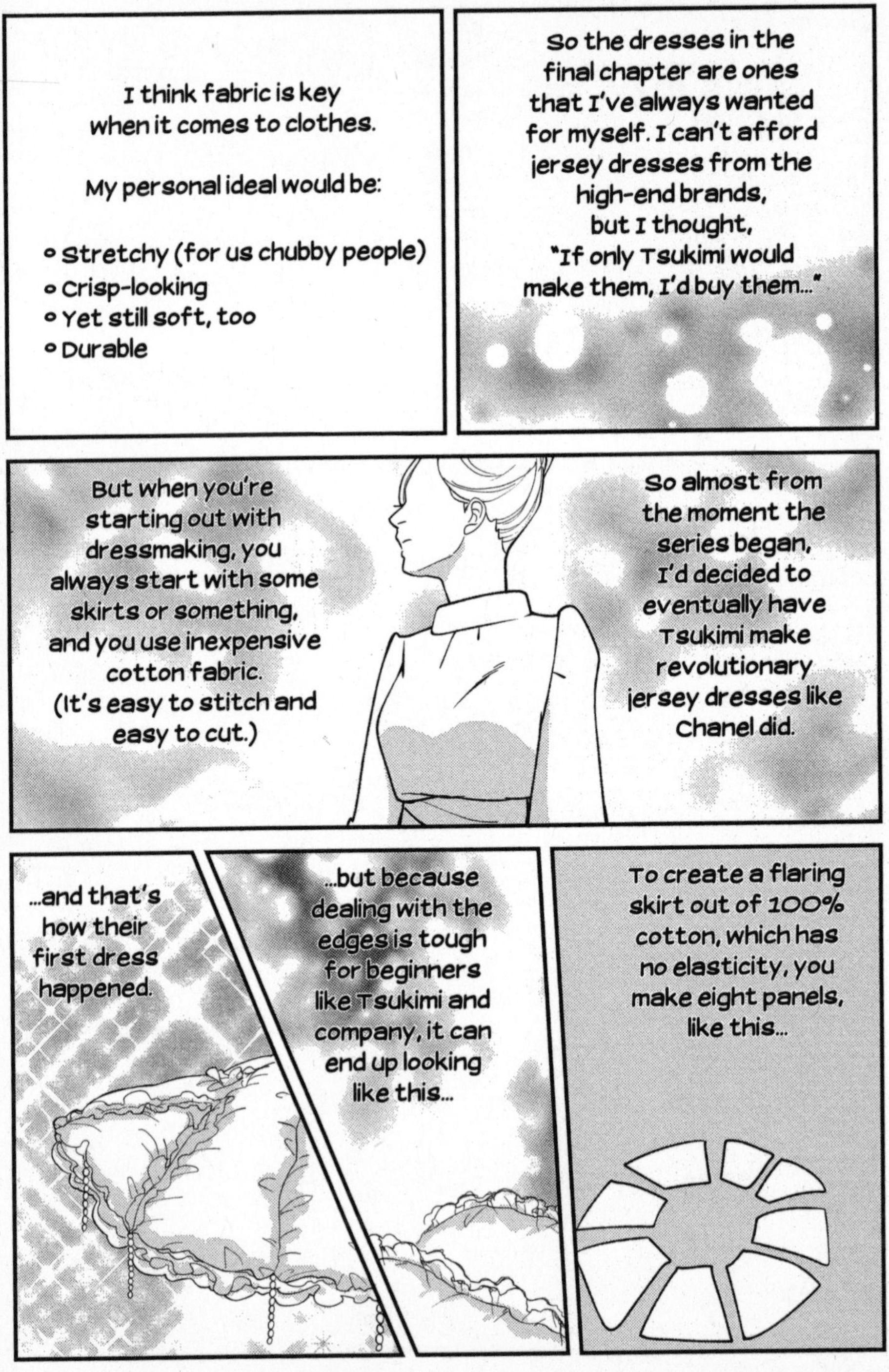
So the dresses in the final chapter are ones that I've always wanted for myself. I can't afford jersey dresses from the high-end brands, but I thought, "If only Tsukimi would make them, I'd buy them..."
I think fabric is key when it comes to clothes.
My personal ideal would be:
∘ Stretchy (for us chubby people)
∘ Crisp-looking
∘ Yet still soft, too
∘ Durable
So almost from the moment the series began, I'd decided to eventually have Tsukimi make revolutionary jersey dresses like Chanel did.
But when you're starting out with dressmaking, you always start with some skirts or something, and you use inexpensive cotton fabric. (It's easy to stitch and easy to cut.)
To create a flaring skirt out of 100% cotton, which has no elasticity, you make eight panels, like this...
...but because dealing with the edges is tough for beginners like Tsukimi and company, it can end up looking like this...
...and that's how their first dress happened.

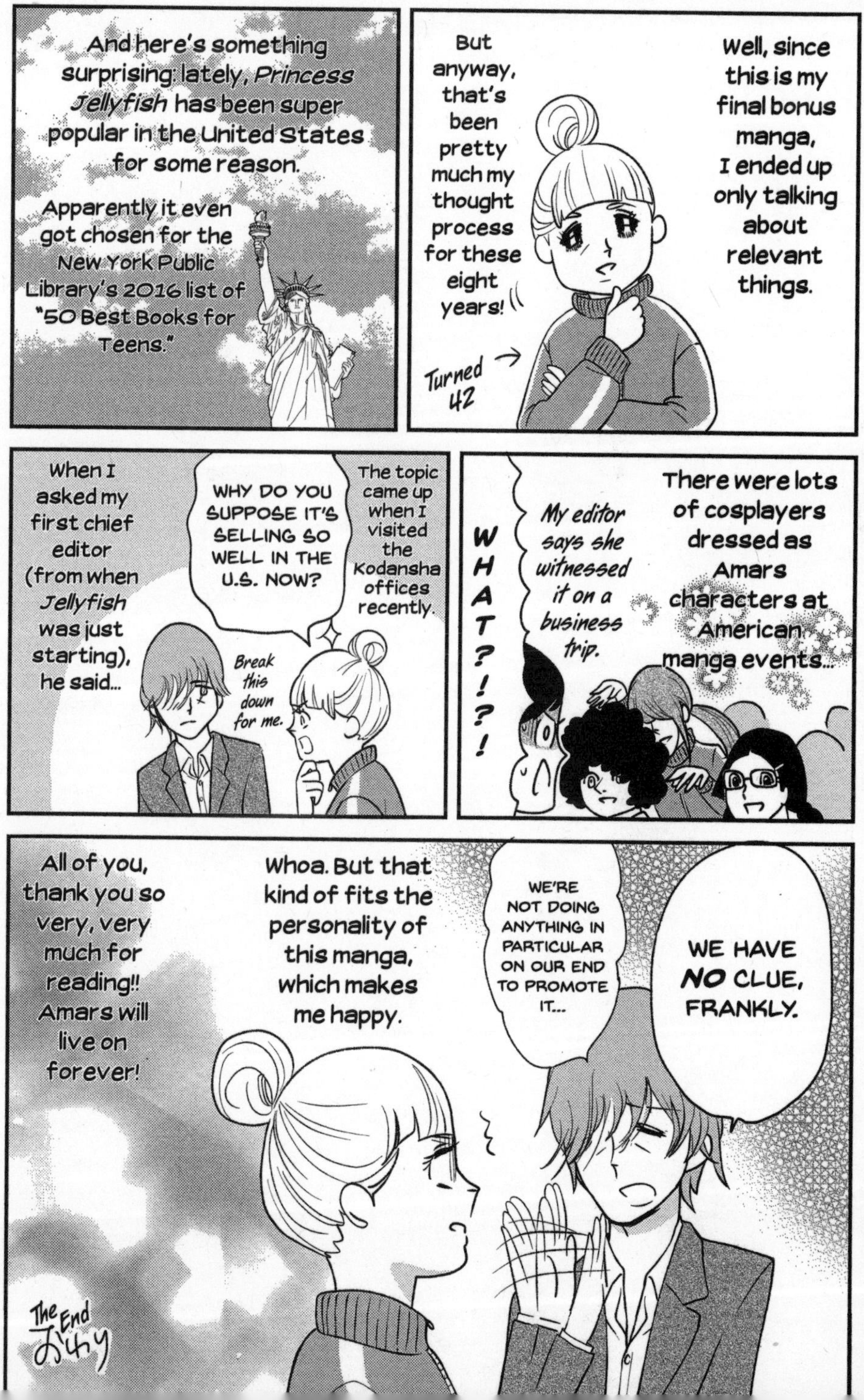
Well, since this is my final bonus manga, I ended up only talking about relevant things.
But anyway, that's been pretty much my thought process for these eight years!
Turned 42
And here's something surprising: lately, *Princess Jellyfish* has been super popular in the United States for some reason.
Apparently it even got chosen for the New York Public Library's 2016 list of "50 Best Books for Teens."
There were lots of cosplayers dressed as Amars characters at American manga events...
My editor says she witnessed it on a business trip.
WHAT?!?!
The topic came up when I visited the Kodansha offices recently.
WHY DO YOU SUPPOSE IT'S SELLING SO WELL IN THE U.S. NOW?
Break this down for me.
When I asked my first chief editor (from when *Jellyfish* was just starting), he said...
WE HAVE **NO** CLUE, FRANKLY.
WE'RE NOT DOING ANYTHING IN PARTICULAR ON OUR END TO PROMOTE IT...
Whoa. But that kind of fits the personality of this manga, which makes me happy.
All of you, thank you so very, very much for reading!! Amars will live on forever!
The End
おわり

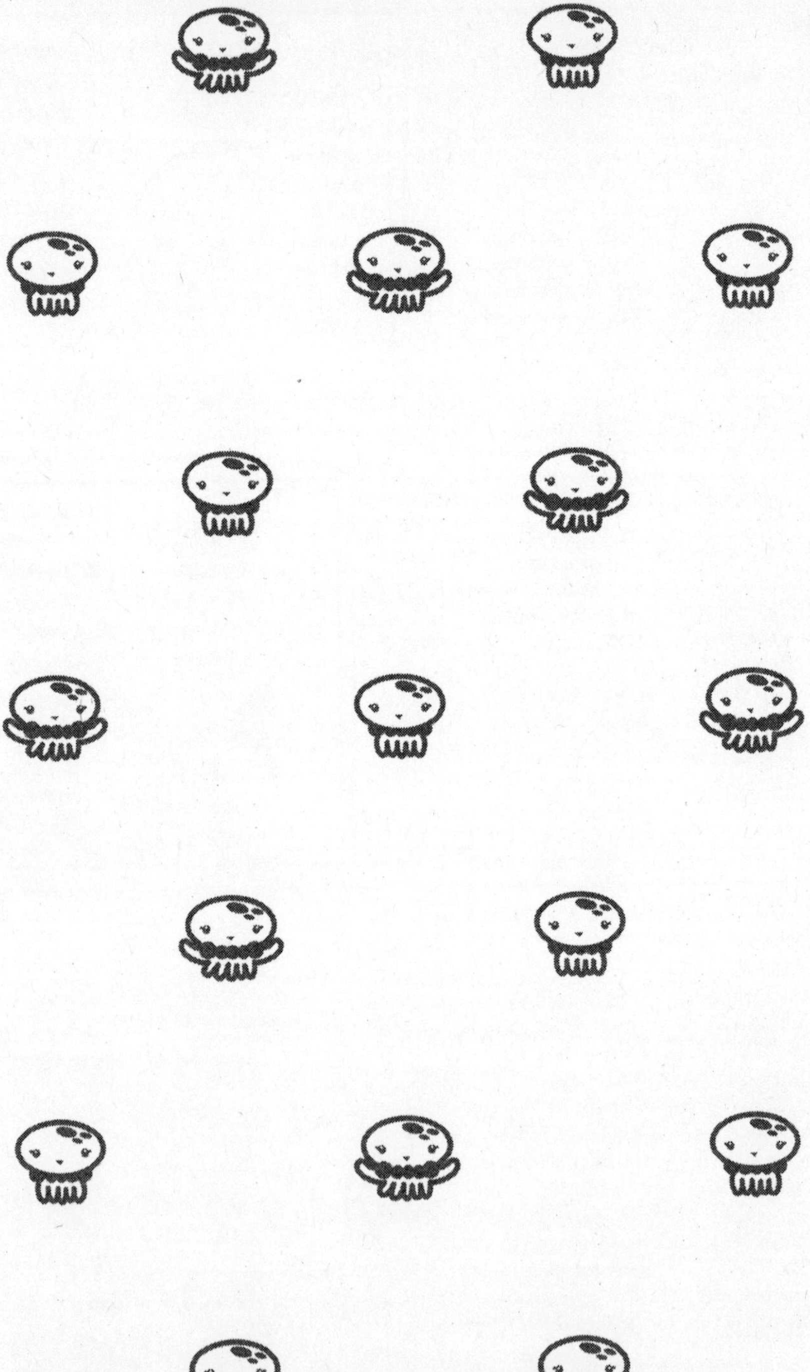

Translation Notes

2- Dresses, page 5
This title is a reference to Anne Fletcher's 2008 film *27 Dresses*.

Hentai Clothes, page 11
In Japanese, *hentai* is a homonym for both "metamorphosis" and "pervert." Unfortunately, Tsukimi is so focused on the metamorphosis of the jellyfish life cycle that she's not quite able to internalize Kuranosuke's concerns about marketing their dresses with a name like that. It's a good thing she's not in charge of public relations!

Let me go home to the forest!, page 16
Banba may be role-playing a Japanese rhinoceros beetle here. These large forest-dwelling insects are popular pets for Japanese children, who often capture them and keep them in small plastic aquariums. Defenders of these captive beetles advocate returning them to the forest and setting them free.

MEXT, page 30
MEXT is the official acronym for the Ministry of Education, Culture, Sports, Science and Technology. Now, that's a mouthful! Japan has had a Ministry of Education since 1871, but over the years, various related government agencies were merged or reorganized, ultimately leading to the establishment of MEXT in 2001.

They're like clothes from the Yayoi Period, page 39
You may remember the Yayoi Period (approx. 300 BCE-300 CE) from Volume 6. Banba is thinking of the same poncho-like *kantoui* discussed there.

Hey! Spring of Trivia, page 44
This is the title of the Spike TV adaptation of a Japanese program called *Toribia no Izumi*, described by PR Newswire in a November 4, 2004 article as "a high-speed procession of fascinating trivia and outrageous information." While *Hey! Spring of Trivia* only ran on Spike for one season in 2004-2005, the original Japanese series lasted on Fuji TV for a decade, ending with a special episode on New Year's Day of 2012.

Kuranosuke, the Dong Zhuo of Dressmaking, page 54
Dictator Kuranosuke's list of errands here includes stops in Asakusabashi for supplies and Sendagaya for dress forms. Asakusabashi in east Tokyo is certainly a good place to shop for sewing and crafting supplies, but Chieko would know the neighborhood far better than Banba or Mayaya—it's a prime destination for high-end Japanese doll shops. Getting from there to Sendagaya is a trek of at least half an hour, so it is indeed a bit tyrannical. Attractions near Sendagaya Station include the beautiful Shinjuku Imperial Gardens as well as a collection of fashion-and apparel-related businesses.

Mayaya's Math Moment, page 54
The "invention of zero" is slightly more complex than Mayaya is making out here, but she got the gist of it exactly right. Mathematicians in India were the first to define zero as a number, thereby revolutionizing mathematical thinking and bringing a truly robust math system to the world.

Why should we have to run this tedious errand?, page 55
In the Japanese, rather than a scavenger hunt, she's referring to a book and TV show called *Hajimete no Otsukai*. This 1976 picture book by Yoriko Tsutsui and Akiko Hayashi was translated into English in 2006 as *Miki's First Errand*, and the story follows a young girl being sent to perform an errand alone for the very first time. It was the inspiration for a popular Japanese TV show of the same name, which is a documentary-esque variety show featuring Japanese children running their own "first errands" as the TV crew and their parents observe their progress from somewhere unseen. Various safety measures are taken, of course, and each child is also given a wireless mic hidden inside a good-luck charm.

I used the machine to stitch that sashiko-style., page 66
Sashiko is a style of traditional Japanese stitching used in quilting and embroidery, often for household garments such as coats. It can be functional, decorative, or both. Since it has become popular with crafters in the West as well, you can search the web for "sashiko" to find English-language patterns and how-to guides.

Banba Channels Coach Hara, page 67
The Japanese national baseball team is known as "Samurai Japan." Their coach for the year 2009 was Tatsunori Hara, and they scored a great victory. Hara congratulated the players by saying, "You've become truly great samurai!"

Will she salt and dry it?!, page 71
Mayaya is riffing on a way of preparing fish called "hiraki." *Hiraki* literally means "open," and refers to the shape the salted fish are served in. Instead of cutting the fish into two parts while gutting it, the chef cuts it almost in half so that the two halves are still connected to each other, "opening" the fish like a book.

This dress is easy to move around in, and I give it very high marks., page 75
Mayaya is suddenly speaking more seriously and formally than she ever has in any similar situation. We can tell that she's regarding this comfy dress as worthy of a thoughtful comment in the way she would consider a new book about Three Kingdoms to be worthy of a thoughtful comment.

Naniwaya, page 78
Naniwaya's main shop in Azabu Juban, Tokyo has an impressive claim to fame as the first *taiyaki* shop. *Taiyaki* is a classic Japanese street food. It is like a stuffed waffle shaped like a fish. It's made of fried dough on the outside and filled with sweet red bean paste on the inside.

"Girl" Is the Right Answer?, page 80
In the literal Japanese, Hanamori is saying that, in line with the conversation, it's obviously more likely that Kuranosuke wishes that Kuranosuke had been born a girl. But as you probably know, Japanese lends itself to more grammatical ambiguity than English. So, since this conflicts with what Banba and Mayaya think they know, and the Japanese Hanamori uses is *just* grammatically ambiguous enough that it *almost* makes sense for them to misunderstand, they are briefly confused trying to figure out what Hanamori is talking about and which gender he's considering Kuranosuke to be—hence the need to ask, "Whose perspective are you talking from?"

This is no time for us to be reheating taiyaki over the fire!!, page 107

Since *taiyaki* are shaped like fish, as we discussed a couple of notes ago, clearly Mayaya and Banba need to reheat them over an open fire, the same way you would roast fish on a camping trip. It just makes sense (if you're Mayaya and Banba, that is).

Tasty Hokkaido Souvenirs, page 115

Hokkaido is the northernmost of Japan's large islands, and is famous for its farmland, including the crops of sweet corn and potatoes. It's also known as the heart of Japan's dairy industry, making cheesecakes another sought-after food item.

Matsu-san did say "let it go," after all, page 126

Hanamori is apparently referring to Takako Matsu's performance of the Japanese version of the song "Let It Go" from Disney's *Frozen*. The Japanese song title meant "Just As I Am," so Hanamori's line literally translates as "Matsu-san did say to be exactly who you are." In other words, don't worry about painting your face.

"A schemer falls prey to his own schemes," page 152

This is a common Japanese proverb these days, but Mayaya is correct that some attribute it to Kong Ming and say that he was referring to Cao Cao. The idea is that Kong Ming would have said this at around the same point he declared that it was easy to defeat Cao Cao because Cao Cao always suspected everything.

Skytree, page 157

The Tokyo Skytree debuted in 2012 as the world's tallest free-standing tower at 634 meters (2080.05 feet) tall. It is a radio broadcast tower in Sumida, Tokyo that also features observation decks as well as shops and restaurants. The surrounding neighborhood called "Tokyo Skytree Town" is also packed with numerous attractions. One of which, is the Sumida Aquarium, where you can see jellies, penguins, and lots of other aquatic wildlife.

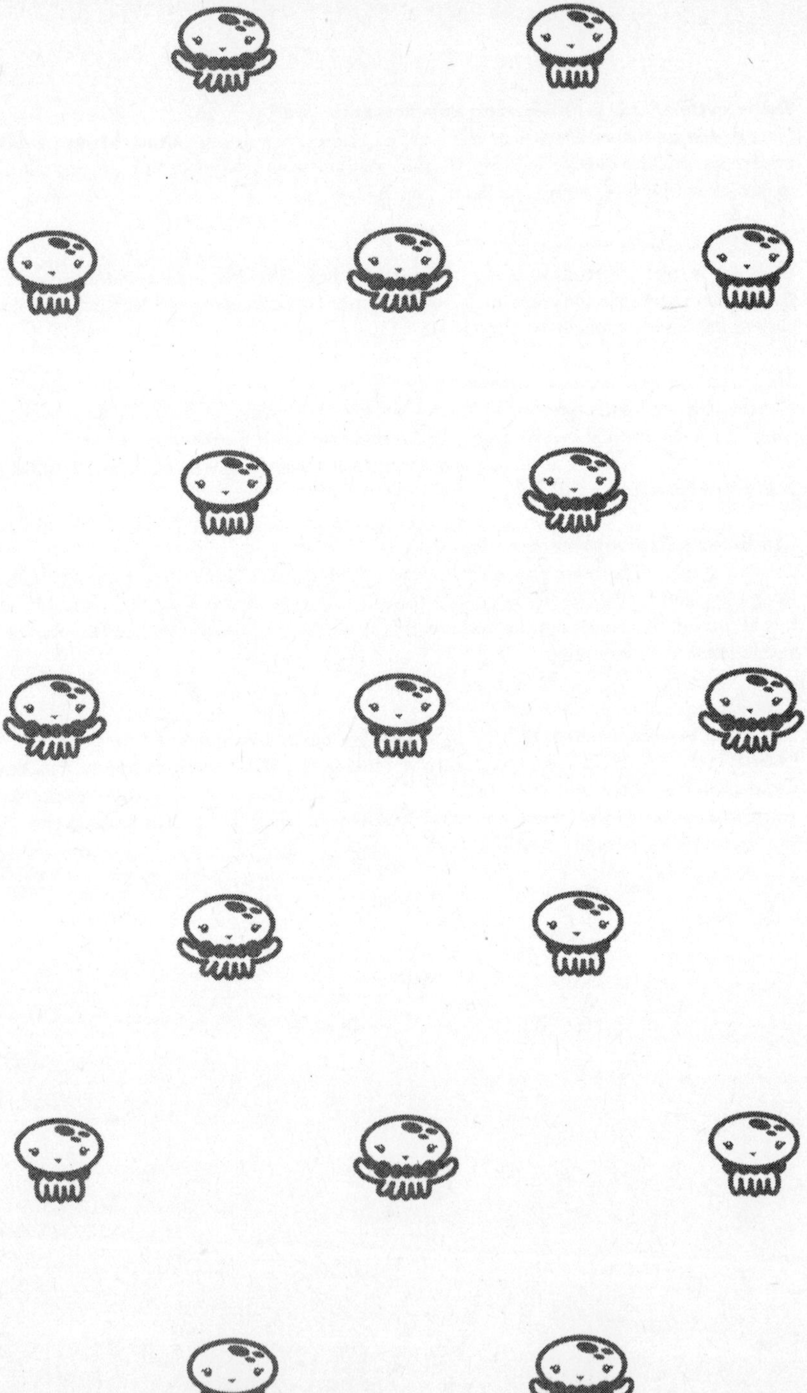

I HAVE TO SAY, ARRIVING AT THE FINAL CHAPTER...
...EVEN I'M FEELING ALL THE EMOTIONS. I'M TEARING UP!
OMG!! BRAVO, HIGASHIMURA-AAA-SENSEI!!
I'm seriously moved!
WHOA! WHO'S THIS?
OH, THE JELLY FROM CHAPTER ONE?
WHY NOW?!

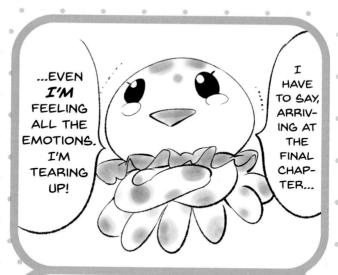

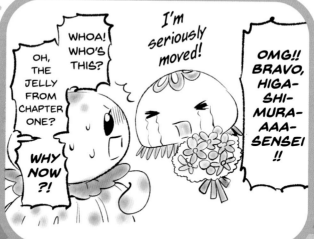

NWAAAAH! YOU HAVE BEEN BLESSED WITH A FEW WORDS BY BANBA!!
THE SHARP CURVE BY THE OMOKAGE-BASHI STATION ON THE TODEN ARAKAWA LINE IS SERIOUSLY WICKED!

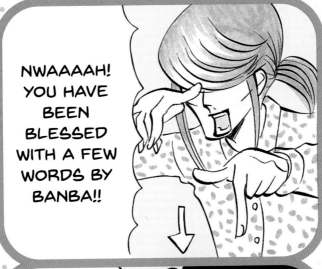

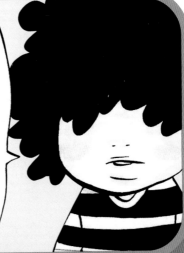

WOO! ☆ I'VE GOT A QUESTION FOR YOU! WHAT IS MY JOB?! YAY! ♥
ぴあ、え？
FWAAH ?!
Correct Answer:
PRIME MINISTER OF JAPAN

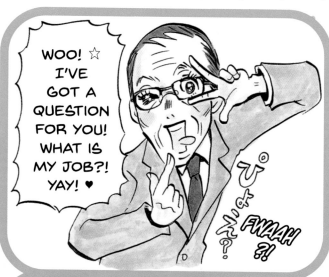

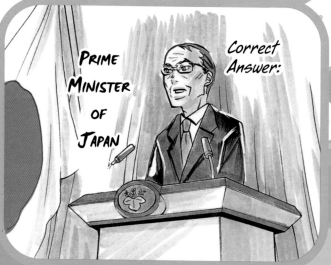

Princess Jellyfish

Akiko
Higashimura
presents...

The Color
Illustration
Gallery!

Did you know...?

Higashimura-sensei sometimes asks
her assistants to strike a pose for
a photo so she can use them as
references for her characters' stances!

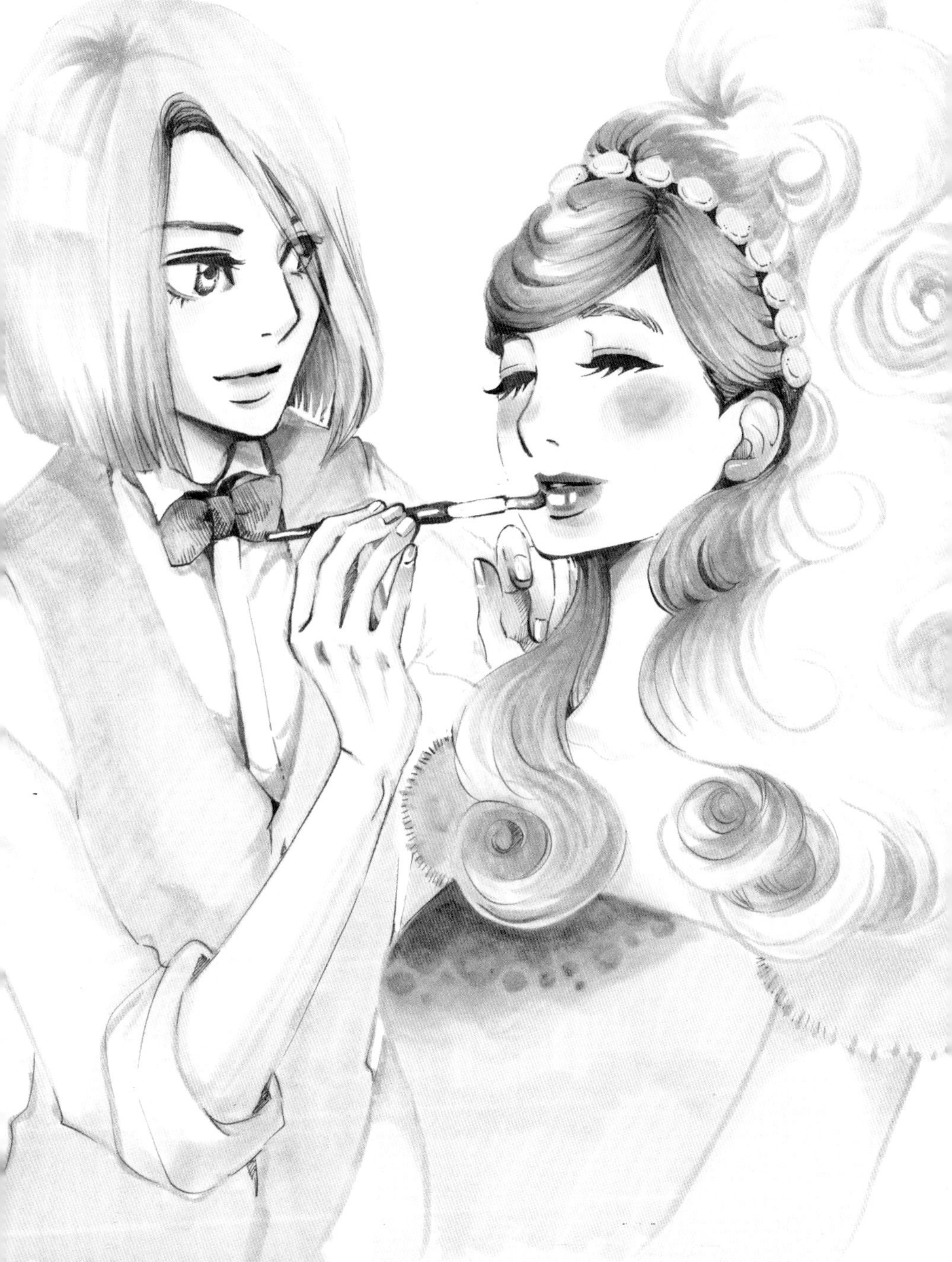

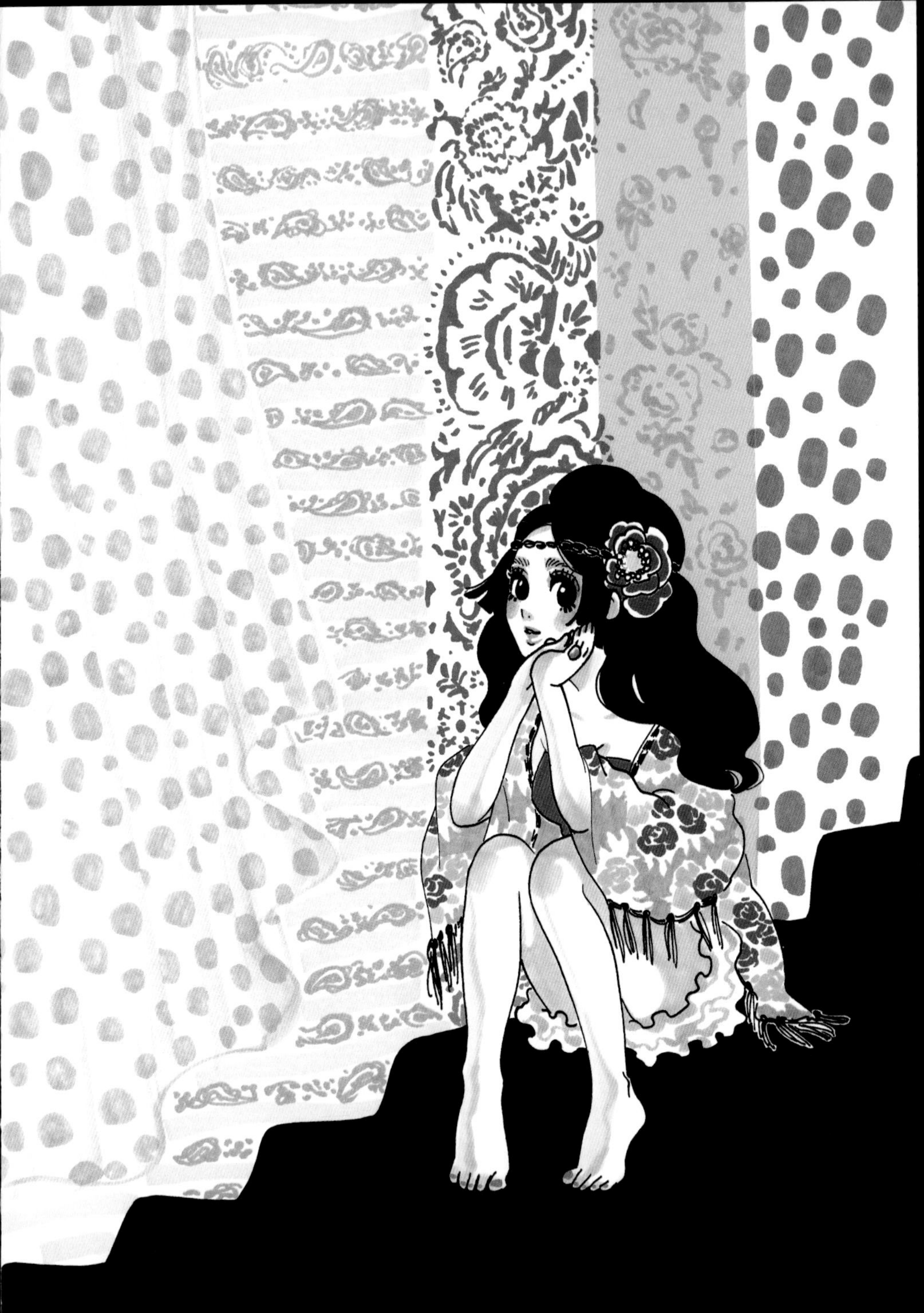

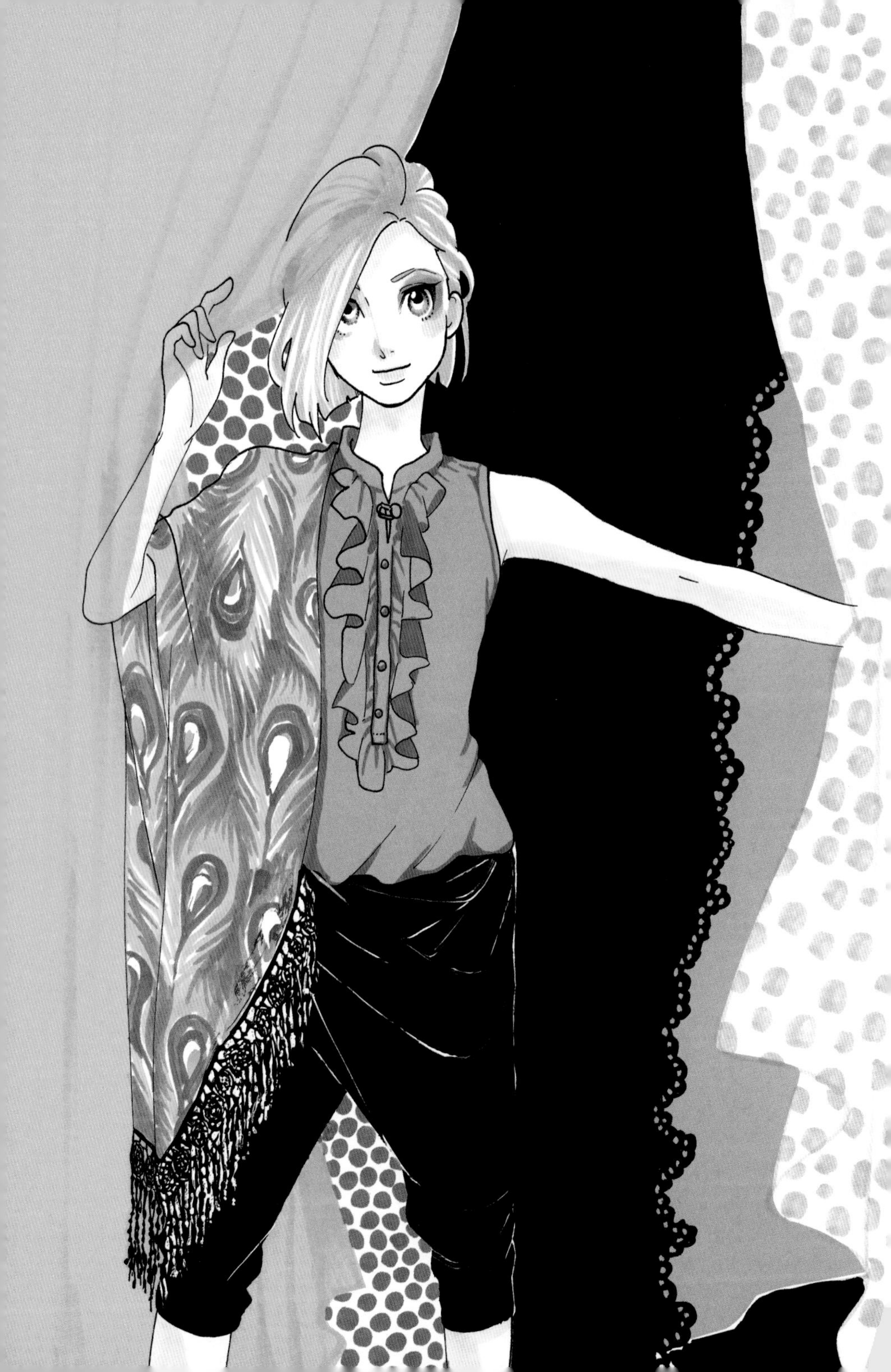

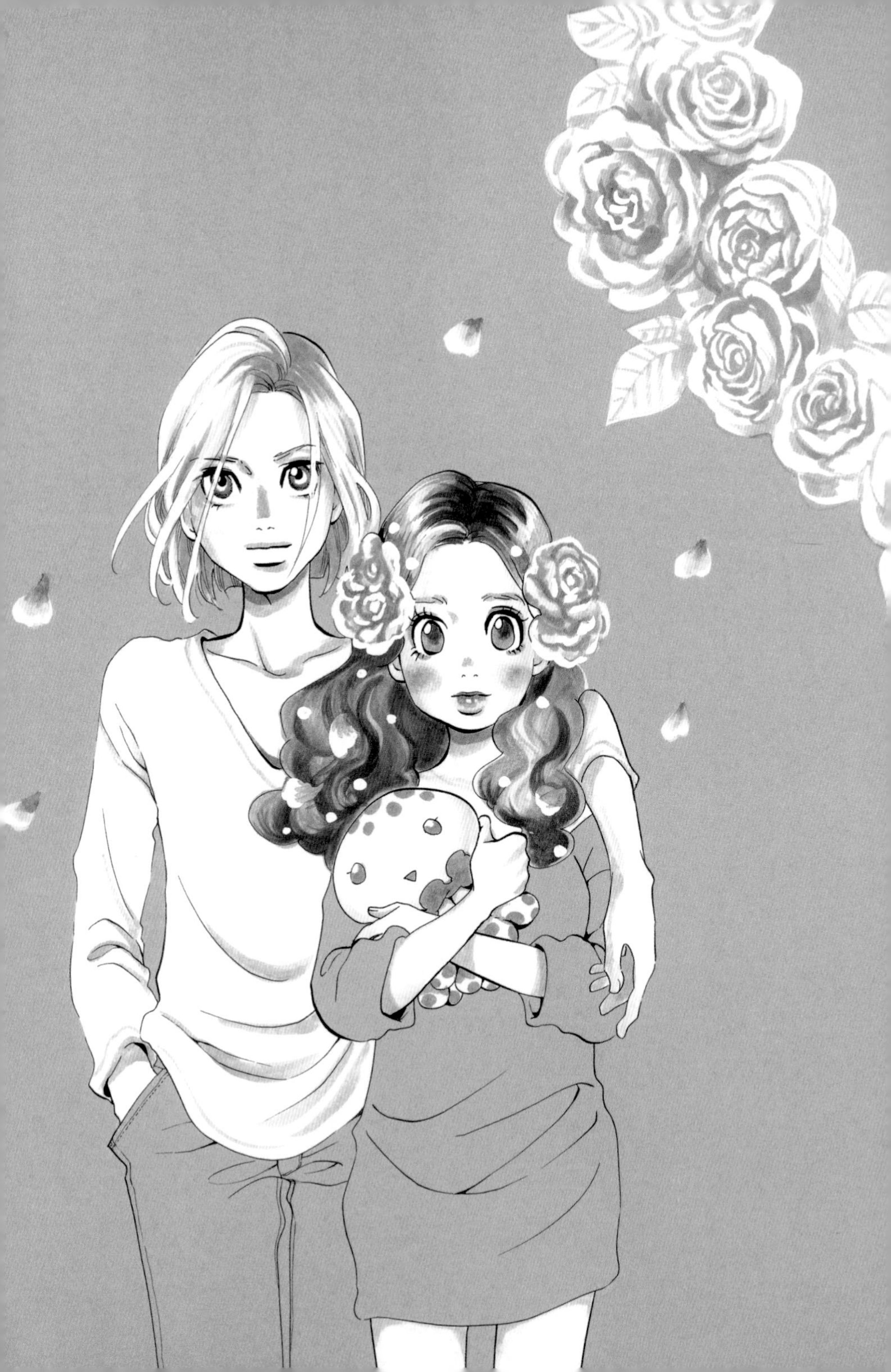

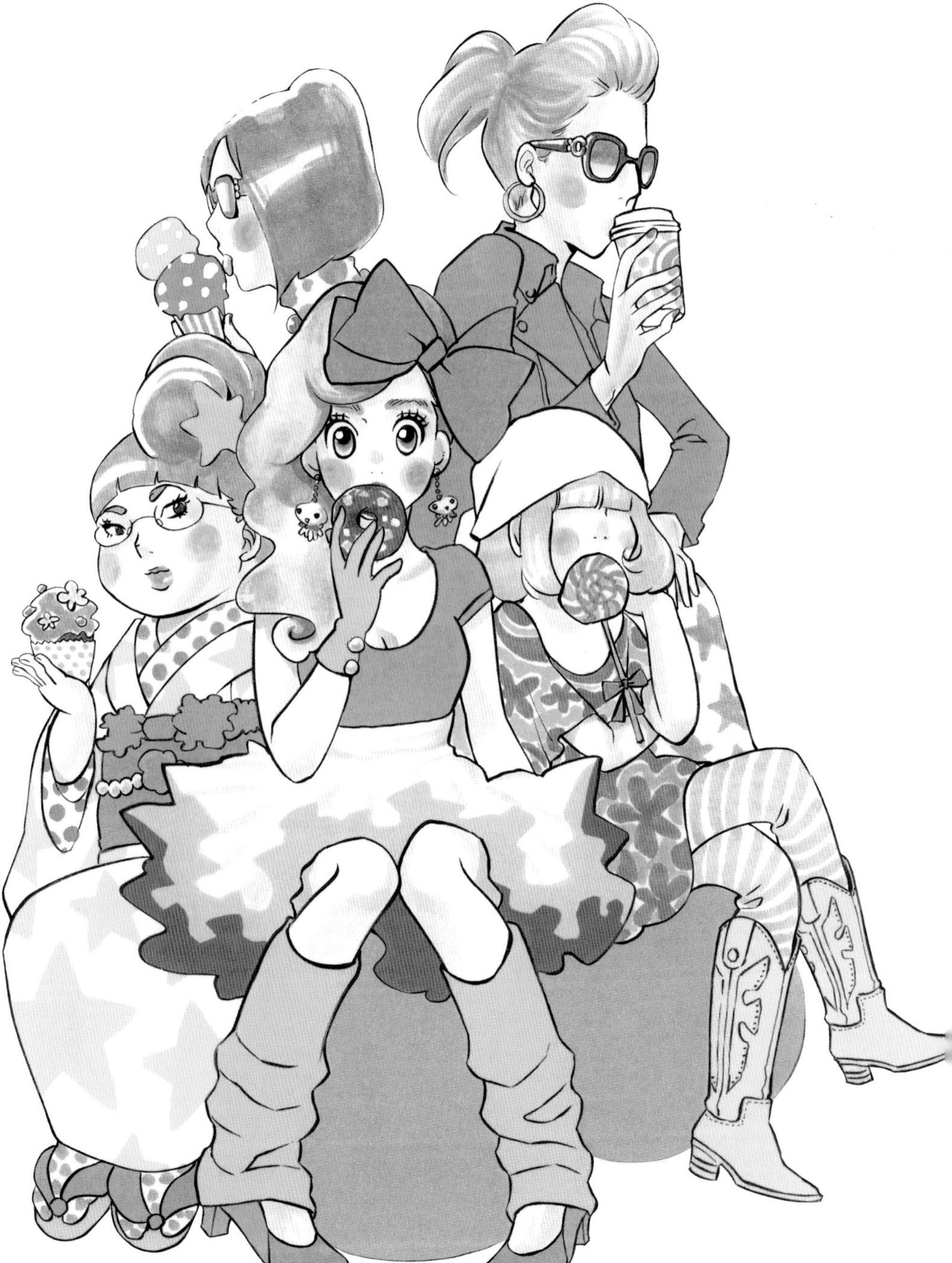

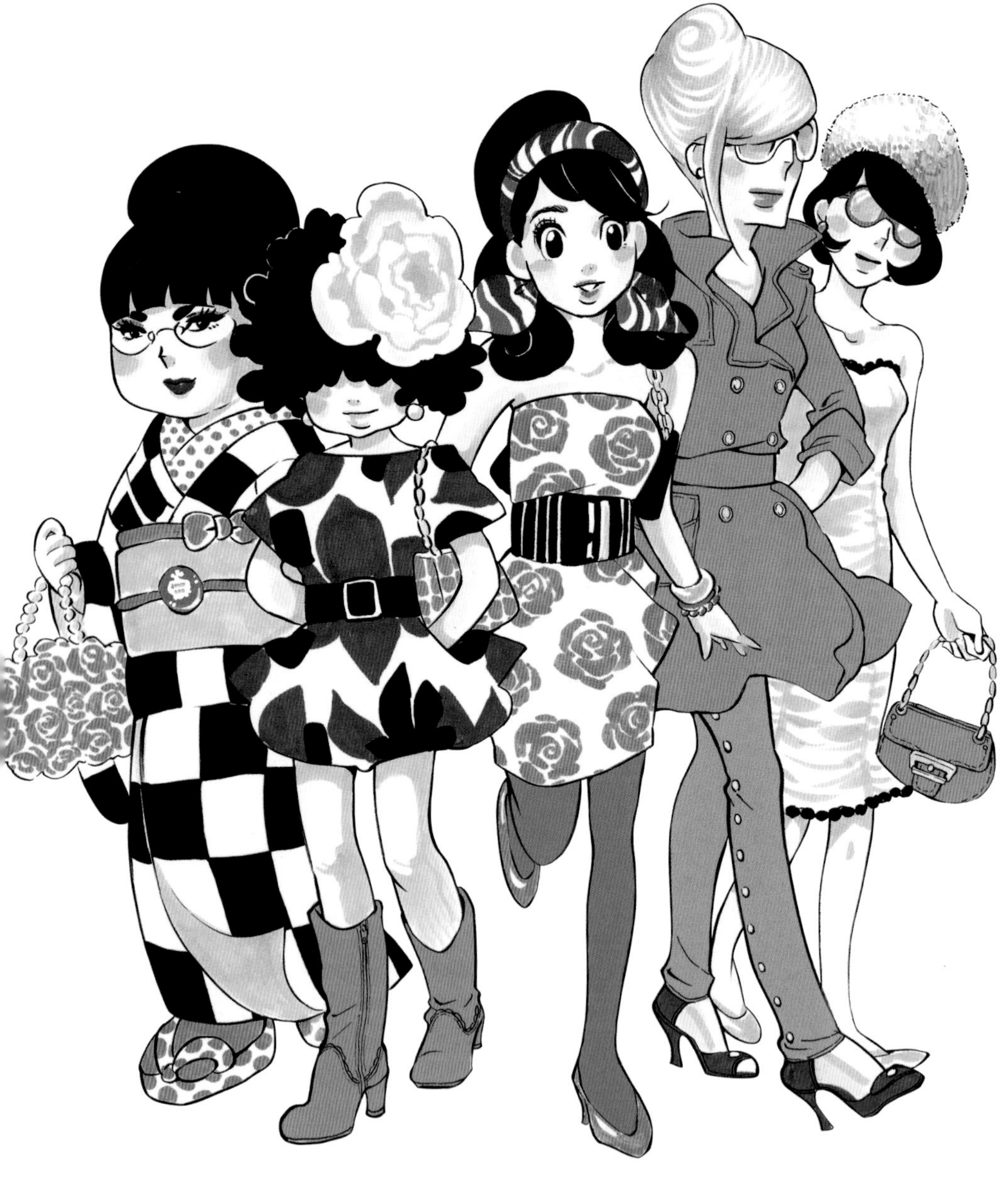

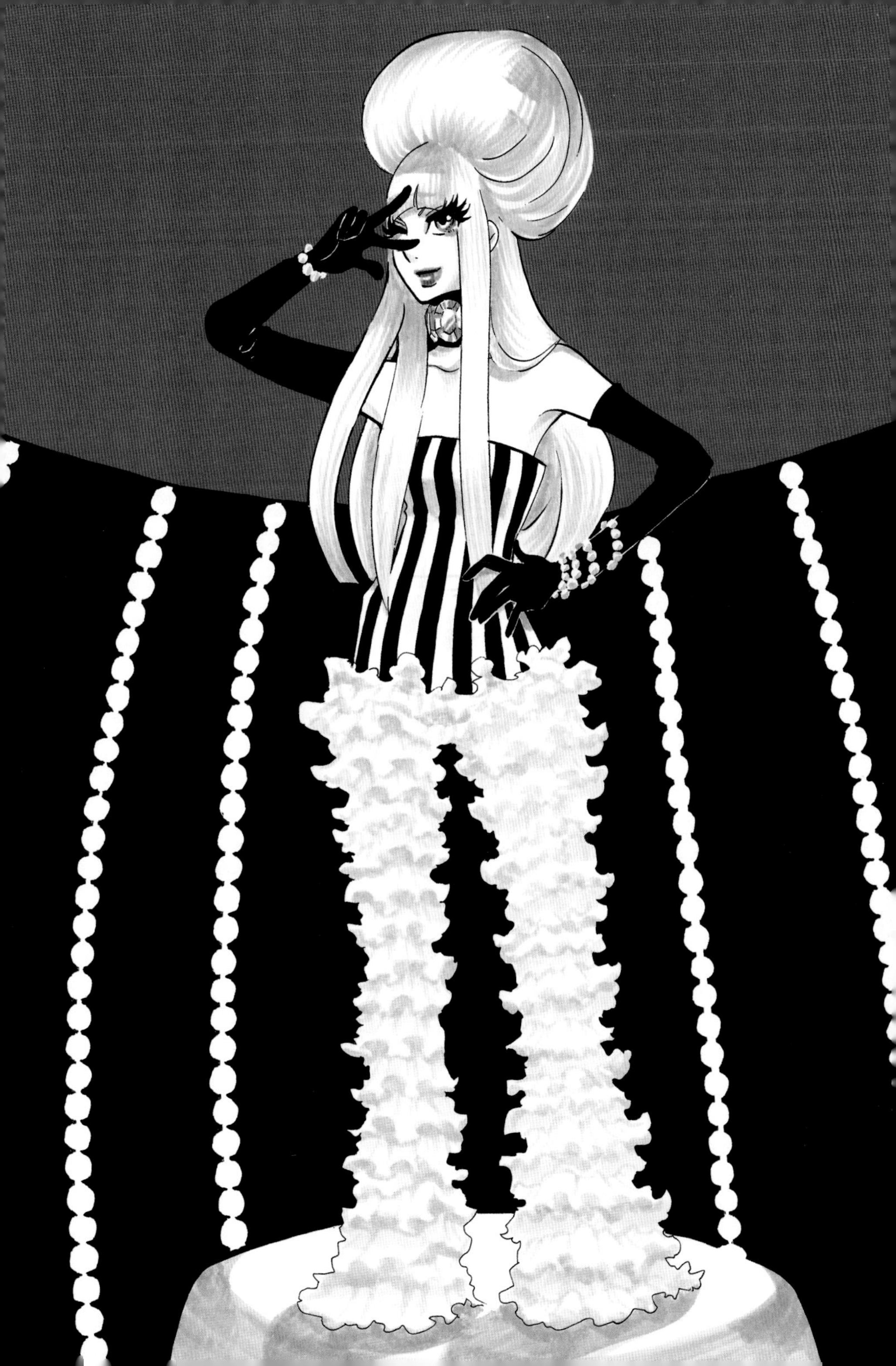

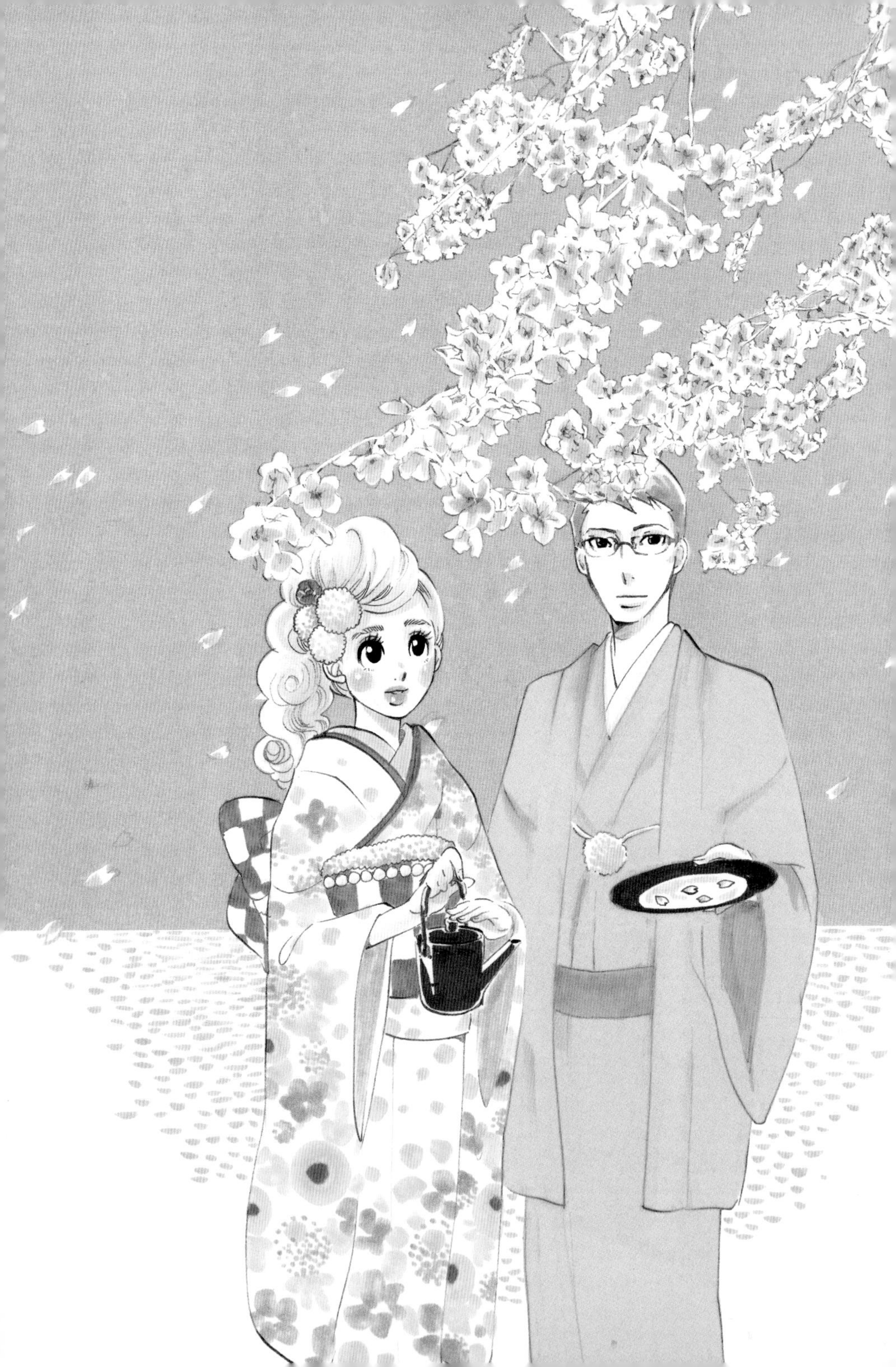

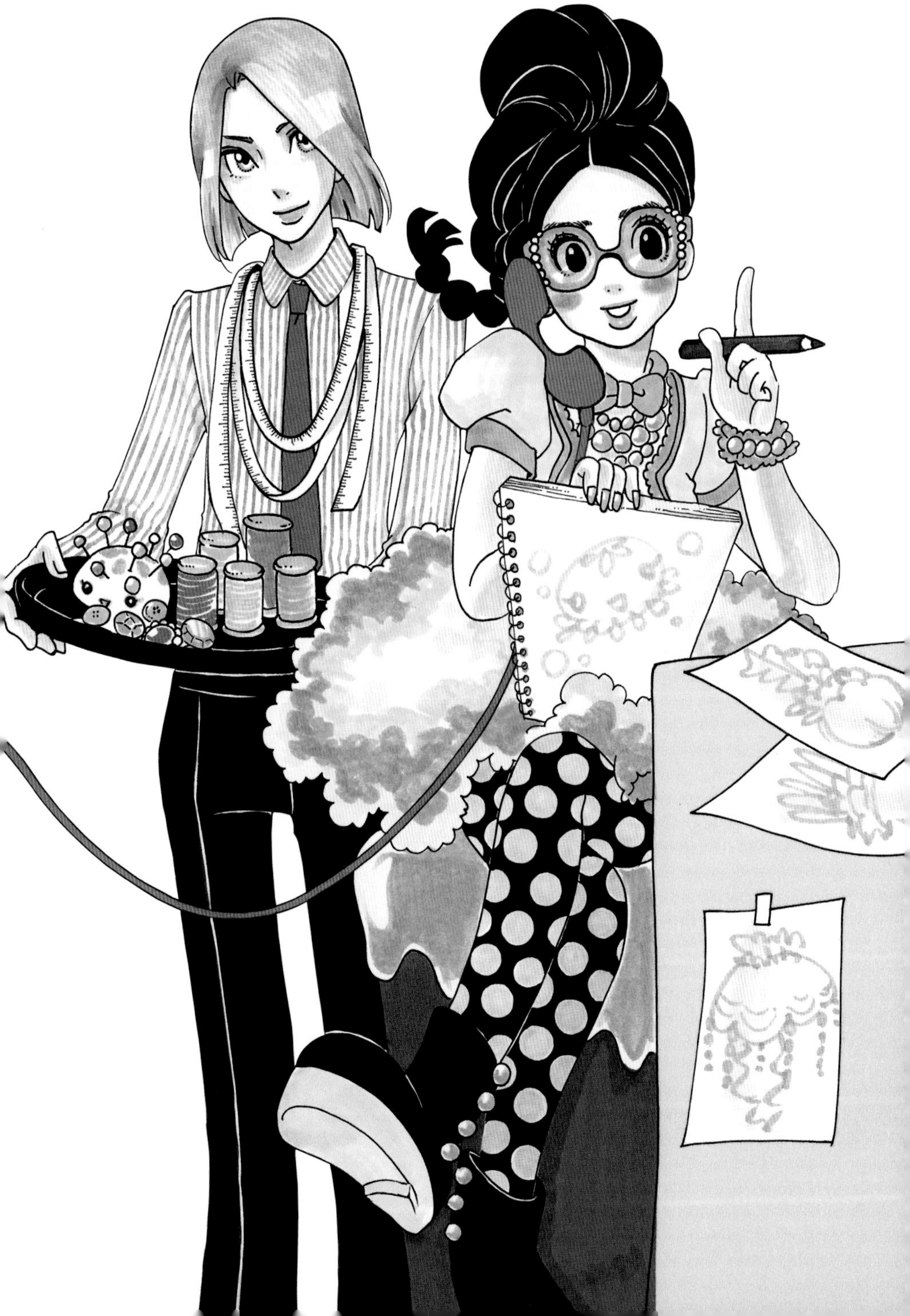

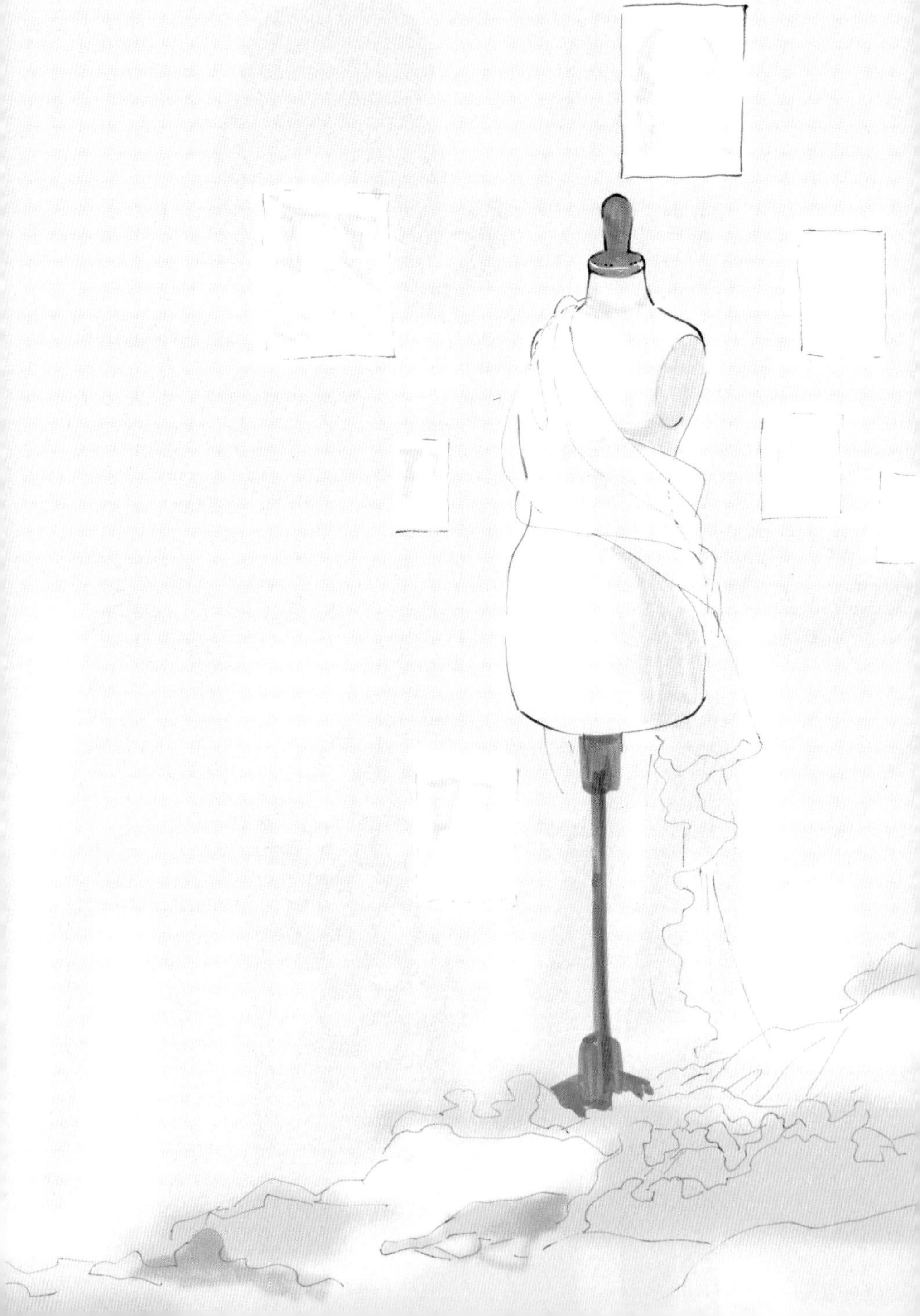

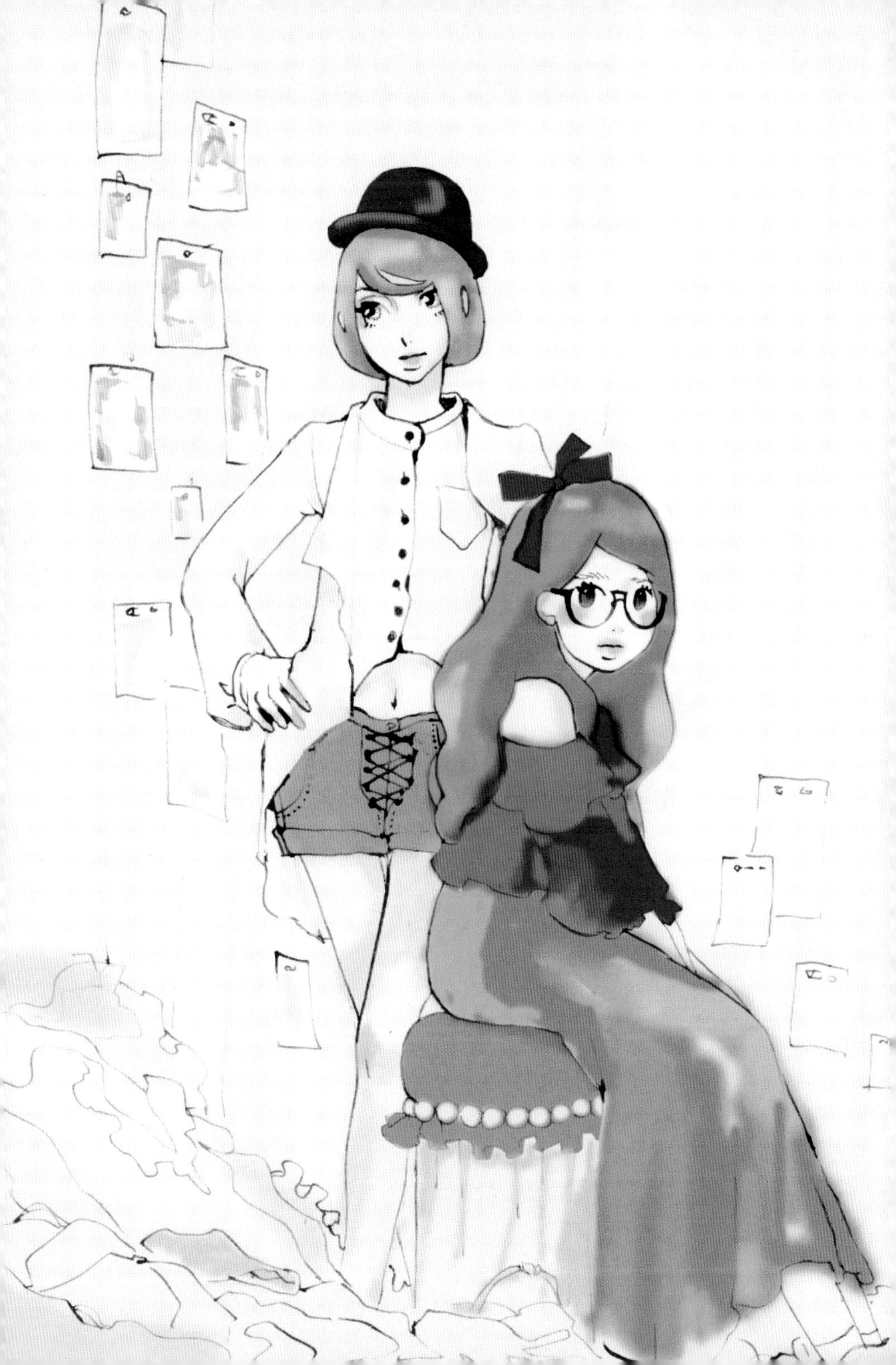

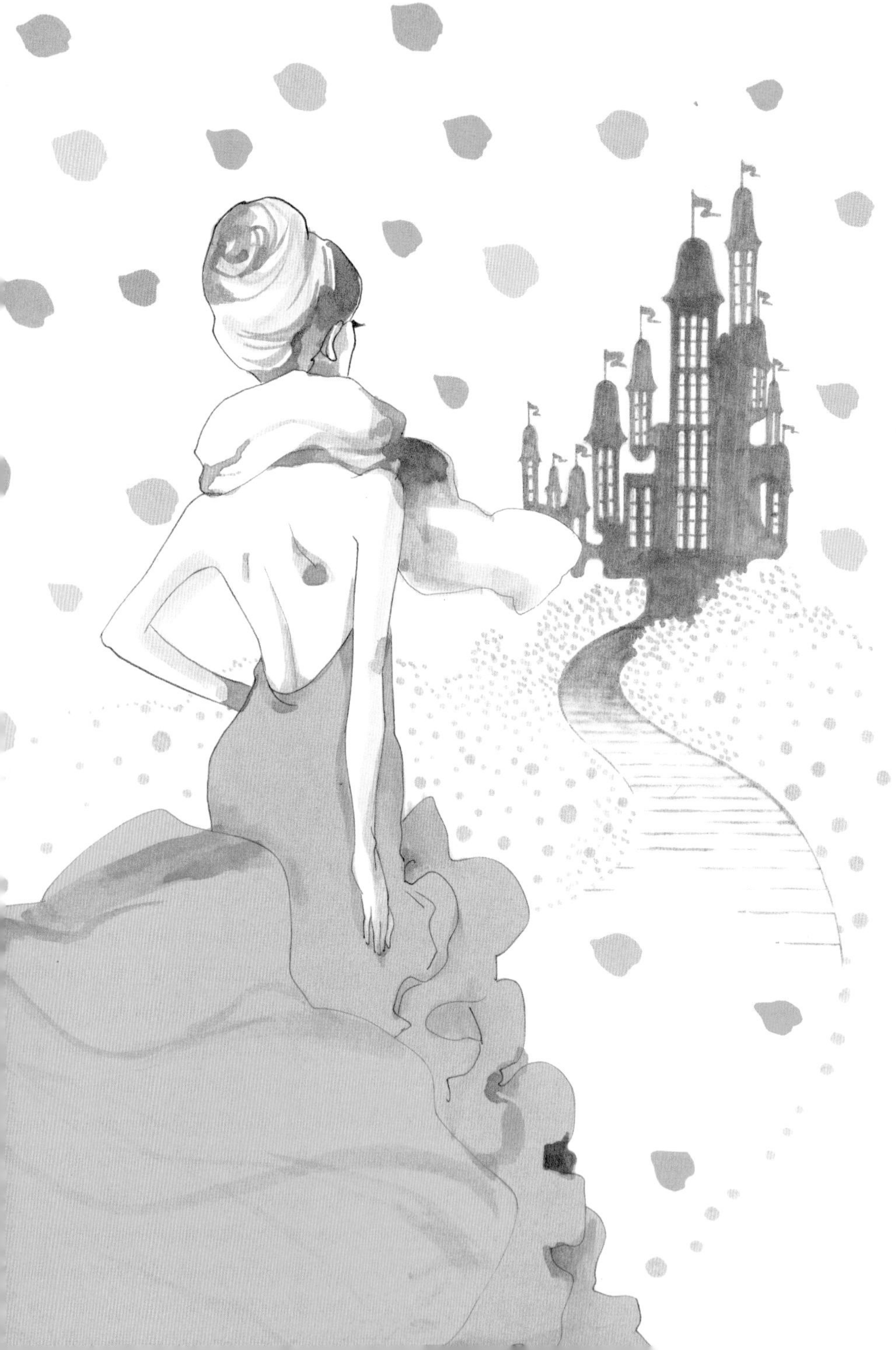

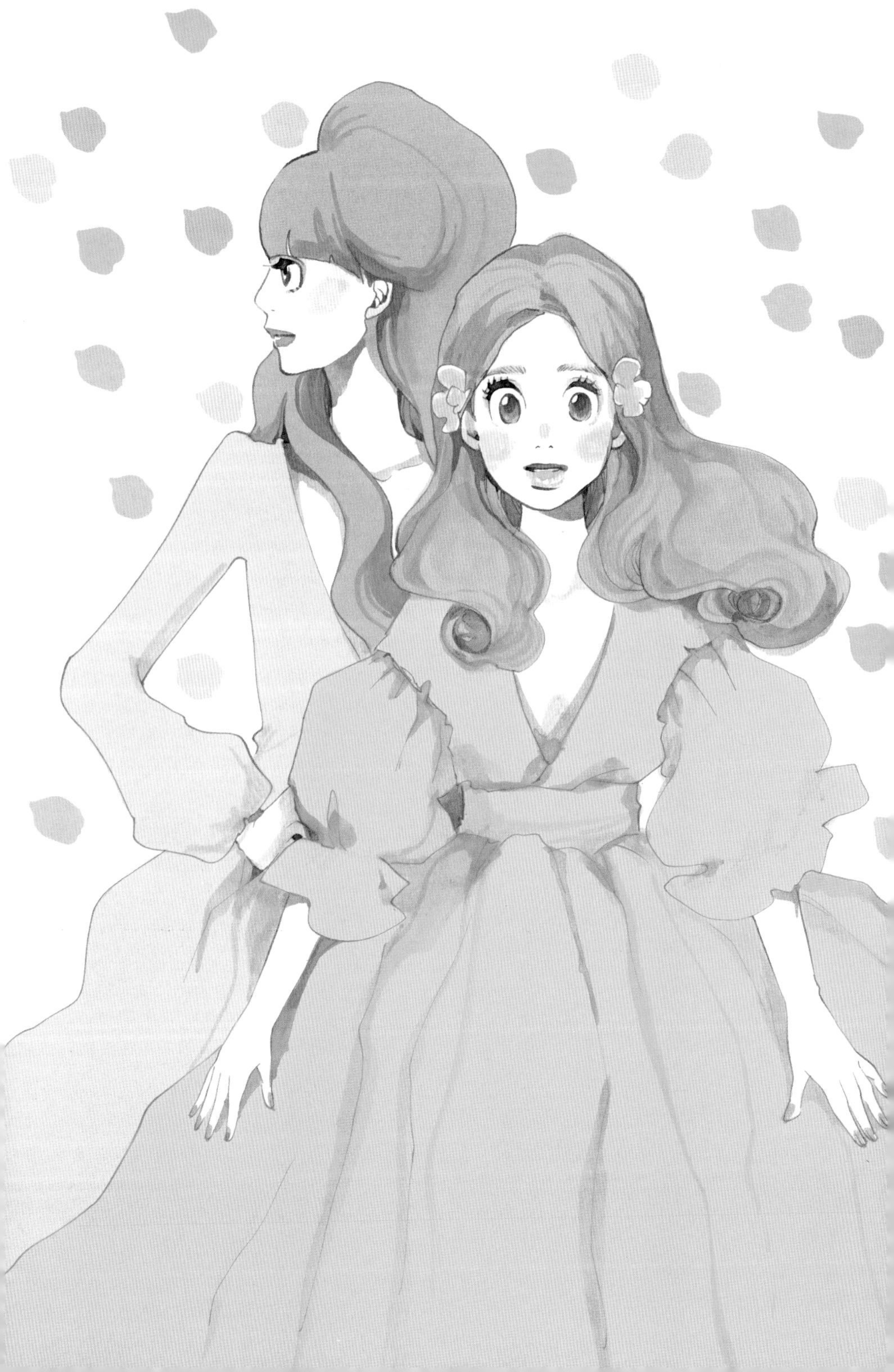

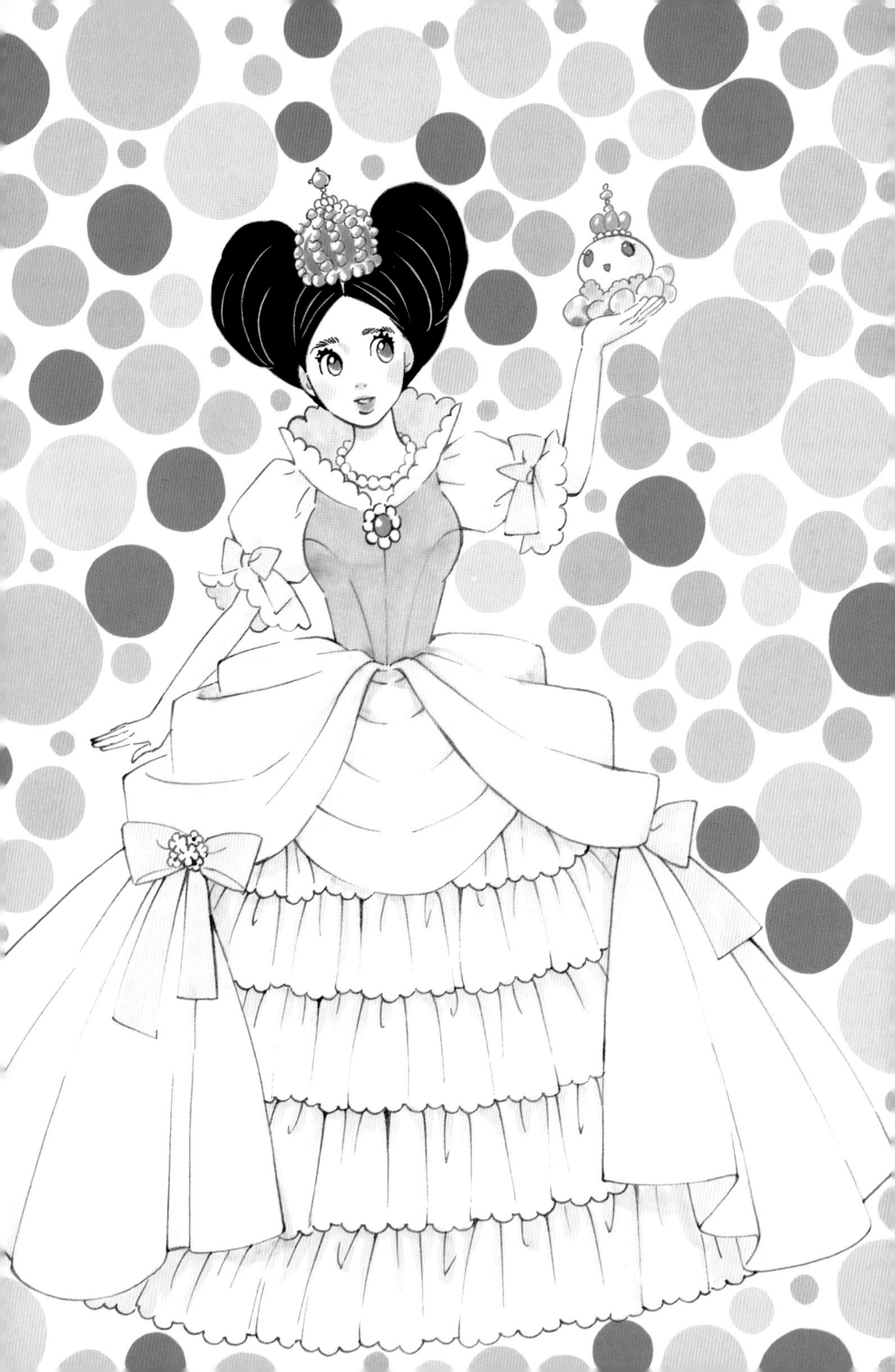

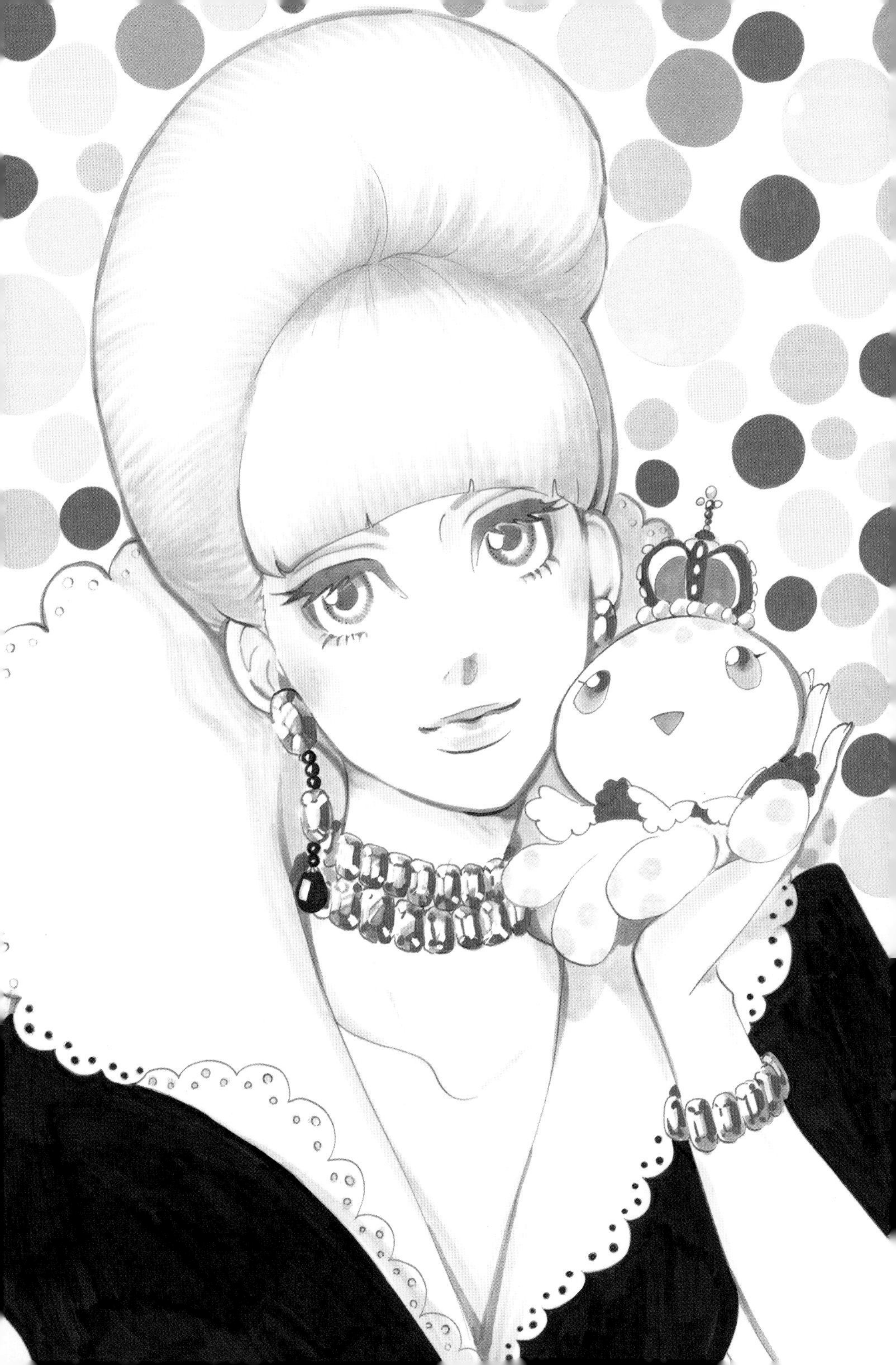

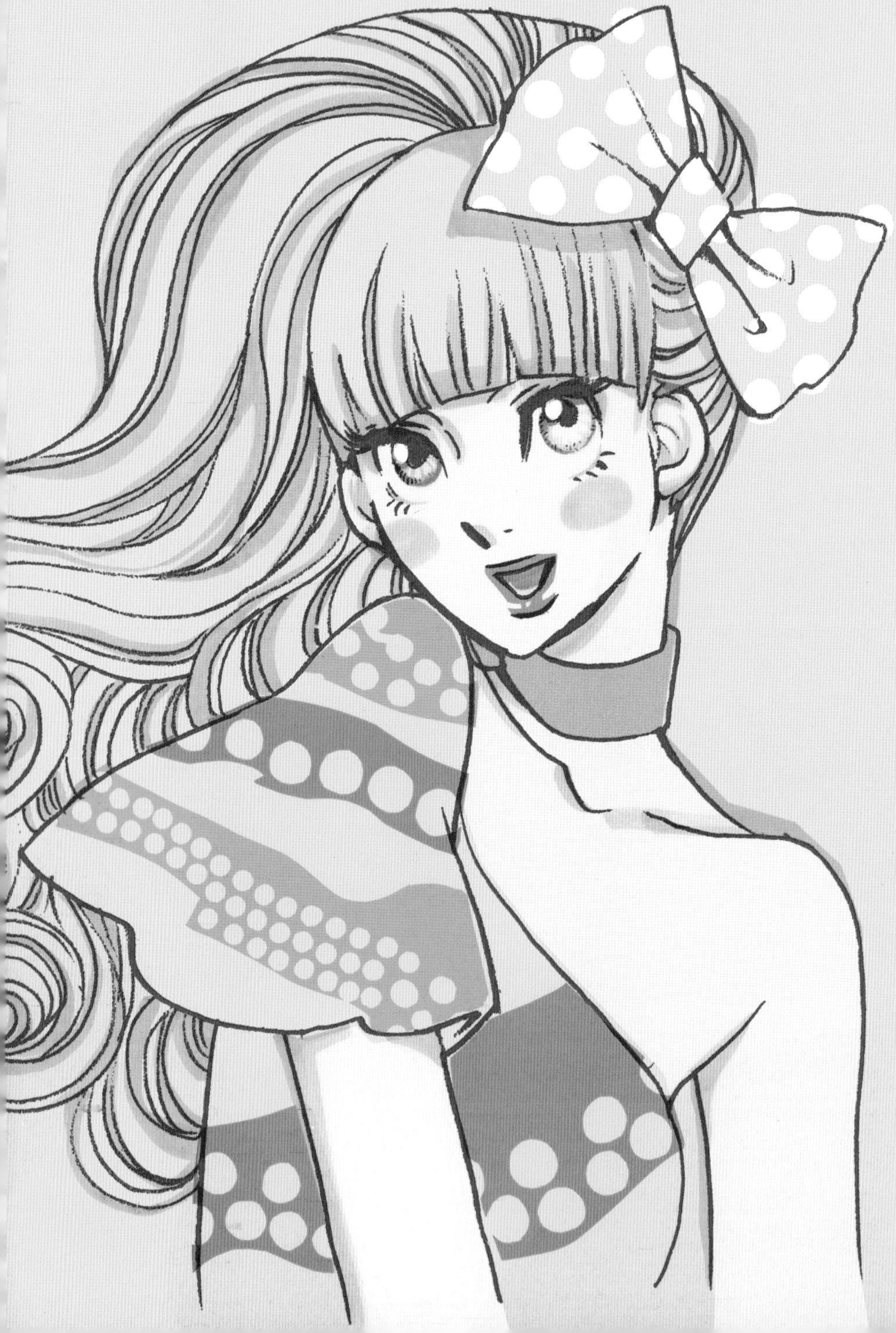

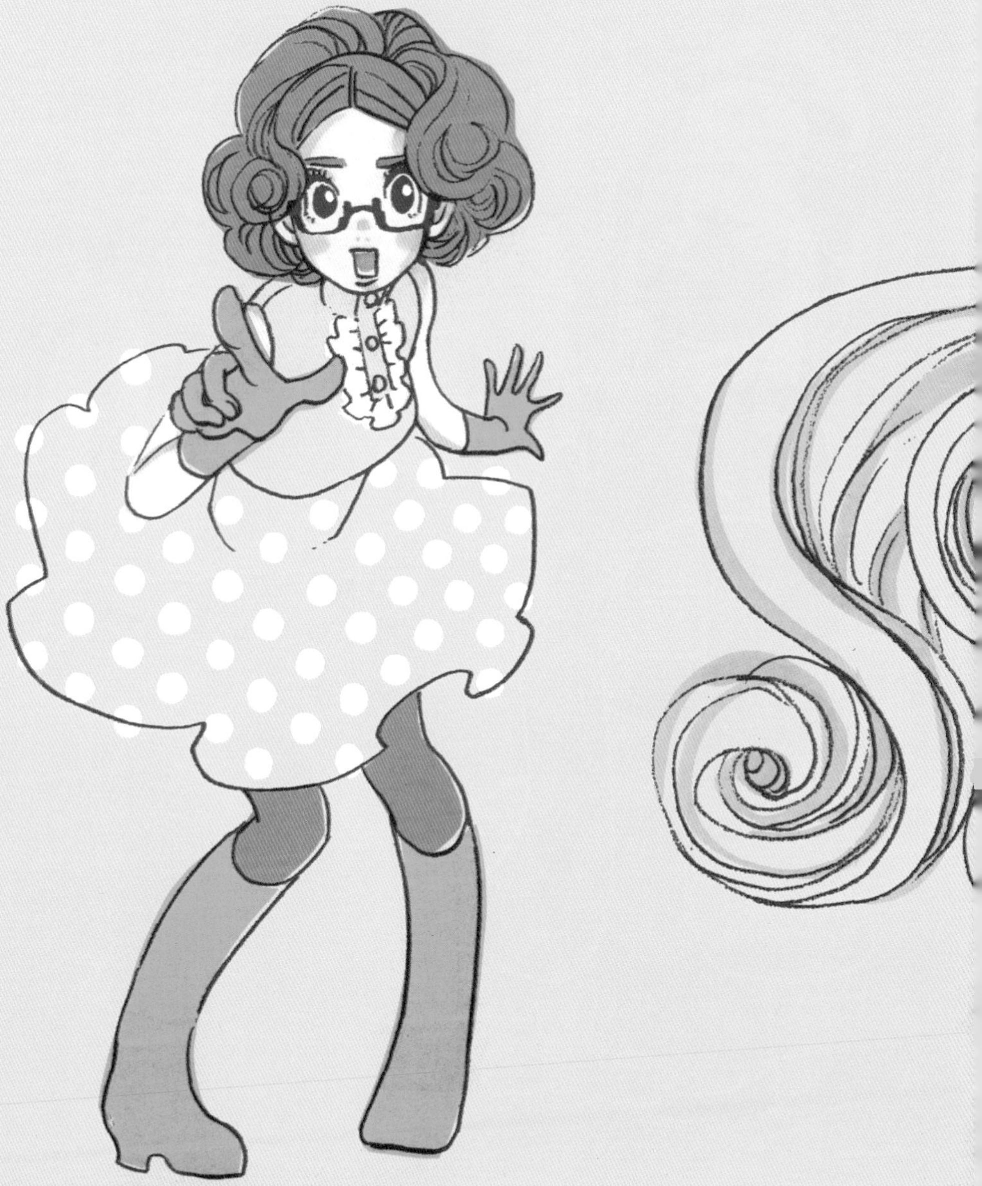

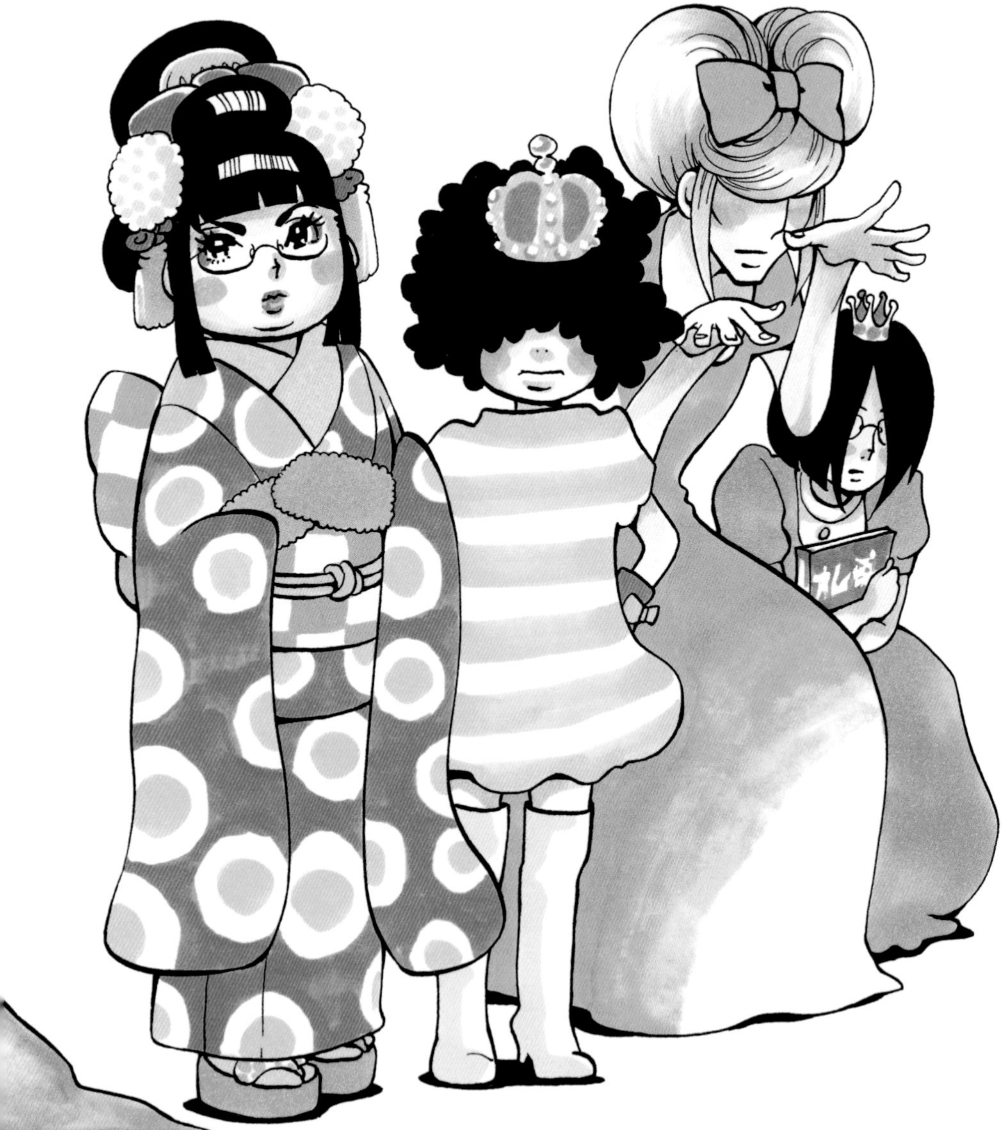

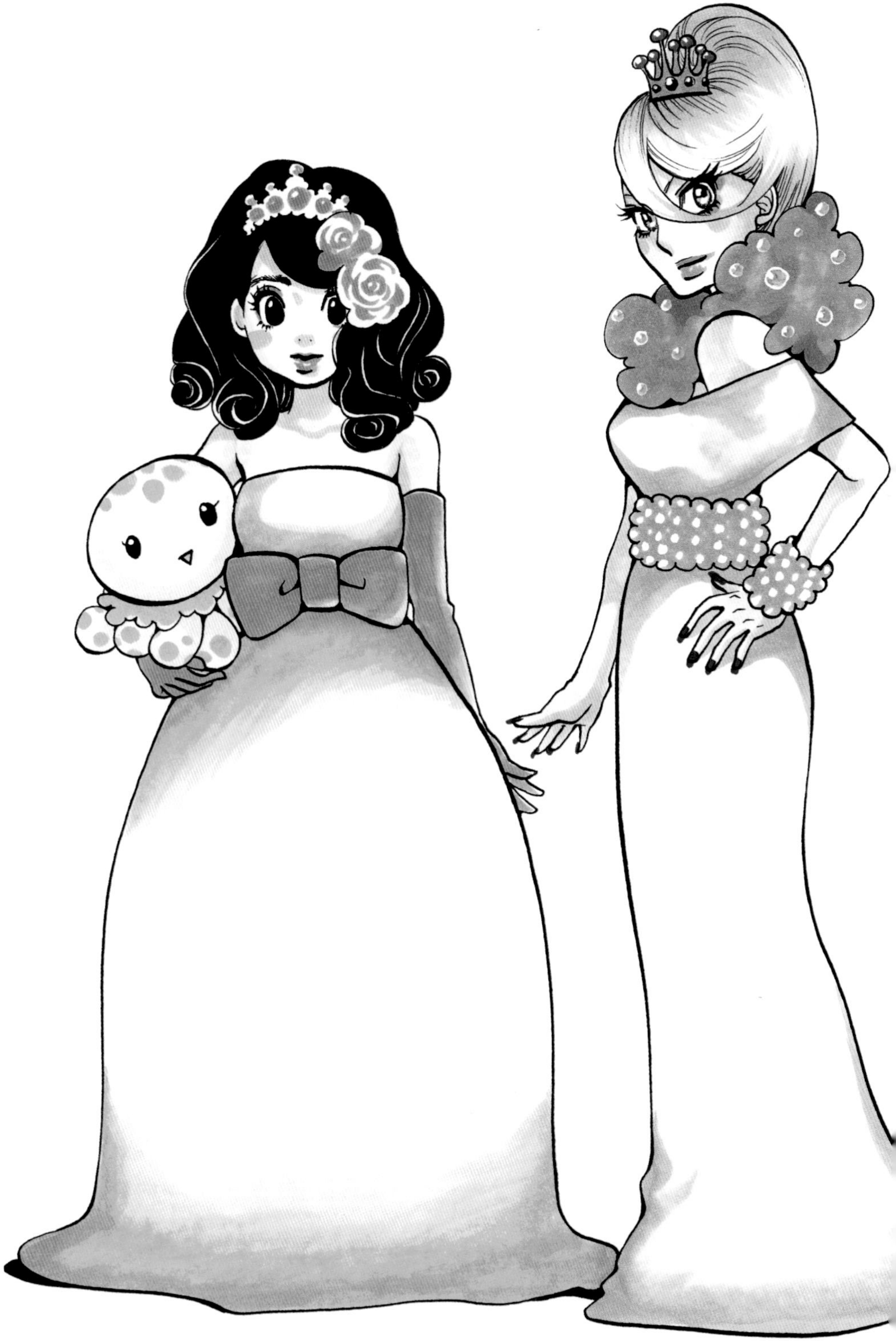

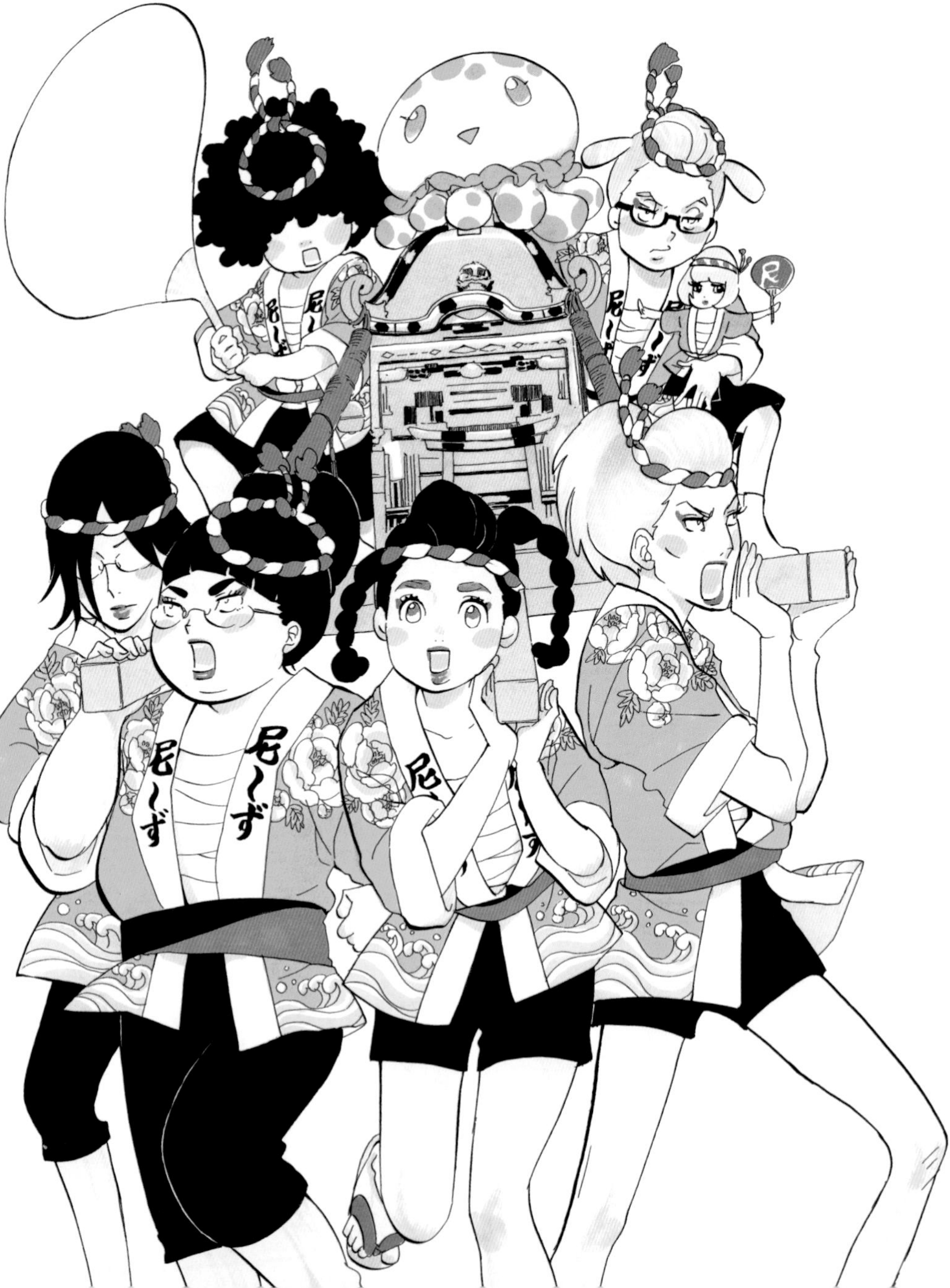
尼〜ず
尼〜ず
尼〜ず
尼〜ず

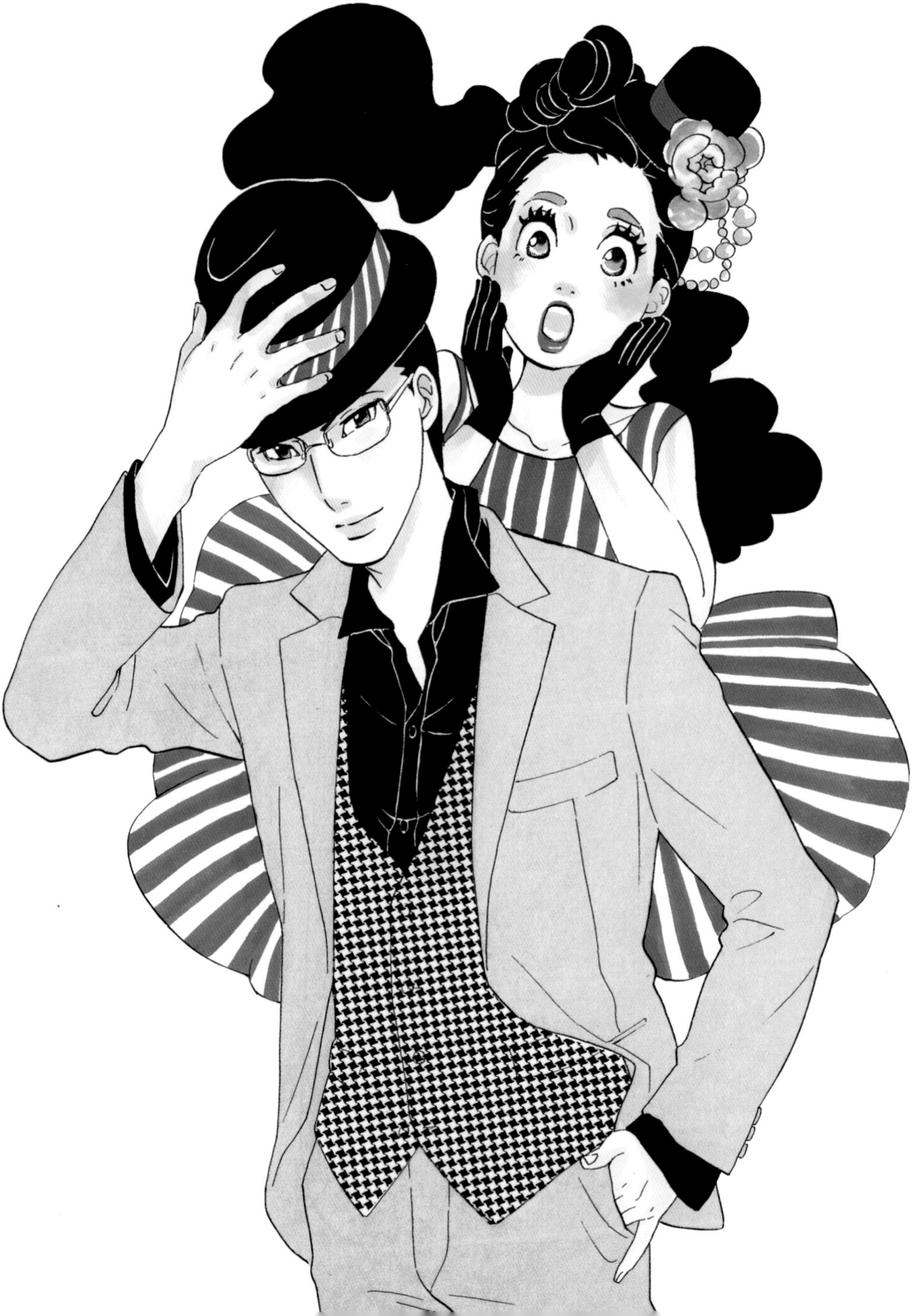

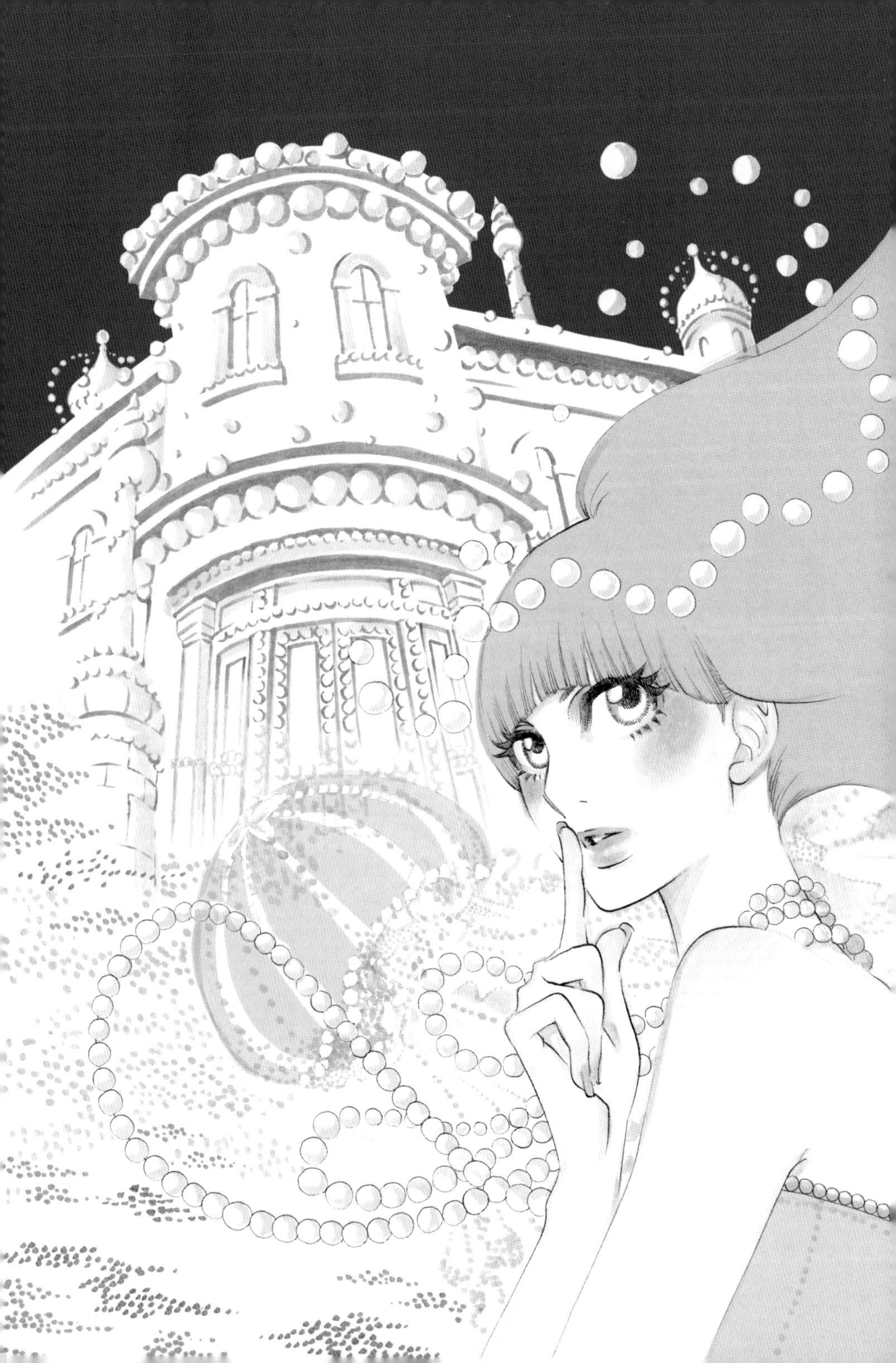

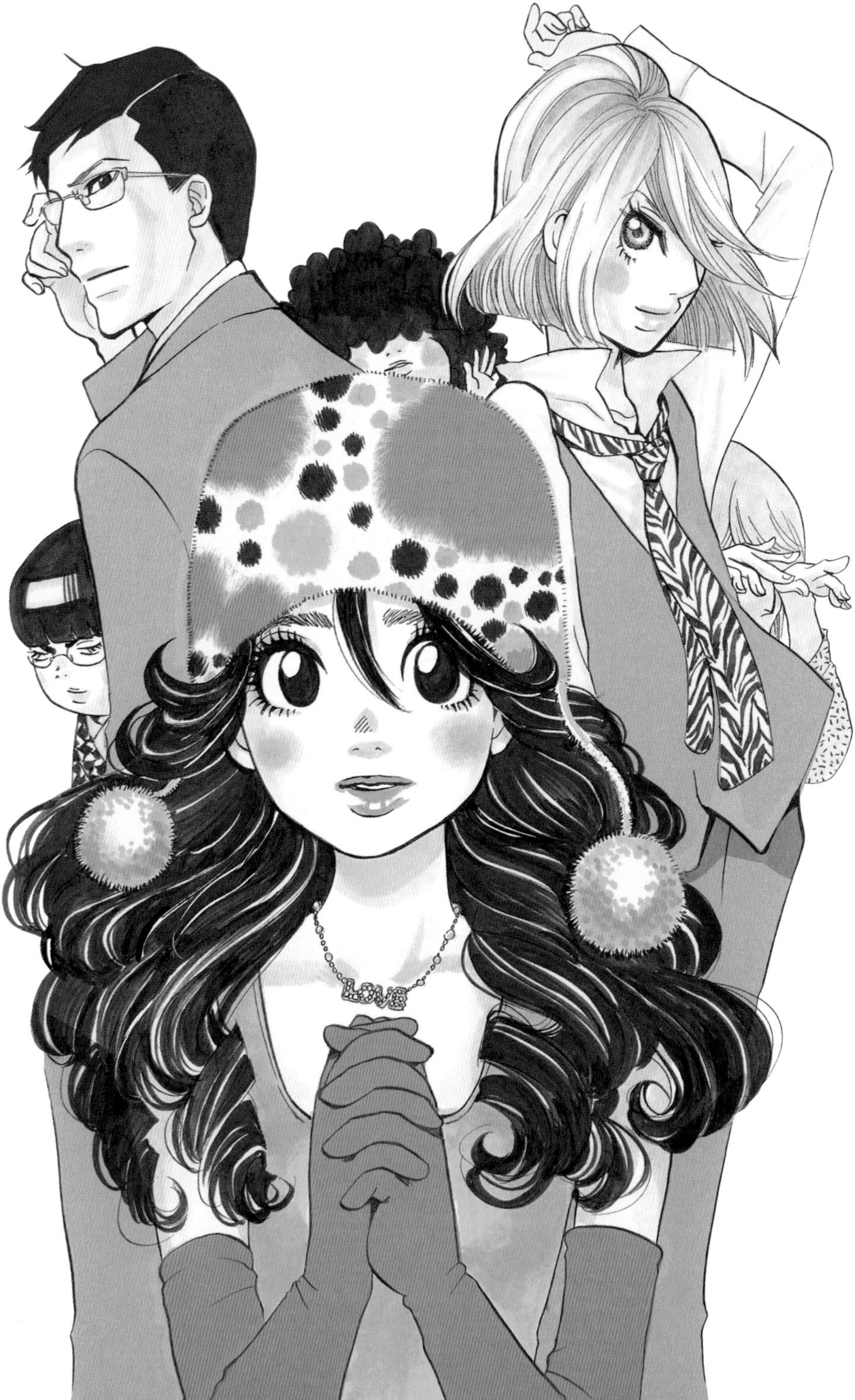
LOVE

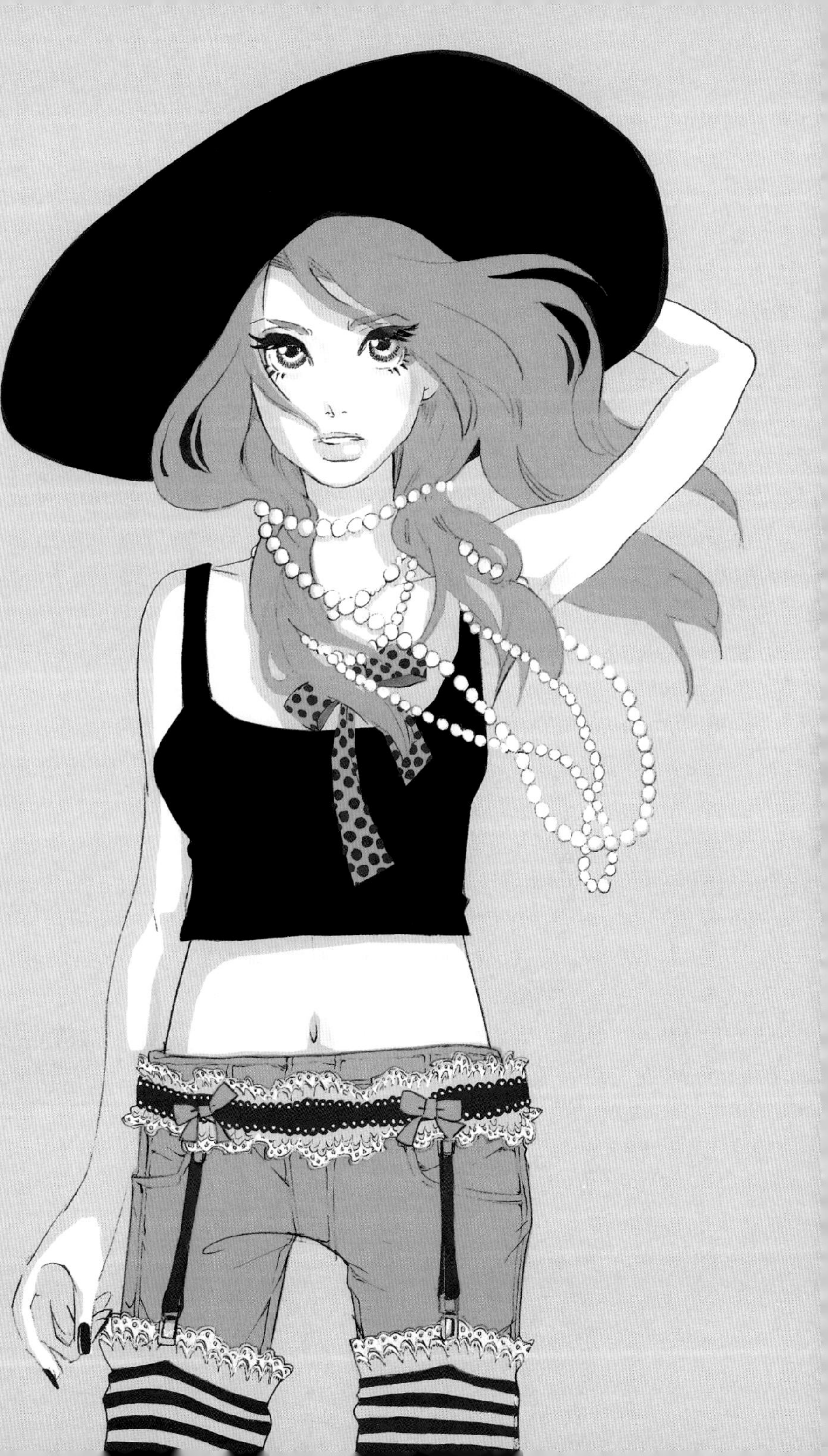

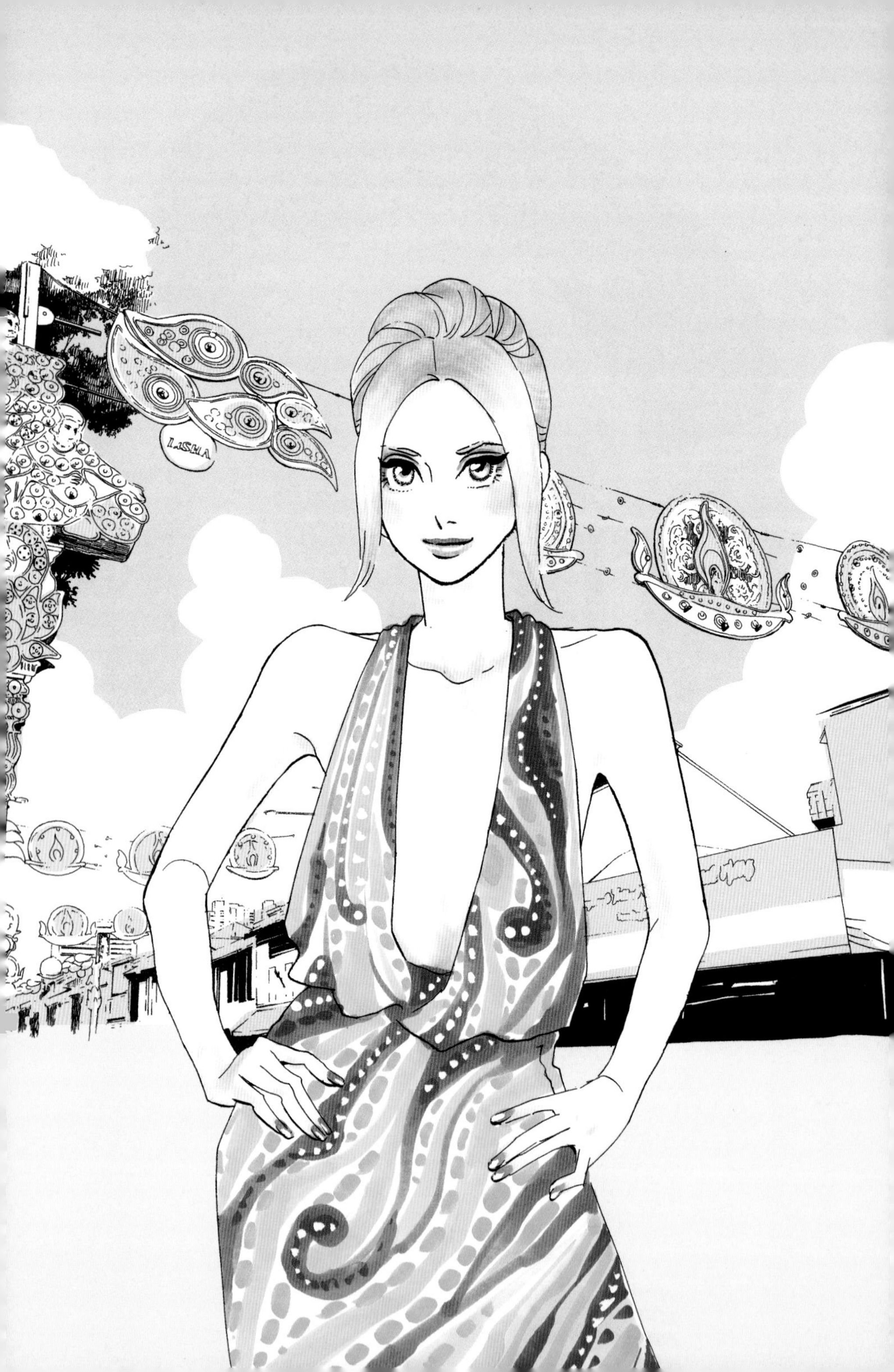
LaSHA

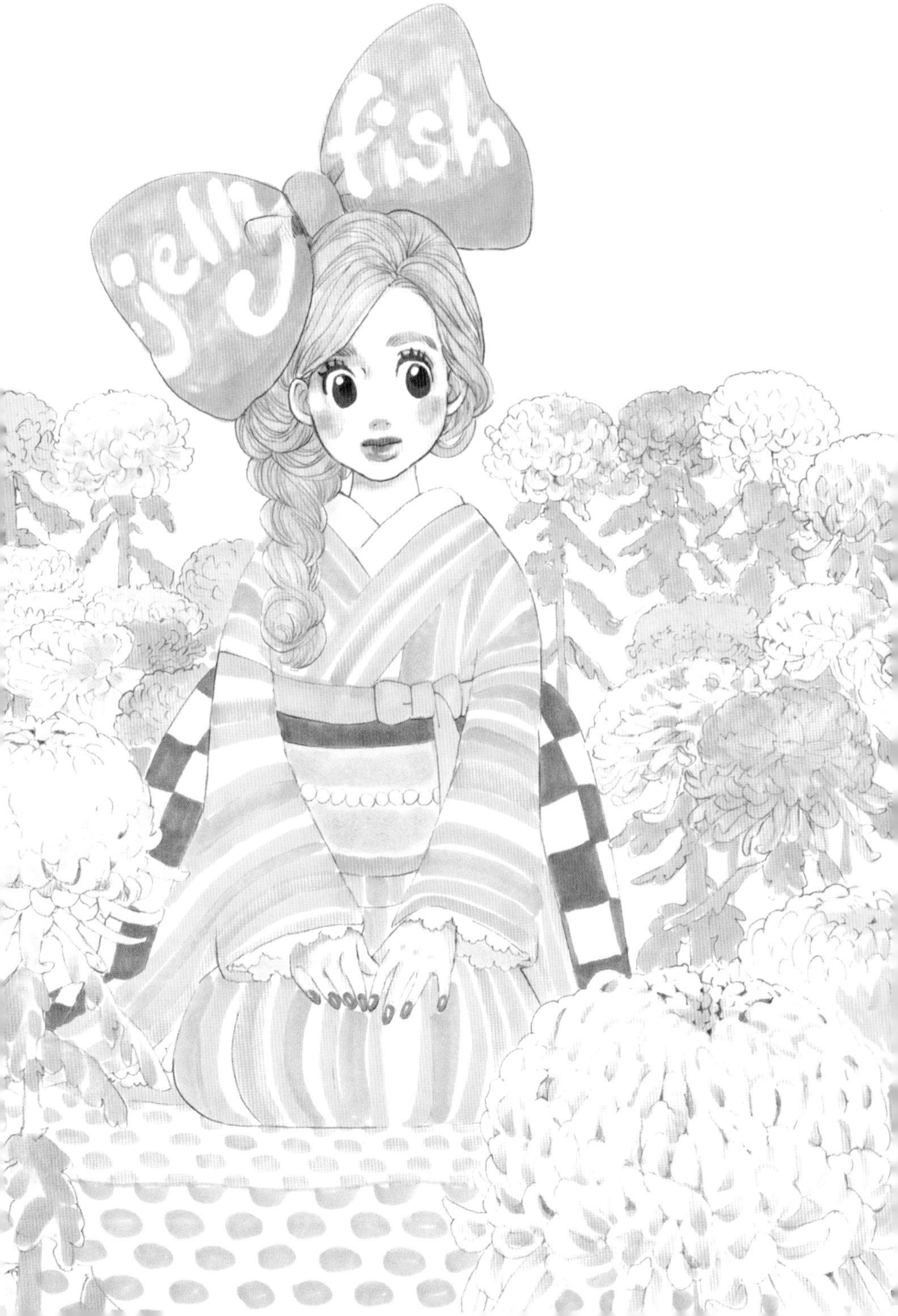
jelly fish

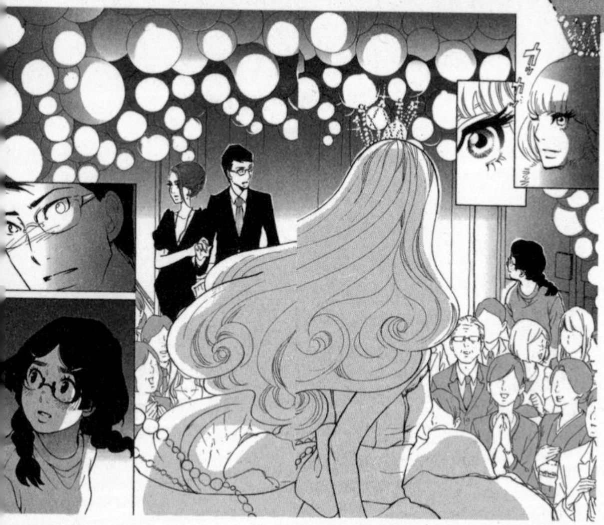

Princess Jellyfish

The first "quintessential romantic comedy" Akiko Higashimura drew in earnest?!

Geek Girls × Romance × Fashion = Princess Jellyfish!

As of Volume 14, the bound volumes of *Princess Jellyfish* have sold over 3.25 million copies. In 2010, it was a winner in the 34th annual Kodansha Manga Awards and got an anime adaptation in Fuji TV's noitaminA time block. Then, just in time for New Year's 2015, it was made into a popular live-action film starring Rena Nounen. The main character is a jellyfish otaku and emphatically non-stylish girl named Tsukimi. To pursue her dream of becoming an illustrator, she moved from Kagoshima to Tokyo, where she lives in the Amamizukan apartment house (no boys allowed) with a group of fellow otaku girls who call themselves "Amars."

One day, Tsukimi meets a beautiful cross-dressing boy named Kuranosuke. Kuranosuke initially starts giving her pretty-girl makeovers just for kicks, but then his older brother Shu falls in love with Tsukimi in her "transformed" state, and even Kuranosuke himself starts feeling drawn to her... When Kuranosuke establishes a fashion brand with Tsukimi and other Amars, the story expands from "otaku girl slice-of-life in a retro, Showa Era apartment house" to "a grand tale told on the global stage" that even exposes the dark underbelly of the fashion industry.

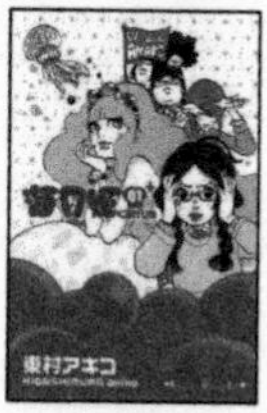
東村アキコ

- 17 volumes total
- Serialized in Kodansha's *Kiss* magazine beginning with Issue 21, 2008

If I were a girl as pretty as a princess...

WHY AM I THE ONLY ONE IN MY REGULAR CLOTHES?

All the Fun of a Quintessential Shojo Manga!

According to Akiko Higashimura, "I'd loved shojo manga ever since I was small, and *Princess Jellyfish* is what happened when I sat down and really drew a shojo manga in earnest." It's packed to the brim with all the shojo manga tropes: a stylish girl (or in this case a boy dressed as one) giving an unpopular girl a makeover; boy meets girl; falling for someone's surprising hidden side; female friendships; and even a series of new romantic rivals; and a girl learning and growing in a harsh new world.

And yet, by spicing up this classic shojo recipe by including elements like a boy who cross-dresses and otaku girls, Akiko Higashimura has achieved a manga that men and boys happily read, too. Right from the early planning stages, she was thinking through how to make it something that as many people as possible could enjoy, including male readers. This is truly Higashimura-sensei's masterpiece, where we see how much she can do when she goes all-out.

A classic romantic comedy about hopes and dreams!

In this manga you won't find any of Higashimura's usual incidents based on real-life events or characters who ignore the story and run wild. This is a classic romantic comedy where girls' wishes to *transform* and *be princesses* are fulfilled.

Their first love confession, with the night skyline in the background.

A stylish manga where the main characters are otaku?!

Most of the major characters are otaku girls, self-proclaimed *Amars* living a "life with no use for men." A number of distinctive characters cross their path, including a cross-dressing boy, an attractive businessman, a prime minister (!), and even a maiden-like middle-aged political secretary.

Otaku girls with no social skills but plenty of specialized expertise unite!

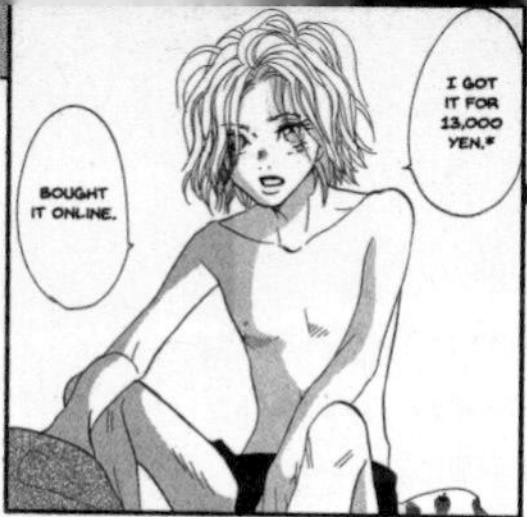
I GOT IT FOR 13,000 YEN.*
BOUGHT IT ONLINE.

The panel where you find out Kuranosuke is male. Can you believe he was originally going to be female?

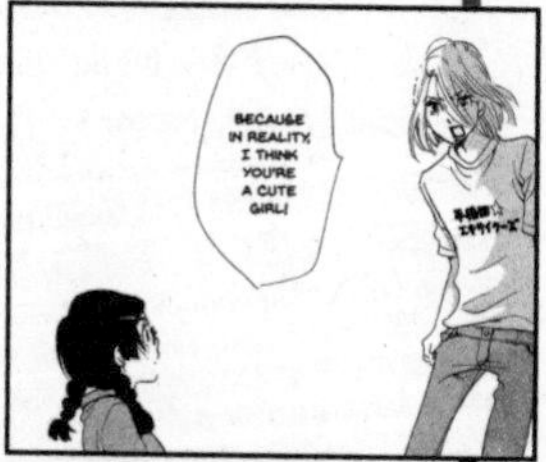
BECAUSE IN REALITY, I THINK YOU'RE A CUTE GIRL!

Kuranosuke telling Tsukimi, "You're cute." This, plus how flustered he gets afterward, set my heart aflutter.

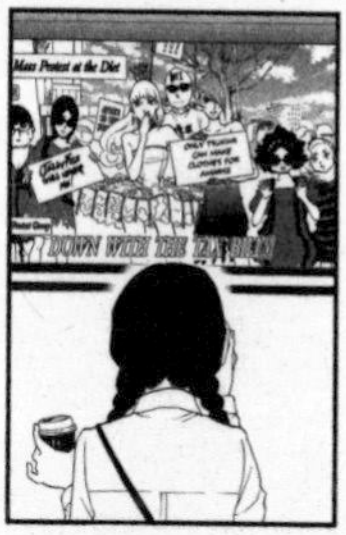

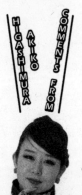

The deep bonds of otaku girl friendship never die, even with Tsukimi in Singapore!

COMMENTS FROM AKIKO HIGASHIMURA

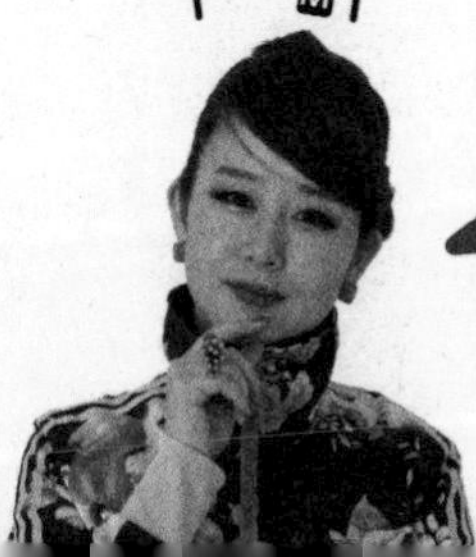

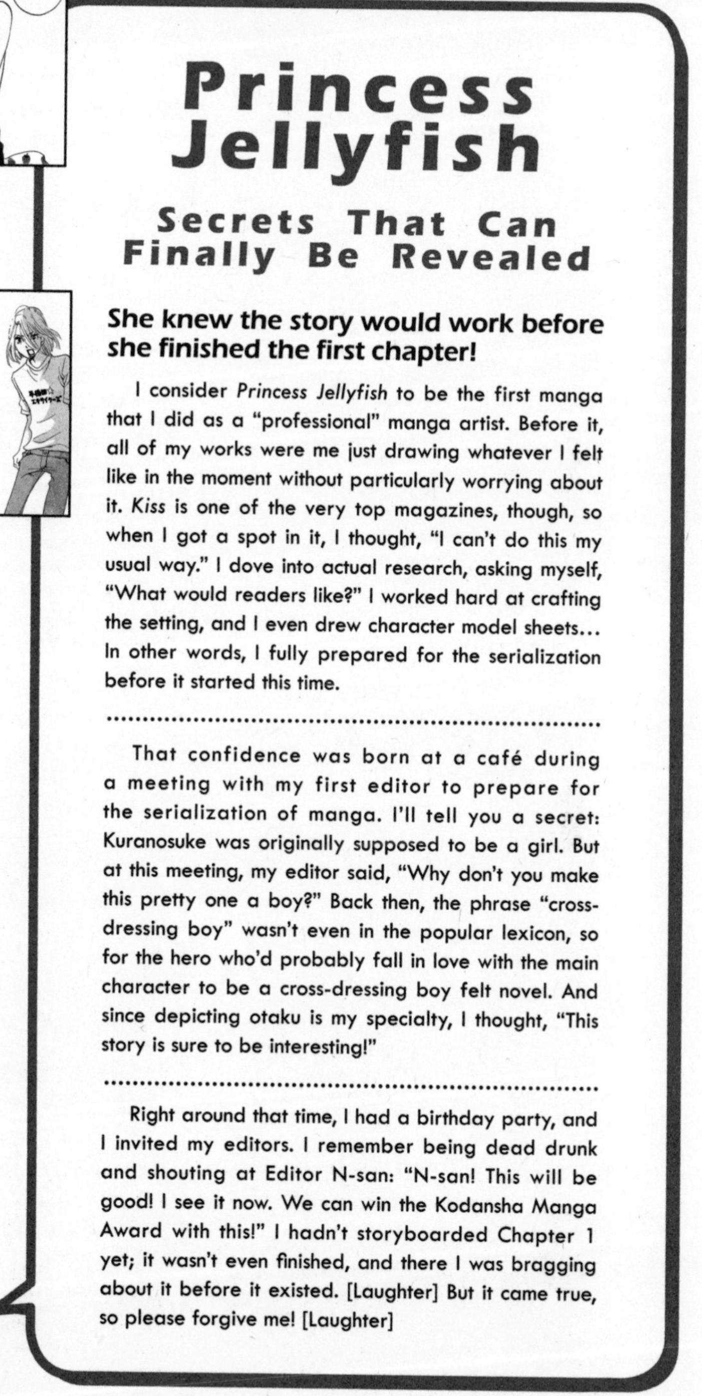

Princess Jellyfish

Secrets That Can Finally Be Revealed

She knew the story would work before she finished the first chapter!

I consider *Princess Jellyfish* to be the first manga that I did as a "professional" manga artist. Before it, all of my works were me just drawing whatever I felt like in the moment without particularly worrying about it. *Kiss* is one of the very top magazines, though, so when I got a spot in it, I thought, "I can't do this my usual way." I dove into actual research, asking myself, "What would readers like?" I worked hard at crafting the setting, and I even drew character model sheets... In other words, I fully prepared for the serialization before it started this time.

That confidence was born at a café during a meeting with my first editor to prepare for the serialization of manga. I'll tell you a secret: Kuranosuke was originally supposed to be a girl. But at this meeting, my editor said, "Why don't you make this pretty one a boy?" Back then, the phrase "cross-dressing boy" wasn't even in the popular lexicon, so for the hero who'd probably fall in love with the main character to be a cross-dressing boy felt novel. And since depicting otaku is my specialty, I thought, "This story is sure to be interesting!"

Right around that time, I had a birthday party, and I invited my editors. I remember being dead drunk and shouting at Editor N-san: "N-san! This will be good! I see it now. We can win the Kodansha Manga Award with this!" I hadn't storyboarded Chapter 1 yet; it wasn't even finished, and there I was bragging about it before it existed. [Laughter] But it came true, so please forgive me! [Laughter]

Are the jellyfish in *Princess Jellyfish* real?

JELLY CATALOG

Narrated by Tsukimi

Princess Jellyfish Edition

For all of you wondering what the jellyfish in *Princess Jellyfish* really look like, Tsukimi is about to explain!

Photo credit: Tsuruoka City Kamo Aquarium

Chrysaora pacifica

(Japanese Sea Nettle)

Tsukimi Note

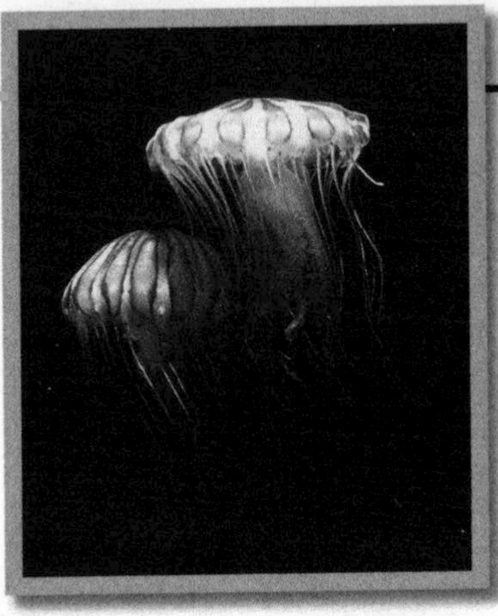

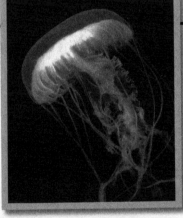

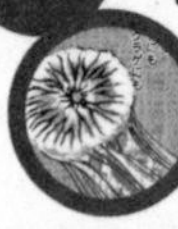

AKA the "battle flag jelly" and the "atchoo jelly."

Their 16 red stripes are pretty. ♥ Their venom packs a punch. I've read that ninja used to grind its desiccated tentacles into a powder that they used to make enemies sneeze.

They've been in our oceans since long before humanity existed!

Fewer than 20 species of jellyfish appear in *Princess Jellyfish*, but jellies live all around the world in environments ranging from inland marshes to deep-sea waters. There are over 3,000 different kinds! They first appeared somewhere between 600 million to 1 billion years ago. Over that mind-blowing length of time, they've been adapting to environmental changes to survive and thrive. Isn't that incredible? ♥ And most importantly of all, they're so beautiful! I'm enchanted...

Photo credit: Tsuruoka City Kamo Aquarium

Sanderia malayensis

(Amakusa Jellyfish)

Tsukimi Note

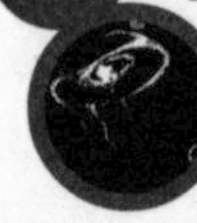

Never put in a tank with other jellies!

These jellies from the Amakusa region eat other species of jellyfish. Even when you raise them in captivity, you feed them jellyfish, but they're smart kids who never eat one of their own kind?!

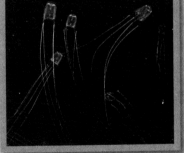

Photo credit: Tsuruoka City Kamo Aquarium

Carybdea brevipedalia

(a type of Box Jelly)

Tsukimi Note

I SKETCHED A DIFFERENT CARYBDEA BREVIPEDALIA, SOME COMB JELLIES, AN ELEGANT JELLY, AND SOME BOX JELLIES...

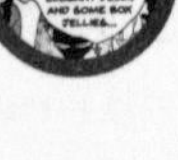

The jelly of summer—and the one who stung you?

Have you heard people say "If you go swimming in the ocean at the end of the summer, you'll get stung by a jelly"? The most likely culprit is one of these jellies. They tend to gather in places with lots of light.

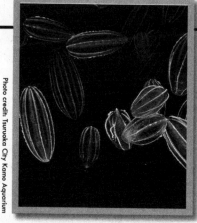

Photo credit: Tsuruoka City Kamo Aquarium

Beroe cucumis

(a type of Comb Jelly)

Tsukimi Note

I SKETCHED A DIFFERENT CARYBDEA BREVIPEDALIA, SOME COMB JELLIES, AN ELEGANT JELLY, AND SOME BOX JELLIES...

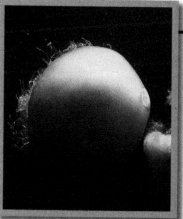

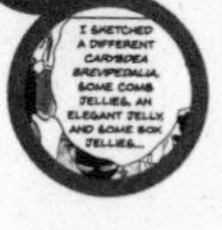

A big-mouthed jelly with no tentacles.

These cucumber-shaped jellies don't have any tentacles. They eat their fellow ctenophores. They have giant mouths, and their magnificent eating style of swallowing prey whole is out of this world!♥

Photo credit: Tsuruoka City Kamo Aquarium

Stomolophus nomurai

(Nomura's Jellyfish)

Tsukimi Note

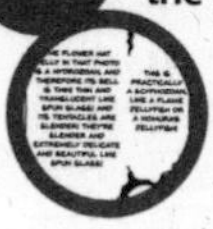

A sometimes troublesome jelly in the world's largest size class.

These king-sized jelly have bells 2m in diameter and can weigh over 200kg. They're problem children who harm the fishing industry when they get caught in stationary nets.

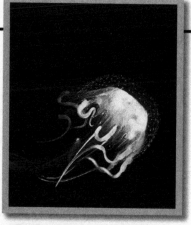

Photo credit: Tsuruoka City Kamo Aquarium

Pelagia noctiluca

(Purple Jelly)

Tsukimi Note

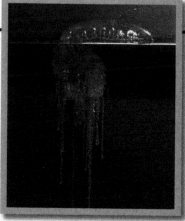

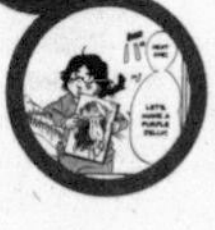

I love the pretty colors like pink and mauve!

The pretty pink color stands out, making these jellies fun to watch! But a large swarm of them has appeared in the Mediterranean Sea, and they can sting people trying to swim there.

Photo credit: New Enoshima Aquarium

Physalia physalis

(Portuguese Man-of-War)

Tsukimi Note

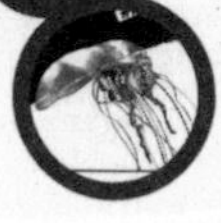

AKA "the floating terror." It uses the wind to move.

This is "the floating terror," whose sting hurts like you wouldn't believe. The pneumatophore above its tentacles catches the wind to help it float along.

References: Lindsay, D. J., & Miyake, H. (2013). *Saishin kurage zukan: Hyakujisshu no kurage no fushigi na seitai*. Seibundoshinkosha.
Namikawa, H., & Soyama, I. (2004). Kurage gaidobukku: Jellyfish in Japanese Waters. CCC Media House.

Photo credit: Tsuruoka City Kamo Aquarium

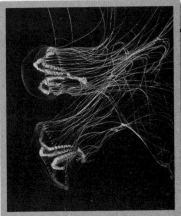

Photo credit: Tsuruoka City Kamo Aquarium

Cyanea capillata

(Lion's Mane Jelly)

Tsukimi Note

The jelly world's No. 1 eater; brightly colored, too.

In Japanese, this red-brown jelly is called the "northern ghost," and in English it's a "lion's mane." It lives in relatively deep water and is a voracious eater, even more so than other jelly-eating jellies.

Tima formosa

(Elegant Jellyfish)

Tsukimi Note

A very beautiful jellyfish. If you want a pet, choose this one!

I saw some twining their long tentacles together at the aquarium, and it was so pretty! These jellies are as beautiful as their name suggests, and easy to keep at home, too.

Photo credit: Tsuruoka City Kamo Aquarium

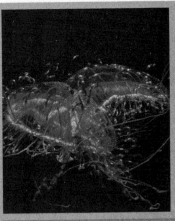

Photo credit: Tsuruoka City Kamo Aquarium

Mastigias papua

(Spotted Jelly)

Tsukimi Note

It's got a cute mushroom-like shape. Popular at aquariums!

My pet Clara is one of these. The Japanese name *tako kurage* comes from how its eight oral arms make it look like a *tako* (octopus). The white polka dots are so pretty.

Olindias formosus

(Flower Hat Jelly)

Tsukimi Note

These pink, yellow, and green tentacles are popular overseas, too.

Their tentacles are so colorful. Flower hat jellies have been exported from Japan to aquariums overseas, where they're quite popular.

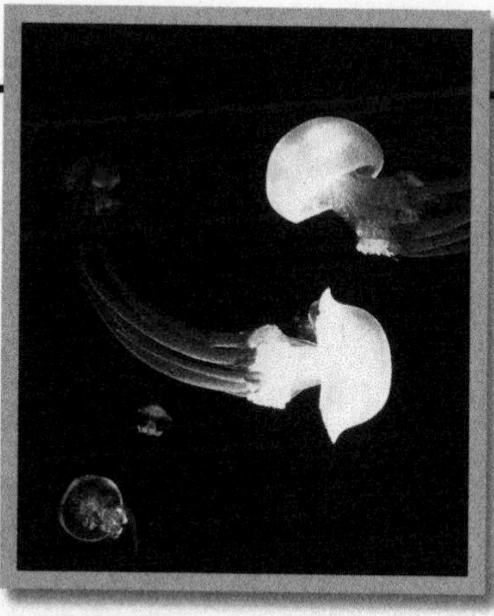

Photo credit: Tsuruoka City Kamo Aquarium

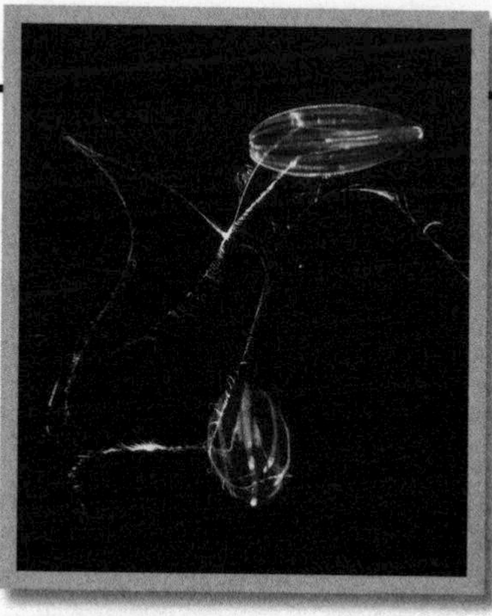

Photo credit: Tsuruoka City Kamo Aquarium

Rhopilema esculentum

(Flame Jellyfish)

Tsukimi Note

An edible jellyfish once considered a fitting gift for the Imperial Court.

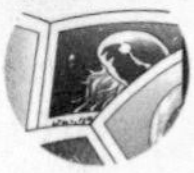

In Japanese, these jellies are named after the Bizen area in Okayama Prefecture. They're ranked highly among the jellies served as food, and I've heard that there are records of them being gifted to the Imperial Court during the Nara period.

Hormiphora palmata

(a type of Cydippid Jellyfish)

Tsukimi Note

It bobs through the water dangling its long tentacles.

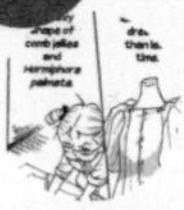

These are 3cm jellies, with bodies shaped like rugby balls and long tentacles with lateral branches. They wrap these tentacles around their prey to capture and eat it.

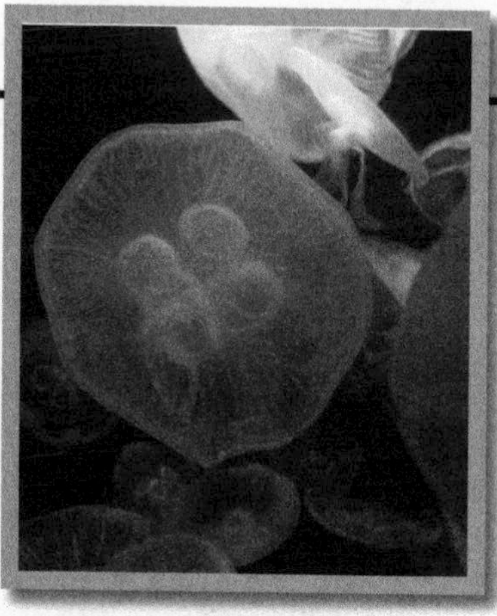

Photo credit: Tsuruoka City Kamo Aquarium

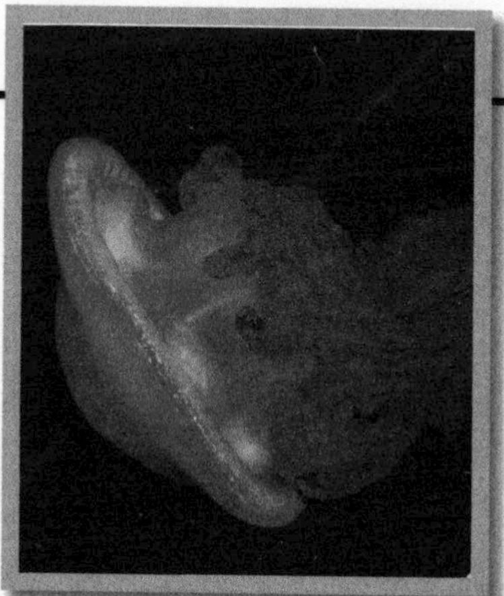

Photo credit: Tsuruoka City Kamo Aquarium

Aurelia aurita

(Moon Jelly)

Tsukimi Note

The most commonly seen jelly in Japanese waters.

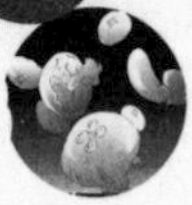

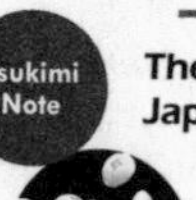

Moon jellies are tricky pets, but they're extremely popular at aquariums, and they are better researched than any other jelly. Just remember, never put one in a tank with a spotted jelly!

Thysanostoma thysanura

(a type of Rhizostome jellyfish)

Tsukimi Note

It looks like a spotted jelly, but in a beautiful purple.

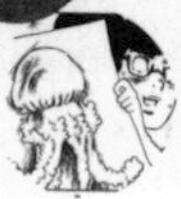

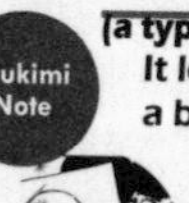

Although in Japanese we call these "*murasaki* (purple) jellies," they also come in other colors, like yellowish-brown. By the way, there are still a lot of scientific mysteries about jellyfish body colors.

Top-Secret Long Interview

AKIKO HIGASHIMURA

Akiko Higashimura Long Interview

Part 1

How did manga artist Akiko Higashimura come to be, and how has she survived the manga industry...? We did a long interview with her, beginning with a look back at her childhood! It's full of statements both surprising and unsurprising.

Her elementary school life, when she aimed to make it safely through each year

—As I understand it, you're from Miyazaki, but you bounced between several elementary schools in Kyushu.

Higashimura: I transferred five times in elementary school and twice in middle school. We hardly even furnished our homes, because we knew we'd just move again anyway.

....

We had a sort of "temporary residence" lifestyle. I still have some trauma related to moving, and I have nightmares about packing. [Laughs] So I don't want my own child to have to transfer schools much. The different Kyushu prefectures all have different dialects, and I hated that, too. But along the way, I gave up and just went with it. I'd read the social cues and do my best not to stir up trouble—to make it safely through each year, basically.

....

—Did you make friends easily?

Higashimura: I was a lively kid, so I did make them easily, but I was also kind of like, "I know I'll just make my next friends at the next place I move to, so..." Maybe this sounds cold, but I was careful to be practical and consider whoever happened to be living nearby to be my friends at the time.

—Do you think your experiences and feelings from back then influence your manga now?

Higashimura: Hmm... I suppose I haven't written superficial things like, "We'll always be together!" or "We'll still be friends even if we're far apart!"

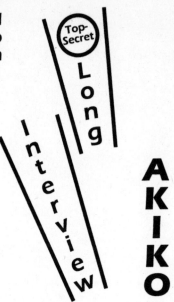

"I don't write superficial manga that says things like 'We'll always be together!'"

The "How glorious I am, reading a jellyfish field guide" attitude is mortifying to think of!

Her high school life as a "fool" for complicating things

—Your fans are familiar with this from *Himawari: Kenichi Legend*, but you were a Hideaki Tokunaga addict.

Higashimura: I think I was in sixth grade. I thought it was really sexy how he managed to be so handsome even with those uneven teeth. I fell for him hard. I'm talking about a "Yep, this is the man I'm gonna marry!" level of crush. I spent my New Year's money buying up all of his merchandise. I created my own original posters, too.

—How did you do that?

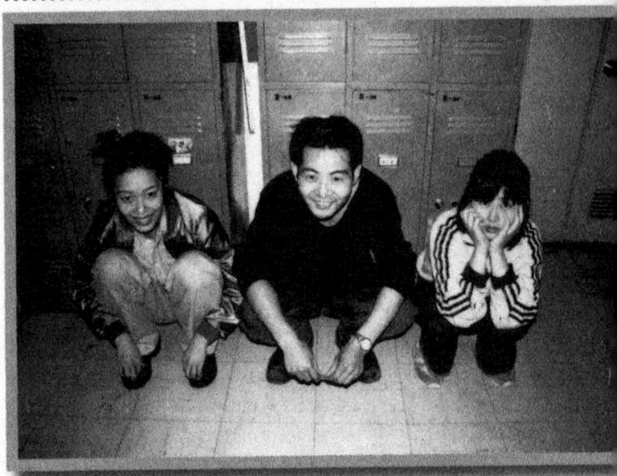

Higashimura-sensei (right) in her second year of art college. She claims to have skipped all her classes to sit in the oil painting studio hallway.

Higashimura: Huh? You never did that? I'd cut photos out of magazines and paste them on big sheets of imitation vellum. There'd be about 150 Tokunagas per poster. [Laughs]

—As for other famous people you got hooked on, in high school there was the marathon runner Koichi Morishita.

Higashimura: That was during the Barcelona Olympics, so I would've been in my second year of high school. It ended with him getting married. [Laughs] And the bride was the daughter of the best friend of a friend of a friend of mine, or something like that.

—So you were close in the sense of "not utterly unconnected," then.

Higashimura: If only he'd married a celebrity! [Laughs] Not that I was even close, really. I was a kid, after all.

—Was that around the time you got hooked on jellyfish, too?

Higashimura: Yes. I've been hooked on them ever since I visited that Kagoshima aquarium on a friend outing.

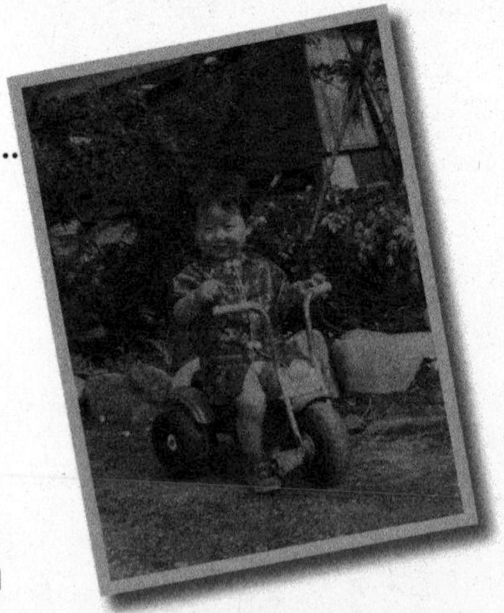

Joyriding through the garden in the outfit her father brought her from a trip to China.

Even though there was no festival that day, her father dressed her in a happi coat and took a snapshot. She says she doesn't remember ever being in a single local festival.

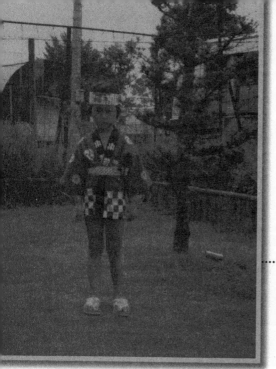

I really did like them, but it's mortifying to think of how that "I'm not like other people, you know!" sentiment was mixed in there. So uncool, right? Like, "Look at how glorious I am, reading a jellyfish field guide like this." When the actual truth is, is that the people reading normal stuff like *nonno* fashion magazine were living life as a girl so much better! I was the fool for complicating things!!

She took it for granted that she'd become a manga artist

—Have you liked to draw since you were a child?

Higashimura: Yes. And I'm grateful to my parents, because they always gave me the freedom to draw like I wanted to. You know, I had eight years of piano lessons, and the only thing I can play now is "*Neko Funjatta*." Once, I started spinning around on the piano stool so fast that I got thrown off of it and bled from a head wound. It took four stitches to close up. And that's all I remember about piano lessons. [Laughs] I think drawing and music may be genetic to some extent. Even if you train hard, you can't do what you can't do, I think.

—When did you start wanting to become a manga artist?

Higashimura: I'd always figured that's what would happen, since before I can remember. I took it for granted.

—When did you draw your first manga?

Higashimura: Fifth grade. It was a gag manga, with my classmates as the characters. I only showed it to the kids I was friends with, but it was stupidly popular with them. They were dying for sequels, so I just kept on going.

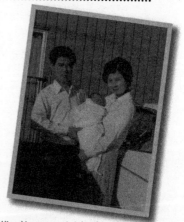

Higashimura-sensei right after she was born in 1975, with her parents, of course.

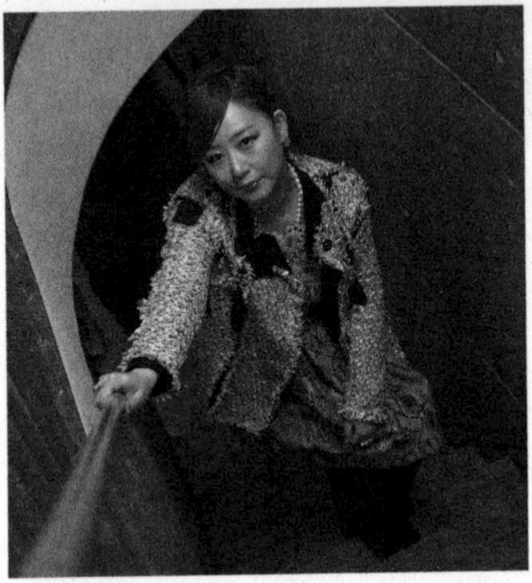

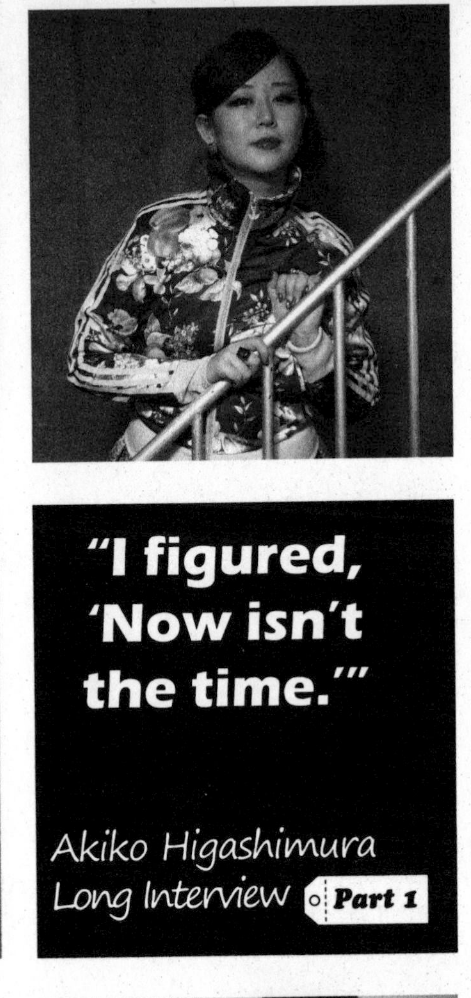

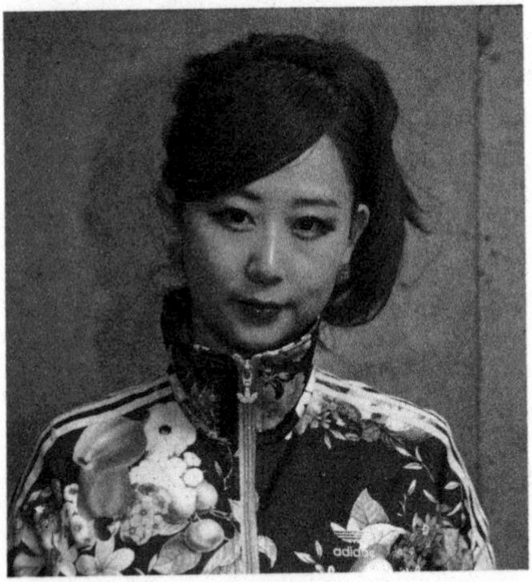

"I figured, 'Now isn't the time.'"

Akiko Higashimura
Long Interview **Part 1**

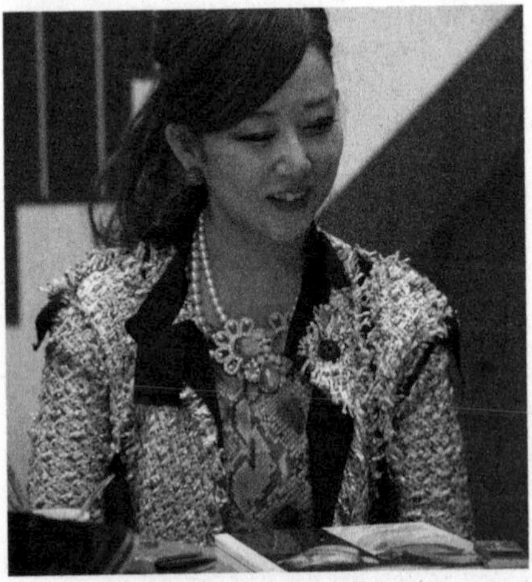

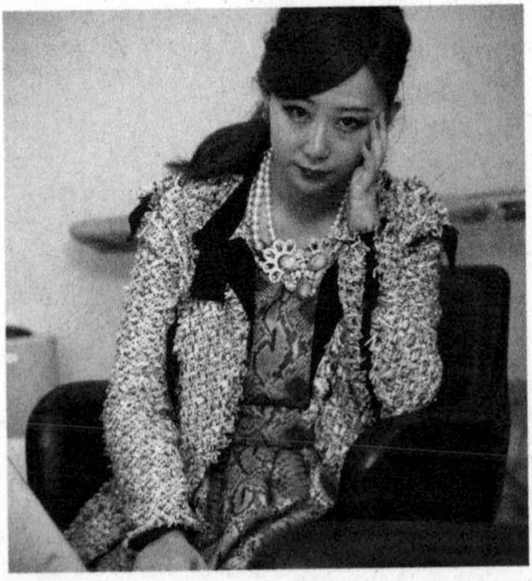

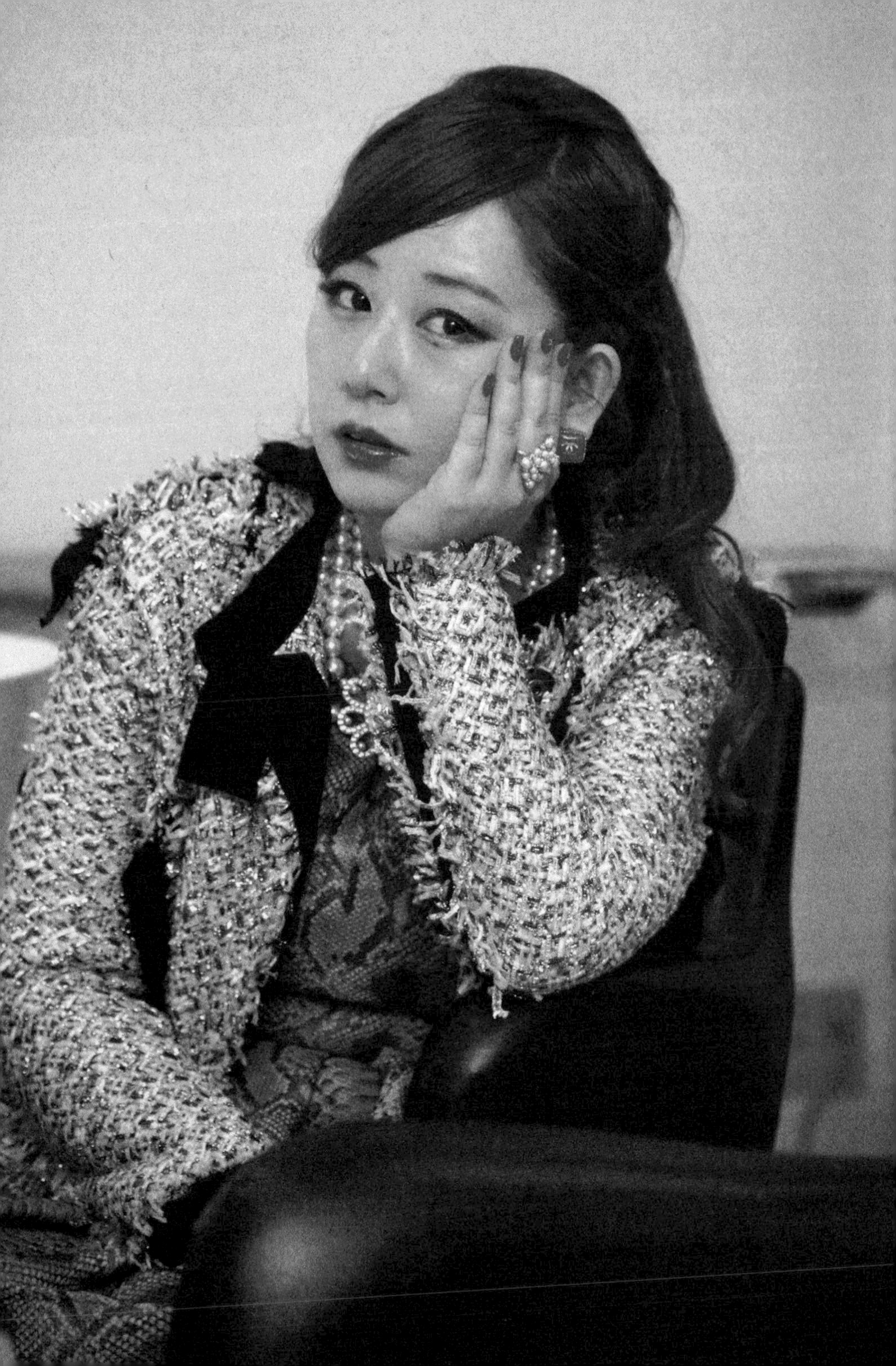

She didn't draw a single page of manga in middle or high school.

I was uncommonly influenced by A-min Okada, so it was a jokes-about-freaks type manga. I think that around this time, a concept of humor formed inside me that wasn't just about manga. These days, when I watch a comedy program on TV, if none of the comedians strike me as being from A-min World, I just don't find it funny.

—A-min World, eh?

Higashimura: I suppose you could call it comedy that isn't a fool-and-straight-man setup, and isn't surreal, either.

—During middle and high school, and even after you entered the Kanazawa College of Art, you didn't draw manga.

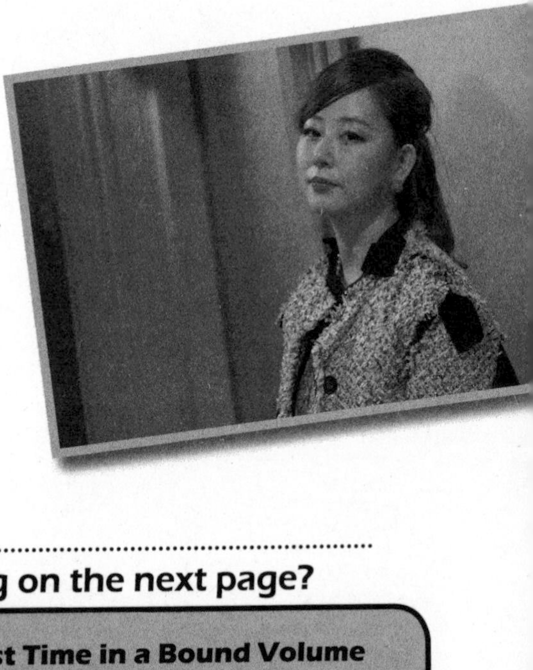

Higashimura: Not even a single page. It's like... I believed I could draw a masterpiece when the time was right, but I thought, "now isn't the time." I told myself, "It'll be my debut work, so when I draw it, I'd better draw it at the right time, in an environment where I can give it my all, and make it a true masterpiece." ...Which is the classic thought process of a deadbeat who never actually starts drawing, isn't it? [Laughs]

—But it didn't end there...

(To be continued in Part 2!)

What's starting on the next page?

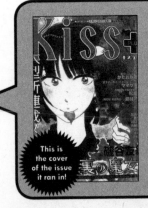

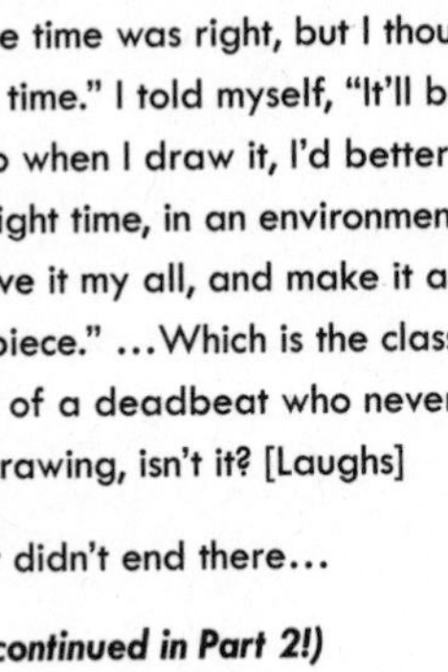
Kiss
This is the cover of the issue it ran in!

First Time in a Bound Volume
Princess Jellyfish Heroes☆

(From the Jan. 2010 issue of Kiss PLUS)

An elusive chapter of the *Princess Jellyfish* side-stories

Starting on the next page is a chapter of *Princess Jellyfish Heroes*☆ that never made it into the collected manga because it was the basis for an anime DVD extra. Please enjoy Chieko—Traditional-Japan Otaku, the Conscience of Amars—along with all her ***profound*** troubles!

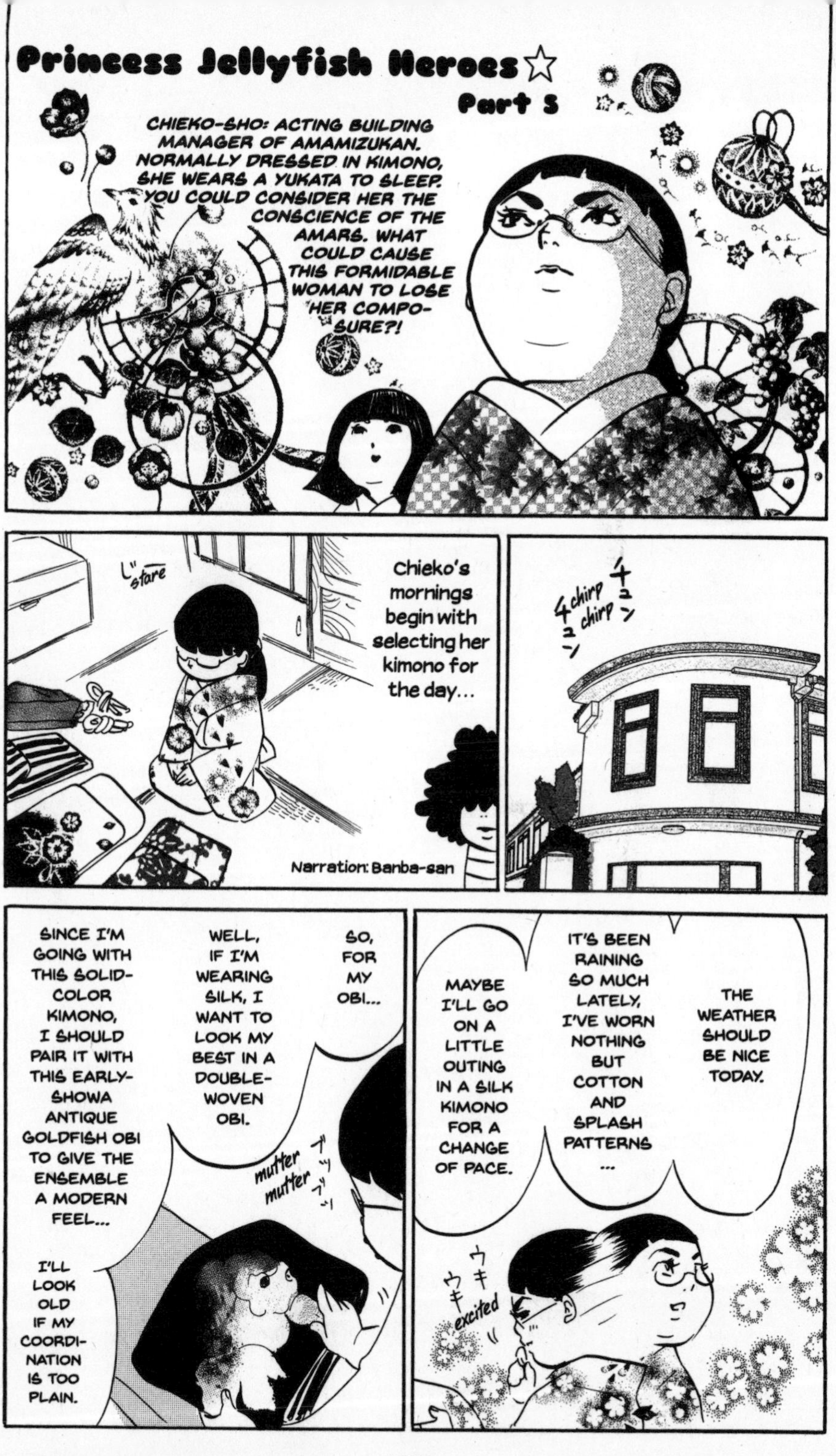
Princess Jellyfish Heroes☆
Part 5
CHIEKO-SHO: ACTING BUILDING MANAGER OF AMAMIZUKAN. NORMALLY DRESSED IN KIMONO, SHE WEARS A YUKATA TO SLEEP. YOU COULD CONSIDER HER THE CONSCIENCE OF THE AMARS. WHAT COULD CAUSE THIS FORMIDABLE WOMAN TO LOSE HER COMPOSURE?!
chirp chirp
Chieko's mornings begin with selecting her kimono for the day...
stare
Narration: Banba-san
THE WEATHER SHOULD BE NICE TODAY.
IT'S BEEN RAINING SO MUCH LATELY, I'VE WORN NOTHING BUT COTTON AND SPLASH PATTERNS...
MAYBE I'LL GO ON A LITTLE OUTING IN A SILK KIMONO FOR A CHANGE OF PACE.
excited
SO, FOR MY OBI...
WELL, IF I'M WEARING SILK, I WANT TO LOOK MY BEST IN A DOUBLE-WOVEN OBI.
SINCE I'M GOING WITH THIS SOLID-COLOR KIMONO, I SHOULD PAIR IT WITH THIS EARLY-SHOWA ANTIQUE GOLDFISH OBI TO GIVE THE ENSEMBLE A MODERN FEEL...
mutter mutter
I'LL LOOK OLD IF MY COORDINATION IS TOO PLAIN.

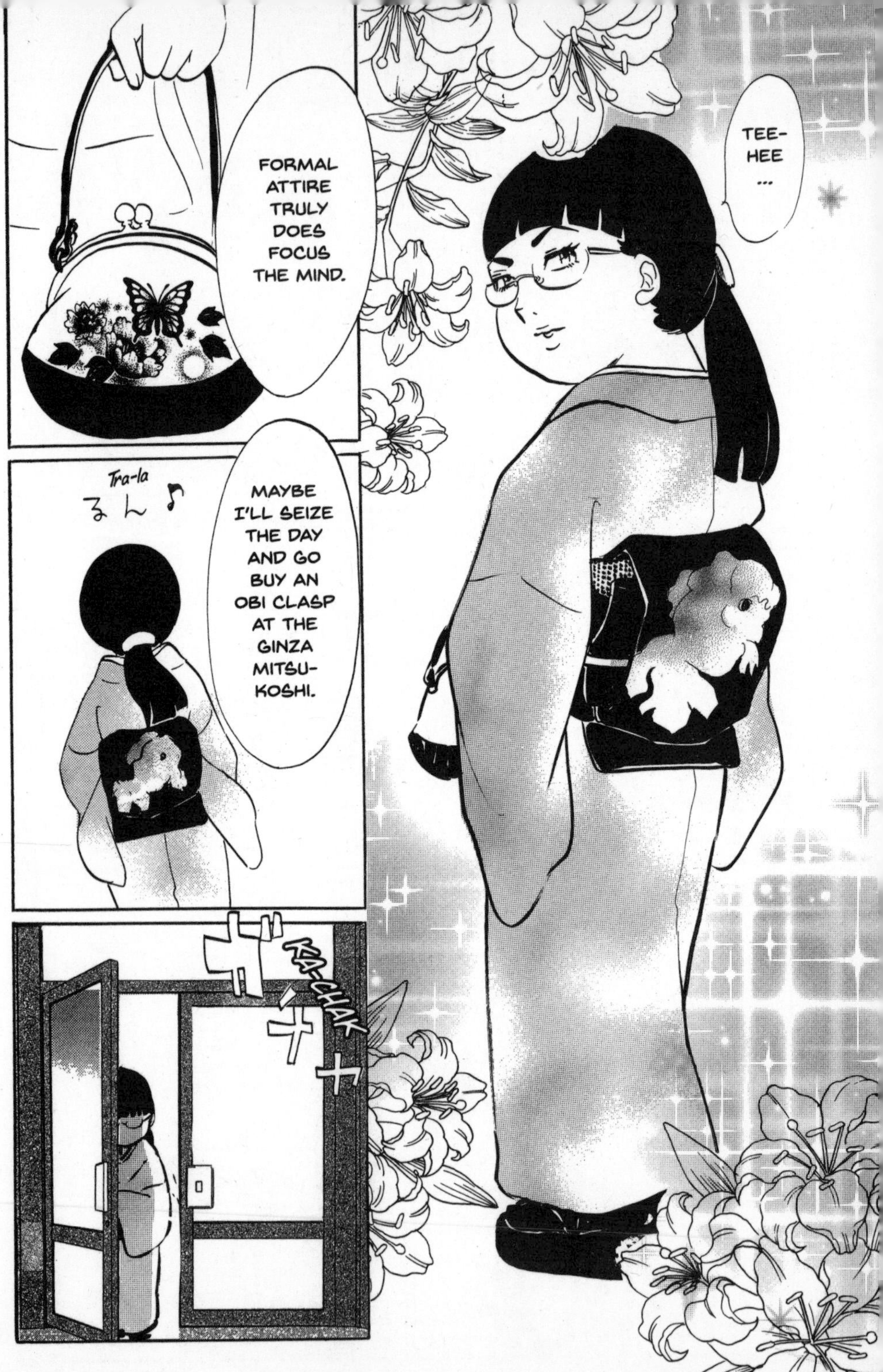
TEE-HEE ...
FORMAL ATTIRE TRULY DOES FOCUS THE MIND.
Tra-la
るん♪
MAYBE I'LL SEIZE THE DAY AND GO BUY AN OBI CLASP AT THE GINZA MITSU-KOSHI.
KA-CHAK

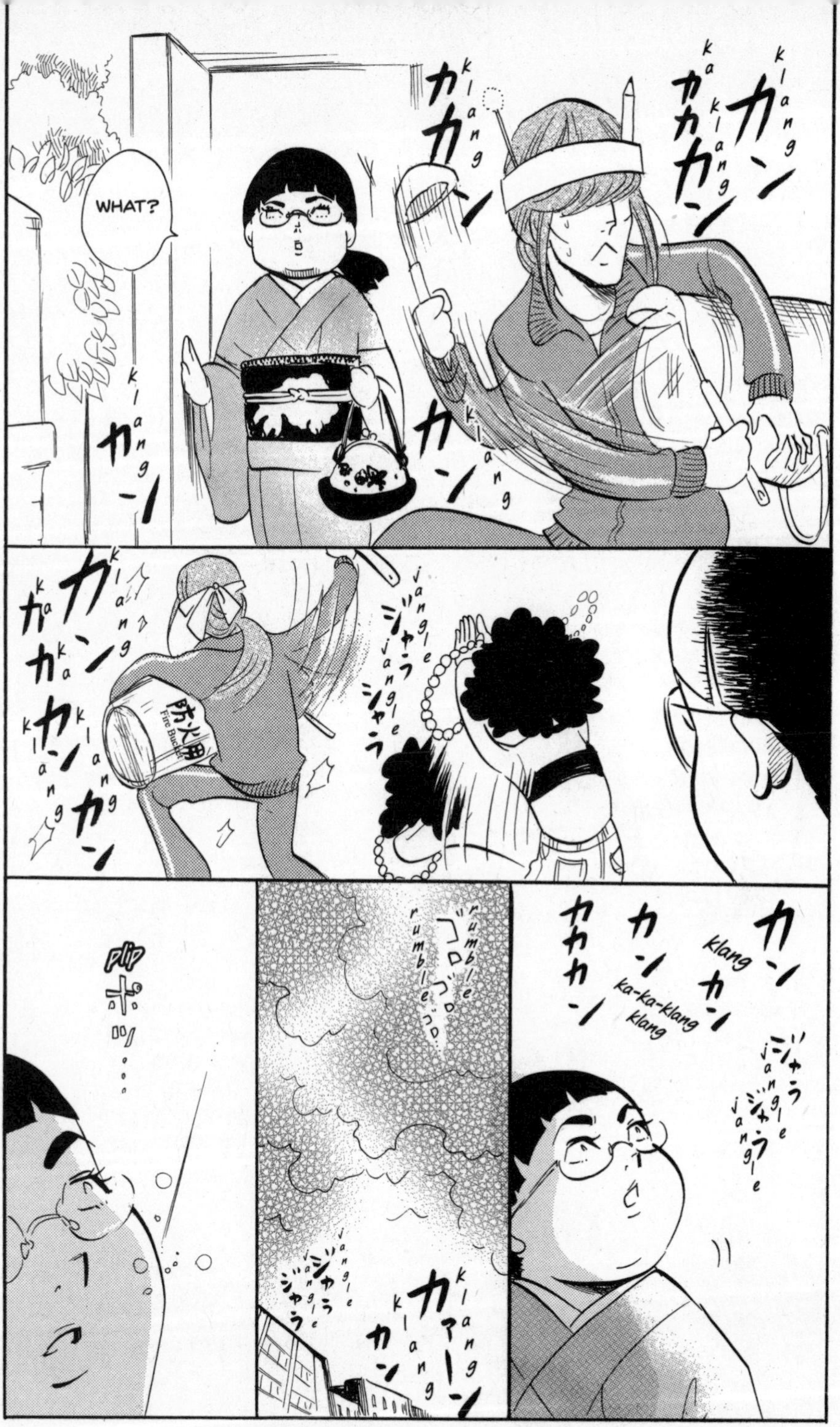

カン klang
カカカン ka-klang-klang
カカン klang
WHAT?
カン klang
カン klang
カン klang
カカカン ka-ka-klang
カン klang
防火用
Fire Bucket
ジャラジャラ jangle jangle
カン klang
カン klang
ka-ka-klang klang
カカカン
ジャラジャラ jangle jangle
ゴロゴロ… rumble rumble
カァーン klang
カン klang
ジャラジャラ jangle jangle
plip
ポツ…

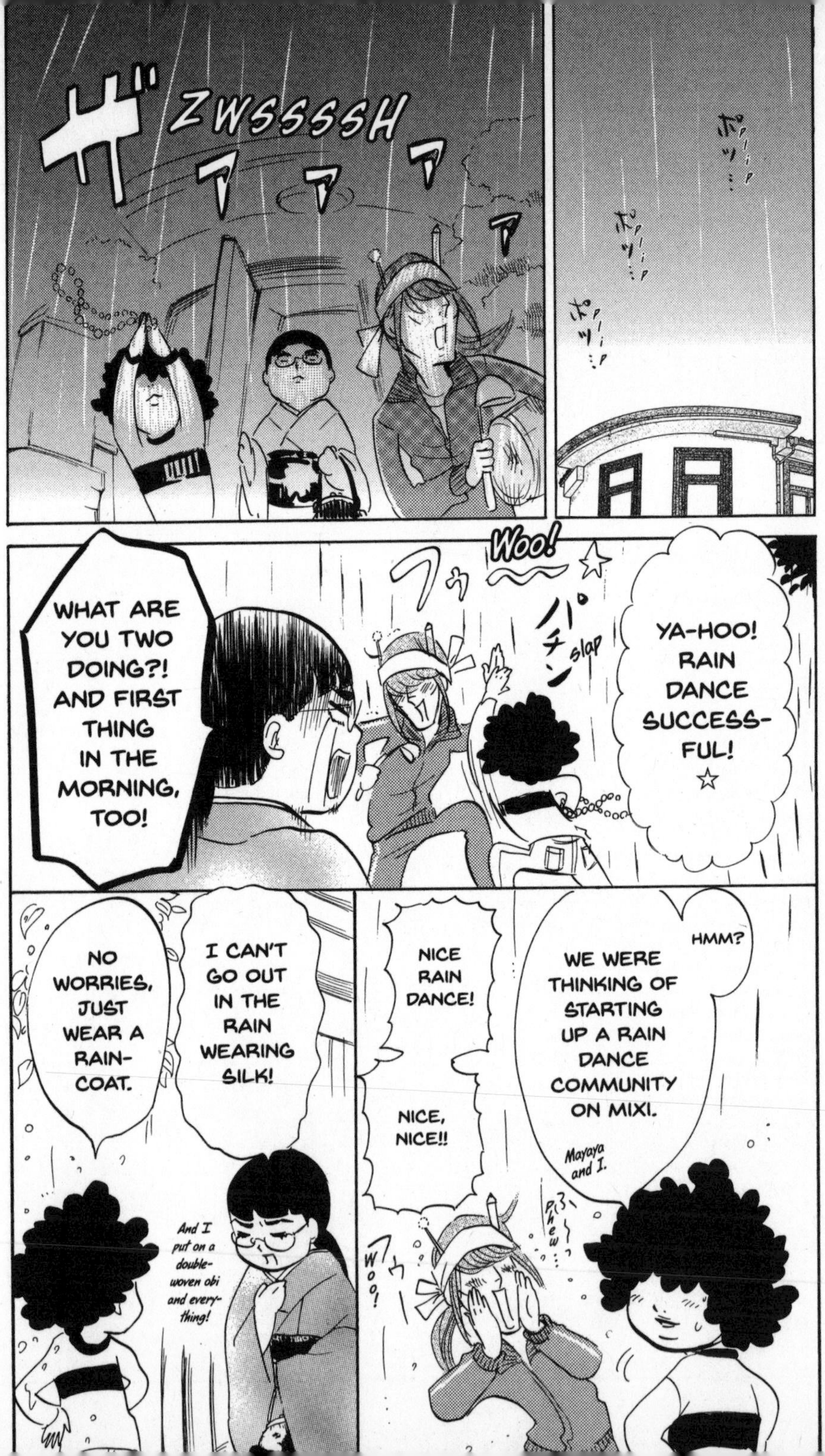
ポツ… p p p
ポツ… p p p
ポツ… p p p
ザァァァァ ZWSSSSH
YA-HOO! RAIN DANCE SUCCESSFUL! ☆
Woo! ☆
パチン slap
WHAT ARE YOU TWO DOING?! AND FIRST THING IN THE MORNING, TOO!
HMM?
WE WERE THINKING OF STARTING UP A RAIN DANCE COMMUNITY ON MIXI.
Mayaya and I.
NICE RAIN DANCE!
NICE, NICE!!
Phew
Woo!
I CAN'T GO OUT IN THE RAIN WEARING SILK!
And I put on a double-woven obi and everything!
NO WORRIES, JUST WEAR A RAIN-COAT.

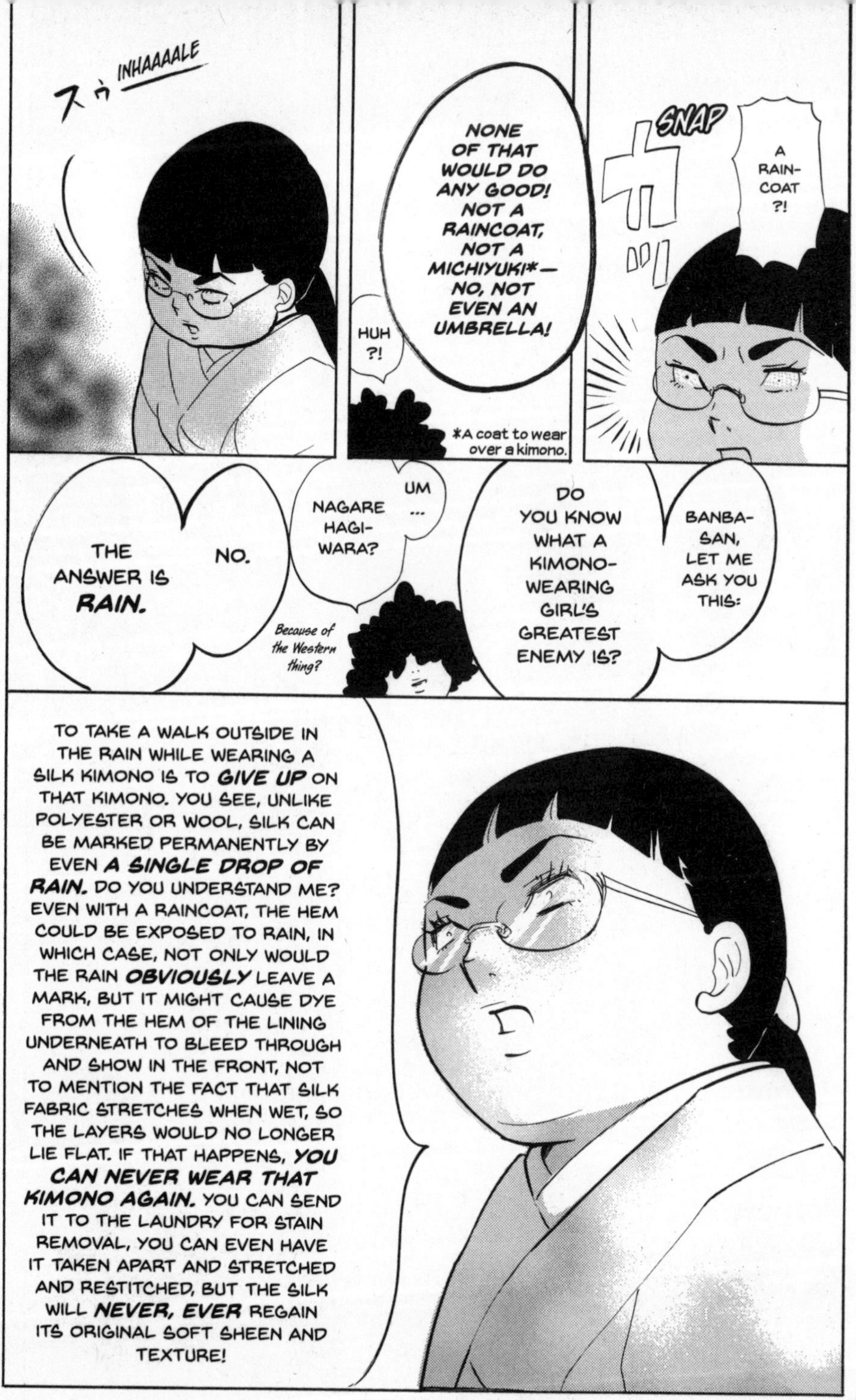
SNAP
A RAINCOAT ?!
NONE OF THAT WOULD DO ANY GOOD! NOT A RAINCOAT, NOT A MICHIYUKI*— NO, NOT EVEN AN UMBRELLA!
HUH ?!
*A coat to wear over a kimono.
スゥ INHAAAALE
BANBA-SAN, LET ME ASK YOU THIS:
DO YOU KNOW WHAT A KIMONO-WEARING GIRL'S GREATEST ENEMY IS?
UM ...
NAGARE HAGIWARA?
Because of the Western thing?
NO.
THE ANSWER IS RAIN.
TO TAKE A WALK OUTSIDE IN THE RAIN WHILE WEARING A SILK KIMONO IS TO GIVE UP ON THAT KIMONO. YOU SEE, UNLIKE POLYESTER OR WOOL, SILK CAN BE MARKED PERMANENTLY BY EVEN A SINGLE DROP OF RAIN. DO YOU UNDERSTAND ME? EVEN WITH A RAINCOAT, THE HEM COULD BE EXPOSED TO RAIN, IN WHICH CASE, NOT ONLY WOULD THE RAIN OBVIOUSLY LEAVE A MARK, BUT IT MIGHT CAUSE DYE FROM THE HEM OF THE LINING UNDERNEATH TO BLEED THROUGH AND SHOW IN THE FRONT, NOT TO MENTION THE FACT THAT SILK FABRIC STRETCHES WHEN WET, SO THE LAYERS WOULD NO LONGER LIE FLAT. IF THAT HAPPENS, YOU CAN NEVER WEAR THAT KIMONO AGAIN. YOU CAN SEND IT TO THE LAUNDRY FOR STAIN REMOVAL, YOU CAN EVEN HAVE IT TAKEN APART AND STRETCHED AND RESTITCHED, BUT THE SILK WILL NEVER, EVER REGAIN ITS ORIGINAL SOFT SHEEN AND TEXTURE!

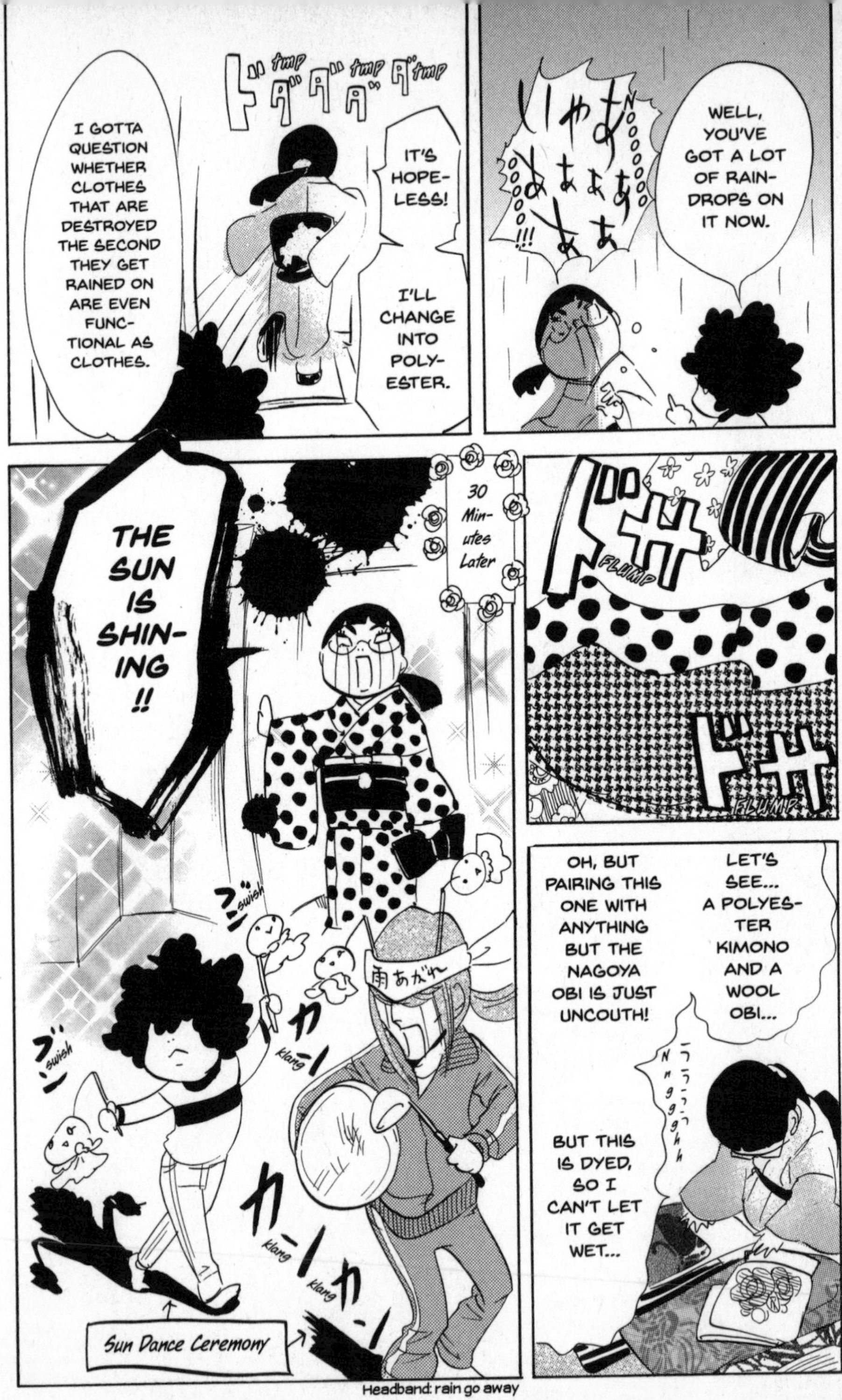
Noooooooooooo!!!
WELL, YOU'VE GOT A LOT OF RAIN-DROPS ON IT NOW.
tmp tmp tmp tmp
IT'S HOPE-LESS!
I'LL CHANGE INTO POLY-ESTER.
I GOTTA QUESTION WHETHER CLOTHES THAT ARE DESTROYED THE SECOND THEY GET RAINED ON ARE EVEN FUNC-TIONAL AS CLOTHES.
FLUMP
FLUMP
LET'S SEE... A POLYES-TER KIMONO AND A WOOL OBI...
OH, BUT PAIRING THIS ONE WITH ANYTHING BUT THE NAGOYA OBI IS JUST UNCOUTH!
Nngggghh
BUT THIS IS DYED, SO I CAN'T LET IT GET WET...
30 Minutes Later
THE SUN IS SHIN-ING!!
swish
swish
klang
klang
klang
Sun Dance Ceremony
雨あがれ

Headband: rain go away

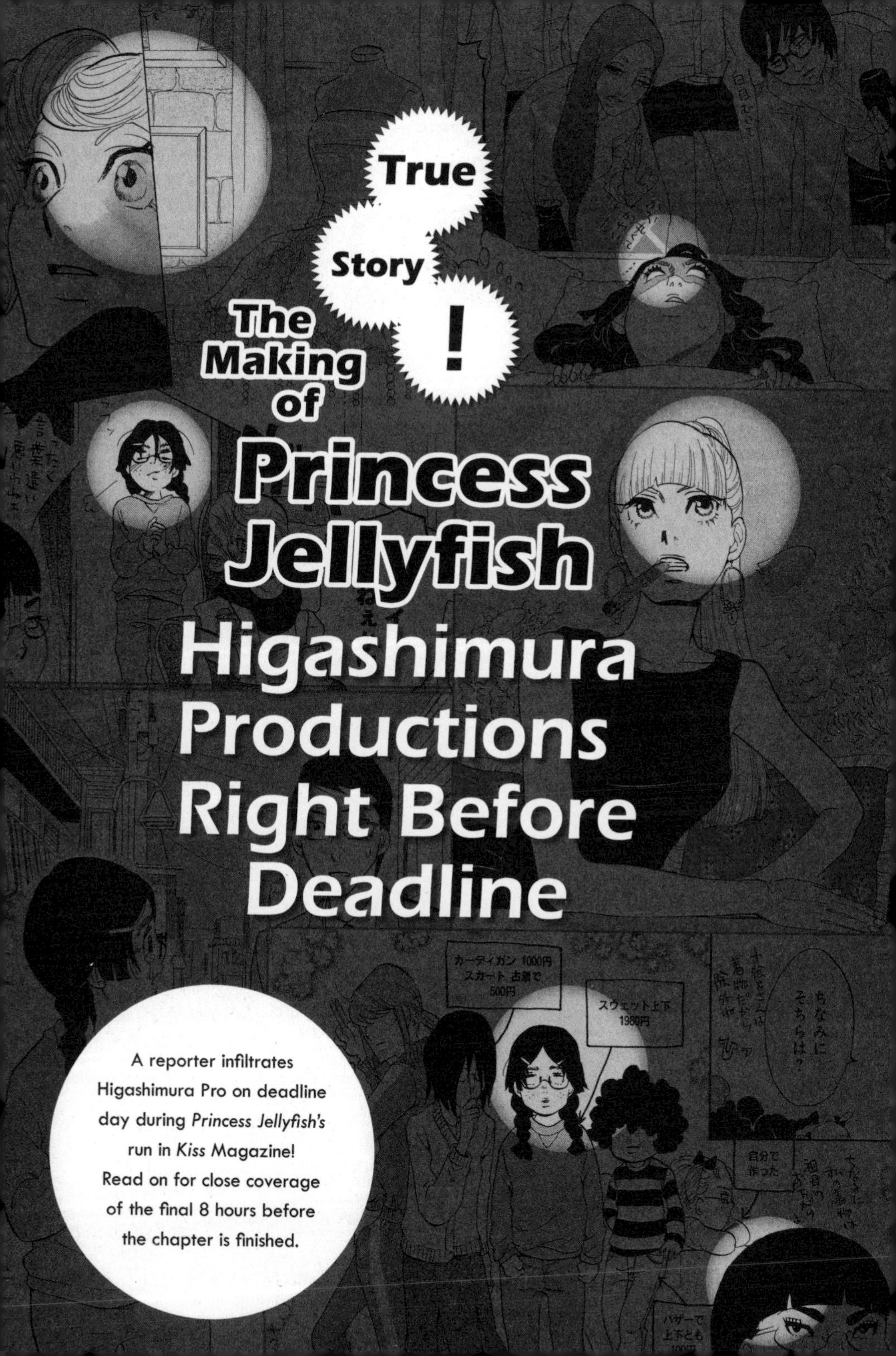
カーディガン 1000円
スカート 古着で
500円
スウェット上下
1980円
ちなみに
そちらは？
自分で
作った

True Story!

The Making of *Princess Jellyfish*

Higashimura Productions Right Before Deadline

A reporter infiltrates Higashimura Pro on deadline day during *Princess Jellyfish's* run in *Kiss* Magazine! Read on for close coverage of the final 8 hours before the chapter is finished.

1

What does PJ look like before I see it?

Princess Jellyfish storyboards revealed for the first time!

Storyboarding is like making a blueprint for your manga. Higashimura-sensei takes just one or two days to draft a full 30-page chapter. What's more, apparently she can storyboard "during meetings" or "while chitchatting."

10% Complete

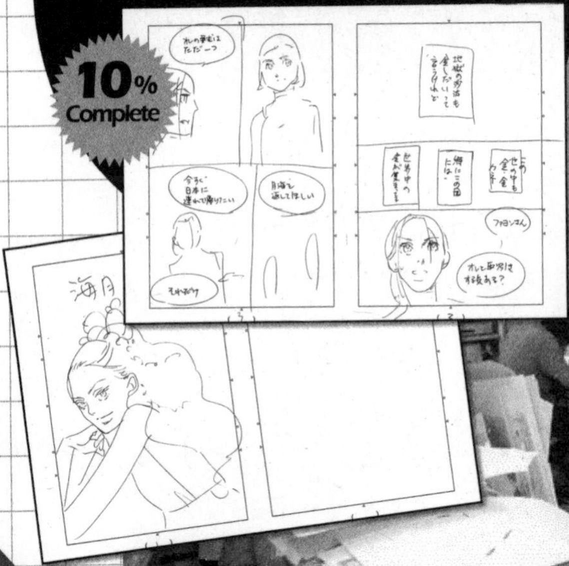

I expected a disaster zone this close to deadline...but it was unexpectedly harmonious and peaceful.

More than 10 assistants are at Higashimura Pro on deadline day. As Higashimura-sensei finishes inking each page, it gets handed to assistants who handle the spot blacks, screen tones, and various other processes that bring the work closer to the finish line. It is Higashimura-sensei's policy that Higashimura Pro working hours are from 11:00 a.m. to 7:00 p.m. Their work stays on schedule to a surprising degree, and watching it actually made me feel good.

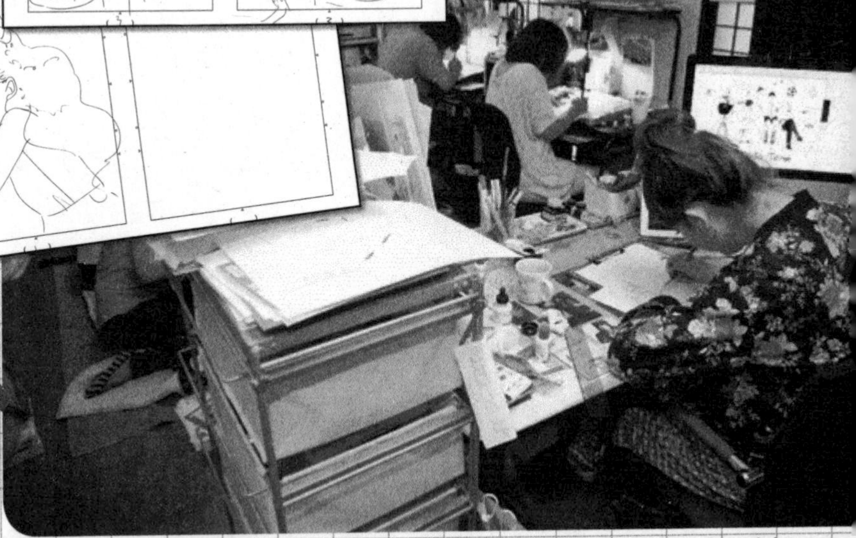

She draws her base sketch according to the storyboard, then inks one frame after another. Rumor has it she's one of the fastest in the industry.

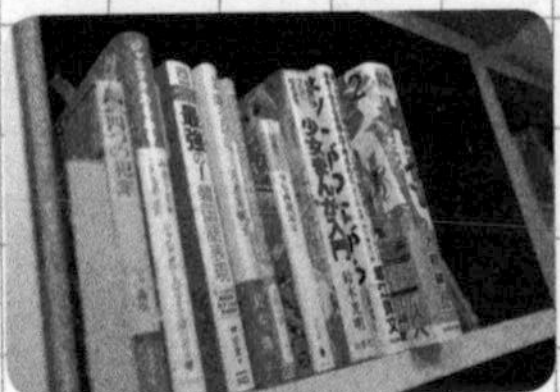

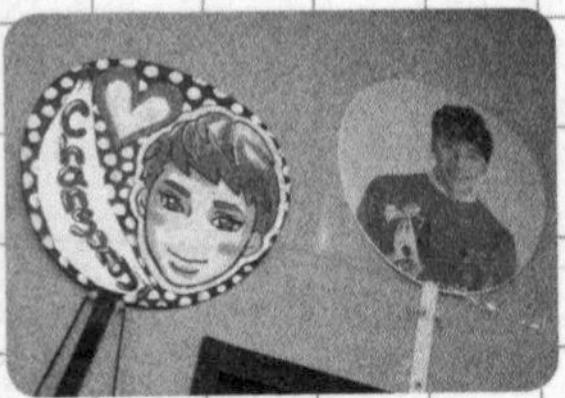

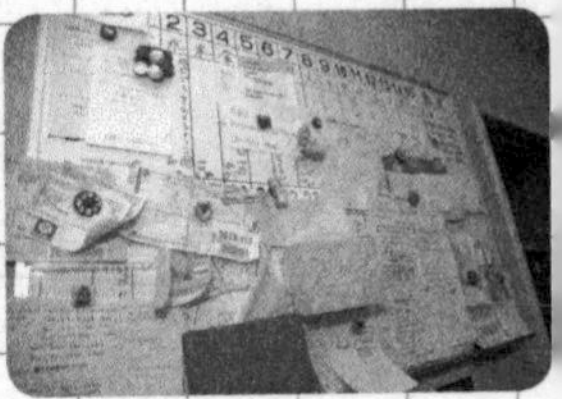

Her studio bookshelves contain manga she's hooked on, and the walls are adorned with fans featuring Korean stars, as well as a scheduling calendar.

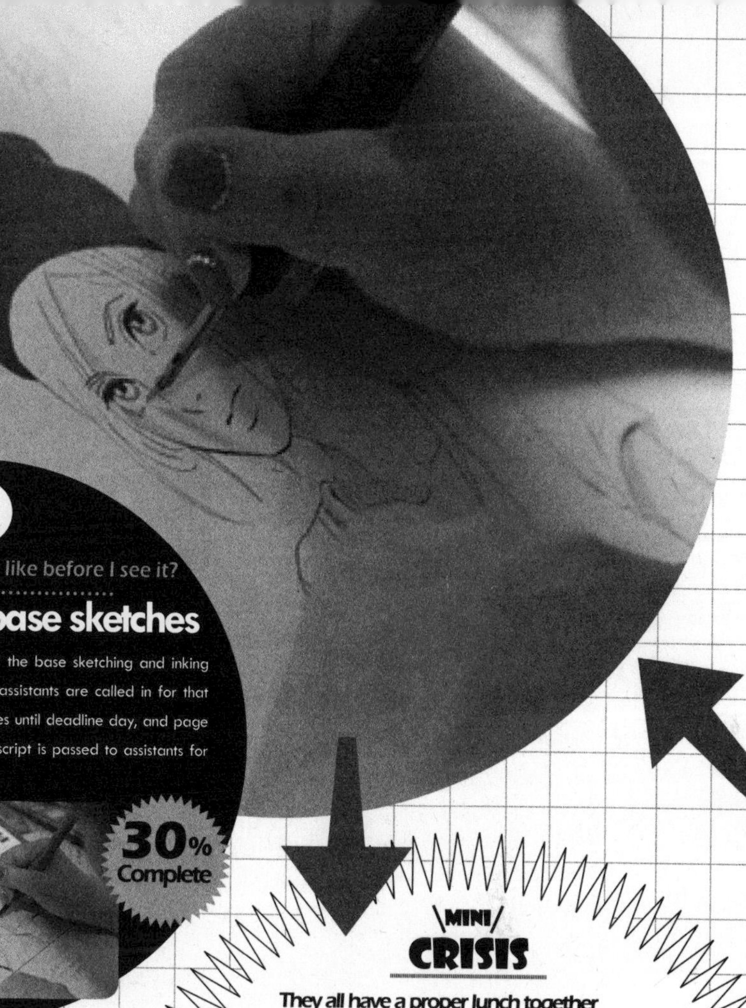

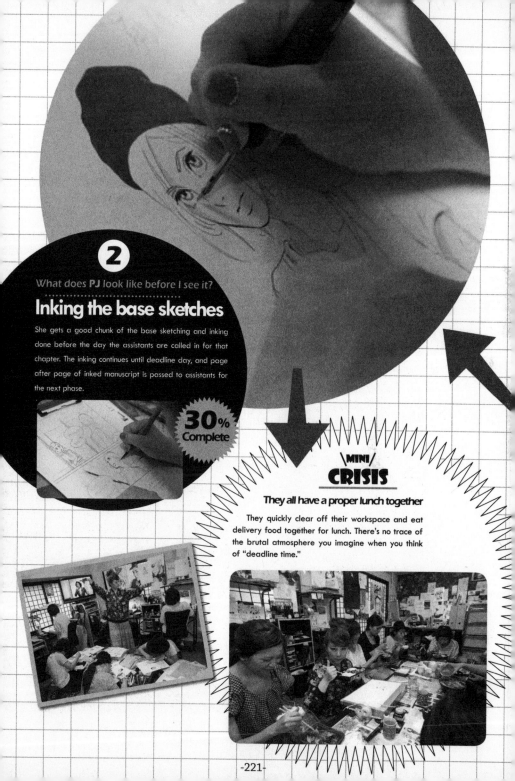

2

What does **PJ** look like before I see it?

Inking the base sketches

She gets a good chunk of the base sketching and inking done before the day the assistants are called in for that chapter. The inking continues until deadline day, and page after page of inked manuscript is passed to assistants for the next phase.

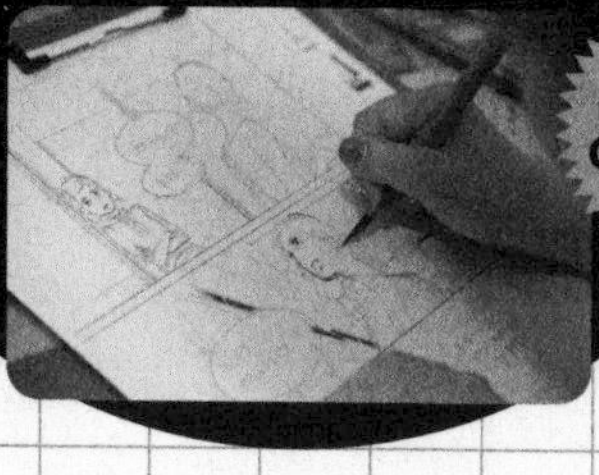

30%
Complete

MINI

CRISIS

They all have a proper lunch together

They quickly clear off their workspace and eat delivery food together for lunch. There's no trace of the brutal atmosphere you imagine when you think of "deadline time."

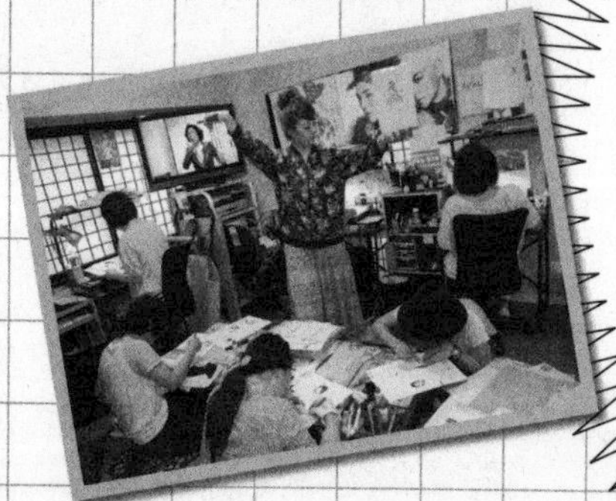

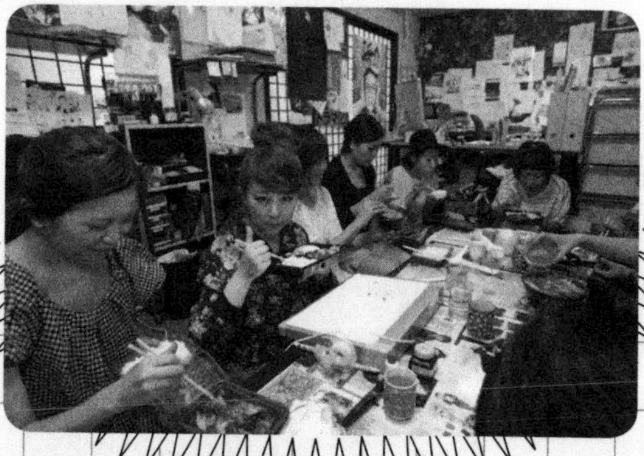

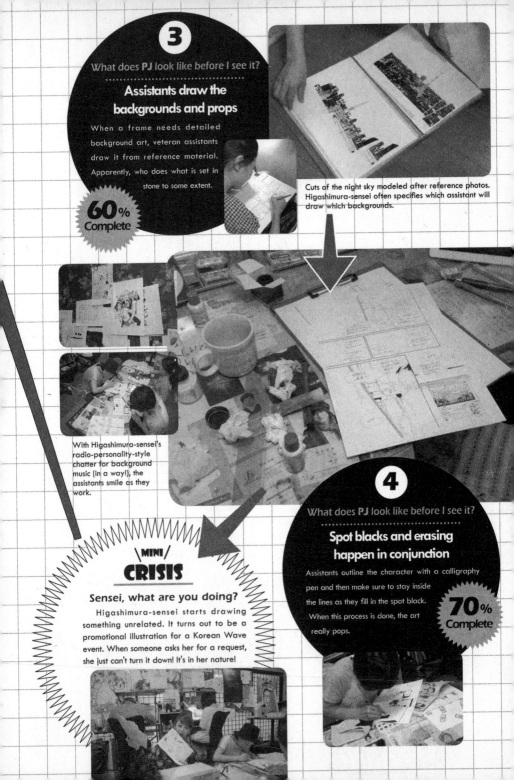

3

What does **PJ** look like before I see it?

Assistants draw the backgrounds and props

When a frame needs detailed background art, veteran assistants draw it from reference material. Apparently, who does what is set in stone to some extent.

60% Complete

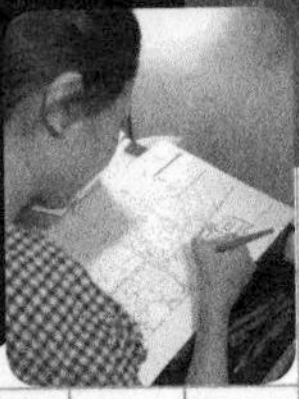

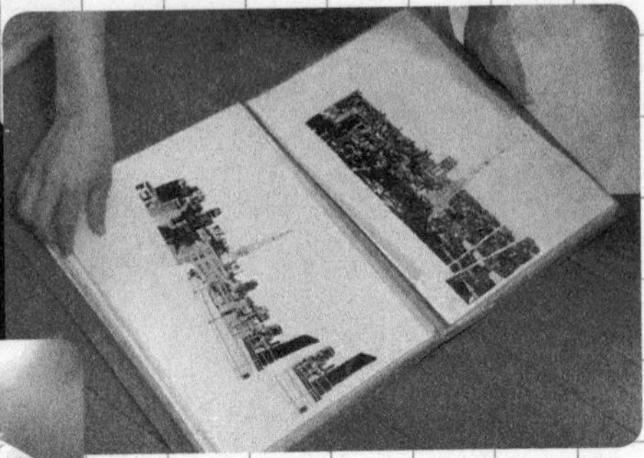

Cuts of the night sky modeled after reference photos. Higashimura-sensei often specifies which assistant will draw which backgrounds.

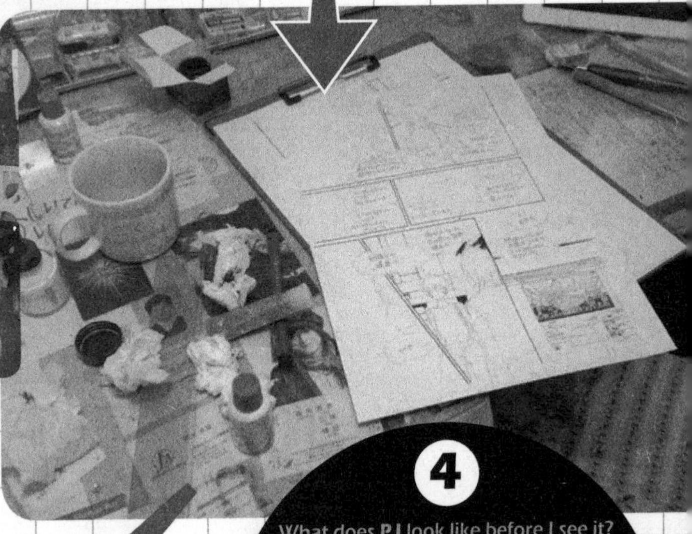

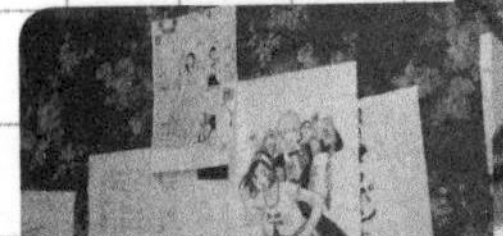

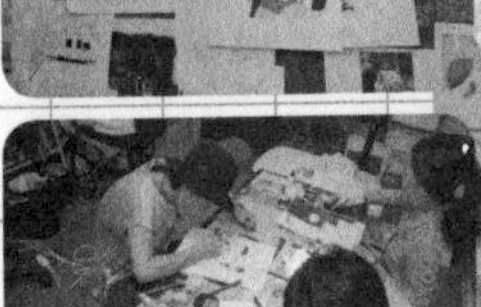

With Higashimura-sensei's radio-personality-style chatter for background music (in a way!), the assistants smile as they work.

\MINI/

CRISIS

Sensei, what are you doing?

Higashimura-sensei starts drawing something unrelated. It turns out to be a promotional illustration for a Korean Wave event. When someone asks her for a request, she just can't turn it down! It's in her nature!

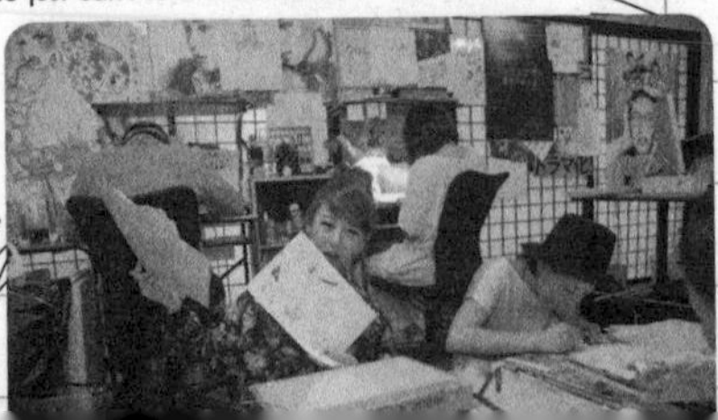

4

What does **PJ** look like before I see it?

Spot blacks and erasing happen in conjunction

Assistants outline the character with a calligraphy pen and then make sure to stay inside the lines as they fill in the spot black. When this process is done, the art really pops.

70% Complete

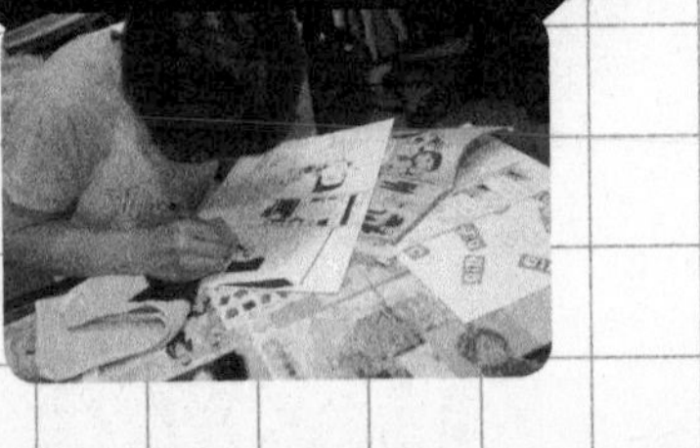

5

What does **PJ** look like before I see it?

Screen tones as designated

Princess Jellyfish uses screen tones more often than Higashimura-sensei's other works. The patterns are cut and applied to the designated areas at a tremendous speed.

80% Complete

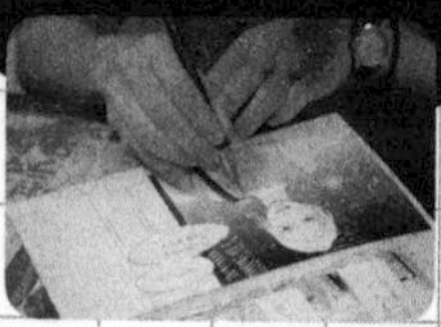

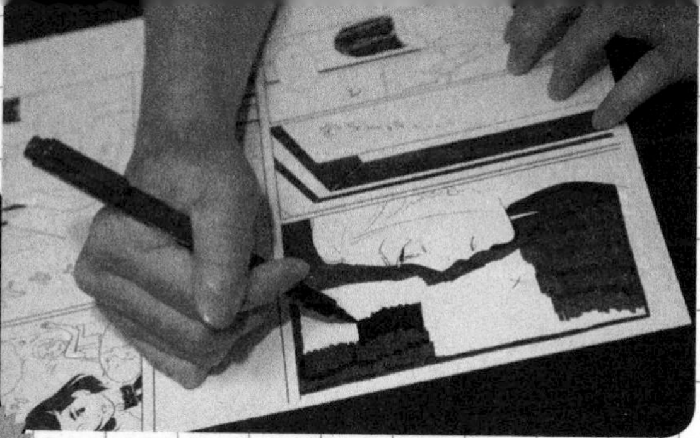

As evening falls and the 7:00 p.m. deadline looms, a sense of urgency gradually builds. There's less talking, and work continues in silence.

MINI

CRISIS

Group snack time

When the assistants are more or less done with their parts, everyone pauses to enjoy some sweets provided by the editor. The manuscript enters its final check by Higashimura-sensei.

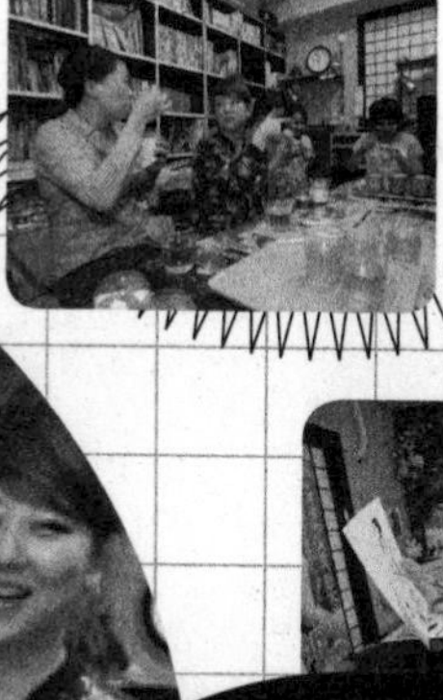

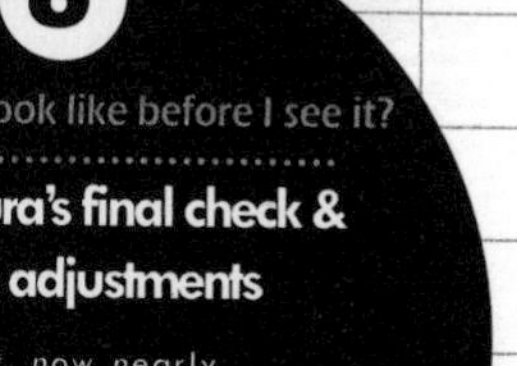

6

What does **PJ** look like before I see it?

Higashimura's final check & minute adjustments

The manuscript, now nearly complete, returns to Higashimura-sensei for a final check. Adjustments are made to small details like the tips of a character's hair.

90% Complete

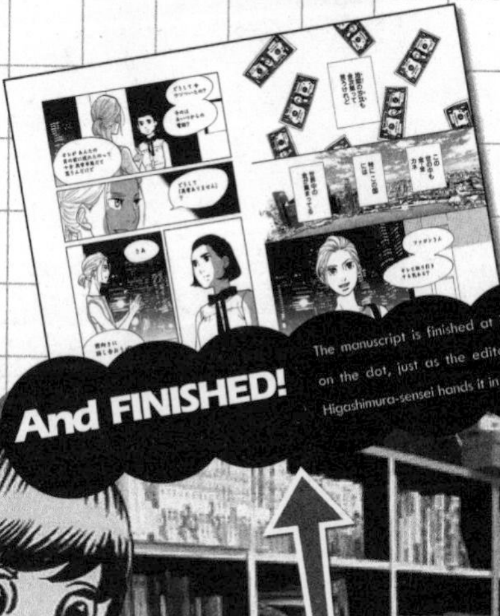

And FINISHED!

The manuscript is finished at 7:00 p.m. on the dot, just as the editor arrives! Higashimura-sensei hands it in personally.

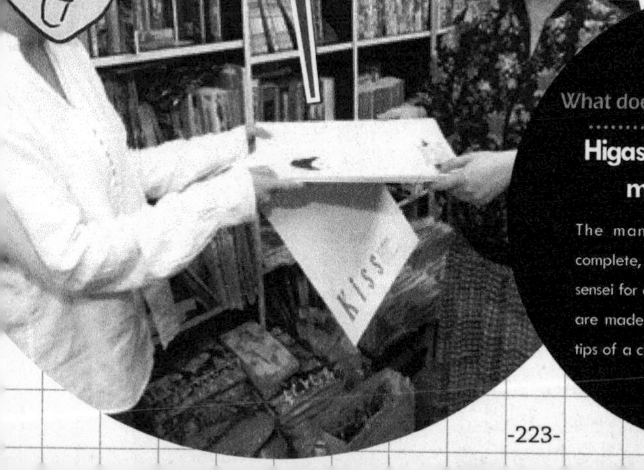

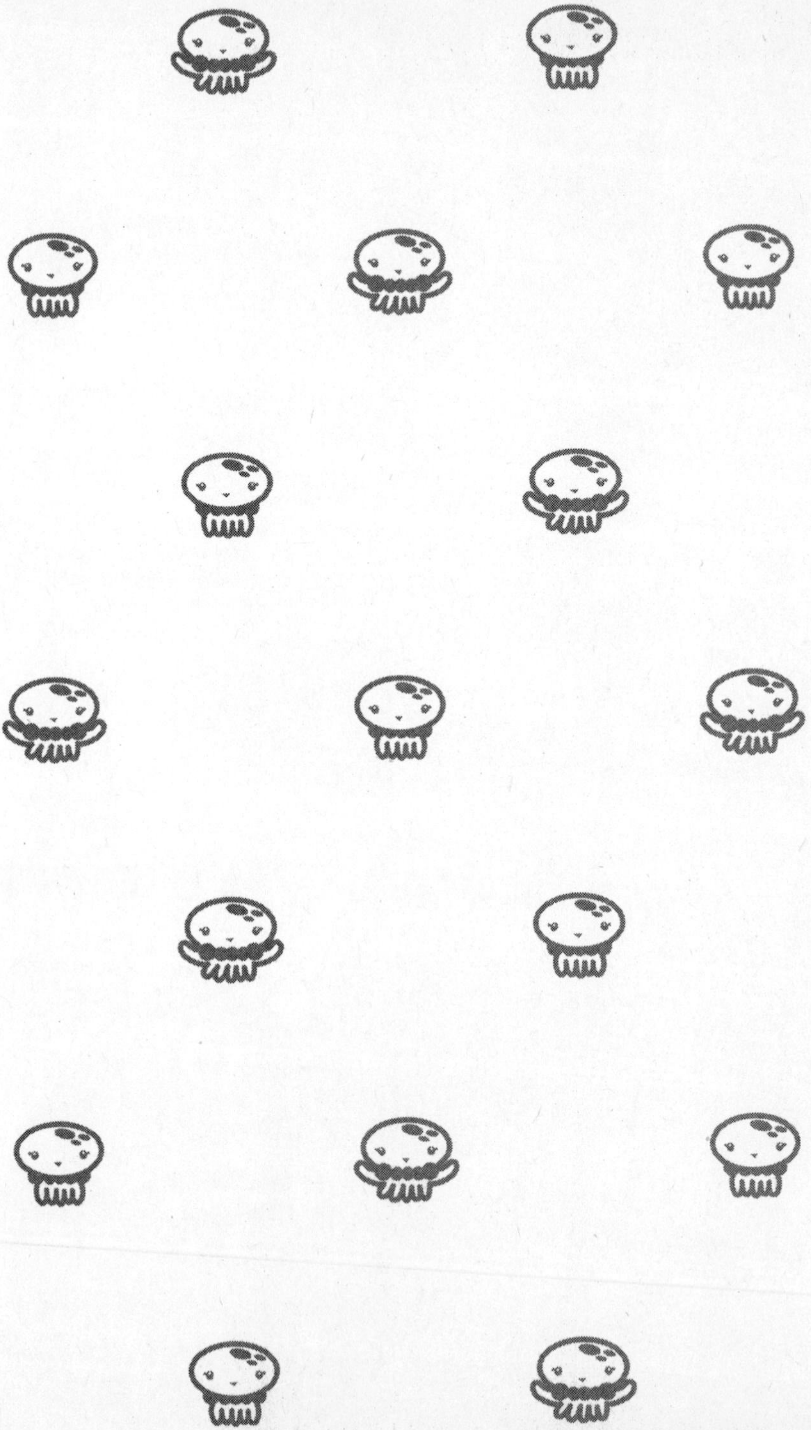

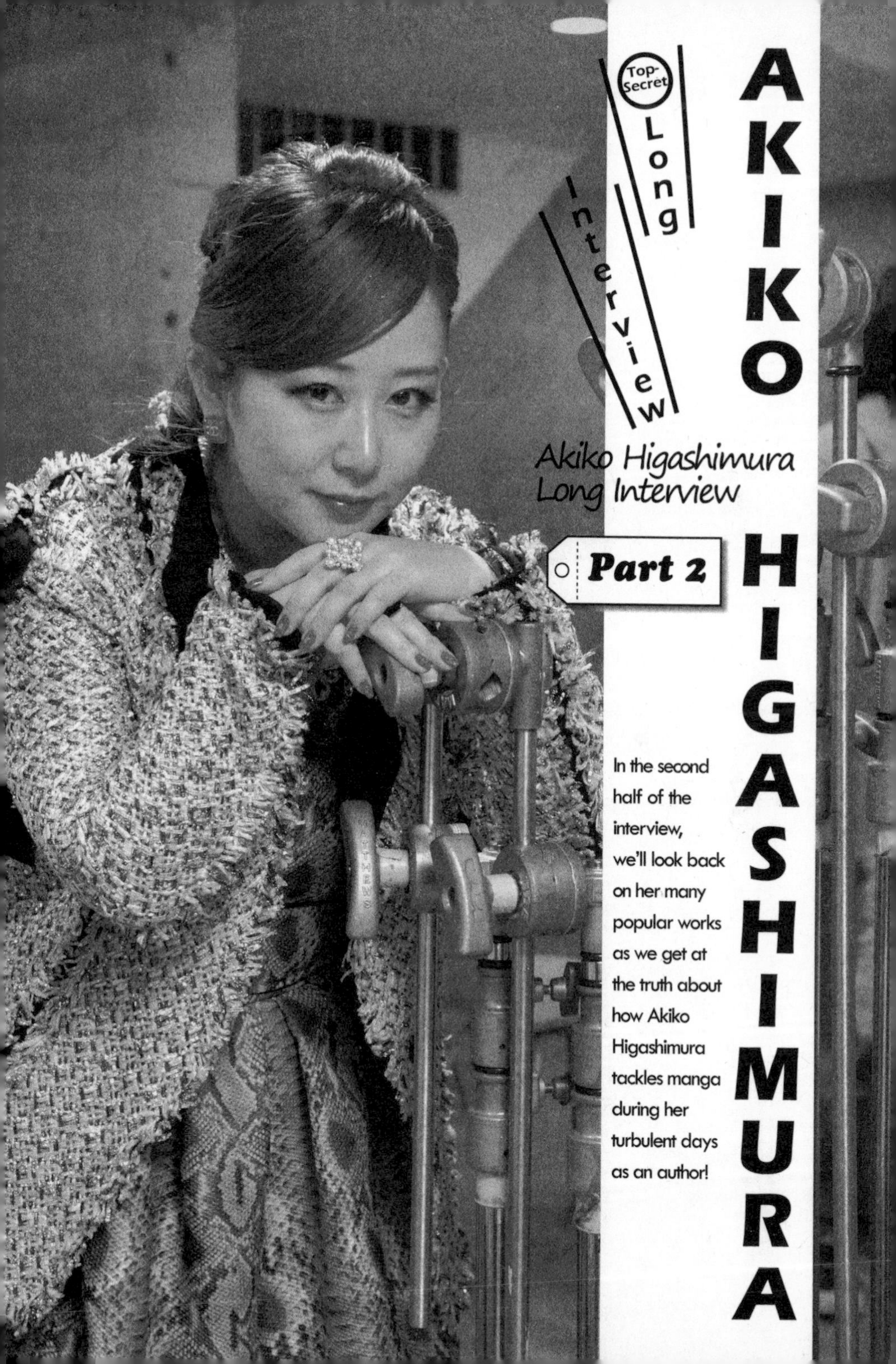

AKIKO HIGASHIMURA

Top-Secret Long Interview

Akiko Higashimura Long Interview

Part 2

In the second half of the interview, we'll look back on her many popular works as we get at the truth about how Akiko Higashimura tackles manga during her turbulent days as an author!

I'm not sure there's any meaning to drawing manga while you're a blank slate as a person.

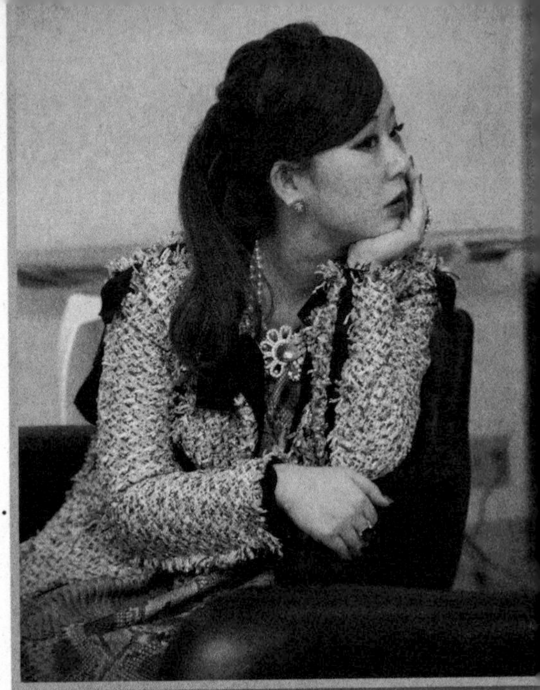

Grueling art training showed her what she could do

—After you graduated from the Kanazawa College of Art, you went back to Miyazaki and got an office job. That's when you finally began to draw manga.

Higashimura: Yes, even though some people debut in their teens. My motivation to draw manga at the time was, "I really wanna quit this job!" [Laughs]

—Do you wish you'd started in your teens?

Higashimura: Hmm… If you want to draw something realistic, I'm not sure there's any meaning to doing it before you have much life experience, while you're still a blank slate as a person. I think it was probably good that I spent my teens doing lots of interesting things and being put through my paces studying art.

From *Kisekae Yuka-chan*. Classic Higashimura gags like short performances by weirdos started here!

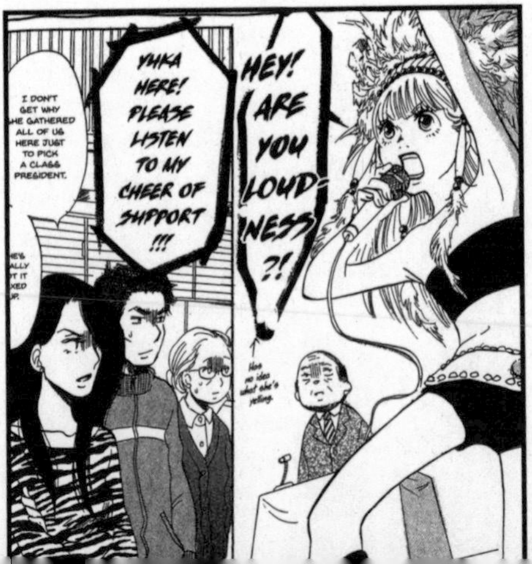
HEY! ARE YOU LOUDNESS?!
YUKA HERE! PLEASE LISTEN TO MY CHEER OF SUPPORT!!!
I DON'T GET WHY HE GATHERED ALL OF US HERE JUST TO PICK A CLASS PRESIDENT.
Has no idea what she's yelling.

—You've depicted in your autobiographical manga *Kakukaku Shikajika* that the strict "Hidaka-sensei," whose classes you took to get into art college, pounded the fundamentals of drawing into you.

Higashimura: I learned to draw quickly, and it was also good for me because it showed me what I was capable of as an artist. Thanks to that training, I can tell right away when I've hit my ceiling and spending more time won't help me achieve better results.

—Your drawings really seem like they're "moving."

Higashimura: That's because I hate it when they look stationary. Sometimes people look at my work and say, "That's sloppy!" But "sloppy" or not, I still like it to have motion. Even when my sketches go totally off the rails, I think to myself, "Hey, it's manga, so maybe off the rails is actually the best way to go sometimes." [Laughs]

So this is what it's like to have a hit!

—Your debut manga was *Fruits Koumori*, a love story with an office worker as the main character.

Higashimura: I was told by the editor who saw my initial submission that the art was so bad I needed to redraw it all. So I did it in three days, while still working my day job. It was basically the same stuff I draw now.

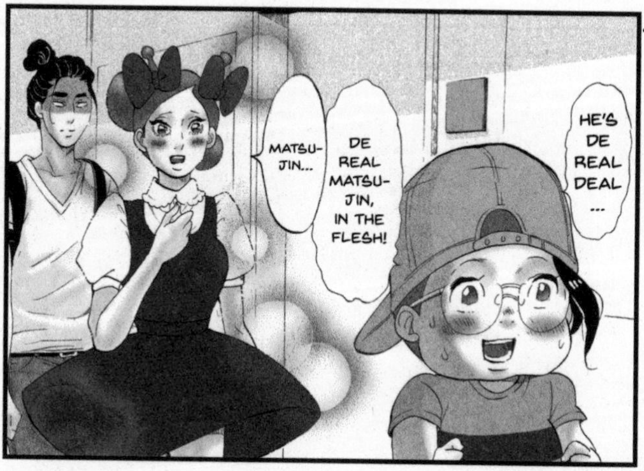
HE'S DE REAL DEAL...
DE REAL MATSU-JIN, IN THE FLESH!
MATSU-JIN...

From *Meropondashi!* Per Higashimura: "Part of the inspiration for this one was that Gocchan was still so cute back then; I really wanted to draw him into my manga."

—And your first serialization was *Kisekae Yuka-chan*. Partway through that one, the type of sharp jokes you do now started coming to the fore.

Higashimura: I drew a gag bit, and it was a hit with the editorial department.

At that point, I was still busy at my day job, and I was teaching at Hidaka-sensei's art school on the weekends, too, so I was slammed. So it was partly me being like, "Oh, gags are what work for you? Okay, I'll do that!" [Laughs]

—You quit your company job later in *Yuka-chan's* run and moved from Miyazaki to Osaka for a while. Then you came to Tokyo, you had a baby... And so your turbulent life as an author began. You started with *Himawari: Kenichi Legend*, which was both your first work in a seinen magazine and your first weekly serial.

Higashimura: Storyboarding started the week after I gave birth... I was always tired!

—Your "child-rearing essays" manga *Mama wa Temparist* started at around the same time. That one became a huge hit.

Higashimura: The people around me and I were flying high when that happened. It was a really fun time. I thought, "Oh, so this is what it's like to have a hit!" I suddenly realized that when what you do matches up with what the world seeks, you can make money... In other words, I finally achieved an adult's mentality.

She'll be the namahage of the late-20s to early-40s world!

—And then *Princess Jellyfish* began, and it became a big hit, too.

Higashimura: It'd be fair to call *Princess Jellyfish* my professional debut. Before that, I shot from the hip as a creator, but for *Jellyfish*, I was deliberate and meticulous in my setup. You see, when I got offered a serial in *Kiss*, to me it felt the same as being told, "Go do a prime-time TV show for a channel everybody watches!" I love magazines, so I'm the type to be hyper-conscious of matching my work to the unique tone of the magazine it's in.

If I only did sympathy-grabbing manga, I'd bore myself!

From *Princess Jellyfish*. Watching the Amars otaku girls work together to make clothes, and thereby begin their journey to the outside world, moved readers.

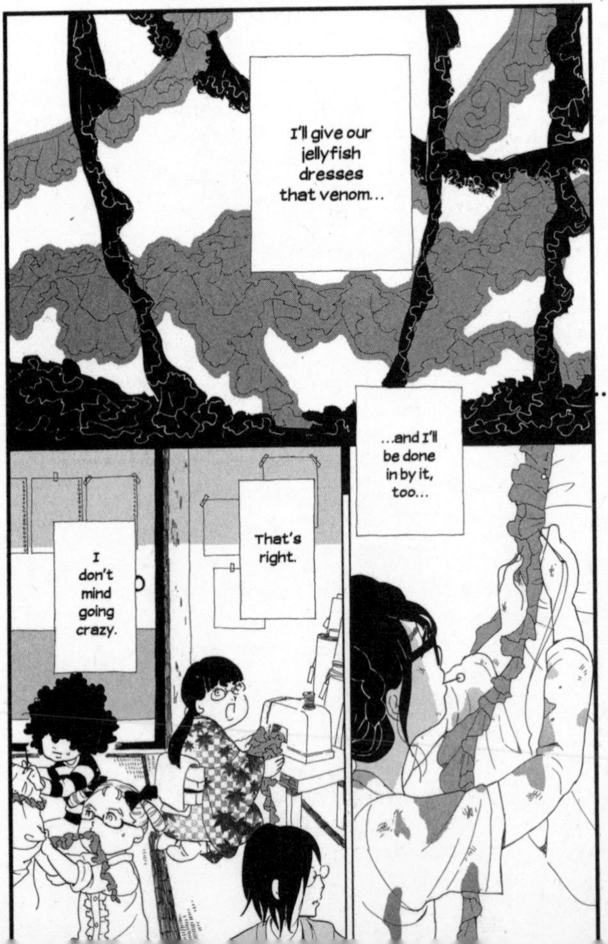
I'll give our jellyfish dresses that venom...
...and I'll be done in by it, too...
That's right.
I don't mind going crazy.

—In terms of seinen magazines, you went on to do *Omo ni Naitemasu* and *Meropondashi!* after *Himawari*.

Higashimura: I made the *Meropon* main character an alien for some reason....

Which was a huge blunder. [Laughs] It brought home to me all over again that people want to see "an extension of everyday life that they can sympathize with." But I had this feeling that if I only did sympathy-grabbing manga, I'd bore myself.

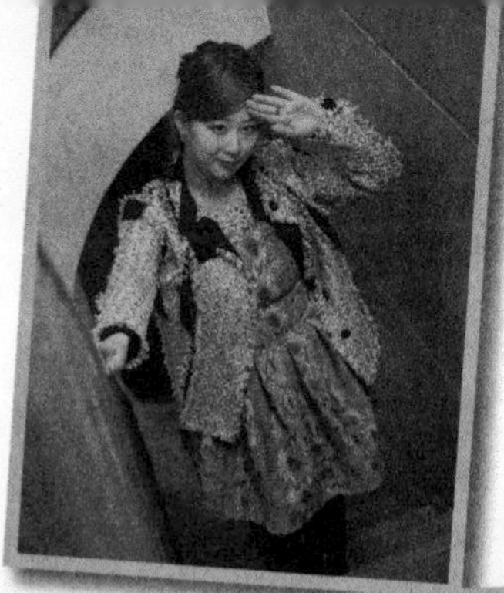

I want to do stuff like **Meropon**, too, and I personally really like **Meropon**.

—Your newest work [at press time] is *Tokyo Tarareba Girls*, the story of a young thirtysomething who can't get married.

Higashimura: Having learned my lesson with *Meropon* [Laughter], I knew I had to do an everyday-life story and really sock it to all the troubled people out there.

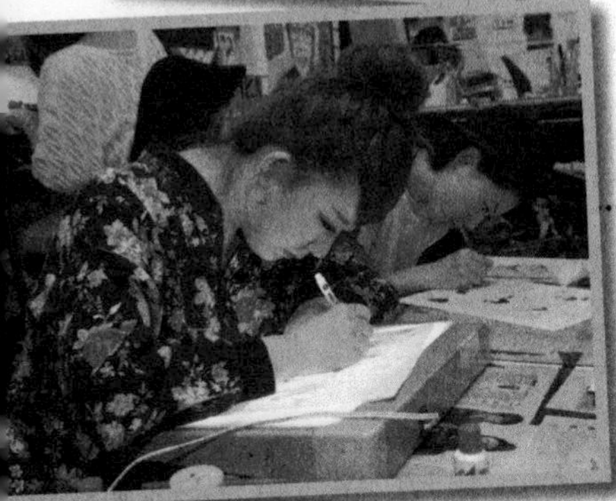

You know, I get a ton of requests for advice from the women around me in their late 20s to early 40s. Maybe they think I'll tell them, "I know the right man for you is out there! Want me to introduce you to someone?"... But this is me telling them that I'm not going to say that. I don't intend to be anyone's savior with this manga! I only plan to depict reality. I intend to be the *namahage* of the late-20s to early-40s world! I'm at your front door asking you, "Who here participates in Girls' Nights?!" [Laughs]

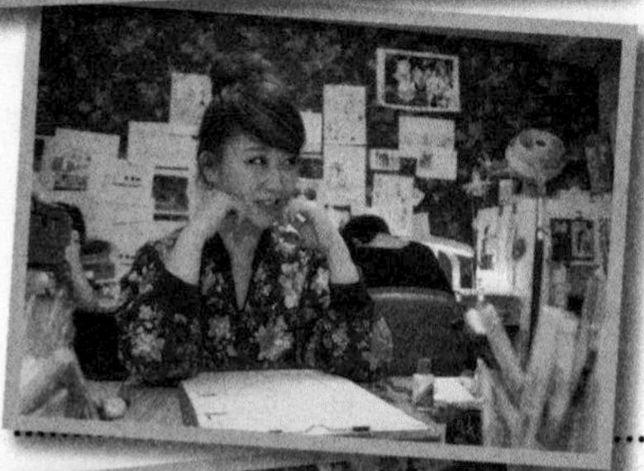

She just loves shojo manga!

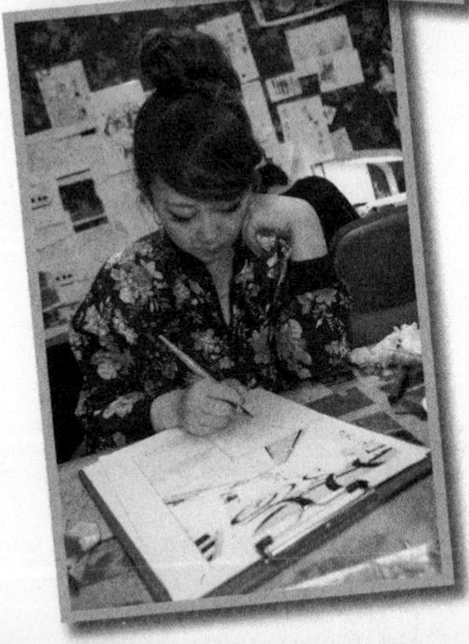

—You once said in an interview that you felt no stress and no pressure about drawing manga.

Higashimura: When someone runs a dango shop, they don't feel pressure every time they make a new batch of dango, do they? They just quietly roll their dango and set them aside. They have deadlines, and when they think, "I gotta make 100 dango by this time tomorrow," I assume they just get a move on and start. I think it's probably the same thing for me.

—Spoken like a true pro.

Higashimura: Maybe it's different for things like novels and films, but people go from one manga to the next very quickly. In a way, they're something you read once and then discard. When we went through my list of one-shot manga earlier, I was surprised at the number. "I can't believe how many one-shots I've done!" I could only even remember drawing about a third of them. The thing is, if I'm not satisfied with something I did, I just forget about it. I don't carry the disappointment around with me.

—Some authors say that once they've built a career, the pressure increases every year and they stop being able to draw manga. But for you, it's almost the opposite...

Higashimura: My output increases every year. [Laughs] I'll be starting a new shojo manga serial next year, so I'm thinking I'll go back to being a "shojo manga author." I want to draw the sort of shojo manga I've been wanting to do for a while: the type you'd show in the liminal time "between" spaces, like an intermission, so to speak. You know, I just *really* love shojo manga. Also...someday when I retire from being a manga author, I think I'll move to Hong Kong and start a chicken nanban business!

—That's the famous dish from Miyazaki Prefecture!

Higashimura: That's right. I'll start by selling it from a cart in the street!

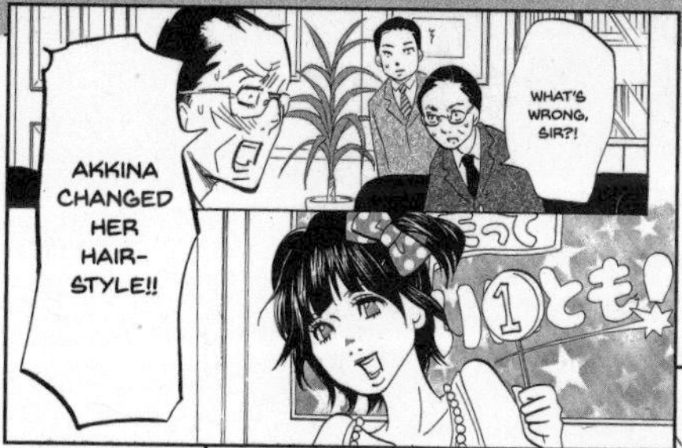
WHAT'S WRONG, SIR?!
AKKINA CHANGED HER HAIR-STYLE!!

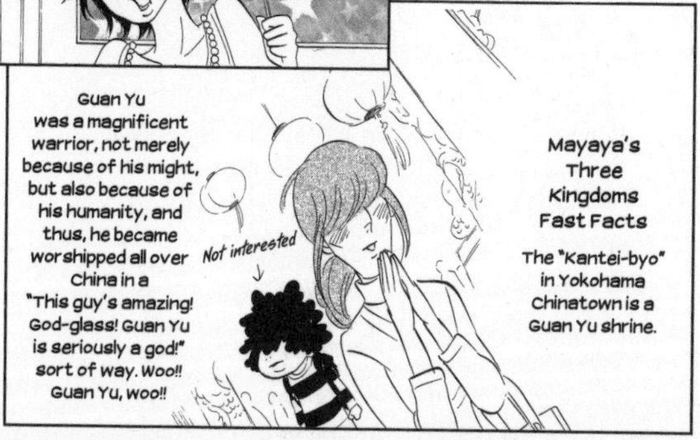
Mayaya's Three Kingdoms Fast Facts
The "Kantei-byo" in Yokohama Chinatown is a Guan Yu shrine.
Not interested
Guan Yu was a magnificent warrior, not merely because of his might, but also because of his humanity, and thus, he became worshipped all over China in a "This guy's amazing! God-glass! Guan Yu is seriously a god!" sort of way. Woo!! Guan Yu, woo!!

Princess Jellyfish Heroes☆

- Ran in Kodansha's *Kiss* magazine from May 2009 to May 2011
- Included periodically in the collected volumes

The supporting characters are even livelier here than in the main story!

At around six pages per chapter, this short spinoff focused the spotlight on Amars and other intense secondary characters who lend their larger-than-life presence to *Princess Jellyfish*. In the latter half of its serialization, it turned into the story of Chieko Mama (Chiyoko) and her band of Korean drama addicts (the Clover Club), which was later collected into one bound volume and retitled *BARAKURA ~Bara no aru Kurashi~*. Chapters before *BARAKURA* were included in order at the end of *Princess Jellyfish*'s bound volumes.

COMMENTS FROM AKIKO HIGASHIMURA

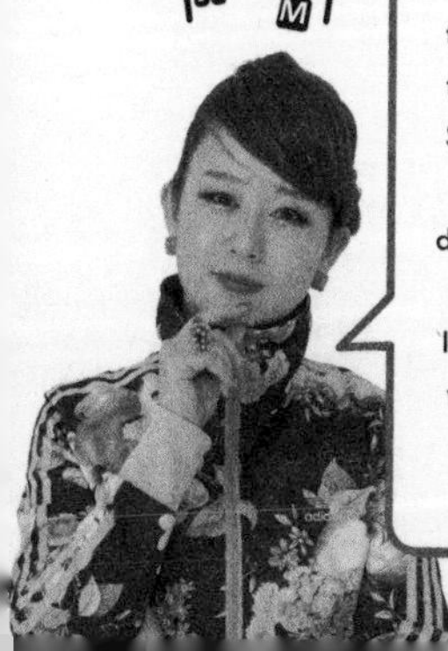

The spinoff spun out of control...

When *Kiss PLUS* magazine launched, they told me, "Do something for this magazine, too." So I ended up drawing a spinoff about the daily lives of Amars and friends. At the time, I never imagined that it would end up evolving into *BARAKURA*, too. [Laughs]

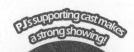

PJ's supporting cast makes a strong showing!

In each chapter, one of the intensely individual characters making up the flanks of the *PJ* army takes their turn being main character. Each episode packs a punch as it gives us a close-up of their respective otaku benders and transformations.

Mayaya, Saburota Negishi, and more

The star of the first chapter is Mayaya, the Three Kingdoms otaku. The second chapter features the Prime Minister.

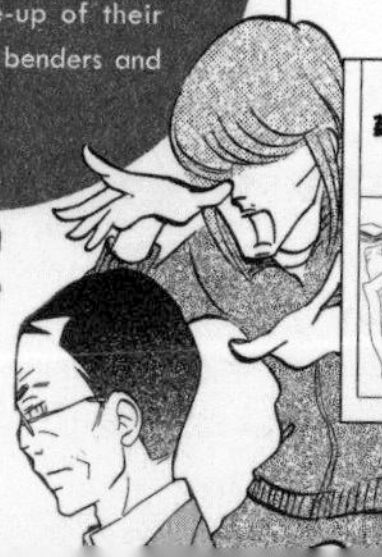

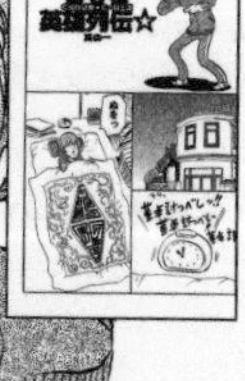

Translation Notes

noitaminA, page 199
noitaminA ("Animation" spelled backwards) is a time slot on Fuji TV which tends to feature anime that are outside of the standard fare. According to Fuji TV's webpage describing the noitaminA show *PSYCHO-PASS*, this backwards spelling is intended "to symbolize an 'upending' to everything you thought you knew about anime." Besides *Princess Jellyfish* and *PSYCHO-PASS*, other notable noitaminA shows include *Ping Pong, Kids on the Slope, Eden of the East*, and *Nodame Cantabile*.

Rena Nounen, page 199
The actress Rena Nounen, who played Tsukimi in the live-action *Princess Jellyfish* film, is also known for her award-winning roles in the film *Hot Road* and the TV drama *Amachan*. She also goes by the stage name "Non."

"Neko Funjatta," page 209
"Neko Funjatta" is a children's song where the singer accidentally steps on a cat, who scratches or jumps (depending on the verse) and must be soothed. The tune is the same one we know by the English name "The Flea Waltz" or the German name "Der Flohwalzer." Just like "The Flea Waltz," it's a beginner's piano piece. When Higashimura-sensei says this is the only song she can play, it's similar to an American piano student saying they can only play "Chopsticks." And, in fact, some English-speaking regions refer to "The Flea Waltz" as "Chopsticks"!

A-min World, page 212
Manga author A-min Okada published shojo comedies in the 1980s and 90s. One of her signature traits, which Higashimura-sensei evidently greatly appreciated, was that many of her characters were total weirdoes. Okada-sensei's representative works include *Papa wa Shinpaishou* and *Lunatic Zatsugidan*.

Nagare Hagiwara, page 217
Nagare Hagiwara, born Mitsuo Hagiwara (1953 – 2015), was a Japanese theater and television actor who did everything from period dramas to variety shows. But when fans picture him, they often picture him not in costume, but in his everyday clothes...because his everyday clothes were cowboy hats, boots, and all the classic trappings of the American Old West. His wife reports that he first adopted this personal style after being inspired by Steve McQueen, and some celebrity gossip sources further specify that the inspiration was Steve McQueen in *The Magnificent Seven*. If so, this would be both offensive to Chieko and hilarious to film buffs, since *The Magnificent Seven* was an American remake of Akira Kurosawa's film *Seven Samurai*, where, of course, the characters wore traditional Japanese attire.

Kimono Hems in the Rain, page 217
The phenomenon Chieko is talking about where the layers of a kimono don't lie flat after getting wet is due to uneven drying of the fabric. Any warping of the fabric which causes a disparity between the length of the lining and the outer layer results in a baggy/wrinkly appearance near the hem. A kimono professional can usually fix this problem to the average wearer's satisfaction, so a non-perfectionist could wear it again...but Chieko is no average wearer.

Namahage, page 228-229
A *namahage* is a type of ogre from Japanese folklore. These menacing beings appear in a New Year's ritual that Akita Prefecture is particularly famous for. People dressed up in *namahage* masks and straw coats make the rounds of local homes, barging in uninvited and checking for naughty or lazy family members by screaming things like, "Any bad kids around here?!" So when Higashimura-sensei becomes the *namahage* of the late-20s to early-40s world, she'll scream, "Who here participates in Girls' Nights?!"

Chicken Nanban, page 230
Chicken nanban is indeed a Miyazaki specialty. While there are many variations, this dish most often includes fried chicken topped with both a vinegar-based sweet and sour sauce and a tartar sauce.

We are pleased to present you with a preview of
Akiko Higashimura's *Tokyo Tarareba Girls!*

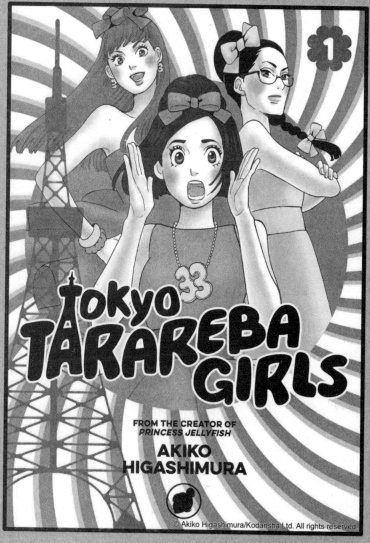

Rinko has done it all right. She hustled her way through her 20s to make it as a
screenwriter, renting her own office in a trendy Tokyo neighborhood. Everything
should have gone according to plan... So at 33, she can't help but lament over
the fact that her career's plateaued, she's still painfully single, and spends most
of her nights drinking with her two best friends in their favorite pub. One night,
drunk and delusional, Rinko swears to get married by the time the Tokyo Olympics
roll around in 2020. But finding a man—or love—may be a cutthroat, dirty job for
a romantic at heart!

**NOW AVAILABLE DIGITALLY AND COMING TO PRINT
6/26/2018!**

TOKYO TARAREBA GIRLS

1

AKIKO HIGASHIMURA

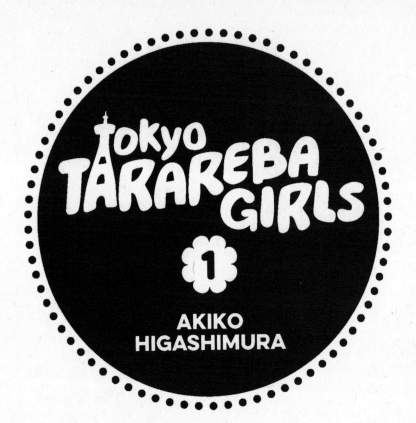

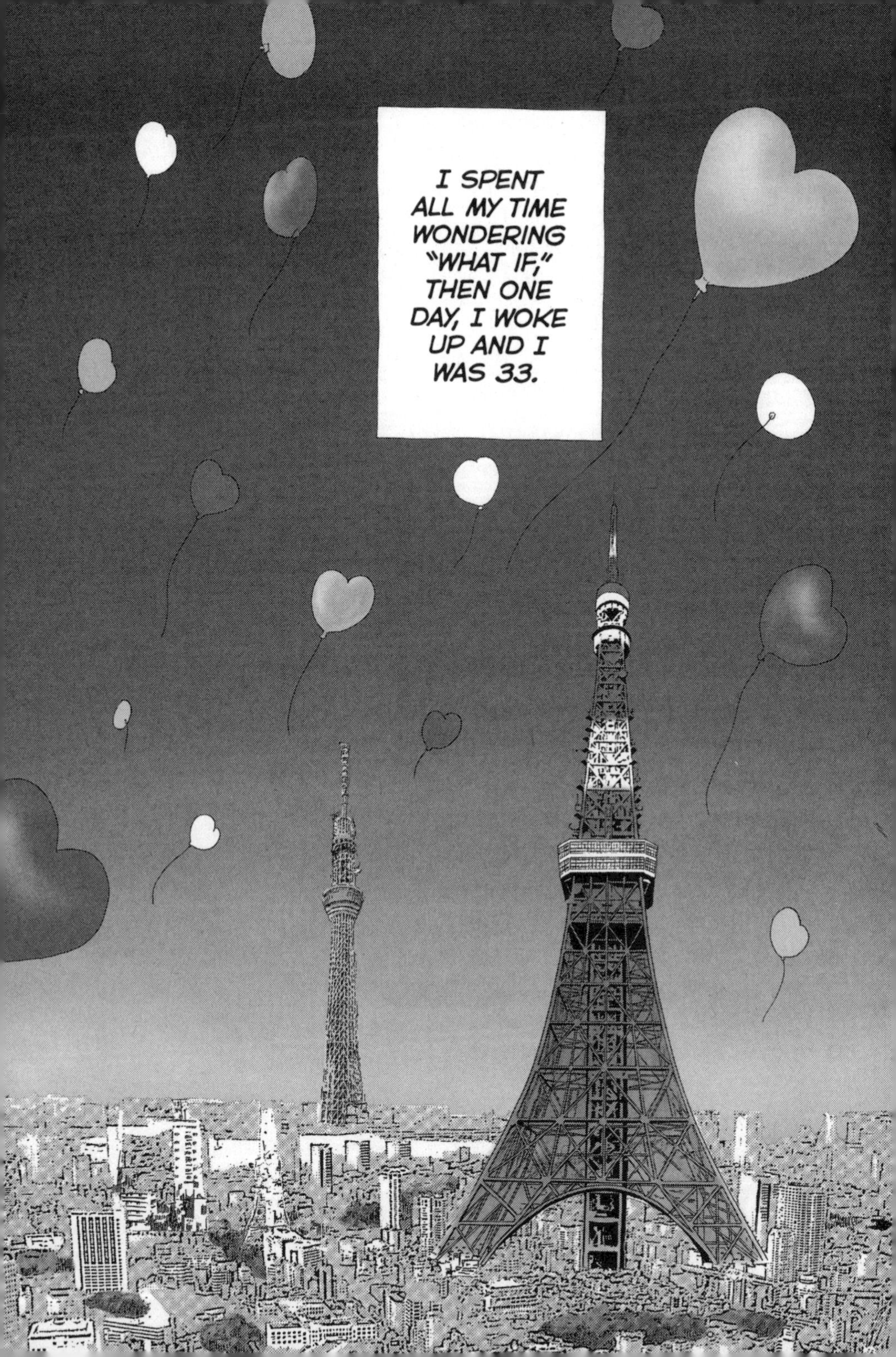
I SPENT ALL MY TIME WONDERING "WHAT IF," THEN ONE DAY, I WOKE UP AND I WAS 33.

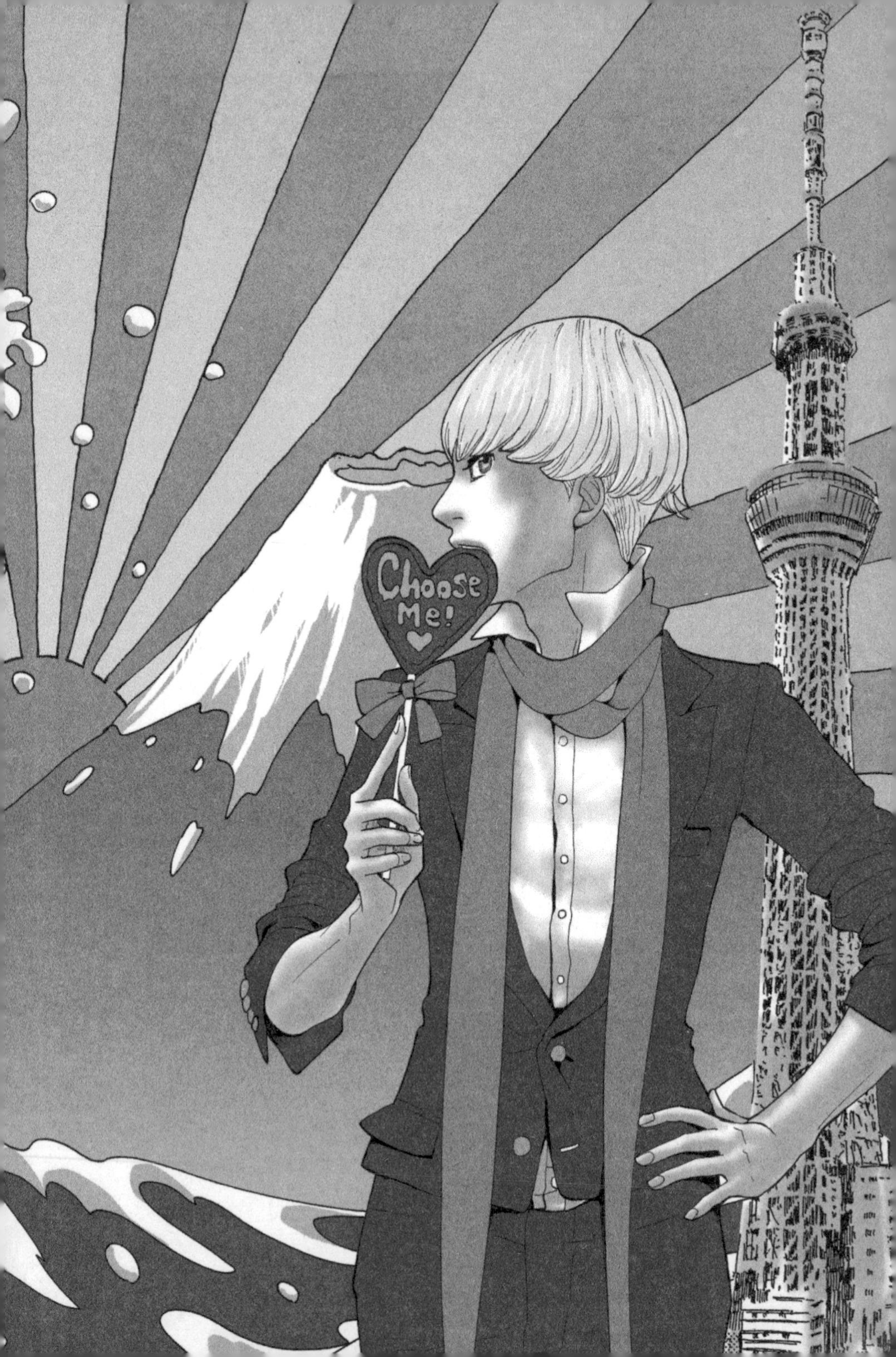
Choose Me!

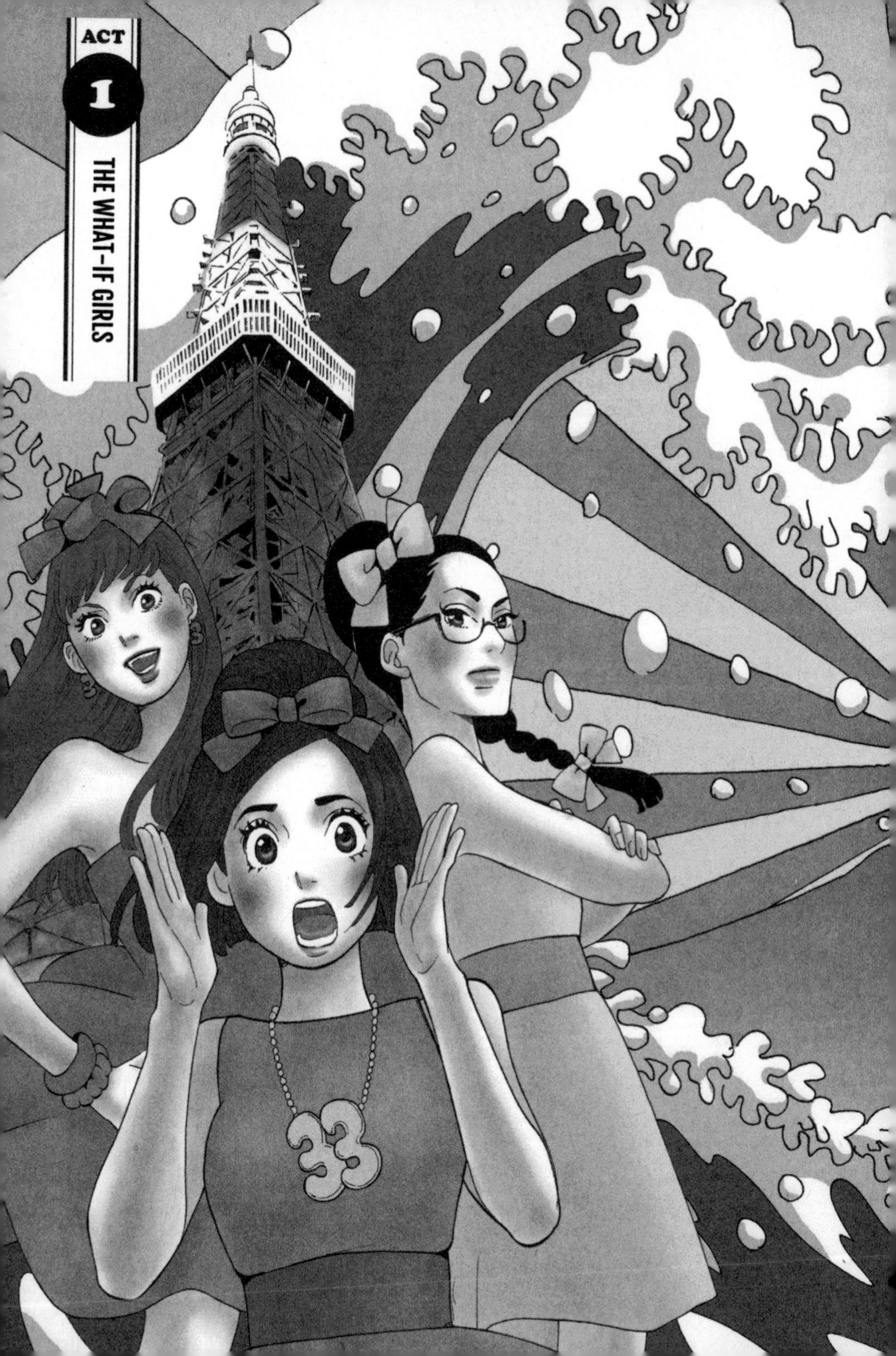
ACT
1
THE WHAT-IF GIRLS

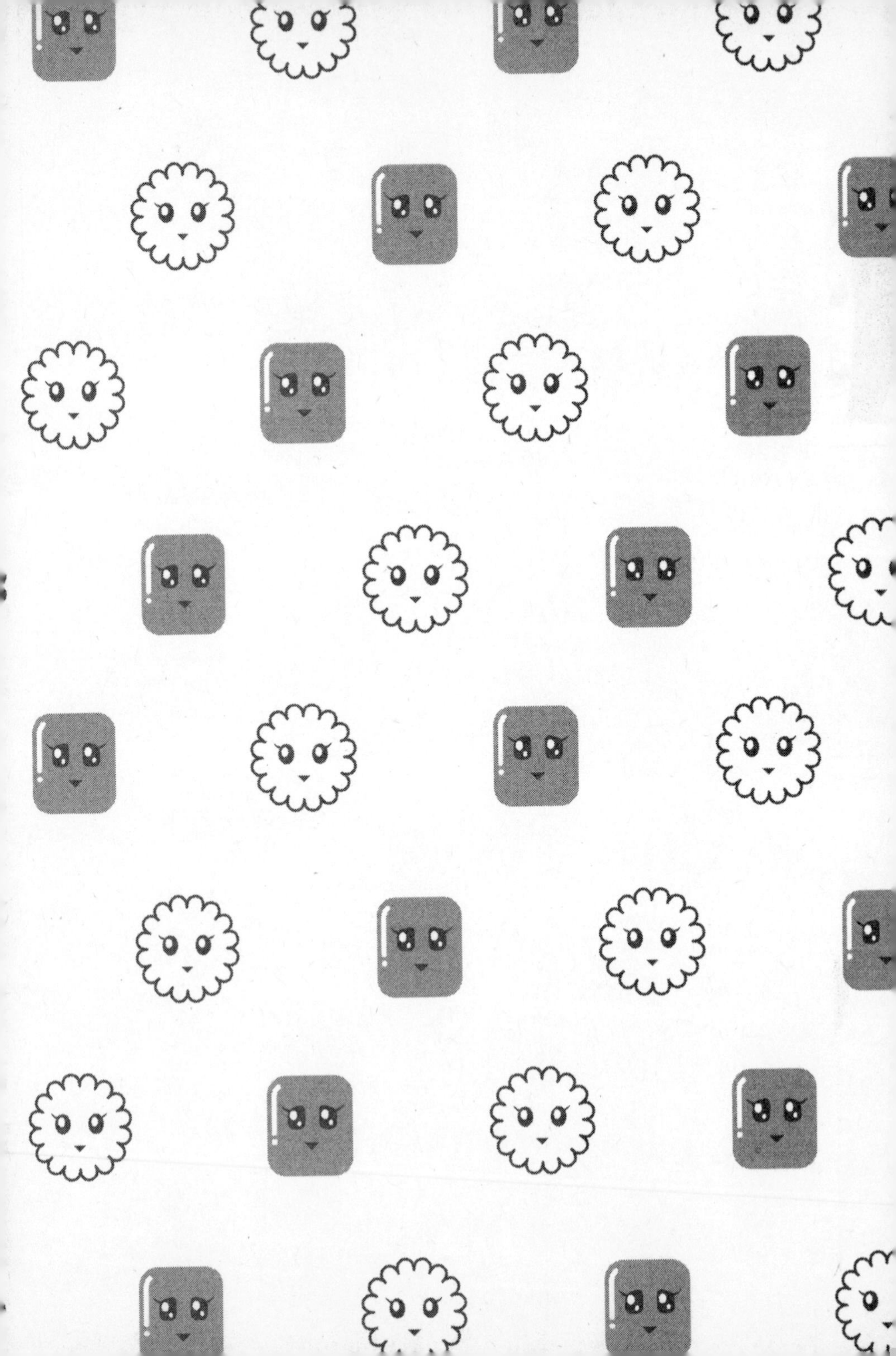

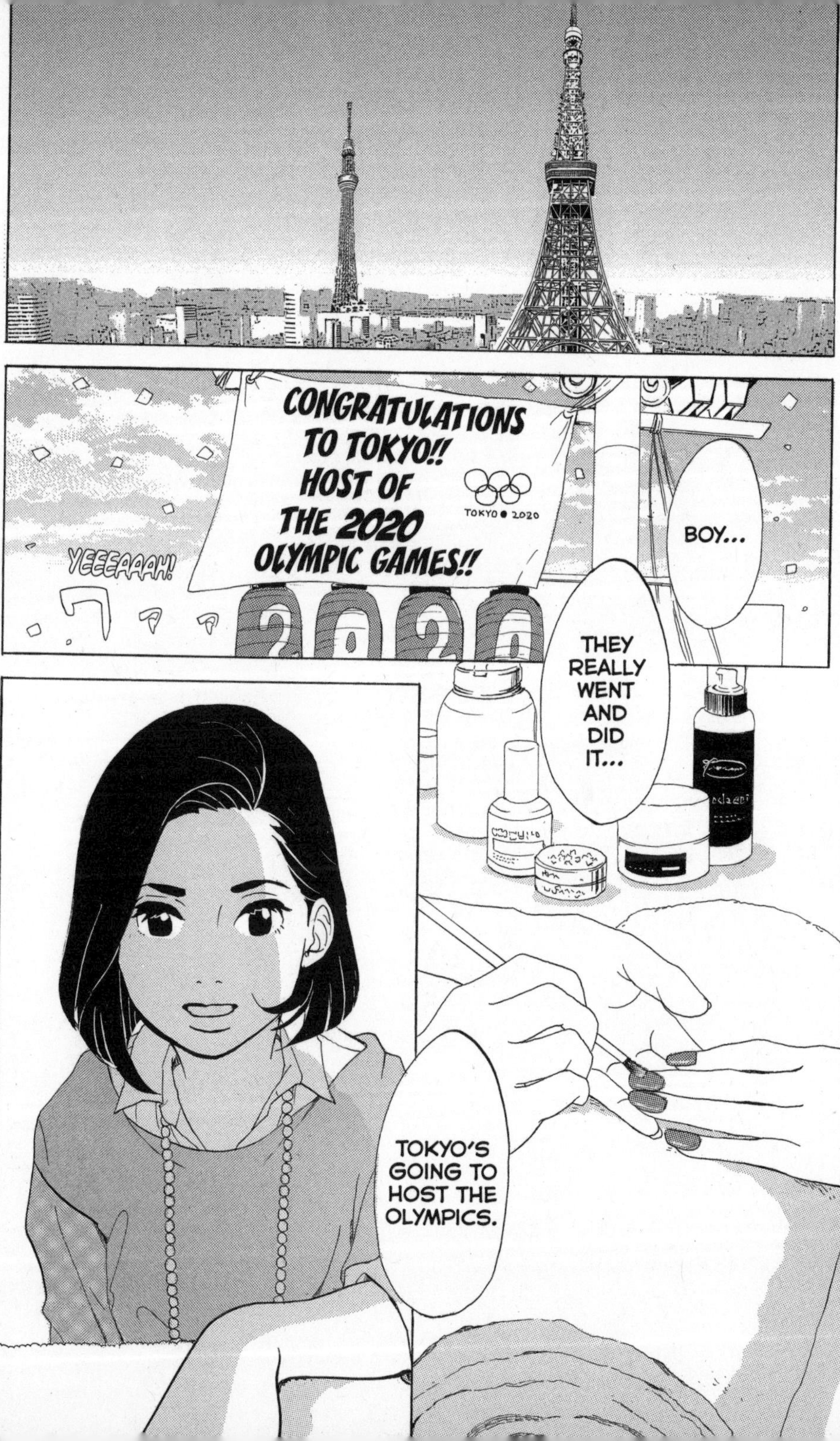
CONGRATULATIONS TO TOKYO!! HOST OF THE 2020 OLYMPIC GAMES!!
TOKYO 2020
BOY...
THEY REALLY WENT AND DID IT...
YEEEAAAH!
2020
TOKYO'S GOING TO HOST THE OLYMPICS.

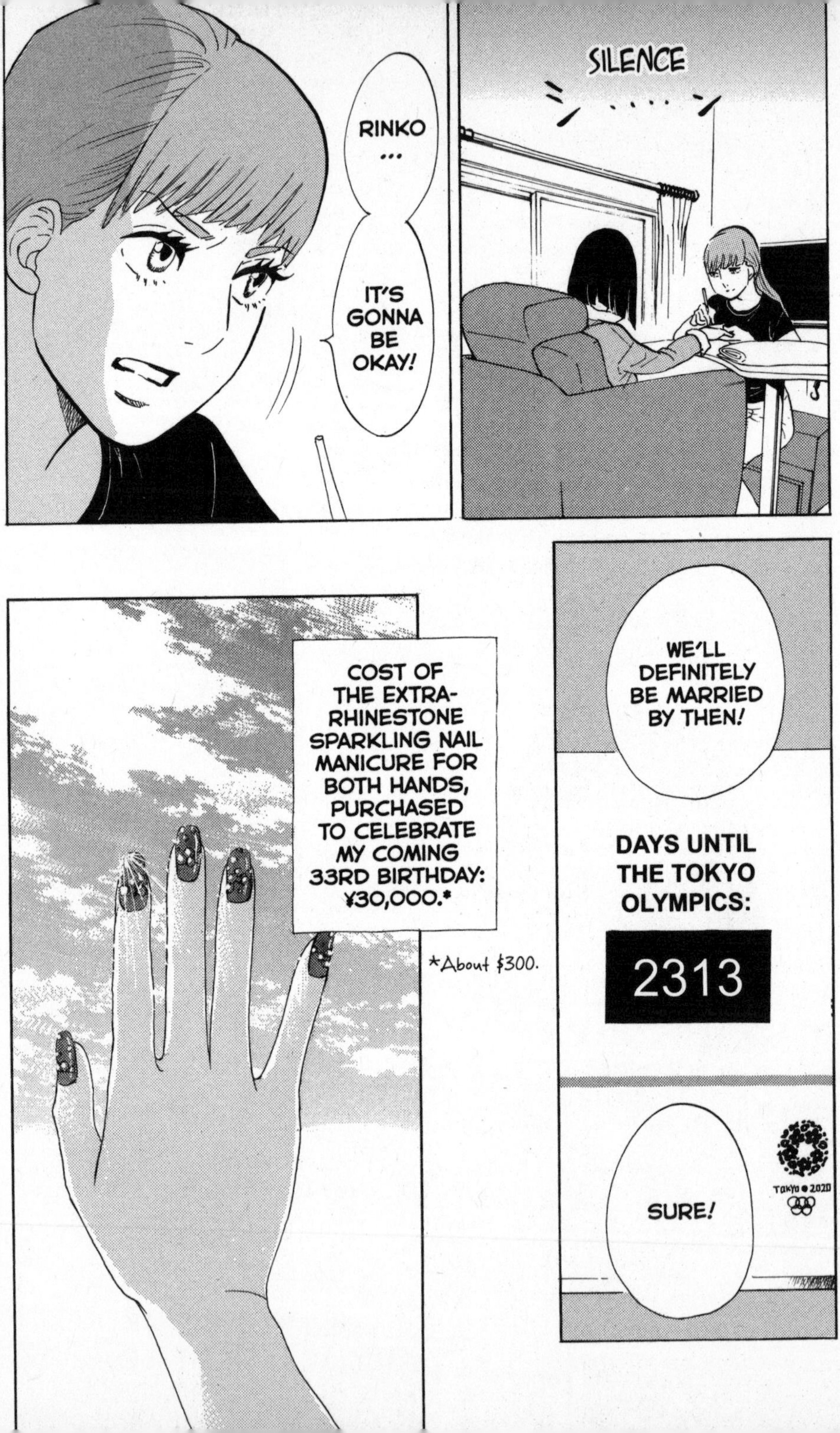
SILENCE
...
RINKO ...
IT'S GONNA BE OKAY!
WE'LL DEFINITELY BE MARRIED BY THEN!
DAYS UNTIL THE TOKYO OLYMPICS:
2313
TOKYO 2020
SURE!
COST OF THE EXTRA-RHINESTONE SPARKLING NAIL MANICURE FOR BOTH HANDS, PURCHASED TO CELEBRATE MY COMING 33RD BIRTHDAY: ¥30,000.*
*About $300.

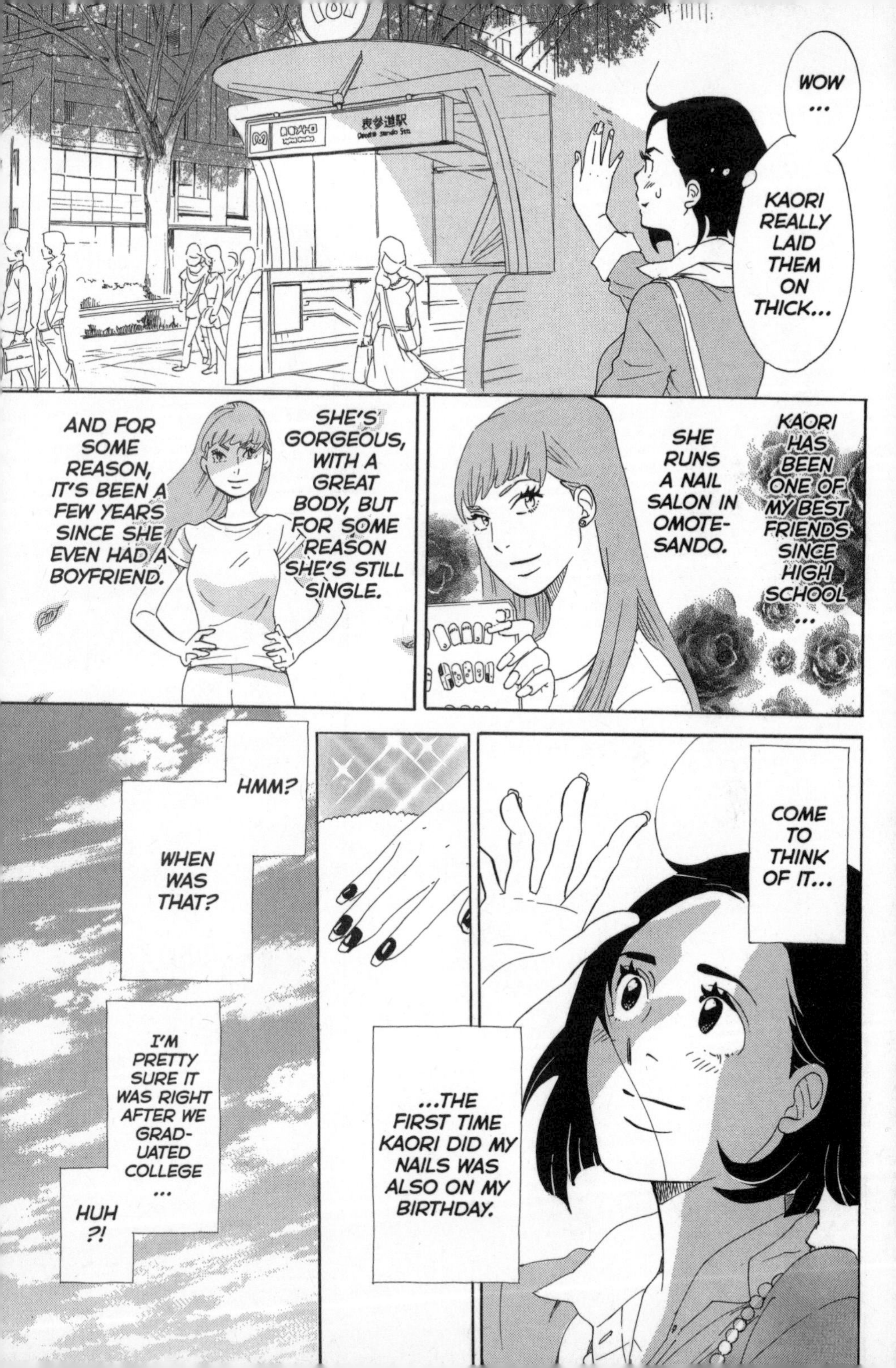
表参道駅
WOW ...
KAORI REALLY LAID THEM ON THICK...
KAORI HAS BEEN ONE OF MY BEST FRIENDS SINCE HIGH SCHOOL ...
SHE RUNS A NAIL SALON IN OMOTE-SANDO.
SHE'S GORGEOUS, WITH A GREAT BODY, BUT FOR SOME REASON SHE'S STILL SINGLE.
AND FOR SOME REASON, IT'S BEEN A FEW YEARS SINCE SHE EVEN HAD A BOYFRIEND.
COME TO THINK OF IT...
...THE FIRST TIME KAORI DID MY NAILS WAS ALSO ON MY BIRTHDAY.
HMM?
WHEN WAS THAT?
I'M PRETTY SURE IT WAS RIGHT AFTER WE GRAD-UATED COLLEGE ...
HUH ?!

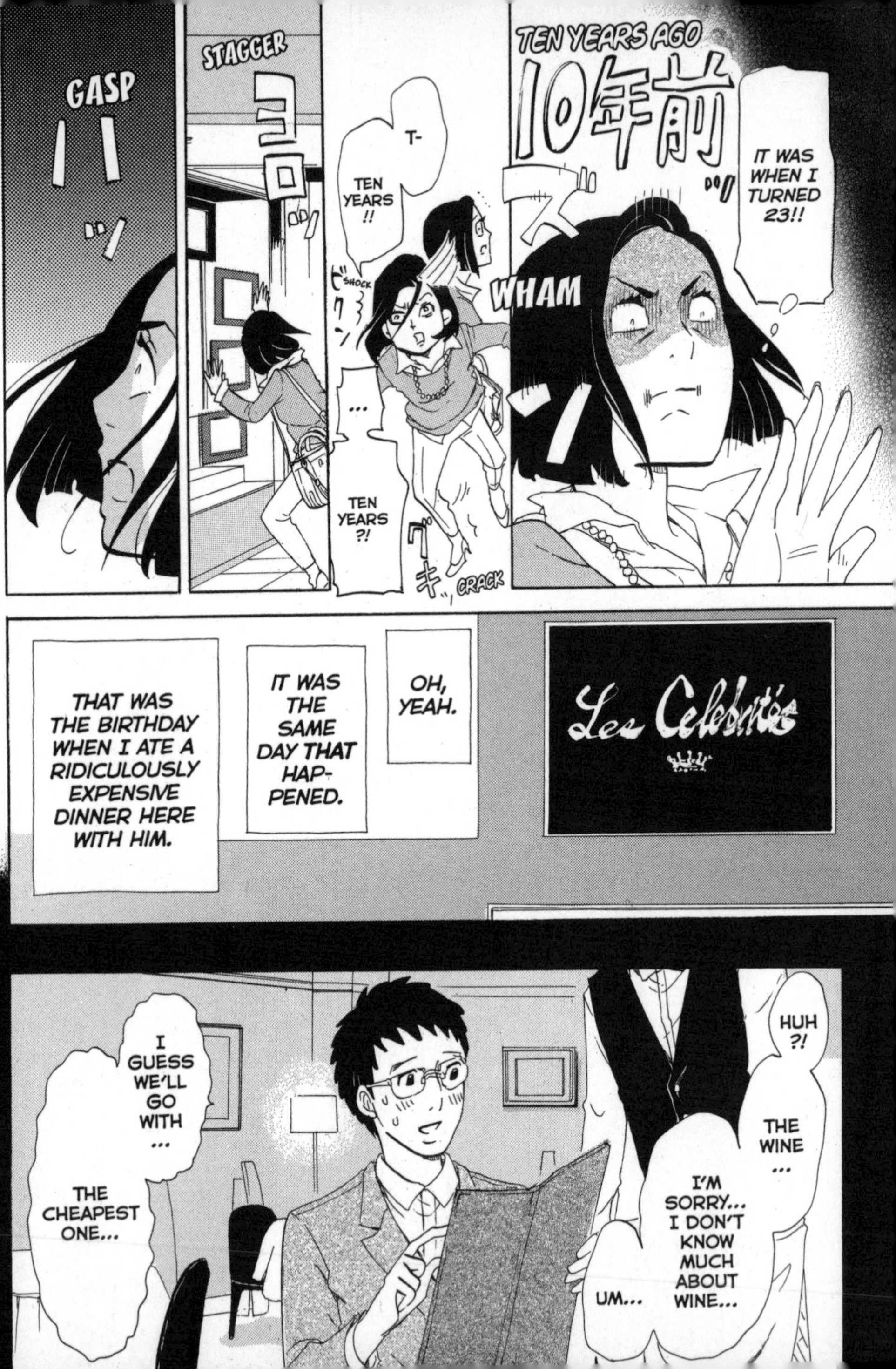
TEN YEARS AGO
10年前
IT WAS WHEN I TURNED 23!!
WHAM
T-
TEN YEARS !!
SHOCK
...
TEN YEARS ?!
CRACK
STAGGER
GASP
Les Celebrités
OH, YEAH.
IT WAS THE SAME DAY THAT HAPPENED.
THAT WAS THE BIRTHDAY WHEN I ATE A RIDICULOUSLY EXPENSIVE DINNER HERE WITH HIM.
HUH ?!
THE WINE ...
I'M SORRY... I DON'T KNOW MUCH ABOUT WINE...
UM...
I GUESS WE'LL GO WITH ...
THE CHEAPEST ONE...

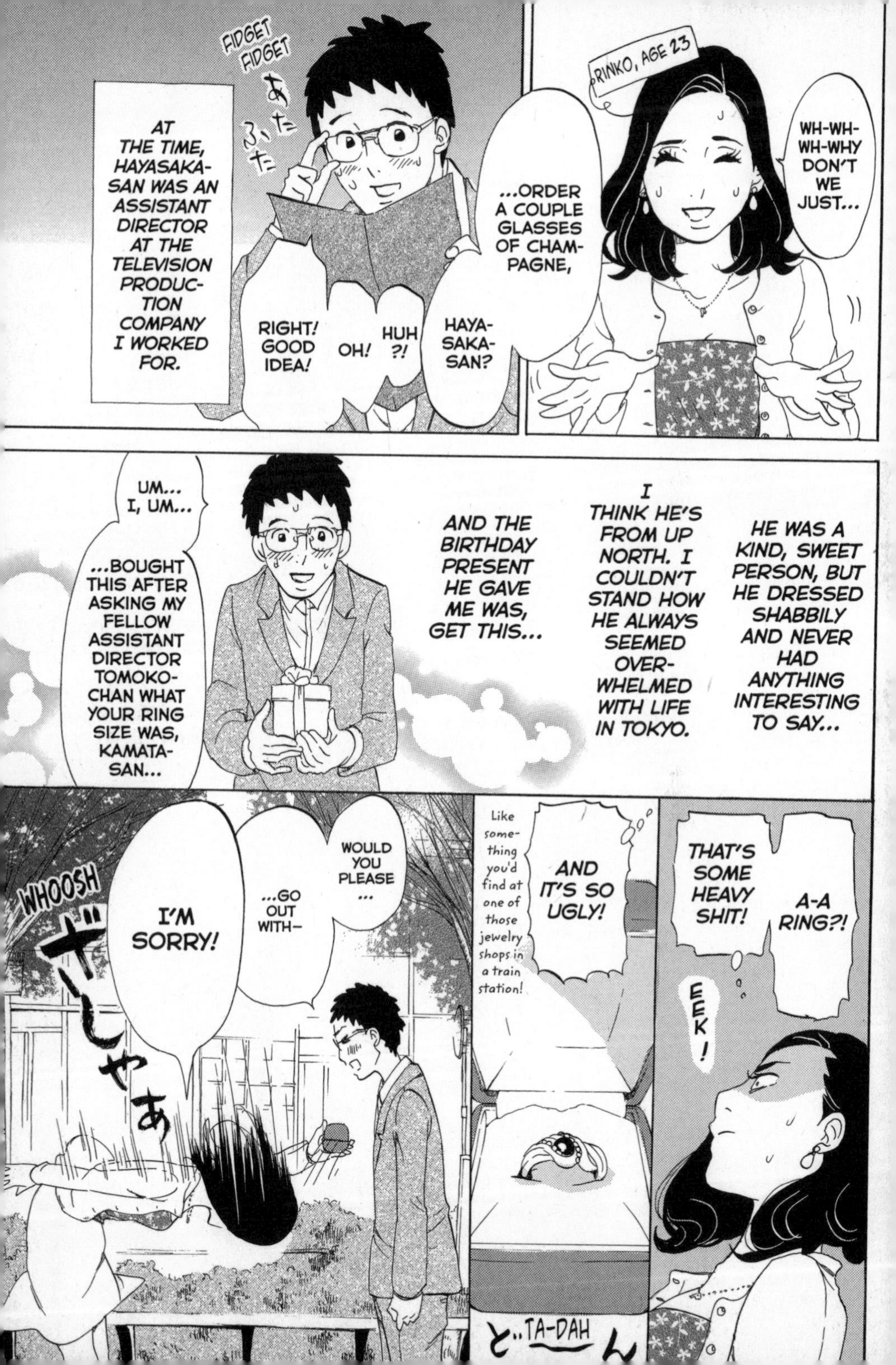
RINKO, AGE 23
WH-WH-WH-WHY DON'T WE JUST...
...ORDER A COUPLE GLASSES OF CHAMPAGNE,
FIDGET FIDGET
あたふた
HAYA-SAKA-SAN?
HUH?!
OH!
RIGHT! GOOD IDEA!
AT THE TIME, HAYASAKA-SAN WAS AN ASSISTANT DIRECTOR AT THE TELEVISION PRODUCTION COMPANY I WORKED FOR.
HE WAS A KIND, SWEET PERSON, BUT HE DRESSED SHABBILY AND NEVER HAD ANYTHING INTERESTING TO SAY...
I THINK HE'S FROM UP NORTH. I COULDN'T STAND HOW HE ALWAYS SEEMED OVER-WHELMED WITH LIFE IN TOKYO.
AND THE BIRTHDAY PRESENT HE GAVE ME WAS, GET THIS...
UM... I, UM...
...BOUGHT THIS AFTER ASKING MY FELLOW ASSISTANT DIRECTOR TOMOKO-CHAN WHAT YOUR RING SIZE WAS, KAMATA-SAN...
A-A RING?!
THAT'S SOME HEAVY SHIT!
EEK!
AND IT'S SO UGLY!
Like something you'd find at one of those jewelry shops in a train station!
と..TA-DAH ん
WOULD YOU PLEASE ...
...GO OUT WITH–
I'M SORRY!
WHOOSH
ざしゃあ

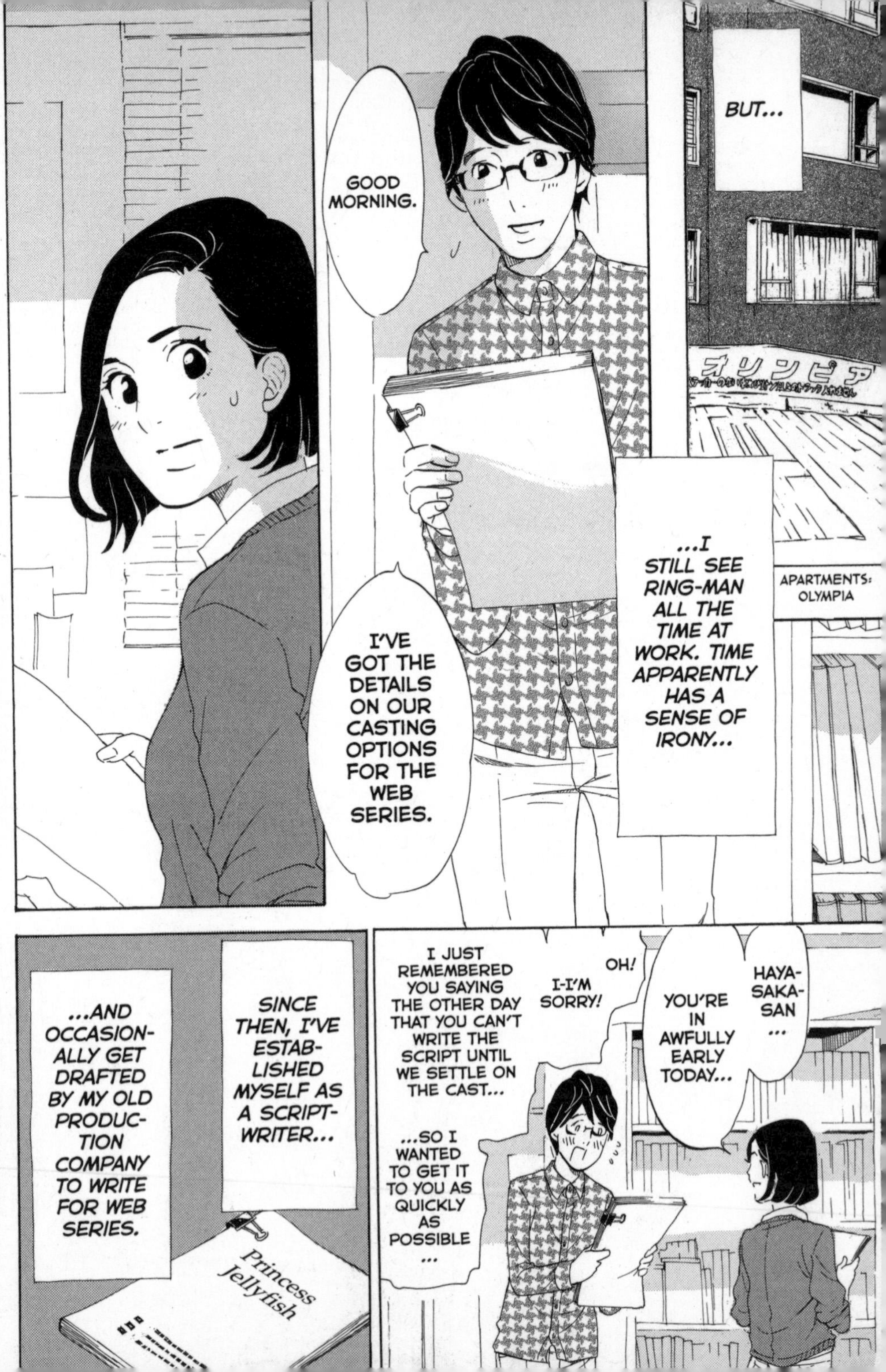
BUT...
オリンピア
APARTMENTS: OLYMPIA
...I STILL SEE RING-MAN ALL THE TIME AT WORK. TIME APPARENTLY HAS A SENSE OF IRONY...
GOOD MORNING.
I'VE GOT THE DETAILS ON OUR CASTING OPTIONS FOR THE WEB SERIES.
HAYASAKA-SAN...
YOU'RE IN AWFULLY EARLY TODAY...
OH!
I-I'M SORRY!
I JUST REMEMBERED YOU SAYING THE OTHER DAY THAT YOU CAN'T WRITE THE SCRIPT UNTIL WE SETTLE ON THE CAST...
...SO I WANTED TO GET IT TO YOU AS QUICKLY AS POSSIBLE...
SINCE THEN, I'VE ESTABLISHED MYSELF AS A SCRIPTWRITER...
...AND OCCASIONALLY GET DRAFTED BY MY OLD PRODUCTION COMPANY TO WRITE FOR WEB SERIES.
Princess Jellyfish

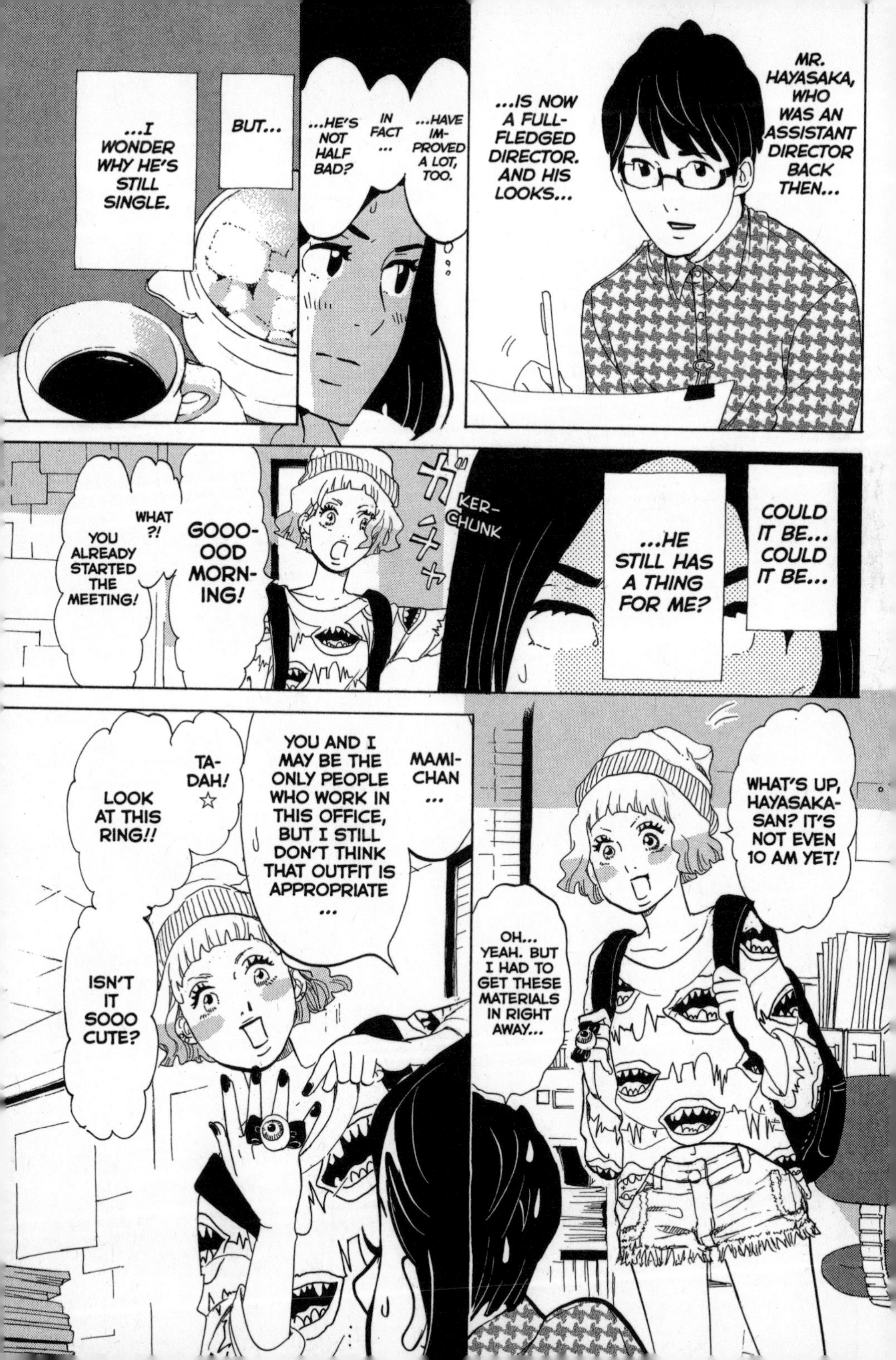
MR. HAYASAKA, WHO WAS AN ASSISTANT DIRECTOR BACK THEN...
...IS NOW A FULL-FLEDGED DIRECTOR. AND HIS LOOKS...
...HAVE IMPROVED A LOT, TOO.
IN FACT...
...HE'S NOT HALF BAD?
BUT...
...I WONDER WHY HE'S STILL SINGLE.
COULD IT BE... COULD IT BE...
...HE STILL HAS A THING FOR ME?
KER-CHUNK
GOOOOOD MORNING!
WHAT?!
YOU ALREADY STARTED THE MEETING!
WHAT'S UP, HAYASAKA-SAN? IT'S NOT EVEN 10 AM YET!
OH... YEAH. BUT I HAD TO GET THESE MATERIALS IN RIGHT AWAY...
MAMI-CHAN...
YOU AND I MAY BE THE ONLY PEOPLE WHO WORK IN THIS OFFICE, BUT I STILL DON'T THINK THAT OUTFIT IS APPROPRIATE...
TA-DAH! ☆
LOOK AT THIS RING!!
ISN'T IT SOOO CUTE?

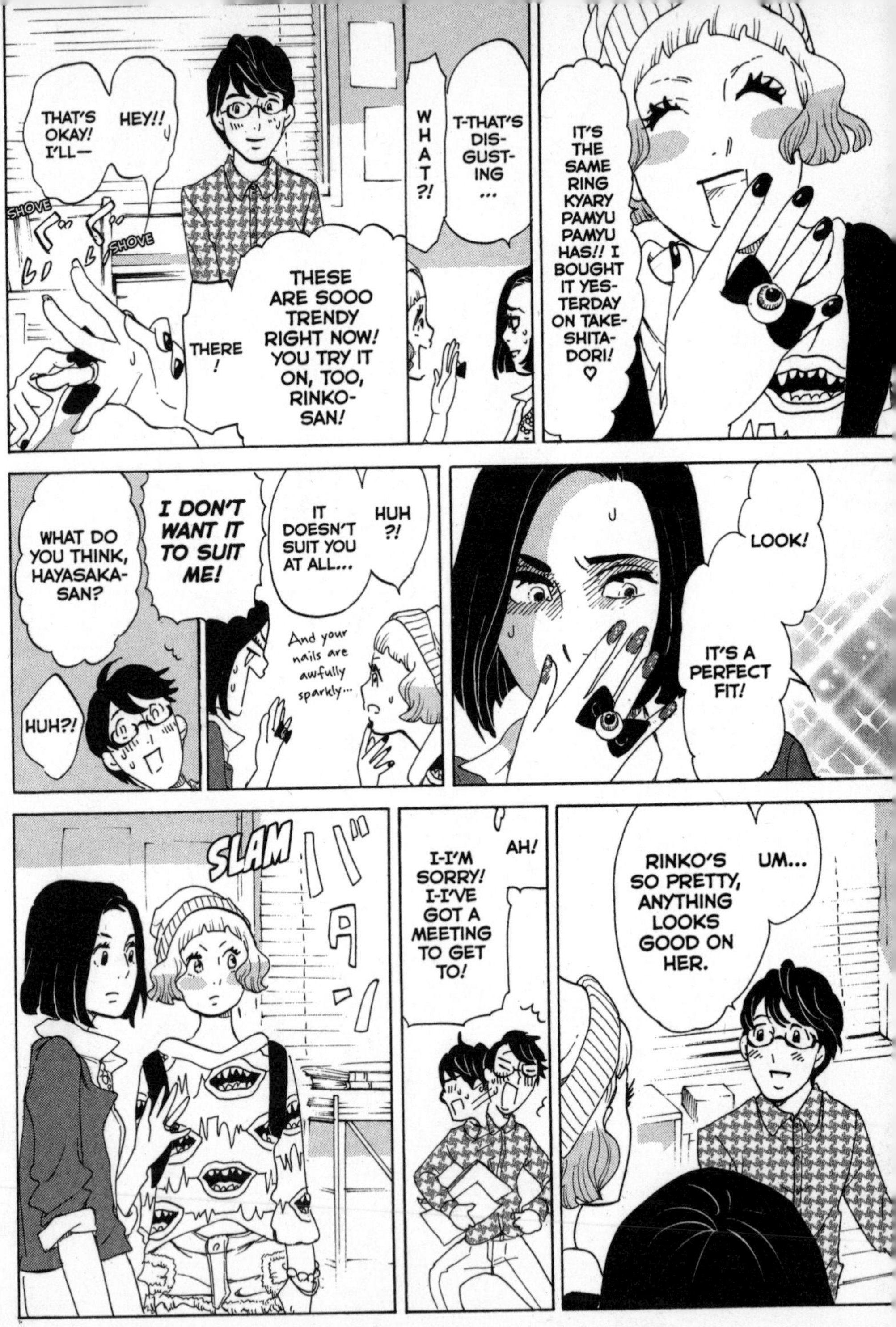
IT'S THE SAME RING KYARY PAMYU PAMYU HAS!! I BOUGHT IT YESTERDAY ON TAKESHITA-DORI! ♡
T-THAT'S DISGUSTING...
WHAT?!
THESE ARE SOOO TRENDY RIGHT NOW! YOU TRY IT ON, TOO, RINKO-SAN!
HEY!!
THAT'S OKAY! I'LL—
SHOVE
SHOVE
THERE!
LOOK!
IT'S A PERFECT FIT!
HUH?!
IT DOESN'T SUIT YOU AT ALL...
And your nails are awfully sparkly...
I DON'T WANT IT TO SUIT ME!
WHAT DO YOU THINK, HAYASAKA-SAN?
HUH?!
UM...
RINKO'S SO PRETTY, ANYTHING LOOKS GOOD ON HER.
AH!
I-I'M SORRY! I-I'VE GOT A MEETING TO GET TO!
SLAM

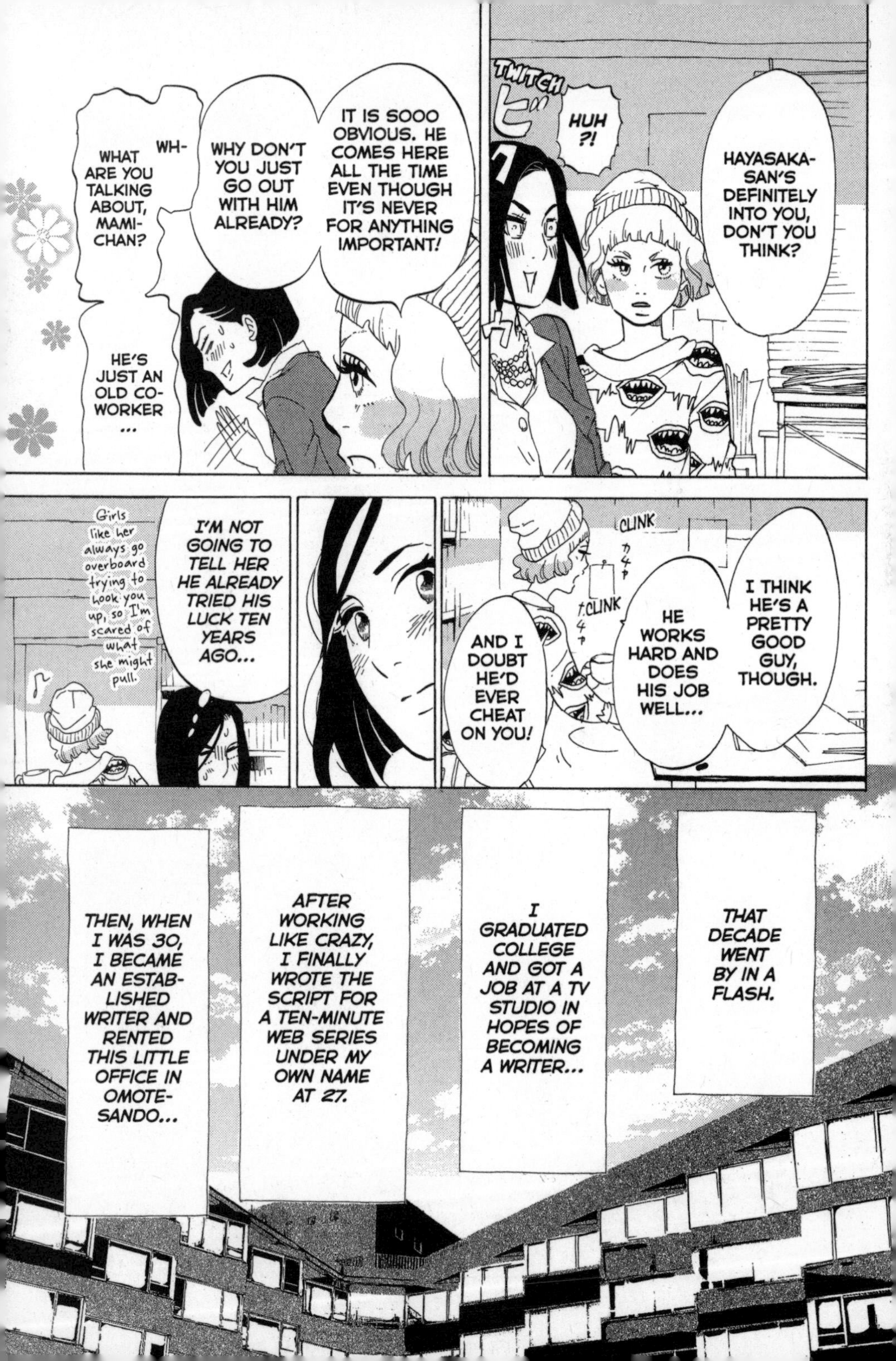
HAYASAKA-SAN'S DEFINITELY INTO YOU, DON'T YOU THINK?
HUH ?!
TWITCH
IT IS SOOO OBVIOUS. HE COMES HERE ALL THE TIME EVEN THOUGH IT'S NEVER FOR ANYTHING IMPORTANT!
WHY DON'T YOU JUST GO OUT WITH HIM ALREADY?
WH-
WHAT ARE YOU TALKING ABOUT, MAMI-CHAN?
HE'S JUST AN OLD CO-WORKER...
I THINK HE'S A PRETTY GOOD GUY, THOUGH.
HE WORKS HARD AND DOES HIS JOB WELL...
CLINK
CLINK
AND I DOUBT HE'D EVER CHEAT ON YOU!
I'M NOT GOING TO TELL HER HE ALREADY TRIED HIS LUCK TEN YEARS AGO...
Girls like her always go overboard trying to hook you up, so I'm scared of what she might pull.
THAT DECADE WENT BY IN A FLASH.
I GRADUATED COLLEGE AND GOT A JOB AT A TV STUDIO IN HOPES OF BECOMING A WRITER...
AFTER WORKING LIKE CRAZY, I FINALLY WROTE THE SCRIPT FOR A TEN-MINUTE WEB SERIES UNDER MY OWN NAME AT 27.
THEN, WHEN I WAS 30, I BECAME AN ESTABLISHED WRITER AND RENTED THIS LITTLE OFFICE IN OMOTE-SANDO...

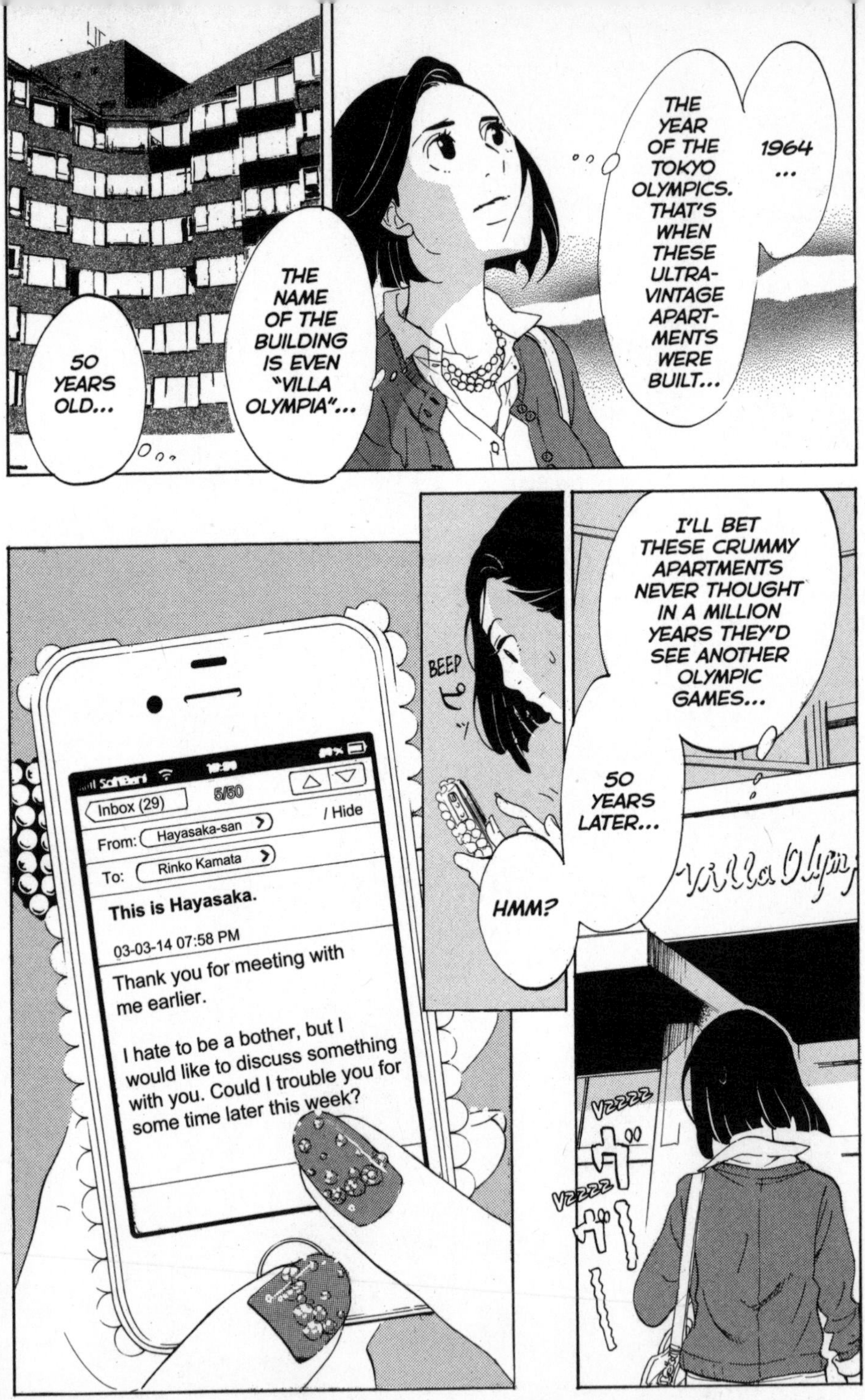
1964...
THE YEAR OF THE TOKYO OLYMPICS. THAT'S WHEN THESE ULTRA-VINTAGE APARTMENTS WERE BUILT...
THE NAME OF THE BUILDING IS EVEN "VILLA OLYMPIA"...
50 YEARS OLD...
I'LL BET THESE CRUMMY APARTMENTS NEVER THOUGHT IN A MILLION YEARS THEY'D SEE ANOTHER OLYMPIC GAMES...
50 YEARS LATER...
VZZZZ
VZZZZ
BEEP
HMM?
Inbox (29)
5/50
/ Hide
From: Hayasaka-san
To: Rinko Kamata
This is Hayasaka.
03-03-14 07:58 PM
Thank you for meeting with me earlier.
I hate to be a bother, but I would like to discuss something with you. Could I trouble you for some time later this week?

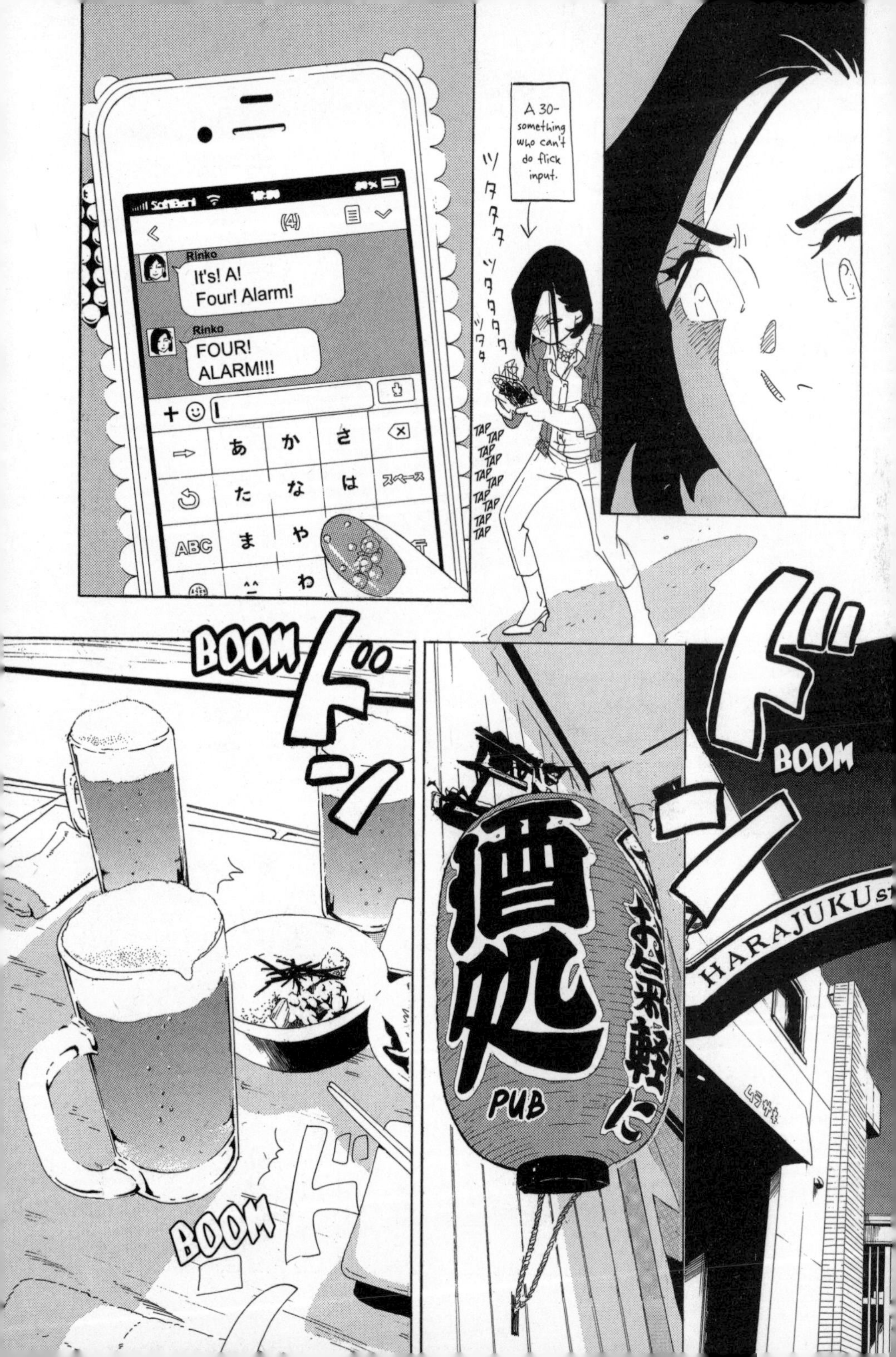

A 30-something who can't do flick input.
ツタタタ
ツタタタタ
ツタタ
TAP TAP TAP TAP TAP TAP TAP TAP TAP TAP TAP
(4)
Rinko
It's! A! Four! Alarm!
Rinko
FOUR! ALARM!!!
あ か さ
た な は スペース
ABC ま や
わ
ドーン
BOOM
酒処
お気軽に
PUB
HARAJUKU st
ムラサキ
BOOM
ドーン
ドーン
BOOM

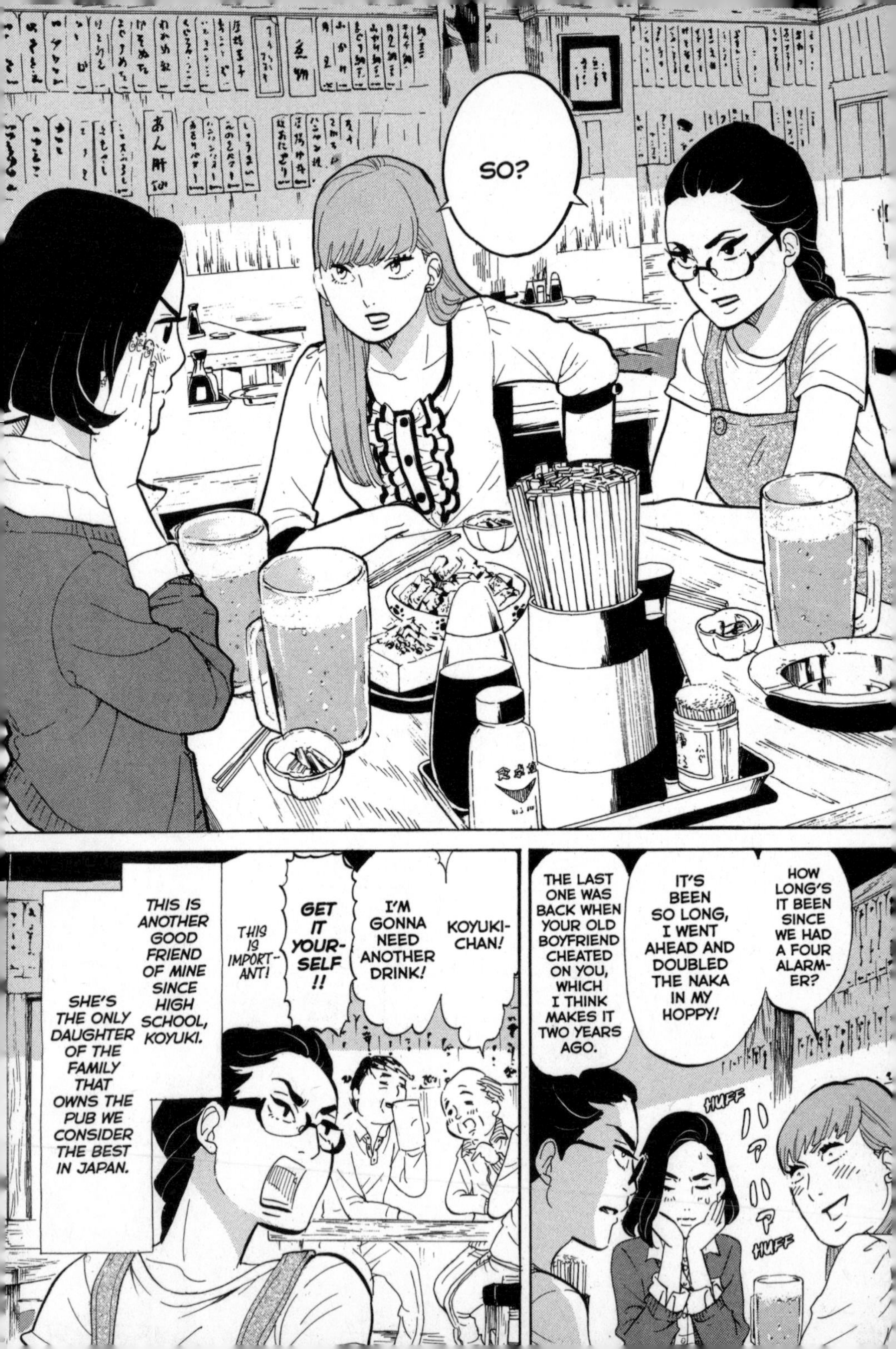
SO?
HOW LONG'S IT BEEN SINCE WE HAD A FOUR ALARMER?
IT'S BEEN SO LONG, I WENT AHEAD AND DOUBLED THE NAKA IN MY HOPPY!
THE LAST ONE WAS BACK WHEN YOUR OLD BOYFRIEND CHEATED ON YOU, WHICH I THINK MAKES IT TWO YEARS AGO.
HUFF
HUFF
KOYUKI-CHAN!
I'M GONNA NEED ANOTHER DRINK!
GET IT YOURSELF!!
THIS IS IMPORTANT!
THIS IS ANOTHER GOOD FRIEND OF MINE SINCE HIGH SCHOOL, KOYUKI.
SHE'S THE ONLY DAUGHTER OF THE FAMILY THAT OWNS THE PUB WE CONSIDER THE BEST IN JAPAN.

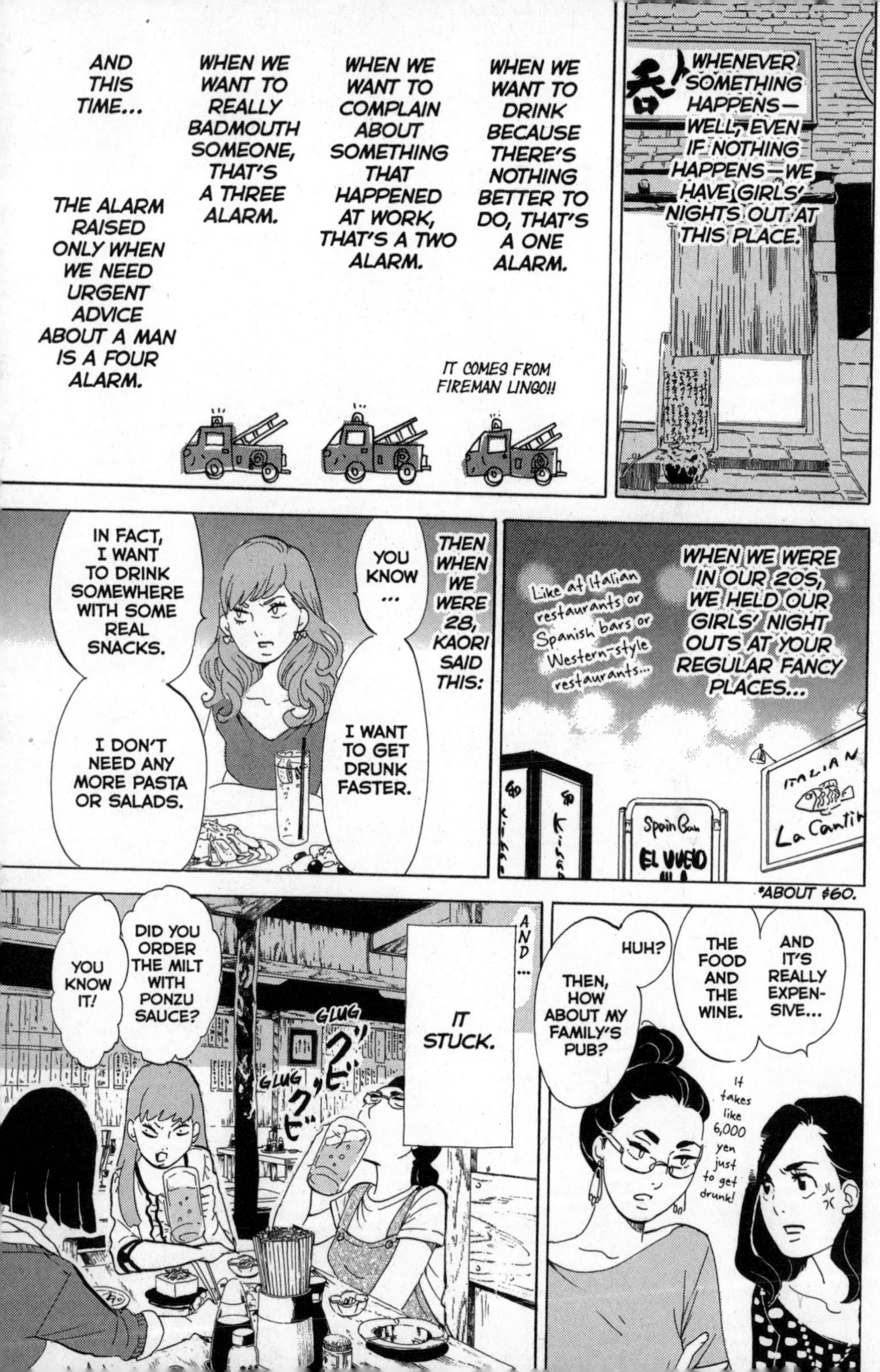
WHENEVER SOMETHING HAPPENS—WELL, EVEN IF NOTHING HAPPENS—WE HAVE GIRLS' NIGHTS OUT AT THIS PLACE.
WHEN WE WANT TO DRINK BECAUSE THERE'S NOTHING BETTER TO DO, THAT'S A ONE ALARM.
WHEN WE WANT TO COMPLAIN ABOUT SOMETHING THAT HAPPENED AT WORK, THAT'S A TWO ALARM.
WHEN WE WANT TO REALLY BADMOUTH SOMEONE, THAT'S A THREE ALARM.
AND THIS TIME...
THE ALARM RAISED ONLY WHEN WE NEED URGENT ADVICE ABOUT A MAN IS A FOUR ALARM.
IT COMES FROM FIREMAN LINGO!!
WHEN WE WERE IN OUR 20S, WE HELD OUR GIRLS' NIGHT OUTS AT YOUR REGULAR FANCY PLACES...
Like at Italian restaurants or Spanish bars or Western-style restaurants...
ITALIAN
La Cantin
Spain Bar
EL VUELO
THEN WHEN WE WERE 28, KAORI SAID THIS:
YOU KNOW ...
I WANT TO GET DRUNK FASTER.
IN FACT, I WANT TO DRINK SOMEWHERE WITH SOME REAL SNACKS.
I DON'T NEED ANY MORE PASTA OR SALADS.
AND IT'S REALLY EXPENSIVE...
THE FOOD AND THE WINE.
HUH?
THEN, HOW ABOUT MY FAMILY'S PUB?
It takes like 6,000 yen just to get drunk!
AND ...
IT STUCK.
GLUG
GLUG
DID YOU ORDER THE MILT WITH PONZU SAUCE?
YOU KNOW IT!

*ABOUT $60.

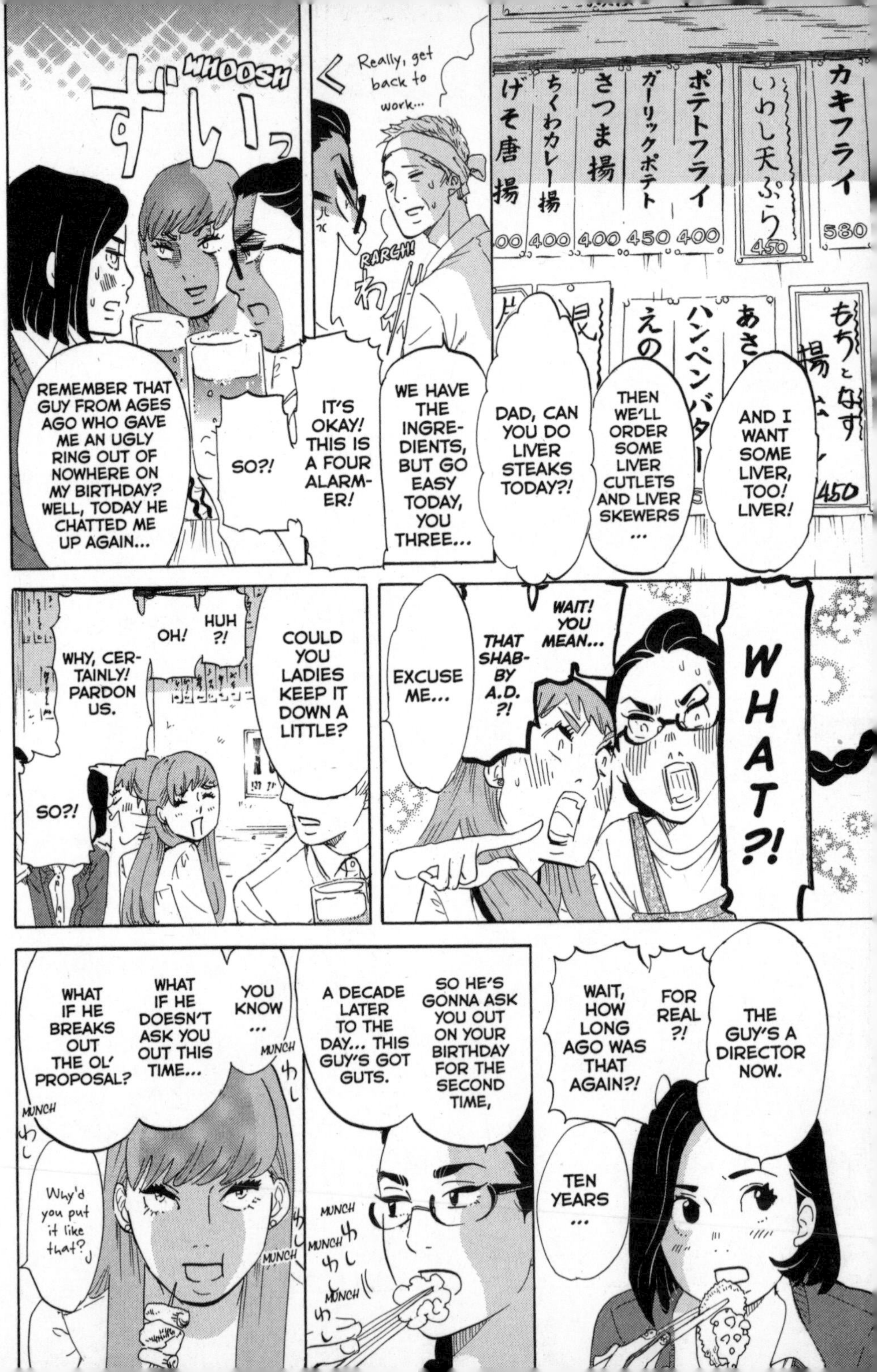
カキフライ 580
いわし天ぷら 450
ポテトフライ 400
ガーリックポテト 450
さつま揚 400
ちくわカレー揚 400
げそ唐揚 400
もちとなす揚
ハンペンバター
450
AND I WANT SOME LIVER, TOO! LIVER!
THEN WE'LL ORDER SOME LIVER CUTLETS AND LIVER SKEWERS ...
DAD, CAN YOU DO LIVER STEAKS TODAY?!
Really, get back to work...
RARGH!
わ
WE HAVE THE INGREDIENTS, BUT GO EASY TODAY, YOU THREE...
WHOOSH
ずいーっ
IT'S OKAY! THIS IS A FOUR ALARMER!
SO?!
REMEMBER THAT GUY FROM AGES AGO WHO GAVE ME AN UGLY RING OUT OF NOWHERE ON MY BIRTHDAY? WELL, TODAY HE CHATTED ME UP AGAIN...
WHAT?!
WAIT! YOU MEAN...
THAT SHABBY A.D. ?!
EXCUSE ME...
COULD YOU LADIES KEEP IT DOWN A LITTLE?
HUH ?!
OH!
WHY, CERTAINLY! PARDON US.
SO?!
THE GUY'S A DIRECTOR NOW.
FOR REAL ?!
WAIT, HOW LONG AGO WAS THAT AGAIN?!
TEN YEARS ...
SO HE'S GONNA ASK YOU OUT ON YOUR BIRTHDAY FOR THE SECOND TIME,
A DECADE LATER TO THE DAY... THIS GUY'S GOT GUTS.
MUNCH
MUNCH
MUNCH
MUNCH
YOU KNOW ...
WHAT IF HE DOESN'T ASK YOU OUT THIS TIME...
WHAT IF HE BREAKS OUT THE OL' PROPOSAL?
MUNCH
Why'd you put it like that?

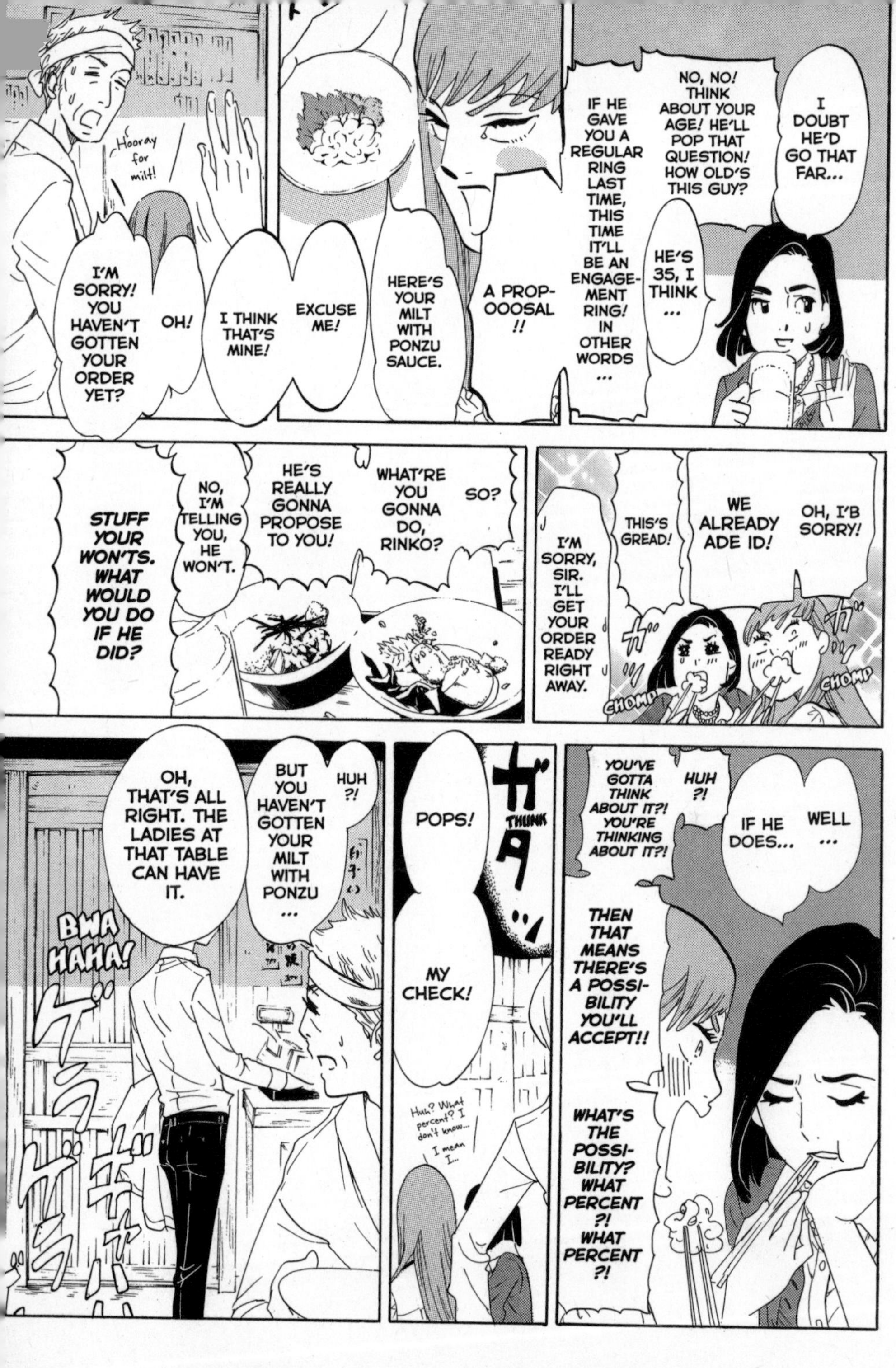
I DOUBT HE'D GO THAT FAR...
NO, NO! THINK ABOUT YOUR AGE! HE'LL POP THAT QUESTION! HOW OLD'S THIS GUY?
HE'S 35, I THINK...
IF HE GAVE YOU A REGULAR RING LAST TIME, THIS TIME IT'LL BE AN ENGAGEMENT RING! IN OTHER WORDS...
A PROPOOOSAL!!
HERE'S YOUR MILT WITH PONZU SAUCE.
EXCUSE ME!
I THINK THAT'S MINE!
Hooray for milt!
OH!
I'M SORRY! YOU HAVEN'T GOTTEN YOUR ORDER YET?
OH, I'B SORRY!
WE ALREADY ADE ID!
THIS'S GREAD!
I'M SORRY, SIR. I'LL GET YOUR ORDER READY RIGHT AWAY.
CHOMP
CHOMP
SO?
WHAT'RE YOU GONNA DO, RINKO?
HE'S REALLY GONNA PROPOSE TO YOU!
NO, I'M TELLING YOU, HE WON'T.
STUFF YOUR WON'TS. WHAT WOULD YOU DO IF HE DID?
WELL...
IF HE DOES...
HUH?!
YOU'VE GOTTA THINK ABOUT IT?! YOU'RE THINKING ABOUT IT?!
THEN THAT MEANS THERE'S A POSSIBILITY YOU'LL ACCEPT!!
WHAT'S THE POSSIBILITY? WHAT PERCENT?! WHAT PERCENT?!
THUNK
POPS!
MY CHECK!
Huh? What percent? I don't know... I mean I...
HUH?!
BUT YOU HAVEN'T GOTTEN YOUR MILT WITH PONZU...
OH, THAT'S ALL RIGHT. THE LADIES AT THAT TABLE CAN HAVE IT.
BWA HAHA!

IN TOKYO, NO ONE CARES IF YOUNG WOMEN DRINK IN SOME CHEAP PUB.

BWAHA HAHAHA

HUH?

WHAT, REALLY?

YOU GIRLS WERE SO LOUD YOU RAN OFF A CUSTOMER!

HEY!

OH MAN!

THUNK

I ENJOYED THE MEAL.

SORRY ABOUT THE NOISE, SIR.

...MAKES DRINKING SO FUN...

IT MAKES THE DRINKS TASTE SO GOOD...

I LOVE DRINKING WITH THE GIRLS.

AND I LOVE TOKYO.

HMM?

WIGGLE

もぞ‥

もぞ‥‥

WIGGLE

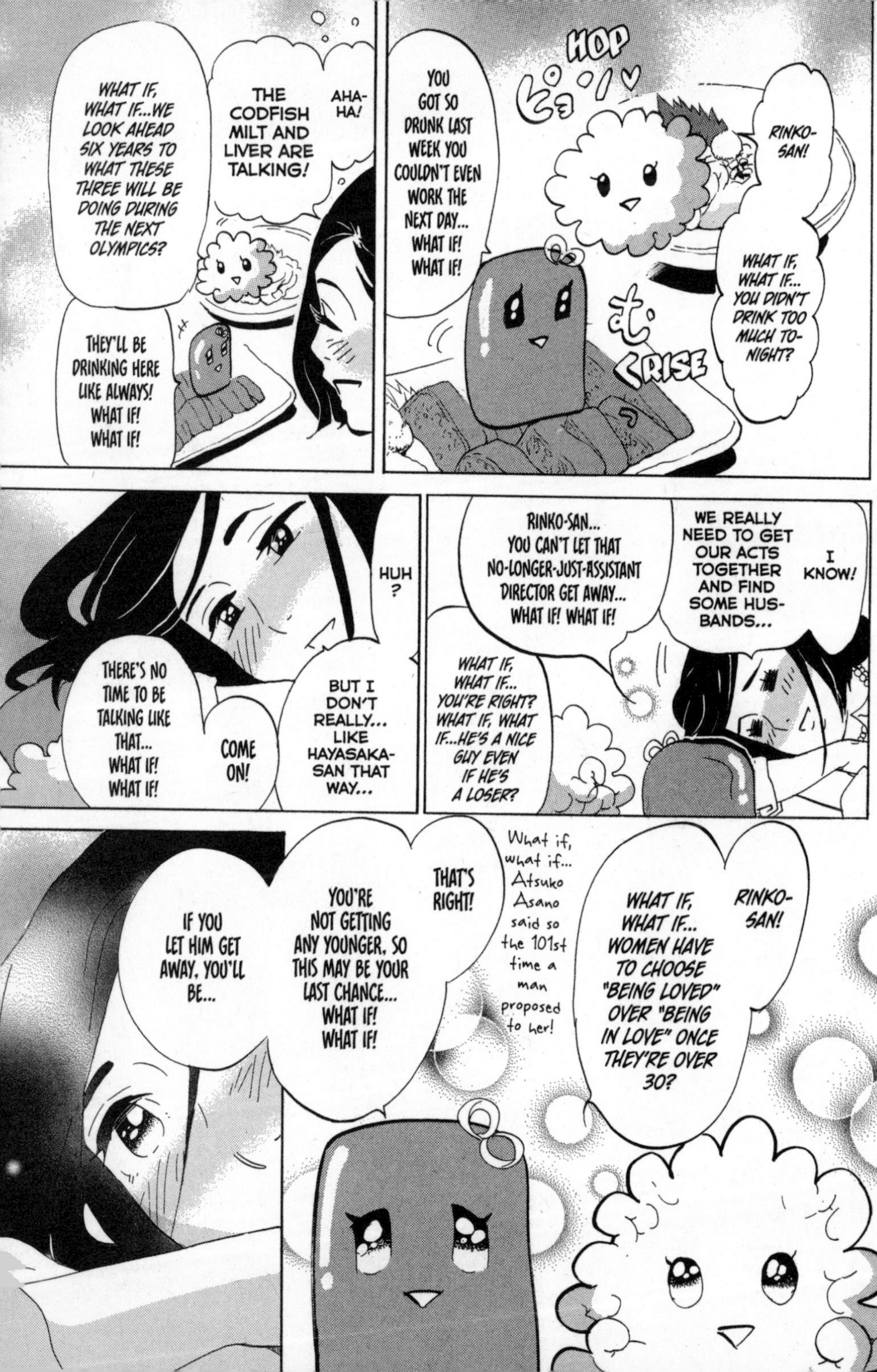
HOP
RINKO-SAN!
YOU GOT SO DRUNK LAST WEEK YOU COULDN'T EVEN WORK THE NEXT DAY... WHAT IF! WHAT IF!
WHAT IF, WHAT IF... YOU DIDN'T DRINK TOO MUCH TO-NIGHT?
RISE
AHA-HA!
THE CODFISH MILT AND LIVER ARE TALKING!
WHAT IF, WHAT IF...WE LOOK AHEAD SIX YEARS TO WHAT THESE THREE WILL BE DOING DURING THE NEXT OLYMPICS?
THEY'LL BE DRINKING HERE LIKE ALWAYS! WHAT IF! WHAT IF!
I KNOW!
WE REALLY NEED TO GET OUR ACTS TOGETHER AND FIND SOME HUS-BANDS...
RINKO-SAN... YOU CAN'T LET THAT NO-LONGER-JUST-ASSISTANT DIRECTOR GET AWAY... WHAT IF! WHAT IF!
WHAT IF, WHAT IF... YOU'RE RIGHT? WHAT IF, WHAT IF...HE'S A NICE GUY EVEN IF HE'S A LOSER?
HUH?
BUT I DON'T REALLY... LIKE HAYASAKA-SAN THAT WAY...
COME ON!
THERE'S NO TIME TO BE TALKING LIKE THAT... WHAT IF! WHAT IF!
RINKO-SAN!
WHAT IF, WHAT IF... WOMEN HAVE TO CHOOSE "BEING LOVED" OVER "BEING IN LOVE" ONCE THEY'RE OVER 30?
What if, what if... Atsuko Asano said so the 101st time a man proposed to her!
THAT'S RIGHT!
YOU'RE NOT GETTING ANY YOUNGER, SO THIS MAY BE YOUR LAST CHANCE... WHAT IF! WHAT IF!
IF YOU LET HIM GET AWAY, YOU'LL BE...

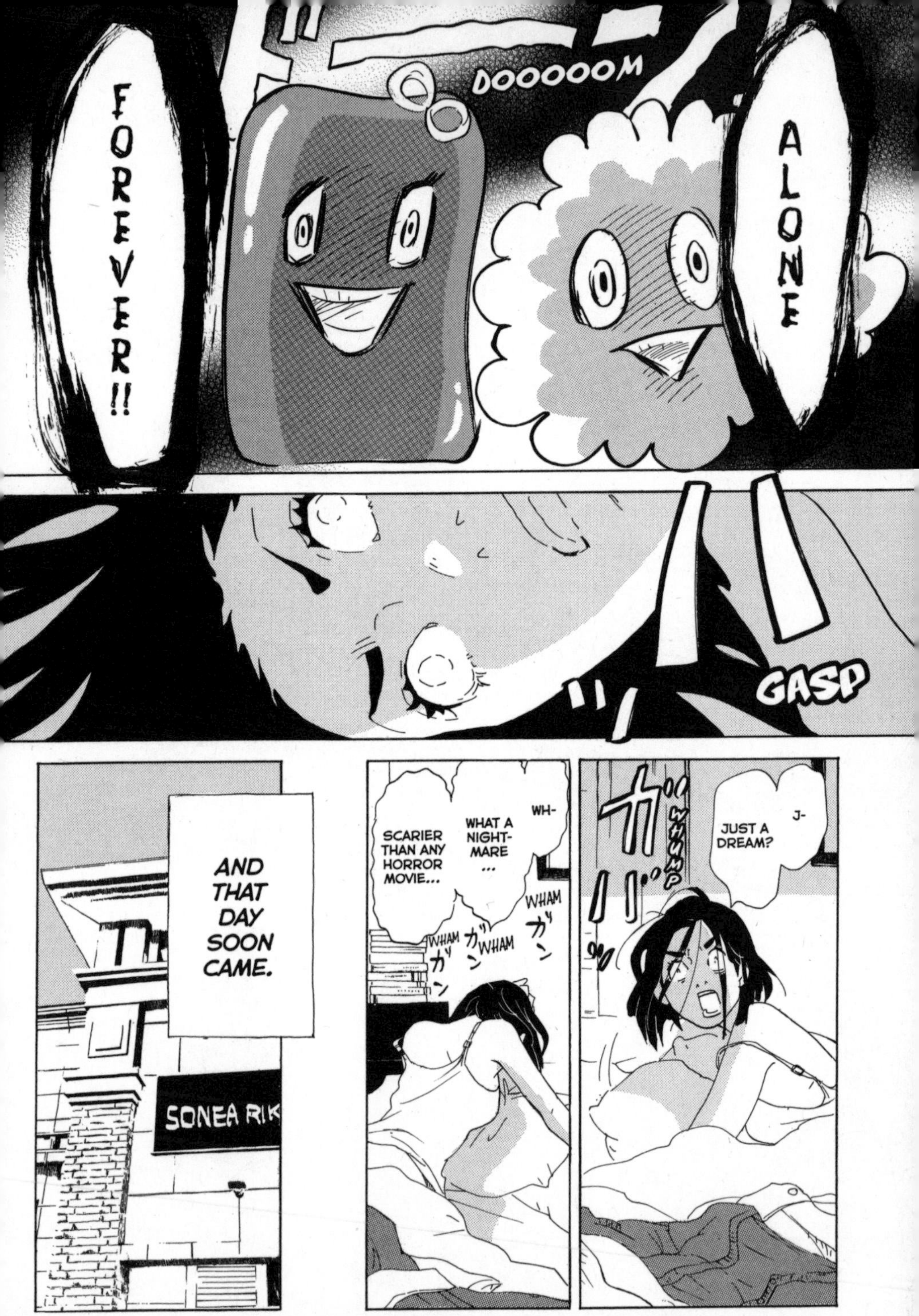
ALONE
DOOOOOM
FOREVER!!
GASP
J-
JUST A DREAM?
WHUMP
WH-
WHAT A NIGHTMARE...
SCARIER THAN ANY HORROR MOVIE...
WHAM
WHAM
WHAM
AND THAT DAY SOON CAME.
SONEA RIK

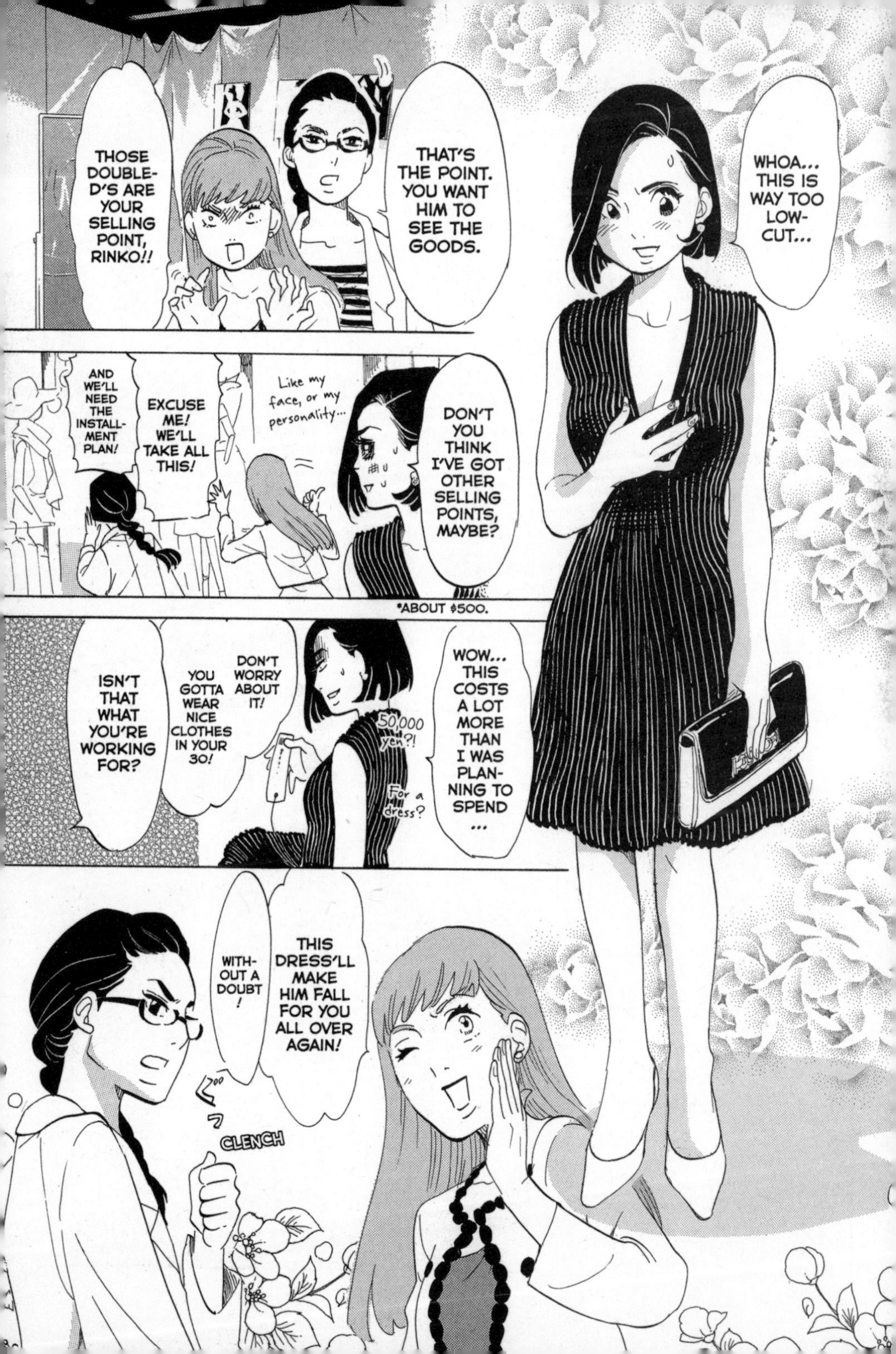
WHOA... THIS IS WAY TOO LOW-CUT...
THAT'S THE POINT. YOU WANT HIM TO SEE THE GOODS.
THOSE DOUBLE-D'S ARE YOUR SELLING POINT, RINKO!!
DON'T YOU THINK I'VE GOT OTHER SELLING POINTS, MAYBE?
Like my face, or my personality...
EXCUSE ME! WE'LL TAKE ALL THIS!
AND WE'LL NEED THE INSTALLMENT PLAN!
WOW... THIS COSTS A LOT MORE THAN I WAS PLANNING TO SPEND...
50,000 yen?!
For a dress?
DON'T WORRY ABOUT IT!
YOU GOTTA WEAR NICE CLOTHES IN YOUR 30!
ISN'T THAT WHAT YOU'RE WORKING FOR?
THIS DRESS'LL MAKE HIM FALL FOR YOU ALL OVER AGAIN!
WITHOUT A DOUBT!
CLENCH

*ABOUT $500.

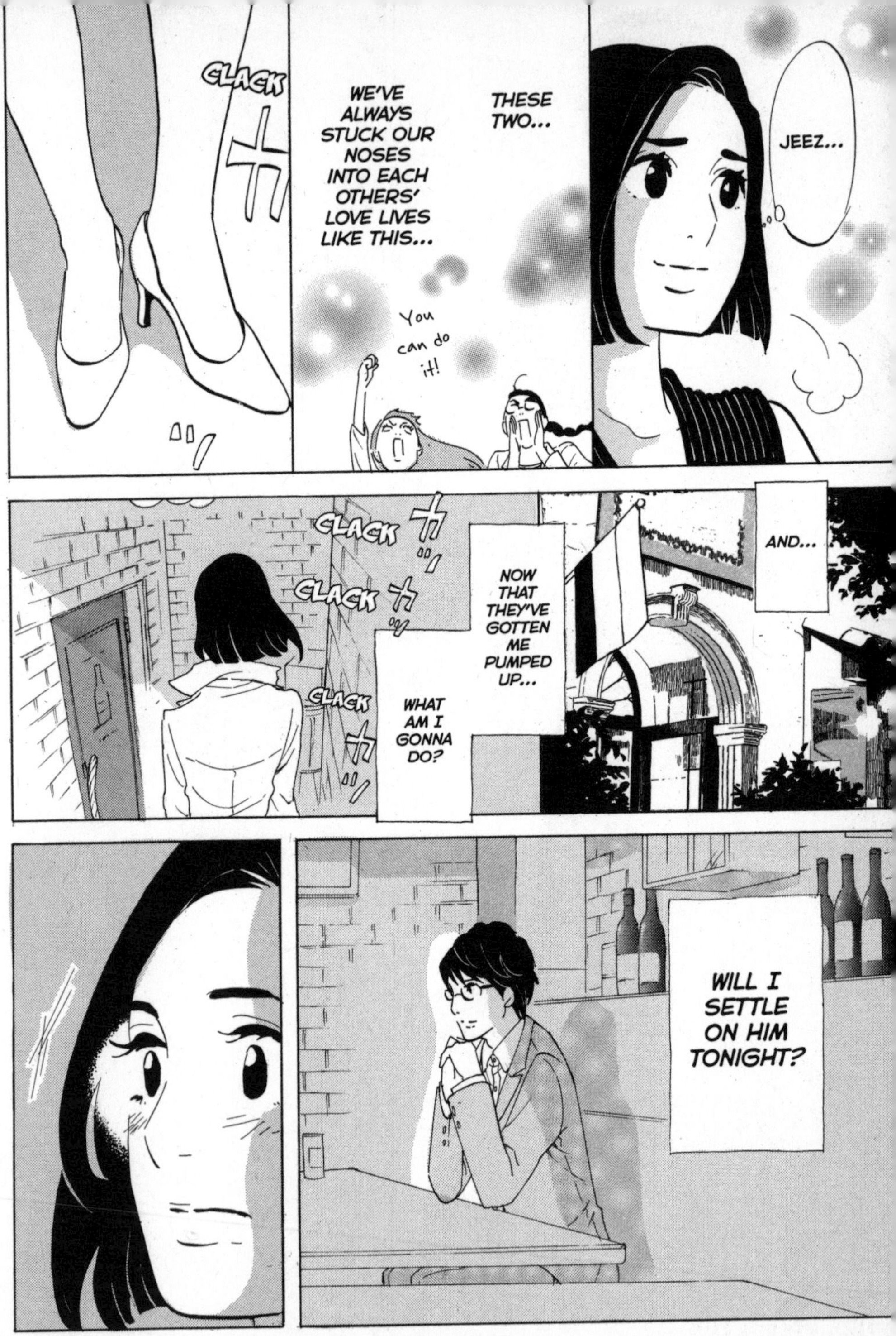

JEEZ...
THESE TWO...
WE'VE ALWAYS STUCK OUR NOSES INTO EACH OTHERS' LOVE LIVES LIKE THIS...
You can do it!
CLACK
AND...
NOW THAT THEY'VE GOTTEN ME PUMPED UP...
WHAT AM I GONNA DO?
CLACK
CLACK
CLACK
WILL I SETTLE ON HIM TONIGHT?

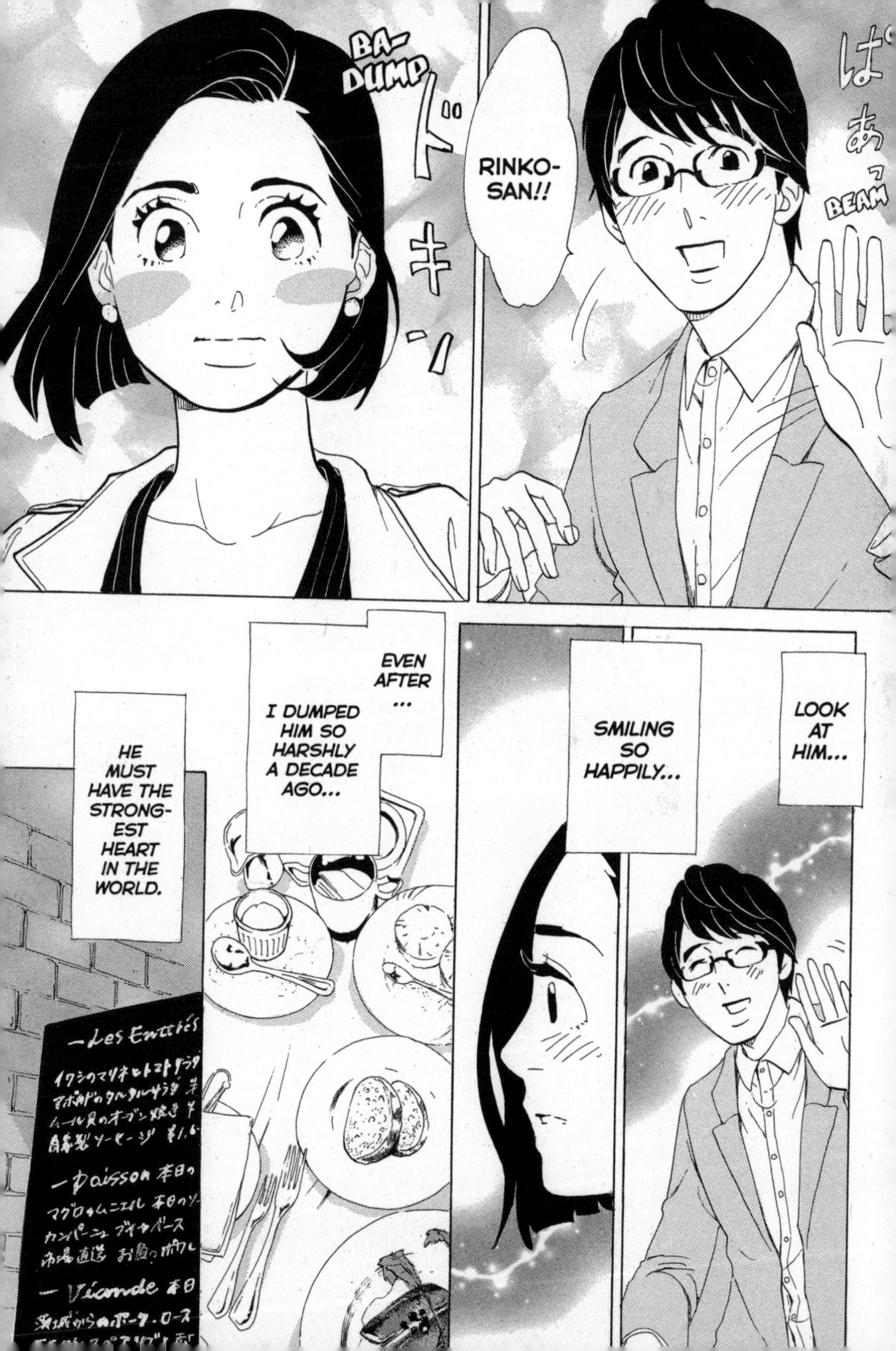
ぱあっ
BEAM
RINKO-SAN!!
BA-DUMP
ドキーン
LOOK AT HIM...
SMILING SO HAPPILY...
EVEN AFTER...
I DUMPED HIM SO HARSHLY A DECADE AGO...
HE MUST HAVE THE STRONGEST HEART IN THE WORLD.
Les Entrées
Poisson
Viande

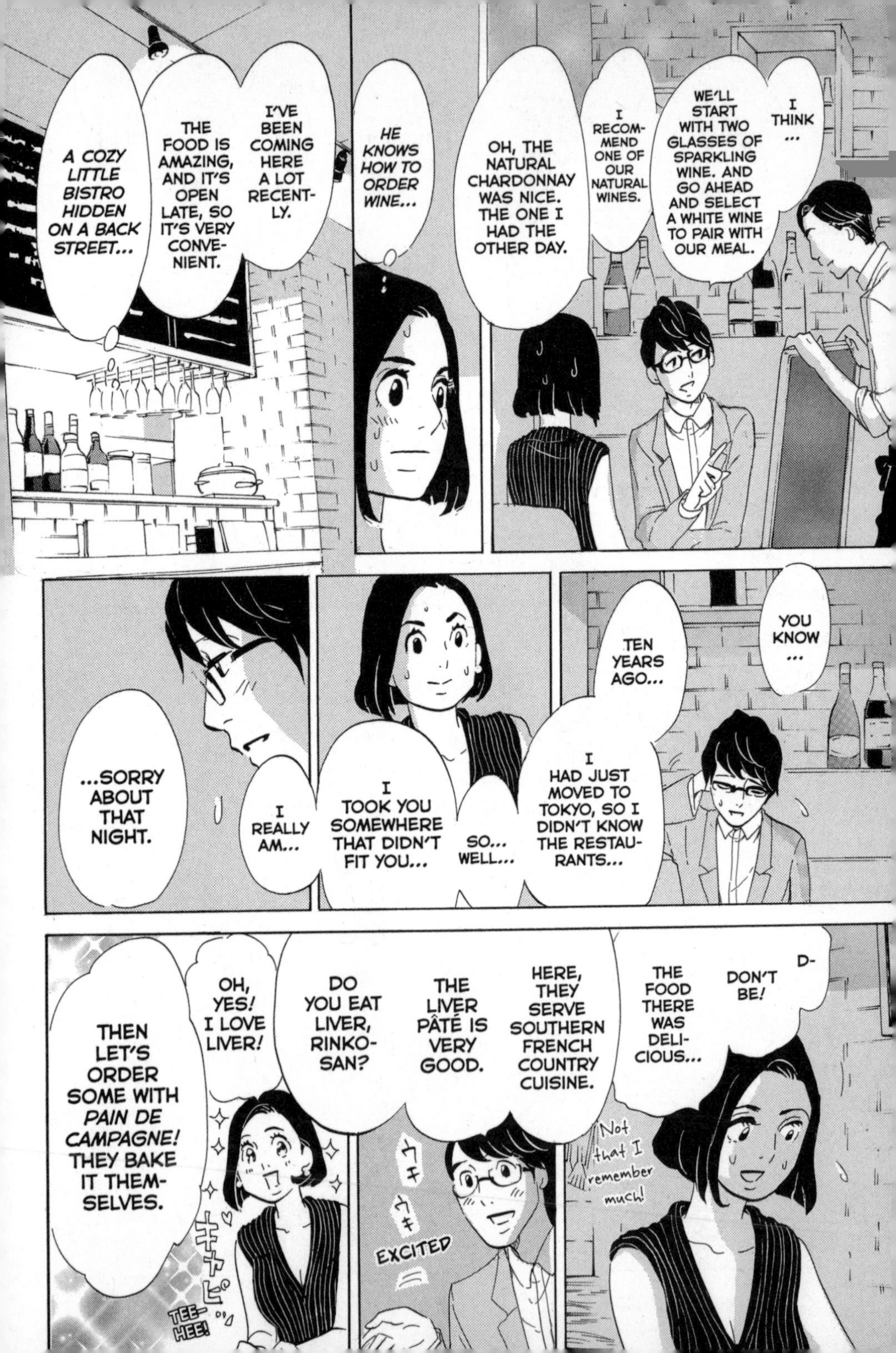
I THINK...
WE'LL START WITH TWO GLASSES OF SPARKLING WINE. AND GO AHEAD AND SELECT A WHITE WINE TO PAIR WITH OUR MEAL.
I RECOMMEND ONE OF OUR NATURAL WINES.
OH, THE NATURAL CHARDONNAY WAS NICE. THE ONE I HAD THE OTHER DAY.
HE KNOWS HOW TO ORDER WINE...
I'VE BEEN COMING HERE A LOT RECENTLY.
THE FOOD IS AMAZING, AND IT'S OPEN LATE, SO IT'S VERY CONVENIENT.
A COZY LITTLE BISTRO HIDDEN ON A BACK STREET...
YOU KNOW...
TEN YEARS AGO...
I HAD JUST MOVED TO TOKYO, SO I DIDN'T KNOW THE RESTAURANTS...
SO... WELL...
I TOOK YOU SOMEWHERE THAT DIDN'T FIT YOU...
I REALLY AM...
...SORRY ABOUT THAT NIGHT.
D- DON'T BE!
THE FOOD THERE WAS DELICIOUS...
Not that I remember much!
HERE, THEY SERVE SOUTHERN FRENCH COUNTRY CUISINE.
THE LIVER PÂTÉ IS VERY GOOD.
DO YOU EAT LIVER, RINKO-SAN?
ウキ ウキ
EXCITED
OH, YES! I LOVE LIVER!
THEN LET'S ORDER SOME WITH *PAIN DE CAMPAGNE!* THEY BAKE IT THEMSELVES.
キャピ
TEE-HEE!

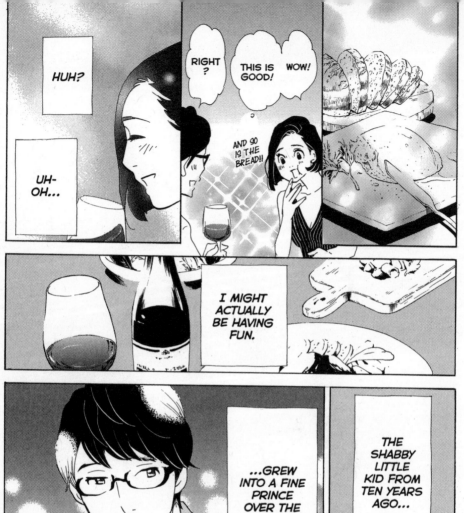

WOW!
THIS IS GOOD!
RIGHT?
AND SO IS THE BREAD!!
HUH?
UH-OH...
I MIGHT ACTUALLY BE HAVING FUN.
THE SHABBY LITTLE KID FROM TEN YEARS AGO...
...GREW INTO A FINE PRINCE OVER THE COURSE OF A DECADE...

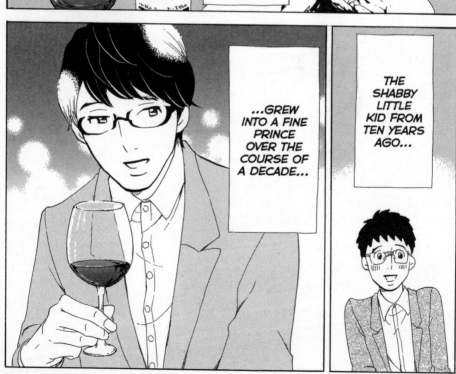

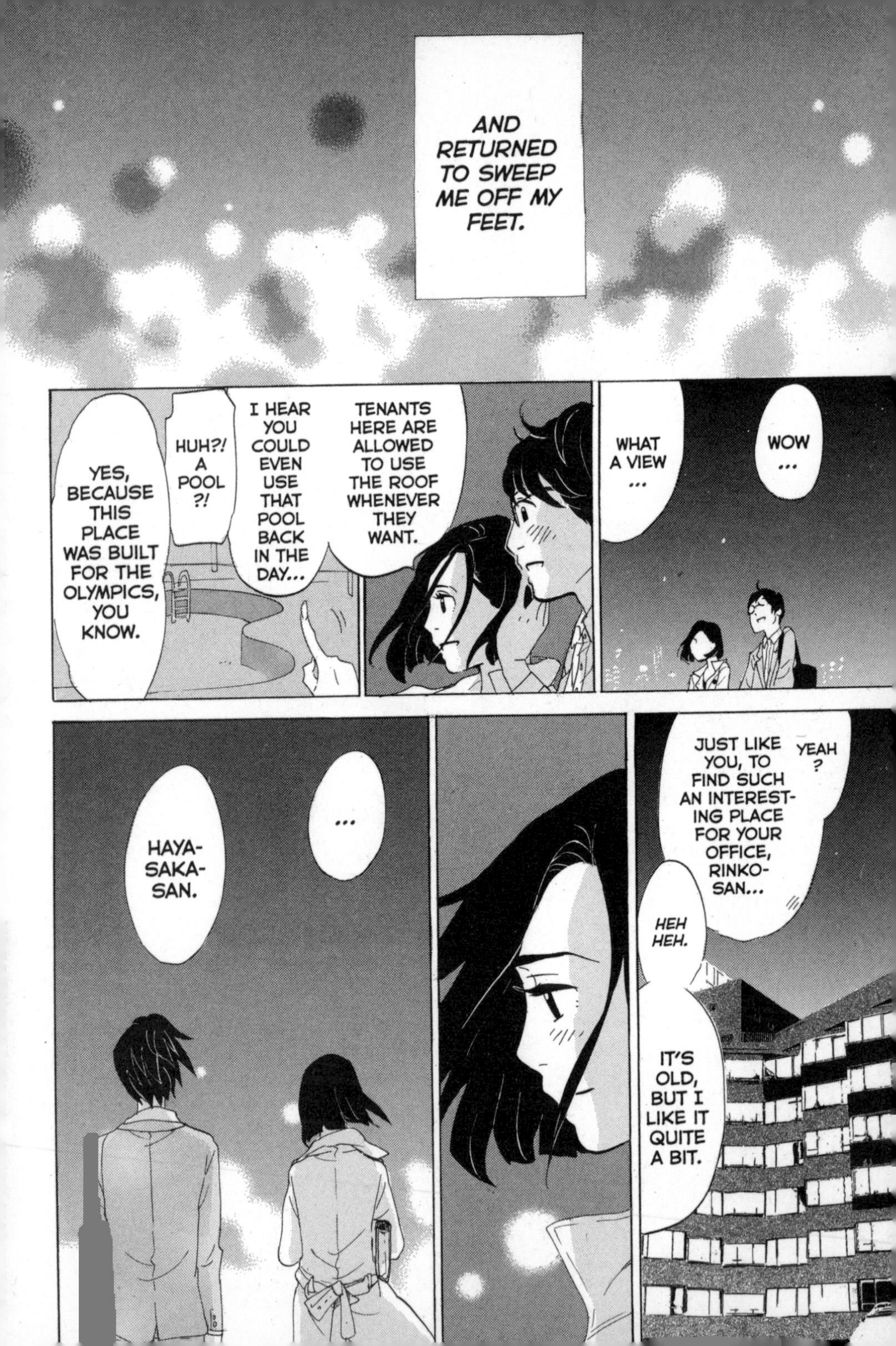
AND RETURNED TO SWEEP ME OFF MY FEET.
WOW ...
WHAT A VIEW ...
TENANTS HERE ARE ALLOWED TO USE THE ROOF WHENEVER THEY WANT.
I HEAR YOU COULD EVEN USE THAT POOL BACK IN THE DAY...
HUH?! A POOL ?!
YES, BECAUSE THIS PLACE WAS BUILT FOR THE OLYMPICS, YOU KNOW.
YEAH ?
JUST LIKE YOU, TO FIND SUCH AN INTERESTING PLACE FOR YOUR OFFICE, RINKO-SAN...
HEH HEH.
IT'S OLD, BUT I LIKE IT QUITE A BIT.
...
HAYA-SAKA-SAN.

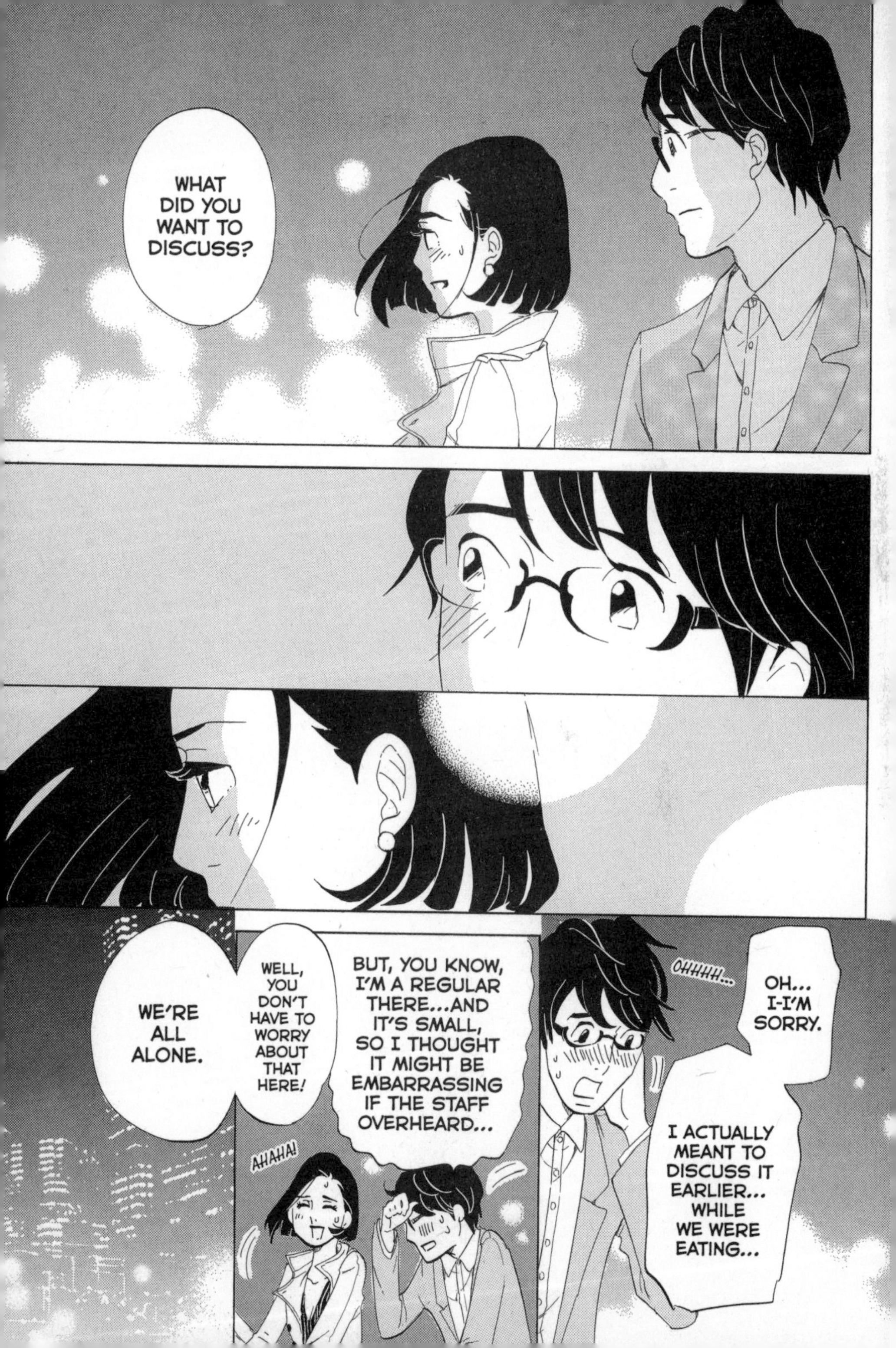
WHAT DID YOU WANT TO DISCUSS?
OH... I-I'M SORRY.
OHHHH...
I ACTUALLY MEANT TO DISCUSS IT EARLIER... WHILE WE WERE EATING...
BUT, YOU KNOW, I'M A REGULAR THERE...AND IT'S SMALL, SO I THOUGHT IT MIGHT BE EMBARRASSING IF THE STAFF OVERHEARD...
WELL, YOU DON'T HAVE TO WORRY ABOUT THAT HERE!
AHAHA!
WE'RE ALL ALONE.

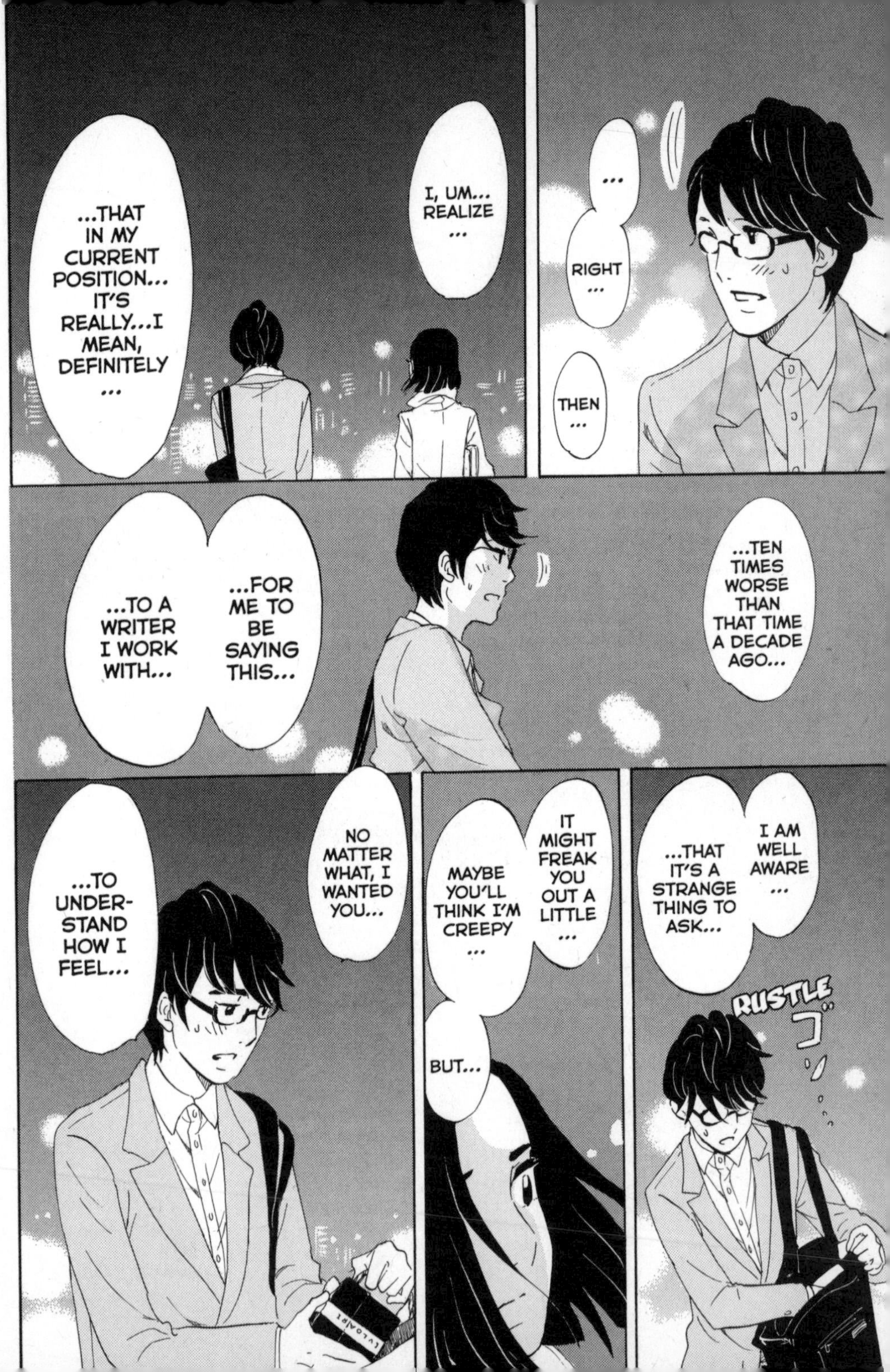
...
RIGHT...
THEN...
I, UM... REALIZE...
...THAT IN MY CURRENT POSITION... IT'S REALLY...I MEAN, DEFINITELY...
...TEN TIMES WORSE THAN THAT TIME A DECADE AGO...
...FOR ME TO BE SAYING THIS...
...TO A WRITER I WORK WITH...
I AM WELL AWARE...
...THAT IT'S A STRANGE THING TO ASK...
RUSTLE
IT MIGHT FREAK YOU OUT A LITTLE...
MAYBE YOU'LL THINK I'M CREEPY...
BUT...
NO MATTER WHAT, I WANTED YOU...
...TO UNDER-STAND HOW I FEEL...

RINKO-SAN.

PLEASE DON'T LAUGH...

BA-DUMP

IS THAT... ANOTHER RING??

I WON'T LAUGH ANY MORE!

I'M SORRY!

ALL RIGHT!

WHAP

AH!

YOU'RE ALREADY LAUGHING!

...

PFFT!

ALL RIGHT.

I...

RINKO-SAN ...

R-

...

GO AHEAD.

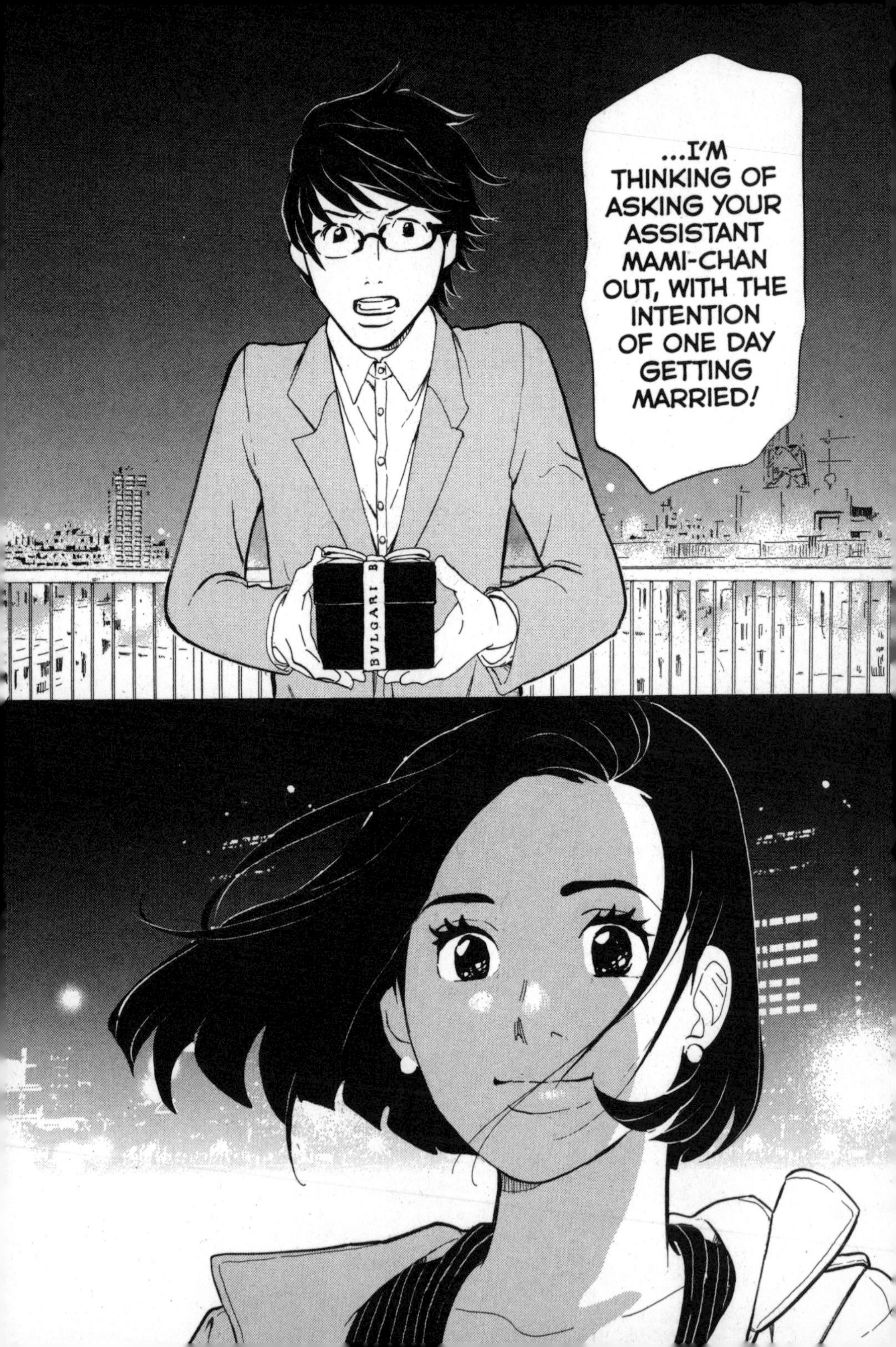
...I'M THINKING OF ASKING YOUR ASSISTANT MAMI-CHAN OUT, WITH THE INTENTION OF ONE DAY GETTING MARRIED!
BVLGARI
BVLGARI

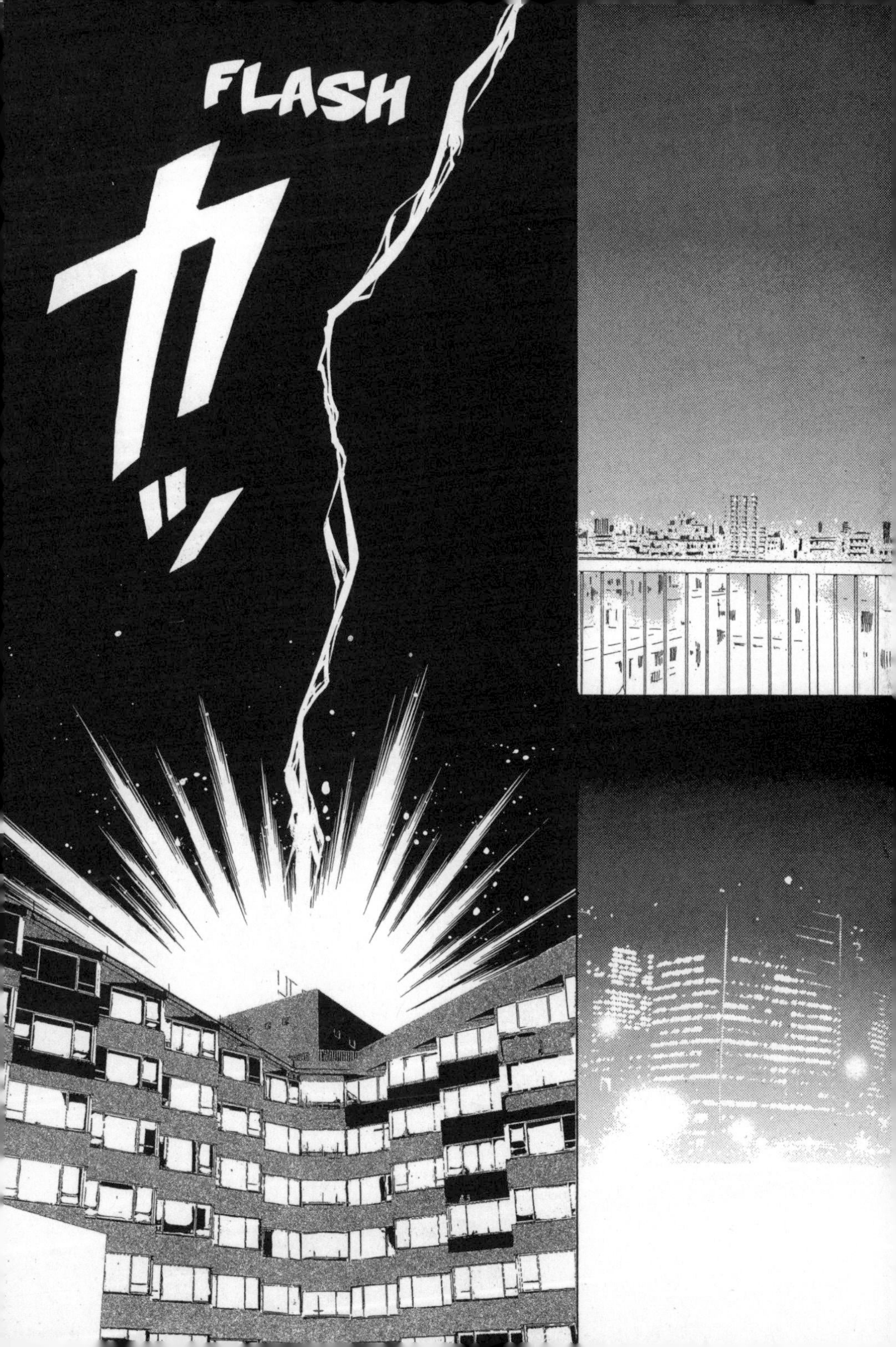
FLASH
カッ

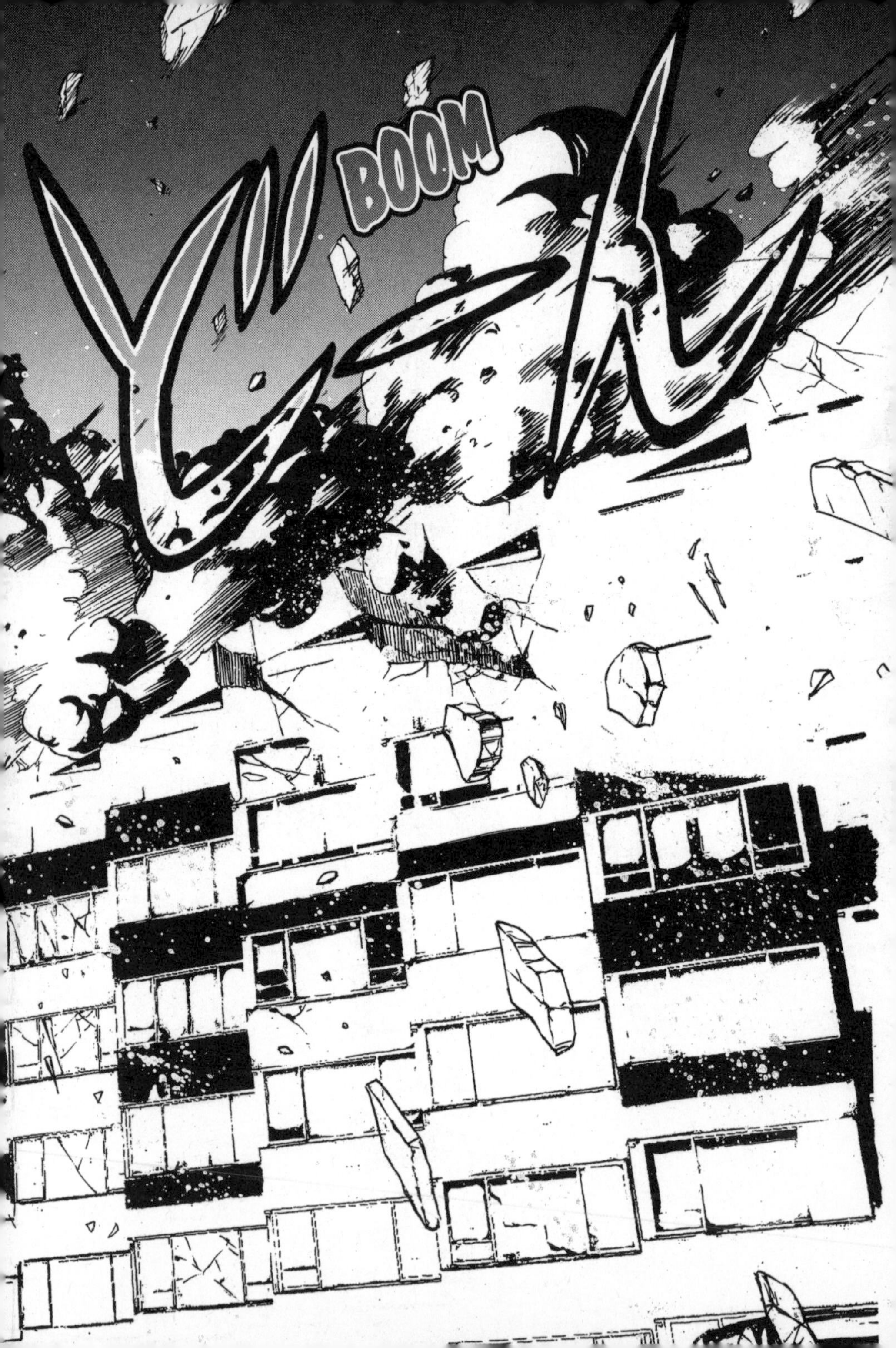
BOOM

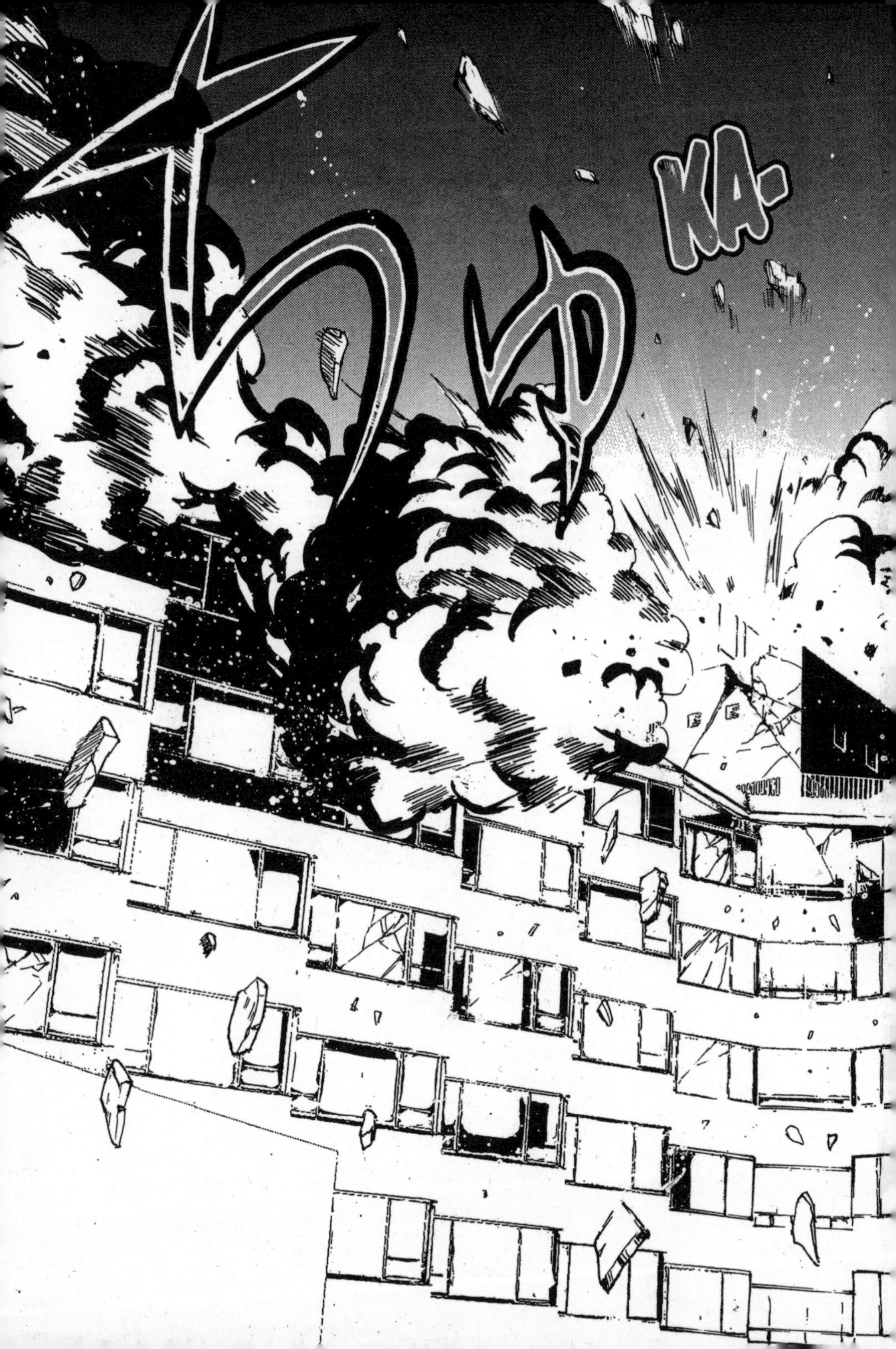
KA-

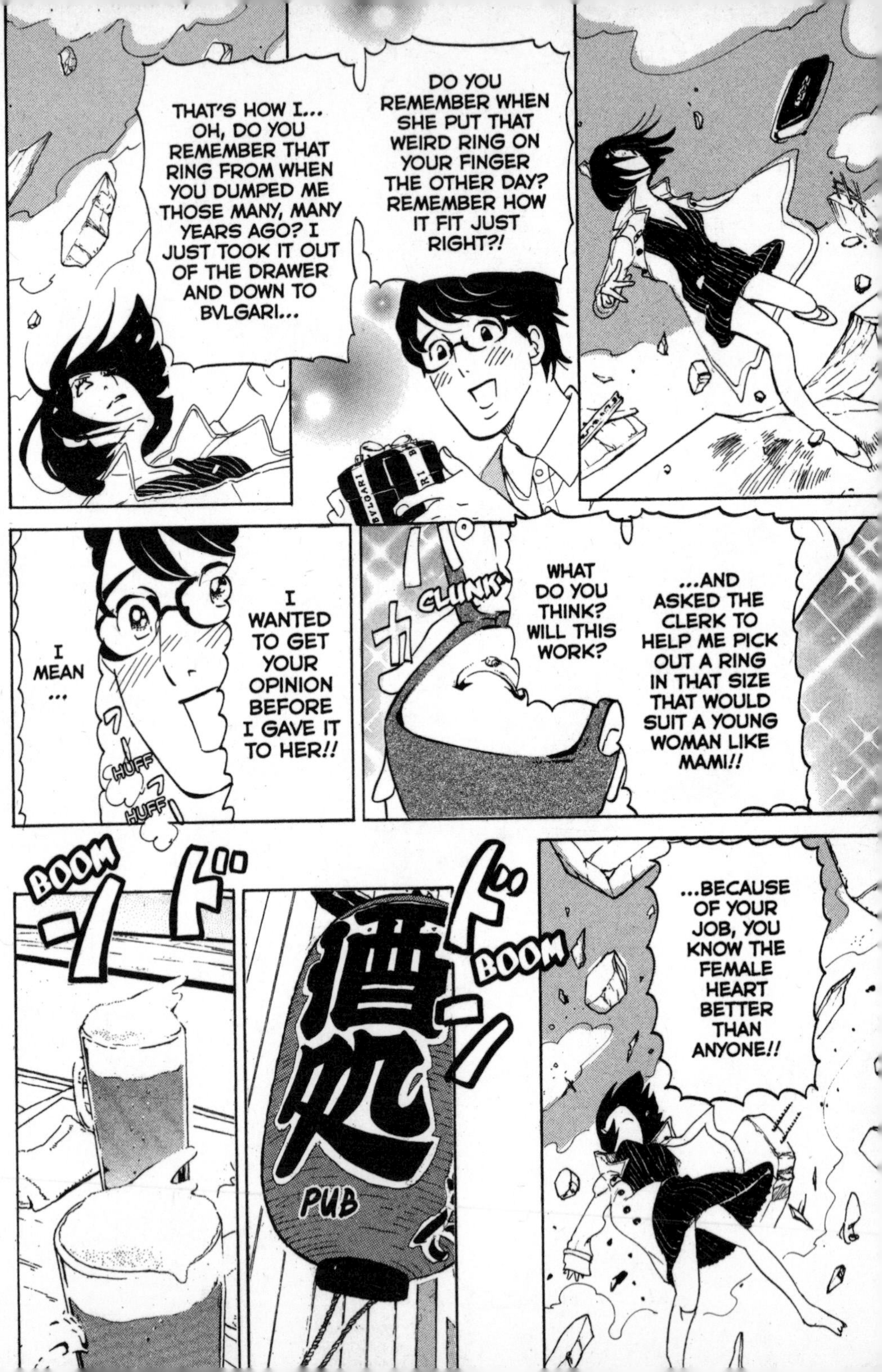
DO YOU REMEMBER WHEN SHE PUT THAT WEIRD RING ON YOUR FINGER THE OTHER DAY? REMEMBER HOW IT FIT JUST RIGHT?!
THAT'S HOW I... OH, DO YOU REMEMBER THAT RING FROM WHEN YOU DUMPED ME THOSE MANY, MANY YEARS AGO? I JUST TOOK IT OUT OF THE DRAWER AND DOWN TO BVLGARI...
BVLGARI
...AND ASKED THE CLERK TO HELP ME PICK OUT A RING IN THAT SIZE THAT WOULD SUIT A YOUNG WOMAN LIKE MAMI!!
WHAT DO YOU THINK? WILL THIS WORK?
GLUNK
I WANTED TO GET YOUR OPINION BEFORE I GAVE IT TO HER!!
I MEAN...
HUFF
HUFF
...BECAUSE OF YOUR JOB, YOU KNOW THE FEMALE HEART BETTER THAN ANYONE!!
BOOM
PUB
BOOM

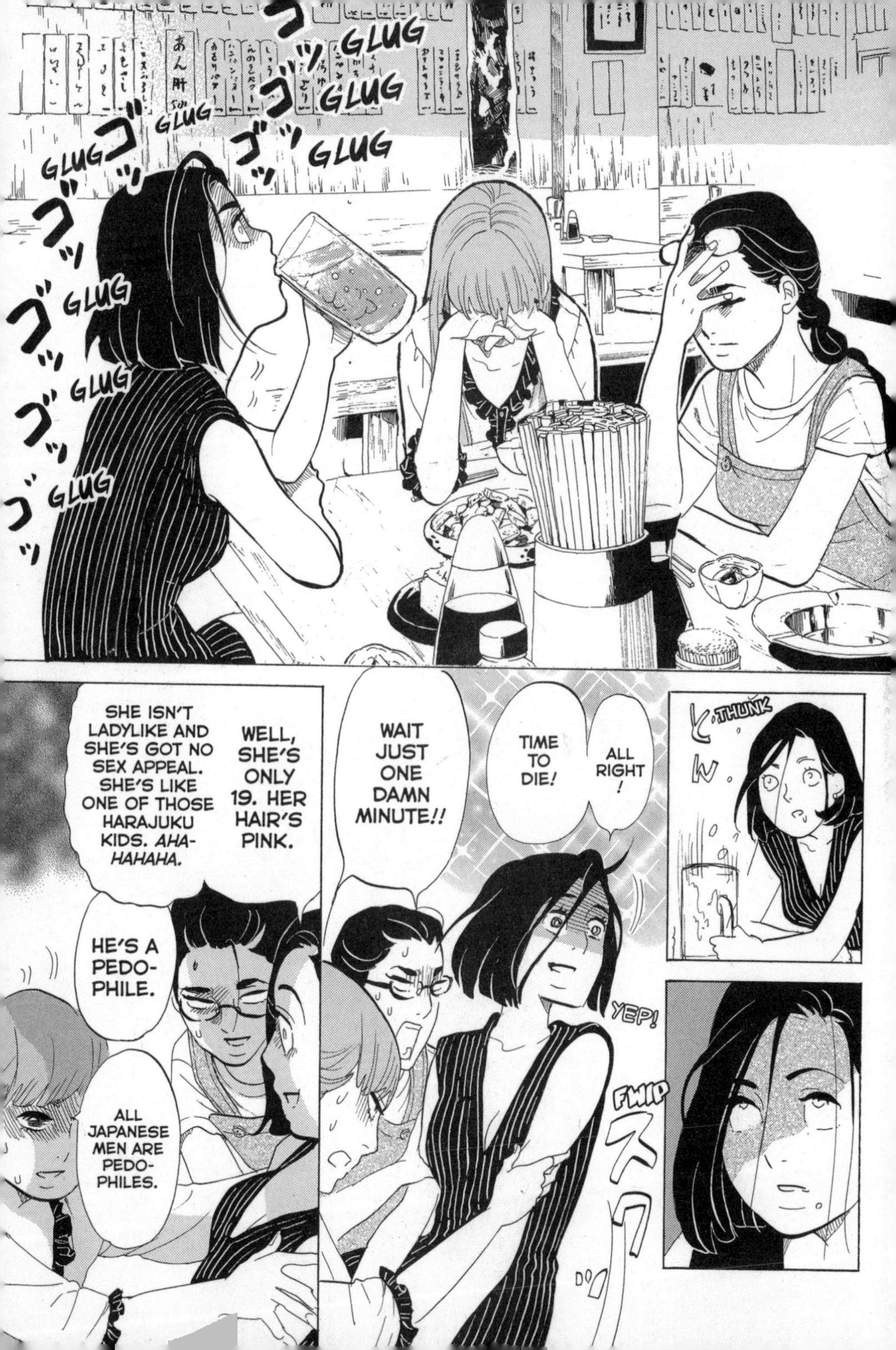
ゴッ GLUG
ゴッ GLUG
ゴッ GLUG
ゴッ GLUG
ゴッ GLUG
ゴッ GLUG
ゴッ GLUG
ゴッ
ドン THUNK
ALL RIGHT!
TIME TO DIE!
WAIT JUST ONE DAMN MINUTE!!
YEP!
スッ FWIP
WELL, SHE'S ONLY 19. HER HAIR'S PINK.
SHE ISN'T LADYLIKE AND SHE'S GOT NO SEX APPEAL. SHE'S LIKE ONE OF THOSE HARAJUKU KIDS. *AHAHAHAHA.*
HE'S A PEDOPHILE.
ALL JAPANESE MEN ARE PEDOPHILES.

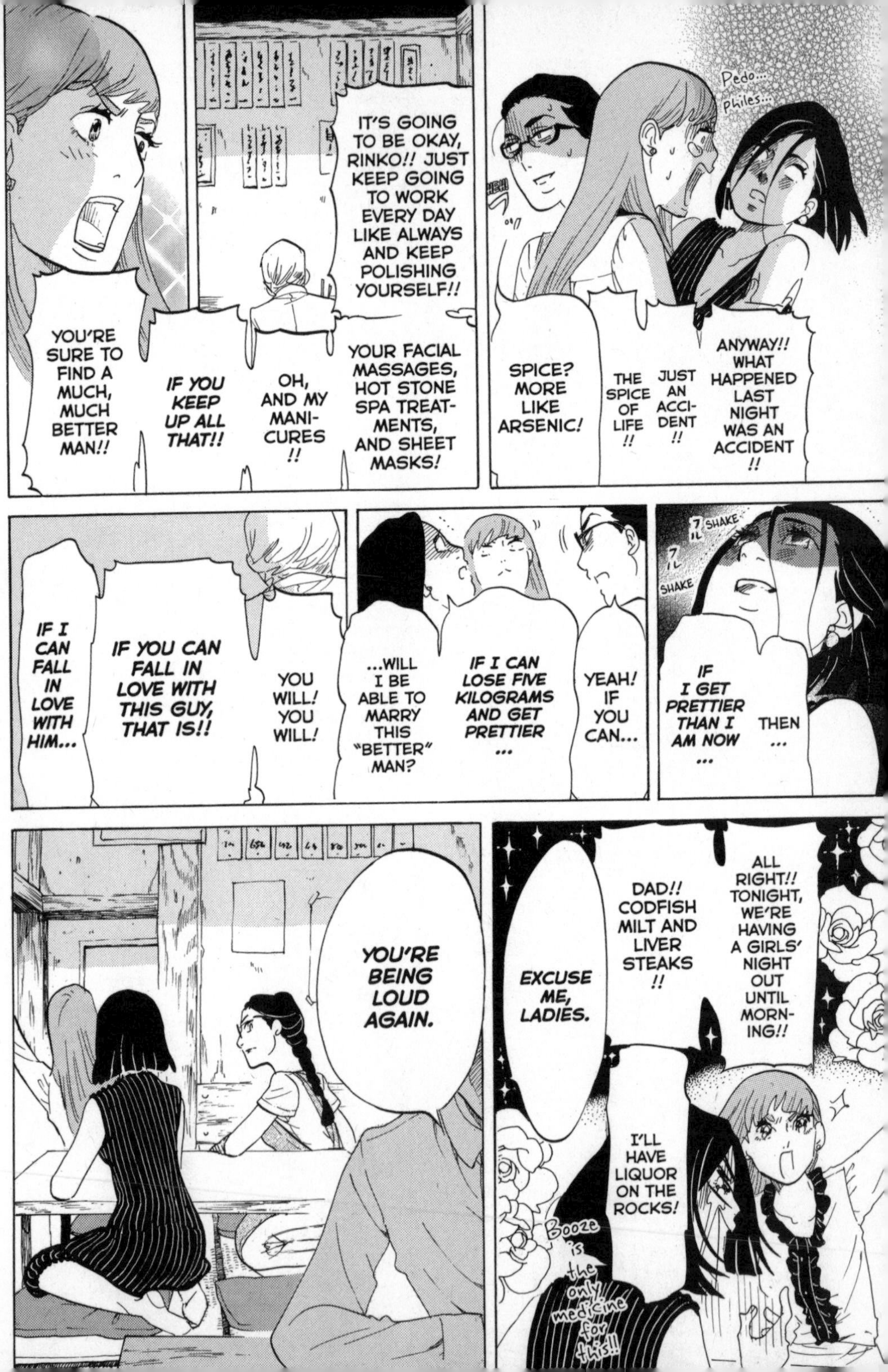
Pedo... philes...
HEH!
ANYWAY!! WHAT HAPPENED LAST NIGHT WAS AN ACCIDENT!!
JUST AN ACCIDENT!!
THE SPICE OF LIFE!!
SPICE? MORE LIKE ARSENIC!
IT'S GOING TO BE OKAY, RINKO!! JUST KEEP GOING TO WORK EVERY DAY LIKE ALWAYS AND KEEP POLISHING YOURSELF!!
YOUR FACIAL MASSAGES, HOT STONE SPA TREAT-MENTS, AND SHEET MASKS!
OH, AND MY MANI-CURES!!
IF YOU KEEP UP ALL THAT!!
YOU'RE SURE TO FIND A MUCH, MUCH BETTER MAN!!
SHAKE
SHAKE
THEN...
IF I GET PRETTIER THAN I AM NOW...
YEAH! IF YOU CAN...
IF I CAN LOSE FIVE KILOGRAMS AND GET PRETTIER...
...WILL I BE ABLE TO MARRY THIS "BETTER" MAN?
YOU WILL! YOU WILL!
IF YOU CAN FALL IN LOVE WITH THIS GUY, THAT IS!!
IF I CAN FALL IN LOVE WITH HIM...
ALL RIGHT!! TONIGHT, WE'RE HAVING A GIRLS' NIGHT OUT UNTIL MORN-ING!!
DAD!! CODFISH MILT AND LIVER STEAKS!!
EXCUSE ME, LADIES.
I'LL HAVE LIQUOR ON THE ROCKS!
Booze is the only medicine for this!!
YOU'RE BEING LOUD AGAIN.

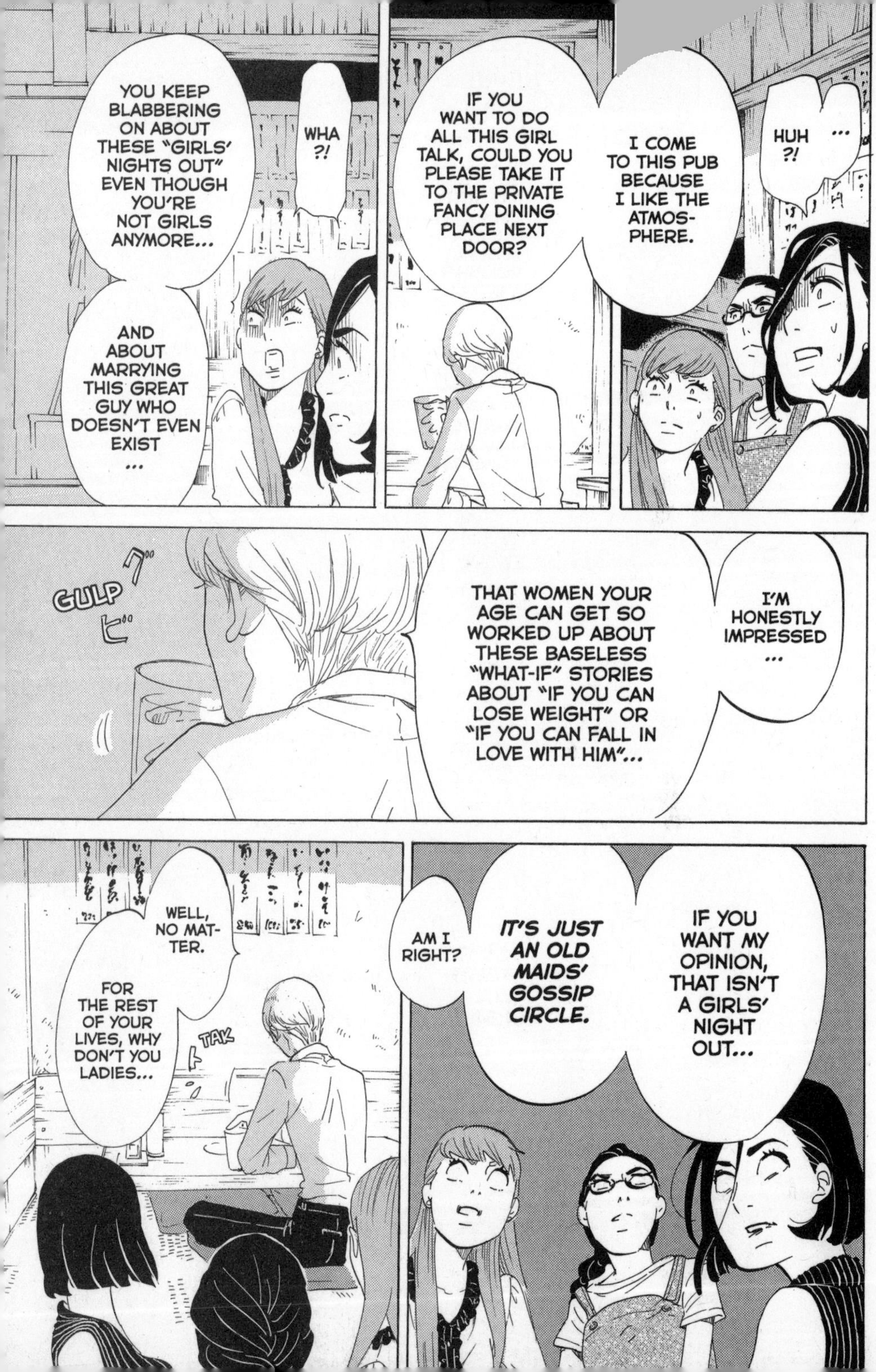
...
HUH ?!
I COME TO THIS PUB BECAUSE I LIKE THE ATMOSPHERE.
IF YOU WANT TO DO ALL THIS GIRL TALK, COULD YOU PLEASE TAKE IT TO THE PRIVATE FANCY DINING PLACE NEXT DOOR?
WHA ?!
YOU KEEP BLABBERING ON ABOUT THESE "GIRLS' NIGHTS OUT" EVEN THOUGH YOU'RE NOT GIRLS ANYMORE...
AND ABOUT MARRYING THIS GREAT GUY WHO DOESN'T EVEN EXIST ...
I'M HONESTLY IMPRESSED ...
THAT WOMEN YOUR AGE CAN GET SO WORKED UP ABOUT THESE BASELESS "WHAT-IF" STORIES ABOUT "IF YOU CAN LOSE WEIGHT" OR "IF YOU CAN FALL IN LOVE WITH HIM"...
GULP
IF YOU WANT MY OPINION, THAT ISN'T A GIRLS' NIGHT OUT...
IT'S JUST AN OLD MAIDS' GOSSIP CIRCLE.
AM I RIGHT?
WELL, NO MATTER.
TAK
FOR THE REST OF YOUR LIVES, WHY DON'T YOU LADIES...

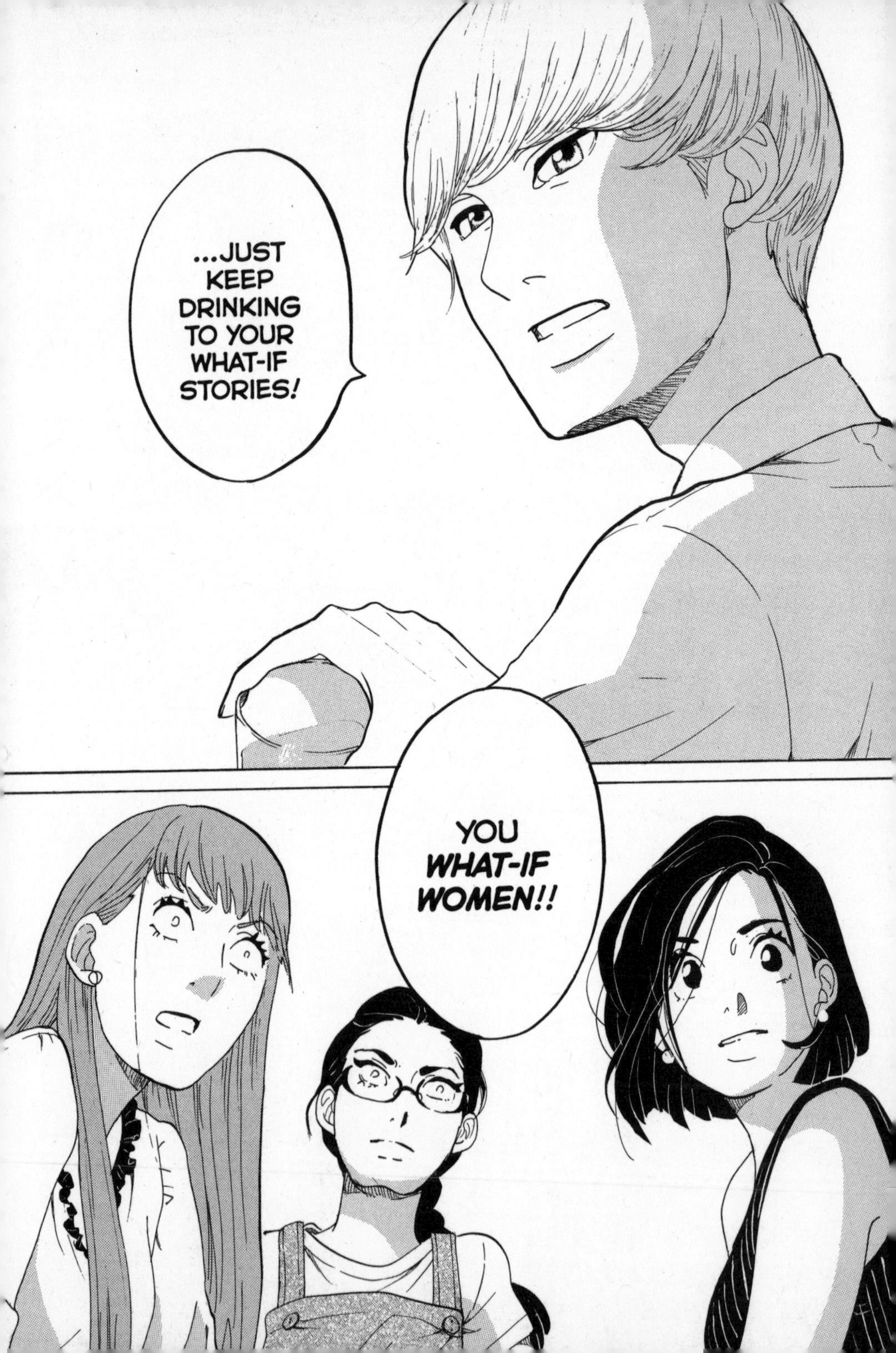
...JUST KEEP DRINKING TO YOUR WHAT-IF STORIES!
YOU *WHAT-IF WOMEN!!*

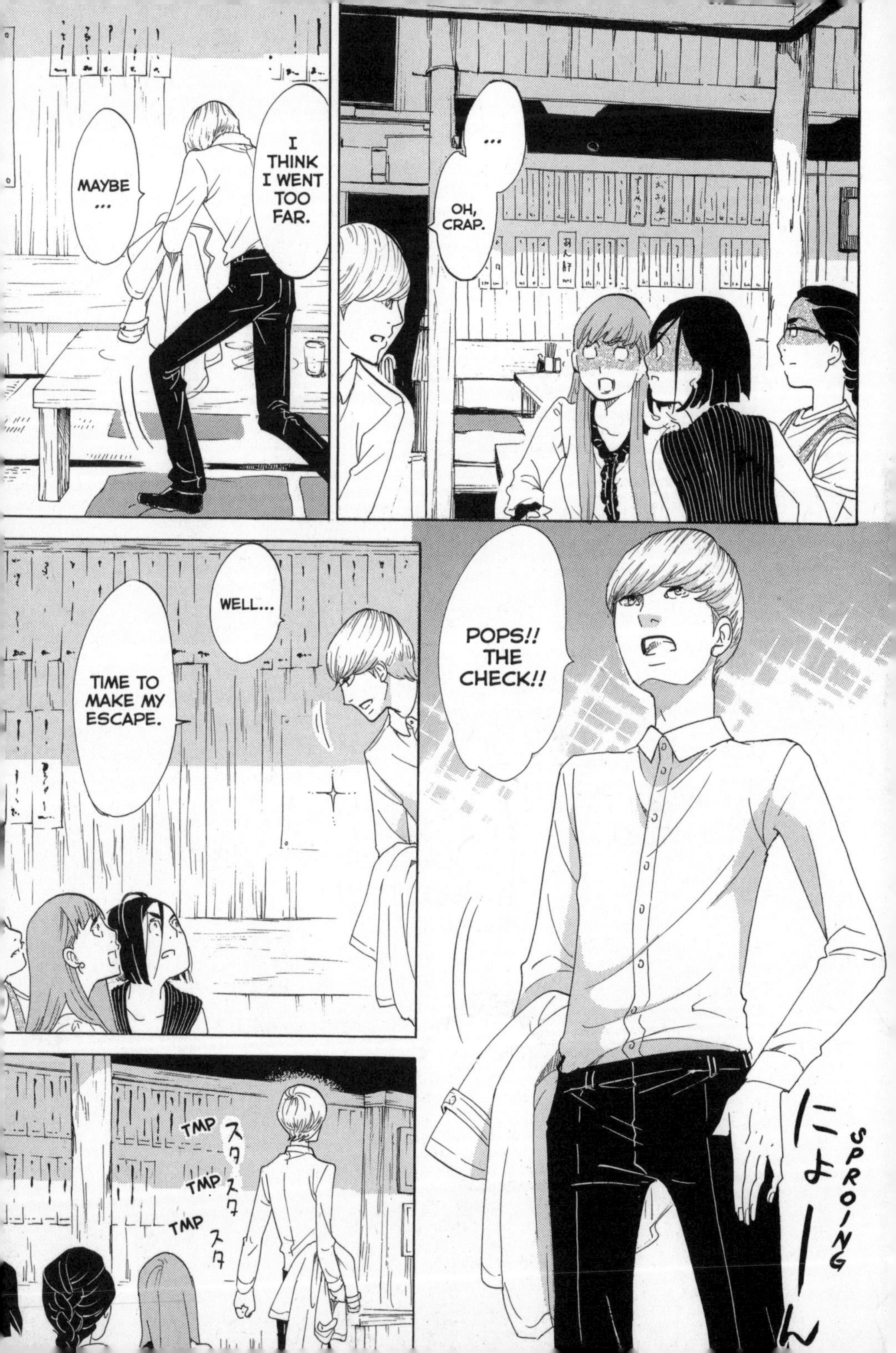
...
OH, CRAP.
I THINK I WENT TOO FAR.
MAYBE...
POPS!! THE CHECK!!
にょーん
SPROING
WELL...
TIME TO MAKE MY ESCAPE.
TMP スタ
TMP スタ
TMP スタ

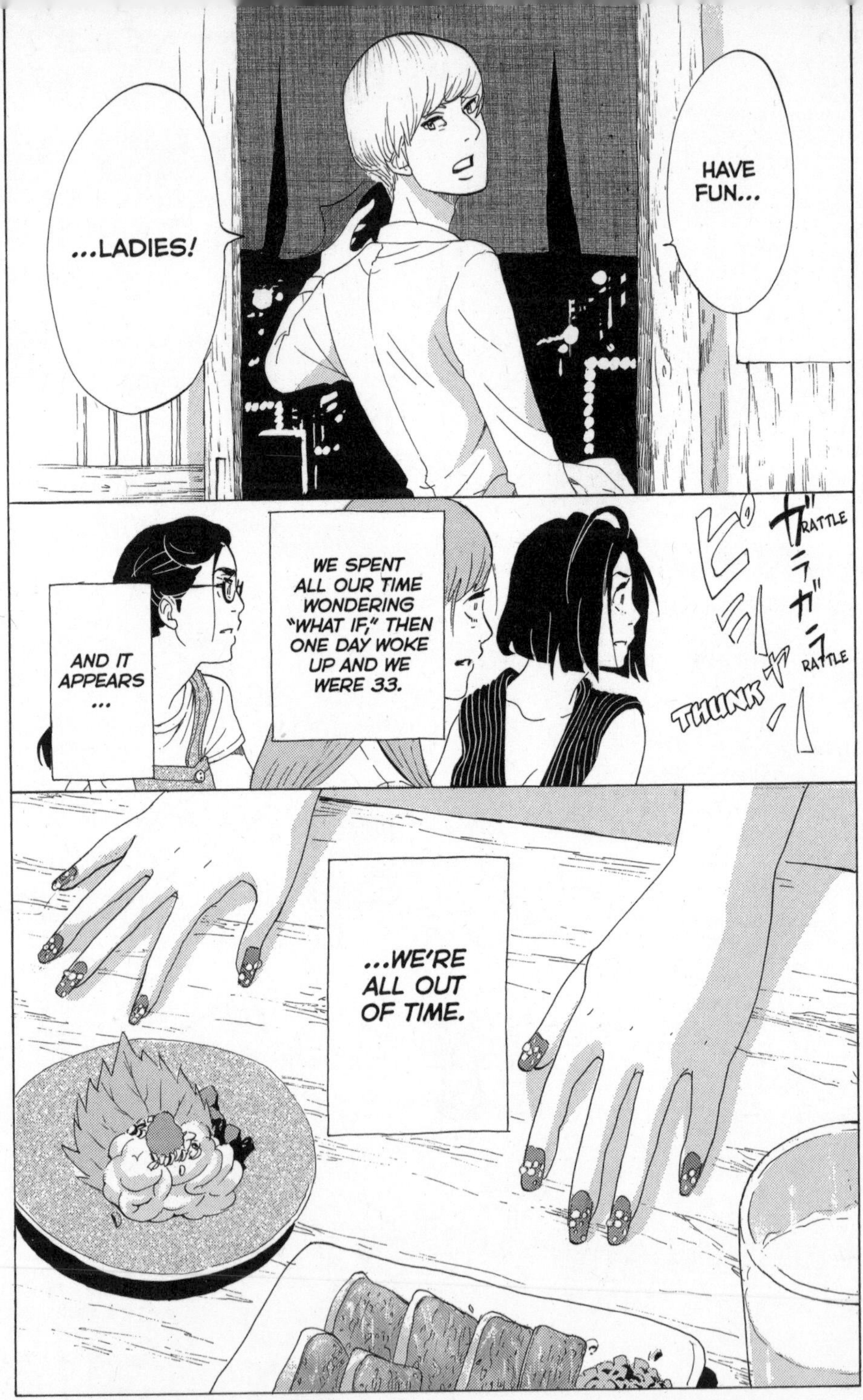
HAVE FUN...
...LADIES!
ガラガラ
RATTLE
RATTLE
ピシャ
THUNK
WE SPENT ALL OUR TIME WONDERING "WHAT IF," THEN ONE DAY WOKE UP AND WE WERE 33.
AND IT APPEARS ...
...WE'RE ALL OUT OF TIME.

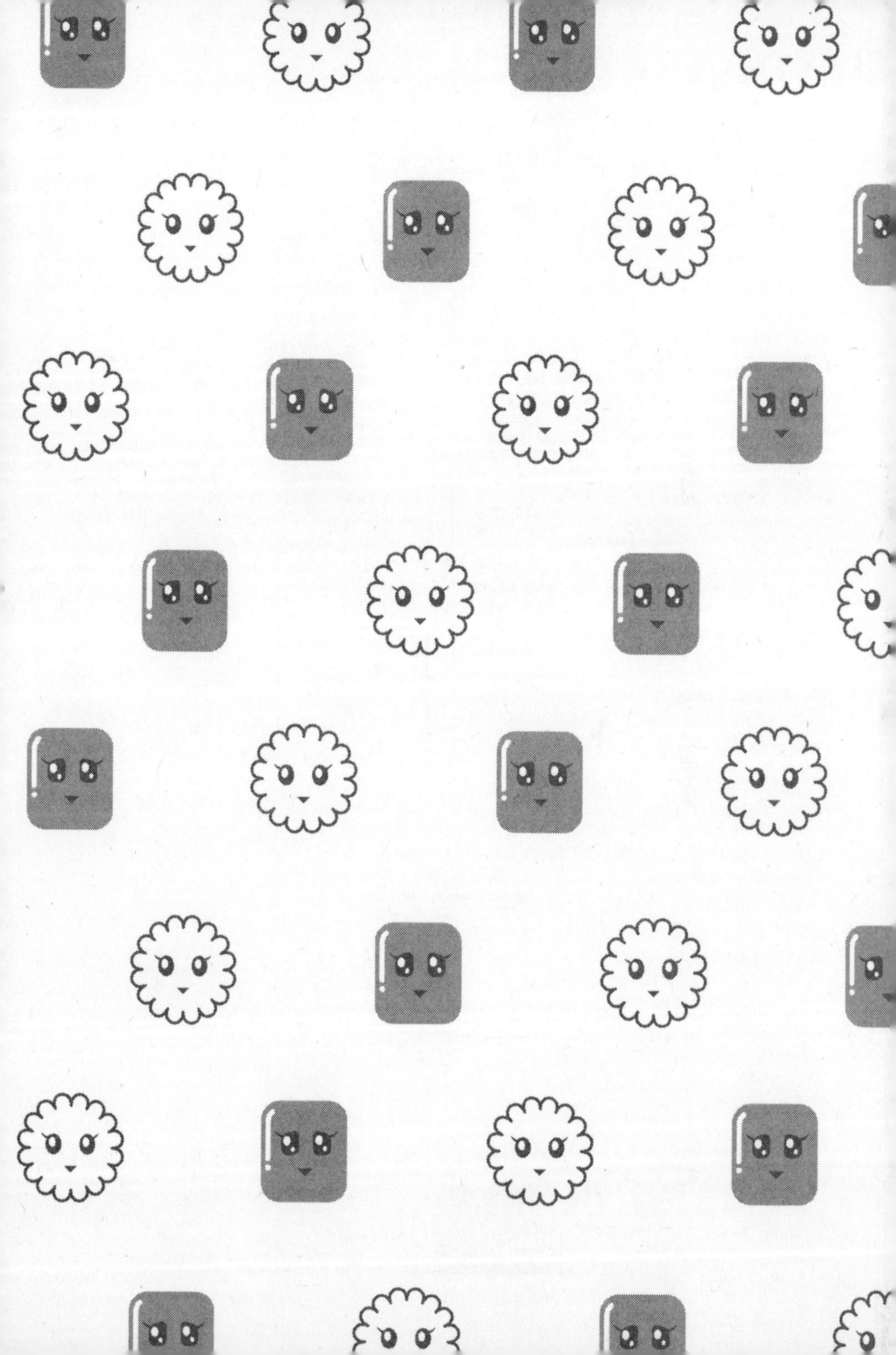

Princess Jellyfish volume 9 is a work of fiction. Names, characters, places, and incidents are the products of the author's imagination or are used fictitiously. Any resemblance to actual events, locales, or persons, living or dead, is entirely coincidental.

A Kodansha Comics Trade Paperback Original.

Princess Jellyfish volume 9 copyright © 2014, 2017 Akiko Higashimura
English translation copyright © 2018 Akiko Higashimura

All rights reserved.

Published in the United States by Kodansha Comics,
an imprint of Kodansha USA Publishing, LLC, New York.

Publication rights for this English edition arranged through Kodansha Ltd., Tokyo.

First published in Japan in 2017 by Kodansha Ltd., Tokyo,
as *Kuragehime* volume 17.
Excerpts first published in Japan in 2014 by Kodansha Ltd., Tokyo,
from *Higashimura Akiko Kaitai Shinsho*.

ISBN 978-1-63236-564-4

Icon design by UCHIKOGA tomoyuki & RAITA ryoko (CHProduction Inc.)

Printed in the United States of America.

www.kodanshacomics.com

9 8 7 6 5 4 3 2 1

Translation: Sarah Alys Lindholm
Lettering: Carl Vanstiphout
Additional Layout and Lettering: Belynda Ungurath
Editing: Haruko Hashimoto
Kodansha Comics Edition Cover Design: Phil Balsman